The Wiley-Blackwell Handbook of The Treatment of Childhood and Adolescent Anxiety

The Wiley-Blackwell Handbook of The Treatment of Childhood and Adolescent Anxiety

Edited by Cecilia A. Essau
and Thomas H. Ollendick

WILEY-BLACKWELL

A John Wiley & Sons, Ltd., Publication

This edition first published 2013
© 2013 John Wiley & Sons, Ltd.

Wiley-Blackwell is an imprint of John Wiley & Sons, formed by the merger of Wiley's global Scientific, Technical and Medical business with Blackwell Publishing.

Registered Office
John Wiley & Sons Ltd, The Atrium, Southern Gate, Chichester, West Sussex, PO19 8SQ, UK

Editorial Offices
350 Main Street, Malden, MA 02148-5020, USA
9600 Garsington Road, Oxford, OX4 2DQ, UK
The Atrium, Southern Gate, Chichester, West Sussex, PO19 8SQ, UK

For details of our global editorial offices, for customer services, and for information about how to apply for permission to reuse the copyright material in this book please see our website at www.wiley.com/wiley-blackwell.

The right of Cecilia A. Essau and Thomas H. Ollendick to be identified as the author of the editorial material in this work has been asserted in accordance with the UK Copyright, Designs and Patents Act 1988.

Library of Congress Cataloging-in-Publication Data

The Wiley-Blackwell handbook of the treatment of childhood and adolescent anxiety / edited by Cecelia [i.e. Cecilia] A. Essau and Thomas H. Ollendick.
    p. cm.
  Includes bibliographical references and index.
  ISBN 978-0-470-66735-4 (cloth)
  1. Anxiety in children.   2. Anxiety in adolescence.   3. Child psychotherapy.   4. Adolescent psychotherapy.   5. Evidence-based psychotherapy.   I. Essau, Cecilia.   II. Ollendick, Thomas H.   III. Title: Handbook of the treatment of childhood and adolescent anxiety.
  RJ506.A58W55 2013
  618.92′8522–dc23

                                                                        2012030891

A catalogue record for this book is available from the British Library.

Cover image: © Tim Robberts / Getty Images.
Cover design by Cyan Design.

Set in 10/12.5 pt Galliard by Aptara Inc., New Delhi, India
Printed in Singapore by Ho Printing Singapore Pte Ltd

1   2013

Contents

Section III

Section IV

Section V

About the Editors

Cecilia A. Essau, PhD obtained her undergraduate and MA degrees in Psychology from Lakehead University (Canada), her PhD from the University of Konstanz (Germany), and her post-doctoral degree (Qualification for tenure-track professorships in Germany) from the University of Bremen (Germany). She has held numerous academic positions in Canadian, Austrian, and German universities before joining the University of Roehampton in 2004 as a Professor of Developmental Psychopathology. At the University of Roehampton, she is also the Director of the Centre for Applied Research and Assessment in Child and Adolescent Wellbeing (CARACAW).

With research grants from numerous national and international institutions, her research has focused on understanding the interacting factors that can lead children and adolescents to have serious emotional and behavioural problems and using this research to (a) enhance the assessment of childhood and adolescent psychopathology and (b) design more effective interventions to prevent and treat such problems. She has published more than 180 articles in either peer-reviewed journals or book chapters in edited volumes, and 15 books.

Thomas H. Ollendick, PhD, is University Distinguished Professor in Clinical Psychology and Director of the Child Study Center at Virginia Polytechnic Institute and State University, Blacksburg, Virginia, USA. He is the author or co-author of over 300 research publications, 75 book chapters, and 25 books. He is the past Editor of the *Journal of Clinical Child Psychology*, past Associate Editor of the *Journal of Consulting and Clinical Psychology*, current Editor of *Behavior Therapy*, and founding Co-Editor of *Clinical Child and Family Psychology Review*. He also serves on the editorial boards of 12 other journals. In addition, he is Past-President of the Association for the Advancement of Behavior Therapy (1995), the Society of Clinical Psychology (1999), the Society of Clinical Child and Adolescent Psychology (2003), and most recently the Society for the Science of Clinical Psychology (2010). The recipient of several NIMH grants, his clinical and research interests range from the study of diverse forms of child psychopathology to the assessment, treatment, and prevention of these child disorders from a social learning/social cognitive theory perspective. He is a frequent speaker at national and international conferences. He holds an honorary adjunct position at Roehampton University.

List of Contributors

Candice A. Alfano, University of Houston, USA

Xenia Anastassiou-Hadjicharalambous, University of Nicosia, Cyprus

Frank Andrasik, University of Memphis, USA

Tony Attwood, The Asperger's Syndrome Clinic, Queensland, Australia

Mirte J. Bakker, St. Radboud University Medical Centre, Nijmegen, The Netherlands

Paula Barrett, Pathways Health and Research Centre, Queensland, Australia

Emily M. Becker, University of Miami, USA

Deborah C. Beidel, University of Central Florida, USA

Courtney L. Benjamin, Temple University, Philadelphia, USA

Boris Birmaher, University of Pittsburgh Medical Center, USA

Frits Boer, Academic Medical Centre (AMC), University of Amsterdam & Department of Child and Adolescent Psychiatry, AMC-de Bascule, The Netherlands

Brian E. Bunnell, University of Central Florida, USA

David M. Clark, Institute of Psychiatry, London, UK

Mary Coffman, Independent Practice, West Union, South Carolina, USA

Maria J. W. Cowart, Virginia Polytechnic Institute and State University, USA

Michael J. Cunningham, Macquarie University, Sydney, Australia

Jill Ehrenreich-May, University of Miami, Florida, USA

Constantina Demetriou, University of Roehampton, UK

Thalia C. Eley, MRC Social Genetic and Developmental Psychiatry Centre, Institute of Psychiatry, King's College London, UK

Cecilia A. Essau, University of Roehampton, UK

Andy Field, University of Sussex, UK

Martin E. Franklin, University of Pennsylvania School of Medicine, USA

Jennifer Freeman, Alpert Medical School of Brown University & Rhode Island Hospital, USA

Jheanell Gabbidon, Institute of Psychiatry, London, UK

Jessica L. Gahr, University of Toledo, Ohio, USA

Alice M. Gregory, Goldsmiths, University of London, UK

David A. Heyne, Leiden University Institute of Psychology, The Netherlands

Cristina Akiko Iizuka, Pathways Health and Research Centre, Queensland, Australia

Shin-ichi Ishikawa, Doshisha University, Japan

Amanda Jensen-Doss, University of Miami, USA

Philip C. Kendall, Temple University, Philadelphia, USA

Kristen L. Lavallee, University of Basel, Switzerland

Ramon J.L. Lindauer, Academic Medical Centre (AMC), University of Amsterdam & Department of Child and Adolescent Psychiatry, AMC-de Bascule, The Netherlands

Elena Longhi, Università degli Studi di Milano-Bicocca, Italy

Katharina Manassis, The Hospital for Sick Children, Toronto, Canada

John March, Duke University Medical Center, USA

Bryce D. McLeod, Virginia Commonwealth University, USA

Phoebe S. Moore, University of Massachusetts Medical School, USA

Kate Morris, Pathways Health and Research Centre, Queensland, Australia

Peter Muris, Maastricht University, The Netherlands

Matthew P. Mychailyszyn, Temple University, Philadelphia, USA

Beatriz Olaya, CIBER en Salud Mental (CIBERSAM), Spain

Thomas H. Ollendick, Virginia Polytechnic Institute and State University, USA

Sean Perrin, Institute of Psychiatry, London, UK

Katere Pourseied, University of Roehampton, UK

Alexander H. Queen, University of Miami, Florida, USA

Ronald M. Rapee, Macquarie University, Sydney, Australia

Kendra L. Read, Temple University, Philadelphia, USA

Dara Sakolsky, University of Pittsburgh Medical Center, USA

Floor M. Sauter, Leiden University Institute of Psychology, The Netherlands

Silvia Schneider, University of Bochum, Germany

Laura D. Seligman, University of Toledo, Ohio, USA

Patrick Smith, Institute of Psychiatry, London, UK

Kate Sofronoff, The University of Queensland, Australia

Chiaying Wei, Temple University, Philadelphia, USA

Emily Wheat, Virginia Commonwealth University, USA

Viviana M. Wuthrich, Macquarie University, Sydney, Australia

William Yule, Institute of Psychiatry, London, UK

Jasper B. Zantvoord, Academic Medical Centre (AMC), University of Amsterdam & Department of Child and Adolescent Psychiatry, AMC-de Bascule, The Netherlands

Helena M. S. Zavos, MRC Social Genetic and Developmental Psychiatry Centre, Institute of Psychiatry, King's College London, UK

Preface

Anxiety disorders are among the most common mental health problems affecting children and adolescents in the general population. It is estimated that up to 10% of children and up to 20% of adolescents meet criteria for an anxiety disorder. In addition to being common, anxiety disorders co-occur frequently with numerous other psychiatric disorders. Anxiety is also associated with impairment in various life domains and may serve as a risk factor for the development of severe mental disorders in adulthood including depression and substance abuse. Moreover, when left untreated, anxiety disorders that begin early in life can become chronic and are often associated with a negative course and outcome.

In response to the growing awareness of the significance of the problem associated with anxiety and its disorders, various prevention and intervention programs for childhood and adolescent anxiety have been developed in the past few decades. Related to this development is the accumulating number of studies that have examined the effectiveness of these interventions for anxiety disorders. As a result, the literature on the prevention and intervention programs for childhood and adolescent anxiety and the studies which have examined the effectiveness of these programs have been accumulating at a rapid pace in recent years. Our aim in this volume is to present the most up-to-date research on child and adolescent anxiety and to present the most common evidence-based interventions for these disorders in a single, comprehensive, and authoritative volume.

This volume is divided into five sections. Section 1 covers an introduction to the field of childhood and adolescent anxiety, including classification, epidemiology, comorbidity, and course and outcome. Section 2 focuses on factors that have been associated with elevated risk of anxiety disorders, including genetic, environmental, neurobiological, interpersonal, social, cognitive (i.e., information biases and processes), and cultural factors.

Section 3 gives an overview about interventions, including evidence-based assessment and case formulation, and on empirically supported psychosocial treatments. This section also contains one chapter on pharmacotherapy, and two chapters on innovative methods to treat childhood and adolescent anxiety (i.e., computerized interventions and bibliotherapy).

Section 4 contains eight chapters on treatment strategies for specific anxiety disorders and problems, including separation anxiety disorder, social phobia, specific phobia, generalized anxiety disorder, obsessive-compulsive disorder, panic disorder, posttraumatic stress disorder, and school refusal. These treatment strategies are based largely on cognitive-behavioral therapy (CBT). By combining two distinct schools of psychotherapy (behavioral and cognitive therapy), these CBT-based treatment programs address the cognitive and behavioral deficits of adolescents with anxiety disorders and problems. Many of these treatments also address the affective and emotional correlates of these disorders. Finally, Section 5 contains three chapters on the prevention of anxiety disorders in specific populations. One chapter covers anxiety prevention in children and adolescents in schools, one among youth with autism spectrum disorders, and another one for those young people with Williams Syndrome. Each of the chapters in sections 4 and 5 begins with a description of the theoretical background underlying the respective intervention programs, the therapeutic goals and methods, and the way in which the interventions are delivered. Available studies that have examined the efficacy are also presented and discussed.

This book is written for advanced students, researchers, and clinicians that include psychologists, psychiatrists, social workers, paediatricians, counsellors, and other mental health professionals who are interested in anxiety disorders, particularly on its treatment. The wealth of information concerning the risk factors and various types of treatment programs for childhood and adolescent anxiety, will make this volume a valuable reference for both the novice and the expert, and to both the clinician and the researcher interested in this field.

We are most grateful to the authors who have contributed to this volume, all of whom have made major contribution to the prevention and treatment of anxiety disorders in children and adolescents. We are honored by their contributions and dedication to this book project. Without them, a comprehensive scholarly coverage of the various types of treatment for anxiety disorders would not have been possible. Finally, we would also like to acknowledge the support and patience of the staff at Wiley-Blackwell.

Cecilia A. Essau and Thomas H. Ollendick

Acknowledgments

I (Cecilia Essau) feel very honoured to have this opportunity to co-edit this volume with my highly respected colleague, Tom Ollendick. Tom has always been a great inspiration to me: he is to me an excellent mentor, scientist, clinician, and a really good friend who is always very patient and full of understanding. I wish to thank my family in Malaysia, Canada, and Germany, especially my husband, Juergen, and our daughter, Anna, for their continuing support and inspiration. I dedicate this work to my late parents, Essau Indit and Runyan Megat, whose courage, love and belief in me had made me become who I am. Had they still be alive, they would have been most proud of this accomplishment.

I (Tom Ollendick) wish to give thanks to my friend and highly esteemed colleague, Cecilia Essau, who planted the seed for this project and who invited me to serve as co-editor with her. This has been a fun project and one that would not have been possible without her vision, dedication, and persistence. I also wish to thank my wife, Mary, our daughters, Laurie Kristine and Kathleen Marie, and our grandchildren, Braden Thomas, Ethan Ray, Calvin David, and Addison Haley. Without them, life would be incredibly less interesting and less enjoyable. Life is good with them, and I thank them for their support over the years. To them, I dedicate this work.

1

Classification of Anxiety Disorders in Children and Adolescents

Cecilia A. Essau[1], Beatriz Olaya[2],
and Thomas H. Ollendick[3]

[1]University of Roehampton, UK
[2]CIBER en Salud Mental (CIBERSAM), Spain
[3]Virginia Polytechnic Institute and State University, USA

Anxiety is a mood state characterized by strong negative emotion in response to threatening events or situations – either real or imagined (Barlow, 1988). It is part of the human condition and is observed in infancy and early childhood. Anxiety is a complex phenomenon which is expressed through three interrelated response systems: physical, cognitive, and behavioral systems. At the cognitive level, the situation is perceived as either threatening or dangerous. Cognitive components of anxiety include anxiety thoughts in response to negative distortions in attention and interpretation, such as worry, fear of being unable to cope with the situation, and uncertainty about the future (Beck, 1976). At the physical level, the perception or anticipation of danger involves the activation of the sympathetic nervous system, which produces both chemical and physical effects that help to mobilize the body for action (Rapee, Craske, & Barlow, 1995). At the behavioral level, the urge that accompanies the fight/flight response is a desire to escape the situation. Behavioral responses include nail-biting and foot-tapping. The most common behavioral symptom, however, is avoidance of the fearful stimuli (e.g., tunnel) or situations (e.g., speaking in a group). Although avoidance results in temporary relief of the anxiety symptoms, it keeps anxiety going and may cause impairment in various life domains.

All children experience anxieties and fears as a normal part of growing up (Table 1.1). However, fears and anxieties change throughout childhood and adolescence and correspond to the child's cognitive development in recognizing and interpreting situations as dangerous. Anxiety serves as a biological warning system and readies the child for action. As such, anxiety can have adaptive value when a child is actually confronted by dangerous stimuli. In fact, moderate levels of anxiety enhance performance and facilitate important developmental transitions. Although normal anxiety can be acutely distressing, in most children it is usually transient. However, because all children show anxiety in some situations and because anxiety is normative at certain developmental periods, it is often difficult to differentiate "normal" from "abnormal" anxiety (or an anxiety disorder). An anxiety is classified as a

The Wiley-Blackwell Handbook of The Treatment of Childhood and Adolescent Anxiety, First Edition.
Edited by Cecilia A. Essau and Thomas H. Ollendick.
© 2013 John Wiley & Sons, Ltd. Published 2013 by John Wiley & Sons, Ltd.

Table 1.1   Common fears in infancy, childhood and adolescence.

Age	Developmental issues	Feared objects/situations	Corresponding DSM-IV anxiety disorders
0–6 months	Biological regulation	Loud noises Loss of physical support	—
6–18 months	Object permanence Formation of attachment relationship	Strangers Separation from parents Sudden and unexpected objects	Separation anxiety disorder
2–3 years	Exploration of the world Magical thinking	Animals Dark Imaginary creatures	Specific phobia Separation anxiety disorder
3–6 years	Autonomy Self-control	Fear of the dark Fear of storms Fear of loss of caregivers	Specific phobia
6–10 years	School adjustment Concrete operations: inference of cause-effect relations and anticipation of dangerous events	School Worry Dark Bodily injury and physical danger Being alone Germs Supernatural being	Generalized anxiety disorder Obsessive-compulsive disorder
10–12 years	Social understanding Friendship	Social concerns Physical appearance Thunder and lightning	Social phobia Specific phobia
13–18 years	Identity Formal operations: catastrophizing about physical symptoms Sexual relationships Physical changes	Social anxiety Peer rejection Personal appearance	Social phobia

Source: Adapted from Klein and Last (1989) and Warren and Stroufe (cited in Ollendick & March, 2004, pp. 92–115).

disorder that should be treated when: (1) the duration and intensity does not correspond to the real danger of the situation; (2) it occurs in "harmless" situations; (3) it is chronic (i.e., lasts over a long period of time); and (4) causes impairment and interferes with psychological, academic, and social functioning (Essau, 2007).

Our current classification systems – the Diagnostic and Statistical Manual (DSM) currently in its fourth edition (DSM-IV) (APA, 2000) and the International Classification of Diseases (ICD) currently in its 10th revision (ICD-10) (WHO, 1992) –

make an explicit distinction between "normal" and "abnormal" anxiety based on the number, severity, persistence, and impairment of symptoms. Additionally, the symptoms cannot be better accounted for by other mental disorders, a general medical condition, or as a result of substance use.

Categorical Classification Systems: DSM-IV and ICD-10

Both DSM-IV and ICD-10 classification systems use categorical approaches to classification. The basic assumption of this approach is that emotional, behavioral, cognitive, and physiological symptoms of psychopathology cluster together to form discrete disorders that are distinct from each other (APA, 2000). The DSM-IV criteria were established, for the most part, by empirical studies via systematic field trials and then balanced by expert opinion. In contrast, the diagnostic criteria in the ICD-10 are based primarily on expert consensus that was later tested with field trials in various countries (WHO, 1992). Although the most recent versions of these systems have increasingly resulted in greater convergence between them, some differences remain (Table 1.2).

Several changes have taken place in the categorization of anxiety disorders in childhood in DSM-IV (APA, 1994). Except for separation anxiety disorder (SAD), all the other anxiety disorders are classified in one category regardless of the age in which the disorder first manifests. Two anxiety disorders that are specific to childhood in DSM-III-R – avoidant disorder and overanxious disorder – were subsumed under social phobia and generalized anxiety disorder (GAD), respectively, in DSM-IV. The decision was to increase consistency with the ICD; furthermore, the decision was based on the lack of evidence that avoidant disorder and overanxious disorder are sufficiently different from their adult counterparts (Kendall & Warman, 1996). Children and adolescents with avoidant disorder do not differ significantly in sociodemographic features (e.g., race, socioeconomic status) from those with social phobia, and there was considerable overlap between these two disorders (Francis, Last, & Strauss, 1992).

In DSM-IV, anxiety disorders can be categorized into eight separate major diagnostic syndromes, which are applicable to children, adolescents, and adults. These include: social phobia, specific phobia, GAD, obsessive-compulsive disorder (OCD), panic disorder, post-traumatic stress disorder (PTSD), and agoraphobia. The common characteristics of all these anxiety disorders are extensive anxiety, physiological anxiety symptoms, and behavioral disturbances (e.g., extreme avoidance of feared objects or situations) which cause significant impairment in functioning. They differ in relation to the nature of the feared stimulus and the anxiety response produced by it. The content of anxious thoughts or worries, and the anticipated harm also varies across anxiety disorders. For example, the main content of worry or anxious thoughts experienced by children with OCD may be contamination, and the anticipated fear is contracting a disease (Keeley & Storch, 2009). Among children with SAD, the content of worry is related to being separated from the caregiver, and the anticipated fear is harm to self or the caregiver (Seligman & Ollendick, 2011).

For almost all anxiety disorders, any differences in diagnostic criteria for children, adolescents, and adults are provided within the criteria set. These differences are

Table 1.2   Classification of anxiety disorders according to ICD-10 and DSM-IV.

ICD-10	*DSM-IV*
F40 Phobic anxiety disorders	
F40.0 Agoraphobia	300.22 Agoraphobia
.00 Without panic disorder	without history of panic
.01 With panic disorder	disorder
F40.1 Social phobias	300.23 Social phobia
F40.2 Specific (isolated) phobias	300.29 Specific phobia
F40.8 Other phobic anxiety disorders	
F40.9 Phobic anxiety disorder, unspecified	
F41 Other anxiety disorders	
F41.0 Panic disorder [episodic paroxysmal anxiety]	300.21 Panic disorder with
F41.1 Generalized anxiety disorder	agoraphobia
F41.2 Mixed anxiety and depressive disorder	300.01 Panic disorder
F41.3 Other mixed anxiety disorders	without agoraphobia
F41.8 Other specified anxiety disorders	300.02 Generalized
F41.9 Anxiety disorder, unspecified	anxiety disorder
	300.00 Anxiety disorder NOS
F42 Obsessive-compulsive disorder	
F42.0 Predominantly obsessional thoughts or ruminations	300.3 Obsessive-
F42.1 Predominantly compulsive acts [obsessional rituals]	compulsive disorder
F42.2 Mixed obsessional thoughts and acts	
F42.8 Other obsessive-compulsive disorders	
F42.9 Obsessive-compulsive disorder, unspecified	
F43 Reaction to severe stress, and adjustment disorders	
F43.0 Acute stress reaction	
F43.1 Post-traumatic stress disorder	308.3 Acute stress disorder
F43.2 Adjustment disorders	309.81 Posttraumatic
F43.8 Other reactions to severe stress	stress disorder
F43.9 Reaction to severe stress, unspecified	

usually related to duration, symptom types, or the extent to which children possess enough insight into the excessiveness or inadequacy of fear (APA, 2000). Specifically, for example, in order to minimize overdiagnosis of normal developmental fears, the symptoms must be present for at least 6 months in specific and social phobias (APA, 2000). Children may also express their anxiety through crying, tantrums, and clinging. For OCD, specific and social phobias, children do not have to acknowledge their fears as being unreasonable or excessive.

In ICD-10, childhood anxiety disorders are classified in a single category, with subcategories that comprise separation anxiety disorder, phobic anxiety disorder, social anxiety disorder, and sibling rivalry disorder; these disorders differ from anxiety disorders in adults by being exaggerations of normal developmental fears (WHO, 1992). ICD also has a category called "other" which includes identity disorder and overanxious disorder.

In this chapter, we will review the major characteristics of anxiety disorders as listed in DSM-IV and their differences from ICD-10.

Separation Anxiety Disorder (SAD)

SAD is defined as a developmentally inappropriate and excessive anxiety regarding separation from those to whom the individual is attached (APA, 2000). In order to meet the DSM-IV criteria for SAD at least three of the following eight criteria must be met: (i) recurrent excessive distress when separation from home or major attachment figures occurs or is anticipated; (ii) persistent and excessive worry about losing, or about possible harm befalling, major attachment figures; (iii) persistent and excessive worry that an untoward event will lead to separation from a major attachment figure (e.g., getting lost or kidnapped); (iv) reluctance or refusal to go to school or elsewhere because of fear of separation; (v) persistently and excessively fearful or reluctance to be alone or without major attachment figures at home or without significant adults in other settings; (vi) persistent reluctance or refusal to go to sleep without being near a major attachment figure or to sleep away from home; (vii) repeated nightmares involving the theme of separation; and (viii) repeated complaints of physical symptoms (e.g., headaches, stomach aches, nausea, or vomiting) when separation from major attachment figures occurs or is anticipated (APA, 2000). Furthermore, the symptoms must last at least 4 weeks and the onset of the symptoms must be before 18 years of age.

Both DSM-IV and ICD-10 are similar in terms of the specific indicator for SAD; however, they differ in criteria related to impairment, age of onset, and symptoms duration. Specifically, DSM-IV requires that the symptoms result in impairment in the academic, familial, social, and other domains. ICD-10, on the other hand, requires impairment only in the social domain. In terms of age of onset, DSM-IV specifies an onset anytime before the age of 18 years whereas ICD-10 states that separation concerns need to be present during the preschool years and should these concerns persist, SAD is diagnosed during later childhood and adolescence. The symptoms must have been present for at least 4 weeks in DSM-IV. ICD-10 does not specify any criteria for minimum duration.

Specific Phobia

The main feature of a specific phobia (formerly called simple phobia in DSM-III and DSM-III-R) is a marked and persistent fear of a specific object or situation that poses little or no danger (APA, 2000). The presence or anticipation of a specific object/situation almost always leads to an immediate anxiety response which might reach the severity threshold of situational bound panic attack. The situations or objects are avoided whenever possible or endured with intense anxiety. The fear and the avoidance behavior have to interfere significantly with the child's normal life or to be associated with clinically significant suffering (Ollendick, King, & Muris, 2004).

DSM-IV modified three criteria that are used for children, namely that (i) panic-like features might be manifested with different emotional responses and may take the form of crying, tantrums, freezing or clinging; (ii) children are not required to consider their fear as irrational or excessive; and (iii) the duration in children must be at least of 6-month duration to warrant a diagnosis.

The DSM-IV differentiates between four subtypes of specific phobia: animal type (fear cued by animals or insects), natural-environment type (fear cued by natural environment such as water, heights, storm), blood-injection-injury type (fear cued by seeing blood, or receiving an injection), situational type (fear cued by specific situations such as flying in an airplane, going through a tunnel), and a residual category (fear cued by other stimuli such as choking, vomiting, loud sounds, and costumed characters). The main feature of each subtype of specific phobia is that fear is circumscribed to a specific object. Thus, when confronted with a feared object, the child with specific phobia will become immediately frightened. The fear is related to concern about dreadful things happening or fear of consequences related to being exposed to the feared object. The decision to differentiate between various types of phobia arises from research suggesting that each type has distinct features, including different gender distribution, age of onset, physiological response, and comorbidity patterns (Antony, Brown, & Barlow, 1997; Lipsitz, Barlow, Mannuzza, et al., 2002; Ollendick, Raishevich, Davis, Sirbu, & Ost, 2010).

The diagnostic criteria of ICD-10 are similar to that of DSM-IV, except that ICD-10 does not classify specific phobic into specific types. Furthermore, ICD-10 does not specify a duration criterion whereas DSM-IV indicates duration of at least 6 months.

Social Phobia

Social phobia (or social anxiety disorder) is characterized by a persistent fear of social (e.g., social gatherings, oral presentation) or performance (e.g., oral presentation) situations that involve possible scrutiny of others (APA, 2000). The individuals fear they will act in a way (or show anxiety symptoms) that will be humiliating or embarrassing. As a result, the feared situations are avoided or are endured with distress. Exposure to the feared social situations generally produces high levels of anxiety and is associated with a wide range of symptoms such as stammering, trembling, and blushing. DSM-IV provides a specifier for social phobia: the specific and the generalized type (APA, 2000). Individuals with the specific type of social phobia have a fear of specific, circumscribed social situations, while those with generalized social phobia fear being in most social situations. As such, the latter tends to be more disabling and severe (Ollendick, 2009).

ICD-10 and DSM-IV differ in several points. First, ICD-10 requires the predominance of avoidance. Second, ICD-10 has an additional diagnostic category for social phobia that is specific to childhood (i.e., before the age of 6 years). Although DSM-IV does not have specific diagnostic criteria for social anxiety disorder of childhood, four of its diagnostic criteria have been modified for children. These modifications include the following: (i) there must be evidence that children are capable of showing age-appropriate social relations with familiar people and show social anxiety in peer settings, not just with adults; (ii) the anxiety may be expressed by crying, tantrums, freezing, or shrinking from social situations with unfamiliar people; (iii) children do not have to recognize that their fear is excessive or unreasonable; and (iv) the duration must be at least 6 months to warrant a diagnosis (APA, 2000). Third, DSM-IV requires that there must be evidence in children that the social anxiety occurs in peer situations, not just in interactions with adults. This requirement does not exist in ICD-10. In fact, the diagnosis criteria for social anxiety disorder of childhood note that the symptoms can be limited to situations that are mainly with adults, or with peers, or with both.

Generalized Anxiety Disorder (GAD)

The main feature of a GAD in DSM-IV is the presence of uncontrollable, unrealistic worry about a number of events or activities (APA, 2000). The anxiety and worry are accompanied by at least three of the following six physiological symptoms: restlessness or feeling keyed up or on edge; being easily fatigued; difficulty concentrating or mind going blank; irritability; muscle tension; and sleep disturbance. These symptoms must be persistent for at least 6 months and be distressing or cause impairment in social, academic, occupational, or other important areas of functioning. DSM-IV modifies the number of somatic symptoms that must be present in children. Specifically, only one instead of three out of the six physiological symptoms is required (APA, 2000).

In DSM-IV, the duration in which the symptoms must be present is specified to be 6 months, while in ICD-10, the duration is less explicit by indicating that the anxiety symptoms be present "for several months" (WHO, 1992, p. 140). DSM-IV requires that the GAD symptoms cause significant distress and impairment in various life domains, whereas in ICD-10, the impairment is not included as one of the criteria. Another difference between the two classification systems is related to the way they handle comorbid disorders. ICD-10 does not allow for the dual diagnosis of GAD with depression, panic disorder, obsessive-compulsive disorder, or a phobic disorder. By contrast, DSM-IV allows the presence of these comorbid disorders.

GAD was first diagnosed in children and adolescents in DSM-IV where, as noted earlier, it subsumes the DSM-III-R-defined overanxious disorder. This change was made to reflect the developmental continuum of the disorder (APA, 1987, 1994; Liebowitz, Barlow, Ballenger, et al., 1998). GAD differs from overanxious disorder in terms of putting greater emphasis on somatic symptoms. In GAD, worry is described as a future focused-worry or anxious apprehension, whereas in overanxious disorder, worry also includes past performance and behavior (Ollendick & Seligman, 2005).

Obsessive-compulsive Disorder (OCD)

The essential feature of OCD in DSM-IV is the presence of obsessions and compulsions (APA, 2000) that cause significant distress, are time-consuming (take more than 1 hour a day), or debilitating and result in interferences in normal functioning that significantly affects the person's life (Piacentini & Bergman, 2000). Obsessions are persistent thoughts, images or impulses that are intrusive, inappropriate, and distressing that must be differentiated from excessive worries about real-life problems.

Individuals with OCD attempt to ignore or suppress the obsessions and recognize them as a product of their own mind. Some common examples of obsessions include fear of dirt or contamination by germs, fear of causing harm to self and others, and religious or sexual preoccupations (Geller, Warner, Williams, & Zimerman, 1998; Masi, Mucci, Nicoletta, Bertini, Milantoni, & Arcangeli, 2005).

Compulsions are repetitive behaviors or mental acts that are performed in response to an obsession and often according to rigid rules. Compulsions are meant to reduce distress or to prevent some dreaded event from occurring. Some common compulsive themes are repeatedly cleaning or decontamination rituals (e.g., bathing, excessive washing), repeatedly checking things (e.g., locks), counting, straightening, and arranging things in a certain way (Geller et al., 1998; Masi et al., 2005). Rituals may provide temporary reduction in anxiety; however, they do not lead to long-term relief because the images and thoughts return persistently and recurrently. Consequently, children with OCD become more and more trapped in a time-consuming and vicious cycle of obsessions and compulsions (Carter & Pollock, 2000). The individual recognizes that the obsessions or compulsions are excessive or unreasonable. However, this criterion does not apply to children. DSM-IV requires that the obsessions or compulsions are not better accounted for by another disorder.

The two classification systems differ significantly in their definition of OCD. First, in DSM-IV, OCD is classified in the section of anxiety disorders, which reflects the fact that it shares the core symptom of anxiety. Specifically, anxiety is often associated with obsessions, and that anxiety is often relieved temporarily by giving way to compulsions. In ICD-10, OCD is not classified as an anxiety disorder, but in the section on Neurotic, Stress-related, and Somatoform disorders, which is within the same larger category as anxiety disorders. Second, they also differ in the way obsessions and compulsions are defined. Obsessions are defined in DSM-IV as recurrent and persistent thoughts, images, or impulses; compulsions are repetitive behaviors or mental acts; thus, compulsions can also be cognitive events. Obsessions are considered to cause anxiety or distress, whereas compulsions are aimed at preventing or reducing distress. In this respect, obsessions and compulsions are assumed to have a functional relationship. In ICD-10, an obsession is defined as a thought, idea, or image, whereas compulsion is defined as an act. Obsessions and compulsions have a common feature of being repetitive and unpleasant. Third, the threshold for OCD in DSM-IV is higher than that in ICD-10 in that its symptoms need to be time-consuming and must be present more than 1 hour per day.

Panic Disorder with or without Agoraphobia

Panic disorder is characterized by recurrent, unexpected panic attacks (APA, 2000). To meet the diagnosis of a panic disorder, an individual must additionally experience at least 1 month in which he or she is concerned about having additional attacks, is worried about the consequences of the attacks, or changes his or her behavior because of the attacks.

DSM-IV defines a panic attack as a discrete period of fear or discomfort that reaches a peak within 10 minutes. It is accompanied by 4 out of 13 autonomic or cognitive symptoms: (1) palpitations, pounding heart, or accelerated heart rate; (2) sweating;

(3) trembling or shaking; (4) sensations of shortness of breath or smothering; (5) feeling of choking; (6) chest pain or discomfort; (7) nausea or abdominal distress; (8) feeling dizzy, unsteady, lightheaded, or faint; (9) derealization or depersonalization; (10) fear of losing control or going crazy; (11) fear of dying; (12) paresthesias (numbness or tingling situations); and (13) chills or hot flushes (APA, 2000). The attacks must not stem from the direct effects of a substance, or a general medical condition. Panic disorder is diagnosed if the attacks continue even when the precipitant is no longer present. It is not diagnosed if the panic attacks are better accounted for by another psychiatric disorder.

Panic disorder is frequently associated with agoraphobia, which is anxiety about being in places or situations in which escape might be difficult or help unavailable in the event of an unexpected panic attack or experience of panic-like symptoms. Some common examples of agoraphobic fears include being outside the home alone; being in a crowd or a shopping center; and travelling in a bus or train. In DSM-IV, individuals can receive a diagnosis of (a) panic disorder without agoraphobia, (b) panic disorder with agoraphobia, or (c) agoraphobia without history of panic disorder.

Although DSM-IV and ICD-10 are similar in the way the diagnostic features of panic disorder are defined (i.e., the recurrence/intensity and unexpected nature of panic attacks), they differ in two areas. First, DSM-IV requires a minimum 1-month period in which there is a change in behavior as a result of the attacks or that the individual has a fear of additional attacks or their implications. For this reason, the core of the panic disorder in DSM-IV is the so-called 'fear of fear'; in ICD-10, it is the presence of panic attacks that constitutes the panic disorder (Ollendick & Seligman, 2005). Second, in DSM-IV, agoraphobia is considered in the diagnosis of panic disorder, with three possible outcomes: panic disorder without agoraphobia, panic disorder with agoraphobia, and agoraphobia without history of panic. This association is not made in the ICD-10. This difference is related to the way in which agoraphobia is defined. DSM-IV defines agoraphobia as involving avoidance of situations or having excessive anxiety about being in situations in which a panic attack might take place or in which it would be difficult to escape should an attack occur. In ICD-10, agoraphobia is defined as the fear of open or crowded places or a fear of situations in which escape might be difficult.

Post-traumatic Stress Disorder (PTSD) and Acute Stress Disorder

PTSD is an anxiety disorder that may develop after the person has been exposed to an extremely traumatic event that involves actual or threatened death or serious injury to the self or others (APA, 2000). The person responds to the traumatic event with intense fear, helplessness, or horror (Criterion A). However, children may respond by disorganized or agitated behavior.

PTSD symptoms are organized into three clusters: intrusive recollection, avoidant/numbing, and hyper-arousal. In order to meet the diagnosis, symptoms from each of these three clusters must be present. DSM-IV requires that the traumatic event is persistently re-experienced (Criterion B: intrusive recollection) in at least one of the following ways: (a) recurrent and intrusive recollections, (b) recurrent nightmares of the events, (c) acting or feeling as if the trauma were recurring, (d) intense psychological distress upon exposure to internal or external cues that represent or are similar to an aspect of the traumatic event, and (e) physiological reactivity upon exposure to external or internal cues that represent or are similar to an aspect of the traumatic event (APA, 2000). Of these five symptoms, three have been modified to make them applicable to children. First, recurrent and intrusive recollections may be expressed through repetitive play that contains themes or aspects of the trauma. Second, instead of having recurrent distressing dreams of the event, children may have frightening dreams without recognizable content. Finally, children may experience trauma-specific re-enactment, instead of acting or feeling as if the traumatic event were recurring.

Criterion C (avoidant and numbing) requires the presence of at least three symptoms related to persistent avoidance and numbing of general responsiveness to stimuli associated with the trauma; these symptoms were not present before the trauma. These include: (a) efforts to avoid thoughts, feelings, or discussions of the trauma; (b) efforts to avoid activities, places, or people that arouse recollections of the trauma; (c) unable to recall an important aspect of the trauma; (d) significant reduction in interest or participation in activities; (e) feelings of detachment or disengagement from others; (f) restricted range of affect; and (g) a sense of a foreshortened future.

Criterion D (hyper-arousal) requires that at least two symptoms of increasing arousal be present that were not present before the traumatic event. These include sleep disturbance; irritability or outbursts of anger; concentration difficulty; hyper-vigilance; and exaggerated startle response. In order to meet the diagnosis of PTSD, symptoms (in Criteria B, C, and D) must be present for at least 1 month and cause significant distress and impairment in important areas of functioning.

Acute Stress Disorder (ASD) is an anxiety disorder that occurs within a month of a traumatic event. The main criterion is the same as for PTSD and that the diagnosis requires the presence of symptoms of re-experiencing, persistent avoidance, and hyper-arousal. However, unlike PTSD, dissociative symptoms such as derealization and depersonalization are emphasized in ASD.

DSM-IV and ICD-10 differ in the way the main criterion of PTSD is defined. Specifically, ICD-10 states that the person must have been exposed to a "stressful event or situation of an exceptionally threatening or catastrophic nature, which is likely to cause pervasive distress in almost anyone" (WHO, 1992, p. 147). Furthermore, ICD-10 does not specify the minimum number of symptoms that is required for the diagnosis to be met.

The diagnostic guidelines for ICD-10 state that the disorder should only be diagnosed after 6 months from the time of exposure to the trauma and the symptoms cannot be better accounted for by another disorder.

Problems with the DSM and ICD in the Classification of Anxiety Disorders in Children and Adolescents

Despite the widespread application of DSM-IV and ICD-10 in diagnosing anxiety disorders in children and adolescents, there are a number of limitations. These include: lack of developmental consideration, high comorbidity rates, reliability and validity issues, and vagueness of the criterion threshold.

Lack of developmental consideration

Except for separation anxiety disorder, all of the anxiety disorders in DSM-IV are grouped together regardless of their age of onset. This means that the same criteria can be applied to children, adolescents, and adults, although the decision for this continues to attract much debate. The focus of the debate lies around DSM-IV's insensitivity to the developmental aspects of anxiety disorders (Whiteside & Ollendick, 2009). As shown by several authors, anxiety/worry tends to change in its magnitude and character due to differences in cognitive, emotional, and social development across age. For example, common fears among toddlers include dark and separation from attached figures, whereas among school-aged children, these include fear of injury and natural disasters (Muris, Merckelbach, & Collaris, 1997). Among adolescents, the fears are mostly related to rejection from others (Muris et al., 1997). Studies have also shown that fears decrease with age (Ollendick, Matson, & Helsel, 1985), whereas some anxiety disorders such as social phobia (Essau, Conradt, & Petermann, 1999) increase with age.

DSM-IV acknowledges this limitation by modifying some symptom features for some disorders which are unique for certain age groups (Beesdo, Knappe, & Pine, 2009). For example, the threshold for GAD is lower in children compared to adults, in that only one instead of three out of six symptoms is required to meet GAD. In ICD-10, children are given different (than adults) diagnostic coding for anxiety disorders that show deviation from normal developmental trends (Beesdo et al., 2009).

High comorbidity

Comorbidity seems to be the rule rather than the exception among children and adolescents with anxiety disorders, with up to 72% of those who meet the diagnosis of anxiety disorders meeting criteria for at least one other psychiatric disorder (Angold, Costello, & Erkanli, 1999; Essau, Conradt, & Petermann, 2000; Feehan, McGee, Nada-Raja, & Williams, 1994; Lewinsohn, Zinbarg, Seeley, Lewinsohn, & Sack, 1997; Kashani & Orvaschel, 1988; Strauss & Last, 1993). The most common comorbid disorder with anxiety is that of depression (Anderson, Williams, McGee, & Silva, 1987; Lewinsohn et al., 1997; McGee, Feehan, Williams, Partridge, Silva, & Kelley, 1990). Among those with anxiety and depression, anxiety generally occurs first before that of depression (Lewinsohn et al., 1997; McGee et al., 1990).

The underlying assumption of the categorical approach is that each anxiety disorder can be recognized as qualitatively different from other disorders. However, the high comorbidity rate has raised questions about the meaningfulness of our current classification systems because it seems to suggest that disorders may not be distinct or, in the least, have not been sufficiently differentiated from one another (Seligman & Ollendick, 1999).

Regardless of the meaning of comorbidity in terms of classification, the presence of comorbid disorders presents a challenge to the clinician as it could cloud the focus of treatment. In the presence of comorbid disorders, clinicians need to decide which disorder should be given priority in terms of treatment (e.g., severity versus order of onset). Answers to these questions may help us design effective treatment for anxiety disorders with comorbid disorders (Brown & Barlow, 2009). Curry, Wells,

Lochman, Craighead, and Nagy (2003) argued that comorbidity necessitates the choice of one of three systematic approaches: sequential treatment (i.e., treating the primary disorder first, and the comorbid disorder second); common process treatment (i.e., targeting common process of both disorders); and modular treatment (i.e., an integrative approach to both disorders that involves addressing the processes which are specific to each disorders). Some other authors have argued (Kendall, Kortlander, Chansky, & Brady, 1992; Oei & Loveday, 1997) that complete treatment is needed to address the principal and comorbid disorders and that we should not expect that the treatment of any one disorder will necessarily produce positive outcomes for the comorbid disorders.

Criterion threshold

A further criticism of the categorical approach is the seemingly arbitrary and dichotomous nature of diagnoses, which specifies that a certain symptomatic threshold criterion (i.e., number of symptoms, their duration, persistence) and clinical significance must be present before diagnoses can be made. Therefore, if a child reports a range of symptoms but falls short of one criterion, a diagnosis will not be made (or meet a nonspecific classification of, for example, anxiety disorder not otherwise specified). This one criterion could be related to number of symptoms (i.e., two symptoms instead of three), duration (five months instead of six), persistence (three instead of four); in still other instances, all the symptoms criteria may be met but these symptoms fail to cause significant impairment (Beesdo et al., 2009; Shear, Bjelland, Beesdo, Gloster, & Wittchen, 2007; Wakefield & First, 2003). For this reason, some authors (Beesdo et al., 2009), have proposed to lower the threshold for children in order to allow early detection of children with anxiety problems so that adequate treatment can be provided.

In DSM-IV the "clinically significant distress and impairment" criterion was introduced to reduce the false-positive problem (Wakefield & First, 2003). However, the introduction of this criterion has been criticized because of the lack of uniform criteria for determining impairment across the lifespan (Wittchen & Jacobi, 2005). It has been argued that the early stage of some anxiety disorders (e.g., specific phobia) may be easier to detect than at the later stage where avoidance behavior has led to periods of not experiencing severe anxiety reactions and impairment (Wittchen & Jacobi, 2005).

The inclusion of "clinically significant distress and impairment" criterion influences both the prevalence and probable course and outcome of anxiety disorders. This point is clearly illustrated in a study by Zimmerman and colleagues (2004) who showed that the addition of this criterion significantly reduced the prevalence of anxiety disorders (specific phobia, PTSD, GAD). Similarly in a study by Shaffer, Fisher, Dulcan, and Davies (1996), the prevalence of anxiety significantly increased when the clinical significance criterion threshold was lowered or omitted.

Bittner, Goodwin, Wittchen, Beesdo, Höfler, and Lieb (2004) examined the extent to which anxiety disorders and impairment associated with anxiety disorders predict major depression. Their findings showed that GAD in early adolescence was the best predictor of major depression in young adulthood, followed by panic disorder, agoraphobia, specific and social phobia. Greater risk of developing a major depression was associated with impairment in one or more social roles. Furthermore, the vagueness in the definition of "clinically significant" has been considered as being responsible for the lack of reliability of anxiety disorders reported in some early studies (Hodges, Cools, & McKnew, 1989). Another related issue is the way in which anxiety symptoms manifest themselves differently in different age groups. In this case, the clinician must make a judgment whether the behavior falls outside developmentally appropriate behavior in a child. Therefore, a clearer definition of this threshold would improve diagnostic reliability (Albano, Chorpita, & Barlow, 2003; Whiteside & Ollendick, 2009).

Reliability and validity issues

Classification systems provide a common language and facilitate communication, guide treatment, and inform research (Lewis & Araya, 2001). However, in order for these functions to be useful, psychiatric diagnoses such as anxiety disorders need to be reliable and valid (Lewis & Araya, 2001). Diagnostic reliability is normally assessed using test–retest (i.e., stability of diagnoses over time) or inter-rater reliability (i.e., agreement of child's diagnosis across assessors) methods.

Inter-rater reliability of the anxiety disorders in children and adolescents used to be poor, with kappa values ranging from 0.24 to 0.84, with a mean of 0.52 (Hodges et al., 1989). However, the development of structured or semi-structured diagnostic interview schedules such as the Diagnostic Interview Schedule for Children (DISC; Shaffer, Schwab-Stone, Fisher et al., 1993) and the Anxiety Disorders Interview Schedule for Children (ADIS; Silverman & Albano, 1996) has greatly enhanced inter-rater reliability of anxiety disorders. For example, Lyneham, Abbott, and Rapee (2007) examined the inter-rater agreement on diagnoses achieved using the parent and child versions of the ADIS-IV in 7- to 16-year-old children with anxiety disorder. The level of agreement for principal diagnosis (kappa = 0.92) and for the individual anxiety disorders (kappa = 0.80–1.0) was excellent when information from parent and child interviews was combined. Agreement ranged from good to excellent when the analysis was done separately for child or parent interviews; inter-rater agreement was not affected by the participant's age or gender.

Some other studies have, however, showed less positive results. For example, Rapee, Barrett, Dadds, and Evans (1994) examined parent–children agreement for the DSM-III-R anxiety disorders and for each specific anxiety disorder (separation anxiety disorder, overanxious disorder, social phobia, specific phobia). Their results showed poor parent–child agreement for overall anxiety disorders and for each anxiety disorder. Levels of agreement between parents and children were affected by the child's age and gender. Specifically, high agreement was reported for older compared to younger, and for boys compared to girls on the overall anxiety category and for social phobia specifically. Grills and Ollendick (2003) similarly found poor levels of parent–child agreement for specific phobia, social phobia, separation anxiety disorder, and GAD. Parent-consensus agreement varied from poor (for specific and social phobia) to good (separation anxiety disorder and GAD). The level of agreement was higher for parent-consensus compared to child-consensus. This finding suggested that clinicians were more inclined to favor information from the parents than from the children. In line with previous findings (Rapee et al., 1994), Grills and Ollendick (2003) also found higher agreement for older than for younger children. In terms of gender, parents showed higher agreement on social phobia and separation anxiety with their sons than did parents of daughters.

The test–retest reliability of anxiety disorders seems to differ across diagnostic interview schedules (Angold, 2002), with values ranging from 0.59 for K-SADS and DISC-IV to 0.82 for intraclass agreement. Silverman, Saavedra and Pina (2001) examined the test–retest reliability of the DSM-IV anxiety symptoms and disorders in children with the ADIS. The children and their parents were interviewed using the ADIS for DSM-IV with an interval of 7–14 days. Results showed excellent reliability in symptoms for SAD, social phobia, specific phobia, and GAD. Good to excellent reliability was also obtained when diagnoses of these disorders are combined.

Despite these limitations with agreement among informants, categorical systems such as the DSM and ICD are important for guiding research, education/training, and clinical practice. Moreover, in clinical settings, the two systems are often associated with reimbursement for treatment services.

Dimensional approach of classification

In the dimensional system, anxiety is defined as a set of emotions and behaviors which occur together in a specific pattern. Anxiety is viewed as existing on a continuum, with children experiencing varying levels of anxiety. In addition to the children themselves, their parents and teachers are often asked questions about the children's behavior in order to derive anxiety symptoms and their severity levels. The threshold between normal and abnormal anxiety is derived using various statistical methods such as factor analysis and confirmatory factor analysis. Assessment in a dimensional approach relies on rating scales.

A major advantage of a dimensional compared to a categorical approach is that it more readily accounts for developmental changes in children, is easier to administer, and is therefore less costly (Essau, Petermann, & Feehan, 1997). It also provides normative data which could be differentiated by gender and age groups. More importantly, it helps to provide sufficient coverage of symptom presentation that may be of clinical significance when criteria for diagnostic categories are not met (Brown & Barlow, 2009). As such, the dimensional approach to classification of anxiety is useful as a screening instrument, particularly in community surveys. An example of a screening instrument is the Spence Children's Anxiety Scale (SCAS; Spence, 1998). The SCAS is a self-report questionnaire, designed to assess children and adolescent's perception of the frequency with which they experience symptoms relating to DSM-IV SAD, social phobia, panic disorder and agoraphobia, GAD, OCD, and fears of physical injury (i.e., specific phobia). The internal consistency of the SCAS has been reported to be excellent, with Cronbach Alpha for the total score reported to be 0.92 (Spence, 1998). The test–retest reliability coefficients have also been reported to be high, ranging from 0.60 to 0.86, for retest intervals between 2 and 12 weeks (Ishikawa, Sato, & Sasagawa, 2009; Mellon & Moutavelis, 2007; Spence, 1998).

Studies (Spence, 1997, 1998; Spence, Barrett, & Turner, 2003) that examined the factor structure of SCAS have provided strong support for a six-correlated factor model which involved six factors related to separation anxiety disorder, social phobia, panic disorder and agoraphobia, GAD, OCD, and fears of physical injury. In terms of its validity, studies have demonstrated differences between anxious children and non-anxious children on the SCAS (Spence, 1998; Whiteside & Brown, 2008). The convergent validity of the SCAS has been established through its positive correlations with measures that purport to assess the construct of anxiety such as the Revised Children's Manifest Anxiety Scale (Reynolds & Richmond, 1978) and depression such as the Children's Depression Inventory (Kovacs, 1985) and the Depression Self-Rating Scale (Birleson, 1981) (Essau, Muris, & Ederer, 2002; Ishikawa et al., 2009; Spence et al., 2003).

Another example of a self-report questionnaire that is commonly used to measure the frequency and severity of anxiety in children and adolescents is the Screen for Child Anxiety Related Emotional Disorders (SCARED; Birmaher, Khetarpal, Brent, et al., 1997). Exploratory factor analysis of the SCARED has revealed five factors, of which four measure anxiety disorder symptoms as conceptualized in the DSM-IV classification of anxiety disorders (panic/somatic, generalized anxiety, separation anxiety, and social phobia). The fifth subscale measures school phobia, which is a common type of childhood problem, but not necessarily anxiety related (King, Ollendick, & Tonge, 1995). The internal consistency of the SCARED has been reported to be good to excellent, with Cronbach Alphas ranging from 0.78 to 0.90 (Birmaher et al., 1997; Birmaher, Brent, Chiappetta, Bridge, Monga, & Baugher, 1999); moreover, the test–retest reliability on an average of 5 weeks has been reported to be moderate, with intraclass correlation coefficients ranging from 0.70 to 0.90. In terms of its validity, the SCARED has been reported to correlate significantly with other measures for anxiety in children and adolescents such as with the SCAS (Essau et al., 2002), the Revised Children's Manifest Anxiety Scale (Muris, Merckelbach, Mayer, et al., 1998), and with the internalizing subscale of the Child Behavior Checklist (Su et al., 2008). Finally, studies that focused on the factor structure of the SCARED have revealed a five-factor solution: panic/somatic, generalized anxiety, separation anxiety, social phobia, and school phobia (Birmaher et al., 1997, 1999; Crocetti, Hale III, Fermani, Raaijmakers, & Meeus, 2009; Hale III, Raaijmakers, Muris, & Meeus, 2005). As dimensional rating scales, the SCAS and the SCARED can be used to provide information about the severity of anxiety symptoms, which could assist with diagnosis, treatment planning, and measuring treatment outcomes (Silverman & Ollendick, 2008).

A problem with the dimensional approach, however, is that it does not allow the formulation of a clinical diagnosis of anxiety and, relatedly, the cut-off used to indicate "caseness" can be arbitrary (Essau et al., 1997). Furthermore, the results obtained may depend on the type of statistical procedures, the number and content of items, and the number of children and adolescents examined in the analyses.

Adding Dimensional Features of Anxiety to DSM/ICD?

In view of the above findings and debates, nosological systems need to consider (a) differences in the expression of anxiety symptoms across developmental stage and gender; (b) differences across informants; and (c) children's tendency to show various problems that are anxiety related (Hudziak, Achenbach, Althoff, & Pine, 2007). It is therefore important to have a system that enables the inclusion of categorical descriptors (e.g., anxiety disorders) and dimensional profiles (i.e., deviation for anxiety problems) (Hudziak et al., 2007). Hopefully, a dimensional profile would give evidence-based information to determine changes in children's categorical descriptions (i.e., the presence or absence of anxiety disorders) and the extent to which the core and associated symptoms (e.g., avoidance, impairment) have changed. Furthermore, as argued by some authors, when studying childhood anxiety, knowledge of age-related expression of anxiety or other mood states that are considered normal is important because these states can be considered abnormal at one age and normal at another (Hudziak et al., 2007).

Additionally, the use of multiple sources of information (i.e., parents, teachers, children) often make it difficult to categorize children as having "normal" or "abnormal" anxiety because of lack of agreement among informants when reporting children's level of anxiety. In this case, it is important to consider whether decisions need to be made by using averages of anxiety symptoms across informants or based on the most severe problems as reported by any one or combination of informants (Hudziak et al., 2007). Brown and Barlow (2005, 2009) have also convincingly argued for the introduction of dimensional severity ratings to the extant diagnostic categories because such information should help to address some of the disadvantages of using only the categorical approach.

Conclusion

Our review has shown two major approaches to classifying anxiety disorders. This review has made us aware of numerous problems with our current classification systems of anxiety disorders in children and adolescents which warrant consideration in future studies:

- Categorical systems of classification (i.e., DSM-IV and ICD-10) make little attempt to adequately address the developmental perspectives in anxiety disorders, which is surprising given substantial age differences in the occurrence and expression of anxiety.
- The validity of using DSM-IV and ICD-10 diagnostic criteria which have been designed for adults to diagnose anxiety disorders in children and adolescents is yet to be fully determined.
- Adding dimensional features of anxiety to complement the categorical aspects of DSM/ICD is recommended.

References

Albano, A., Chorpita, B., & Barlow, D. (2003). Childhood anxiety disorders. In E. Mash & R. Barkley (Eds.), *Child Psychopathology*, 2nd edn. (pp. 279–329). New York: Guilford Press.

Anderson, J. C., Williams, S., McGee, R., & Silva, P. A. (1987). DSM-III disorders in preadolescent children. Prevalence in a large sample from the general population. *Archives of General Psychiatry, 44,* 69–76.

Angold, A. (2002). Diagnostic interviews with parents and children. In M. Rutter, E. Taylor (Eds.), *Child and Adolescent Psychiatry: Modern Approaches*, 4th edn (pp. 32–51). Oxford: Blackwell Scientific.

Angold, A., Costello, E. J., & Erkanli, A. (1999). Comorbidity. *Journal of Child Psychology and Psychiatry and Allied Disciplines, 40,* 57–87.

Antony, M. M., Brown, T. A., & Barlow, D. H. (1997). Heterogeneity among specific phobia types in DSM-IV. *Behaviour Research and Therapy, 35,* 1089–1100.

American Psychiatric Association (1987). *Diagnostic and Statistical Manual of Mental Disorders,* 3rd edn. Washington, DC: American Psychiatric Association.

American Psychiatric Association (1994). *Diagnostic and Statistical Manual of Mental Disorders,* 4th edn. Washington, DC: American Psychiatric Association.

American Psychiatric Association (2000). *Diagnostic and Statistical Manual of Mental Disorders,* text revision, 4th edn. Washington, DC: American Psychiatric Press.

Barlow, D. H. (1988). *Anxiety and its Disorders.* New York: Guilford Press.

Beck, A. T. (1976). *Cognitive Therapy and the Emotional Disorders.* Penguin Books.

Beesdo, K., Knappe, S., & Pine, D. S. (2009). Anxiety and anxiety disorders in children and adolescents: Developmental issues and implications for DSM-V. *Psychiatric Clinics of North America, 32,* 483–524.

Birleson, P. (1981). The validity of depressive disorder in childhood and the development of self-rating scale. *Journal of Child Psychology and Psychiatry, 22,* 73–88.

Birmaher, B., Brent, D., Chiappetta, L., Bridge, J., Monga, S., & Baugher, M. (1999). Psychometric properties of the Screen for Child Anxiety Related Emotional Disorders (SCARED): A replication study. *Journal of the American Academy of Child and Adolescent Psychiatry, 38,* 1230–1236.

Birmaher, B., Khetarpal, S., Brent, D., Cully, M., Balach, L., Kaufman, J., & McKenzie Neers, S. (1997). The Screen for Child Anxiety Related Emotional Disorders (SCARED): Scale construction and psychometric characteristics. *Journal of the American Academy of Child and Adolescent Psychiatry, 36,* 545–553.

Bittner, A., Goodwin, R. D., Wittchen, H.-U., Beesdo, K., Höfler, M., & Lieb, R. (2004). What characteristics of primary anxiety disorders predict subsequent major depressive disorder? *Journal of Clinical Psychiatry, 65,* 618–626.

Brown, T. A., & Barlow, D. H. (2005). Dimensional versus categorical classification of mental disorders in the fifth edition of the diagnostic and statistical manual of mental disorders and beyond: comment on the special section. *Journal of Abnormal Psychology, 114,* 551–556.

Brown, T. A., & Barlow, D. H. (2009). A proposal for a dimensional classification system based on the shared features of the DSM-IV anxiety and mood disorders: Implications for assessment and treatment. *Psychological Assessment, 21* (3), 256–271.

Carter, A. S., Pollock, R. A. (2000). Obsessive compulsive disorder in childhood. *Current Opinion in Pediatry, 12,* 325–330.

Crocetti, E., Hale, W. W., III, Fermani, A., Raaijmakers, Q., & Meeus, W. (2009). Psychometric properties of the Screen for Child Anxiety Related Emotional Disorders (SCARED) in the general Italian adolescent population: A validation and a comparison between Italy and The Netherlands. *Journal of Anxiety Disorders, 23,* 824–829.

Curry, J. F., Wells, K. C., Lochman, J. E., Craighead, W. E., & Nagy, P. D. (2003). Cognitive-behavioral intervention for depressed, substance-abusing adolescents: Development and pilot testing. *Journal of the American Academy of Child & Ado-lescent Psychiatry, 42,* 656–665.

Essau, C. A. (2007). Editorial: Anxiety in children: When is it classed as a disorder that should be treated? *Expert Review of Neurotherapeutics, 7,* 909–911.

Essau, C. A., Conradt, J., & Petermann, F. (1999). Frequency, comorbidity, and psychosocial impairment of social phobia and social fears in adolescents. *Behaviour Research and Therapy, 37,* 831–843.

Essau, C. A., Conradt, J., & Petermann, F. (2000). Frequency, comorbidity, and psychosocial impairment of anxiety disorders in adolescents. *Journal of Anxiety Disorders, 14,* 263–279.

Essau, C. A., Muris, P., & Ederer, E. M. (2002). Reliability and validity of the "Spence Children's Anxiety Scale" and the "Screen for Child Anxiety Related Emotional

Disorders" in German children. *Journal of Behavior Therapy and Experimental Psychiatry, 33*, 1–18.

Essau, C. A., Petermann, F., & Feehan, M. (1997). Research methods and designs. In C. A. Essau & F. Petermann (Eds.), *Developmental Psychopathology: Epidemiology, Diagnostics, and Treatment* (pp. 63–95). London: Harwood Academic Publishers.

Feehan, M., McGee, R., Nada-Raja, S., & Williams, S. M. (1994). DSM-III-R disorders in New Zealand 18-year-olds. *Australian and New Zealand Journal of Psychiatry, 28,* 87–99.

Francis, G., Last, C. G., & Strauss, C. C. (1992). Avoidant personality disorder and social phobia in children and adolescents. *Journal of the American Academy of Child and Adolescent Psychiatry, 31,*1086–1089.

Grills, A. E., & Ollendick, T. H. (2003). Multiple informant agreement and the Anxiety Disorders Interview Schedule for parents and children. *Journal of the American Academy of Child and Adolescent Psychiatry, 42,* 30–40.

Geller, B., Warner, K., Williams, M., & Zimerman, B. (1998). Prepubertal and young adolescent bipolarity versus ADHD: Assessment and validity using the WASH-U-KSADS, CBCL and TRF. *Journal of Affective Disorders, 51,* 93–100.

Hale, W. W. III, Raaijmakers, Q., Muris, P., & Meeus, W. (2005). Psychometric properties of the Screen for Child Anxiety Related Emotional Disorders (SCARED) in the general adolescent population. *Journal of the American Academy of Child and Adolescent Psychiatry, 44,* 283–290.

Hodges, K., Cools, J., & McKnew, D. (1989). Test-retest reliability of a clinical research interview for children: The Child Assessment Schedule. *Psychological Assessment, 10,* 173–189.

Hudziak, J. J., Achenbach, T. M., Althoff, R. R., & Pine, D. S. (2007). A dimensional approach to developmental psychopathology. *International Journal of Methods in Psychiatric Research, 16,* 16–23.

Ishikawa, S., Sato, H., & Sasagawa, S. (2009). Anxiety disorder symptoms in Japanese children and adolescents. *Journal of Anxiety Disorders, 23,* 104–111.

Kashani, J. H., & Orvaschel, H. (1988). Anxiety disorders in mid-adolescence: A community sample. *American Journal of Psychiatry, 145,* 960–964.

Keeley, M., & Storch, E. A. (2009). Anxiety disorders in youth. *Journal of Pediatric Nursing, 24,* 26–40.

Kendall, P. C., Kortlander, E., Chansky, T. E., & Brady, E. U. (1992). Comorbidity of anxiety and depression in youth: treatment implications. *Journal of Consulting and Clinical Psychology, 60,* 869–880.

Kendall, P. C., & Warman, M. J. (1996). Anxiety disorders in youth: Diagnostic consistency across DSM-III-R and DSM-IV. *Journal of Anxiety Disorders, 10,* 453–463.

King, N. J., Ollendick, T. H., & Tonge, B. J. (1995). *School refusal: Assessment and treatment.* Boston: Allyn & Bacon.

Klein, R. G., & Last, C. G. (1989). *Anxiety disorders in children.* Newbury Park, CA: Sage.

Kovacs, M. (1985). The Interview Schedule for Children. *Psychopharmacology Bulletin, 21,* 991–994.

Lewinsohn, P. M., Zinbarg, R., Seeley, J. R., Lewinsohn, M., & Sack, W. H. (1997). Lifetime comorbidity among anxiety disorders and between anxiety disorders and other mental disorders in adolescents. *Journal of Anxiety Disorders, 11,* 377–394.

Lewis, G., & Araya, R. (2001). Classification, disability and the public health agenda. *British Medical Bulletin, 57,* 3–15

Liebowitz, M. R., Barlow, D. H., Ballenger, J. C., Davidson, J., Foa, E. B., Fyer, A. J., Koopman, C., Kozak, M. J., & Spiegel, D. (1998). DSM-IV anxiety disorders: Final overview. In T. A. Widiger, A. J. Frances, H. A. Pincus, R. Ross, M. B. First, W. Davis, & M. Kline (Eds.), *DSM-IV sourcebook (Volume 4)* (pp. 1047–1076), Washington, D. C: American Psychiatric Association.

Lipsitz, J. D., Barlow, D. H., Mannuzza, S., et al. (2002). Clinical features of four DSM-IV specific phobia subtypes. *Journal of Nervous and Mental Disorders, 190*, 471–478.

Lyneham, H. J., Abbott, M. J., & Rapee, R. M. (2007). Interrater reliability of the Anxiety Disorders Interview Schedule for DSM-IV: child and parent version. *Journal of the American Academy of Child and Adolescent Psychiatry, 46*, 731–736.

Masi, G., Mucci, M., Nicoletta, B., Bertini, N., Milantoni, L., & Arcangeli, F. (2005). A naturalistic study of referred children and adolescents with obsessive-compulsive disorder. *Journal of the American Academy of Child and Adolescent Psychiatry, 44*, 673–681.

McGee, R., Feehan, M., Williams, S., Partridge, F., Silva, P. A., & Kelly, J. (1990). DSM-III disorders in a large sample of adolescents. *Journal of the American Academy of Child and Adolescent Psychiatry, 29*, 611–619.

Mellon, R. C., & Moutavelis, A. G. (2007). Structure, developmental course, and correlates of children's anxiety disorder-related behaviour in a Hellenic community sample. *Journal of Anxiety Disorders, 21*, 1–21.

Muris, P., Merckelbach, H., & Collaris, R. (1997). Common childhood fears and their origins. *Behaviour Research and Therapy, 35*, 929–937.

Muris, P., Merckelbach, H., Mayer, B., van Brakel, A., Thissen, S., Moulaert, V., & Gadet, B. (1998). The Screen for Child Anxiety Related Emotional Disorders (SCARED) and traditional childhood anxiety measures. *Journal of Behavior Therapy and Experimental Psychiatry, 29*, 327–339.

Oei, T. P. S., & Loveday, W. A. L. (1997). Management of co-morbid anxiety and alcohol disorders: parallel treatment of disorders. *Drug and Alcohol Review, 16*, 261–274.

Ollendick, T. H. (2009). Social anxiety disorder in youth: An ecological-developmental analysis. In J. A. Mancini & K. A. Roberto (Eds.), *Pathways of human development* (pp. 95–112). New York: Lexington Books.

Ollendick, T. H., King, N. J., & Muris, P. (2004). Phobias in children and adolescents. In M. Maj, H. S. Akiskal, J. J. Lopez-Ibor, & Okasha, A. (Eds.), *Phobias* (pp. 245–279). London: John Wiley & Sons, Inc. Ollendick, T, H., & March, J. S. (Eds.) (2004). *Phobic and anxiety disorders: A clinician's guide to effective psychosocial and pharmacological interventions.* New York: Oxford University Press.

Ollendick, T. H., & March, J. S. (eds.) (2003). *Phobic and Anxiety Disorders: A Clinician's Guide to Effective Psychosocial and Pharmacological Interventions.* New York: Oxford University Press.

Ollendick, T. H., Matson, J. L., & Helsel, W. J. (1985). Fears in children and adolescents: Normative data. *Behaviour Research and Therapy, 23*, 465–467.

Ollendick, T. H., Raishevich, N., Davis, T. E. III., Sirbu, C., & Ost, L.-G. (2010). Phenomenology and psychological characteristics of youth with specific phobias. *Behavior Therapy, 41*, 133–141.

Ollendick, T. H., & Seligman, L. D. (2005). Anxiety disorders. In C. Gillberg, R. Harrington, & H.-C. Steinhausen (Eds.), *A Clinician's handbook of child and adolescent psychiatry* (pp. 144–187). Cambridge: Cambridge University Press.

Piacentini, J., & Bergman, R. L (2000). Obsessive-compulsive disorder in children. *Psychiatric Clinics of North America, 23*, 519–533.

Rapee, A. A., Barrett, P. M., Dadds, M. R., & Evans, L. (1994). Reliability of the DSM-III-R childhood anxiety disorders using structured interview: interrater and parent-child agreement. *Journal of the American Academy of Child and Adolescent Psychiatry, 33*, 984–992.

Rapee, R. M., Craske, M. G., & Barlow, D. H. (1995). Assessment instrument for panic disorder that includes fear of sensation-producing activities: The Albany Panic and Phobia Questionnaire. *Anxiety, 1*, 114–122.

Rapee, R. M., Craske, M. G., Brown, T. A., & Barlow, D. H. (1996). Measurement of perceived control over anxiety related events. *Behaviour Therapy, 27*, 279–293.

Reynolds, C. R., & Richmond, B. O. (1978). What I think and feel: A revised measure of children's manifest anxiety. *Journal of Abnormal Child Psychology, 6,* 271–280.

Schniering, C. A., Hudson, J. L., & Rapee, R. M. (2000). Issues in the diagnosis and assessment of anxiety disorders in children and adolescents. *Clinical Psychology Review, 20,* 453–478.

Seligman, L. D., & Ollendick, T. H. (1999). Anxiety disorders. In H. C. Steinhauser & F. Verhulst (Eds.), *Risks and outcomes in developmental psychopathology* (pp. 103–120). New York: Oxford University Press.

Seligman, L. D., & Ollendick, T. H. (2011). Cognitive Behavior Therapy for anxiety disorders in children and adolescents. *Psychiatric Clinics of North America, 20,* 217–238.

Shaffer, D., Fisher, P., Dulcan, M. K., & Davies, M. (1996). The NIMH Diagnostic Interview Schedule for Children Version 2.3 (DISC-2.3): Description, acceptability, prevalence rates, and performance in the MECA study. *Journal of the American Academy of Child & Adolescent Psychiatry, 35,* 865–877.

Shaffer, D., Schwab-Stone, M., Fisher, P. W., Cohen, P., Piacentini, J., Davies, M., Conners, C. K., & Regier, D. (1993). The Diagostic Interview Schedule for Children—Revised version (DISC-R): I. Preparation, field testing, interrater reliability, and acceptability. *Journal of the American Academy of Child and Adolescent Psychiatry, 32,* 643–650.

Shear, M. K., Bjelland, I., Beesdo, K., Gloster, A. T., & Wittchen, H.-U. (2007). Supplementary dimensional assessment in anxiety disorders. *International Journal of Methods in Psychiatric Research,16* (Suppl 1), 52–64.

Silverman, W. K., & Albano, A. M. (1996). *Anxiety Disorders Interview Schedule for DSM-IV: Child and Parent Versions.* San Antonio, TX: Psychological Corporation.

Silverman, W. K., & Ollendick, T. H. (2008). Assessment of child and adolescent anxiety disorders. In J. Hunsley & E. Mash (Eds.), *A guide to assessments that work* (pp. 181–206). New York: Oxford University Press.

Silverman, W. K., Saavedra, L. M., & Pina, A. A. (2001). Test-retest reliability of anxiety symptoms and diagnoses with anxiety disorders interview schedule for DSM-IV: child and parent versions. *Journal of the American Academy of Child and Adolescent Psychiatry, 40,* 937–944.

Spence, S. H. (1997). The structure of anxiety symptoms among children: A confirmatory factor analytic study. *Journal of Abnormal Psychology, 106,* 280–297.

Spence, S. H. (1998). A measure of anxiety symptoms among children. *Behavior Research and Therapy, 36,* 545–566.

Spence, S. H., Barrett, P. M., & Turner, C. M. (2003). Psychometric properties of the Spence Children's Anxiety Scale with young adolescents. *Journal of Anxiety Disorders, 17,* 605–625.

Strauss, C. C., & Last, C. G. (1993). Social and simple phobias in children. *Journal of Anxiety Disorders, 7,* 141–152.

Su, L., Wang, K., Fan, F., Su, Y., & Gao, X. (2008). Reliability and validity of the Screen for Child Anxiety Related Emotional Disorders (SCARED) in Chinese children. *Journal of Anxiety Disorders, 22,* 612–621.

Wakefield, J. C., & First, M. B. (2003). Clarifying the distinction between disorder an nondisorder. Confronting the overdiagnosis (false-positives) problem in DSM-V. In K. Phillips, M. B. First, H. A. Pincus (Eds.), *Advancing DSM. Dilemmas in psychiatric diagnosis* (pp. 23–55). Arlington (VA): American Psychiatric Association.

Whiteside, S. P., & Brown, A. M. (2008). Exploring the utility of the Spence Children's Anxiety Scales parent- and child-report forms in a North American sample. *Journal of Anxiety Disorders, 22,* 1440–1446.

Whiteside, S. P., & Ollendick, T. H. (2009). Developmental perspectives on anxiety classification. In D McKay, J. S. Abramowitz, S. Taylor, & G. J. Asmundson (Eds.), *Current perspectives on the anxiety disorders: Implications for DSM-V and beyond* (pp. 303–325). New York: Springer.

Wittchen, H.-U., & Jacobi, F. (2005). Size and burden of mental disorder in Europe: A critical review and appraisal of 27 studies. *European Neuropsychopharmacology, 15,* 357–376.

WHO (1992). *The ICD-10 classification of mental and behavioral disorders.* Geneva: World Health Organization.

Zimmerman, M., Chelminski, I., & Young, D. (2004). On the threshold of disorder: a study of the impact of the DSM-IV clinical significance criterion on diagnosing depressive and anxiety disorders in clinical practice. *Journal of Clinical Psychiatry, 65,* 1400–1405.

2

Epidemiology, Comorbidity and Mental Health Services Utilization

Cecilia A. Essau[1] and Jheanell Gabbidon[2]

[1]University of Roehampton, UK
[2]Institute of Psychiatry, UK

Anxiety and fear in children used to be considered as a mild and transitory disturbance which would fade over time as part of normal development. However, studies in the past two decades have shown that a high proportion of children who experience anxiety continue to do so into adolescence and adulthood (Ollendick & King, 1994). In the majority of children, these fears and anxieties are short-lived; however, for some these problems may be excessive and debilitating and may develop into an anxiety disorder (Cohen, Cohen, Kasen et al., 1993; Feehan, McGee, & Williams, 1993; Essau, Conradt, & Petermann, 2000).

In this chapter, the lifetime prevalence, age of onset, use of mental health services, and comorbidity of anxiety disorders in children and adolescents will be presented. The review focuses on findings from large general population studies relating to the following anxiety disorders: separation anxiety disorder (SAD), social phobia, specific phobia, generalized anxiety disorder (GAD), obsessive-compulsive disorder (OCD), panic disorder, post-traumatic stress disorder (PTSD) and agoraphobia.

Epidemiology

Information on the epidemiology of anxiety disorders in children and adolescents has accumulated over the past two decades. This increase is related to the development of diagnostic criteria in our classification systems – International Classification of Diseases (ICD) and Diagnostic and Statistical Manual (DSM) – which make it possible to operationalize and develop highly structured diagnostic interview schedules based on these criteria. Diagnostic interviews such as the Anxiety Disorder Interview Schedule for Children (Silverman & Albano, 1996) not only reduce the observer, information, and criteria variance when using less structured diagnostic instruments, but also allow for comparison of results across studies. Due to their highly structured forms, less

The Wiley-Blackwell Handbook of The Treatment of Childhood and Adolescent Anxiety, First Edition.
Edited by Cecilia A. Essau and Thomas H. Ollendick.
© 2013 John Wiley & Sons, Ltd. Published 2013 by John Wiley & Sons, Ltd.

clinical judgement is needed and many of them can be administered by trained layman interviewers. Another related development is the application of a lifetime approach in addition to several levels of cross-sectional diagnoses when estimating the prevalence of psychiatric disorders. This approach enables the determination of the occurrence, clustering, and sequence of syndromes and disorders over the person's lifespan. Such an approach, originally introduced and used in the Epidemiologic Catchment Area study (Regier, Meyer, Kramer et al., 1984), has been adopted in child epidemiologic studies. Further progress in epidemiological studies involving children and adolescents is related to the introduction of systematic coordination of information from various informants such as from parents, teachers, clinicians, and the children or adolescents themselves (Verhulst, 1995). Thus, for example, we now have parallel versions of diagnostic interview schedules that can be used to interview children with anxiety disorders and their parents.

Before reviewing the prevalence of anxiety disorder, it is important to highlight several issues: (a) Almost all of the studies have used two versions of the DSM (i.e., the DSM-III-R and DSM-IV), as well as the ICD-10. Although the diagnostic criteria for some anxiety disorders only differ slightly in DSM-IV and ICD-10 classification systems and between DSM-III-R and DSM-IV, they have an impact on the over-all prevalence and comorbidity rates of anxiety disorders (Kessler, Ruscio, Shear, & Wittchen, 2009). For example, in ICD-10, SAD is diagnosed if the symptoms are present before the age of six, while in DSM-IV they should be evident before the age of 18 years. ICD-10 criteria also state that no SAD and social phobia diagnoses should be given if the child has GAD. (b) Age of onset is based on retrospective reports of the children and adolescents who are asked whether or not they have experienced a particular syndrome. As such, age of onset information may be subject to recall bias although less than would be expected in adults. (c) Furthermore, some questions in interview schedules may be hard to understand, particularly for younger children, which may lead to underreporting biases (Kessler, Berglund, Demler, Jin, & Walters, 2005). (d) Some studies collect information from both the children themselves and from their parents. As there are no agreed rules on how best to use information from various informants, studies vary in the way in which they combine information in order to estimate prevalence rates (Fleming, Offord & Boyle, 1989; Roberts, Attkisson, & Rosenblatt, 1998). (e) Diagnostic systems change over time, and in DSM-IV, there is the additional requirement for an impairment criterion. Studies have indicated that the application of an impairment criterion lowers the prevalence rates of psychiatric disorders, particularly anxiety disorders (Bird et al., 1988; Leung, Hung, Ho et al., 2008; Roberts, Roberts, & Chen, 1997; Shaffer, Fisher, Dulcan, & Davies, 1996). Furthermore, there is lack of agreement on how to operationalize an impairment cri-terion, with different operational definitions producing different prevalence rates. For example, the use of global scales such as the Child Global Assessment Scale, and the clinical vignette approach in assessing impairment tend to give lower prevalence esti-mates than those dependent on disorder-specific impairment in Diagnostic Interview Schedule for Children – version 4 (DISC-IV) (McArdle, Prosser, & Kolvin, 2004; Roberts, Roberts, & Xing, 2007). (f) Studies also differ in the number and subtype of anxiety disorders included in the summary category of "any anxiety disorders."

All these points may contribute to variations in the prevalence of anxiety disorders across studies so that caution should be made when comparing the prevalence rates of anxiety disorders across studies. Thus, differences in the prevalence of anxiety disorders may not be a true reflection of regional differences in these disorders. However, it should also be noted that with few exception (Adewuya, Ola, & Adewumi, 2007; Gau, Chong, Chen, & Cheng, 2005; Leung, Hung, Ho et al., 2008), most community studies on the prevalence of anxiety disorders have been conducted in Western, industrialized countries.

Large community studies have consistently indicated that anxiety disorders are one of the most common psychiatric disorders in children and adolescents. The lifetime prevalence of any anxiety disorders in children and adolescents range from 15 to 31.9% (Table 2.1). A recent finding from the National Comorbidity Survey Replication – Adolescent Supplement (NCS-A) (Merikangas, He, Burstein et al., 2010) showed 31.9% of the adolescents met the lifetime prevalence of any anxiety disorders. The period prevalence (1 year or 6-months) for any anxiety disorders are not significantly lower than the lifetime rates, with values ranging from 3.1 to 18%. Within the subtypes of anxiety disorders, the most common are specific phobia, whereas panic disorder, PTSD, OCD, and GAD are less common (Table 2.2). For example, in the Bremen Adolescent Study (Essau et al., 2000), the lifetime rates of phobias were about 3%; the rates of PTSD and OCD were less than 2%, and that of panic disorder and GAD were less than 1%.

It is interesting to note that the prevalence of anxiety disorders varied depending on whether an impairment criterion is applied. For example, in a study by Leung, Hung, Ho et al. (2008) in Hong Kong, the point prevalence for "any disorder" was 16.4%, down from 38.4% when only symptom criteria were used (57% reduction). Among diagnostic groupings, anxiety disorders were most affected. The prevalence of "any anxiety disorder" was 6.9%, down from 30.2%, indicating a 77% reduction. Within the specific types of anxiety disorders, the point prevalence for agoraphobia, specific phobia, OCD, social phobia, GAD, and SAD were respectively 0.4, 3.4, 0.7, 2.6, 0.4, and 0.7%, which dropped from 4.4, 22.0, 2.0, 7.2, 0.9, and 1.5%.

Among children and adolescents in clinical settings, the prevalence of anxiety disorders based on ICD-10 criteria plus impairment rating was 5.7% (Esbjørn, Hoeyer, Dyrborg, Leth, & Kendall, 2010). Of those with any anxiety disorders, "other disorder" was the most common, with a prevalence of 42.8%, followed by GAD (26.5%), and social phobia (18.7%). The lowest was found for SAD (6.6%). It should be noted that in ICD-10, "other disorder" includes nine anxiety disorders: phobic anxiety disorders; other phobic anxiety disorders; phobic anxiety disorder, unspecified; other anxiety disorders; panic disorder; mixed anxiety and depressive disorder; other mixed anxiety disorders; other specified anxiety disorders; and anxiety disorder, unspecified.

Gender: Anxiety disorders are significantly more common in girls than in boys, with a 2:1 to 3:1 female preponderance (Costello, Mustillo, Erkanli, et al., 2003; Essau et al., 2000); this gender difference remains throughout adulthood. Gender difference in anxiety disorders generally occurs at an early age in that by the age of six years, twice as many girls than boys have experienced an anxiety disorder (Lewinsohn, Gotlib, Lewinsohn, Seeley, & Allen, 1998). Girls were also over-represented among those with current and past anxiety disorders (Lewinsohn et al., 1998). However, for those with an anxiety disorder, no gender differences were found as to when they experienced their first anxiety episode (i.e., age of onset) and the duration of their first anxiety episode. Consistent with Lewinsohn et al.'s (1998) findings, Essau et al.

Table 2.1 Prevalence (%) of anxiety disorders in children and adolescents.

Authors	Country	Diagnostic criteria	N	Age (years)	Informants	Lifetime	Point
Essau et al. (2000)	Germany	DSM-IV	1035	12–17	Child/adolescents	18.6	11.3 +
Wittchen et al. (1998)	Germany	DSM-IV	3021	14–24	Child/adolescents	14.4	9.3 +
Wittchen et al. (1999)	Germany	DSM-IV	1395	14–17	Child/adolescents	21.3	14.5 +
Verhulst et al. (1997)	Netherlands	DSM-III-R	780	13–18	Child/adolescents	—	10.0 ++
					Parent	—	16.5 ++
Steinhausen et al. (1998)	Switzerland	DSM-III-R	379	6–17	Parent	—	11.4 ++
Leung et al. (2008)	China	DSM-IV	541	Mean = 13.8 years	Child & Parent	—	30.2* +
					Parent	—	6.9** +
Gau et al. (2005)	Taiwan	DSM-IV	1070	7th Grade	Child/adolescents	—	9.2 +++
			1051	8th Grade	Child/adolescents	—	7.4 +++
			1035	9th Grade	Child/adolescents	—	3.1 +++
Wells et al. (2006)	New Zealand	DSM-IV	12,992	16–24	Child/adolescents	—	17.7
Romano et al. (2001)	Canada	DSM-III-R	1201	14–17	Child/adolescents	—	8.9 ++
					Parent	—	6.5 ++
					Parent/child/ adolescents	—	14.0 ++
Canino et al. (2004)	Puerto Rico	DSM-IV	1897	4–16	Parent/child/ adolescents	—	9.5* +
					adolescents	—	6.9** +
Lewinsohn et al. (1993)	USA	DSM-III-R	1710	13–19	Child/adolescents	8.8	—
Costello et al. (1996)	USA	DSM-III-R	4500	9, 11, 13	Child/adolescents	—	5.69 +++
Merikangas et al. (2010)	USA	DSM-IV	10,123	13–18	Child/adolescents	31.9	—

* = Symptom criteria only; ** = symptom + impairment criteria; + = 12 months; ++ = 6 months; +++ = 3 months.

Table 2.2 Prevalence (%) of subtypes of anxiety disorders in children and adolescents.

Authors	Informants	Specific phobia		Social phobia		Agoraphobia		Panic disorder		GAD/OAD		SAD	
		L	P	L	P	L	P	L	P	L	P	L	P
Essau et al. (2000)	C/A	3.5	2.7	1.6	1.4	4.1	2.7	0.5	0.5	0.4	0.2	—	—
Witchen et al. (1998)	C/A	2.3	1.8	3.5	2.6	2.6	1.6	1.6	1.2	0.8	0.5	—	—
Witchen et al. (1999)	C/A	17.1	10.9	3.7	2.9	2.8	2.1	0.7	0.3	0.3	0.2	—	—
Verhulst et al. (1997)	C/A	—	9.2	—	6.3	—	1.9	—	0.3	—	0.7	—	—
Steinhausen et al. (1998)	P	—	4.5	—	3.7	—	0.7	—	0.2	—	0.6	—	—
	P	—	5.8	—	4.7	—	1.9	—	—	—	0.5	—	0.75
Gau et al. (2005)	C/A	—	5.0	—	3.4	—	0.2	—	0.2	—	0.7	—	0.3
	C/A	—	5.6	—	1.8	—	0.0	—	0.1	—	0.3	—	0.1
	C/A	—	0.7	—	2.0	—	0.0	—	0.0	—	0.4	—	0.0
Wells et al. (2006)	C/A	—	7.3	—	5.1	—	0.6	—	1.7	—	2.0	—	—
Canino et al. (2004)	C/A/P	—	—	—	2.5	—	—	—	0.5	—	2.2	—	5.7*
		—	—	—	2.8	—	—	—	0.7	—	2.4	—	3.1**
Lewinsohn et al. (1993)	C/A	1.99	1.40	1.46	0.94	0.70	0.41	0.82	0.35	1.29	0.47	4.21	0.18
Costello et al. (1996)	C/A	—	3.49	—	0.27	—	0.07	—	0.03	—	1.67	—	3.49
Merikangas et al. (2010)	C/A	19.3	—	9.1	—	2.4	—	2.3	—	2.2	—	7.6	—
Adewuya et al. (2007)	C	—	2.5	—	4.8	—	—	—	2.4	—	3.6	—	2.1

L = Lifetime; P = Point; * = symptom criteria only; ** = symptom + impairment criteria; + = 12 months; ++ = 6 months; +++ = 3 months; C = child; A = adolescent; P = parent.

(2000) reported girls to have a significantly higher rate of anxiety disorders than boys. GAD was the only disorder to affect an equal number of boys and girls (Essau et al., 2000). In the NCS-A, the greatest gender difference was found for PTSD (Merikangas et al., 2010). Similar to findings in studies conducted in Western countries, a study in Taiwan found girls to have higher rates of anxiety disorders than boys, particularly, higher rates of specific phobia and social phobia.

Several speculations have been offered to explain this gender difference. First, it is assumed that gender differences are genetically and biologically determined (Lewinsohn et al., 1998). Second, because of the common co-occurrence of anxiety and depression, it has been argued that the preponderance of anxiety disorder among girls may be related to their general tendency to be ruminative about current and future events (Lewinsohn et al., 1998). Third, this may be due to gender difference in experiences and social roles in boys and girls (Lewinsohn et al., 1998). To examine this hypothesis, Lewinsohn et al. (1998) investigated a wide range of psychosocial factors that could help explain the female preponderance for anxiety disorders. Ten out of 13 psychosocial factors examined were associated with both anxiety and gender. These factors were: major life events, self-consciousness, low self-esteem, low social self-competence, poor coping skills, low family social support, physical illness, lifetime physical symptoms, and emotional reliance. Significant gender differences remained after controlling for these psychological variables. It was concluded that gender differences in anxiety disorders cannot be fully explained by differing social roles and experiences. They argued that the female vulnerability to anxiety is "associated with some type of genetic, rather than purely environmentally determined, gender differences" (p. 113). Based on her review of the literature on gender differences in psychopathology, Seeman (1997) agreed and stated that "the estrogens are neuro-protective with respect to neuronal degeneration, growth, and susceptibility to toxins. The cyclic fluctuations of estrogens and progesterone enhance the response to stress, which confers susceptibility to depression and anxiety" (p. 1641).

Age: Findings on the prevalence of anxiety disorders by age vary across studies. In the recent NCS-A study (Merikangas et al., 2010), anxiety disorders were equally distributed across age groups; however, considerable variations were found within the subtypes of anxiety disorders. That is, PTSD, GAD, panic disorder, and social phobia demonstrated a consistent increase with age (Merikangas et al., 2010). In the Bremen Adolescent Study (Essau et al., 2000), the prevalence of anxiety disorders increased with age, with the greatest increase occurring between age 12–13 and 14–15 years. Among those in the clinical settings, SAD, GAD, and social phobia have been found to increase with age from preschool to school age (Esbjørn et al., 2010).

Gender and age differences seem to differ across subtypes of anxiety disorders (Beesdo, Knappe, & Pine, 2009). In the Early Developmental Stages of Psychopathology study (EDSP), the prevalence of specific phobia showed a clear gender difference in childhood, with a ratio 3:1 by age 10 years. Agoraphobia had a strong and steady increase for females after the age of 6, whereas among males, a less clear pattern was seen. Specifically, agoraphobia showed a slight increase of incidence between the ages of 15 and 20, and a leveling off after the age of 25 years. Panic disorder revealed an increased incidence in females between the ages of 13 and 26 years; males displayed lower rates of panic disorder and that the period of increased incidence was less pronounced. In a longitudinal study by Costello et al. (2003), by the age of 12 years, SAD had almost disappeared, particularly in boys. The results further indicated an increase in rates of social phobia in girls at the onset of adolescence which was not observed in boys. The mid-adolescent years revealed a slight increase in GAD and panic disorder across both boys and girls.

When analyzing the rates of disorders by age and gender, Essau and colleagues (2000) showed significant gender difference beginning at age 14, with significantly higher rates found in females than in males. Some authors have found a similar increase in the prevalence of anxiety disorders after puberty (Rutter, 1986). This higher prevalence of anxiety disorders appeared to be associated with physical maturity. As shown in a study by Hayward and colleagues (1992) (Hayward, Killen, Hammer, Litt, Wilson, Simmonds, & Taylor, 1992), sexual maturity tended to be highly correlated with an increase in panic attack.

Age of onset. Anxiety disorders have their onset generally in childhood (Beesdo, Pine, Lieb, & Wittchen, 2010; Kessler, Berglund, Demler et al., 2005; Last, Perrin, Hersen, & Kazdin, 1996), with the earliest age of onset being found for SAD. Most children and adolescents with some specific phobias (animal, blood injection injury, and environmental type) also reported the onset of their disorders before the age of 12 years, followed by the onset of social phobia in late childhood and throughout adolescence (Kessler et al., 2005). On average, the first onset of panic disorder, agoraphobia, and GAD is in late adolescence or in early adulthood (Beesdo et al., 2010; Kessler et al., 2005). Similar findings have been reported in the NCS-A in that of all the psychiatric disorders examined, anxiety disorders occurred the earliest (Merikangas et al., 2010). Specifically, about half (50%) of the adolescents with any anxiety disorder had their onset by the age of six. The onset leveled off after age 12 years; the median age of onset for anxiety disorders was 6 years. Furthermore, in a prospective study conducted in New Zealand, more than one-third of the persons who had an anxiety disorder at 32 years of age had an anxiety disorder before the age of 15 years (Gregory, Caspi, Moffitt, Koenen, Eley, & Poulton, 2007). The onset of PTSD is more varied as it depends on the age when the trauma occurred.

Psychosocial Impairment

A high majority of those with anxiety disorders were severely impaired in their daily life and activities (at school/work, social, and leisure time) during the worst episode of their disorders (Essau et al., 2000). The most impaired were children with specific phobia, followed by those with GAD. Wittchen et al. (1998) similarly found specific phobia, GAD, and panic disorder to be associated with severe psychosocial impairment during the worst episode of their disorders. A recent study by Lack, Storch, Keeley et al. (2009) showed that the presence of OCD was associated with poorer quality of life compared to those with other disorders, more so among females than males. This finding was interpreted as indicating that OCD has a larger impact on ratings of quality of life for girls than for boys.

Children with anxiety disorders also had a poor relationship with their peers (Bowen, Offord, & Boyle, 1990; Messer & Beidel, 1994; Strauss, Lahey, Frick, Frame, & Hynd, et al., 1988). In a study by Ezpeleta, Keeler, Erkanli, et al. (2001), the largest impact of child anxiety is on family interaction. Studies have also reported children with anxiety disorders to be impaired in their social activities and in school activities; interestingly, it was the teachers, and not the parents that reported these impairments in the children (Benjamin et al., 1990). Two studies by Ialongo and colleagues (Ialongo, Edelsohn, Wertharmer-Larsson, Crockett, & Kellam, 1994, 1995) have also found the presence of anxiety symptoms to be associated with low achievement in reading and in mathematics.

Mental Health Services Utilization

Despite the availability of effective treatments, only a small proportion of children and adolescents with an anxiety disorder receive mental health services. For example, in one American study (Whitaker, Johnson, Shaffer et al., 1990), only about half of the adolescents with an anxiety disorder made some type of consultation for emotional problems from a general health provider and mental health professional. Most of these visits were made by those with GAD (60%) and OCD (25%), and less frequently by those with panic disorder (14%). In another American study (Keller, Lavori, Wunder, Beardslee, Schwartz, & Roth, 1992), only 24% of the children with anxiety received treatment for these anxiety disorders. Of those who sought treatment, 13% received individual counseling, 5% received family counseling, and 5% received psychological evaluation (without treatment). In the Great Smoky Mountain Study (Burns, Costello, Angold et al., 1995), the main demographic predictors for the utilization of mental health services were being male and living in poverty. No differences were identified between children living in rural areas and those living in urban areas irrespective of the decreased accessibility to services in rural areas. In a study in New Zealand (Fergusson, Horwood, & Lynskey, 1993), even fewer (9%) of the children with anxiety or mood disorder used some forms of health services for their conditions. The use of health services was significantly affected by the presence of comorbid disorders, with service utilization rates increasing significantly with the increased number of comorbid disorders.

Among German adolescents, only 18.2% of those adolescents that met the diagnostic criteria for anxiety disorders used mental health services (Essau, 2005); this low rate of mental health utilization was surprising because of the comprehensive coverage and the non-gatekeeper system in the German health system at the time of the study. Adolescents who sought mental health services, compared to those without any treatment, had significantly higher scores on psychological distress, as measured by the SCL-90-R. That is, adolescents who received mental health services compared to those that did not receive such services had significantly higher scores on the global severity index, and on the following subscales of the SCL-90-R: obsessive-compulsive behavior, interpersonal sensitivity, depression, anger-hostility, paranoid ideation, and psychoticism.

Within the anxiety disorders, adolescents with PTSD (47.1%) had the highest rate of mental health services utilization, followed by those with OCD (30.8%) and GAD (25%) (Essau, 2005). Most treatment was carried out in outpatient settings (88.3%), with almost half of the adolescents seeking help from school psychologists (Essau, 2005). Treatment received at an inpatient setting was rare: Only 5.9% of the adolescents sought treatment in an inpatient setting. About 5.9% received help from "other social services," such as telephone counseling (e.g., tele-care) and self-help groups. Mental health services utilization was associated with past suicide attempt, parental anxiety, parental depression, older age, and the presence of comorbid disorders. The frequency of any mental health services increased with the number of comorbid disorders. About 10.6% of the pure anxiety cases reported having sought mental health services, compared to 22.9% of those with one comorbid disorder, and 32.1% of those with at least two comorbid disorders. However, when males and females were analyzed separately, the presence of comorbid disorders was significantly associated with the use of mental health services only for males, whereas no such association was found for females. This study also indicated that 84.3% of the chronic anxiety cases had never received mental health services.

According to Burns et al. (1995), the educational sector played a major role in addressing the needs of children with mental health problems. Specifically, 70–80% of the children who reported seeking help for a mental health problem including anxiety were seen by guidance counselors or school psychologists. The study also revealed that there are a substantial number of children diagnosed as having a psychiatric disorder and functional impairment whose needs are not being met.

Comorbid Patterns

Since the seminal paper on comorbidity by Caron and Rutter (1991), a large body of research has been conducted on comorbidity in psychopathology. One of the most consistent findings in childhood and adolescent psychopathology is the high comorbidity rates. As reported by Anderson and colleagues (1987), about 60% of children and adolescents with a diagnosable condition have two or more additional disorders. Angold and Costello (1992) similarly found, after reviewing six community studies, that the presence of one disorder in adolescents increased the probability for another disorder by at least 20 times.

In addition to being prevalent, anxiety disorders frequently co-occur both within anxiety disorders (i.e., homotypic) and with other mental disorders (i.e., heterotypic), with up to 72% of those who meet the diagnosis of anxiety disorders meeting criteria for at least one other psychiatric disorder (Angold, Costello, & Erkanli, 1999; Essau et al., 2000; Feehan, McGee, Nada-Raja, & Williams, 1994; Lewinsohn, Zinbarg, Seeley, Lewinsohn, Sack, 1997; Kashani & Orvaschel, 1988; Strauss & Last, 1993). As shown by Lewinsohn and colleagues (1997), having an anxiety disorder was significantly associated with six of the nine other psychiatric disorders. The disorders that commonly co-occur with anxiety disorders include depression, substance use, and disruptive behavior disorders.

In the section that follows, we review the comorbidity between anxiety and other psychiatric disorders, as well as the impact of comorbidity on assessment and treatment.

Comorbidity within anxiety disorders

Lewinsohn and colleagues (1997) examined lifetime comorbidities of anxiety disorders in a general population sample of adolescents aged 14–19 years. Among those with a lifetime anxiety disorder, 81.3% had only one anxiety disorder, 15.7% had two, and 3% had three anxiety disorders. Of all the 15 pairs of anxiety disorders,

10 were significant. The highest comorbidity rates were found for panic and OCD, followed by OCD and overanxious, as well as social phobia and OCD. Similar findings have been reported by Essau (2003) when investigating the comorbidity of anxiety disorders in German adolescents aged 12–17 years old. The results revealed a relatively low comorbidity rate of 14.1% within the anxiety disorders. Conversely, there was a high comorbidity rate between anxiety disorders and other psychiatric disorders, where 51% of the adolescents diagnosed as having an anxiety disorder had other psychiatric disorders. The finding that homotypic comorbidity is less common than heterotypic comorbidity has also been replicated in clinical settings. As reported by Esbjørn et al. (2010), only 2.8% of children and adolescents with any anxiety disorders had received more than one anxiety diagnosis, compared to 42.9% of those with heterotypic comorbidity.

Almost all of those with more than one anxiety disorder were females (i.e., two males and 23 females) (Lewinsohn et al., 1997). Females' higher rates of intra-anxiety comorbidity compared to males were explained in terms of gender differences in behavioral inhibition (Biederman, Rosenbaum, Chaloff, & Kagan, 1995). It was argued that females' greater risk of having multiple anxiety disorders may be mediated by their higher levels of behavioral inhibition, and that behavioral inhibition may be associated with the occurrence of intra-anxiety comorbidity (Biederman et al., 1995).

The number of children and adolescents with only one anxiety disorder decreases with age; by late adolescence or early adulthood, the co-occurrence of multiple anxiety disorders is more common (Wittchen, Lecrubier, Beesdo et al., 2003). The number of anxiety disorders also significantly predicted the development of secondary disorder (Woodward & Fergusson, 2001). Specifically, the number of anxiety disorders in adolescence was significantly associated with risk of development of substance dependence and suicidal behavior in adulthood, as well as with other negative developmental outcomes (e.g., educational underachievement).

Overall, the findings above showed that the comorbidity rates within the anxiety disorders have been reported to be lower than the rates between anxiety and other psychiatric disorders (Essau, 2003; Lewinsohn et al., 1997).

Depressive disorders

Depressive disorders are characterized by the presence of depressed moods together with a set of additional symptoms, persisting over time, and causing disruption and impairment of function. Two depressive disorders commonly reported in adolescents are major depressive disorder and dysthymic disorder (APA, 1994). Major depressive disorder denotes a severe and acute form of depressive disorder. Dysthymic disorder is a chronic, but less severe form of depressive disorder.

The most common comorbid disorder with anxiety is depression, with comorbidity rates ranging from 50 to 72% (Anderson, Williams, McGee, & Silva, 1987; Lewinsohn et al., 1997; McGee, Feehan, Williams, et al., 1990). The common comorbidity between anxiety and depressive disorders has been interpreted as giving support to the tripartite model (Clark & Watson, 1991) which suggested that both disorders contain significant overlap and differentiability. The overlap aspect suggests that anxiety and depression share a nonspecific component of generalized affective distress or negative affect. The differentiability component considers anhedonia or diminished positive affect to be a factor that contains features that are specific to depression, whereas the physiological symptoms of hyperarousal component contains a factor that is specific to anxiety.

Among those with both anxiety and depression, anxiety generally occurs before depression (Lewinsohn et al., 1997; McGee, Feehan, & Williams, 1990). For example, data of the Oregon Adolescent Depression Project have shown (Rohde, Lewinsohn, & Seeley, 1991) that 85% of comorbid cases in their study of adolescents had an anxiety disorder before they developed depression. Follow-up of their sample 1 year later (Orvaschel, Lewinsohn, & Seeley, 1995) provided supportive evidence. Whereas 42% of the T1 anxiety disorder cases had a major depression at Time 2, only 6.5% of the Time 1 depressed cases had an anxiety disorder diagnosis at Time 2. However, there are variations within the anxiety disorders, in that specific phobia, SAD, overanxious disorder, and social phobia come before depression, but less so for panic and OCD (Lewinsohn et al., 1997). These findings suggest that in many cases the anxiety disorder may play a role in the chain of events leading to depression.

In the Bremen Adolescent Study (Essau, 2003), most adolescents with both anxiety and depression had anxiety before depression (72%), 12% had depression before anxiety, and 16% reported the onset of these disorders within the same year. Within the anxiety disorders, half of those with agoraphobia, anxiety NOS (not otherwise specified), and generalized anxiety disorder first had these disorders before major depression. All of those with social and specific phobia, first had these two subtypes of anxiety disorders before depression. About half of those with panic disorder and depression experienced the onset of these disorders within the same year.

Some studies have examined the characteristics of anxiety disorders which predict the development of depression. Features of anxiety disorders that increased the risk of depression included: the presence of more than one anxiety disorder, severe impairment due to the anxiety disorder, and comorbid panic disorder (Bittner, Goodwin, Wittchen et al., 2004). In a study by Beesdo, Bittner, Pine et al. (2007), the characteristics of social anxiety disorder that predicted an increased risk to develop depression were degree of impairment, persistence, and several indicators of greater severity of social anxiety disorder such as a higher number of social anxiety situations and anxiety cognitions, occurrence of panic attacks, the fear of an anxiety attack in social situations, and a higher Symptom Checklist-90-Revised phobic anxiety subscale score.

Substance use disorders

SUD includes substance dependence and substance abuse, the former refers to a physiological and/or psychological dependence on a substance. The latter is a less severe symptom presentation than substance dependence. A person with a substance abuse disorder may continue using the substance despite problems in various life domains.

High comorbidity rates between anxiety disorders and SUD have been reported in both clinical samples and in the general population. For example, in the Bremen Adolescent Study (Essau, 2003), 11.5% of the adolescents who met the diagnosis of any anxiety disorders also met the diagnosis of any SUD. Within the SUD, the disorders that most commonly co-occur with anxiety disorders were alcohol use disorders

(8.85%) and cannabis use disorders (8.33%). Amphetamine (1.04%) and hallucinogen use disorders (1.04%) co-occurred less frequently with anxiety disorders. In the Oregon Adolescent Depression Project (OADP), 11.9% of the anxiety cases also had alcohol abuse/dependence (Lewinsohn et al., 1997). In a study by Clark and Jacob (1992), 50% of the adolescents with SUD had at least one lifetime anxiety disorder. The temporal sequence of anxiety and SUD is variable, depending on the type of anxiety disorders. Social phobia and agoraphobia usually precede alcohol abuse, while panic disorder and generalized anxiety disorder tend to follow the onset of alcohol abuse (Kushner, Abram, & Borchardt, 2000).

As anxiety disorders – particularly social anxiety and SUD – co-occur frequently, three models have been put forward to explain the comorbidity between social anxiety and SUD: (i) tension reduction theory (i.e., alcohol use to relieve tension in social situations; Conger, 1956); (ii) stress response dampening model (i.e., use of alcohol to reduce reactivity to stressful situations; Khantzian, 1997); and the (iii) self-medication hypothesis (i.e., the psychotropic effects of alcohol on an individual's anxiety symptoms could lead to the development of alcohol dependence). However, studies that attempt to test these models have reported inconsistent findings.

Disruptive behavior disorders

Disruptive behavior disorders include three separate disorders: conduct disorder, oppositional defiant disorder, and attention-deficit/hyperactivity disorder (ADHD). Conduct disorder is a persistent behavior pattern in which the basic rights of others or age-appropriate societal norms are repeatedly violated (APA, 1994). Oppositional defiant disorder (ODD) is a recurring pattern of defiant, disobedient, negativistic, and hostile behavior toward authority figures. ADHD is a persistent pattern of inattention and/or hyperactivity-impulsivity which is more severe and frequent than is commonly seen in persons of similar age and developmental level.

Several studies have shown anxiety disorders to occur frequently in children and adolescents with conduct disorder, ODD, and ADHD (Benjamin, Rosenbaum, Hirshfeld et al., 1990; Bird, Gould, & Staghezza, 1993; Cohen et al., 1993). In a study by Mancini, Van Ameringen, Oakman, and Figueiredo (1999), the prevalence of anxiety disorders comorbid with ADHD has been reported to be as high as 50% (Mancini et al., 1999). Among children with ADHD, high rates of agoraphobia, simple phobias, separation anxiety disorders, social phobias, and OCD have also been reported (Spencer, Biederman, & Wilens, 1998). However, some other studies failed to find a significant association between anxiety disorders and disruptive disorders (Lewinsohn et al., 1997). Costello et al.'s (2003) longitudinal study also showed significant comorbidity between anxiety disorders and behavioral disorders; however, these associations disappeared after controlling for other forms of comorbidity (Costello et al., 2003).

Meaning and Impact of Comorbidity

Despite the high comorbidity rates between addictive problems and other psychiatric disorders, the meaning of comorbidity for psychopathology and classification issues remains unclear. There has been much debate as to whether comorbidity is "real" or an artifact. Artifactual explanations include methodological and assessment biases.

Methodological biases include treatment or sampling bias in which adolescents with two or more disorders have a greater chance to be hospitalized or treated. As such, the clinic samples generally comprised individuals with comorbid disorders. This phenomenon arises because the chance of being referred to mental health services is higher for adolescents with a comorbid disorder than for those with only one disorder (i.e., Berkson's bias). Comorbidity found in clinical settings could reflect severe psychopathology and psychosocial impairment; thus, adolescents with comorbid disorders are more likely to be referred than those with non-comorbid disorders.

Assessment bias may include the lack of discrete diagnostic definitions in which a large degree of symptom overlap exists between two diagnostic categories, or the application of diagnostic hierarchies which may mask an association between disorders (Widiger & Ford-Black, 1994). As argued by Maj (2005), comorbidity may occur as a by-product of some specific features of our current classification systems, and claimed "If demarcations are made where they do not exist in nature, the probability that several diagnosis have to be made in an individual case will obviously increase" (p. 182). He further argued that by artificially splitting a clinical problem into pieces not only prevents a holistic approach to the individual, but also encourages unwarranted polypharmacy.

However, there are also some indicators to support the presence of "true" comorbidity. Rutter (1986), for example, has argued that the core of every disorder is a struggle for adaptation, but the way in which the phenotype is expressed depends on environmental conditions and person–environment interactions. According to Merikangas (1989) the co-occurrence of disorders could be etiologic in that one disorder causes the second disorder (i.e., causal association), or that the two disorders are manifestations of the same underlying etiologic factors (i.e., common etiology), or that it may reflect different stages of the same disease, or that one disorder lowers the threshold for the expression of the other.

Regardless of the meaning of comorbidity, knowledge on the impact of comorbid disorders on the treatment outcome of anxiety disorders in children and adolescents is important. However, studies in this area are rare despite the number of studies showing the high prevalence of psychiatric disorders in children and adolescents with anxiety disorders. As discussed earlier, the presence of comorbid disorders is generally associated with higher levels of severity and impairment than is the case for a single disorder (Manassis & Hood, 1998). It is therefore logical to assume that the effectiveness of therapy for anxiety disorders may be reduced among children with comorbid disorders (Rapee, 2003).

An early study by Kendall, Brady, and Verduin (2001) failed to find any significant difference in the treatment outcome among children with one anxiety disorder, compared to those with comorbid anxiety disorders, and children with comorbid externalizing disorders. A similar finding was reported by Rapee (2003) in that the treatment outcome for children and adolescents with anxiety disorders with and without comorbid disorders did not significantly differ at the end treatment; positive gain was maintained at 12-month follow-up. Overall, these studies indicated that the effects of treatment were not negatively affected by the presence of comorbid disorders.

Ollendick, Öst, Reuterskiöld, and Costa (2010) recently examined the effect of comorbid specific phobias and other anxiety disorders on treatment outcomes of children with various kinds of specific phobia (i.e., animal, natural environment, situational, and "other" types of phobia). Their findings showed that the presence of comorbid phobias or anxiety disorders did not affect treatment outcomes. Although the treatment was developed for specific phobias, the clinical severity of comorbid phobia and anxiety disorders (i.e., GAD, SAD, and social phobia) was significantly reduced at post-treatment and 6-month follow-up. These findings suggest that comorbid phobias responded similarly to the CBT treatment independent of the type of phobia that was the focus of treatment.

Assessment Implications of Comorbidity

The high comorbidity rates among the anxiety disorders suggest that when assessing children and adolescents with these disorders, a wide range of other disorders should be assessed routinely, especially because some of the symptoms of anxiety disorders do resemble physical symptoms. As such, anxiety disorders are often misdiagnosed or underdiagnosed. Another issue is related to difficulties in differentiating impairment due to anxiety from impairment due to other psychiatric disorders. It is therefore important to use diagnostic interview schedules because of their comprehensive coverage of psychiatric disorders and their ability to help reduce variability through clear specification, definition, and instruction of the items involved.

In many settings, evaluation of psychiatric symptoms occurs only at in-take; however, because comorbid psychiatric disorders may emerge and develop at a different pace and severity during the treatment period, the presence of a wide variety of psychiatric symptoms should be monitored. This means that assessment should be made on an ongoing basis or at specific intervals to capture the emergence of any new disorders as well as any clinical changes in the primary diagnosis. This in turn may help to understand the sequencing of disorders and to tailor treatment for anxiety disorders and their interaction with other disorders (Piotrowski, 2007).

Anxiety disorders with comorbid disorders will naturally take more time to administer assessments. Both due to the complexity and time-consuming nature of administration and interpretation, the cost of assessing comorbid disorders will be higher than when assessing anxiety disorders only (Piotrowski, 2007).

Treatment Implications of Comorbidity

The cost of treating comorbid disorder also tends to be higher due to the burden of needing more services and integrated care. For example, Kessler and colleagues (1994) reported that six out of ten individuals with multiple comorbid disorders received treatment. Findings such as this stresses the importance of improving our intervention programs so that those with comorbid disorders could be treated effectively. Treatment of anxiety disorders with comorbid disorders also require knowledge on how treatment for one disorder may interact with treatment of other disorders (Ollendick, Jarrett, Grills-Taquechel, Hovey, & Wolff, 2008).

As reported earlier, anxious children and adolescents with comorbid disorders tend to report more severe psychosocial impairment in diverse areas of life than those with only anxiety disorders (Kelly, Cornelius, & Clark, 2004). For this reason, treatment needs to be multifaceted by not focusing only on the anxiety disorders, but also on the comorbid disorders and a range of interrelated problems. It also needs to be decided which disorder takes precedence and how treatment of comorbid disorders may affect the anxiety disorder.

Conclusion

Anxiety disorders have been reported as the most common psychiatric disorder in children and adolescents, affecting up to 31.9% of those in this age group. These disorders occur significantly more common among girls than boys. Anxiety disorders have their onset generally in childhood, with the earliest age of onset being found for SAD. Anxiety disorders are not only common, they also co-occur with several other psychiatric disorders such as with depression, SUD and disruptive disorders. Despite the frequency of comorbidity among children and adolescents with anxiety disorders, the meaning of comorbidity is unclear. However, it seems to have important implications on treatment management and assessment.

References

Adewuya, A. O., Ola, B. A., & Adewumi, T. A. (2007). The 12-month prevalence of DSM-IV anxiety disorders among Nigerian secondary school adolescents aged 13–18 years. *Journal of Adolescents, 30,* 1071–1076.

Anderson, J. C., Williams, S., McGee, R., & Silva, P. A. (1987). DSM-III disorders in preadolescent children. Prevalence in a large sample from the general population. *Archives of General Psychiatry, 44,* 69–76.

Angold, A., & Costello, E. J. (1992). Comorbidity in children and adolescents with depression. *Child and Adolescent Psychiatric Clinics of North America, 1,* 31–51.

Angold, A., Costello, E. J., & Erkanli, A. (1999). Comorbidity. *Journal of Child Psychology and Psychiatry and Allied Disciplines, 40* (1), 57–87.

American Psychiatric Association (1994). *Diagnostic and Statistical Manual of Mental Disorders,* 4th edn. *(DSM-IV).* Washington, DC: American Psychiatric Association.

Beesdo, K., Bittner, A., Pine, D. S., et al. (2007). Incidence of social anxiety disorder and the consistent risk for secondary depression in the first three decades of life. *Archives General of Psychiatry, 64,* 903–912.

Beesdo, K., Knappe, S., & Pine, D. S. (2009). Anxiety and Anxiety Disorders in Children and adolescents: Developmental Issues and Implications for DSM-V. *Psychiatric Clinics of North America, 32,* 483–524.

Beesdo, K., Pine, D. S., Lieb, R., & Wittchen, H.-U. (2010). Incidence and Risk Patterns of Anxiety and Depressive Disorders and Categorization of Generalized Anxiety Disorder. *Archives of General Psychiatry, 67,* 47–57.

Benjamin, R. S., Costello, E. J., & Warren, M. (1990). Anxiety disorders in a pediatric sample. *Journal of Anxiety Disorders, 4,* 293–316.

Biederman, J., Rosenbaum, J. F., Hirshfeld, D. R., Faraone, S. V., Bolduc, E. A., Gersten, M., Meminger, S. R., Kagan, J., Snidman, N., & Reznick, J. S. (1990). Psychiatric correlates of behavioral inhibition in young children of parents with and without psychiatric disorders. *Archives of General Psychiatry, 47* (1), 21–26.

Biederman, J., Rosenbaum, J., Chaloff, F., & Kagan, J. (1995). Behavioral inhibition as a risk factor for anxiety disorders. In J. S. March (Ed.), *Anxiety disorders in children and adolescents* (pp. 61–81). New York: Guilford.

Biederman, J., Rosenbaum, J. F., Hirschfeld, D. R., Faraone, S. V., Bolduc, E. A., Gersten, M., Merninger, S. R., Kagan, J., Snidman, N., & Reznick, S. (1990). Psychiatric correlates of behavioral inhibition in young children of parents with and without psychiatric disorders. *Archives of General Psychiatry, 47* (1), 21–26.

Bird, H. R., Gould, M. S., & Staghezza, B. M. (1993). Patterns of diagnostic comorbidity in a community sample of children aged 9 through 16 years. *Journal of the American Academy of Child and Adolescent Psychiatry, 32,* 361–368.

Bird, H., Canino, G., Rubio-Stipec, M., Gould, M. S., Ribera, J., Sesman, M., Woodbury, M., Huertas-Goldman, S., Pagan, A., Sanchez-Lacay, A., & Moscoso, M. (1988). Estimates of the prevalence of childhood maladjustment in a community survey in Puerto Rico. *Archives of General Psychiatry, 45,* 1120–1126.

Bittner, A., Goodwin, R. D., Wittchen, H.-U., Beesdo, K., Höfler. M., & Lieb, R. (2004). What characteristics of primary anxiety disorders predict subsequent major depressive disorder? *Journal of Clinical Psychiatry, 65,* 618–626.

Bowen, R. C., Offord, D. R., & Boyle, M. H. (1990). The prevalence of overanxious disorder and separation anxiety disorder: Results from the Ontario Child Health Study. *Journal of the American Academy of Child and Adolescent Psychiatry, 29,* 753–758.

Burns, B. J., Costello, E. J., Angold, A.,Tweed, D., Stangl, D., Farmer, E. M., & Erkanli, A. (1995). Children's Mental Health Service Use Across Service Sectors. *Health Affairs, 14* (3), 147–159.

Canino, G., Shrout, P. E., Rubio-Stipec, M., et al. (2004). The DSM-IV rates of child and adolescent disorders in Puerto Rico: Prevalence, correlates, service use, and the effects of impairment. *Archives of General Psychiatry. 61,* 85–93.

Caron, C., & Rutter, M. (1991). Comorbidity in child psychopathology: Concepts, issues and research strategies. *Journal of Child Psychology and Psychiatry, 32,* 1063–1080.

Clark, L. A., & Watson, D. (1991). Tripartite model of anxiety and depression: Psychometric evidence and taxonomic implications. *Journal of Abnormal Psychology, 100,* 316–336.

Clark, D. B., & Jacob, R. G. (1992). Anxiety disorders in 30 adolescents with alcohol abuse and dependence. *Alcoholism, Clinical and Experimental Research, 16,* 371.

Cohen, P., Cohen, J., Kasen, S., Velez, C. N., Hartmark, C., Johnson, J., Rojas, M., Brook, J., & Streuning, E. L. (1993). An epidemiological study of disorders in late childhood and adolescence—I: Age- and gender-specific prevalence. *Journal Child Psychology and Psychiatry, 34,* 851–866.

Conger, J. (1956). Reinforcement theory and the dynamics of alcoholism. *Quarterly Journal of Studies on Alcohol, 17,* 296–305.

Costello, E. J., Angold, A., Burns, B. J., Stangl, D. K., Tweed, D. L., Erkanli, A., et al. (1996). The Great Smoky Mountains Study of Youth: Goals, designs, methods, and the prevalence of DSM-III-R disorders. *Archives of General Psychiatry, 53,* 1129–1136.

Costello, E. J., Mustillo, S., Erkanli, A., Keeler, G., & Angold, A. (2003). Prevalence and Development of Psychiatric Disorders in Childhood and Adolescence. *Archives of General Psychiatry, 60,* 837–844.

Esbjørn, B. H., Hoeyer, M., Dyrborg, J., Leth, I., & Kendall, P. C. (2010). Prevalence and comorbidity among anxiety disorders in a national cohort of psychiatrically referred children and adolescents. *Journal of Anxiety Disorders, 24* (8), 866–872.

Essau, C. A., & Conradt, J., & Petermann, F. (2000). Frequency, comorbidity, and psychosocial impairment of anxiety disorders in German adolescents. *Journal of Anxiety Disorders, 14* (3), 263–279.

Essau, C. A. (2003). Comorbidity of anxiety disorders in adolescents. *Depression and Anxiety, 18,* 1–6.

Essau, C. A. (2005). Frequency and patterns of mental health services utilisation among adolescents with anxiety and depressive disorders. *Depression and Anxiety, 22,* 130–137.

Ezpeleta, L., Keeler, G., Erkanli, A., Costello, E. J., & Angold, A. (2001). Epidemiology of psychiatric disability in childhood and adolescence. *Journal of Child Psychology and Psychiatry, 42,* 901–914.

Feehan, M., McGee, R., & Williams, S. M. (1993). Mental health disorders from age 15 to age 18 years. *Journal of the American Academy of Child and Adolescent Psychiatry, 32,* 1118–1126.

Feehan, M., McGee, R., Nada-Raja, S., & Williams, S. M. (1994). DSM-III-R disorders in New Zealand 18-year-olds. *Australian and New Zealand Journal of Psychiatry, 28,* 87–99.

Fergusson, D. M., Horwood, L. J., & Lynskey, M. T. (1993). Prevalence and comorbidity of DSM-III-R diagnoses in a birth cohort of 15 year olds. *Journal of the American Academy of Child and Adolescent Psychiatry, 32,* 1127–1134.

Fleming, J. E., Offord, D. R., & Boyle, M. H. (1989). Prevalence of childhood and adolescent depression in the community: Ontario Child Health Study. *British Journal of Psychiatry, 155,* 647–654.

Gau, S. S., Chong, M. Y., Chen, T. H., & Cheng, A. T. (2005). A 3-year panel study of mental disorders among adolescents in Taiwan. *The American Journal of Psychiatry, 162,* 1344–1350.

Gregory, A. M., Caspi, A., Moffitt, T. E., Koenen, K., Eley, T. C., & Poulton, P. (2007). Juvenile mental health histories of adults with anxiety disorders. *American Journal of Psychiatry, 164,* 301–308.

Hayward, C., Killen, J. D., Hammer, L. D., Litt, I. F., Wilson, D. M., Simmonds, B., & Taylor, C. B. (1992). Pubertal stage and panic attack history in sixth- and seventh-grade girls. *American Journal of Psychiatry, 149,* 1239–1243.

Ialongo, N., Edelsohn, G., Werthamer-Larsson, L, Crockett, L., & Kellam, S. (1994). The significance of self-reported anxious symptoms in first grade children. *Journal of Abnormal Child Psychology, 22,* 441–456.

Ialongo, N., Edelsohn, G., Werthamer-Larsson, L., Crockett, L., & Kellam, S. (1995). The significance of self-reported anxious symptoms in first grade children: Prediction to anxious symptoms and adaptive functioning in fifth grade. *Journal of Child Psychology and Psychiatry, 36,* 427–437.

Kashani, J. H., & Orvaschel, H. (1988). Anxiety disorders in mid-adolescence: a community sample. *American Journal of Psychiatry, 145,* 960–964.

Keller, M. B., Lavori, P., Wunder, J., Beardslee, W. R., Schwartz, C. E., & Roth, J. (1992). Chronic course of anxiety disorders in children and adolescents. *Journal of the American Academy of Child and Adolescent Psychiatry, 31,* 595–599.

Kelly, T. M., Cornelius, J. R., & Clark, D. B. (2004). Psychiatric disorders and attempted suicide among adolescents with substance use disorders. *Drug and Alcohol Dependence, 73,* 87–97.

Kendall, P. C., Brady, E. U., & Verduin, T. L. (2001). Comorbidity in childhood anxiety disorders and treatment outcome. *Journal of the American Academy of Child and Adolescent Psychiatry, 40* (7), 787–794.

Kessler, R. C., Berglund, P., Demler, O., Jin, R., & Walters, E. E. (2005). Lifetime prevalence and age-of-onset distributions of DSM-IV disorders in the National Comorbidity Survey Replication. *Archives of General Psychiatry, 62,* 593–602.

Kessler, R. C., & McGonagle, K. A., & Zhao, S., & Nelson, C. B., & Hughes, M., & Eshleman, S., & Wittchen, H-U., & Kendler, K. (1994). Lifetime and 12-Month Prevalence of DSM-III-R Psychiatric Disorders in the United States. *Archives of General Psychiatry, 51,* 8–19.

Kessler, R. C., Ruscio, A. M., Shear, K., & Wittchen, H.-U. (2009). Epidemiology of anxiety disorders. In Antony, M. M., & Stein, M. B. (eds), *Oxford Handbook of Anxiety and Related Disorders* (pp. 19–33). New York: Oxford University Press.

Khantzian, E. (1997). The self-medication hypothesis of substance use disorders: a reconsideration and recent applications. *Harv Rev Psychiatry 4,* 231–244.

Kushner, M. G., Abram, K., & Borchardt, C. (2000). The relationship between anxiety disorders and alcohol use disorders: A review of the major perspectives and findings. *Clinical Psychiatric Review 20,* 149–171.

Lack, C. W., Storch, E. A., Keely, M., Geffken, G. R., Ricketts, E., et al. (2009). Quality of life in children and adolescents with obsessive-compulsive disorder. *Social Psychiatry and Psychiatric Epidemiology, 44,* 935–942.

Last, C. G., Perrin, S, Hersen, M, & Kazdin, A. E. (1996). A prospective study of childhood anxiety disorders. *Journal of the American Academy of Child and Adolescent Psychiatry, 35,* 1502–1510.

Leung, P. W. L., Hung, S. F., Ho, T. P., Lee, C. C., Liu, W. S., et al. (2008). Prevalence of DSM-IV disorders in Chinese adolescents and the effects of an impairment criterion: A pilot community study in Hong Kong. *European Child, & Adolescent Psychiatry, 17,* 452–461.

Lewinsohn, P. M., Gotlib, I. H., Lewinsohn, M., Seely, J. R., & Allen, N. B. (1998). Gender differences in anxiety disorders and anxiety symptoms in adolescents. *Journal of Abnormal Psychology, 107*(1), 109–117.

Lewinsohn, P. M., Hops, H., Roberts, R. E., Seeley, J. R., & Andrews, J. A. (1993). Adolescent psychopathology: I. Prevalence and incidence of depression and other DSM-III-R disorders in high school students. *Journal of Abnormal Psychology, 102,* 133–144.

Lewinsohn, P. M., Zinbarg, R., Seeley, J. R., Lewinsohn, M., & Sack, W. H. (1997). Lifetime comorbidity among anxiety disorders and between anxiety disorders and other mental disorders in adolescents. *Journal of Anxiety Disorders, 11,* 377–394.

Maj, M. (2005). 'Psychiatric comorbidity': an artefact of current diagnostic systems? *British Journal of Psychiatry, 186,* 182–184.

Manassis, K., & Hood, J. (1998). Individual and familial predictors of impairment in childhood anxiety disorders. *Journal of the American Academy of Child and Adolescent Psychiatry, 37,* 428–434.

Mancini, C., Van Ameringen, M., Oakman, J. M., & Figueiredo, D. (1999). Childhood attention deficit/hyperactivity disorder in adults with anxiety disorders. *Psychological Medicine, 29,* 515–525.

McArdle, P., Prosser, J., & Kolvin, I. (2004). Prevalence of psychiatric disorder: with and without psychosocial impairment. *European Child & Adolescent Psychiatry, 13,* 347–353.

Roberts, R. F., Roberts, C. R., & Xing, Y. (2007). Comorbidity of substance use disorders and other psychiatric disorders among adolescents: evidence from an epidemiologic survey. *Drug and Alcohol Dependence, 88,* S4–13.

McGee, R., Feehan, M., Williams, S., Partridge, F., Silva, P. A., & Kelly, J. (1990). DSM-III disorders in a large sample of adolescents. *Journal of the American Academy of Child and Adolescent Psychiatry, 29,* 611–619.

Merikangas, K. R. (1989). Comorbidity for anxiety and depression: Review of family and genetic studies. In J. D. Maser, & C. R. Cloninger (Eds.), *Comorbidity of Mood and Anxiety Disorders* (pp. 331–348). Washington, DC: American Psychiatric Press, Inc.

Merikangas, K. R., He, J. P., Burstein, M., Swanson, S. A., Avenevoli, S., Cui, L., Benjet, C., Georgiades, K., & Swendsen, J. (2010). Lifetime Prevalence of Mental Disorders in U.S. Adolescents: Results from the National Comorbidity Survey Replication–Adolescent Supplement (NCS-A). *Journal of the American Academy of Child and Adolescent Psychiatry, 49,* 980 –989.

Messer, S. C., & Beidel, D. C. (1994). Psychosocial correlates of childhood anxiety disorders. *Journal of the American Academy of Child Psychiatry, 33,* 975–983.

Ollendick, T. H., Jarrett, M. A., Grills-Taquechel, A. E., Hovey, L. D., & Wolff, J. (2008). Comorbidity as a predictor and moderator of treatment outcome in youth with anxiety, affective, AD/HD, and oppositional/conduct disorders. *Clinical Psychology Review, 28,* 1447–1471.

Ollendick, T. H., & King, N. J. (1994). Diagnosis, assessment, and treatment of internalizing problems in children: The role of longitudinal data. *Journal of Consulting and Clinical Psychology, 62,* 918–927.

Ollendick, T. H., Öst, L. G., Reuterskiöld, L., & Costa, N. (2010). Comorbidity in youth with specific phobias: Impact of comorbidity on treatment outcome and the impact of treatment on comorbid disorders. *Behaviour Research and Therapy, 48,* 827–831.

Orvaschel, H., Lewinsohn, P. M., & Seeley, J. R. (1995). Continuity of psychopathology in a community sample of adolescents. *Journal of the American Academy of Child and Adolescent Psychiatry, 34,* 1525–1535.

Piotrowski, N. A. (2007). Comorbidity and psychological science: Does one size fit all? *Clinical Psychology: Science and Practice, 14,* 6–19.

Rapee, R. M. (2003). The influence of comorbidity on treatment outcome for children and adolescents with anxiety disorders. *Behavior Research and Therapy, 41,* 105–112.

Regier, D. A., Meyer, J. K., Kramer, M., Robins, L. N., Blazer, D. G., Hough, R. L., Eaton, W. W., & Locke, B. Z. (1984). The NIMH Epidemiologic Catchment Area (ECA) Program: Historical context, major objective, and study population characteristics. *Archives of General Psychiatry, 41,* 934–941.

Roberts, R. E., Attkisson, C., & Rosenblatt, A. (1998). Prevalence of psychopathology among children and adolescents. *American Journal of Psychiatry, 155* (6), 715–725.

Roberts, R. E., Roberts, C. R., & Chen, Y. R. (1997). Ethnocultural differences in prevalence of adolescent depression. *American Journal of Community Psychology, 25,* 95–110.

Rohde, P., Lewinsohn, P. M., & Seeley, J. R. (1991). Comorbidity of unipolar depression: II. Comorbidity with other mental disorders in adolescents and adults. *Journal of Abnormal Psychology, 100,* 214–222.

Romano, E., Tremblay, R. E., & Vitaro, F. (2001). Prevalence of psychiatric diagnoses and the role of perceived impairment: Findings from an adolescent community sample. *Journal of Child Psychology and Psychiatry, 42,* 451–461.

Rutter, M. (1986). The developmental psychopathology of depression: Issues and perspectives. In M. Rutter, C. E. Izard, & P. B. Read (Eds.), *Depression in Young People* (pp. 3–30). New York: Guilford Press.

Seeman, M. V. (1997). Psychopathology in women and men: focus on female hormones. *Amerian Journal of Psychiatry, 154,* 1641–1647.

Shaffer, D., Fisher, P., Dulcan, M. K., & Davies, M. (1996). The NIMH Diagnostic Interview Schedule for Children Version 2 ± 3 (DISC 2 ± 3): Description, acceptability, prevalence rates, and performance in the MECA study. *Journal of the American Academy of Child and Adolescent Psychiatry, 35,* 865–877.

Silverman, W. K., & Albano, A. M. (1996). *The Anxiety Disorders Interview Schedule for DSM-IV-Child and Parent Versions.* London: Oxford University Press.

Spencer, T. J., Biederman, J., & Wilens, T. (1998). Pharmacotherapy of ADHD with antidepressants. In R. A. Barkley (Ed.), *Attention-deficit hyperactivity disorder. A handbook for diagnosis and treatment* (pp. 552–563). New York: Guilford Press.

Steinhausen, H.-C., Metzke, C. W., Meier, M., & Kannenberg, R. (1998). Prevalence of child and adolescent psychiatric disorders: the Zurich Epidemiological Study. *Acta Psychiatrica Scandinavia, 98,* 262–271.

Strauss, C. C., & Last, C. G. (1993). Social and simple phobias in children. *Journal of Anxiety Disorders, 7,* 141–152.

Strauss, C. C., Lahey, B. B., Frick, P., Frame, C. L., & Hynd, G. W. (1988). Peer social status of children with anxiety disorders. *Journal of Consulting and Clinical Psychology, 56,* 137–141.

Verhulst, F. C. (1995). The epidemiology of child and adolescent psychopathology: Strengths and limitations. In F. C. Verhulst, & H. M. Koot (Eds.), *The Epidemiology of Child and Adolescent Psychopathology* (pp. 1–21). Oxford: Oxford University Press.

Verhulst, F. C., van der Ende, J., Ferdinand, R. F., & Kasius, M. C. (1997). The prevalence of DSM-III-R diagnoses in a national sample of Dutch adolescents. *Archives of General Psychiatry, 54,* 329–336.

Wells, J. E., Oakley Browne, M. A., Scott, K. M., McGee, M. A., Baxter, J., & Kokaua, J. (2006). Prevalence, interference with life and severity of 12 month DSM-IV disorders in Te Rau Hinengaro: The New Zealand Mental Health Survey. *Australian and New Zealand Journal of Psychiatry, 40* (10), 845–854.

Whitaker, A., Johnson, J., Shaffer, D., Rapoport, J. L., Kalikow, K., Walsh, B. T., Davies, M., Braiman, S., & Dolinsky, A. (1990). Uncommon troubles in young people: Prevalence estimates of selected psychiatric disorders in a nonreferred population. *Archives of General Psychiatry, 47,* 487–496.

Widiger, T. A., & Ford-Black, M. M. (1994). Diagnoses and disorders. *Clinical Psychology: Science and Practice, 1,* 84–87.

Wittchen, H.-U., Nelson, C. B., & Lachner, G. (1998). Prevalence of mental disorders and psychosocial impairments in adolescents and young adults. *Psychological Medicine 28,* 109–126.

Wittchen, H.-U., Lecrubier, Y., Beesdo, K., & Nocon, A. (2003). Relationships among anxiety disorders: patterns and implications. In D. J. Nutt & J. C. Ballenger (Eds.), *Anxiety Disorders* (pp. 25–37). Oxford: Blackwell Science.

Wittchen, H.-U., Nelson, C. B., & Lachner, G. (1998). Prevalence of mental disorders and psychosocial impairments in adolescents and young adults. *Psychological Medicine, 28,* 109–126.

Woodward, L. J., & Fergusson, D. M. (2001). Life course outcomes of young people with anxiety disorders in adolescence. *Journal of the American Academy of Child and Adolescent Psychiatry, 40,* 1086–1093.

3

Course and Outcome of Child and Adolescent Anxiety

Laura D. Seligman and Jessica L. Gahr

University of Toledo, Ohio, USA

Over the past three decades, much of the research on the prevalence and incidence of anxiety disorders in youth has begun to take a developmental perspective; these studies in both clinical and general community samples have greatly extended our knowledge regarding the course and outcome of anxiety disorders in children and adolescents. The present chapter provides a synthesis of this literature as it relates to the onset, maintenance, and remission of anxiety disorders. More specifically, we review data on age of onset, homotypic comorbidity, and heterotypic comorbidity to evaluate stability and change in pediatric anxiety. Additionally, we review diagnostic and non-diagnostic outcomes of children and adolescents with anxiety disorders as well as potential predictors and moderators of outcome. Particular attention is paid to recent developmental epidemiological studies that have documented the course of anxiety disorders in representative samples of youth in multiple countries over extended periods of time.

Age of Onset

In addition to providing a useful description of the typical course of a disorder, age of onset data can be used to develop estimates of lifetime prevalence, cumulative morbidity (i.e., the number of individuals who have had a disorder at least once in their lifetime), and projected lifetime risk (i.e., the percent of individuals who will have a disorder by the end of their lives) (see Kessler, Berglund, Demler, Jin, Merikangas, & Walters, 2005). Importantly, such estimates allow for prediction about the need for treatment and societal burdens such as treatment costs and lost productivity (Kessler et al., 2005). As such, these data, taken in the larger context of course, impairment, and treatment studies can help establish research and training priorities and provide insight into the etiology of anxiety disorders. Furthermore, research on age of onset allows for enhanced and specifically targeted prevention and intervention programs.

The Wiley-Blackwell Handbook of The Treatment of Childhood and Adolescent Anxiety, First Edition.
Edited by Cecilia A. Essau and Thomas H. Ollendick.
© 2013 John Wiley & Sons, Ltd. Published 2013 by John Wiley & Sons, Ltd.

Given its importance, it is surprising that age of onset has been relatively neglected, and that many studies of age of onset have used adult samples and relied on retrospective reports. Retrospective reports are especially problematic when estimating age of onset in that the validity of reports may be related to age of onset; that is, less reliable data may be available for disorders with an earlier age of onset because of the deterioration related to the need for the longer length of recall (Costello, Egger, & Angold, 2005). This may be especially problematic for the anxiety disorders in that retrospective studies of adults suggest that anxiety disorders have a relatively early age of onset (Kessler et al., 2005). For example, utilizing data from the National Comorbidity Survey-Replication (NCS-R), Kessler et al. (2005) found that the median age of onset for anxiety disorders was 11 years as compared to 20 years and 30 years for substance use and mood disorders, respectively. Anxiety disorders also evidence a relatively narrow range for age of onset, with interquartile ranges between 6 and 12 years (Kessler et al., 2005). Findings from the NCS-R are consistent with previous studies which found anxiety disorders to have an early age of onset. For example, Keller, Lavori, Wunder, Beardslee, Schwartz, and Roth (1992) found that the mean age of onset for anxiety disorders was 10 years of age while Orvaschel, Lewinsohn, and Seely (1995) reported an even earlier age of onset for anxiety disorders, 7.2 years of age, in a sample of 236 adolescents from the Oregon Adolescent Depression Project (OADP). Similar results for early age of onset were found in the World Health Organization's Mental Health Initiative survey which surveyed adults aged 16 years and older from 17 countries (Kessler et al., 2007). More specifically, Kessler, Angermeyer, Anthony et al. (2007) found that anxiety disorders evidenced two patterns for age of onset such that specific phobias and separation anxiety disorder (SAD) had early age of onset distributions ranging from 7 to 14 years of age whereas generalized anxiety disorder (GAD), panic disorder (PD), and post-traumatic stress disorder (PTSD) evidenced later age of onset distributions, ranging from 24 to 50 years of age. Although few other studies have examined age of onset for the specific anxiety disorders, below we review the data that are available for GAD, SAD, and social anxiety disorder.

Generalized anxiety disorder

Estimates for the age of onset for GAD are somewhat varied. The Diagnostic and Statistical Manual of Mental Disorders, Fourth Edition-Text Revision (DSM-IV-TR) recognizes this variability by reporting that more than half of those diagnosed with GAD report age of onset in childhood or early adolescence but that adult onset is not uncommon (American Psychiatric Association [APA], 2000; Wittchen, Lieb, Schuster, & Oldehinkel, 2000b). In a community sample of young adults ($n = 591$), the mean age of onset for GAD was 15.6 years with 75% of cases occurring before the age of 20 (Angst, Gamma, Baldwin, Ajdacic-Gross, & Rssler, 2009). In a large community sample, Beesdo, Pine, Lieb, and Wittchen (2010) found a delayed age of onset distribution for GAD as compared to the other anxiety disorders with age of onset for GAD occurring mostly during adolescence and early adulthood, while other anxiety disorders commonly developed in childhood. In fact, Beesdo et al. (2010) found that age of onset for GAD was more similar to depression than the other anxiety disorders.

Separation anxiety disorder

By definition, to meet diagnostic criteria for SAD, age of onset must be prior to age 18 with early age of onset defined as onset prior to 6 years of age (APA, 2000). Kessler et al. (2005) found that SAD had the earliest median age of onset of all anxiety disorders (i.e., 7 years) and also had a limited range of onset with interquartile ranges of 4–7 years. Epidemiological studies consistently support a relatively early age of onset for this disorder ranging from 7 to 14 years of age (Kessler et al., 2005, 2007). However, despite its categorization as a childhood disorder in the *Diagnostic and Statistical Manual*, 4th edition (DSM-IV; APA, 2000), research indicates that individuals may experience adult-onset separation anxiety. In fact, Shear, Jin, Ruscio, Walters, and Kessler (2006) examined the prevalence and age of onset distributions for child and adult separation anxiety within the National Comorbidity Study and found that adult onset of SAD may be relatively common. More specifically, 77.5% of participants who reported lifetime SAD and 75.2% who reported SAD in the past 12 months had adult onset SAD. However, 80% of SAD diagnoses still occurred prior to 30 years of age, with most individuals experiencing onset by their late teens to early 20s (Shear et al., 2006).

Social anxiety disorder

Epidemiological studies support a relatively early age of onset for social anxiety disorder with a median age of onset at 13 years (Kessler et al., 2005). However, this figure may be misleading because some research supports a bimodal pattern for age of onset for social phobia with both an early onset and an adolescent onset pattern. For example, in an epidemiological sample of individuals with social anxiety disorder, Schneier, Johnson, Hornig, Liebowitz, and Weissman (1992) found two distinct patterns for age of onset with one group reporting an age of onset prior to 5 years of age (21%) and the second group evidencing onset between the ages of 11 and 15 years (26%). More recent research suggests that social anxiety disorder evidences a unique pattern for age of onset. Beesdo, Bittner, Pine et al. (2007) investigated the incidence of social phobia in a 10-year longitudinal study of 3021 adolescents in a Munich community sample and found that the incidence of social anxiety disorder increased dramatically after 9 years of age and later began to gradually decrease. The age point at which the gradual decrease began differed between girls and boys such that boys began to report a decrease in the incidence of social phobia at 17 years compared to a decrease after 19 years in girls. As such, the research on age of onset of social anxiety disorder is somewhat unclear but suggests that there may be several distinct patterns that may have implications for the course of disorder. Obviously, more research is needed to clarify discrepancies amongst studies; however, one thing seems to be consistent – most individuals who will experience significant problems with social anxiety first evidence symptoms before reaching adulthood.

Conclusions

Overall, the anxiety disorders, perhaps with the exception of GAD, evidence an earlier age of onset relative to other classes of disorders (e.g., mood disorder and personality disorders). However, much of the data on age of onset comes from retrospective studies conducted with adults. Moreover, extant research generally considers anxiety disorders as a class rather than examining each of the specific anxiety disorders – despite some data suggesting that there may be important differences in age of onset patterns within the anxiety disorders. Additional prospective studies with samples large enough to examine each of the anxiety disorders individually are necessary to resolve the discrepancies in the literature and to draw more definitive conclusions.

Homotypic Continuity – Chronicity versus Remission

Homotypic continuity refers to the ongoing or repeated presence of a specific disorder or class of disorders. Stability of disorder is of both theoretical and practical significance. Understanding the stability of a cluster of symptoms can help in determining whether these symptoms constitute a clinically significant syndrome. In clinical practice, knowledge of stability can help in informing families about prognosis.

When youth are followed prospectively, general community and epidemiological studies show surprisingly consistent and high rates of remission for anxiety disorders as a class (i.e., collapsing over the specific anxiety disorders). For example, in the Early Developmental Stages of Psychopathology Study (EDSP) – which enrolled adolescents and young adults in Munich, Germany, who were between the ages of 14 and 24 years at baseline – approximately 80% of participants classified as threshold cases with an anxiety disorder at baseline were no longer classified as such at the next assessment about 20 months later (Wittchen, Lieb, Pfister, & Schuster, 2000a). Similarly, Essau, Conradt and Petermann (2000) found that approximately 77% of their non-selected sample of adolescents with an anxiety disorder had recovered 15 months later. Moreover, rates of remission seem to be similar in clinical samples, with about 80% of youth no longer evidencing their primary anxiety disorder after about 3–4 years (Last, Perrin, Hersen, & Kazdin, 1996). However, this of course means that about 20% of youth presenting with an anxiety disorder could be expected to have continuing, clinically significant problems. Moreover, for the significant minority of youth with stable and enduring disorder, the course of their illness may be quite protracted. In fact, Keller and colleagues report that the mean duration of illness for youth with anxiety disorders in their sample was 4 years and that about half of these youth could be expected to remain ill for about 8 years after the onset of their disorder (Keller et al., 1992). Additionally, relapse rates of approximately 30% suggest that even for those children and adolescents whose disorder remits, clinically significant levels of anxiety may continue to be a problem (Keller et al., 1992). This is supported by the fact that in the Great Smoky Mountains Study (GSMS), which followed youth over a longer period of time – the youngest children in the sample were enrolled at age 9 years and the sample was followed until age 19 – found at least some degree of continuity of anxiety disorders in about 30% of their sample (Bittner, Egger, Erkanli, Costello, Foley, & Angold, 2007).

Of note, remission has typically been defined as no longer meeting full diagnostic criteria for a disorder, so we know little about whether those youth defined as recovered or remitted are relatively free of their original anxiety symptoms or whether these symptoms continue on a subclinical level and result in considerable distress. Studies that examine anxiety dimensionally suggest a good deal of continuity which may mean that youth whose anxiety disorder remits continue to experience high levels of symptoms. For example, Crocetti, Klimstra, Keijsers, Hale and Meeus (2009) measured anxiety in a sample of over 1300 adolescents for 5 years and found that the trajectory of anxiety symptoms for these youth could be best defined by two patterns: youth whose initial levels of anxiety were relatively low and decreased over time and youth who initially reported high levels of anxiety whose symptoms increased over time. Moreover, in one of the few studies to report a fine-grained analysis of severity of diagnostic status and symptoms, Wittchen et al. (2000a,b) found that of the youth defined as threshold cases at time 1, as indicated above, 19.7% continued to have a threshold anxiety diagnosis at time 2 but an additional 15.8% were considered subthreshold cases, 26.3% were symptomatic and only 38.2% were classified as well.

With more long-term data from a growing number of longitudinal, general community samples becoming available, continuity of anxiety disorders has also been examined using follow-back analysis. In these analyses, the group of interest is defined by those who have a disorder at a certain point in time (e.g., young adulthood) and the diagnostic history of this group is established by examining earlier diagnostic assessments. Although earlier studies have been able to do these types of analyses retrospectively, follow-back analyses using longitudinal data avoid the biases that may influence the retrospective reports of those with a disorder. When continuity is assessed in this way, stability is high – in other words, consistent with what we know from studies of age of onset, most individuals with an anxiety disorder in late adolescence or early adulthood have experienced clinically significant anxiety during youth. For example, Orvaschel and colleagues found that of the adolescents diagnosed with anxiety disorder at time 2 in their study, 56.3% had been classified as having an anxiety disorder at time 1 (Orvaschel et al., 1995). This rate of continuity was higher than that found for other disorders and the high relative risk for continued anxiety remained even after controlling for the base rate of disorders. Additionally, when participants from the Dunedin Multidisciplinary Health and Development Study (DMHS), a long-term longitudinal study of a complete birth cohort in Dunedin, New Zealand, were assessed at 21 years, those with anxiety disorder were significantly more likely to have experienced an anxiety disorder than another disorder at previous assessments and they were significantly more likely to have been diagnosed with anxiety disorder than no disorder (Newman, Moffitt, Caspi, Magdol, Dilva, & Stanton, 1996). Specifically, 61.5% of the sample of young adults with an anxiety disorder at 21 years had reported symptoms consistent with an anxiety disorder at an earlier assessment (Newman et al., 1996). Further, 85% of the participants in the Dunedin sample diagnosed with an anxiety disorder at age 26 had experienced a disorder in a previous diagnostic assessment and, more specifically, they were almost three times more likely to have had an anxiety disorder in late childhood and early adolescence (Kim-Cohen, Caspi, Moffitt, Harrington, Milne, & Poulton, 2003).

In summary, these data suggest that for many youth with an anxiety disorder, the disorder will remit over time but that many of these youth may relapse or continue to evidence subclinical levels of anxiety symptoms. Moreover, follow-back analyses suggest a good deal of continuity for those who evidence an anxiety disorder in adulthood and these types of analyses support retrospective studies in adults that suggest that anxiety disorders often begin during childhood and adolescence. Taken together these data suggest a good deal of homotypic comorbidity across the anxiety disorders; however, studies that have examined stability across a number of specific anxiety disorders have found a good deal of variability (Last et al., 1996; Wittchen et al., 2000a); therefore, where sufficient data exist we discuss the stability of specific anxiety disorders.

Generalized anxiety disorder and overanxious disorder

With the DSM-III-R (APA, 1987), generalized and pervasive worry and anxiety in youth could be diagnosed as either GAD or overanxious disorder (OAD), one of the three anxiety disorders specific to childhood. With the advent of DSM-IV (APA, 1994, 2000), OAD was eliminated from the diagnostic system as it was hypothesized that youth that would have been diagnosed with OAD would be captured by the revised definition of GAD. The absence of OAD is likely to continue in the fifth edition of the DSM (American Psychiatric Assocation, 2010). While some studies do indeed suggest that these two disorders may be comparable, this finding has not been entirely consistent (e.g., Breslau, Davis, & Prabucki, 1987); therefore, examining the stability of GAD and OAD across time may be somewhat hampered by these changes in definition. Nevertheless, several studies have examined the stability of one or both of these disorders and we report these findings together, pointing out similarities and differences where possible. However, it must be recognized that stability estimates may be affected by this diagnostic shift.

In terms of length of illness, Keller and colleagues found that OAD in youth lasted an average of $4^1/_2$ years (Keller et al., 1992) and although the EDSP examined GAD but not OAD, GAD was found to have one of the lowest complete remission rates (Wittchen et al., 2000a). However, Wittchen and colleagues defined complete remission as the absence of all diagnoses not just the index diagnosis; therefore, this low rate could be driven by stability of GAD or its relationship with other disorders. In a more specific analysis, but with a much smaller sample, Last et al. (1996) found the 3- to 4-year recovery rate for OAD to be around 80% – similar to the rate of anxiety disorders in general (Last et al., 1996).

The GSMS was one of the few studies to examine both OAD and GAD at multiple assessments in a large epidemiological sample and results suggest a much different picture of the stability of GAD as compared to OAD, with much lower stability found for GAD in youth. For example, while about 29% of youth with OAD were found to evidence the disorder at multiple assessments, only 4.3% of those with GAD met criteria at more than one assessment (Bittner et al., 2007). Moreover, in logistic regression analyses, while OAD in childhood significantly predicted OAD in adolescence even when controlling for comorbidity among the anxiety disorders, childhood GAD was *not* associated with adolescent GAD (Bittner et al., 2007). This lack of stability for GAD is also supported by a study of German youth that found that none of the youth (ages 12–17 years) diagnosed with GAD at the initial assessment continued to have GAD again 15 months later (Essau, Conradt, & Petermann, 2002). However, it should be noted that only two participants (out of 523 interviewed at both time points) in this study were diagnosed with GAD at the initial assessment and the reliability of the GAD module of the diagnostic interview used was low ($\kappa = 0.45$). Therefore, it is unclear whether the low stability for GAD is a true characteristic of the disorder or whether these findings may be at least partially driven by a low base rate in childhood coupled with problems in diagnostic assessments of the disorder.

Contrary to these problematic findings in the stability of GAD, some evidence has been found for greater stability when OAD and GAD are considered together. For example, in the New York Longitudinal Study (NYLS) the odds were three times higher that youth with an OAD diagnosis would later develop GAD (Pine, Cohen, Gurley, Brook, & Ma, 1998), and in the DMHS the presence of OAD at 11–15 years predicted GAD at age 32 (Gregory, Caspi, Moffitt, Koenen, Eley, & Poulton, 2007).

Panic disorder

Many epidemiological studies of youth have not examined PD although the data that do exist suggest that PD may be among the most stable of the anxiety disorders in youth. For example, Last and colleagues found one of the lowest recovery rates within the anxiety disorders was for PD (Last et al., 1996). Similarly, PD was found to be the most stable anxiety disorder in the EDSP with about 44% of youth evidencing PD at the initial assessment reporting PD again approximately 20 months later (Wittchen et al., 2000a). Other studies have not examined full-blown PD but have instead examined panic attacks; here too studies have found considerable stability (Goodwin, Lieb, Hoefler et al., 2004; Pine et al., 1998).

Separation anxiety disorder

Data on the stability of SAD are mixed with some studies reporting very high rates of recovery or remission while others suggest a good deal of stability. For example, only 6% of adolescents in the OADP diagnosed with SAD before age 16 years still had an SAD diagnosis at age 17 (Lewinsohn, Holm-Denoma, Small, Seeley, & Joiner, 2008). This is consistent with a recovery rate of about 96% reported in clinical samples (Last et al., 1996). On the other hand, childhood SAD predicted adolescent SAD in the GSMS and this relationship remained significant even when controlling for other anxiety disorders (Bittner et al., 2007). Moreover, of the adolescents diagnosed with SAD in the GSMS, 18% met criteria for the diagnosis at multiple assessments (Bittner et al., 2007) and a similar rate was found in the Virginia Twin Study for Adolescent Behavioral Development (VTSABD; Foley, Pickles, Maes, Silberg, & Eaves, 2004). In fact, Foley et al. (2004) found that the odds of an SAD diagnosis were eight times higher for youth who had had a previous diagnosis of SAD.

SAD has long been thought to be a diagnosis restricted to childhood and early adolescence so continuity into adulthood was considered nonexistent. However, as indicated previously some relatively recent research suggests that there may be a clinically significant form of SAD that is found in adults (Manicavasagar, Silove, Curtis, & Wagner, 2000; Seligman & Wuyek, 2007; Shear et al., 2006; Silove, Man-icavasagar, & Drobny, 2002). Moreover, retrospective reports suggest that some of these adult cases may be childhood cases that have persisted into adulthood (Manicavasagar et al., 2000). In fact, data from the NCS-R suggest that adult SAD may be much more common than previously realized and that about a quarter of adult cases are childhood-onset SAD that have persisted (Shear et al., 2006). Moreover, this type of persistent SAD seems to be related to functional impairment (Seligman &

Wuyek, 2007; Shear et al., 2006). Thus, although relatively rare, this persistent form of SAD may warrant further attention.

Social anxiety disorder/social phobia

Although the stability of social phobia or social anxiety disorder is somewhat lower than the stability of other anxiety disorders (Wittchen et al., 2000a) studies have still found significant relationships between social anxiety disorder in childhood and social anxiety disorder in adolescence on the one hand (Bittner et al., 2007) and social anxiety disorder in adolescence and social anxiety disorder in young adulthood on the other (Pine et al., 1998). These relationships remain even when statistical techniques are used to control for comorbidity among social anxiety disorder and the other anxiety disorders. In fact, in the GSMS over 14% of cases of social anxiety disorder evidenced the disorder at more than one assessment (Bittner et al., 2007) and Essau et al. (2000) found that 10% of the adolescents they diagnosed with social anxiety disorder at an initial assessment continued to have social anxiety disorder at follow-up.

Specific phobias

Specific or simple phobias have often been thought to be transient or inconsequential; however, the data do not support such a contention. In fact, the opposite seems to be true. In the EDSP, specific phobias were among the anxiety disorders showing the greatest stability with 30% of youth evidencing a specific phobia at the initial assessment meeting criteria again 20 months later (Wittchen et al., 2000a). Essau and colleagues report a similar, although somewhat higher rate of stability; 36% of their sample that reported a specific phobia at time 1 was again diagnosed with a specific phobia at a 15 month follow-up (Essau et al., 2002). Looking at these data from the opposite prospective, Last et al. (1996) report a recovery rate of 70% for specific phobias.

Similarly, epidemiological studies have found that specific phobias are stable over a relatively long period of time with the odds of a child or adolescent diagnosed with a specific phobia continuing to have a specific phobia being around $3^1/_2$ times greater 9 years later and over 8 times greater when the time between assessments was 7 years (Pine et al., 1998). Moreover, specific phobias in youth are predictive of specific phobia in adulthood (Gregory et al., 2007).

Summary

In sum, studies suggest a good deal of homotypic comorbidity for anxiety disorders in youth, although the majority of children and adolescents with an anxiety disorder will recover before adulthood – at least to some degree. Specific rates of stability and recovery vary within the anxiety disorders with disorders such as PD and specific phobias showing the highest levels of homotypic comorbidity and social anxiety showing somewhat lower rates of stability.

Although studies have used different methodologies to assess stability (e.g., different diagnostic interviews, different algorithms to weight parent and child reports) and have assessed youth from varying geographic locations (e.g., New York State,

New Zealand, Germany) and for different lengths of time, results are often surprisingly consistent, suggesting that although there are still many questions to be answered, we know much more about the stability of anxiety disorders in youth and the homotypic comorbidity of anxiety in youth and anxiety in adulthood than we did even 10 or 15 years ago.

Heterotypic Comorbidity

Heterotypic comorbidity is when an individual manifests two or more different disorders or classes of disorders over time. Four reasons for heterotypic comorbidity have been suggested in the literature (Frances, Widiger, & Fyer, 1990), including those related to measurement and definition artifacts and those that reflect the true nature of the disorders in question. First, two or more disorders may appear to be comorbid at higher than chance rates because the measurement tools used to assess the disorders contain a good deal of overlap – this may be particularly problematic when assessment tools focus on associated as opposed to core features of a disorder (Seligman & Ollendick, 1998; Silverman & Ollendick, 2005). Second, comorbidity may arise because disorders representing one unified underlying construct have been artificially split in the diagnostic system. Third, common, or related risk factors could cause multiple disorders; therefore, if the risk factor is present the probability of manifesting multiple disorders is increased. Finally, one disorder could cause or put one at risk for other disorders. Therefore, knowledge of heterotypic comorbidity not only allows us to make informed statements about the long-term prognosis of youth and to plan on an individual and societal scale, it also provides a "jumping off" point for research into the diagnostic nomenclature, diagnostic measurement, and etiology of disorder by pointing out potential problems and development pathways.

For childhood anxiety disorders, clinical studies have for some time suggested high rates of heterotypic comorbidity. For example, Last et al. (1996) found that approximately 30% of clinically-referred youth with an anxiety disorder developed a new disorder within 3 or 4 years; this was significantly higher than the rate of new disorder observed in the non-diagnosed (at initial assessment) control group. Further, more recently, the relationship between anxiety disorders in youth and the development of later psychopathology was confirmed by developmental epidemiology. More specifically, there seems to be particularly strong evidence for the relationship between anxiety disorders and later mood disorder and substance use disorders.

For example, of 62 German adolescents in a general community sample initially diagnosed with an anxiety disorder, approximately 18% had an affective disorder and over 6.5% had a substance abuse disorder at a 15-month follow-up (Essau et al., 2002). Interestingly, over 27% of these adolescents also developed a somatoform disorder; however, it is not possible to determine whether this is a reliable finding given that many studies do not systemically assess for somatoform disorders. Similarly, early anxiety disorder was related to increased risk of subsequent dysthymia and substance abuse in the OADP (Orvaschel et al., 1995), and anxiety disorders as a group were also related to the development of affective disorders in the GSMS (Bittner, Goodwin, Wittchen, Beesdo, Hfler, & Lieb, 2004). In a more specific analysis, adolescents with anxiety disorders in the Christchurch Health and Development Study (CHDS) in New

Zealand were at increased risk of later major depression, nicotine dependence, alcohol dependence, and illicit drug dependence, as well as suicidal behavior (Woodward & Fergusson, 2001).

The results from the DMHS reveal a somewhat different picture. For affective disorders, findings from the sample are relatively consistent with those from other epidemiological samples; follow-back analyses suggest that participants who were diagnosed with depression at age 26 were more likely to have had an anxiety diagnosis in youth (Kim-Cohen et al., 2003). Similarly, about 27% of those diagnosed with major depressive disorder (MDD) by age 32 had a previous anxiety disorder and 41% of the sample who were diagnosed with an anxiety disorder prior to age 32 developed MDD (Moffitt, Harrington, Caspi et al., 2007). However, somewhat conflicting findings were revealed for substance disorders. While 29% of the DMHS sample diagnosed with a substance disorder at 21 years had met criteria for an anxiety disorder at a previous assessment (Newman et al., 1996), follow-back analyses of the sample did not find a significant relationship between juvenile anxiety disorders and substance disorders in young adulthood at 26 years of age (Kim-Cohen et al., 2003). On the other hand, adult schizophreniform disorder, not assessed in many other studies, was associated with anxiety disorder in childhood and adolescence in this sample (OR adjusted for sex = 2.5; Kim-Cohen et al., 2003).

In sum, strong evidence has been found for the heterotypic comorbidity of anxiety and depression, with anxiety disorders preceding the affective disorder in the majority of cases (Essau et al., 2000; Roza, Hofstra, van der Ende, & Verhulst, 2003). Additionally, although there have been some discrepancies, relatively consistent findings suggest that youth with anxiety disorders are at increased risk for the later development of substance use disorders (e.g., Newman et al., 1996). Moreover, these findings do not seem to reflect a wide-ranging tendency of youth with anxiety disorders to be at increased risk for psychopathology in general. Although caution should be used when interpreting null results, youth with anxiety disorders have not been found to be at increased risk for adult psychopathology such as eating disorders, antisocial disorder, or mania (e.g., Kim-Cohen et al., 2003). Moreover, these data do not seem to reflect a general tendency for any type of psychopathology to increase risk for affective disorders and substance use as studies with psychiatric control groups have found differences in the course of anxiety disorders in youth as opposed to other disorders. However, rate of heterotypic comorbidity as well as specific patterns vary somewhat by specific anxiety diagnosis (e.g., Last et al., 1996; Lewinsohn, Zinbarg, Seeley, Lewinsohn, & Sack, 1997), so we now turn to reviews of the specific anxiety disorders where sufficient data exist to draw conclusions. We include here a review of heterotypic continuity within the anxiety disorders as well.

Generalized anxiety disorder and overanxious disorder

Interestingly, despite its deletion from current versions of the DSM, childhood OAD has proven to be predictive of various forms of psychopathology at relatively high rates. In fact, Last et al. (1996) found that 35% of the youth with OAD in their sample developed another disorder during the 3–4 years they followed them. In general, studies have found a link between childhood OAD and the development of later anxiety disorders and depression. For example, OAD has been linked to elevated risk for PD, panic attacks, and agoraphobia (Biederman, Petty, Faroane et al., 2005; Bittner et al., 2007; Gregory et al., 2007; Pine et al., 1998); in fact, some evidence suggests that OAD may be one of the best predictors of clinically significant PD in adulthood (Biederman et al., 2005). Moreover, studies have found an association between OAD and the development of social anxiety disorder (Gregory et al., 2007; Pine et al., 1998), with data from the NYLS suggesting that, compared to youth without OAD, the odds were close to seven times greater that a child or adolescent with OAD would develop social anxiety disorder (Pine et al., 1998). OAD has also been consistently linked with the development of affective disorders including MDD (Bittner et al., 2007; Pine et al., 1998) and bipolar disorder (Henin, Biederman, Mick et al., 2007). Interestingly, there is also some evidence that childhood OAD and GAD may be related to the subsequent development of conduct disorder in youth (Bittner et al., 2007; Pine et al., 1998).

Panic disorder and agoraphobia

Compared to other anxiety disorders, PD in youth has been linked to one of the highest rates of development of subsequent disorder (Last et al., 1996). However, because PD is very uncommon in young children, few studies have had large enough samples of youth with full-blown PD or PD with agoraphobia to conduct adequately powered statistical analysis. Therefore, some studies have investigated the developmental course of panic attacks as opposed to full-blown PD or agoraphobia. For example, the NYLS examined the course of fearful spells, defined as "brief, spontaneous, crescendo anxiety" (Pine et al., 1998, p. 57) and found that early fearful spells predicted later social anxiety disorder, specific phobias, GAD, and MDD. Similarly, youth with panic attacks in the EDSP were found to be at increased risk for the development of social anxiety disorder, specific phobias, GAD, somatoform disorders, and substance disorders (Goodwin et al., 2004). Moreover these youth were more likely than those without panic attacks at the initial assessment to develop multiple anxiety disorders as well as multiple substance use disorders. Interestingly, remitted panic attacks seem to be as predictive as active panic in predicting substance disorders (Goodwin et al., 2004; Zimmermann, Wittchen, Hfler, Pfister, Kessler, & Lieb, 2003). Further, Biederman and colleagues, although not studying PD directly, found that agoraphobic avoidance predicted GAD even when controlling for comorbid anxiety disorders and parental psychopathology (Biederman, Petty, Hirschfeld-Becker et al., 2007). Finally, in one of the few studies we found examining heterotypic comorbidity of psychopathology in youth and physiologic disorders, Scott and colleagues found that PD and agoraphobia predicted adult onset asthma and this risk of adult onset asthma in those with PD was elevated even when controlling for demographic characteristics and smoking status (Scott, Von Korff, Alonso et al., 2008).

Separation anxiety disorder

Findings on the heterotypic comorbidity of SAD are somewhat conflicting. For example, studying short-term course (i.e., approximately 18 months), Foley et al. (2004) found that about 60% of the youth with SAD in their sample had no diagnosis at follow-up. Similarly, youth in the GSMS with childhood SAD were more likely to have SAD in adolescence but childhood SAD did not predict the occurrence of other disorders despite the fact that some of the sample was already entering young adulthood at follow-up (Bittner et al., 2007). On the other hand, Lewinsohn et al. (2008) found that close to 80% of youth with childhood SAD had a diagnosable psychiatric disorder in adulthood.

Moreover, there has been considerable speculation about a specific link between childhood SAD and PD in adulthood (e.g., Gittelman & Klein, 1984). According to Gittelman and Klein (1984), conjecture about the relationship between these disorders stems from clinical observations starting as early as the 1960s (e.g., Klein, 1964); and although this hypothesis is consistent with some early developmental theories, systematic observation has been equivocal. For example, a study of adults found that those with self-reported PD symptoms scored higher on retrospective measures of childhood SAD than those with more general types of anxiety symptoms (Silove & Manicavasagar, 1993). Additionally, a similar retrospective study found that adults with anxiety disorders reported more childhood SAD symptoms. Furthermore, those with PD reported significantly more symptoms than those with other anxiety disorders (Silove, Harris, Morgan et al., 1995). It should be noted though that there was significant comorbidity in the PD group and this was not controlled for. Again, however, in a study of adults who feared school as children, there was a trend for those retrospectively reporting more childhood SAD to have a higher likelihood of PD with agoraphobia (Silove et al., 2002). Similarly, using classification and regression trees, Biederman and colleagues found childhood SAD to be an independent predictor of PD in both referred and nonreferred adults (Biederman et al., 2005; Biederman, Petty, Faroane et al., 2006). Also, youth in the OADP with SAD in childhood or adolescence were at increased risk for the development of PD in adulthood even when controlling for demographic characteristics and comorbid psychopathology (Lewinsohn et al., 2008). Additionally, in prospective analyses of youth enrolled in the EDSP, childhood SAD was strongly associated with the development of later PD with agoraphobia, with a hazard ratio of 18.1 (Brückl, Wittchen, Höfler, Pfister, Scneider, & Lieb, 2006). The link between SAD and the development of PD was also found in a 5-year prospective study of youth, including those at high risk for PD (Biederman et al., 2007). However, several other prospective studies have failed to find this link. For example, when youth treated for anxiety disorders were assessed 7 years later, those with a history of SAD did not have a higher incidence of PD than those with other childhood anxiety disorders; this was true regardless of whether or not SAD had remitted as a result of treatment (Aschenbrand, Kendall, Webb, Safford, & Flannery-Schroeder, 2003). Moreover, no relationship was found between a SAD diagnosis at baseline and a PD diagnosis at follow-up in the NYLS (Pine et al., 1998), and SAD was not associated with either cued or uncued panic attacks (too few cases of full-blown PD were present to conduct analyses) in the GSMS (Bittner et al., 2007). Similarly, youth in the DMHS diagnosed with SAD between the ages of 11 and 15 years were not found to be at increased risk for PD at age 32 (Gregory et al., 2007). Furthermore, even in those studies that have found a link between SAD and PD, many have not found this to be a specific link as originally hypothesized, with other childhood disorders predicting later PD and SAD predicting later non-panic symptoms and disorders (e.g., Biederman et al., 2005, 2006; Brückl et al., 2006).

Relatedly, several studies have found a link between early SAD and later affective disorders. In fact, 75% of youth diagnosed with SAD in the OADP were later diagnosed with MDD; when controlling for comorbidity, youth with SAD were more likely to develop MDD compared to youth with no disorder or youth with a non-anxiety disorder but not when compared to youth with other anxiety disorders (Lewinsohn et al., 2008). In addition, Biederman et al. (2007) found that SAD predicted later MDD even when controlling for comorbid anxiety disorders at baseline and parental PD and MDD. SAD, particularly, persistent SAD, was also associated with depression in the VTSABD, with about 10% of those with transient SAD and 28% of persistent SAD cases evidencing either major or minor depression at follow-up (Foley et al., 2004). Interestingly, in at least two studies, SAD has also been associated with bipolar disorder (Brückl et al., 2006; Henin et al., 2007).

Several studies have also found evidence for a link between early SAD and the development of later anxiety disorders other than PD – particularly GAD/OAD, social anxiety disorder, and specific phobias, with some evidence of a link between SAD and later OCD (Brückl et al., 2006; Foley et al., 2004; Gregory et al., 2007; Pine et al., 1998). However, it should be noted that while studies have generally found that youth with SAD in childhood are at increased risk of later anxious pathology, studies have not been entirely consistent about the specific anxiety disorders that develop subsequent to SAD. Finally, as with anxiety disorders in general, there is some evidence for a link between SAD and later substance use disorders (Brückl et al., 2006).

Social anxiety disorder/social phobia

Retrospective studies of adults have found social anxiety disorder to be predictive of MDD (Alpert, Maddocks, Rosenbaum, & Fava, 1994; Kessler, Stang, Wittchen, Stein, & Walters, 1999). In fact, in a study of 116 adults with MDD by age 18, social anxiety disorder was the most common premorbid diagnosis, with approximately 18% of the sample reporting clinically significant social anxiety prior to the onset of the MDD (Alpert et al., 1994). Additionally prospective studies have also found a link between social anxiety disorder and the development of depression (Beesdo et al., 2007; Stein, Fuetsch, Müller, Hfler, Lieb & Wittchen, 2001; see however Pine et al. 1998), with social anxiety disorder comorbid with depression predicting a particularly problematic course (e.g., higher likelihood of suicidal ideation and longer duration of depressive episode). Moreover, social anxiety disorder has been related to more severe and persistent mood disorder (Kessler et al., 1999).

In addition, social anxiety disorder in youth has been associated with the development of substance disorders and may in fact, be largely responsible for the relationship between anxiety disorders as a group and substance disorder. For example, youth in the OADP diagnosed with social anxiety disorder were at greater risk for developing alcohol or cannabis dependence even when controlling for comorbidity with other anxiety disorders (Buckner, Schmidt, Lang, Small, Schlauch, & Lewinsohn, 2008). Moreover, some evidence for the specificity of this link was found other anxiety disorders (nor mood disorders) were not found to be related to increased risk when controlling for comorbidity. Similarly, youth in the EDSP with a social anxiety disorder diagnosis at baseline were more likely to report regular alcohol consumption as well as consumption at hazardous levels at follow-up (Zimmermann et al., 2003). The presence of social anxiety disorder was also positively related to the persistence of substance dependence disorders (Zimmermann et al., 2003). Importantly, the link between social anxiety disorder and substance disorders may be present even when the social anxiety disorder remits (Zimmermann et al., 2003).

Some studies have also described an interesting relationship between social anxiety disorder and the development of externalizing disorders. For example, Bittner et al. (2007) found a significant bivariate relationship between social phobia and attention deficit hyperactivity disorder (ADHD); however, in logistic regressions controlling for comorbidity, the relationship was no longer significant. Moreover, some evidence suggests that social phobia may serve as a protective factor in the development of externalizing disorder, with youth exhibiting more social anxiety symptoms being less likely to evidence later conduct disorder (Pine, Cohen, Cohen, & Brook, 2000).

Specific phobias

In general, the prognosis for youth with specific phobias seems to be somewhat brighter than for youth with other anxiety disorders – at least when looking at the development of new disorder. Several studies have found that specific phobias in childhood are not predictive of later psychopathology (e.g., Biederman et al., 2007; Bittner et al., 2004). In fact, Last and colleagues found that, of the anxiety disorders, specific phobias in youth were associated with the lowest rate of new disorder (Last et al., 1996). However, this may be true for "pure" specific phobia but not specific phobias comorbid with other disorders (Bittner et al., 2004). Additionally, most studies that have examined the course of specific phobias have only examined diagnostic outcomes within the anxiety disorders or affective disorders, so we know little about the relationship – or lack of relationship – between specific phobias and later non-internalizing disorders (e.g., substance abuse). Moreover, even examining these limited outcomes, studies are not entirely consistent. For example, in the DMHS, specific phobias diagnosed in late childhood and early adolescence were predictive of adult GAD, social phobia, agoraphobia, OCD, and PTSD (Gregory et al., 2007); however, it should be noted that these analyses did not control for comorbidity. Additionally, some evidence was found for a link between specific phobias and the development of later GAD in the NYLS study (Pine et al., 1998). Findings have been particularly conflicted around the relationship with specific phobias and later PD, with some studies finding no relationship (Gregory et al., 2007) while others have found a link (Biederman et al., 2006) even when controlling for comorbidity with other anxiety disorders and other disorders in general.

Summary

Although there are some discrepancies across studies, research has generally found support for heterotypic comorbidity within the anxiety disorders. However, more specific links that have been hypothesized – such as the one between SAD in childhood and PD in adulthood – have not been widely supported. There also seems to be strong support for the heterotypic comorbidity of early anxiety disorder and subsequent depression, a claim which has been echoed in the clinical literature for some time (Kovacs, Gatsonis, Paulauskas, & Richards, 1989; Mitchell, McCauley, Burke, & Moss, 1988; Strauss, Last, Hersen, & Kazdin, 1988b). Given that this relationship is well established, more research needs to be conducted to determine the underlying reasons. Additionally, anxiety disorders, particularly social anxiety disorder, have been linked with substance use disorders. While this link may at first seem counterintuitive – that those with anxiety disorders would be adverse to the risks associated with substance use – some studies suggest that those with social anxiety disorder may begin using substances in social situations as a way of self-medicating (Norberg, Norton, Olivier, & Zvolensky, 2010), or that they may be sensitive to the social rewards that substance use can bring (Kashdan, Collins, & Elhai, 2006; Kashdan, Elhai, & Breen, 2008). Finally, some research suggests that although most individuals with social anxiety do exhibit low risk-taking behavior, there may exist a subgroup that is characterized by increased novelty seeking (Kashdan & Hofmann, 2008); it may be this group that goes on to experiment with alcohol and other drugs and eventually develop substance disorders.

Predictors and Moderators of Outcome

Although studies suggest a significant minority of youth with anxiety disorders will continue to have clinically significant psychopathology into adulthood, most studies conclude that most child and adolescent anxiety disorders will not continue into adulthood but that, on the other hand, most adults with an internalizing disorder will have been previously ill with an internalizing disorder in childhood or adolescence. Thus, it would seem that prevention efforts targeting youth with the most persistent anxiety disorders could have significant effects on the prevalence of adult psychopathology. The obvious question, then, is whether we can predict which youth manifesting anxiety disorders in childhood or adolescence will have persistent psychopathology. Several potential predictors of the course of childhood anxiety disorders have been investigated with mixed results.

Age of onset has been one such putative predictor examined across several studies. However, in general, age of onset has not been found to predict persistence of anxiety disorders. For example, Orvaschel et al. (1995) found no relationship between age of onset of disorder and either recovery or recurrence of anxiety disorder in the OADP. Similarly, Last et al. (1996) found that age of onset of failed to predict recovery or the development of new disorder. Although few studies have examined whether age of onset predicts the course of particular anxiety disorders, the studies that we are aware of examine SAD and the findings have been somewhat contradictory. Lewinsohn and colleagues found that the age of onset of SAD was not related to the development of new disorder (Lewinsohn et al., 2008); however, recent research indicates that age of onset for SAD may help clarify the relationship between SAD and PD. More specifically, Doerfler, Toscano, and Connor (2008) analyzed records for children referred to a medical university who presented with SAD with and without comorbid PD. When comparing children with SAD ($n = 63$) to those with SAD and PD ($n = 31$), children with SAD and PD evidenced a later age of onset of SAD (mean age = 6.9 years) relative to children with SAD only (mean age = 4.7) (Doerfler et al., 2008). So, while it has often been postulated that youth who manifest anxiety disorders early in their development will be most at risk for ongoing psychopathology, empirical studies do not seem to support this.

Similarly, although several studies have examined whether there are sex differences in the course of anxiety disorders, most have found limited support for sex as a predictor or moderator of disease course. For example, sex did not predict the persistence of SAD nor did it moderate the effects of other potential predictors of course (e.g., impairment, socioeconomic status, parental conflict) in the VTSABD (Foley et al., 2004), nor was sex found to be a significant predictor of continuity or discontinuity in the OADP sample (Lewinsohn et al., 2008; Orvaschel et al., 1995). Similarly, sex also did not predict internalizing disorder persistence in the NYLS (Pine et al., 1998). However, Bittner et al. (2007) found that sex did moderate the course of GAD such that the relationship between childhood GAD and adolescent substance abuse was significantly and substantially stronger for girls than for boys (ORs 16.0 and 0.4, respectively). Additionally, there is some evidence that sex moderated the outcome for youth with internalizing disorders in the DMHS, with girls with internalizing disorders evidencing greater risk for continuing internalizing problems and boys with internalizing disorders being at greater risk for externalizing problems (McGee, Feehan, Williams, & Anderson, 1992). Thus, most studies find little evidence that sex predicts the outcome of anxiety disorders or that it moderates the effects of other potential predictors. The one possible exception may be in the relationship between anxiety disorders and subsequent substance disorders or externalizing behaviors (see however, Zimmermann et al., 2003). Interestingly, some recent research suggests that girls and boys suffering with anxiety symptoms or anxiety disorders may engage in substance use for different reasons – with anxious girls more likely to use substances to ameliorate negative affect and anxious boys more likely to use substances to enhance positive affect (Norberg et al., 2010). This may place anxious girls more at risk for overuse and risky use. Further research is needed to examine sex as a moderator of the course of disorder and, specifically, the link between early anxiety disorders and subsequent externalizing disorders in boys as it is unclear that this is a reliable finding.

Severity of disorder has also been examined as a predictor of course with the hypothesis that the most severely ill youth will be the ones to evidence persistent anxiety and develop new disorders. In general this hypothesis has been supported. For example, Bittner et al. (2004) found that level of impairment was among the best predictors of depression in youth with anxiety disorders. Similarly, results from the EDSP suggest that severity of impairment and symptom severity are related to an increased risk for persistent anxiety disorder as well as the development of an affective disorder (Bittner et al., 2004; Wittchen et al., 2000a). Studies examining symptoms of anxiety and depression dimensionally have also found that more severe anxiety predicts subsequent affective symptoms (Hale, Raaijmakers, Muris, van Hoof, & Meeus, 2008). Additionally, severity and impairment seems to be related to the likelihood that youth with SAD will go on to develop a substance disorder (Lewinsohn et al., 2008); however, it may not be related to the persistence of SAD (Foley et al., 2004). Further, comorbidity that is somewhat correlated with severity, has also been shown to predict the course of pediatric anxiety disorders. For example, Essau and colleagues found that comorbidity with a non-anxiety disorder was related to persistence of anxiety (Essau et al., 2002). More specifically, they found that while 31.6% of youth who evidenced only anxiety disorders at an initial assessment continued to have an anxiety disorder 15 months later, 68.4% of those comorbid with a non-anxiety disorder at the initial assessment evidenced persistent anxiety disorder. Moreover, in regression analyses predicting persistence, the presence of somatoform disorders and substance use disorders at the initial assessment were significant predictors of ongoing anxiety disorder (Essau et al., 2002). Additionally, Pine et al. (1998) found that the presence of multiple anxiety disorders or multiple internalizing disorders present during adolescence was related to increased risk of anxiety disorder and internalizing disorder in young adulthood. Similarly, the risk of later depression seems to be elevated for youth who have more than one anxiety disorder; although this effect may be largely driven by the differences in risk for youth with specific phobias alone versus the risk for youth with specific phobias comorbid with other anxiety disorders (Bittner et al., 2004).

Parental psychopathology, implicated in the development of anxiety disorders by learning theories, cognitive theories, and psychodynamic theories has also been examined as a predictor of the course of anxiety disorders in youth and surprisingly most studies fail to find significant effects for parental psychopathology or a family history of anxiety disorders (e.g., Essau et al., 2002; Foley et al., 2004; Kessler, Davis, & Kendler, 1997; Knappe, Beesdo, Fehm, Hfler, Lieb, & Wittchen, 2009; Last et al., 1996). Somewhat related though, mixed results have been found for family functioning. For example, marital conflict and family functioning (e.g., affective overinvolvement and family communication) has been related to persistence of anxiety disorders (Foley et al., 2004; Knappe et al., 2009) but attachment and parental overprotection, warmth, and rejection have generally not been related to the course of pediatric anxiety disorders (Essau et al., 2002; Knappe et al., 2009). Moreover, studies of the effects of stressors and negative life events, which have sometimes been defined to include exposure to parental psychopathology and negative family functioning, have also been somewhat mixed. For example Kessler et al. (1997) found relatively weak associations between life stressors and the development of anxiety disorders in youth and negative life events did not predict the course of anxiety disorders. On the other hand, Essau and colleagues found that the number of negative life events experienced by youth with anxiety disorders did predict persistence of disorder (Essau et al., 2002). However, it should be noted that few studies have examined problematic family functioning and negative life events more generally as predictors of course, so it is difficult to know whether these findings, or lack of findings, will be replicated.

Similarly, few studies have examined the effects of ethnicity, race, or socioeconomic factors on the course of pediatric anxiety disorders; the ones that have done so have found limited support for these sociocultural variables as predictors or moderators of the course of anxiety disorders in youth (e.g., Bittner et al., 2007); however, given the scarcity of research investigating these questions and the fact that some studies have found differences in the expression of anxiety disorders across different ethnic groups (Beidel, Turner, & Trager, 1994; Compton, Nelson, & March, 2000; Glover, Pumariega, Holzer, Wise, & Rodriguez, 1999), this is an important avenue for future research.

Finally, although treatment would obviously be hypothesized to have a strong relationship with the course of disorder, surprisingly, research has not shown this to be the case – at least not in the expected direction. For example, having received treatment has not been related to persistence or recovery from SAD (Foley et al., 2004), nor anxiety disorders in general (Last et al., 1996). In fact, Last and colleagues found that, although treatment was not related to recovery from anxiety disorders, treatment was related to the development of new disorder – with youth receiving treatment for their initial anxiety disorder being almost six times *more* likely to develop a new disorder when compared to those who did not receive treatment (Last et al., 1996). While it might be hypothesized that the children who received treatment were those with the most severe symptoms and that this drove the relationship with new disorders, severity did not emerge as a significant predictor of disorder persistence or new disorder in this study, suggesting something else might be responsible for this relationship as well as the lack of relationship between treatment and recovery. However, it may be that the type of treatments commonly offered to youth with anxiety disorders is responsible for this effect. Several studies suggest that the treatment youth typically receive in non-research settings differs in important ways from those treatments that have been found to be efficacious and that very few children and adolescents receive an evidence based treatment (e.g., Weiss, Catron, Harris, & Phung, 1999; Weisz, Han, & Valeri, 1996; Weisz, Jensen-Doss, & Hawley, 2006). In fact, non-research based psychotherapy for youth has been associated with a small *negative* effect on outcome (Weiss et al., 1999). Given this, it is perhaps not surprising that treatment is not related to recovery from anxiety disorder or that at least one study has found treatment to be related to negative prognosis. For this reason, it will be important to carefully examine current efforts to disseminate evidence based treatments and to examine their effects on the course of anxiety disorders in youth.

Non-Diagnostic Outcomes for Youth with Anxiety Disorders

Youth with anxiety disorders experience a wide range of psychosocial sequelae, sometimes well into adulthood. When anxiety symptoms are at their worst, the associated impairment and interference in daily life seems to be significant (Essau et al., 2000). In fact, in one study, 100% of those with PD reported that their symptoms engendered significant impairment in their daily lives (Newman et al., 1996). More specifically, young adults with a history of anxiety disorders in youth may be less likely than those without childhood disorders to live independently and they may get less education and training than their non-anxious peers (Last, Hansen, & Franco, 1997; Woodward & Fergusson, 2001). Children with anxiety disorders have also been found to be more lonely and less socially skilled than children without a psychiatric disorder (Strauss, Lease, Kazdin, Dulcan, & Last, 1989) and they appear to suffer social neglect in settings with peers (e.g., Strauss, Lahey, Frick, Frame, & Hynd, 1988a).

Of note, comorbidity seems to significantly affect psychosocial impairment across several studies. For example, examining impairment in youth and young adults with a variety of mental disorders, Wittchen and colleagues found that comorbidity substantially affected workplace absenteeism, with 35% of the sample with one disorder reporting missing work because of their psychiatric symptoms and over 60% of those with at least two disorders reporting being absent from work due to the impairment associated with their disorders (Wittchen, Nelson, & Lachner, 1998). Additionally, Woodward and Fergusson (2001) found that as the number of anxiety disorders experienced during mid-adolescence (i.e., between 14 and 16 years of age) increased, the likelihood going to college decreased and the likelihood of becoming a parent at a young age increased. In fact, they found that non-anxious participants in the CHDS were $2^{1}/_{2}$ times more likely to attend college than those youth with an anxiety disorder. Similarly, youth with a history of anxiety disorder comorbid with an affective disorder are less likely to be employed or in school as young adults (Last et al., 1997).

Given the prevalence of anxiety disorders and the associated impairment, the negative consequences have effects on the societal as well as the individual level. In fact, studies in the United States and abroad have investigated the economic burden to society of anxiety disorders and the figures are quite remarkable. For example, Bodden, Dirksen, and Bögels (2008) found that clinical levels of anxiety in youth cost the Dutch society approximately 20 million Euros per year. Similarly, data from the NCS in the 1990s suggests that anxiety disorders cost the United States over 42 billion dollars annually or about $1542 per person with an anxiety disorder (Greenberg, Sisitsky, Kessler et al., 1999). Similarly, Andlin-Sobcoki and Wittchen (2005) found that costs related to anxiety disorders in Europe ranged from about 500 euro to 1600 euro per case. Moreover, while the personal and societal costs associated with anxiety disorders are great, the likelihood of those with an anxiety disorder seeking treatment are low (Ravens-Sieberer, Wille, Erhart et al., 2008) and, perhaps even more importantly, the probability of getting effective treatment may be even lower (e.g., Nutt, Kessler, Alonso et al., 2007; Weiss et al., 1999)

Conclusions

In sum, while most youth with an anxiety disorder will recover at least to some degree, anxiety disorders seem to be a problem of childhood and adolescence in that for most individuals who experience an anxiety disorder anytime in their lives, the symptoms become apparent well before adulthood. Further, anxiety disorders in youth are predictive of later affective disorder as well as substance use disorders. Unfortunately, aside from severity and comorbidity, we currently know little about what predicts or moderates the course of anxiety disorders and it seems that the treatments that have been commonly used outside research setting in the past several decades have not been affective in producing a more positive course for youth with anxiety disorders. Therefore it seems that many youth will recover to some degree on their own but for those who do not many of the most commonly available treatments do not better their chances. While the field has made considerable advancements in the treatment of anxiety disorders, whether these treatments can be effectively disseminated and whether effective dissemination can have a positive effect on the course of anxiety in youth remains to be seen. Moreover, it is unclear whether effective treatment can prevent some of the negative psychosocial sequelae (e.g., poor educational outcomes and early parenthood) associated with anxiety disorders in youth. These are important questions for the next generation of epidemiological studies to address as it is becoming increasingly clear that the anxiety disorders and those disorders that anxiety portends exact a significant toll on the individuals affected as well as society as a whole.

References

Alpert, J. E., Maddocks, A., Rosenbaum, J. F., & Fava, M. (1994). Childhood psychopathology retrospectively assessed among adults with early onset major depression. *Journal of Affective Disorders, 31* (3), 165–171. doi: 10. 1016/0165-0327(94)90025-6

APA (Producer). (2010, August 4, 2010). *DSM-5: The Future of Psychiatric Diagnosis.* American Psychiatric Association. Retrieved from http://www. dsm5. org/Pages/Default. aspx

APA (1987). *Diagnostic and Statistical Manual of Mental Disorders,*(3rd revised edn. Washington, DC: American Psychiatric Association.

APA (1994). *Diagnostic and Statistical Manual of Mental Disorders*, 4th edn. Washington, DC: American Psychiatric Association.

APA (2000). *Diagnostic and Statistical Manual of Mental Disorders*, 4th revised edn). Washington, DC: American Psychiatric Assocation.

Andlin-Sobocki, P., & Wittchen, H. U. (2005). Cost of anxiety disorders in Europe. *European Journal of Neurology, 12*(s1), 39–44. doi: 10.1111/j.1468-1331.2005.01196.x

Angst, J., Gamma, A., Baldwin, D. S., Ajdacic-Gross, V., & Rssler, W. (2009). The generalized anxiety spectrum: Prevalence, onset, course and outcome. *European Archives of Psychiatry and Clinical Neuroscience, 259* (1), 37–45. doi: 10.1007/s00406-008-0832-9.

Aschenbrand, S. G., Kendall, P. C., Webb, A., Safford, S. M., & Flannery-Schroeder, E. (2003). Is childhood separation anxiety disorder a predictor of adult panic disorder and agoraphobia? A seven-year longitudinal study. *Journal of the American Academy of Child & Adolescent Psychiatry, 42* (12), 1478–1485. doi: 10.1097/00004583-200312000-00015

Beesdo, K., Bittner, A., Pine, D. S., Stein, M. B., Hofler, M., Lieb, R., & Wittchen, H.-U. (2007). Incidence of social anxiety disorder and the consistent risk for secondary depression in the first three decades of life. *Archives of General Psychiatry, 64* (8), 903–912. doi: 10.1001/archpsyc.64.8.903

Beesdo, K., Pine, D. S., Lieb, R., & Wittchen, H.-U. (2010). Incidence and risk patterns of anxiety and depressive disorders and categorization of generalized anxiety disorder. *Archives of General Psychiatry, 67* (1), 47–57. doi: 10.1001/archgenpsychiatry.2009.177

Beidel, D. C., Turner, M. W., & Trager, K. N. (1994). Test anxiety and childhood anxiety disorders in African American and White school children. *Journal of Anxiety Disorders, 8* (2), 169–179. doi: 10.1016/0887-6185(94)90014-0.

Biederman, J., Petty, C., Faraone, S. V., Hirshfeld-Becker, D. R., Henin, A., Rauf, A., et al. (2005). Childhood antecedents to panic disorder in referred and nonreferred adults. *Journal of Child and Adolescent Psychopharmacology, 15* (4), 549–562. doi: 10.1089/cap.2005.15.549

Biederman, J., Petty, C. R., Faraone, S. V., Hirshfeld-Becker, D. R., Henin, A., Brauer, L., et al. (2006). Antecedents to panic disorder in nonreferred adults. *Journal of Clinical Psychiatry, 67*(8), 1179–1186.

Biederman, J., Petty, C. R., Hirshfeld-Becker, D. R., Henin, A., Faraone, S. V., Fraire, M., et al. (2007). Developmental trajectories of anxiety disorders in offspring at high risk for panic disorder and major depression. *Psychiatry Research, 153* (3), 245–252. doi: 10.1016/j.psychres.2007.02.016.

Bittner, A., Egger, H. L., Erkanli, A., Costello, E. J., Foley, D. L., & Angold, A. (2007). What do childhood anxiety disorders predict? *Journal of Child Psychology and Psychiatry, 48* (12), 1174–1183. doi: 10.1111/j.1469–7610.2007.01812.x.

Bittner, A., Goodwin, R. D., Wittchen, H.-U., Beesdo, K., Hfler, M., & Lieb, R. (2004). What characteristics of primary anxiety disorders predict subsequent major depressive disorder? *Journal of Clinical Psychiatry, 65* (5), 618–626.

Bodden, D. H., Dirksen, C. D., & Bögels, S. M. (2008). Societal burden of clinically anxious youth referred for treatment: A cost-of-illness study. *Journal of Abnormal Child Psychology: An official publication of the International Society for Research in Child and Adolescent Psychopathology, 36* (4), 487–497. doi: 10.1007/s10802-007-9194-4.

Breslau, N., Davis, G. C., & Prabucki, K. (1987). Searching for evidence on the validity of generalized anxiety disorder: Psychopathology in children of anxious mothers. *Psychiatry Research, 20* (4), 285–297. doi: 10.1016/0165-1781(87)90089-8.

Brückl, T. M., Wittchen, H.-U., Höfler, M., Pfister, H., Schneider, S., & Lieb, R. (2006). Childhood separation anxiety and the risk of subsequent psychopathology: Results from a community study. *Psychotherapy and Psychosomatics, 76* (1), 47–56. *doi: 10.1159/000096364.*

Buckner, J. D., Schmidt, N. B., Lang, A. R., Small, J. W., Schlauch, R. C., & Lewinsohn, P. M. (2008). Specificity of social anxiety disorder as a risk factor for alcohol and cannabis dependence. *Journal of Psychiatric Research, 42* (3), 230–239. doi: 10.1016/j.jpsychires.2007.01.002.

Compton, S. N., Nelson, A. H., & March, J. S. (2000). Social phobia and separation anxiety symptoms in community and clinical samples of children and adolescents. *Journal of the American Academy of Child & Adolescent Psychiatry, 39* (8), 1040–1046. doi: 10.1097/00004583-200008000-00020

Costello, E. J., Egger, H. L., & Angold, A. (2005). The developmental epidemiology of anxiety disorders: Phenomenology, prevalence, and comorbidity. *Child and Adolescent Psychiatric Clinics of North America, 14* (4), 631–648. doi: 10.1016/j.chc.2005.06.003.

Crocetti, E., Klimstra, T., Keijsers, L., Hale, W. W., & Meeus, W. (2009). Anxiety trajectories and identity development in adolescence: A five-wave longitudinal study. *Journal of Youth and Adolescence, 38* (6), 839–849. doi: 10.1007/s10964-008-9302-y.

Doerfler, L. A., Toscano, P. F., & Connor, D. F. (2008). Separation anxiety and panic disorder in clinically referred youth. *Journal of Anxiety Disorders, 22* (4), 602–611. doi: 10.1016/j.janxdis.2007.05.009.

Essau, C. A., Conradt, J., & Petermann, F. (2000). Frequency, comorbidity, and psychosocial impairment of anxiety disorders in German adolescents. *Journal of Anxiety Disorders, 14* (3), 263–279. doi: 10. 1016/s0887–6185(99)00039–0

Essau, C. A., Conradt, J., & Petermann, F. (2002). Course and outcome of anxiety disorders in adolescents. *Journal of Anxiety Disorders, 16* (1), 67–81. doi: 10.1016150887-6185(01)00091-3.

Foley, D. L., Pickles, A., Maes, H. M., Silberg, J. L., & Eaves, L. J. (2004). Course and short-term outcomes of separation anxiety disorder in a community sample of twins. *Journal of the American Academy of Child & Adolescent Psychiatry, 43* (9), 1107–1114. doi: 10.1097/01.chi.0000131138.16734.f4.

Frances, A. J., Widiger, T. A., & Fyer, M. R. (1990). The influence of classification methods on comorbidity. In J. D. Maser & C. R. Cloninger (Eds.), *Comorbidity of Mood and Anxiety Disorders,* (pp. 41–59). Washington, DC: American Psychiatric Association.

Gittelman, R., & Klein, D. F. (1984). Relationship between separation anxiety and panic and agoraphobic disorders. *Psychopathology, 17* (Suppl 1), 56–65. doi: 10.1159/000284078.

Glover, S. H., Pumariega, A. J., Holzer, C. E. I., Wise, B. K., & Rodriguez, M. (1999). Anxiety symptomatology in Mexican-American adolescents. *Journal of Child & Family Studies, 8* (1), 47–57. doi: 10.1023/A:1022994510944.

Goodwin, R. D., Lieb, R., Hoefler, M., Pfister, H., Bittner, A., Beesdo, K., & Wittchen, H.-U. (2004). Panic attack as a risk factor for severe psychopathology. *The American Journal of Psychiatry, 161* (12), 2207–2214. doi: 10.1176/appi.ajp.161.12.2207.

Greenberg, P. E., Sisitsky, T., Kessler, R. C., Finkelstein, S. N., Berndt, E. R., Davidson, J. R. T., et al. (1999). The economic burden of anxiety disorders in the 1990s. *Journal of Clinical Psychiatry, 60* (7), 427–435.

Gregory, A. M., Caspi, A., Moffitt, T. E., Koenen, K., Eley, T. C., & Poulton, R. (2007). Juvenile mental health histories of adults with anxiety disorders. *The American Journal of Psychiatry, 164* (2), 301–308. doi: 10. 1176/appi.ajp.164.2.301.

Hale, W. W., Raaijmakers, Q., Muris, P., van Hoof, A., & Meeus, W. (2008). Developmental trajectories of adolescent anxiety disorder symptoms: A 5-year prospective community study. *Journal of the American Academy of Child & Adolescent Psychiatry, 47* (5), 556–564. doi: 10.1097/CHI.0b013e3181676583.

Henin, A., Biederman, J., Mick, E., Hirshfeld-Becker, D. R., Sachs, G. S., Wu, Y., et al. (2007). Childhood antecedent disorders to bipolar disorder in adults: A controlled study. *Journal of Affective Disorders, 99* (1–3), 51–57. doi: 10.1016/j.jad.2006.09.001

Kashdan, T. B., Collins, R. L., & Elhai, J. D. (2006). Social anxiety and positive outcome expectancies on risk-taking behaviors. *Cognitive Therapy and Research, 30* (6), 749–761. doi: 10. 1007/s10608–006–9017-x

Kashdan, T. B., Elhai, J. D., & Breen, W. E. (2008). Social anxiety and disinhibition: An analysis of curiosity and social rank appraisals, approach-avoidance conflicts, and disruptive risk-taking behavior. *Journal of Anxiety Disorders, 22* (6), 925–939. doi: 10.1016/j.janxdis.2007.09.009.

Kashdan, T. B., & Hofmann, S. G. (2008). The high-novelty-seeking, impulsive subtype of generalized social anxiety disorder. *Depression and Anxiety, 25* (6), 535–541. doi: 10.1002/da.20382.

Keller, M. B., Lavori, P. W., Wunder, J., Beardslee, W. R., Schwartz, L. E., & Roth, J. (1992). Chronic course of anxiety disorders in children and adolescents. *Journal of the American Academy of Child & Adolescent Psychiatry, 31* (4), 595–599. doi: 10.1097/00004583-199207000-00003.

Kessler, R. C., Angermeyer, M., Anthony, J. C., De Graaf, R., Demyttenaere, K., Gasquet, I., et al. (2007). Lifetime prevalence and age-of-onset distributions of mental disorders in the World Health Organization's World Mental Health Survey Initiative. *World Psychiatry, 6* (3), 168–176.

Kessler, R. C., Berglund, P., Demler, O., Jin, R., Merikangas, K. R., & Walters, E. E. (2005). Lifetime prevalence and age-of-onset distributions of DSM-IV disorders in the National Comorbidity Survey Replication. *Archives of General Psychiatry, 62* (6), 593–602. doi: 10.1001/archpsyc.62.6.593.

Kessler, R. C., Davis, C. G., & Kendler, K. S. (1997). Childhood adversity and adult psychiatric disorder in the US National Comorbidity Survey. *Psychological Medicine: A Journal of Research in Psychiatry and the Allied Sciences, 27* (5), 1101–1119. doi: 10.1017/s0033291797005588.

Kessler, R. C., Stang, P., Wittchen, H. U., Stein, M., & Walters, E. E. (1999). Lifetime comorbidities between social phobia and mood disorders in the US National Comorbidity Survey. *Psychological Medicine: A Journal of Research in Psychiatry and the Allied Sciences, 29* (3), 555–567. doi: 10.1017/s0033291799008375.

Kim-Cohen, J., Caspi, A., Moffitt, T. E., Harrington, H., Milne, B. J., & Poulton, R. (2003). Prior juvenile diagnoses in adults with mental disorder: Developmental follow-back of a prospective-longitudinal cohort. *Archives of General Psychiatry, 60* (7), 709–717. doi: 10.1001/archpsyc.60.7.709.

Klein, D. (1964). Delineation of two drug-responsive anxiety syndromes. *Psychopharmacologia, 3*, 397–408.

Knappe, S., Beesdo, K., Fehm, L., Hfler, M., Lieb, R., & Wittchen, H.-U. (2009). Do parental psychopathology and unfavorable family environment predict the persistence of social phobia? *Journal of Anxiety Disorders, 23* (7), 986–994. doi: 10.1016/j.janxdis.2009.06.010.

Kovacs, M., Gatsonis, C., Paulauskas, S., & Richards, C. (1989). Depressive disorders in childhood IV. A longitudinal study of comorbidity with and risk for anxiety disorders. *Archives of General Psychiatry, 46*, 776–782.

Last, C. G., Hansen, C., & Franco, N. (1997). Anxious children in adulthood: A prospective study of adjustment. *Journal of the American Academy of Child & Adolescent Psychiatry, 36* (5), 645–652. doi: 10.1097/00004583-199705000-00015.

Last, C. G., Perrin, S., Hersen, M., & Kazdin, A. E. (1996). A prospective study of childhood anxiety disorders. *Journal of the American Academy of Child & Adolescent Psychiatry, 35* (11), 1502–1510. doi: 10.1097/00004583-199611000-00019.

Lewinsohn, P. M., Holm-Denoma, J. M., Small, J. W., Seeley, J. R., & Joiner, T. E. (2008). Separation anxiety disorder in childhood as a risk factor for future mental illness. *Journal of the American Academy of Child & Adolescent Psychiatry, 47* (5), 548–555. doi: 10.1097/CHI.0b013e31816765e7.

Lewinsohn, P. M., Zinbarg, R. E., Seeley, J. R., Lewinsohn, M., & Sack, W. H. (1997). Lifetime comorbidity among anxiety disorders and between anxiety disorders and other mental disorders in adolescents. *Journal of Anxiety Disorders, 11* (4), 377–394. doi: 10.1016/S0887-6185(97)00017-0

Manicavasagar, V., Silove, D., Curtis, J., & Wagner, R. (2000). Continuities of separation anxiety from early life into adulthood. *Journal of Anxiety Disorders, 14* (1), 1–18. doi: 10.016/s0887-6185(99)00029-8

McGee, R., Feehan, M., Williams, S., & Anderson, J. (1992). DSM-III disorders from age 11 to age 15 years. *Journal of the American Academy of Child and Adolescent Psychiatry, 31* (1), 50–59.

Mitchell, J. R., McCauley, E., Burke, P. M., & Moss, S. J. (1988). Phenomenology of depression in children and adolescents. *Journal of the American Academy of Child & Adolescent Psychiatry, 27* (1), 12–20.

Moffitt, T. E., Harrington, H., Caspi, A., Kim-Cohen, J., Goldberg, D., Gregory, A. M., & Poulton, R. (2007). Depression and generalized anxiety disorder: Cumulative and sequential comorbidity in a birth cohort followed prospectivity to age 32 years. *Archives of General Psychiatry, 64* (6), 651–660. doi: 10.1001/archpsyc.64.6.651.

Newman, D. L., Moffitt, T. E., Caspi, A., Magdol, L., Silva, P. A., & Stanton, W. R. (1996). Psychiatric disorder in a birth cohort of young adults: Prevalence, comorbidity, clinical significance, and new case incidence from ages 11 to 21. *Journal of Consulting and Clinical Psychology, 64* (3), 552–562. doi: 10.1037/0022-006x.64.3.552.

Norberg, M. M., Norton, A. R., Olivier, J., & Zvolensky, M. J. (2010). Social anxiety, reasons for drinking, and college students. *Behavior Therapy, 41* (4), 555–566. doi: 10.1016/j.beth.2010.03.002.

Nutt, D. J.,Kessler, R. C., Alonso, J., Benbow, A., Lecrubier, Y., Lpine, J.-P., et al. (2007). Consensus statement on the benefit to the community of ESEMeD (European Study of the Epidemiology of Mental Disorders) survey data on depression and anxiety. *Journal of Clinical Psychiatry, 68* (Suppl 2), 42–48.

Orvaschel, H., Lewinsohn, P. M., & Seeley, J. R. (1995). Continuity of psychopathology in a community sample of adolescents. *Journal of the American Academy of Child and Adolescent Psychiatry, 34* (11), 1525–1535. doi: 10.1097/00004583-199511000-00020.

Pine, D. S., Cohen, E., Cohen, P., & Brook, J. S. (2000). Social phobia and the persistence of conduct problems. *Journal of Child Psychology & Psychiatry & Allied Disciplines, 41* (5), 657–665. doi: 10.1111/1469- 7610.00652.

Pine, D. S., Cohen, P., Gurley, D., Brook, J., & Ma, Y. (1998). The risk for early-adulthood anxiety and depressive disorders in adolescents with anxiety and depressive disorders. *Archives of General Psychiatry, 55* (1), 56–64. doi: 10.1001/archpsyc.55.1.56.

Ravens-Sieberer, U., Wille, N., Erhart, M., Bettge, S., Wittchen, H. -U., Rothenberger, A., . . . Bella study group, G. (2008). Prevalence of mental health problems among children and adolescents in Germany: Results of the BELLA study within the National Health Interview and Examination Survey. *European Child & Adolescent Psychiatry, 17* (Suppl 1), 22–33. doi: 10.1007/s00787-008-1003-2.

Roza, S. J., Hofstra, M. B., van der Ende, J., & Verhulst, F. C. (2003). Stable prediction of mood and anxiety disorders based on behavioral and emotional problems in childhood: A 14-year follow-up during childhood, adolescence, and young adulthood. *The American Journal of Psychiatry, 160* (12), 2116–2121. doi: 10.1176/appi.ajp.160.12.2116.

Schneier, F. R., Johnson, J., Hornig, C. D., Liebowitz, M. R., & Weissman, M. M. (1992). Social phobia: Comorbidity and morbidity in an epidemiologic sample. *Archives of General Psychiatry, 49* (4), 282–288.

Scott, K. M., Von Korff, M., Alonso, J., Angermeyer, M. C., Benjet, C., Bruffaerts, R., et al. (2008). Childhood adversity, early-onset depressive/anxiety disorders, and adult-onset asthma. *Psychosomatic Medicine, 70* (9), 1035–1043. doi: 10.1097/PSY. 0b013e318187a2fb.

Seligman, L. D., & Ollendick, T. H. (1998). Comorbidity of anxiety and depression in children and adolescents: An integrative review. *Clinical Child and Family Psychology Review, 1* (2), 125–144. doi: 10.1023/a:1021887712873.

Seligman, L. D., & Wuyek, L. A. (2007). Correlates of separation anxiety symptoms among first-semester college students: An exploratory study. *Journal of Psychology: Interdisciplinary and Applied, 141* (2), 135–145. doi: 10.3200/jrlp.141.2.135-146.

Shear, K., Jin, R., Ruscio, A. M., Walters, E. E., & Kessler, R. C. (2006). Prevalence and correlates of estimated DSM-IV child and adult separation anxiety disorder in the National Comorbidity Survey Replication. *American Journal of Psychiatry, 163* (6), 1074–1083. doi: 10.1176/appi.ajp.163.6.1074.

Silove, D., Harris, M., Morgan, A., Boyce, P., Manicavasagar, V., Hadzi-Pavlovic, D., & Wilhelm, K. (1995). Is early separation anxiety a specific precursor of panic disorder-agoraphobia? A community study. *Psychological Medicine, 25* (2), 405–411. doi: 10.1017/s0033291700036291.

Silove, D., & Manicavasagar, V. (1993). Adults who feared school: Is early separation anxiety specific to the pathogenesis of panic disorder? *Acta Psychiatrica Scandinavica, 88* (6), 385–390. doi: 10. 1111/j.1600-0447.1993.tb03478.x.

Silove, D., Manicavasagar, V., & Drobny, J. (2002). Associations between juvenile and adult forms of separation anxiety disorder: A study of volunteers with histories of school refusal. *Journal of Nervous & Mental Disease, 190* (6), 413–414. doi: 10.1097/00005053-200206000-00013.

Silverman, W. K., & Ollendick, T. H. (2005). Evidence-based assessment of anxiety and its disorders in children and adolescents. *Journal of Clinical Child and Adolescent Psychology, 34* (3), 380–411. doi: 10.1207/s15374424jccp3403_2.

Stein, M. B., Fuetsch, M., Müller, N., Hfler, M., Lieb, R., & Wittchen, H.-U. (2001). Social anxiety disorder and the risk of depression: A prospective community study of adolescents and young adults. *Archives of General Psychiatry, 58* (3), 251–256. doi: 10.1001/archpsyc.58.3.251.

Strauss, C. C., Lahey, B. B., Frick, P., Frame, C. L., & Hynd, G. W. (1988). Peer social status of children with anxiety disorders. *Journal of Consulting & Clinical Psychology, 56* (1), 137–141. doi: 10.1037/0022-006x.56.1.137.

Strauss, C. C., Last, C. G., Hersen, M., & Kazdin, A. E. (1988). Association between anxiety and depression in children and adolescents with anxiety disorders. *Journal of Abnormal Child Psychology, 16* (1), 57–68. doi: 10.1007/BF00910500.

Strauss, C. C., Lease, C. A., Kazdin, A. E., Dulcan, M. K., & Last, C. G. (1989). Multimethod assessment of the social competence of children with anxiety disorders. *Journal of Clinical Child Psychology, 18* (2), 184–189. doi: 10.1037/0022-006x.62.1.100.

Weiss, B., Catron, T., Harris, V., & Phung, T. M. (1999). The effectiveness of traditional child psychotherapy. *Journal of Consulting and Clinical Psychology, 67* (1), 82–94.

Weisz, J. R., Han, S. S., & Valeri, S. M. (1996). What can we learn from Fort Bragg. *Journal of Child and Family Studies, 5* (2), 185–190. doi: 10.1007/BF02237941.

Weisz, J. R., Jensen-Doss, A., & Hawley, K. M. (2006). Evidence-based youth psychotherapies versus usual clinical care: a meta-analysis of direct comparisons. *American Psychologist, 61* (7), 671–689. doi: 10.1037/0003-066x.61.7.671.

Wittchen, H.-U., Lieb, R., Pfister, H., & Schuster, P. (2000). The waxing and waning of mental disorders: Evaluating the stability of syndromes of mental disorders in the population. *Comprehensive Psychiatry, 41* (2, Suppl 1), 122–132. doi: 10.1016/s0010-440x(00)80018-8.

Wittchen, H.-U., Lieb, R., Schuster, P., & Oldehinkel, A. J. (2000). When is onset? Investigations into early developmental stages of anxiety and depressive disorders *Childhood Onset* of *"Adult" Psychopathology: Clinical and Research Advances* (pp. 259–302). Washington, DC: American Psychiatric Press.

Wittchen, H.-U., Nelson, C. B., & Lachner, G. (1998). Prevalence of mental disorders and psychosocial impairments in adolescents and young adults. *Psychological Medicine: A Journal of Research in Psychiatry and the Allied Sciences, 28* (1), 109–126. doi: 10.1017/s0033291797005928.

Woodward, L. J., & Fergusson, D. M. (2001). Life course outcomes of young people with anxiety disorders in adolescence. *Journal of the American Academy of Child & Adolescent Psychiatry, 40* (9), 1086–1093. doi: 10.1097/00004583-200109000-00018.

Zimmermann, P., Wittchen, H.-U., Hfler, M., Pfister, H., Kessler, R. C., & Lieb, R. (2003). Primary anxiety disorders and the development of subsequent alcohol use disorders: A 4-year community study of adolescents and young adults. *Psychological Medicine: A Journal of Research in Psychiatry and the Allied Sciences, 33* (7), 1211–1222. doi: 10.1017/s0033291703008158.

4

Genetic and Environmental Influences on Child and Adolescent Anxiety

Helena M.S. Zavos[1], Thalia C. Eley[1], and
Alice M. Gregory[2]

[1]MRC Social Genetic and Developmental Psychiatry Centre, Institute of Psychiatry,
King's College London, UK
[2]Goldsmiths, University of London, UK

Anxiety disorders are the most commonly occurring class of psychiatric disorders in youth, with an estimated prevalence of between 5 and 18% (Costello & Angold, 1995). Anxiety can be debilitating, affecting children's functioning with peers, school, and recreation (Essau, Conradt & Petermann, 2000). It is, therefore, important to understand how these difficulties develop. One way of increasing understanding of the etiology of anxiety is to investigate its genetic and environmental influences. Research in this field has moved away from simply estimating the level of genetic and environmental influences on anxiety to considering more complex issues, including the extent to which genetic (and environmental) influences are common across disorders (for example anxiety and depression), how these influences might change over time, and how genes and environment interact.

This chapter provides an overview of quantitative and molecular genetic research in this area. We present a series of analyses which combine multiple methods and include assessment of genetic risks, cognitive vulnerability, and environmental stress on the development of anxiety. It is hoped that this type of research will lead to a greater understanding of the way in which genes and environment contribute to anxiety, and that this information will eventually lead to preventative methods and individually targeted and tailored methods being developed.

Methods Used to Investigate Genetic and Environmental Factors

It has long been recognized that traits, such as anxiety, run in families with family members tending to resemble one another. Family studies of anxiety have highlighted a higher than chance incidence of anxiety among first degree relatives of those with anxiety disorders (e.g., Weissman, Leckman, Merikangas, Gammon & Prusoff, 1984). Although genetic relatedness may be one reason why anxiety disorders cluster within family members, this method cannot tease apart similarity dues to genetic influences

The Wiley-Blackwell Handbook of The Treatment of Childhood and Adolescent Anxiety, First Edition.
Edited by Cecilia A. Essau and Thomas H. Ollendick.
© 2013 John Wiley & Sons, Ltd. Published 2013 by John Wiley & Sons, Ltd.

from those due to shared environmental influences (i.e., those environmental influences that act to make individuals within a family alike). This is because members of the same family are likely to share, in addition to their genes, the same family environment. In contrast to family studies, twin and adoption studies are particularly useful in estimating the influence of genetic and environmental factors on traits.

Both twin and adoption studies are able to disentangle familiarity into genetic and environmental components by using different assumptions. Twin studies, for example, decompose variance into genetic and environmental sources by comparing within-pair similarity for monozygotic (MZ) twins and dizygotic (DZ) twins who both have in common their shared environment but differ in their genetic relatedness. MZ twins share 100% of their genetic make-up whereas DZ twins share on average half their segregating genes (Plomin, Defries, McClearn & McGuffin, 2008). In the standard twin design, variance in a phenotype (Vp) is divided into three latent variables: additive genetic (A) effects (involving alleles or loci 'adding up'), common or shared environmental (C), influences (making family members alike) and non-shared environmental (E), influences (which act to make children within a family different) ($Vp = A + C + E$). The non-shared environmental component (E) will also include any measurement error.

Resemblance within MZ twin pairs (r_{MZ}) is due to genes as well as shared environment hence $r_{MZ} = A + C$. Resemblance within DZ (r_{DZ}) pairs is expressed as $r_{DZ} = {}^1/_2(A) + C$. This is because DZ twins share only half their segregating genes but share the same shared environment. Additive genetics refers to the proportion of phenotypic variation in a population that is attributable to genetic variation among individuals. In the twin design, heritability (the proportion of variance due to additive genetic effects) is calculated as twice the difference between MZ and DZ correlations ($A = 2 (r_{MZ}-r_{DZ})$). Shared environment can be estimated as the difference between the MZ correlation and the heritability (i.e., $rMZ - A = C$). As non-shared environment is the only thing makes MZ twins different from one another, it can be calculated as the total phenotypic variance (which is typically standardized to 1 for ease of interpretation) minus the MZ correlation (i.e., $Vp - rMZ = E$).

Twin studies have been described as "the perfect natural experiment" (Martin, Boomsma & Machin, 1997); however, such studies are associated with certain limitations. First, the twin method assumes that the environment will not be more similar for MZ twins than DZ twins (the equal environments assumption). This assumption can be tested using a number of approaches (reviewed by Kendler, Neale, Kessler, Heath & Eaves, 1993). Some studies have challenged this assumption suggesting MZ twins are in fact treated more similarly than DZ twins (e.g., Loehlin & Nicholls, 1976). However, for the most part, this assumption holds true with regard psychiatric traits. For example, research has demonstrated that MZ twins mislabeled as DZ twins are treated as similarly as correctly labeled MZ twins (Goodman & Stevenson, 1991). Other areas of discussion include the influence on estimates of genetic and environmental influence on traits of: chronionicity (whether twins share the same placental sac during pregnancy) and assortative mating ("birds of a feather flock together": the suggestion that individuals mate with others that are similar to them, therefore reducing the range of variation). Furthermore, it has been argued that it is not possible to generalize findings from twins to the non-twin population (for a discussion see Plomin et al., 2008). Limitations, such as the ones mentioned above, are likely to have small effects on estimates and work in different directions, some inflating and others deflating heritability. As such, derived estimates of heritability and environmental influences should be taken only as indicative rather than absolute.

Adoption designs provide another way of investigating the genetic and environmental structure of a disorder. They can provide further support for estimates of heritability. With adoption, genetically related individuals receive a distinct family environment and individuals who are not genetically related share environments. Any resemblance between the former individuals implies genetic influences to the trait. By comparing adopted children to their adoptive relatives (with whom they share environment but not genes) the influence of shared environment can be tested as any resemblance between them would have to be due to environmental influences as they are not genetically related. Three main problems arise from the adoption paradigm. The first of these problems is that families involved in adoption are unlikely to be representative of the population. Second, similarity between the biological mother and child could be increased as a function of the 9 months in which the biological mother provides the pre-natal environment (this would artificially inflate estimates of heritability). Third, the selective placement of adopted children into families that are matched on certain characteristics to the biological parents could artificially inflate the estimations of shared environment. As with heritability estimates from twin studies, those derived from adoption studies should be interpreted broadly.

Once a trait has been demonstrated to be under genetic influence, the next step is usually to establish which genes are important for this trait. The techniques used for molecular genetic investigations are ever evolving. We describe three main approaches; linkage, candidate gene association, and genome-wide association studies.

Linkage approaches systematically scan the genome, requiring only a few hundred DNA markers (known sequences of DNA) looking for violations of Mendel's law of independent assortment between a disorder and a marker. Genetic linkage occurs when a disease causing variant and a marker are inherited together from parent to offspring at a level greater than expected under independent inheritance (Teare & Barrett, 2005). Linkage studies can be used to identify chromosomal regions where susceptibility genes may lie. Linkage analysis is often the first step in the genetic investigation of a trait as it can identify broad regions of the genome which may contain a disease gene and it can be carried out in the absence of a hypothesis regarding specific genes.

Affected sibling-pair linkage designs are generally used to study complex disorders as they have a greater power to detect genes of smaller effect size. In a sibling-pair design, families where two siblings are affected are used. The term "affected" can refer to a variety of things; it can mean that both siblings meet the criteria for a diagnosis or that both siblings have an extreme score on a certain quantitative trait. The method is based on allele sharing – whether affected siblings share 0, 1, or 2 alleles for a DNA marker (Plomin et al., 2008). Thus if a marker is linked to a gene that influences the disorder, more than 25% of the affected individuals will share the two alleles for the marker. When a marker is not linked to a gene implicated in the disorder, the probability of them co-occurring is 25%.

Anxiety – like other psychiatric problems – is a quantitative trait, meaning it is due to multiple genes (and environmental influences), each having a relatively small effect size rather than a single gene. This means that linkage approaches, although systematic, are not the best design of molecular genetic investigations of anxiety. This is because linkage for genes of small effect size, which are expected for most complex disorders, cannot be detected without vast samples (Risch, 2000). A useful analogy for viewing linkage studies is a telescope which scans the horizon for distant mountains (large genotypic effects) but that the telescope goes out of focus when trying to detect nearby hills (small genotypic effects) (Plomin et al., 2008). Linkage studies are therefore rarely used to identify the genes influencing anxiety.

Association studies have the statistical power to detect quantitative trait loci (QTLs; genes involved in a multiple gene system) of small effect size but, unlike linkage studies, associations can only be detected if a DNA marker is itself the QTL or very close to it. As a result, the candidate gene approach has tended to be used, as tens of thousands of DNA markers would be needed to scan the genome thoroughly. A candidate gene is normally selected based on biological function and *a priori* evidence to suggest it plays a part in the expression of a trait. Genes involved in the regulation of the serotonin system have been the focus of much research attention within this field as this system has been implicated in both the etiology and treatment of anxiety. Association studies take advantage of linkage disequilibrium. Linkage disequilibrium occurs when linkage between two alleles is so tight that it leads to an association at the population level. This is unlike simple linkage where the two loci tend to be further apart and the chance of recombination at any single meiosis is greater. At a population level, every time recombination occurs between the loci, linkage disequilibrium is weakened. It is only maintained if the loci are very close together. This is why association studies focus on more specific regions. Although association studies have been more successful than linkage studies in the search for risk loci involved in complex disorders such as anxiety, the literature is still teeming with reports of associations that cannot be replicated or that are not supported by linkage studies. Common problems in association studies include small sample size, poorly matched control group, over-interpretation of results, and positive publication bias.

More recently, genome-wide association (GWA) studies have been conducted to investigate genetic variants associated with psychiatric difficulties (see Psychiatric GWAS Consortium Coordinating Committee., 2009a, 2009b for review). This method offers a hypothesis-free approach. In GWA studies, researchers tend to compare cases (people with an illness) to controls (unaffected individuals). Highly powered GWA studies show great promise in the identification of risk alleles that are associated with psychiatric problems. However, multiple testing issues remain a considerable challenge, and much larger samples are needed than are typically used currently. Replication in an independent sample is often the only practical way of separating out true findings from false positives.

To What Extent Is Anxiety Heritable?

Although a seemingly simple question, the heritability of anxiety varies according to a number of factors. This is in part because heritability is a population statistic, which means that it applies to the particular population under investigations. It can therefore change depending on the population being studied. It also varies according to the definition of anxiety being used as well as the rater and sex of the participant.

Anxiety can be defined in numerous ways. Studies range from considering anxiety as an aspect of temperament to investigating anxiety disorders. Behavioral genetic research has considered a range of anxiety related phenotypes, including behavioral inhibition (Robinson, Kagan, Reznick & Corley, 1992), neuroticism (Thapar & McGuffin, 1996) and shyness and emotionality (Van Hulle, Lemery-Chalfant, & Goldsmith, 2007). Other studies have shown genetic influence on symptoms of anxiety (Eley, Gregory, Clark, & Ehlers, 2007) as well as anxiety disorders (Eaves, Silberg, Meyer et al., 1997).

Twin studies are able to investigate possible sex differences in the effects of genes or environment on anxiety. Differences can either be quantitative or qualitative. Quantitative differences refer to variation in the extent to which genetic or environmental factors influence traits for girls versus boys. Where qualitative differences are found, it suggests that the risk factors affecting males and female are different. Generally, there is little evidence of sex differences with regards to anxiety, but where sex differences are found they tend to be quantitative in nature – with higher heritability for girls as compared to boys (Feigon, Waldman, Levy, & Hay, 2001).

Heritability estimates may also be influenced by who is rating the anxiety (i.e., the parent, teacher, or the child herself or himself). Review studies of anxiety and depression have suggested that estimates of heritability based on parental self-report are higher than heritabilities based on child self-report (Gregory & Eley, 2007; Rapee, Schniering, & Hudson, 2009; Rice, Harold, & Thapar, 2002).

Behavioral genetic studies have also examined the possibility of sibling interaction. This occurs when the behavior of one twin influences the behavior of the other. This interaction can be co-operative or competitive depending on whether the behavior of one sibling facilitates or inhibits the behavior of the other. Co-operation will lead to increased phenotypic resemblance amongst MZ and DZ twins where as competition will lead to a decrease in resemblance. Interestingly, studies of child and adolescent anxiety find no evidence of sibling interaction effects (van den Oord, Boomsma, & Verhulst, 1994; van der Valk, Verhulst, Stroet, & Boomsma, 1998). This is in contrast to externalizing behaviors such as ADHD where sibling interaction is found, particularly in parent report (Price, Simonoff, Asherson, et al., 2005).

Influence of Genetic and Environmental Factors Over Time

Longitudinal studies of anxiety have established that anxiety disorders during childhood and adolescence are moderately stable and are predictive of other mental health problems in later life (for review see Rapee et al., 2009). There are two main questions with regard to investigation of genetic and environmental influences over time. First does the structure of influence change through development and second to what extent are the influences continuous? The first question can use cross-sectional data whereas the second requires longitudinal data.

Different heritability estimates have been found when looking at participants of different ages. One of the clearest examples of this is when looking at the contribution of shared environment to anxiety through development. Shared environment is often found to influence anxiety in childhood; however, this influence often disappears by adolescence. For example, the stability of symptoms of anxious/depression was examined in participants from early to late childhood (3–12 years) (Bartels, van Beijsterveldt, Derks et al., 2007). In this study it was found that genetic and shared environment influences were most important. Using the same sample, authors analyzed measures of anxious-depressive behavior and noted significant age-related changes from early to late adolescence (Lamb, Middeldorp, van Beijsterveldt, Bartels, et al., 2010). The authors found that at age 12, familial clustering was explained by genetic and shared environmental factors much like in childhood. However, by age 14, genetic factors were sufficient to explain familial clustering. The authors propose that the decrease in the influence of shared environment with age could be due to gradual attenuation of the level of parental control and time spent at home and together with the co-twin.

Along with evidence of the decline in importance of the shared environment, some studies have also found that the heritability of anxiety increases with age. In the aforementioned study, heritability was found to increase from 12 to 14 but did not increase from 14 to16 years (Lamb et al., 2010). Many other studies have found that heritability increases with age (Feigon et al., 2001) and this has been supported by a meta-analysis (Bergen, Gardner & Kendler, 2007). One explanation for this increasing heritability with age is the possibility of gene–environment correlation (to be discussed in more detail later in the chapter) whereby as children grow up, they increasingly select, modify, and create their own experiences in part based on their genetic propensities (Haworth, Wright, Luciano et al., 2010).

To investigate the pattern of genetic and environmental effects on anxiety over time, longitudinal designs are required. Generally, studies of psychopathology have found evidence of genetic continuity with environmental specificity (Kendler, Gardner, Annas & Lichtenstein, 2008a; Kendler, Gardner, Annas, Neale, Eaves & Lichtenstein, 2008b; Lau & Eley, 2006). One such study investigated the genetic and environmental architecture of fear symptoms from 8 to 20 years old (Kendler et al., 2008b). Results indicated genetic continuity across middle childhood, although new genetic influences also emerged throughout adolescence and adulthood. Of note, the genetic factor influencing continuity attenuated over time, with new genetic influences coming on board during adolescence, suggesting that the effects of early genetic factors acting on fear diminish over time. Substantial genetic continuity with some genetic change has also been found for other anxiety-related measures. For example, this pattern was found on the level of anxiety and depression in a population based cohort from age 8 to 20 years (Kendler, Gardner, & Lichtenstein, 2008c). The authors also found that the influence of shared environment decreases over time whereas non-shared environment was increasingly important with age.

Comorbidity

Anxiety commonly co-occurs with a number of other psychiatric difficulties. Most notabily there seems to be substantial comorbidity between anxiety and depression. More recently studies have also demonstrated a link between anxiety and sleep disturbances, autism, and externalizing problems (Gregory, Eley, O'Connor, Rijsdijk &

Plomin, 2005b; Gregory, Eley & Plomin, 2004a; Hallett, Ronald & Happe, 2009; Thapar & McGuffin, 1997). By using twin studies, it is possible to determine whether two traits covary for genetic or environmental reasons.

Both anxiety and depression have been shown to be moderately heritable (Franic, Middeldorp, Dolan, Ligthart & Boomsma, 2010; Gregory & Eley, 2007; Rice, 2009). Genes have been shown to be a driving force behind the high co-occurence between these difficulties; whereas environmental influences tend to be more specific to the individual phenotypes (Eley & Stevenson, 1999; Middeldorp, Cath, Van Dyck & Boomsma, 2005; Thapar & McGuffin, 1997). To illustrate the point, identical twins may share genetic risk for developing an emotional problem. However, one may have experiences related to anxiety (such as life events involving danger), which may lead to the development of anxiety, whereas the other twin may experience events which make them more susceptible to depression (for a discussion of life events related to anxiety or depression see Eley & Stevenson, 2000; Kendler, Hettema, Butera, Gardner & Prescott, 2003).

Researchers have also investigated the links between anxiety and sleep difficulties. In one study, persistent sleep problems, measured at 5, 7 and 9 years were found to predict anxiety (but not depression) in young adulthood (Gregory, Caspi, Eley, Moffitt, Oconnor & Poulton, 2005a). Using the twin method, the etiology of this relationship can be examined. In one such study of over 6000 twin pairs aged 3–4 years, the overlap between sleep problems and anxiety was mainly due to shared environmental influences (Gregory et al., 2005b).

Studies have suggested that children with autism spectrum disorders (ASD) are significantly more anxious than typically developing children (Kim, Szatmari, Bryson, Streiner & Wilson, 2000; Sukhodolsky, Scahill, Gadow et al., 2008). A recent meta-analysis has suggested that up to 84% of children with ASD also experience anxiety (White, Oswald, Ollendick & Scahill, 2009). Behavioral genetic analysis has revealed that the association between anxiety and autistic like traits are explained in a small part by shared genetic factors, however, genetic factors were found to be mostly specific (Hallett et al., 2009).

Others have addressed the overlap between internalizing and externalizing symptoms, and a recent study explored the role of early temperament on this association (Rhee, Cosgrove, Schmitz, Haberstick, Corley & Hewitt, 2007). For boys, shared environmental influences on emotionality **and** shyness in infancy helped to explain the association between internalizing and externalizing problems in childhood. For the girls, shared environmental influences on emotionality helped to explain most of the subsequent association between internalizing and externalizing problems. An important role for the shared environment was also found when the link between anxiety and conduct difficulties was examined in a sample of twins (Gregory, Eley & Plomin, 2004b).

Evidence of genetic correlation between different disorders can be taken as support for the generalist genes hypothesis (see Eley, 1997; Kovas & Plomin, 2006). The generalist genes hypothesis suggests that the same genes are involved in ability as are involved in disability. It also suggests that the same genes influence one difficulty, for example anxiety, also influence another difficulty, for example depression. This is supported by the high genetic correlation between, for example, anxiety and depression. Interestingly, the genetic correlation between anxiety and autism is fairly low suggesting that although there is a degree of genetic overlap, there is also evidence of genetic specificity.

Specific Genes Involved in Development of Anxiety – Evidence from Molecular Genetic Studies

Although research using twin studies suggests that anxiety is moderately heritable, relatively little is known about the specific genes involved. There are several reasons for this; however, one of the most likely is that – as with other difficulties – anxiety is influenced by many genes of small effect, which are therefore difficult to identify. Despite this, there are several plausible candidates that we discuss below. We will review research in both adult and child/adolescent samples.

The serotonin transporter (5-HT) represents a good functional candidate for anxiety as the serotonin system is involved in mood, and is also the site of action of the selective serotonin re-uptake inhibitors (SSRIs), which are a successful pharmacological intervention in the treatment of anxiety. A major finding in this area has been the discovery of genetic variation in a crucial regulatory molecule within the serotonin *5-HT* system, the *5-HT* transporter (5-HTT). The most widely explored polymorphism (a section of DNA that varies between individuals) is the serotonin transporter polymorphism (5-HTTLPR). The 5-HTTLPR was initially considered bi-allelic. Individuals may be homozygous for the long allele (L) (which is more expressing), homozygous for the short allele (S) (associated with reduced 5-HT expression), or heterozygous (LS) (i.e. carry one copy of the long allele and one copy of the short allele).

Generally, individuals who have one or two copies of the short allele have been found to have higher anxiety-related personality scores than those with no copies of this allele (Lesch, Bengel, Heils et al., 1996). This is far from a consistent finding, with replication sometimes proving successful (Katsuragi, Kunugi, Sano et al., 1999) and sometimes not (Jorm, Henderson, Jacomb et al., 1998). Less research has been conducted in samples of younger people; however, a similar trend and inconsistent replications are also the norm here. Indeed, one study found that having two copies of the short allele is associated with shyness in Caucasian children (Battaglia, Ogliari, Zanoni et al., 2005). Another study found that children with one or more copy of the short allele were more nervous during a laboratory assessment of temperament and were rated as shyer by their mothers (Hayden, Dougherty, Maloney et al., 2007). In contrast to these findings, a further study found that the long version of the allele was associated with shyness in children (Arbelle, Benjamin, Golin, Kremer, Belmaker & Ebstein, 2003). A recent investigation into anxious depression (A/D) in childhood and adolescence found no consistent effect of serotonergic genes (Middeldorp, Slof-Op 't Landt, Medland et al., 2010).

Catechol-O-methyltransferase (COMT) has also been widely investigated in relation to anxiety and a number of other psychiatric problems (Craddock, Owen, & O'Donovan, 2006; Tunbridge, Harrison, & Weinberger, 2006). COMT is the enzyme involved in the inactivation of catecholamines ("fight or flight" hormones released by the brain in response to stress). Lowered COMT activity results in higher concentrations of dopamine being available. Dopamine has many functions in the brain, including important roles in behavior, cognition, and motivation. The COMT gene contains a common functional polymorphism that produces an amino acid change from valine to methionine commonly known as val158met (Lundstrom, Salminen, Jalanko, Savolainen & Ulmanen, 1991). There is a significant difference in the level of COMT enzymatic activity between the two alleles (val and met). The val allele has been associated with higher activity (decreasing the amount of dopamine available) whereas the met form is less active (Lachman, Papolos, Saito, Yu, Szumlanski, & Weinshilboum, 1996). COMT genotype is beneficial or detrimental depending on the nature of question (Bilder, Volavka, Lachman, & Grace, 2004). The met allele, for example, is generally beneficial in working memory tasks but has been linked to a number of negative affective states such as obsessive compulsive disorder in men (Karayiorgou, Altemus, Galke et al., 1997), increased anxiety in women (Enoch, Schuckit, Johnson & Goldman, 2003) and panic disorder (Woo, Yoon, Choi, Oh, Lee, & Yu, 2004). Some research has found different effects of COMT on males and females. In female mice, COMT disruption lead to changes in anxiety-related behaviors, whereas in male mice, disruption leads to increased aggression (Gogos, Morgan, Luine et al., 1998).

Corticotropin-releasing hormones (CRH) are involved in the hypothalamic pituitary adrenal (HPA) axis, which is involved in reactions to stress. Studies in mice have demonstrated a replicable association between CRH and anxiety (see Bakshi & Kalin, 2000). Research in humans is more mixed. For example, one study found an association between the CRH gene and behavioral inhibition (Smoller, Yamaki, Fagerness et al., 2005). This was not replicated in another study of CRH and neuroticism (Tochigi, Kato, Otowa et al., 2006)

Other candidate genes for anxiety include those associated with brain-derived neurotrophic factors (BDNF). BDNF is a neuroprotective protein which has been associated with depression (Karege, Perret, Bondolfi, Schwald, Bertschy, & Aubry, 2002) and more recently, anxiety in mice (Chen, Jing, Bath et al., 2006). The estrogen receptor (ESR) has also been considered as a candidate gene based on the finding that oestrogen plays a role in mood and cognitive functioning. Polymorphisms of this gene have been found to account for between 1.6% and 2.8% of the variance in anxiety in children and adolescents (Prichard, Jorm, Prior et al., 2002).

Recently, epigenetic processes have been explored as possible mediators for the risk of mental illness. "Epigenetics" refers to the reversible regulation of gene expression mediated principally through changes in DNA methylation (involving chemical modification of DNA) and histone modification (referring to the DNA and protein complex making up chromosomes). Epigenetic processes are essential for normal cellular development and differentiation, and allow the regulation of gene function through non-mutagenic mechanisms. Unlike the DNA sequence, which is stable and strongly conserved, epigenetic processes are tissue-specific, developmentally regulated, and relatively dynamic. For example, mounting evidence suggests that epigenetic processes can be influenced by exposure to a range of external environmental factors, either globally or at specific loci. Specific epigenetic processes have yet to be identified in relation to anxiety. However, work has provided some interesting insights into the effects of early life stress (Weaver, Champagne, Brown et al., 2005). In a study of rats, for example, it was found that pups that experience greater maternal care (licking and grooming) were more resilient to stress. Later studies showed that this effect was mediated by differences in methylation of the glucocorticoid receptor promoter in the hippocampus (Weaver, Meaney & Szyf, 2006).

Way in Which Environment and Genes Might Act Together

Gene–environment correlation

Gene–environment correlation (rGE) refers to genetic influence on individual variation in *exposure* to particular environments. There are three types of gene–environment correlations: passive, evocative, and active (Plomin, DeFries, & Loehlin, 1977). "Passive" rGE occurs because parents generally pass on to their children both genes and environmental experiences. Thus, as an example, offspring of anxious mothers may receive both a genetic vulnerability for the condition and the environmental effects of an anxious parenting style. Evocative gene–environment correlations occur when a child's phenotype (which is influenced by their genes) evokes a certain reaction from others. Indeed, an infant who cries easily or shows irritability may be more likely to elicit negative reactions from caregivers, which may impact on parenting style, influencing the child's development. Intermediate phenotypes, such as temperament, may mediate these effects. Finally, active gene–environment correlations occur when the individual actively selects and adapts experiences according to their genetic propensity. Here, it is possible that a behaviorally inhibited or shy individual may be less likely to seek out friends choosing instead to engage in solitary activities, thus ultimately influencing social development.

It is possible to investigate rGE using twin studies. This involves using a bivariate model with an environmental measure and a measured phenotype (e.g., anxiety). In this type of model, both variables are decomposed into genetic and environmental factors. If the genetic factor influencing the environmental measure is correlated with the genetic factor influencing anxiety, then rGE is implied.

Evidence suggests that there is a reciprocal relationship between parental and child behaviors in the development and maintenance of anxiety (Hudson & Rapee, 2001). As temperamental characteristics are genetically influenced, this could mean that a genetic influence (from the child) is evoking controlling behaviors in the parent. By investigating rGE, in scenarios such as the one discussed above, the processes involved in the development of anxiety can be better understood. One study examined this link using an etch-a-sketch task (Eley, Napolitano, Lau, & Gregory, 2010). The researchers found that that children who experienced maternal controlling behavior coded as "extreme" in a videotaped interaction task, reported higher levels of anxiety than those who did not experience such high levels of control. They found there was a large genetic component to the observed ratings of extreme control. Furthermore, the association between maternal control and child anxiety was largely genetically mediated – suggesting a gene–environment correlation.

Traditional child twin data cannot disentangle whether an rGE is active, passive, or evocative. To do so requires data from the children of twins (Narusyte, Neiderhiser, D'Onofrio et al., 2008a). This design uses genetic information to determine whether inter-generational transmission occurs through genetic or environmental routes. The logic of the approach is that children from identical twin pairs are as similar genetically to their aunt/uncle as they are to their own parent. The rearing environment is provided by their own parent. Therefore, the extent to which children more closely resemble their MZ parent than their aunt/uncle gives an estimate of environmental transmission. One of the few studies to use this type of design investigated the genetic and environmental influences on the transmission of parental depression to depression and conduct problems in children (Silberg, Maes, & Eaves, 2010). The authors sought to investigate the extent to which parental depression on child depression was environmentally mediated or due to a shared genetic liability between parents and child. Parental depression was found to operate via environmental mechanisms to influence child depression. Of note, the links between parent and child symptoms are likely to be mediated by complex interactions of influences, and another study found that the internalizing problems of adolescents that were genetically influenced evoked maternal over-involvement (Narusyte, Neiderhiser, D'Onofrio et al., 2008b).

Gene–environment interaction

Interactions refer to the differential effect of one variable at different levels of another variable. Gene–environment interactions occur when environmental risks change as a function of genetic risk (or conversely that genetic risks are only expressed in the certain environments). In terms of risk mechanisms, interactions may refer to genetic influences on reactivity towards the environment or when a stressor elicits (latent or estimated) genetic susceptibilities.

Gene–environment interactions can be investigated using twin data – and also using measured genes and environments. Using the first approach, gene–environment interactions were found between negative life events and female adolescent anxiety (Silberg, Rutter, Neale, & Eaves, 2001). Another study looked at a range of environmental adversity measures in relation to internalizing disorders in adolescents (Hicks, DiRago, Iacono et al., 2009). In this study, genetic factors played a greater role in the etiology of internalizing symptoms when in low stress environments, with non-shared environmental influences increasing with greater environmental adversity. This does not mean that individuals with increased genetic risk should avoid low-stress environments but rather suggests that in the absence of environmental stress, inherited characteristics play a greater role in the emergence of internalizing symptoms. This is an interesting finding and not necessarily in line with other studies of internalizing disorder which tend to find that environmental risks exacerbates genetic effects on self-reported internalizing symptoms (Lau & Eley, 2008).

A seminal paper by Caspi and colleagues (2003) neatly demonstrated an interaction between a measured genotype and the environment. The authors showed that the effect of life stress on depression was moderated by variation in the serotonin transporter gene (5-HTT). This effect was partially replicated in a younger sample (Eley, Sugden, Corsico et al., 2004). In this study, girls with two copies of the short allele (SS) for 5-HTTLPR who were also high for environmental risk scores were almost twice as likely to be in the severe depression group as compared to those who had the SS genotype but were low for environmental risk (Eley et al., 2004).

Fewer studies have been carried out with child anxiety. However, one such study found evidence for an interaction between 5-HTTLPR and the environment on fear and anxiety in children (Fox, Nichols, Henderson et al., 2005). They found that children with one or more copy of the S allele (risk allele) with low social support had an increased risk for behavioural inhibition. A study in infants also found that variation in 5-HTTLPR moderates the influence of the mother's anxiety on infant irritability (Ivorra, Sanjuan, Jover et al., 2010).

Recently it has been suggested that in addition to the more well-described risk for poor outcome which is associated with many genotypes in situations of high stress, these same genotypes may confer some advantage in beneficial environments (Belsky, Jonassaint, Pluess, Stanton, Brummett, & Williams, 2009). This hypothesis, know as the "differential susceptibility hypothesis", suggests that some genes could be conceptualised as "plasticity genes" responding to environments differentially. Researchers reviewed several studies and found evidence of a cross-over interaction in line with this hypothesis.

Pathways by Which Genetic and Environmental Factors May Influence Anxiety

Internalizing disorders such as anxiety tend to be associated with cognitive biases. There are three levels of bias described in cognitive models of anxiety: attention, interpretation and memory (see Muris & Field, 2008). In this section, studies that have assessed biases associated with anxiety in child anxiety and in the context of a genetically informative design are described.

One such bias of both attention and interpretation is anxiety sensitivity, originally proposed to explain variation in panic (Clark, 1986). This bias has consistently been found to be predictive of anxiety in both clinical and non-clinical samples (BenÃ-tez, Shea, Raffa et al., 2009; Plehn & Peterson, 2002; Schmidt, Keough, Mitchell et al., 2010). Anxiety sensitivity refers to the belief that the experience of anxiety or anxiety-related sensations such as increased heart rate or trembling, have negative social, psychological, or physical consequences (Taylor, 1995). Individuals with high levels of anxiety sensitivity fear, for example, having heart palpitations as they believe they may suffer a heart attack. Those with low levels, however, will perceive such sensations as more transient and harmless. Individual differences in anxiety sensitivity are hypothesized to emerge from the combined influence of genetic variation along with learned experiences that lead to acquisition of beliefs about the potentially aversive consequences of anxiety-related states. More recently, interest has turned to considering whether anxiety sensitivity may mediate genetic risk for anxiety disorders. The first twin study of anxiety sensitivity used a large population-based sample of adults and produced a heritability estimate of around 50% (Stein, Jang, & Livesley, 1999), with the remaining variance due to non-shared environment. These findings have been extended to adolescents where heritability of anxiety sensitivity was estimated at 47% (Zavos, Rijsdijk, Gregory, & Eley, 2010) and children where heritability was estimated at 37% (Eley et al., 2007). Multivariate studies in adolescents have shown that the genetic correlation (extent of genetic overlap) between anxiety sensitivity and anxiety ratings is very high, almost as high as that seen between anxiety and depression in this sample (Zavos et al., 2010). This indicates that anxiety sensitivity largely reflects genetic vulnerability to anxiety.

A molecular genetic investigation into anxiety sensitivity found evidence for a gene–environment interaction between 5-HTTLPR genotype and childhood maltreatment

(Stein, Schork, & Gelernter, 2008). Specifically, in a sample of 150 young adults (mean age 18 years) those with the SS genotype *and* childhood emotional (or physical) maltreatment had significantly higher levels of anxiety sensitivity than participants with either the LL or LS genotypes. To our knowledge, molecular genetic analyses of anxiety sensitivity in younger samples have yet to be published, but it seems likely that anxiety sensitivity in younger samples will be associated with this marker, possibly in conjunction with life stress or parenting style.

Cognitive attention theories linking enhanced detection of potentially threatening cues in the environment to anxiety have also been influential and are perhaps more pertinent to anxiety disorders where social interactions and emotional expression are the key problems (e.g. social phobia). Research has suggested that individuals who prioritize attention allocation towards negative or threatening material are more susceptible to internalising disorders. In children, evidence of avoidance of both angry and fearful faces using a dot-probe task was strongest in children with symptoms of social anxiety (Stirling, Eley, & Clark, 2006). In a study of twins (aged 10 years), using a matched cues task, anxious children again showed avoidance of angry faces – although no significant genetic effects on this trait were found (J.Y.F. Lau, A.M. Gregory, E.M. Viding, D.S. Pine, & T.C. Eley, in preparation). More recently, studies have found an effect of 5-HTTLPR on the magnitude of attention bias toward both angry and happy faces (Perez-Edgar, Bar-Haim, McDermott et al., 2010). In another study, children at high risk due to both maternal depression and the S-allele displayed non-significant trend of attentional avoidance to sad but not happy or angry faces compared to children at low risk (Gibb, Benas, Grassia, & McGeary, 2009).

The other major approach to studying information processing is to use neuropsychological tests to assess aspects of brain function. With regard to understanding the development of child anxiety in the context of genetic risk, three main groups of studies have emerged thus far. The first group of studies looks at brain reactivity to processing of emotional facial expressions, generally using fMRI (Battaglia, Ogliari, Zanoni et al., 2005; Hariri, Mattay, Tessitore et al., 2002). The second group uses skin conductance and startle reflex to assess stress reactivity (Craske, Waters, Lindsey Bergman et al., 2008; Merikangas, Avenevoli, Dierker, & Grillon, 1999). Finally, a small number of studies have explored the carbon dioxide challenge test and its association with panic (Pine, Coplan, Papp et al., 1998). This is will be discussed in more detail in chapter four.

Summary and Future Directions

Several decades of research has demonstrated that anxiety in childhood and adolescence is moderately heritable. This area of research is now moving on to try to understand the mechanisms by which genes and environment influence anxiety.

First, studies have looked at anxiety longitudinally, allowing greater understanding of the ways in which genetic and environmental influences change over time. So far, research has indicated that genetic effects are largely continuous, with environmental influences proving more specific and possibly accounting more for change over time (Kendler et al., 2008a, 2008b). That environmental influences are relatively specific makes sense as many stressful life experiences are unlikely to be continuous (Goodyer,

Kolvin, & Gatzanis, 1987). Moving to a new school, for example is likely to have only a short-term effect in the majority of individuals and will therefore only influence mood for limited time. The specificity of these environmental influences also reflects, in part, the varied social environments children and particularly adolescents find themselves in as they are confronted with novel socialization practices both in the family and in their peer group. However, these studies have also shown that genetic influences, although largely stable, are developmentally sensitive with their influences attenuating over time, with new genetic influences becoming evident particularly in adolescence – perhaps in conjunction with the onset of puberty.

The second important development in this field has been work examining the nature of the relationship between anxiety and other psychiatric symptoms such as depression and sleep problems (Gregory, Rijsdijk, Dahl, McGuffin, & Eley, 2006; Thapar & McGuffin, 1997). This research has again highlighted the general way in which genes act, with many studies finding that co-variation between different symptoms are largely due to genetic influences. Third, there is now an increased understanding of the interplay between genes and environment. Two examples were presented: that of gene–environment correlation (mainly quantitative genetic studies); and gene–environment interaction (using both quantitative and molecular method-ologies). The evidence that specific genes interact with environmental influences may have significant implications for treatment. Cognitive behavioral therapy (CBT) is an example of a widely used "environmental" intervention for child anxiety. How-ever, CBT is only effective in approximate 60% of cases (Cartwright-Hatton, Roberts, Chitsabesan, Fothergill, & Harrington, 2004). Several factors have been associated with poor response to CBT including symptom severity and parental psychopathol-ogy (Bodden, Bogels, Nauta et al., 2008; Hudson, Deveney, & Taylor, 2005). Future work from our group will investigate whether certain genotypic markers were able to predict which individuals were going to perform particularly poorly to CBT treatment (Eley, Hudson, Tropeano et al., 2011).

References

Arbelle, S., Benjamin, J., Golin, M., Kremer, I., Belmaker, R. H., & Ebstein, R. P. (2003). Relation of shyness in grade school children to the genotype for the long form of the serotonin transporter promoter region polymorphism. *American Journal of Psychiatry, 160,* 671–676.

Bakshi, V. P. & Kalin, N. H. (2000). Corticotropin-releasing hormone and animal models of anxiety: gene–environment interactions. *Biological Psychiatry, 48,* 1175–1198.

Bartels, M., van Beijsterveldt, C. E., Derks, E. M., Stroet, T. M., Polderman, T. J., Hudziak, J. J., er al. (2007). Young Netherlands Twin Register (Y-NTR): a longitudinal multiple informant study of problem behavior. *Twin Research and Human Genetics, 10,* 3–11.

Battaglia, M., Ogliari, A., Zanoni, A., Citterio, A., Pozzoli, U., Giorda, R., et al. (2005). Influence of the serotonin transporter promoter gene and shyness on children's cerebral responses to facial expressions. *Archives of General Psychiatry, 62,* 85–94.

Belsky, J., Jonassaint, C., Pluess, M., Stanton, M., Brummett, B., & Williams, R., (2009). Vulnerability genes or plasticity genes? *Molecular Psychiatry, 14,* 746–754.

BenÂ-tez, C. I. P., Shea, M. T., Raffa, S., Rende, R., Dyck, I. R., Ramsawh, H. J., et al. (2009). Anxiety sensitivity as a predictor of the clincal course of panic disorder: A 1-year follow-up study. *Depression and Anxiety, 26,* 335–342.

Bergen, S. E., Gardner, C. O., & Kendler, K. S. (2007). Age-related changes in heritability of behavioral phenotypes over adolescence and young adulthood: a meta-analysis. *Twin Research and Human Genetics, 10,* 423–433.

Bilder, R. M., Volavka, J., Lachman, H. M., & Grace, A. A. (2004). The catechol-O-methyltransferase polymorphism: relations to the tonic-phasic dopamine hypothesis and neuropsychiatric phenotypes. *Neuropsychopharmacology, 29,* 1943–1961.

Bodden, D. H., Bogels, S. M., Nauta, M. H., De Haan, E., Ringrose, J., Appelboom, C., et al. (2008). Child versus family cognitive-behavioral therapy in clinically anxious youth: an efficacy and partial effectiveness study. *Journal of the American Academy of Child & Adolescent Psychiatry, 47,* 1384–1394.

Cartwright-Hatton, S., Roberts, C., Chitsabesan, P., Fothergill, C., & Harrington, R. (2004). Systematic review of the efficacy of cognitive behaviour therapies for childhood and adolescent anxiety disorders. *Britsh Journal of Clinical Psychology, 43,* 421–436.

Caspi, A., Sugden, K., Moffitt, T. E., Taylor, A., Craig, I. W., Harrington, H., et al. (2003). Influence of life stress on depression: moderation by a polymorphism in the 5-HTT gene. *Science, 301,* 386–389.

Chen, Z. Y., Jing, D., Bath, K. G., Ieraci, A., Khan, T., Siao, C. J., et al. (2006). Genetic variant BDNF (Val66Met) polymorphism alters anxiety-related behavior. *Science, 314* (5796), 140–143.

Clark, D. M. (1986). A cognitive approach to panic. *Behaviour Research and Therapy 24,* 461–470.

Costello, E. J. & Angold, A. (1995). Epidemiology. In J. S. March (Ed.), *Anxiety Disorders in Children and Adolescents.* New York: Guilford Press, 109–124.

Craddock, N., Owen, M. J., & O'Donovan, M. C. (2006). The catechol-O-methyl transferase (COMT) gene as a candidate for psychiatric phenotypes: evidence and lessons. *Molecular Psychiatry, 11,* 446–458.

Craske, M. G., Waters, A. M., Lindsey Bergman, R., Naliboff, B., Lipp, O. V., Negoro, H., et al. (2008). Is aversive learning a marker of risk for anxiety disorders in children? *Behaviour Research and Therapy, 46,* 954–967.

Eaves, L. J., Silberg, J. L., Meyer, J. M., Maes, H. H., Simonoff, E., Pickles, A., et al. (1997). Genetics and developmental psychopathology: 2. The main effects of genes and environment on behavioral problems in the Virginia Twin Study of Adolescent Behavioral Development. *Journal of Child Psychology and Psychiatry, 38,* 965–980.

Eley, T. C. (1997). General Genes: A new theme in developmental psychopathology. *Current Directions in Psychological Science, 6,* 90–95.

Eley, T. C., Gregory, A. M., Clark, D. M., & Ehlers, A. (2007). Feeling anxious: a twin study of panic/somatic ratings, anxiety sensitivity and heartbeat perception in children. *Journal of Child Psychology and Psychiatry, 48,* 1184–1191.

Eley, T. C., Hudson, J. L., Creswell, C., Tropeano, M., Lester, K.J., Cooper, P., et al. (2012). *Therapygenetics: The* 5HTTLPR *and response to psychological therapy. Molecular Psychiatry, 17* (3), 236–237.

Eley, T. C., Napolitano, M., Lau, J. Y., & Gregory, A. M. (2010). Does childhood anxiety evoke maternal control? A genetically informed study. *Journal of Child Psychology and Psychiatry, 51,* 772–779.

Eley, T. C. & Stevenson, J. (1999). Exploring the covariation between anxiety and depression symptoms: a genetic analysis of the effects of age and sex. *Journal of Child Psychology and Psychiatry, 40,* 1273–1282.

Eley, T. C. & Stevenson, J. (2000). Specific life events and chronic experiences differentially associated with depression and anxiety in young twins. *Journal of Abnormal Child Psychology, 28,* 383–394.

Eley, T. C., Sugden, K., Corsico, A., Gregory, A. M., Sham, P., McGuffin, P., et al. (2004). Gene–environment interaction analysis of serotonin system markers with adolescent depression. *Molecular Psychiatry, 9,* 908–915.

Enoch, M. A., Schuckit, M. A., Johnson, B. A., & Goldman, D. (2003). Genetics of alcoholism using intermediate phenotypes. *Alcoholism: Clinical and Experimental Research, 27,* 169–176.

Essau, C. A., Conradt, J., & Petermann, F. (2000). Frequency, comorbidity, and psychosocial impairment of anxiety disorders in German adolescents. *Journal of Anxiety Disorders, 14,* 263–279.

Feigon, S. A., Waldman, I. D., Levy, F., & Hay, D. A. (2001). Genetic and environmental influences on separation anxiety disorder symptoms and their moderation by age and sex. *Behaviour Genetics, 31,* 403–411.

Fox, N. A., Nichols, K. E., Henderson, H. A., Rubin, K., Schmidt, L., Hamer, D., et al. (2005). Evidence for a gene–environment interaction in predicting behavioral inhibition in middle childhood. *Psychological Science, 16,* 921–926.

Franic, S., Middeldorp, C. M., Dolan, C. V., Ligthart, L., & Boomsma, D. I. (2010). Childhood and adolescent anxiety and depression: Beyond heritability. *Journal of the American Academy of Child & Adolescent Psychiatry, 49,* 820–829.

Gibb, B. E., Benas, J. S., Grassia, M., & McGeary, J. (2009). Children's attentional biases and 5-HTTLPR genotype: potential mechanisms linking mother and child depression. *Journal of Clinical Child and Adolescent Psychology, 38,* 415–426.

Gogos, J. A., Morgan, M., Luine, V., Santha, M., Ogawa, S., Pfaff, D., & Karayiorgou, M. (1998). Catechol-O-methyltransferase-deficient mice exhibit sexually dimorphic changes in catecholamine levels and behavior. *Proceeding of the National Academy of Science USA, 95,* 9991–9996.

Goodman, R. & Stevenson, J. (1991). Parental critism and warmth toward unrecognised monozygotic twins. *Behavioural and Brain Sciences, 14,* 394–395.

Goodyer, I. M., Kolvin, I., & Gatzanis, S. (1987). The impact of recent undesirable life events on psychiatric disorders in childhood and adolescence. *British Journal of Psychiatry, 151,* 179–184.

Gregory, A. M., Caspi, A., Eley, T. C., Moffitt, T. E., Oconnor, T. G., & Poulton, R. (2005a). Prospective longitudinal associations between persistent sleep problems in childhood and anxiety and depression disorders in adulthood. *Journal of Abnormal Child Psychology, 33,* 157–163.

Gregory, A. M. & Eley, T. C. (2007). Genetic influences on anxiety in children: what we've learned and where we're heading. *Clinical Child and Family Psychology Review, 10,* 199–212.

Gregory, A. M., Eley, T. C., O'Connor, T. G., Rijsdijk, F. V., & Plomin, R. (2005b). Family influences on the association between sleep problems and anxiety in a large sample of pre-school aged twins. *Personality and Individual Differences, 39,* 1337–1348.

Gregory, A. M., Eley, T. C., & Plomin, R. (2004a). Exploring the association between anxiety and conduct problems in a large sample of twins aged 2–4. *Journal of Abnormal Child Psychology, 32,* 111–122.

Gregory, A. M., Eley, T. C., & Plomin, R. (2004b). Exploring the association between anxiety and conduct problems in a large sample of twins aged 2–4. *Journal of Abnormal Child Psychology, 32,* 111–122.

Gregory, A. M., Rijsdijk, F. V., Dahl, R. E., McGuffin, P., & Eley, T. C. (2006). Associations between sleep problems, anxiety, and depression in twins at 8 years of age. *Pediatrics, 118,* 1124–1132.

Hallett, V., Ronald, A., & Happe, F. (2009). Investigating the association between autistic-like and internalizing traits in a community-based twin sample. *Journal of the American Academy of Child and Adolescent Psychiatry, 48,* 618–627.

Hariri, A. R., Mattay, V. S., Tessitore, A., Kolachana, B., Fera, F., Goldman, D., et al. (2002). Serotonin transporter genetic variation and the response of the human amygdala. *Science, 297,* 400–403.

Haworth, C. M., Wright, M. J., Luciano, M., Martin, N. G., de Geus, E. J., van Beijsterveldt, C. E., et al. (2010). The heritability of general cognitive ability increases linearly from childhood to young adulthood. *Molecular Psychiatry, 15*, 1112–1120.

Hayden, E. P., Dougherty, L. R., Maloney, B., Emily Durbin, C., Olino, T. M., Nurnberger, J. I., Jr., et al. (2007). Temperamental fearfulness in childhood and the serotonin transporter promoter region polymorphism: a multimethod association study. *Psychiatric Genetics, 17*, 135–142.

Hicks, B. M., DiRago, A. C., Iacono, W. G., McGue, M., Hicks, B. M., DiRago, A. C., et al. (2009). Gene–environment interplay in internalizing disorders: consistent findings across six environmental risk factors. *Journal of Child Psychology and Psychiatry, 50*, 1309–1317.

Hudson, J. L., Deveney, C., & Taylor, L. (2005). Nature, assessment, and treatment of generalized anxiety disorder in children. *Pediatric Annals, 34*, 97–106.

Hudson, J. L. & Rapee, R. M. (2001). Parent–child interactions and anxiety disorders: an observational study. *Behaviour Research and Therapy, 39*, 1411–1427.

Ivorra, J. L., Sanjuan, J., Jover, M., Carot, J. M., Frutos, R., Molto, M. D., et al. (2010). Gene–environment interaction of child temperament. *Journal of Developmental & Behavioral Pediatrics, 31*, 545–554.

Jorm, A. F., Henderson, A. S., Jacomb, P. A., Christensen, H., Korten, A. E., Rodgers, B., et al. (1998). An association study of a functional polymorphism of the serotonin transporter gene with personality and psychiatric symptoms. *Molecular Psychiatry 3*, 449–451.

Karege, F., Perret, G., Bondolfi, G., Schwald, M., Bertschy, G., & Aubry, J. M. (2002). Decreased serum brain-derived neurotrophic factor levels in major depressed patients. *Psychiatry Research, 109* (2), 143–148.

Karayiorgou, M., Altemus, M., Galke, B. L., Goldman, D., Murphy, D. L., Ott, J., et al. (1997). Genotype determining low catechol-O-methyltransferase activity as a risk factor for obsessive-compulsive disorder. *PNAS, 94*, 4572–4575.

Katsuragi, S., Kunugi, H., Sano, A., Tsutsumi, T., Isogawa, K., Nanko, S., et al. (1999). Association between serotonin transporter gene polymorphism and anxiety-related traits. *Biological Psychiatry, 45*, 368–370.

Kendler, K. S., Gardner, C. O., Annas, P., & Lichtenstein, P. (2008a). The development of fears from early adolesence to young adulthood: a multivariate study. *Psychological Medicine, 38*, 1759–1769.

Kendler, K. S., Gardner, C. O., Annas, P., Neale, M. C., Eaves, L. J., & Lichtenstein, P. (2008b). A longitudinal twin study of fears from middle childhood to early adulthood: evidence for a developmentally dynamic genome. *Archives of General Psychiatry*, 421–429.

Kendler, K. S., Gardner, C. O., & Lichtenstein, P. (2008c). A developmental twin study of symptoms of anxiety and depression: evidence for genetic innovation and attenuation. *Psychological Medicine, 38*, 1567–1575.

Kendler, K. S., Hettema, J. M., Butera, F., Gardner, C. O., & Prescott, C. A. (2003). Life event dimensions of loss, humiliation, entrapment, and danger in the prediction of onsets of major depression and generalized anxiety. *Archives of General Psychiatry, 60*, 789–796.

Kendler, K. S., Neale, M. C., Kessler, R. C., Heath, A. C., & Eaves, L. J. (1993). A test of the equal-environment assumption in twin studies of psychiatric illness. *Behavior Genetics, 23*, 21–27.

Kim, J. A., Szatmari, P., Bryson, S. E., Streiner, D. L., & Wilson, F. J. (2000). The prevalence of anxiety and mood problems among children with autism and Asperger syndrome. *Autism, 4*, 117–128.

Kovas, Y. & Plomin, R. (2006). Generalist genes: implications for the cognitive sciences. *Trends in Cognitive Sciences, 10*, 198–203.

Lachman, H. M., Papolos, D. F., Saito, T., Yu, Y. M., Szumlanski, C. L., & Weinshilboum, R. M. (1996). Human catechol-O-methyltransferase pharmacogenetics: description of a functional polymorphism and its potential application to neuropsychiatric disorders. *Pharmacogenetics, 6*, 243–250.

Lamb, D. J., Middeldorp, C. M., van Beijsterveldt, C. E., Bartels, M., van der Aa, N., Polderman, T. J., et al. (2010). Heritability of anxious-depressive and withdrawn behavior: age-related changes during adolescence. *Journal of the American Academy of Child and Adolescent Psychiatry, 49,* 248–255.

Lau, J. Y. & Eley, T. C. (2006). Changes in genetic and environmental influences on depressive symptoms across adolescence and young adulthood. *British Journal of Psychiatry, 189,* 422–427.

Lau, J. Y. & Eley, T. C. (2008). Disentangling gene–environment correlations and interactions on adolescent depressive symptoms. *Journal of Child Psychology and Psychiatry, 49,* 142–150.

Lau, J., Hilbert, K., Goodman, R., Gregory, A. M., Pine, D. S. Viding, E. M., Eley, T. C. (In press) Investigating the genetic and environmental bases of biases in threat recognition and avoidance in children with anxiety problems. Biology of mood & anxiety disorders.

Lesch, K. P., Bengel, D., Heils, A., Sabol, S. Z., Greenberg, B. D., Petri, S., et al. (1996). Association of anxiety-related traits with a polymorphism in the serotonin transporter gene regulatory region. *Science, 274,* 1527–1531.

Loehlin, J. C. & Nicholls, J. (1976). *Heredity, Environment and Personality.* Austin: University of Texas.

Lundstrom, K., Salminen, M., Jalanko, A., Savolainen, R., & Ulmanen, I. (1991). Cloning and characterization of human placental catechol-O-methyltransferase cDNA. *DNA and Cell Biology, 10,* 181–189.

Martin, N., Boomsma, D., & Machin, G. (1997). A twin-pronged attack on complex traits. *Nature Genetics, 17,* 387–392.

Merikangas, K. R., Avenevoli, S., Dierker, L., & Grillon, C. (1999). Vulnerability factors among children at risk for anxiety disorders. *Biological Psychiatry, 46,* 1523–1535.

Middeldorp, C., Slof-Op 't Landt, M., Medland, S., van Beijsterveldt, C., Bartels, M., Willemsen, G., et al. (2010). Anxiety and depression in children and adults: Influence of serotonergic and neurotrophic genes? *Genes, Brain & Behavior, 9,* 808–816.

Middeldorp, C. M., Cath, D. C., Van Dyck, R., & Boomsma, D. I. (2005). The co-morbidity of anxiety and depression in the perspective of genetic epidemiology. A review of twin and family studies. *Psychological Medicine, 35,* 611–624.

Muris, P. & Field, A. P. (2008). Distorted cognition and pathological anxiety in children and adolescents. *Cognition and Emotion, 22,* 395–421.

Narusyte, J., Neiderhiser, J. M., D'Onofrio, B. M., Reiss, D., Spotts, E. L., Ganiban, J., et al. (2008a). Testing different types of genotype–environment correlation: an extended children-of-twins model. *Developmental Psychology, 44,* 1591–1603.

Narusyte, J., Neiderhiser, J. M., D'Onofrio, B. M., Reiss, D., Spotts, E. L., Ganiban, J., et al. (2008b). Testing different types of genotype-environment correlation: an extended children-of-twins model. *Developmental Psychology 44,* 1591–1603.

Perez-Edgar, K., Bar-Haim, Y., McDermott, J. M., Gorodetsky, E., Hodgkinson, C. A., Goldman, D., et al. (2010). Variations in the serotonin-transporter gene are associated with attention bias patterns to positive and negative emotion faces. *Biological Psychology, 83,* 269–271.

Pine, D. S., Coplan, J. D., Papp, L. A., Klein, R. G., Martinez, J. M., Kovalenko, P., et al. (1998). Ventilatory physiology of children and adolescents with anxiety disorders. *Archives of General Psychiatry, 55,* 123–129.

Plehn, K. & Peterson, R. A. (2002). Anxiety sensitivity as a predictor of the development of panic symptoms, panic attacks, and panic disorder: a prospective study. *Journal of Anxiety Disorders, 16,* 455–474.

Plomin, R., DeFries, J. C., & Loehlin, J. C. (1977). Genotype-environment interaction and correlation in the analysis of human behavior. *Psychological Bulletin, 84,* 309–322.

Plomin, R., Defries, J. C., McClearn, G. E., & McGuffin, P. (2008). *Behavioural Genetics,* 5th edn. New York: Worth Publishers.

Price, T. S., Simonoff, E., Asherson, P., Curran, S., Kuntsi, J., Waldman, I., et al. (2005). Continuity and change in preschool ADHD symptoms: longitudinal genetic analysis with contrast effects. *Behavior Genetics, 35,* 121–132.

Prichard, Z., Jorm, A. F., Prior, M., Sanson, A., Smart, D., Zhang, Y., et al. (2002). Association of polymorphisms of the estrogen receptor gene with anxiety-related traits in children and adolescents: a longitudinal study. *American Journal of Medical Genetics, 114*(2), 169–176.

Psychiatric GWAS Consortium Steering Committee (2009a). A framework for interpreting genome-wide association studies of psychiatric disorders. *Molecular Psychiatry, 14,* 10–17.

Psychiatric GWAS Consortium Coordinating Committee (2009b). Genomewide association studies: history, rationale and prospects for psychiatric disorders. *American Journal of Psychiatry, 166,* 540–556.

Rapee, R. M., Schniering, C. A., & Hudson, J. L. (2009). Anxiety disorders during childhood and adolescence: origins and treatment. *Annual Review of Clinical Psychology, 5,* 311–341.

Rhee, S. H., Cosgrove, V. E., Schmitz, S., Haberstick, B. C., Corley, R. C., & Hewitt, J. K. (2007). Early childhood temperament and the covariation between internalizing and externalizing behavior in school-aged children. *Twin Research and Human Genetics, 10,* 33–44.

Rice, F. (2009). The genetics of depression in childhood and adolescence. *Current Psychiatry Reports, 11,* 167–173.

Rice, F., Harold, G. T., & Thapar, A. (2002). Assessing the effects of age, sex and shared environment on the genetic aetiology of depression in childhood and adolescence. *Journal of Child Psychology and Psychiatry, 43,* 1039–1051.

Risch, N. J. (2000). Searching for genetic determinants in the new millennium. *Nature, 405,* 847–856.

Robinson, J. L., Kagan, J., Reznick, J. S., & Corley, R. (1992). The heritability of inhibited and uninhibited behaviour: A twin study. *Developmental Psychology, 28,* 1030–1037.

Schmidt, N. B., Keough, M. E., Mitchell, M. A., Reynolds, E. K., Macpherson, L., Zvolensky, M. J., et al. (2010). Anxiety sensitivity: prospective prediction of anxiety among early adolescents. *Journal of Anxiety Disorders, 24,* 503–508.

Silberg, J., Rutter, M., Neale, M., & Eaves, L. (2001). Genetic moderation of environmental risk for depression and anxiety in adolescent girls. *British Journal of Psychiatry, 179,* 116–121.

Silberg, J. L., Maes, H., & Eaves, L. J. (2010). Genetic and environmental influences on the transmission of parental depression to children's depression and conduct disturbance: an extended Children of Twins study. *Journal of Child Psychology and Psychiatry, 51,* 734–744.

Smoller, J. W., Yamaki, L. H., Fagerness, J. A., Biederman, J., Racette, S., Laird, N. M., et al. (2005). The corticotropin-releasing hormone gene and behavioral inhibition in children at risk for panic disorder. *Biological Psychiatry, 57,* 1485–1492.

Stein, M. B., Jang, K. L., & Livesley, W. J. (1999). Heritability of anxiety sensitivity: a twin study. *The American Journal of Psychiatry 156,* 246–251.

Stein, M. B., Schork, N. J., & Gelernter, J. (2008). Gene-by-environment (serotonin transporter and childhood maltreatment) interaction for anxiety sensitivity, an intermediate phenotype for anxiety disorders. *Neuropsychopharmacology, 33,* 312–319.

Stirling, L. J., Eley, T. C., & Clark, D. M. (2006). Preliminary evidence for an association between social anxiety symptoms and avoidance of negative faces in school-age children. *Journal of Clinical Child and Adolescent Psychology, 35,* 431–439.

Sukhodolsky, D. G., Scahill, L., Gadow, K. D., Arnold, L. E., Aman, M. G., McDougle, C. J., et al. (2008). Parent-rated anxiety symptoms in children with pervasive developmental disorders: frequency and association with core autism symptoms and cognitive functioning. *Journal of Abnormal Child Psychology, 36,* 117–128.

Taylor, S. (1995). Anxiety sensitivity: theoretical perspectives and recent findings. *Behaviour Research and Therapy, 33,* 243–258.

Teare, M. D., & Barrett, J. H. (2005). Genetic linkage studies. *The Lancet, 366,* 1036–1044.

Thapar, A. & McGuffin, P. (1996). A twin study of antisocial and neurotic symptoms in childhood. *Psychological Medicine, 26,* 1111–1118.

Thapar, A. & McGuffin, P. (1997). Anxiety and depressive symptoms in childhood—a genetic study of comorbidity. *Journal of Child Psychology and Psychiatry, 38,* 651–656.

Tochigi, M., Kato, C., Otowa, T., Hibino, H., Marui, T., Ohtani, T., et al. (2006). Association between corticotropin-releasing hormone receptor 2 (CRHR2) gene polymorphism and personality traits. *Psychiatry and Clinical Neuroscience, 60,* 524–526.

Tunbridge, E. M., Harrison, P. J., & Weinberger, D. R. (2006). Catechol-o-methyltransferase, cognition, and psychosis: Val158Met and beyond. *Biological Psychiatry, 60,* 141–151.

van den Oord, E. J., Boomsma, D. I., & Verhulst, F. C. (1994). A study of problem behaviors in 10- to 15-year-old biologically related and unrelated international adoptees. *Behavior Genetics, 24,* 193–205.

van der Valk, J. C., Verhulst, F. C., Stroet, T. M., & Boomsma, D. I. (1998). Quantitative genetic analysis of internalising and externalising problems in a large sample of 3-year-old twins. *Twin Research, 1,* 25–33.

Van Hulle, C. A., Lemery-Chalfant, K., & Goldsmith, H. H. (2007). Genetic and environmental influences on socio-emotional behavior in toddlers: an initial twin study of the infant-toddler social and emotional assessment. *Journal of Child Psychology and Psychiatry, 48,* 1014–1024.

Weaver, I. C., Champagne, F. A., Brown, S. E., Dymov, S., Sharma, S., Meaney, M. J., & Szyf, M. (2005). Reversal of maternal programming of stress responses in adult offspring through methyl supplementation: altering epigenetic marking later in life. *Journal of Neuroscience, 25,* 11045–11054.

Weaver, I. C., Meaney, M. J., & Szyf, M. (2006). Maternal care effects on the hippocampal transcriptome and anxiety-mediated behaviors in the offspring that are reversible in adulthood. *PNAS, 103,* 3480–3485.

Weissman, M. M., Leckman, J. F., Merikangas, K. R., Gammon, G. D., & Prusoff, B. A. (1984). Depression and anxiety disorders in parents and children. Results from the Yale family study. *Archives of General Psychiatry, 41,* 845–852.

White, S. W., Oswald, D., Ollendick, T., & Scahill, L. (2009). Anxiety in children and adolescents with autism spectrum disorders. *Clinical Psychology Review, 29,* 216–229.

Woo, J. M., Yoon, K. S., Choi, Y. H., Oh, K. S., Lee, Y. S., & Yu, B. H. (2004). The association between panic disorder and the L/L genotype of catechol-O-methyltransferase. *Journal of Psychiatric Research, 38,* 365–370.

Zavos, H. M., Rijsdijk, F. V., Gregory, A. M., & Eley, T. C. (2010). Genetic influences on the cognitive biases associated with anxiety and depression symptoms in adolescents. *Journal of Affective Disorders, 124,* 45–53.

5

Neurobiology of Paediatric Anxiety

Jasper B. Zantvoord[1], Ramon J.L. Lindauer[1],
Mirte J. Bakker[2], and Frits Boer[1]

[1]Academic Medical Centre (AMC), University of Amsterdam & Department of
Child and Adolescent Psychiatry, AMC-de Bascule, The Netherlands
[2]St Radboud University Medical Centre, Nijmegen, The Netherlands

The early age of onset of anxiety disorders (Kessler, Berglund, Demler, Jin, Merikangas, & Walters, 2005a) and their often chronic nature (Kessler, Chiu, Demler, Merikangas, Walters, 2005b) emphasize that childhood and adolescence are the main risk phases for the development of an anxiety disorder and suggest a possible developmental nature of these disorders. This has led the DSM-V anxiety disorder taskforce to offer the developmental perspective a more prominent role in the upcoming DSM-V (Beesdo, Knappe, & Pine, 2009; Pynoos, Steinberg, Layne, Briggs, Ostrowski, & Fairbank, 2009). This shift towards a more developmentally oriented classification system will most likely ensure that the developmental perspective will become a more considerable part of daily clinical practice over the coming years. With the growing emphasis on the developmental nature of anxiety disorders, the interest in the fields of developmental neuroscience and biological psychiatry has increased. An integration of both fields seems especially suitable to clarify the underlying mechanism of anxiety disorders in children and adolescents. Both fields have profited to great extent from the emergence of accurate and minimally invasive neuroimaging, and physiological and endocrinological techniques over the past few decades. Studies using these techniques have contributed considerably to our understanding of the normal development of the human brain. Furthermore, studies of adults have established that mental disorders reflect individual differences in brain, physiological, and endocrinological functioning. The increased understanding of normal brain development and the findings from neurobiological studies in adults with anxiety disorders have encouraged scientists to clarify the neurobiological mechanisms underlying anxiety disorders in children and adolescents. In this chapter we will give an overview of the findings that have emerged from these studies so far and place them in an (neuro-)developmental perspective.

We will begin by setting out the components, normal functioning, and interactions of the (neuro-)biological systems which are supposed to be involved in anxiety disorders. The chapter then provides a description of the normal development trajectories of these systems, and presents a summary of findings from preclinical and clinical

The Wiley-Blackwell Handbook of The Treatment of Childhood and Adolescent Anxiety, First Edition.
Edited by Cecilia A. Essau and Thomas H. Ollendick.
© 2013 John Wiley & Sons, Ltd. Published 2013 by John Wiley & Sons, Ltd.

neurobiological research in paediatric anxiety disorders, including post-traumatic stress disorder (PTSD). These findings will be synthesized in a developmental framework. We will also summarize the findings of neurobiological research in obsessive-compulsive disorder (OCD) and compare these findings with those from other anxiety disorders to answer the question of whether OCD is a special kind of anxiety disorder. We will give a rationale for biological treatment outcome studies and present some preliminary findings from this emerging field. We conclude by discussing directions for future research.

Neurobiological Systems Involved in the Fear Response

In order to survive in an ever-changing environment, an organism has to indentify and appropriately respond to situations, persons, and stimuli which pose potential threats to its own integrity or survival. An organism can respond to threat with defensive behaviors such as fighting, fleeing or when both are impossible by freezing. Because children have a limited ability to oversee, evaluate and respond to novel situations, they are largely dependent on their caregivers for the evaluation of novel situations and guidance of their subsequent responses. When a child encounters a novel situation it will, rather than independently judge the situation, look at cues in the facial expression of its caregiver to evaluate the safety of the situation, a phenomenon known as social referencing. Because children will get lost in flight and are likely to lose a fight, they will seek protection from their caregivers when threat arises by showing attachment behavior. In the course of development it is important that a child learns to distinguish relatively safe from potentially threatening situations and learns to respond in a proper way, increasingly independent of its caregivers. This process is called emotional learning and is facilitated by (contextual) fear conditioning and extinction learning.

Fear conditioning and contextual fear conditioning

Fear conditioning is a form of classical Pavlovian conditioning which involves the pairing of an initially neutral stimulus (conditioned stimulus, CS) with an emotionally significant stimulus (unconditioned stimulus, US). Preclinical studies of fear conditioning typically use tone or light as CS and a footshock as US. The US elicits a wide variety of defensive responses. These include defensive behaviors, alternation of reflex expression (increased startle) and autonomous (heart rate) and endocrine (cortisol excretion) alternations. When the US is (repeatedly) presented at the end of the occurrence a neutral CS, conditioning of the CS will occur. After conditioning, the CS will elicit the same fear response (conditioned fear responses, CR) as when the US is presented (Pavlov, 1927).

Researchers studying fear conditioning noticed, that when a rat is returned to the room where conditioning took place, it would show increased defensive behavior (freezing), even when the CS was not presented. This finding led to the notion that context plays an important role in conditioning, in the form of contextual conditioning. For contextual conditioning to occur, background stimuli need to be continuously present during CS and US pairing and remain present when the rat is returned to the chamber where pairing took place (Phillips & LeDoux, 1992).

Over the past decades the relevance of fear conditioning to anxiety disorders has become ever more evident. This led to an increased interest in the neurobiological mechanism underlying fear memory in general and fear conditioning in particular. Several protagonists of neuroscience, such as Nobel laureate Eric Kandel and Joseph Ledoux have contributed greatly to our understanding in this area. With pioneering research, the neurobiological correlates of fear conditioning and contextual fear conditioning have been successfully clarified in rodents and also to a lesser extent in humans. Most studies show that the amygdala plays a central role in both (LeDoux, 2000).

The amygdala consists of a collection of nuclei that can be divided in to several distinct areas. The areas which are involved in (contextual) fear conditioning are mainly the lateral (LA), basal (B), central nuclei (CE), and the connections between them. The LA is the primary sensory gateway of the amygdala. Sensory input reaches the LA through two distinct pathways: the thalamic pathway and sensory cortical pathway. The former is considered to be quick but imprecise while the latter is slow but accurate. In the LA, information from the CS and US converge and is paired. Contextual information is provided to the amygdala through a different pathway. Projections from the hippocampus reach the basal nucleus of the amygdala. The basal nucleus also receives sensory information from the thalamus. This makes it possible for contextual information and sensory information (US or CS) to converge and pair. For long-term pairing of the CS-US or US-context to take place, long-term potentiation (LTP) has to occur, a process involving protein synthesis and synaptic strengthening. Both the lateral nucleus and the basal nucleus project to the central nucleus, the main output region of the amygdala. Through projections to nuclei in the brainstem and to the hypothalamus, the CE controls the behavioral, autonomic, and endocrine fear response, and reflex expression (Debiec & LeDoux, 2009).

Conditioned fear response

Conditioned fear responses enable the organism to face the upcoming danger. Activation of the nuclei in the brainstem mainly the locus coeruleus leads to an increase of sympathetic nervous system (SNS) activation and a release of the hormones/neurotransmitters adrenalin and noradrenalin. Activation of the SNS and release of adrenalin prepares the organism for action by increasing the blood pressure, heart rate and muscle tone. Noradrenalin increases alertness and reduces the tendency to sleep. Furthermore it promotes long-term potentiation, thereby increasing the long-term pairing between the CS and US. Stimulation of the hypothalamus leads to the release of corticotropine releasing hormone (CRH) that binds to CRH receptors in the pituitary, which in turn releases adrenocorticotropic hormone (ACTH) which binds to receptors in the adrenal glands resulting in the release of cortisol. This is known as the hypothalamus-pituitary-adrenal (HPA) axis. Cortisol binds to mineralocorticoid receptors (MR) and glucocorticoid receptors (GR) at various sites throughout the body. Binding of cortisol to the MR and GR increases blood glucose levels and stimulates fat and protein metabolism, resulting in an increased availability of energy resources. Furthermore, binding of cortisol to receptors in the hypothalamus reduces the release of CRH, completing a negative feedback loop (Berridge, 2009).

Fear extinction

Learning to recognize danger through fear conditioning and responding properly to it is essential, but learning when threat ceases and damping the fear responses is equally important. This form of emotional learning is driven by fear extinction. Fear extinction usually occurs when a conditioned stimulus is repeatedly presented in the absence of any aversive event and leads to a decline of the conditioned fear responses (Yehuda & LeDoux, 2007). Fear extinction is not the same as forgetting or unlearning the acquired fear response. Instead it involves new inhibitory learning. Hence the association between the CS and US remains, but is opposed by a new inhibitory association (CS–No US), with no net activation of the CR as a result. This means that an initially extinguished response can return over time, for instance after manipulation of the unconditioned stimulus or a change of context. The latter indicates that fear extinction is context depended, as is the case in fear conditioning (Myers & Davis, 2007). Fear extinction occurs in three successive phases: acquisition, consolidation, and retrieval. Acquisition of extinction occurs when the CS is repeatedly presented without the US during which the CR declines. Followed by the consolidation phase, which last several hours, during which long-term potentiation stabilizes the CS–No US association. Retrieval of extinction is triggered by re-presentation of the CS. Successful extinction is characterized by low conditioned responses during the retrieval phase. During the three extinction phases, different brain regions are involved.

The amygdala seems to be involved in all three phases. During the acquisition phase, the CS stimulus and No US converge and are paired in the lateral and basal nuclei of the amygdala. During consolidation the CS–No US association is strengthened in the LA and B nuclei. During retrieval, activation of the central nucleus by CS is suppressed by the inhibitory neurotransmitter GABA from the LA and B (Quirk & Mueller, 2008). Lesions of the ventromedial prefrontal cortex (vmPFC) impair consolidation of extinction of conditioned fear suggesting a role of the vmPFC in the consolidation phase of extinction. During consolidation, inhibitory connections of the vmPFC with the LA and the CE are established. During retrieval, the vmPFC suppresses the expression of the conditioned fear response via two pathways. In the first pathway the mPFC directly reduces fear expression through descending projections to nuclei in the brainstem and hypothalamus. The second indirect pathway reduces the afferent input (from the LA) to the central nucleus of the amygdala, through the connection established during consolidation. The reduced input to the central nucleus leads to a reduced excitatory output of it to the brainstem and hypothalamus (Sotres-Bayon, Cain, & LeDoux, 2006). Lesion studies in which the hippocampus of rats was inactivated prior to retention showed that when the hippocampus was inactive, the context dependency of extinction was lost, suggesting an important role of the hippocampus in contextual modulation of extinction (Ji & Maren, 2007).

Development of Structures Involved in the Fear Response

In the previous section we have shown that the amygdala, ventromedial prefrontal cortex, and hippocampus are the key brain areas involved in fear conditioning and extinction. Furthermore, we have described the role of the HPA-axis and brain stem nuclei in the execution of the fear response. In this section we will have a closer look at the developmental trajectories of these structures. This will facilitate the integration of the neurobiological findings in pediatric anxiety disorders into a developmental framework, which will be addressed in the following sections. This section will focus on the development of structures involved in fear and is not intended to give a full account of the development trajectories of the complete child and adolescent brain. For that purpose we refer to some more comprehensive reviews.

Up until the 1980s, our knowledge about normal brain development was mostly derived from lesion studies and post-mortem studies. The neuroimaging techniques that have become available over the past 3 decades – especially magnetic resonance imaging (MRI) and functional MRI (fMRI) – have made it possible to study brain development non-invasively and over longer periods of time. This has led to a significant expansion of our knowledge about normal brain development including the amygdala, vmPFC, and hippocampus.

Amygdala

For a child to be capable of detecting threat cues from a caregiver's facial expression through social referencing, the amygdala has to be functional at an early stage of development. This assumption is supported by data from lesion studies in both animals and humans. Amygdala lesions that occur in infancy dramatically impair processing of fearful facial expressions. This leads to an inability to recognize cues that signal safety and therefore increase fear responses during social interactions (Adolphs, Tranel, Damasio, & Damasio, 1995). However, amygdala lesions occurring during adulthood result in unrestrained behavior in social interactions. This finding stresses the importance of the timing of the amygdala lesion and the changing role over time that the amygdala plays in social and emotional learning (Tottenham, Hare, & Casey, 2009).

Longitudinal MRI studies of normal brain development have shown that apart from the importance of time, gender also plays a critical role in amygdala development. While amygdala volumes increased between the age of 4 and 18 in males, female amygdala volumes remained stable over time. This gender specific maturation difference could be explained by the relative high number of androgen (male sex-hormone) receptors in the amygdale (Lenroot & Giedd, 2010).

In contrast with MRI, there is a paucity of longitudinal fMRI studies of brain development. Therefore we still have to rely on cross-sectional studies when we are examining the changes of intact human brain function during development. Nevertheless, the results of these cross-sectional comparisons between age groups yield important insights into amygdala functioning over time. One of the most striking examples is the change of amygdala activity while watching neutral and fearful faces. Adults, adolescents, and children all show amygdala activation during the presentation of fearful faces (Baird, Gruber, Fein et al., 1999; Thomas, Drevets, Whalen et al., 2001b). This indicates that the amygdala is involved in the processing of emotional faces across development. However, contrasting findings occur when amygdala activation in adults and children during the presentation of neutral faces is compared. Thomas and colleagues showed that adults demonstrated a greater amygdala activity for fearful faces relative to neutral faces. Children (mean age 11) on the other hand surprisingly showed greater amygdala activity for neutral faces than for fearful faces (Thomas et al., 2001b). These findings indicate that children might process neutral faces as more threatening than adults would do. A possible explanation for this is that neutral faces have a more ambiguous nature for younger children. The exact consequence of seeing a neutral facial expression is still uncertain and has to be learned through experience (Tottenham et al., 2009). Given the limited ability of children to fight or flight when they encounter danger it is understandable that ambiguous signals are perceived as threatening, better safe than sorry. The question remains which brain structures (and mechanisms) underlie learning that a neutral face signals safety and does not have to elicit fear responses. From the previous paragraph we know that the vmPFC is critical for restraining the fear responses through extinction. This structure thus seems a suitable candidate.

Ventromedial prefrontal cortex

Unlike the amygdala which reaches anatomical and functional maturation in an early stage of development, the vmPFC is developing throughout childhood, adolescences and early adulthood. Recent studies have shown that maturation of the vmPFC even extends well into the third decade of life (Benes, Turtle, Khan, & Farol, 1994). Post mortem and longitudinal MRI studies have shown that three developmental processes play a crucial role in vmPFC maturation namely synaptogenesis, synaptic pruning and myelination. Through synaptogenesis there is a massive overproduction of synapses during the prenatal period and infancy. The synaptic overproduction is followed by a gradual decrease of synaptic connections through synaptic pruning. By synaptic pruning more active synapses are strengthened and less active synapses are weakened or eliminated, this leads to a more efficient set of synaptic connections. The time course of synaptogenesis and pruning varies considerably between different brain areas. The vmPFC reaches its peak of synaptic connections at 3–4 years of age, which is relatively late compared to other brain areas (for instance the number of synapses in the visual cortex peaks at 3–4 months). Not only does the vmPFC obtain its maximum number of synapses relatively late in development but synaptic pruning also persists longer. Synaptic density only reaches adult levels in mid to late adolescence. In comparison, adult synaptic density in the visual cortex is reached at preschool age (Toga, Thompson, & Sowell, 2006). Apart from synaptogenesis and pruning, myelination is crucial for brain maturation. Through myelination the neural signal transmission speed and synchronicity of neural firing patterns increases (Giedd & Rapoport, 2010). Myelin consists of fatty white sheets that wrap around axons and can be seen on MRI scans as white matter, which makes it relatively easy to track developing myelination patterns longitudinally. These MRI studies again show that the vmPFC is late to mature: the onset of myelination is relatively late and extends throughout the third decade.

The findings concerning synaptogenesis, pruning, and myelination all point out that the vmPFC is a late maturing structure. This leads to the conclusion that the degree in which the vmPFC is involved in fear extinction may differ across development. Indeed, studies show that in 24-day-old rats, extinction involved both the vmPFC and amygdala while in 17-day-old rats extinction only involved the amygdala (Kim & Richardson, 2010). To replicate these findings in humans we will need longitudinal fMRI studies using fear conditioning and extinction paradigms in which children are followed throughout development.

Hippocampus

MRI studies have shown that during development, overall hippocampal volumes increase. As in amygdala development, not only is time important in hippocampal development but gender also plays a role. Earlier we have shown that amygdala volumes increase over time in males and remain stable in females. An opposite pattern can be seen with hippocampal volumes. While hippocampal volumes increase over time in females, they stay stable in males. This gender-specific maturation difference can again be explained by difference in sex/hormone levels. The hippocampus namely has a relative high number of estrogen (female sex-hormone) receptors in the hippocampus (Giedd, Snell, Lange et al., 1996). In contrast to the PFC, the hippocampus structure is almost fully developed in early childhood (age 2 years).

Startle Response

The startle reflex is a rapid, involuntary contraction of the skeletal and facial muscles in response to abrupt and intense stimulation (Wilkins, Hallett, & Wess, 1986). It occurs in almost all species and can be elicited in humans starting at 2–4 months of age. The reflex is part of the fear response and has the likely purpose of facilitating the flight reaction and/or protecting the body from a sudden attack. With repeated stimulation, the intensity of the surprise reaction decreases. Animal studies have shown that the amygdala – a structure believed to play a key role in emotional processing – facilitates and decreases the startle reflex (Davis, 1992).

The startle reflex can be provoked by stimuli of different sensory modalities (e.g., sound, light and tactile shocks). It commences proximally with an eye-blink response and facial grimace, and spreads distally to produce upper-limb, truncal, and lower-limb flexion. Electromyographic latencies of onset of startle increase from central to peripheral muscle groups, being 41–58 ms for orbicularis oculi to 110 ms in quadriceps femoris (Wilkins et al., 1986). An eye-blink reflex is always seen, regardless of the presence of a more generalized startle reflex. The initial phase of the startle reflex is followed by a secondary stage that shows much interindividual variation in form and duration (Howard & Ford, 1992; Wilkins et al., 1986).

Although startle is stereotyped, it is not invariant. It shows a relatively high variability that reflects variation in the internal state of the organism. To the extent that these changes are under experimental control, the startle reflex can inform us about this internal state (Grillon & Baas, 2003). Therefore, measurements of the startle reflex have become useful paradigms in the research of mental disorders. In this research, three broad areas of interest can be delineated (Grillon & Baas, 2003): (1) the study of startle reactivity in general as the reflection of interindividual differences in the sensitivity of the fear system; (2) the study of the modulation of the startle reflex by emotional states; (3) the startle reflex as an index of sensorimotor gating, by investigating the inhibition of the startle reflex by sensory stimuli presented shortly before the startle-inducing stimulus (pre-pulse inhibition, or PPI). The PPI approach has especially been used in schizophrenia research, whereas the first two are typically used in the investigation of anxiety disorders in adults and children.

A sudden loud sound is the most frequently used stimulus in anxiety research, leading to an acoustic startle reflex (ASR). There are several other ways to elicit startle in research, for instance by applying an electric shock, or (alternatively in children) an air puff. It is important, however, to choose a stimulus that is on the one hand intense enough to elicit a startle, but on the other hand does not induce a maximum response, thereby creating a ceiling effect that hides individual differences.

In humans, the ASR is most often operationalized by electromyogram (EMG) measurement of the reflex following a brief and intense auditory stimulus with a fast rising time. Because of its resistance to habituation and therefore easily inducible several times within a short period, the eye-blink reflex is the most commonly used measure of startle in human research today. However, there are doubts whether the blink response is the best parameter to measure the anxiety-related ASR. One study (Bakker, 2009) of 27 normally developing children (age 8–17 years) showed that the blink response and the whole-body startle response (the combined response of multiple muscles) following auditory stimuli have markedly different habituation patterns. The expected physiological habituation occurs when multiple muscles are analyzed, but not when only the blink response is taken into account. Although in need of replication, this study suggests that measurement of the ASR over multiple muscles provides a more valid and reliable impression of the startle reflex.

Neurobiological Findings in Child and Adolescent Anxiety Disorders

In the previous section we have described the development and underlying neurobiological mechanisms of the normal fear response. A normal functioning fear response enables an individual to appropriately respond to threat and is beneficiary for its survival. However, disturbances of the fear response can lead to excessive or inappropriate fear. Excessive fear can be maladaptive; it limits an individual's behavior and thus causes functional impairment. Maladaptive fear is an important component of most anxiety disorders. In the current paragraph we will shift our attention from the normal development and normal function of the fear response to the neurobiological mechanisms underlying behavioral inhibition, stress, and the different anxiety disorders in children. We will begin by reviewing the available neurobiological data regarding two risk factors for the development of anxiety disorders namely: behavioral inhibition and stress. We then summarize the findings of neurobiological studies on the different anxiety disorders in children. Finally, we will propose developmental model of anxiety disorders based on the findings of the current and previous paragraphs.

Behavioural inhibition

When interacting with (young) groups of children, one cannot fail to notice that some children appear to be timid with unfamiliar persons or objects while others tend to approach novelty more spontaneously. The ways in which children react when novelty arises is shaped by their temperament. Temperament refers to the stable set of behavioral profiles and moods observed in infancy and toddlerhood (Schwartz, Wright, Shin, Kagan, & Rauch, 2003). Following the longitudinal and empirical studies on childhood development performed in the 1950s by Chess and Thomas (Chess, Thomas, Birch, & Hertzig, 1960), interest in childhood temperaments and their implications for psychopathology have radically increased. Since then, two temperamental constructs have come forward as particularly relevant to (child and adolescent) psychiatry; namely the inhibited and uninhibited temperament.

Kagan and Snidman (1999) compared children with an inhibited temperament with children with an uninhibited temperament and followed their development throughout childhood and adolescence. Inhibited children were characterized by high reactivity to novel situations in their infancy and reticence in the company of people or objects during childhood. The uninhibited children showed the opposite behavioral pattern of low reactivity to novelty during infancy and minimal fear or avoidance of unfamiliar persons or objects during childhood. A high reactive infant displays vigorous limb movement and crying when it encounters an unfamiliar event; low reactive infants show minimal limb movement and no crying in unfamiliar situations. Both limb movement and crying in unfamiliar situations are controlled by the amygdala, the former through projections from the basal lateral amygdala to the ventral striatum, the latter by projections from the amygdala to the anterior cingulate cortex. Kagan showed that children who were high-reactive during infancy showed enhanced behavioral (failure to approach unfamiliar person or object, crying and decreased smiling during novelty) and physiological (increased sympathetic tone and HPA axis reactivity) fear reactions during social and non-social events throughout their childhood compared to their low-reactive peers. Children who were classified as behaviorally inhibited during childhood had a moderately increased risk of developing a social anxiety disorder during adolescence. During the past two decades these findings have been replicated and a number other studies have shown that behavioral inhibition not only predisposes children for SAD but also for other anxiety disorders and depression (Chronis-Tuscano, Degnan, Pine et al., 2009; Perez-Edgar & Fox, 2005; Prior, Smart, Sanson, & Oberklaid, 2000).

Kagan and colleagues expressed the relevance of the structure and function of the fear circuitry to the concept of behavioral inhibition. They proposed a model in which behavioral inhibition reflects increased reactivity of the amygdala (Kagan, Reznick, & Snidman, 1988). In the past few years this model has been used as a starting point for neurobiological studies of behavioral inhibition. We will present an overview of the main finding derived from these studies.

Schwartz et al. (2003) compared adults who were behaviorally inhibited at age 2 years with adults who were uninhibited at their second year of life. They used fMRI to measure amygdala activation during the presentation of novel and familiar faces. Adults who had been categorized as behaviorally inhibited showed greater amygdala activity to novel faces versus familiar faces compared with uninhibited controls. These findings were replicated by Perez-Edgar in adolescents (Perez-Edgar, Roberson-Nay, Hardin et al., 2007). They compared adolescents who were labeled behavioral inhibited during toddlerhood and early childhood with adolescents who were labelled uninhibited. The adolescent had to view emotional faces and rate their level of fear while an fMRI scan was performed. The inhibited group showed exaggerated amygdala activity compared to the uninhibited group during fear rating and during the presentation of novel faces. These results emphasize that inhibited and uninhibited infants show different amygdalar responses to novelty and suggest that these differences are preserved from infancy throughout adolescence into early adulthood. Longitudinal neuroimaging studies are necessary to affirm these findings.

Stress

Every day children fall victim to abuse, neglect, acts of violence, (natural) disasters, and other stressful or traumatic life events. The prevalence of such events in children is high. Copeland, Keeler, Angold and Costello (2007) found that in a sample of American children, 67.8% reported exposure to at least one traumatic event. Children who experience stress or trauma have an increased risk of developing anxiety disorders and depression later in life (Pine & Cohen, 2002). Studies in both animals and humans have shown that stress effects brain, cognition, and behavior. These effects are reliant on the nature of the stressor and the duration of exposure. Furthermore, effects are dependent on the brain areas that are developing at the time of exposure. Roughly three distinct periods in which stress takes place can be distinguished: the prenatal period, the postnatal period, and adolescence (Lupien, McEwen, Gunnar, & Heim, 2009).

Prenatal period: Exposure to stress increases glucocorticoids secretion in pregnant women, a portion of these glucocorticoids reach the fetus by passing the placenta. Maternal glucocorticoids increase fetal HPA-axis activity and influence brain development. Research in rats and monkeys has shown maternal glucocorticoids influence HPA-axis and brain development of the offspring in at least three ways. (1) Increased levels of glucocorticoids delays maturation of neurons, vascularization, and myelination in the offspring. Leading to inhibited neurogenesis and disrupted neuronal structure and synapse formation (Seckl, 2008). (2) Increased levels of maternal glucocorticoids decreased the number of glucocoriticoid and mineralocorticoid receptors in the hippocampus of the offspring; this reduces the inhibitory control of the hippocampus on the HPA-axis resulting in increased glucocorticoid secretion in stressful situations later on. (3) Prenatal glucocorticoid exposure increases adult corticotropin releasing hormone levels in the central nucleus of the amygdala, which increases anxiety-related behaviors (Cratty, Ward, Johnson, Azzaro, & Birkle, 1995). Retrospective studies of maternal stress during pregnancy in humans also show increased HPA-axis activity in offspring throughout childhood and increased risk for the development of anxiety disorders (Lupien et al., 2009).

Postnatal period: Studies on the effects of stress during the postnatal period yield contrasting results. The nature and severity of the stressor are important. While maternal separation (out-of-home day care) results in elevated glucocorticoids levels in toddlers and preschoolers, chronic and severe deprivation or abuse result in decreased basal glucocorticoid levels (Gunnar & Donzella, 2002). The decreased basal glucocorticoids levels can be explained by a downregulation of the HPA-axis through chronic heightened CRH levels in the hypothalamus (Fries, Ziegler, Kurian, Jacoris, & Pollak, 2005).

Adolescence: During adolescence distinct changes in sex steroid levels take place. These changes induce an increase of basal and stress-induced HPA-axis activity and glucocorticoid levels (McCormick & Mathews, 2007). The adolescent brain seems to be especially sensitive to the effects of glucocorticoids. This can be explained by the great amount of structural changes which take place in the adolescent brain. Earlier we have shown that the amygdala and PFC continue developing during adolescence. Continuing increased levels of glucocorticoids influence the expression of the growth factor, brain-derived neurotropic factor (BNDF), which is liked with neuronal proliferation and plasticity (van Harmelen, van Tol, van der Wee et al., 2010). Altered expression of BNDF in the amygdala and PFC can disrupt amygdala en PFC development causing decreased regulation from the mPFC of the amygdala resulting in increased fear and anxiety.

From behavioural inhibition and stress to anxiety disorders

Not all individuals who are behaviorally inhibited or exposed to stress during their childhood or adolescence develop psychopathology. However, a significant portion do develop one or more anxiety disorders later in life (Chronis-Tuscano, et al., 2009; Meiser-Stedman, Smith, Glucksman, Yule, & Dalgleish, 2008). The mechanisms that determine which child will and which child will not develop psychopathology are not yet clarified. Neurobiological studies comparing individuals with and without anxiety disorders can give an insight in these mechanisms. These insights can help us to distinguish behaviorally inhibited or stress-exposed children who are very likely to develop anxiety disorders from those who are less likely to develop anxiety disorders.

Neuroimaging studies in children with generalized and social anxiety disorders

The first fMRI study performed in children with anxiety disorders compared 12 children with GAD or panic disorder with 12 healthy comparison children while viewing pictures of fearful and neutral faces (Thomas, Drevets, Dahl et al., 2001b). Children with anxiety disorders showed increased amygdala response to fearful faces. The magnitude of change in amygdala response between fearful and neutral faces was positively correlated with reported anxiety symptoms. In another study, Monk, Nelson, McClure et al. (2006) compared BOLD signal as measured via fMRI of 18 adolescents with GAD with 15 matched healthy adolescents. The participants preformed an emotional dot-probe task in which an angry and neutral face pair was shown for 500 ms as a distracter between the dot and probe presentation. Subjects pressed a button to indicate whether the probe (asterisk) appeared on the same or opposite side of the angry face. Patients with GAD showed greater attention bias *away* from angry faces and increased ventrolateral prefrontal cortex (vlPFC) activation. As vlPFC activity increased, severity of anxiety symptoms decreased. In contrast with the findings by Thomas et al. (2001b), this study did not find differences in amygdala activity between adolescents with GAD and healthy controls. Based on these findings, the authors hypothesize that vlPFC activity might serve as a compensatory response to heightened amygdala activity. This hypothesis was tested by the same research group in a case control study in which 17 adolescents with GAD were compared with 12 healthy controls (Monk, Telzer, Mogg et al., 2008). The researchers used the same emotional dot-probe task but this time the distracting face pairs were masked and presented only for 17 ms so that the participants were not aware of the nature of the faces. Patients showed an attention bias *towards* threatening faces and did show increased (right) amygdala activation compared to healthy comparisons. A functional connectivity analysis showed a negative coupling of amygdala activity with vlPFC activity in both groups. To summarize these findings:

1. Adolescents with GAD show an increased amygdala response which is positively correlated with symptom severity and attention bias towards threat when angry faces are presented briefly.
2. Adolescent with GAD demonstrate increased vlPFC activity which is negatively correlated with symptom severity and attention bias away from threat when angry faces are presented for a longer period of time.
3. Amygdala and vlPFC activity are negatively correlated in both patients and controls.

These findings suggest that in pediatric GAD, the compensatory function of the vlPFC falls short to effectively modulate the amygdala's hyper-response to threatening stimuli.

In another line of research, McClure, Monk, Nelson et al. (2007) studied the effects of specific attention states on neural activity in the fear circuitry. In a case control study, 15 adolescents with GAD were compared to 20 controls. The participants completed a face-attention paradigm in which they viewed neutral and emotional (angry, fearful, and happy) faces over a longer period (several seconds) of time. During face presentation three different attention states were evoked by asking participants to rate: how afraid they felt, the nose width of each face and the hostility of each face. During the "how afraid" attention state, patients showed altered activation to fearful faces than to happy faces in a network consisting of the amygdala, vlPFC, and anterior cingulate cortex. These findings indicate that pathological fear circuitry activation is particularly evident during focus on subjectively experienced fear. The interaction of attention states with neural activity in the amygdala ventral PFC network was also found in children diagnosed with social anxiety disorder. Guyer, Lau, McClure-Tone et al. (2008) compared 14 socially anxious adolescents with 14 matched control subjects. During an fMRI scan, participants classified pictures of peers as ones with whom they did or did not want to interact. Participants were told that their decision would be passed on to the peer shown in the picture. Compared to healthy controls, adolescents with SAD showed increased amygdala activity and perturbed amygdala and vlPFC connectivity when they anticipated evaluation from pears rated as undesirable for interaction.

Startle response in children with anxiety disorders

Children with anxiety disorders (AD) are hypothesized to have a highly sensitive fear system, including an augmented startle reflex (ASR) (Bakker, 2009). There is evidence of an association between AD and an enlarged ASR, but the results are equivocal for AD in adults (Grillon & Baas, 2003). Research in AD children is limited. One study examined startle reactivity in anticipation of a mild anxiogenic laboratory procedure in school-age children with current AD and in those at-risk for AD due to parental anxiety. Blink-reflex magnitude in anticipation of anxiogenic procedures increased across the 7–12 year age range in children at-risk for AD, whereas elevations in startle reactivity were already manifest from a younger age in children with AD. In control children, age had no effect on the size of the reflex. The findings suggest an underlying vulnerability that becomes manifest with development in offspring of anxious parents as the risk for anxiety disorders increases (Waters, Craske, Bergman, Naliboff, Negoro, & Ornitz, 2008). A longitudinal study of temperament (behavioral inhibition) in children demonstrated that only adolescents with high levels of behavioral inhibition together with a lifetime occurrence of AD, showed increased blink startle reactivity, but neither behavioral inhibition as such nor diagnosis was related to startle reactivity during threat cues. The authors conclude that the blink startle reflex may be a potential risk marker for the development of anxiety disorders among behaviorally inhibited adolescents (Reeb-Sutherland, Helfinstein, Degnan et al., 2009). Note however that another study of behaviorally inhibited children showed these children displayed smaller eye-blink magnitudes in response to novel slides than uninhibited children (van Braker, Murris, & Bogels, 2006).

Bakker (2009) argued that the inconsistent results of studies of the startle reflex in anxious children may be due to the eye-blink methodology adopted in these studies. Bakker and colleagues performed a couple of studies in AD children, employing a measurement over multiple muscles instead. In a case-control study of 25 clinically referred children (age 8–17 years) with one or more AD the auditory startle reflex measured over multiple muscles proved to be enlarged in the AD group, whereas the blink response was normal in patients, compared to healthy controls (Bakker, 2009). Of the AD children 20 were re-examined after 12 weeks of cognitive behavioral therapy (CBT). This showed that ASR in AD children normalizes with the reduction of the anxiety symptoms. In contrast, the multiple muscle ASR significantly increased or remained stable in treatment non-responders. In healthy controls, the ASR remained stable over time. In addition, a positive response to CBT was predicted by a large ASR magnitude before treatment. Again, these results were strictly related to the multiple muscles methodology, and could not be found when measurement was restricted to the eye-blink reflex. The authors point out that replication by other research teams in larger samples is imperative. For now, the results suggest that an increased ASR in AD children is at least partially a state characteristic (as it normalizes upon remission of the disorder), although this does not preclude a contribution by individual vulnerability (trait) as well.

Summary

Children who are behaviorally inhibited or exposed to stress show exaggerated amygdala activity; this leads to increased physiological and HPA-axis (re)activity resulting in a heightened startle response and increased cortisol levels. Increased cortisol levels influence brain development through glucocorticoid and mineralocortiod receptors. The prefrontal cortex is especially prone to the influences of cortisol because it contains high levels of GRs and MRs and is developing throughout childhood and adolescence. Exposure to heightened levels of cortisol during development will cause altered PFC structure in some children. PFC function may be impaired in adolescence and adulthood even when high levels of cortisol subside. Individuals with an impaired PFC function fail to adequately modulate amygdala activity when potential threat arises and when threat ceases to exist, causing pathological activation of the fear circuitry and resulting in sustained anxiety symptoms.

Neurobiological Findings in Child and Adolescent PTSD

In the general population, experiencing extreme life stressors is very common. About 60% of men and 50% of women were exposed to one or more traumatic events (Kessler et al., 2005). Before the age of 18 years, 25–65% of the children experienced one or more traumatic events (Copeland, et al., 2007). Most children and adults recovered spontaneously after experiencing a traumatic event. About 10–35% of these children develop a PTSD. For the PTSD diagnosis, a traumatic event is necessary. The definition of a traumatic event is an event in which one is exposed to serious threat of injury or death and then experiences extreme fear, helplessness, or horror. Three symptom clusters define the disorder. *Symptoms of re-experiencing*: recurrent and intrusive recollections and nightmares of the event, and flashbacks of a part of the event. *Avoidance symptoms*: avoidance of reminders of the event, emotional numbing, and an inability to feel any positive emotions. *Hyperarousal symptoms*: enhanced startle response, difficulty sleeping, concentrating, and hypervigilance for danger. Although exposure to potentially traumatic events is common, development of PTSD is a relatively rare condition. Some children develop PTSD while others exposed to similar threatening events do not. Other factors, biological factors, are also important to understand the etiology of this disorder. In this paragraph, the biological aspects of PTSD will be discussed.

In PTSD, biological changes have been found in the hippocampal volume, cerebral blood flow, level of stress hormones, and more general physiological indicators like heart rate and blood pressure. Genetic and neurotransmitter system studies are sparse in PTSD. Most biological studies have been done in adults (Lindauer, Vlieger, Jalink et al., 2004, 2005). There are some studies in children: psychophysiological, endocrinological and brain volume studies.

Structural brain imaging

Structural brain imaging studies in PTSD have reported smaller hippocampal volume in different adult populations. Reductions in hippocampal volume between 5% and 26% were reported. Other studies did not confirm the finding of smaller hippocampal volume in trauma, for example the study by DeBellis in maltreated children and adolescents (De Bellis, Hall, Boring, Frustaci, & Moritz, 2001). In this study, young subjects in the midst of hippocampal maturation were included and that could have masked the full effect on the hippocampus. Although most volumetric studies in PTSD have specifically measured hippocampal changes, smaller volumes have also been found for the total cerebrum and corpus callosum in maltreated children corpus callosum (De Bellis, Keshavan, Shifflett et al., 2002). The hippocampus is a brain area involved in learning and memory processes. Studies in nonhuman primates and rodents have reported that chronic psychosocial stress leads to specific hippocampal neural atrophy due to an interaction of elevated glucocorticoids and excitatory neurotransmitters (McEwen & Magarinos, 1997). In this light, Bremner has proposed that smaller hippocampal volumes may be a result of neurotoxic effects related to traumatic events and subsequent PTSD (Bremner, 1999). This hypothesis of stress-induced hippocampal damage is one of the possible explanations of the findings of smaller hippocampal volume in PTSD. A second explanation might be that PTSD induces comorbid conditions such as major depression or alcohol abuse, which themselves have been found to damage the hippocampus (Pitman, 2001). A third explanation is that the smaller hippocampal volume may be a pre-existing factor for the development of PTSD (Gilbertson, Shenton, Ciszewski et al., 2002). In recent literature, the last hypothesis is more than likely. Gilbertson et al. have found evidence that severe PTSD twin pairs, both the trauma-exposed and non-exposed members, have significantly smaller hippocampi than non-PTSD pairs. In other words, smaller hippocampi are a risk factor for the development of PTSD.

Functional brain imaging

Stimuli associated with a traumatic event may activate a highly coherent network responsible for the memory structure in PTSD. In different studies, tape-recorded scripts of the personal traumatic event, referred to as script-driven imagery, have been used to successfully provoke PTSD symptoms in psychophysiological assessment as well as in functional brain imaging. Other paradigms used in functional brain imaging have been trauma-related visual stimuli, trauma-related sounds, and pharmacological challenges.

Several different imaging techniques have been used to assess changes in cerebral blood flow, including positron emission tomography (PET), single photon emission computed tomography (SPECT), and fMRI.

On the basis of results from these functional brain imaging studies, the following brain areas are now thought to be involved in the pathophysiology of PTSD: limbic structures, including the amygdala and hippocampus; paralimbic or medical prefrontal structures, including the anterior cingulate and orbitofrontal cortices; prefrontal structures, including the left inferior prefrontal cortex (Broca's area) and dorsolateral prefrontal cortex; and other brain structures, including the posterior cingulate, parietal, visual, visual association and motor cortices as well as the cerebellum. On the basis of neuroanatomical models and functional brain imaging studies reported in PTSD, limbic and cortical brain regions are involved in the pathophysiology of PTSD (Bremner, 2002; Pitman, 2001). The main findings are: (a) dysfunction of the medial prefrontal cortex: the medial prefrontal cortex normally modulates responses to fear, both through inhibitory connections with the amygdala and by attenuating peripheral sympathetic and hormonal responses to stress (LeDoux, 2000); (b) hyperactivation of the amygdala and insula: the amygdala plays a crucial role in the acquisition and extinction of conditioned fear as well as in the expression of the associated autonomic arousal (Pitman, 2001). A reciprocal relationship has been found between medial prefrontal cortex function and amygdala function in PTSD (Shin, Orr, Carson et al., 2004).

Endocrinology

In PTSD, studies found lower cortisol levels, higher corticotropin-releasing factor (CRF) levels, exaggerated suppression of cortisol in response to dexamethasone administration, and increased sensitivity of lymphocyte glucocorticoid receptors, suggesting that the sensitivity of the negative-feedback system is heightened (for a review see Yehuda, 2002). These HPA axis alterations in PTSD have not been reported consistently (Rasmusson, Vythilingam, & Morgan, 2003). The findings of normal or low baseline cortisol levels in PTSD might seem at odds with the glucocorticoid hypothesis that increased cortisol levels lead to hippocampal damage. The cortisol levels measured in all these PTSD studies were still within the normal range.

Psychophysiology/startle response

Studies of the psychophysiological aspects of PTSD have used script-driven imagery to provoke PTSD symptoms and the concomitant increases in autonomic and muscular activity. Studies reported heightened physiological responses during personalized trauma-related imagery (Pitman, Orr, Forgue, de Jong, & Claiborn, 1987), thus confirming one of the defining features of PTSD in DSM-IV-TR, "physiological reactivity on exposure to internal or external cues that symbolize or resemble an aspect of the traumatic event" (PTSD criterion B.5, American Psychiatric Association; APA, 2000). Studies investigating physiological responsivity to specifically trauma-related cues gave reported sensitivities and specificities in the ranges of 60%–90% and 80%–100%, respectively (Orr & Roth, 2000).

An exaggerated startle response is a clinical feature often reported by patients with PTSD, and in fact is one of the hyperarousal or Criteria D symptoms of the DSM-IV (APA, 2000). But in laboratory studies of baseline (that is without creating a fearful situation) acoustic startle responses in subjects with PTSD the results have been mixed. Exaggerated baseline startle responses have been found in combat veterans with PTSD by some researchers, but other investigators were not able to replicate these findings (Lipschitz, Mayes, Rasmusson et al., 2005). Relatively little is known about startle as a clinical phenomenon in children and adolescents. A study of traumatized adolescent girls showed psychological distress at trauma reminders (75%), active attempts to avoid people or places connected to the trauma (70%), and hypervigilance (63%) as most common PTSD symptoms. Only thirty eight percent of this traumatized sample reported an exaggerated startle. To date very few studies have examined acoustic startle responses in children and adolescents with PTSD, and the results are inconsistent, ranging from attenuated (Ornitz & Pynoos, 1989) to normal ASR's (Lipschitz, et al. 2005). All the studies thus far have employed the eye blink paradigm. It is possible that measurement over multiple muscles will yield more constituent results

Obsessive Compulsive Disorder – a Special Kind of Paediatric Anxiety Disorder?

Obsessive-compulsive disorder (OCD) is characterized by recurrent and persistent thoughts, impulses, or images, which cause marked anxiety or distress, and repetitive behaviors or mental acts that the person feels driven to perform in response to an obsession, or according to rules that must be applied rigidly (APA, 2000). In the DSM-IV classification system, OCD is classified in the section of anxiety disorders, but this is controversial (Mataix-Cols, Pertusa, & Leckman, 2007). The DSM-V OCD workgroup proposes to include OCD in a grouping of Anxiety and Obsessive-Compulsive Spectrum Disorders, suggesting both similarity and distinction between anxiety and obsessive compulsive phenomena (www.dsm5.org/proposed_revisions). More importantly, in a paper by members of the work group, it is emphasized that OCD is a clinically heterogeneous disorder, with different symptom dimensions of which symmetry/ordering, contamination/cleaning, and hoarding are supported best by the available evidence (Leckman, Denys, Simpson et al., 2010). It might well be that within this heterogeneity, the symmetry/ordening subtype, with shows a higher comorbidity with tic-disorders, is more akin to a motor disorder, whereas the contamination/cleaning subtype is more similar to an anxiety disorder (Radua, van den Heuvel, Surguladze, & Mataix-Cols, 2010). As we will see in this section, the evidence about the neurobiology of pediatric OCD is still fragmentary, but is also suggestive of similarity as well as distinction with regard to anxiety disorders.

Three types of neurobiological models

In organizing and describing the available neurobiological findings, it is helpful to follow, and where possible, integrate three different types of neurobiological models of the pathophysiology of OCD (Rauch, Whalen, & Dougherty, 1998): (1) corticostriatal circuitry models; (2) amygdalocentric models; and (3) neurochemical models.

Corticostriatal circuitry models. Corticostriatal systems serve multiple normal functions, including processing and/or filtering information (by the striatum) such that it does not reach the conscious domain, as well as the mediation of stereotyped behaviors. A dysfunction of corticostriatal systems is therefore explanatory for the intrusive phenomena and the ritualized repetitive behaviors so typical of OCD. Within this model there is currently believed to be an involvement of a direct and an indirect cortico-striato-thalamic pathway (Mataix-Cols & van den Heuvel, 2006). In the direct pathway, an excitatory glutamatergic signal projects to the striatum, sending an inhibitory gamma-aminobutyric acid (GABA)-ergic signal to the internal part of the globus pallidus. This signal results in a decreased inhibition (disinhibition) of the thalamus and thus an increased excitatory effect on the prefrontal cortex. In the indirect pathway, the striatum projects an inhibitory signal to the external part of the globus pallidus and the subthalamic nucleus, sending an excitatory signal to the internal part of the globus pallidus. The net effect is an increased inhibition of the thalamus and decreased excitation on the prefrontal cortex. It is hypothesized that the direct pathway functions as a self-reinforcing positive feedback loop and contributes to the initiation and continuation of behaviors, whereas the indirect pathway provides a mechanism of negative feedback which is important for the inhibition of behaviors and in switching between behaviors.

Amygdalocentric models. Rauch et al. (1998) point out that the amygdalocentric perspective allows a better understanding of the affective and motivational elements of OCD. The amygdala has a prominent role in the assessment of danger and is critical to an organism's ability to modify the perceived danger value of a given stimulus, as well as the organism's behavior in response to that stimulus. In these functions, the amygdala is interconnected with the corticostriatal system: the amygdala-mediated plasticity relies on its interconnections with the medial frontal cortex, and next to this the amygdala has dense connections with the striatum, that are presumed to support an efficient system for driving automated behaviors in response to danger. In view of the critical role of the amygdala in the neurobiology of anxiety disorders, it is plausible that a better understanding of the role of the amygdala in OCD will be helpful in untangling the similarities and differences between OCD and the more prototypical anxiety disorders.

A recent review of the neuroimaging studies in pediatric OCD (Huyser, Veltman, de Haan, & Boer, 2009) shows that the model of Rauch et al. is partially supported by the available evidence. Based upon 28 neuroimaging studies, including a total of 462 paediatric OCD patients, Huyser et al. conclude that there is ample support for the hypothesis of dysfunctional prefrontal-striatal-thalamic circuitry, and also evidence for involvement of (para)limbic circuitry (amygdala, hippocampus, and insula cortex), frontotemporoparietal and frontocerebellar circuits, as well as the corpus callosum and the pituitary gland. The findings in pediatric OCD to an extent converge with those in adult OCD, but there are also important differences. The involvement of the orbitofrontal cortex (OFC) and caudate nucleus that emerged from a meta-analysis of functional neuroimaging data of adult OCD patients, has only been replicated in one pediatric study for the OFC. Pediatric OCD neuroimaging data point at the involvement of other basal ganglia structures (putamen, globus pallidus) and the thalamus instead. Huyser et al. (2009) point out that a greater involvement of the putamen/globus pallidus and thalamus in pediatric OCD versus prefrontal cortex/caudate nucleus in adult OCD might also explain differences in comorbidity: Tourette syndrome (TS) and pervasive developmental disorder, that co-occur more often with pediatric OCD, have been associated with basal ganglia dysfunction, whereas depression, a more prominent comorbid condition in adult OCD, has been associated with prefrontal dysfunction.

Cross-sectional studies in pediatric OCD patients suggest abnormalities of brain development, with findings of an age-related volume increase of the anterior cingulate cortex (ACC), and a decrease in dorsolateral prefrontal cortex (DLPFC) volume in OCD patients, but not in healthy controls, whereas an age-related volume decrease of the thalamus and an increase in corpus callosum volume was observed in healthy controls but not in OCD patients, which suggests a developmentally mediated network dysplasia due to different patterns of pruning and myelinization among several frontostriatal networks. The frontal regions increase with age where the opposite would be expected, and the thalamus lacks the normal pruning pattern of a decreasing volume with age. However, since these results were obtained exclusively in cross-sectional studies, there is clearly a need for empirical confirmation in longitudinal designs.

Neurochemical models. Neurochemical processes are superimposed over the anatomy described in the first two models, and modulate the neurotransmission within these systems. Abnormalities of serotonergic transmission in OCD are suggested by pharmacological imaging studies, which have shown a reduction in 5-HT synthesis in the ventral prefrontal cortex and caudate in 11 treatment-naive pediatric subjects, which partially normalized following successful treatment (Simpson, Lombardo, Slifstein et al., 2003). The findings for the dopaminergic system are less consistent, with mixed results concerning changes in peripheral dopaminergic markers and the provocation of obsessive symptoms by dopamine agonists (Denys, Zohar, & Westenberg, 2004). Glutamate is the major excitatory neurotransmitter in the frontal-striatal circuitry, and magnetic resonance spectroscopy has demonstrated elevation in levels of glutamate and glutamine in the thalamus of treatment-naive children with OCD (Rosenberg, MacMaster, Keshavan, Fitzgerald, Stewart, & Moore, 2000). There is, thus, some direct support for anomalous serotonergic and glutamatergic neurotransmission and more indirect and somewhat inconsistent evidence of abnormal dopaminergic signaling. These findings do not necessarily imply a causal role. The neurochemical abnormalities may also be epiphenomena of OCD. Furthermore, some of these abnormalities are part of the genetic makeup (trait), whereas others are of a more temporary nature and subside when the OCD clears up (state), as is suggested by findings in treatment studies. In the Rosenberg et al. (2000) study, treatment with paroxetine normalized the increased glutamate concentration. This reduction correlated with treatment response (C-YBOCS scores).

Paediatric Autoimmune Neuropsychiatric Disorders Associated with Streptococcal Infections (PANDAS)

A post-infectious subgroup of pediatric OCD has been postulated, with susceptible individuals developing OCD symptoms and tic disorders as a result of post-infectious autoimmune processes (Leckman et al., 2010). Infections with group A beta hemolytic streptococci (GABHS) have been hypothesized to be responsible. Swedo, Leonard, Garvey et al. (1998) have proposed that this subgroup, identified by the acronym PANDAS, follows a waxing and waning clinical course that is closely temporally linked to GABHS infections. PANDAS remains a controversial area of science, with a significant fraction of experts doubting its existence (Leckman et al., 2010). Supporting evidence that GABHS may be involved in the onset of TS and OCD comes from a case-control study of 144 children who received their first diagnosis of OCD, TS, or tic disorder within a set time interval (3 months to 1 year) (Mell, Davis, & Owens, 2005). Patients with OCD, TS, or tic disorder were significantly more likely than controls to have had streptococcal infection in the 3 months before onset date. These findings were recently replicated in a national sample with five times the number of cases and controls (Leslie, Kozma, Martin et al., 2008). Prospective longitudinal studies have yielded less compelling data (Leckman, King, Gilbert et al., 2011). Brain imaging studies of PANDAS cases have consistently implicated the basal ganglia. Specific findings include the transient enlargement of the striatum and the basal ganglia as a whole (Giedd, Rapoport, Garvey, Perlmutter, & Swedo, 2000).

A special kind of anxiety disorder?

The discussion whether OCD should be considered an anxiety disorder or not is partially hampered by the lack of studies directly comparing the neural substrates of these disorders (Mataix-Cols & van den Heuvel, 2006). Differences in historical background partly explain the limited overlap in the functional imaging paradigms used. Neuroimaging research in OCD has long been dominated by a limited – or at least a predominant – focus on the basal ganglia and the ventral prefrontal-striatal circuits, whereas neuroimaging work in PD consisted largely of pharmacologic-challenge studies to induce panic attacks and ligand studies, and in PTSD research, most experiments followed the classical fear-conditioning model, focusing on the amygdala, hippocampus, and medial prefrontal cortex. In their discussion of the adult literature, Mataix-Cols and van den Heuvel (2006) emphasize that OCD is a compendium of multiple overlapping syndromes rather than a unitary nosologic entity, and state that any viable neurobiological model would need to take into account this heterogeneity. Therefore they propose a multidimensional model in which OCD is understood as multiple, potentially overlapping, syndromes that share etiologic factors but also have unique etiologic factors. In evolutionary terms, general anxiety, which is common to patients who have OCD and indeed other anxiety disorders, may have evolved to deal with nonspecific threats (e.g., increased vigilance, physiological arousal), whereas specific types of anxiety evolved to protect against specific threats. This model could be extended easily to the symptom dimensions of OCD; for instance, cleanliness is important for protection against infections; harming obsessions and checking rituals to keep people safe; and hoarding to help people survive periods of scarcity. Although based upon the adult literature, this model may also serve a source of inspiration for the further research of pediatric OCD.

Neurobiology and Its Consequences for Treatment

In the previous sections, we have shown which neurobiological systems are involved in the development and maintenance of the different anxiety disorders. In this section we will shift our attention from the etiology of anxiety disorders to the neurobiological aspects of treatment. Several psychological and pharmacological treatments for anxiety disorders have been developed over the past decades. Of these, cognitive-behavioral therapy (CBT) and selective serotonin reuptake inhibitors (SSRIs) have shown to be effective. Although most children will benefit from CBT or SSRIs, the number of children who do not show symptom remission during the course of treatment remains alarmingly high (up to 44% non-response) (Ipser, Stein, Hawkridge, & Hoppe, 2009; James, Soler, & Weatherall, 2005). Studies measuring the effects of CBT and SSRIs on the neural circuitry, autonomous nervous system, and HPA-axis render important insights into the working mechanisms of psychotherapy and pharmacotherapy and can thus help to improve treatment strategies, especially for those who do not respond to treatment. Furthermore, treatment outcome studies using neurobiological measures might help to differentiate between children who are likely to remit in CBT from those who are likely to respond to SSRIs. This would lead to lower rates of non-response and shorter times to remission (Siegle, Steinhauer, Friedman, Thompson, & Thase, 2011). From studies in adults with anxiety disorders we know that effective treatments influence activity in frontal (mPFC and DLPFC) and limbic brain structures and physiological reactivity (Linden, 2006). Considering that frontal brain regions do not reach anatomical and functional maturity until well in the third decade of life, shows that results from studies in adult populations cannot be simply extrapolated to children. It is therefore of great importance to investigate neurobiological treatment effects in children and adolescents with anxiety disorders as well. Research on the neurobiological effects of psychotherapies and pharmacotherapy in children with anxiety disorders is still in its infancy and literature on controlled neurobiological treatment studies is still very sparse. To get an idea of this emerging research field we will present the findings of some pioneering studies.

Maslowsky and colleagues (Maslowsky, Mogg, Bradley et al., 2010) compared children with GAD who received either CBT or fluoxetine (SSRI) with age-matched and gender-matched healthy peers. fMRI acquisition during a emotional dot-probe task was performed before and after treatment in patients and at comparable time points in healthy controls. Both children in the CBT and fluoxetine group showed increased ventrolateral prefrontal cortex activity after treatment relative to children in the control group. As we have seen above, vlPFC activity is negatively correlated with symptom severity in children with GAD and may have a compensatory function over the amygdale (Monk et al., 2006). The preliminary results of this small study indicate that both CBT and fluoxetine increase vlPFC compensatory action on the amygdala. Due to a lack of power, a direct comparison of CBT and fluoxetine responders and non-responders was not possible.

Children with social phobia treated with either CBT, citalopram (SSRI), or a neurokinin-1 antagonist showed decreased amygdala, hippocampus, and parahippocampal activity during a stressful public speaking task as compared to children with social phobia on a waitlist. When treatment responders were compared to treatment non-responders, a similar pattern emerged: responders demonstrated decreased activity in these three regions while activity in non-responders stabilized. No differences between treatment groups were described (Furmark, Tillfors, Marteinsdottir et al., 2002; Furmark, Appel, Michelgard et al., 2005). The preliminary conclusion from studies described above should be that both CBT and SSRIs influence frontal and limbic circuits involved in the human fear response in children with GAD and social phobia. Diverging effects of CBT and SSRIs were not yet observed. To unveil such differences between different treatment modalities studies with larger samples sizes are essential.

At our own department we performed an fMRI study with children and adolescents with OCD who were treated with CBT (Huyser, Veltman, Wolters, de Haan, & Boer, 2010). In this study, behavioral performance and associated brain activation during performance of the Tower of London planning task were investigated in medication-free pediatric OCD patients before and after CBT compared to healthy controls (HC). The results showed that pediatric OCD patients compared to healthy controls had longer mean reaction times but similar accuracy during planning, associated with decreased recruitment of frontal-parietal areas. With increasing task load, pediatric OCD patients were found to activate additional brain regions, in particular dorsomedial prefrontal cortex and dorsal anterior cingulate cortex, and insula, compared with control subjects. After CBT, these differences between OCD and HC ceased to be significant, indicating that these abnormalities are state rather than trait features of pediatric OCD. This study supports neurobiological models of OCD characterized by both dysfunction of dorsal frontal-parietal-striatal (cognitive) networks and hyperactivity of medial prefrontal-limbic (affective) circuitry, although the latter was observed only when task demands increased.

Future Research

Neurobiological research of the past decades has made it possible to propose models of the normal fear response, normal brain development, pathophysiology, and treatment of anxiety disorders. Some of the prevailing models have been described in the previous sections. Now that fMRI and non-invasive endocrinological measurements are becoming increasingly more available in (clinical) research settings, it has become easier to test these models and determine their clinical significance. We will propose some future research directions that we think will be fruitful.

There is a great need for longitudinal, large-scale, functional neuroimaging studies of normal brain development. Without the results of these studies as a background, it is impossible to study disrupted brain development. Projects like those performed by Giedd and colleagues (Giedd & Rapoport, 2010) at the national institute of Mental Health are extremely valuable. Studies in which children that are behaviorally inhibited or exposed to stress are followed throughout their development are crucial to determine which factors are protective and which factors increase risk of developing anxiety disorders later in life. An elegant example of such a prospective study in adult war veterans was recently performed by Vermetten and his research group (van Wingen, Geuze, Vermetten, & Fernandez, 2011a, 2011b; van Zuiden, Geuze, Willemen et al., 2011). This type of research is lengthy, costly, and needs a large number of participants and is thus difficult to execute in a single research institution, underscoring the need for long-term cross-institutional cooperation.

The analysis of neuroimaging data is still relatively cumbersome and therefore not yet suitable to be routinely used in a clinical setting. For that reason there is a need for easy-to-use, non-invasive, and reliable biological measures which reflect the activity of frontal and limbic brain structures and are clinically prognostic. Studies using a combination of neuroimaging, physiological measures, endocrinological measures, and clinical assessment in children with anxiety disorders are of great value. A fine example of a study with such a combination of measures was performed by Siegle and colleagues (2011) in adults with major depressive disorder.

Neurobiological studies comparing multiple effective treatments can help to indentify which child is most likely to benefit from which type of treatment and will improve the precision of referrals, resulting in decreased suffering, reduced healthcare burden, and reduced healthcare cost. These studies should use extended follow-up periods to examine if treatment effects are stable over time and which children are at risk of relapsing after initial successful treatment.

Finally, studies combining neurobiological measures with genetic measures can help to further unravel mechanisms involved in anxiety disorders.

References

Adolphs, R., Tranel, D., Damasio, H., & Damasio, A. R. (1995). Fear and the human amygdala. *Journal of Neuroscience, 15* (9), 5879–5891.

APA (2000). *Diagnostic and Statistical Manual of Mental Disorders* 4th edn. Text Revision: DSM-IV-TR. Washington, DC: American Psychiatric Association.

Baird, A. A., Gruber, S. A., Fein, D. A., Maas, L. C., Steingard, R. J., Renshaw, P. F. et al. (1999). Functional magnetic resonance imaging of facial affect recognition in children and adolescents. *Journal of the American Academy of Child and Adolescent Psychiatry, 38* (2), 195–199.

Bakker, M. J. (2009). The startle reflex in children with neuropsychiatric disorders. PhD thesis. Amsterdam: Academic Medical Centre, University of Amsterdam.

Beesdo, K., Knappe, S., & Pine, D. S. (2009). Anxiety and anxiety disorders in children and adolescents: developmental issues and implications for DSM-V. *Psychiatric Clinics of North America, 32* (3), 483–524.

Benes, F. M., Turtle, M., Khan, Y., & Farol, P. (1994). Myelination of a key relay zone in the hippocampal formation occurs in the human brain during childhood, adolescence, and adulthood. *Archives of General Psychiatry, 51* (6), 477–484.

Berridge, G. W. (2009). The locus coeruleus-noradrenergic system and stress: implications for post-traumatic stress disorder. In J. P. Shiromani, T. M. Keane, J. LeDoux (Eds.). *Post-Traumatic Stress Disorder Basic Science and Clinical Practice* (pp. 213–23). New York: Humana Press.

Bremner, J. D. (1999). Does stress damage the brain? *Biological Psychiatry, 45* (7), 797–805.

Bremner, J. D. (2002). Neuroimaging of childhood trauma. *Seminars in Clinical Neuropsychiatry, 7* (2), 104–112.

Chess, S., Thomas, A., Birch, H. G., & Hertzig, M. (1960). Implications of a longitudinal study of child development for child psychiatry. *American Journal of Psychiatry, 117,* 434–441.

Chronis-Tuscano, A., Degnan, K. A., Pine, D. S., Perez-Edgar, K., Henderson, H. A., Diaz, Y. et al. (2009). Stable early maternal report of behavioral inhibition predicts lifetime social anxiety disorder in adolescence. *Journal of the American Academy of Child and Adolescent Psychiatry, 48* (9), 928–935.

Copeland, W. E., Keeler, G., Angold, A., & Costello, E. J. (2007). Traumatic events and posttraumatic stress in childhood. *Archives of General Psychiatry, 64* (5), 577–584.

Cratty, M. S., Ward, H. E., Johnson, E. A., Azzaro, A. J., & Birkle, D. L. (1995). Prenatal stress increases corticotropin-releasing factor (CRF) content and release in rat amygdala minces. *Brain Res, 675* (1–2), 297–302.

Davis, M. (1992). The role of the amygdala in fear-potentiated startle: implications for animal models of anxiety. *Trends in Pharmacological Sciences, 13* (1), 35–41.

De Bellis, M. D., Hall, J., Boring, A. M., Frustaci, K., & Moritz, G. (2001). A pilot longitudinal study of hippocampal volumes in pediatric maltreatment-related posttraumatic stress disorder. *Biological Psychiatry, 50* (4), 305–309.

De Bellis, M. D., Keshavan, M. S., Shifflett, H., Iyengar, S., Beers, S. R., Hall, J. et al. (2002). Brain structures in pediatric maltreatment-related posttraumatic stress disorder: a sociodemographically matched study. *Biological Psychiatry, 52* (11), 1066–1078.

Debiec, J. & Ledoux, J. (2009). The amygdala and the neural pathways of fear. In J. P. Shiromani, T. M. Keane, J. Ledoux (Eds.), *Post-Traumatic Stress Disorder Basic Science and Clinical Practice* (pp. 23–38). New York: Humana Press.

Denys, D., Zohar, J., & Westenberg, H. G. (2004). The role of dopamine in obsessive-compulsive disorder: preclinical and clinical evidence. *Journal of Clinical Psychiatry, 65* (Suppl 14),11–17.

Fries, A. B., Ziegler, T. E., Kurian, J. R., Jacoris, S., & Pollak, S. D. (2005). Early experience in humans is associated with changes in neuropeptides critical for regulating social behavior. *Proceedings of the National Academy of Sciences of the United States of America, 102* (47), 17237–17240.

Furmark, T., Appel, L., Michelgard, A., Wahlstedt, K., Ahs, F., Zancan, S. et al. (2005). Cerebral blood flow changes after treatment of social phobia with the neurokinin-1 antagonist GR205171, citalopram, or placebo. *Biological Psychiatry, 58* (2), 132–142.

Furmark, T., Tillfors, M., Marteinsdottir, I., Fischer, H., Pissiota, A., Langstrom, B. et al. (2002). Common changes in cerebral blood flow in patients with social phobia treated with citalopram or cognitive-behavioral therapy. *Archives of General Psychiatry, 59* (5), 425–433.

Giedd, J. N., Rapoport, J. L., Garvey, M. A., Perlmutter, S., & Swedo, S. E. (2000). MRI assessment of children with obsessive-compulsive disorder or tics associated with streptococcal infection. *American Journal of Psychiatry, 157* (2), 281–283.

Giedd, J. N. & Rapoport, J. L. (2010). Structural MRI of pediatric brain development: what have we learned and where are we going? *Neuron, 67* (5), 728–734.

Giedd, J. N., Snell, J. W., Lange, N., Rajapakse, J. C., Casey, B. J., Kozuch, P. L. et al. (1996). Quantitative magnetic resonance imaging of human brain development: ages 4–18. *Cereb Cortex, 6* (4), 551–560.

Gilbertson, M. W., Shenton, M. E., Ciszewski, A., Kasai, K., Lasko, N. B., Orr, S. P. et al. (2002). Smaller hippocampal volume predicts pathologic vulnerability to psychological trauma. *Nature Neuroscience, 5* (11), 1242–1247.

Grillon, C. & Baas, J. (2003). A review of the modulation of the startle reflex by affective states and its application in psychiatry. *Clinical Neurophysiology, 114* (9), 1557–1579.

Gunnar, M. R. & Donzella, B. (2002). Social regulation of the cortisol levels in early human development. *Psychoneuroendocrinology, 27* (1–2), 199–220.

Guyer, A. E., Lau, J. Y., McClure-Tone, E. B., Parrish, J., Shiffrin, N. D., Reynolds, R. C. et al. (2008). Amygdala and ventrolateral prefrontal cortex function during anticipated peer evaluation in pediatric social anxiety. *Archives of General Psychiatry, 65* (11), 1303–1312.

Howard, R. & Ford, R. (1992). From the jumping Frenchmen of Maine to post-traumatic stress disorder: the startle response in neuropsychiatry. *Psychological Medicine, 22* (3), 695–707.

Huyser, C., Veltman, D. J., de Haan, E., & Boer, F. (2009). Paediatric obsessive-compulsive disorder, a neurodevelopmental disorder? Evidence from neuroimaging. *Neuroscience & Biobehavioral Reviews, 33* (6), 818–830.

Huyser, C., Veltman, D. J., Wolters, L. H., de Haan, E., & Boer, F. (2010). Functional magnetic resonance imaging during planning before and after cognitive-behavioral therapy in pediatric obsessive-compulsive disorder. *Journal of the American Academy of Child and Adolescent Psychiatry, 49* (12), 1238–48, 1248.

Ipser, J. C., Stein, D. J., Hawkridge, S., & Hoppe, L. (2009). Pharmacotherapy for anxiety disorders in children and adolescents. *Cochrane Database Systematic Review,* Issue 3, Art. No. CD005170.

James, A., Soler, A., & Weatherall, R. (2005). Cognitive behavioural therapy for anxiety disorders in children and adolescents. *Cochrane Database Systematic Review,* Issue 4, Art. No.CD004690.

Ji, J. & Maren, S. (2007). Hippocampal involvement in contextual modulation of fear extinction. *Hippocampus, 17* (9), 749–758.

Kagan, J., Reznick, J. S., & Snidman, N. (1988). Biological bases of childhood shyness. *Science, 240,* 167–171.

Kagan, J. & Snidman, N. (1999). Early childhood predictors of adult anxiety disorders. *Biological Psychiatry, 46* (11), 1536–1541.

Kessler, R. C., Berglund, P., Demler, O., Jin, R., Merikangas, K. R., & Walters, E. E. (2005a). Lifetime prevalence and age-of-onset distributions of DSM-IV disorders in the National Comorbidity Survey Replication. *Archives of General Psychiatry, 62* (6), 593–602.

Kessler, R. C., Chiu, W. T., Demler, O., Merikangas, K. R., & Walters, E. E. (2005b). Prevalence, severity, and comorbidity of 12-month DSM-IV disorders in the National Comorbidity Survey Replication. *Archives of General Psychiatry, 62* (6), 617–627.

Kim, J. H. & Richardson, R. (2010). New findings on extinction of conditioned fear early in development: theoretical and clinical implications. *Biological Psychiatry, 67* (4), 297–303.

Leckman, J. F., Denys, D., Simpson, H. B., Mataix-Cols, D., Hollander, E., Saxena, S. et al. (2010). Obsessive-compulsive disorder: a review of the diagnostic criteria and possible subtypes and dimensional specifiers for DSM-V. *Depression and Anxiety, 27* (6), 507–527.

Leckman, J. F., King, R. A., Gilbert, D. L., Coffey, B. J., Singer, H. S., Dure, L. S. et al. (2011). Streptococcal upper respiratory tract infections and exacerbations of tic and obsessive-compulsive symptoms: a prospective longitudinal study. *Journal of the American Academy of Child and Adolescent Psychiatry, 50* (2), 108–118.

LeDoux, J. E. (2000). Emotion circuits in the brain. *Annual Review of Neuroscience, 23,* 155–184.

Lenroot, R. K. & Giedd, J. N. (2010). Sex differences in the adolescent brain. *Brain and Cognition, 72* (1), 46–55.

Leslie, D. L., Kozma, L., Martin, A., Landeros, A., Katsovich, L., King, R. A. et al. (2008). Neuropsychiatric disorders associated with streptococcal infection: a case-control study among privately insured children. *Journal of the American Academy of Child and Adolescent Psychiatry, 47* (10), 1166–1172.

Lindauer, R. J., Vlieger, E. J., Jalink, M., Olff, M., Carlier, I. V., Majoie, C. B. et al. (2004). Smaller hippocampal volume in Dutch police officers with posttraumatic stress disorder. *Biological Psychiatry, 56* (5), 356–363.

Lindauer, R. J., Vlieger, E. J., Jalink, M., Olff, M., Carlier, I. V., Majoie, C. B. et al. (2005). Effects of psychotherapy on hippocampal volume in out-patients with post-traumatic stress disorder: a MRI investigation. *Psychological Medicine, 35* (10), 1421–1431.

Linden, D. E. (2006). How psychotherapy changes the brain—the contribution of functional neuroimaging. *Molecular Psychiatry, 11* (6), 528–538.

Lipschitz, D. S., Mayes, L. M., Rasmusson, A. M., Anyan, W., Billingslea, E., Gueorguieva, R. et al. (2005). Baseline and modulated acoustic startle responses in adolescent girls with posttraumatic stress disorder. *Journal of the American Academy of Child and Adolescent Psychiatry, 44* (8), 807–814.

Lupien, S. J., McEwen, B. S., Gunnar, M. R., & Heim, C. (2009). Effects of stress throughout the lifespan on the brain, behaviour and cognition. *Nature Reviews Neuroscience, 10* (6), 434–445.

Maslowsky, J., Mogg, K., Bradley, B. P., McClure-Tone, E., Ernst, M., Pine, D. S. et al. (2010). A preliminary investigation of neural correlates of treatment in adolescents with generalized anxiety disorder. *Journal of Child and Adolescent Psychopharmacology, 20* (2), 105–111.

Mataix-Cols, D., Pertusa, A., & Leckman, J. F. (2007). Issues for DSM-V: how should obsessive-compulsive and related disorders be classified? *American Journal of Psychiatry, 164* (9), 1313–1314.

Mataix-Cols, D. & van den Heuvel, O. A. (2006). Common and distinct neural correlates of obsessive-compulsive and related disorders. *Psychiatric Clinics of North America, 29* (2), 391–410, viii.

McClure, E. B., Monk, C. S., Nelson, E. E., Parrish, J. M., Adler, A., Blair, R. J. et al. (2007). Abnormal attention modulation of fear circuit function in pediatric generalized anxiety disorder. *Archives of General Psychiatry, 64* (1), 97–106.

McCormick, C. M. & Mathews, I. Z. (2007). HPA function in adolescence: role of sex hormones in its regulation and the enduring consequences of exposure to stressors. *Pharmacology Biochemistry and Behavior, 86* (2), 220–233.

McEwen, B. S. & Magarinos, A. M. (1997). Stress effects on morphology and function of the hippocampus. *Annals of the New York Academy of Sciences, 821,* 271–284.

Meiser-Stedman, R., Smith, P., Glucksman, E., Yule, W., & Dalgleish, T. (2008). The posttraumatic stress disorder diagnosis in preschool- and elementary school-age children exposed to motor vehicle accidents. *American Journal of Psychiatry, 165* (10), 1326–1337.

Mell, L. K., Davis, R. L., & Owens, D. (2005). Association between streptococcal infection and obsessive-compulsive disorder, Tourette's syndrome, and tic disorder. *Pediatrics, 116* (1), 56–60.

Monk, C. S., Nelson, E. E., McClure, E. B., Mogg, K., Bradley, B. P., Leibenluft, E. et al. (2006). Ventrolateral prefrontal cortex activation and attentional bias in response to angry faces in adolescents with generalized anxiety disorder. *American Journal of Psychiatry, 163* (6), 1091–1097.

Monk, C. S., Telzer, E. H., Mogg, K., Bradley, B. P., Mai, X., Louro, H. M. et al. (2008). Amygdala and ventrolateral prefrontal cortex activation to masked angry faces in children and adolescents with generalized anxiety disorder. *Archives of General Psychiatry, 65* (5), 568–576.

Myers, K. M. & Davis, M. (2007). Mechanisms of fear extinction. *Molecular Psychiatry, 12* (2), 120–150.

Ornitz, E. M. & Pynoos, R. S. (1989). Startle modulation in children with posttraumatic stress disorder. *American Journal of Psychiatry, 146* (7), 866–870.

Orr, S. P. & Roth, W. T. (2000). Psychophysiological assessment: clinical applications for PTSD. *Journal Affective Disorders, 61* (3), 225–240.

Pavlov, I. P. (1927). *Conditioned Reflexes: An Investigation of the Physiological Activity of the Cerebral Cortex.* London: Oxford University Press.

Perez-Edgar, K. & Fox, N. A. (2005). Temperament and anxiety disorders. *Child and Adolescent Psychiatric Clinics of North America, 14* (4), 681–706, viii.

Perez-Edgar, K., Roberson-Nay, R., Hardin, M. G., Poeth, K., Guyer, A. E., Nelson, E. E. et al. (2007). Attention alters neural responses to evocative faces in behaviorally inhibited adolescents. *Neuroimage, 35* (4), 1538–1546.

Phillips, R. G. & LeDoux, J. E. (1992). Differential contribution of amygdala and hippocampus to cued and contextual fear conditioning. *Behavioral Neuroscience, 106* (2), 274–285.

Pine, D. S. & Cohen, J. A. (2002). Trauma in children and adolescents: risk and treatment of psychiatric sequelae. *Biological Psychiatry, 51* (7), 519–531.

Pitman, R. K. (2001). Hippocampal diminution in PTSD: more (or less?) than meets the eye. *Hippocampus, 11* (2), 73–74.

Pitman, R. K., Orr, S. P., Forgue, D. F., de Jong, J. B., & Claiborn, J. M. (1987). Psychophysiologic assessment of posttraumatic stress disorder imagery in Vietnam combat veterans. *Archives of General Psychiatry, 44* (11), 970–975.

Prior, M., Smart, D., Sanson, A., & Oberklaid, F. (2000). Does shy-inhibited temperament in childhood lead to anxiety problems in adolescence? *Journal of the American Academy of Child and Adolescent Psychiatry, 39* (4), 461–468.

Pynoos, R. S., Steinberg, A. M., Layne, C. M., Briggs, E. C., Ostrowski, S. A., & Fairbank, J. A. (2009). DSM-V PTSD diagnostic criteria for children and adolescents: A developmental perspective and recommendations. *Journal of Traumatic Stress, 22* (5), 391–398.

Quirk, G. J. & Mueller, D. (2008). Neural mechanisms of extinction learning and retrieval. *Neuropsychopharmacology, 33* (1), 56–72.

Radua, J., van den Heuvel, O. A., Surguladze, S., & Mataix-Cols, D. (2010). Meta-analytical comparison of voxel-based morphometry studies in obsessive-compulsive disorder vs other anxiety disorders. *Archives of General Psychiatry, 67* (7), 701–711.

Rasmusson, A. M., Vythilingam, M., & Morgan, C. A, III. (2003). The neuroendocrinology of posttraumatic stress disorder: new directions. *CNS Spectrums, 8* (9), 651–657.

Rauch, S. L., Whalen, P. J., & Dougherty, D. D. (1998). Neurobiological models of obsessive compulsive disorders. Obsessive compulsive disorders: practical management . Boston: Mosby. Pp. 222–253.

Reeb-Sutherland, B. C., Helfinstein, S. M., Degnan, K. A., Perez-Edgar, K., Henderson, H. A., Lissek, S. et al. (2009). Startle response in behaviorally inhibited adolescents with a lifetime occurrence of anxiety disorders. *Journal of the American Academy of Child and Adolescent Psychiatry, 48* (6), 610–617.

Rosenberg, D. R., MacMaster, F. P., Keshavan, M. S., Fitzgerald, K. D., Stewart, C. M., & Moore, G. J. (2000). Decrease in caudate glutamatergic concentrations in pediatric obsessive-compulsive disorder patients taking paroxetine. *Journal of the American Academy of Child and Adolescent Psychiatry, 39* (9), 1096–1103.

Schwartz, C. E., Wright, C. I., Shin, L. M., Kagan, J., & Rauch, S. L. (2003). Inhibited and uninhibited infants "grown up": adult amygdalar response to novelty. *Science, 300* (5627), 1952–1953.

Seckl, J. R. (2008). Glucocorticoids, developmental 'programming' and the risk of affective dysfunction. *Progres in Brain Research, 167,* 17–34.

Shin, L. M., Orr, S. P., Carson, M. A., Rauch, S. L., Macklin, M. L., Lasko, N. B. et al. (2004). Regional cerebral blood flow in the amygdala and medial prefrontal cortex during traumatic imagery in male and female Vietnam veterans with PTSD. *Archives of General Psychiatry, 61* (2), 168–176.

Siegle, G. J., Steinhauer, S. R., Friedman, E. S., Thompson, W. S., & Thase, M. E. (2011). Remission prognosis for cognitive therapy for recurrent depression using the pupil: utility and neural correlates. *Biological Psychiatry, 69* (8), 726–733.

Simpson, H. B., Lombardo, I., Slifstein, M., Huang, H. Y., Hwang, D. R., Abi-Dargham, A. et al. (2003). Serotonin transporters in obsessive-compulsive disorder: a positron emission tomography study with [(11)C]McN 5652. *Biological Psychiatry, 54* (12), 1414–1421.

Sotres-Bayon, F., Cain, C. K., & LeDoux, J. E. (2006). Brain mechanisms of fear extinction: historical perspectives on the contribution of prefrontal cortex. *Biological Psychiatry, 60* (4), 329–336.

Swedo, S. E., Leonard, H. L., Garvey, M., Mittleman, B., Allen, A. J., Perlmutter, S. et al. (1998). Pediatric autoimmune neuropsychiatric disorders associated with streptococcal infections: clinical description of the first 50 cases. *American Journal of Psychiatry, 155* (2), 264–271.

Thomas, K. M., Drevets, W. C., Dahl, R. E., Ryan, N. D., Birmaher, B., Eccard, C. H. et al. (2001a). Amygdala response to fearful faces in anxious and depressed children. *Archives of General Psychiatry, 58* (11), 1057–1063.

Thomas, K. M., Drevets, W. C., Whalen, P. J., Eccard, C. H., Dahl, R. E., Ryan, N. D. et al. (2001b). Amygdala response to facial expressions in children and adults. *Biological Psychiatry, 49* (4), 309–316.

Toga, A. W., Thompson, P. M., & Sowell, E. R. (2006). Mapping brain maturation. *Trends in Neuroscience, 29* (3), 148–159.

Tottenham, N., Hare, T. A., & Casey, B. J. (2009). A developmental perspective on human amygdala function. In E. Phelps & P. Whalen (Eds.), *The Human Amygdala* (pp. 107–117). New York: The Guilford Press.

van Braker, A. M. L., Murris, P., & Bogels, S. M. (2006). A Multifactorial Model for the Etiology of Anxiety in Non-Clinical Adolescents: Main and Interactive Effects of Behavioral Inhibition, Attachment and Parental Rearing. *Journal of Child and Family Studies, 15,* 568–578.

van Harmelen, A. L., van Tol, M. J., van der Wee, N. J., Veltman, D. J., Aleman, A., Spinhoven, P. et al. (2010). Reduced medial prefrontal cortex volume in adults reporting childhood emotional maltreatment. *Biological Psychiatry, 68* (9), 832–838.

van Wingen, G. A., Geuze, E., Vermetten, E., & Fernandez, G. (2011). Consequences of combat stress on brain functioning. *Molecular Psychiatry, 16* (6), 583.

van Wingen, G. A., Geuze, E., Vermetten, E., & Fernandez, G. (2011). Perceived threat predicts the neural sequelae of combat stress. *Molecular Psychiatry, 16* (6), 664–671.

van Zuiden, M., Geuze, E., Willemen, H. L., Vermetten, E., Maas, M., Heijnen, C. J. et al. (2011). Pre-existing high glucocorticoid receptor number predicting development of post-traumatic stress symptoms after military deployment. *American Journal of Psychiatry, 168* (1), 89–96.

Waters, A. M., Craske, M. G., Bergman, R. L., Naliboff, B. D., Negoro, H., & Ornitz, E. M. (2008). Developmental changes in startle reactivity in school-age children at risk for and with actual anxiety disorder. *International Journal of Psychophysiology, 70* (3), 158–164.

Wilkins, D. E., Hallett, M., & Wess, M. M. (1986). Audiogenic startle reflex of man and its relationship to startle syndromes. A review. *Brain, 109* (Part 3), 561–573.

Yehuda, R. (2002). Post-traumatic stress disorder. *New England Journal of Medicine, 346* (2), 108–114.

Yehuda, R. & LeDoux, J. (2007). Response variation following trauma: a translational neuroscience approach to understanding PTSD. *Neuron, 56* (1), 19–32.

6

Interpersonal and Social Factors in the Treatment of Child and Adolescent Anxiety Disorders

Thomas H. Ollendick[1] and Shin-ichi Ishikawa[2]

[1]Virginia Polytechnic Institute and State University, USA
[2]Doshisha University, Japan

In the *Diagnostic and Statistical Manual of Mental Disorders* (DSM-IV; APA, 1994) and the *International Statistical Classification of Diseases and Related Health Problems* (ICD-10; WHO, 1992), children (as well as adults) can be categorized according to eight major diagnostic syndromes associated with anxiety: panic disorder with agoraphobia, panic disorder without agoraphobia, agoraphobia without history of panic, specific phobia, social phobia, obsessive-compulsive disorder, post-traumatic stress disorder, and generalized anxiety disorder. In addition, both diagnostic systems specify one anxiety disorder unique to childhood: separation anxiety disorder. Earlier versions of the DSM included two additional anxiety diagnoses specific to childhood, namely avoidant disorder and overanxious disorder. In the current revision, avoidant disorder and overanxious disorder have been subsumed under the diagnoses of social phobia and generalized anxiety disorder, respectively.

Epidemiological studies have estimated the prevalence of anxiety disorders in general community samples of children to range from 5.7% to 17.7% (e.g., Costello, Egger, & Angold, 2005). Anxiety disorders also tend to be more prevalent in girls than boys and in older than younger children. Some children may have only one anxiety or phobic disorder as per DSM-IV or ICD10 criteria. However, most children who have one anxiety disorder tend to be comorbid with other anxiety or phobic disorders; as such, it is not uncommon for children to present in epidemiological studies with two, three or more anxiety disorders (Ollendick & Seligman, 2006; Seligman & Ollendick, 2011).

Children in clinic samples frequently exhibit higher levels of comorbidity than children in community samples (see Ollendick, King, & Muris, 2002). It is not uncommon for clinic-referred children with anxiety disorders to not only present with additional anxiety disorders but also major depressive disorder/dysthymia and disruptive behavior disorders including oppositional defiant disorder and attention deficit hyperactivity disorder. Thus, the clinical picture can be quite complex due to the presence of overlapping disorders. Comorbidity appears to be the rule, not the exception.

The Wiley-Blackwell Handbook of The Treatment of Childhood and Adolescent Anxiety, First Edition.
Edited by Cecilia A. Essau and Thomas H. Ollendick.
© 2013 John Wiley & Sons, Ltd. Published 2013 by John Wiley & Sons, Ltd.

Moreover, anxiety disorders have a complex etiology with genetic factors, temperament characteristics (especially behavioral inhibition), parenting practices (attachment histories, socialization of emotions, overprotection), parental psychopathology (anxiety and depression, in particular), specific learning histories (including traumatic and vicarious experiences), information-processing and emotion regulation deficits, impaired peer relationships, and complex societal and cultural factors all being implicated (see other chapters in this volume). Consistent with a developmental psychopathology framework, there may be multiple pathways to any one anxiety disorder or any combination of anxiety disorders. In addition, any combination of protective factors (such as secure attachment, good peer relationships, positive parenting) can serve to prevent anxiety disorders or – in cases where clinical anxiety is present – mitigate the severity of the disorder (see Ollendick, Costa, & Benoit, 2010 for a review).

Unfortunately, DSM-IV and ICD-10 are relatively silent as to the role of interpersonal and social factors in the development and expression of the anxiety disorders in childhood, with the notable exception of social phobia and separation anxiety disorder. In social phobia, there must be the capacity for age-appropriate social relationships and the anxiety must be present in peer settings, not just in interactions with adults. Typically, young children with social phobia appear excessively shy, shrink from contact with others, refuse to participate in group play, and stay on the periphery of social activities. Thus, social phobia is fundamentally an interpersonal disorder. In separation anxiety disorder, the cardinal symptom is the presence of developmentally inappropriate and excessive worry concerning separation from those to whom the child is attached. When separated from attachment figures, these children frequently need to know their whereabouts and need to stay in contact with them (e.g., frequent phone calls, text messaging). Moreover they oftentimes display "clinging" behavior, staying close to and "shadowing" the parent around the home and in community settings. In some instances, the anxiety is so severe they refuse to leave home and go to school. Overall, they display an insecure attachment. As such, separation anxiety disorder – like social phobia – is fundamentally an interpersonal, social disorder. For the other anxiety disorders, however, there is little to no mention of interpersonal or social factors or the interpersonal or social situations that might serve to occasion the disorders or to qualify their expression.

In the present chapter, we have three primary goals: (1) to review normative interpersonal development, (2) explicate interpersonal processes that may lead to the development and expression of anxiety disorders in childhood, and (3) explore the implications of interpersonal processes for the treatment of these disorders in children.

Normative Interpersonal Development

Normative interpersonal development involves four primary processes (Ollendick et al., 2010). The first process entails the ability to form an attachment within the parent–child relationship. The second process involves the ability to regulate emotions through the development of skills such as responding appropriately, being flexible, and resolving conflicts in difficult social situations. The third process consists of the socialization of emotion through parental practices and behaviors. The fourth process provides the foundation for the ability of the developing child to form peer relationships, which frequently play a powerful role in the socialization of emotion, in as much as interactions with peers constitute an important developmental context for children and adolescents (Davila, La Greca, Starr, & Landoll, 2010; Rubin, Bukowski, & Parker, 1998). Each of these processes will be discussed briefly in turn.

The first process involves the ability to form a close, emotional bond or relationship with a caregiver (i.e., an attachment relationship). The parent–child attachment is considered to be one of the most fundamental and important relationships in development. The type of attachment children have is characterized by the quality of the parent–child relationship in terms of the security and trust that children have towards their caregiver (Bowlby, 1973). More specifically, whether a child is securely or insecurely attached to their caregiver is directly related to how safe the child feels when navigating her or his environment. Securely attached children tend to explore their environment more willingly and confidently, and feel like their caregiver is accessible and responsive to their needs (Bowlby, 1973). For example, a young, securely attached child is able to separate from her caregiver and play with other children in the park (with her caregiver nearby) or to leave for preschool with only the slightest reticence. In addition, securely attached children are more self-confident, trusting, and competent in their attachments to other people in their life and have higher self-regulatory abilities, which allows even fearful or inhibited children to confront perceived threat because their caregiver is available to assist them if need be (Thompson, 2001). The feelings that securely attached children have about their own abilities to handle stress or interact with their environment are not thought to be solely "in" the child, but rather embedded in the parent–child relational context. Given this, secure attachment is considered to be an important interpersonal factor that protects the child against the development of anxiety and related disorders.

Attachment in middle childhood (ages 5–10 years) marks the beginning of children starting to use other adults and peers as a secure base to explore their environment. This is mainly due to the introduction of different school environments in which there are increasingly longer periods of separation from caregivers. Whereas physical proximity is the central theme in attachment in the early years, the *availability* of the attachment figure, not proximity, becomes the prevailing theme during middle childhood (Bowlby, 1987). Although children in this age group are developing more cognitive, emotional, and physical skills to begin taking responsibility for their own protection and actions, they are still not making decisions solely on their own. Knowing and having the security that an attachment figure is available to help if need be seems critical to the progression of normative interpersonal development during middle childhood and on into early adolescence, not only because of the direct effects that a secure attachment has on the parent–child relationship, but also because of the indirect effects it has on children's interactions and experiences with other people throughout life. Secure attachment continues to play a role into adolescence as evident in close personal and even romantic relationships (La Greca & Prinstein, 1999).

The next process in interpersonal development – the ability to regulate emotions – has been a central focus of developmental psychology for several years. Research in this area has produced an abundance of work on the specific mechanisms through which children come to regulate their emotions and behavior. While various operational definitions have been put forth for this concept (Eisenberg, 2002), most researchers agree that emotion regulation involves those physiological, cognitive, and behavioral processes that allow individuals to modulate how they experience and express positive and negative emotions.

The main mechanism through which emotion regulation is thought to emerge is effortful control, "the ability to inhibit a dominant response to perform a subdominant response" (Rothbart & Bates, 1998, p. 137). Effortful control includes two primary processes. The first process includes attentional control, the ability to shift and focus attention as required by the situation. Rothbart and colleagues (Rothbart, Posner, & Boylan, 1990) have shown that children exhibit less distress when they are able to fluidly shift focus away from distressing stimuli and deftly focus on non-distressing stimuli. Attentional processes can also be used to redirect attention internally by helping the child think positive thoughts or to distract oneself when faced with a distressing situation, such as when a child focuses on their caregiver when trying out something new for the first time or a pleasant object when confronted by a scary dog. The second process of effortful control is inhibitory control, the ability to suppress inappropriate responses when necessary to do so. This process includes the ability to inhibit aggressive responses when in anger-provoking situations or inhibit avoidant responses when in anxiety-arousing situations, such as when a child offers a comment in class, even though he's anxious that other children in the class might laugh at him.

In addition to these inhibitory functions, Thompson (1994) emphasizes that emotion regulation also involves the ability to enhance and maintain emotion when needed, such as when children increase their anger in order to confront bullies or become brave and courageous in fear-producing situations. This also occurs with positive emotions, such as when children recall pleasant experiences to feel increased levels of positive arousal and resultant happiness. When children successfully master the above processes, they are better able to keep their emotions in check and respond appropriately in interpersonal contexts, demonstrate flexibility in these situations, and resolve conflicts. Such interpersonal skills then lead to more successful interpersonal relationships (Ollendick et al., 2010).

The third process by which children develop interpersonally occurs through the socialization of emotion. Emotion socialization occurs via parental practices and behaviors that influence how a child experiences, expresses, and regulates emotion and emotion-related behaviors (Eisenberg, Cumberland, Spinrad, et al., 2001a; Eisenberg, Iosoya, Fabes, et al., 2001b). This process is closely linked to the second process of emotion regulation discussed above in as much as children often regulate their emotions, at least early in life, primarily through external forces and most often through the efforts of their parents or significant others. The interpersonal relationship between parent and child is important in this regard, as children learn from their parents how to behave competently in social contexts (Thompson, 1994). It has been shown that emotion socialization occurs primarily as a result of processes engaged in by others, such as selective reinforcement and modeling of emotional expressions. Other indirect processes of socialization include social referencing and creating an overall "safe" environment, while direct processes include coaching/teaching, discussing emotions, and establishing contingencies for emotional behavior (Klimes-Dougan & Zeman, 2007). These indirect and direct approaches can be thought of in terms of a tripartite model in which children's socialization of emotions are affected by parents as interactive partners, direct instructors, and providers of opportunity (Parke, Orstein, Rieser, & Zahn-Waxler, 1994).

The emotional competence skills that emerge in children via emotion regulation and socialization have been linked to social competence with peers. Some examples of this include research showing that when parents comfort their children during times of negative emotion, children tend to exhibit more constructive anger reactions with their peers or confront scary situations in a more calm manner (Eisenberg & Fabes, 1994). Children are also more aware and understanding of the emotions of others when their parents willingly discuss emotions with them. Moreover, when fathers comfort and accept emotional distress in their children, the children tend to have more positive peer relationships (Roberts, 1994).

In the fourth process – peer relationships – middle childhood represents a dramatic change in children's social context because interactions with peers steadily increase and take on increasingly greater significance. Peer relationships in middle childhood are characterized by particular behaviors, thoughts, and emotions. For example, Eisenberg and Fabes (1998) report that positive social behaviors such as generosity, helpfulness, or cooperation increase rapidly during this time period. Children's understanding of friendships also changes during middle childhood. Children begin to develop a sense of continuity and reciprocity in their choice of friends. Perspective-taking abilities become salient in that children begin to appreciate the thoughts and feelings of others (Selman & Schultz, 1990).

From a developmental perspective, one of the most important tasks of middle childhood is to learn acceptable ways of interacting with one's peers. Although interpersonal abilities and social skills accrued from a secure attachment relationship and healthy parental socialization of emotions affect this learning, the majority of this learning occurs within the context of peer groups. As such, interactions with peers play an important role in children's interpersonal, social, and cognitive development. Certain social skills are necessary in order for children to form successful peer relationships (Matson & Ollendick, 1988; Rubin et al., 1998). These social skills include, but are not limited to, the ability to: (1) understand the thoughts and feelings of others, (2) begin, maintain, and end interactions in a positive way, (3) appropriately express emotions and behaviors, and (4) inhibit behaviors that might be construed as negative by others. Peer acceptance is thought to be, in part, a function of these social skills. Concerns about peer acceptance take on a significant role during this time period. More importantly, peer acceptance is a significant predictor of short and long-term adjustment. Hence, normative interpersonal development entails children possessing the social skills that enable them to form peer relationships and subsequently be accepted by their peers. Of course, these processes continue to evolve in adolescence. During adolescence, close friends take on increasing importance as they surpass parents as the primary source of social support (La Greca & Prinstein, 1999).

Interpersonal Processes Leading to the Development of Childhood Anxiety Disorders

Thus far, we have focused on normative interpersonal and social development. However, what happens when these normal developmental processes go awry? Although multiple outcomes are possible, one possible and frequent outcome is that the risk for developing psychopathology is heightened in children who do not evince normal interpersonal or social functioning. Support for this possibility has been shown in the area of childhood depression. Interpersonal characteristics such as insecure attachment, poor emotion regulation, negative self perceptions, and lower rates of peer acceptance have all emerged as salient components of the depressive experience in children (e.g., Essau & Ollendick, 2009; Hammen & Goodman-Brown, 1990). Given the demonstrated link between interpersonal development and childhood depression, the purpose of the next part of this chapter is to extend this line of research to childhood anxiety. Specifically, we now examine the applicability of these concepts to childhood anxiety from an interpersonal development perspective (see also Ollendick et al., 2010). We will first review temperament, specifically behavioral inhibition, as this is postulated to be an innate biological characteristic that affects later interpersonal relationships. Second, the proposed interpersonal processes of attachment, emotion regulation, parental socialization of emotions, and peer relationships will be discussed; in doing so, we will emphasize the role they play in the onset and maintenance of childhood anxiety. Lastly, the role of parenting behaviors and operant conditioning will be discussed because these processes not only influence the development of childhood anxiety disorders directly, but also indirectly via interactions with aspects of normative interpersonal development to increase risk for these disorders.

Temperament. Temperament has been defined by Rothbart and Ahadi (1994) as "constitutionally based individual differences in reactivity and self-regulation, influenced over time by heredity, maturation, and experience" (p. 55). The most widely researched temperamental characteristic linked to anxiety problems is behavioral inhibition (BI). BI, defined as an overt representation of a psychological and physiological state of uncertainty, results from exposure to unfamiliar objects, people, and situations (Kagan, 1994). It is often described as the tendency to restrict exploration and avoid novelty, and is characterized by withdrawal, fearfulness, timidity, shyness, and emotional restraint behaviors when exposed to unfamiliar stimuli (Kagan, Reznick, & Gibbons, 1989). BI is also characterized by several physiological reactions such as increases in heart rate, blood pressure, muscle tension, and levels of secreted cortisol (Kagan et al., 1989). The combination of behavioral responses characterized by withdrawal, avoidance, and physiological responses characterized by increased sympathetic arousal is similar to what is seen in the anxiety disorders (Ollendick et al., 2002).

Empirical research affirms the importance of BI as a risk factor in the emergence of anxiety disorders. For example, Biederman and colleagues (1990) examined inhibited and uninhibited infants from two studies undertaken by Kagan and his colleagues (Kagan, Reznick, & Snidman 1987, 1988) when infants were 7–8 years of age. Results indicated that inhibited children were higher in rates of specific anxiety disorders than uninhibited children [i.e., separation anxiety disorder (9.1% vs. 5.3%) and social phobia (31.8% vs. 5.3%)]. Similarly, Hirshfeld and colleagues (1992) reported that children with behavioral inhibition had significantly higher rates of other anxiety disorders than uninhibited children, including the tendency to have more than one anxiety disorder. In these studies, behaviorally inhibited children displayed fears related primarily to interpersonal situations, including speaking in front of the class, being around strangers, and going into crowded situations or places. In as much as BI is characterized by withdrawal, dependence on parents, fearfulness, and shyness when exposed to unfamiliar people, the tendency to exhibit these interpersonal reactions may be a risk factor for other childhood anxiety disorders as well. Consistent with this notion, presence of BI during childhood has been found to predict adolescent anxiety disorders more broadly as well (Dumas, LaFreniere, & Serketich, 1995; Muris & Ollendick, 2005).

Attachment. As noted earlier, Bowlby (1987) theorized that early interpersonal experiences within the parent–child attachment relationship play an important role in interpersonal development in childhood, adolescence, and adulthood. Furthermore, others have demonstrated that attachment style predicts later psychopathology (Mason, Platts, & Tyson, 2005). Given this, attachment theory provides a framework for conceptualizing the influence of interpersonal relationships on the development and course of childhood anxiety (Manassis & Bradley, 1994). The model by Manassis and Bradley, for example, posits that an *insecure* attachment results in an environmental context that influences, promotes, and reinforces the development of trait anxiety and its course over development. Consistent with this model, child insecure attachment has been found to be a risk factor for the development of anxiety disorders in children and adolescents (Manassis, Bradley, Goldberg, Hood, & Swinson, 1994; Mattis & Ollendick, 1997; Warren, Huston, Egeland, & Sroufe, 1997).

Attachment theory posits that insecure attachments convey the message to children that caregivers are unreliable, unavailable, untrustworthy, and largely uncommunicative. Children who receive these types of messages can develop a maladaptive approach to future interpersonal situations or relationships based on the expectation that their needs will not be met by others, causing either low interpersonal contact/avoidance behaviors or high interpersonal contact/demanding behaviors (see Manassis & Bradley, 1994). These behaviors elicit negative reactions from others, which serve to strengthen the distorted beliefs that these insecure children have. This distorted view can be expressed in maladaptive forms of coping and avoidance creating a chronic and persistent state of anxiety within children, thus placing them at higher risk for the development of anxiety disorders (Manassis & Bradley, 1994).

Ample research has supported insecure attachment as a risk factor in the development of anxiety. For example, Warren et al. (1997) examined 172 insecurely attached children at 12 months of age and found that they were more likely to have an anxiety disorder at age 17 years. Manassis et al. (1994) examined attachment patterns in clinically anxious mothers and their children and found that infants of anxious mothers not only displayed insecure attachments but also evidenced higher rates of subsequent anxiety disorders. Similarly, in another study, Manassis and her colleagues (1995) found that insecurely attached children experienced higher levels of anxiety than securely attached children. In addition, Muris and Meesters (2002) demonstrated that insecure attachment accounted for independent and unique predictions of child anxiety as reported by parents and children.

Emotion regulation and parental socialization of emotions. Children's ability to learn how to modulate and enhance emotion increases the chances of successful social interactions. Recent work suggests that children with anxiety disorders have inherent difficulty with this important developmental process, most notably in the areas of interpreting emotionally arousing events and regulating attentional processes (Thompson, 2001). Typically developing children can ordinarily manage their emotional arousal by reinterpreting or reframing situations that evoke strong emotion. Examples of this include re-casting frightening accounts in more calming terms, such as "it's just a story" and there "really is nothing to be afraid of" when watching a scary movie. Parents play an important role in this arena as well, such as when they calm a child before a dental visit by saying it will simply be "tooth tickling" or by giving support and encouragement when a shy child encounters a novel situation (Miller & Green, 1985). However, children with anxiety disorders are different in that their interpretations of the world tend to be biased towards threat and impending doom, even when situations are benign and relatively innocuous. They see a world that is more threatening than non-anxious children, such as when children with separation anxiety disorder fear being kidnapped or worry excessively that their parents are going to be harmed, or children with a specific phobia of dogs fear that all dogs are harmful and will attack them. This persistent focus on negative outcomes makes it difficult for them to reinterpret events in less threatening ways. This is especially true if parents are overprotective or over-controlling and do not encourage alternative and more healthy interpretations in their children. The more they and their children avoid the feared situations, the less likely they are to come to see them in more realistic and "safe" ways.

In the area of attentional processes, attentional control may reduce problems with anxiety by facilitating children's ability to shift attention away from distressing thoughts, events, and objects and thus modulate the level of negative emotional arousal (Hannesdottir & Ollendick, 2007). For example, if children can tolerate delayed rewards by directing their attention away from the desired object and distracting themselves with another activity, less anxiety will likely occur. Parents again act as socialization agents in this regard by distracting children during upsetting events, limiting their child's awareness of distressing information, or focusing their child's attention on the positive aspects of difficult situations. When children are not properly socialized to these modulating processes of emotional control, they seem to be at an increased risk of developing anxiety disorders. As shown by Lemery, Essex, and Smider (2002), low attention focusing is linked to higher levels of anxiety and fearfulness in children. Furthermore, children who develop these problems may attend to many minor stressors at one time and have difficulty shifting attention away from these arousing stimuli. As such, children's inability to shift attention away from minor stressors and distress in general may increase emotional arousal. Persistently high levels of fearful emotional arousal may then lead to childhood anxiety problems. Examples of this include clinically anxious children who selectively shift their attention toward threat-relevant cues, and test anxious children who engage in negative self-talk and are overly concerned with their performance, resulting in increased arousal and interference with test performance (Vasey, Daleiden, Williams, & Brown, 1995). Because of the tendency of these children to have difficulty disengaging from threatening stimuli, it is more difficult for them to regulate their emotions, which can then impact negatively upon their interpersonal relationships.

Peer relationships/social skills. As noted, the ability to form peer relationships is also an important interpersonal process that may be linked with the development of different anxiety disorders. Two characteristics seem to have importance here. The first characteristic is the outlook children have about future interpersonal relationships, which is based largely on the parent–child attachment relationship. The second characteristic is the child's temperament and how it elicits or occasions certain behaviors from others. Both the parent–child attachment relationship and the child's temperament – especially behavioral inhibition – directly and indirectly affect the formation of peer relationships (Ollendick & Hirshfeld-Becker, 2002) and subsequent anxiety disorders (Ollendick, 1998).

The optimal outcome in forming good peer relationships is for children to feel they are accepted and valued by their peers. However, the opposite of being accepted and valued by one's peers is being rejected by them. When children are rejected by their peers, anxiety may develop. Rubin and colleagues (1998) have described this pathway well. Beginning with behavioral inhibition, the pathway to social wariness, withdrawal, and rejection unfolds. Parents dealing with behaviorally inhibited children may have the tendency to become insensitive and unresponsive due to the high frequency of these behaviors and because their attempts to soothe or comfort their children have failed (Rubin, Both, Zahn-Waxer, Cummings, & Wilkinson, 1991). Subsequently, the interaction of the child's behaviors and the parent's behaviors toward the child result in the solidification of an insecure parent–child attachment. It is thought to be this sequence of events that hinders a child's ability to form subsequent good peer relationships.

How does not being able to form peer relationships result in the development of an anxiety disorder? Insecurely attached children are thought to be afraid of rejection; therefore, these children withdraw from their peers in anticipation of avoiding rejection. This social withdrawal, in turn, results in children not being able to learn the requisite social skills and to establish normal social relationships, thereby decreasing their chances of being exposed to normative social behaviors (Rubin et al., 1998). This results in children having increased anxiety when placed in settings with peers, which then results in higher levels of withdrawal in these settings. As children progress through childhood, their withdrawal behaviors become increasingly recognized by peer groups (Younger & Boyko, 1987), which then serves to increase anxiety in the already anxious and withdrawn child. It is evident how the interpersonal process of forming peer relationships can have a dramatic effect on the development of anxiety in childhood, especially social anxiety disorder.

This pattern can also result in the failure to develop appropriate social interaction skills. All of the anxiety disorders bear some relationship to social skills; however, this relationship is most evident with social anxiety disorder (Jewell, Jordan, Hupp, & Everett, 1999). Although not all theorists agree that children with social anxiety disorder have poor social skills and probably some do not (see review Rapee & Spence, 2004), this disorder is at its core related to deficit skills in maintaining conversations, initiating conversations, and perceiving social cues in others (Beidel & Turner, 1998). For instance, Spence, Donovan, and Brechman-Toussaint (1999) showed that socially anxious children evidenced social skills deficits not only by self-reports and parent reports but also by behavioral observations. Furthermore, Beidel and her colleagues indicated that compared with normal peers, children with social anxiety disorder were rated as less socially skilled in various social interaction tasks (Beidel, Turner, & Morris, 1999).

Moreover, children with other anxiety disorders might also display social incompetence and maladjustment. Anxious youth, in general, are socially neglected (Strauss, Lahey, Frick, Frame, & Hynd, 1988), describe themselves as less socially competent (Strauss, Lease, Kazdin, Dulcan, & Last, 1989), feel inadequate in peer relationship (Ishikawa, Oota, & Sakano, 2003), and show social withdrawal behavior in the school (Ishikawa & Sakano, 2006). Ginsburg, La Greca, and Silverman (1998) examined the relationship between social incompetence and social anxiety in children with different anxiety disorders (not just those with social anxiety disorder). They reported that high levels of social anxiety were related to low social acceptance, more negative inter-action with peers, and less assertive and responsible social skills. A laboratory-based study regarding peer perceptions and liking of children with anxiety disorders also confirmed difficulties with social adjustment. In this study by Verduin and Kendall (2008), peer raters watched a video clip of speeches given by anxious or non-anxious children and then reported their reactions on peer-liking scales. Children with various anxiety disorders received significantly higher ratings of disliking than children who had no anxiety disorders.

However, not *all* phobic and anxious children show deficient social skills, at least not all the time or in all situations. Children with generalized anxiety disorders, for example, sometimes show socially desirable behaviors (see Kendall, Krain, & Treadwell, 1999) and can be socially gracious and eager to please in their social interactions with others. Also, children who are recognized by teachers as obedient and following rules (i.e., compliant) compared to children who show lower social skills and problem behaviors tend to show higher anxiety symptoms (Ishikawa & Sakano, 2005). In terms of social anxiety disorder in particular, Cartwright-Hatton and her colleagues showed there was very little correlation between social anxiety symptoms and actual observer ratings of children's social skills (Cartwright-Hatton, Hodges, & Porter, 2003). That is, independent observers were unable to distinguish between the low and high social anxiety group through direct observation (Cartwright-Hatton, Tschernitz, & Gomersall, 2005).

Although, as discussed above, diverse developmental pathways are hypothesized regarding the onset, maintenance, and persistence or desistance of anxiety disorders, social skills deficits can lead to a lack of exposure to social situations throughout development. As a result, children and adolescents have fewer opportunities to learn social skills and they tend to avoid social situations more and more. Such a vicious cycle can worsen their anxiety symptoms.

Parental behaviors. Certain parenting behaviors provide an environmental context that contributes to the development of anxiety disorders in children over time (see Wood, McLeod, Sigman, Hwang, & Chu, 2003). In a meta-analysis of the anxiety and parenting literature, Wood et al. (2003) identified four main parenting behaviors associated with the development of anxiety: (1) psychological control, (2) overprotec-tiveness, (3) rejection/criticism, and (4) modeling or reinforcing anxious or avoidant behaviors. Interestingly, research has shown that both anxious mothers and mothers with anxious children (although they might not be anxious themselves) display the above parenting characteristics during interactions with their children, whereas non-anxious mothers or mothers with non-anxious children do not generally display these characteristics (Whaley, Pinto, & Sigman, 1999).

First, psychological control is defined as intrusive behaviors that inhibit psycho-logical autonomy granting, induce guilt, instill anxiety, and withdraw love (Barber & Harmon, 2001). Dumas et al. (1995) found that psychological control was associated with higher levels of anxiety in children and Siqueland, Kendall, and Steinberg (1996) demonstrated that mothers of children with anxiety disorders were more psycho-logically controlling than mothers of non-anxious children. Other studies examining children's reports of psychological control have found significant associations between perceived parental psychological control and anxiety in both children and adolescents (Costa & Weems, 2005). Finally, Whaley et al. (1999) showed that anxious mothers were more psychologically controlling and that anxious mothers with anxious children were the most psychologically controlling of all.

Second, parental overprotection consists of parental behaviors that are overly restrictive and protective of a child's behaviors and activities, resulting in the child developing less autonomy. In two separate studies, Dadds and Barrett (1996) and Hudson and Rapee (2002) found that mothers with anxious children demonstrated higher levels of domineering and overprotective parenting behaviors. Perceived ratings of behavioral control by children and adolescents have also been shown to be related to high levels of anxiety (Costa & Weems, 2006; Ollendick & Horsch, 2007). Both Whaley et al. (1999) and Moore, Whaley, and Sigman (2004) demonstrated that anxious mothers with anxious children displayed the highest level of maternal behavioral control as compared to anxious mothers with non-anxious children or control mothers and children.

Third, rejection/criticism is characterized by disapproving, judgmental, and dismissive parenting behaviors. It has been hypothesized that parents who criticize and minimize their children's feelings do not promote children's emotion regulation (Wood et al., 2003). Specifically, rejection and criticism do not afford children the opportunity to learn, through trial and error, how to deal with and tolerate negative affect, thereby increasing children's sensitivity to anxiety. Overall, research has shown that higher rates of rejection and criticism are related to higher levels of anxiety in children (Dumas et al. 1995; Silverman & Ginsburg, 1998). Furthermore, research on anxious mothers demonstrates that they exhibit less warmth and positivity than control mothers with non-anxious children (Whaley et al., 1999).

The above parenting behaviors are thought to enhance children's anxiety by: (1) increasing the likelihood that children will cognitively interpret these behaviors as a signal that a particular situation is threatening or dangerous, (2) preventing children from facing fear-provoking events and seeing that their fear is either ultimately unfounded or that their fear does not result in the catastrophic consequence they expect, and (3) hindering children's ability to develop effective solutions to face fear (Rapee, 1997).

The last way that parenting behaviors can increase the risk of children developing anxiety disorders is through the modeling and reinforcement of anxious and avoidant behaviors. The modeling of anxiety by parents occurs when parents actively exhibit avoidance and anxious behaviors in front of their child, who is then seemingly reinforced by these behaviors (Barrett, Rapee, Dadds, & Ryan, 1996b). Furthermore, one of the main reasons why children's fears persist in the above circumstances is because they have limited opportunity to habituate to feared stimuli as their parents frequently fear the same stimuli and shield their children from them (Menzies & Harris, 2001). The reinforcement of anxiety is thought to occur by parents paying attention to, agreeing with, tolerating, and reciprocating avoidant behaviors exhibited by their children (Barrett, et al., 1996b). When parents continually allow and encourage their child to avoid and escape from the situations they fear, that fear gets reinforced. It is the reduction in anxiety that occurs upon escape from the situation that powerfully reinforces that avoidance behavior. The opposite approach of having the child face what they fear leads to anxiety in the short term, but it also is likely to reduce anxiety in the long run by allowing the child to be exposed to the situation (Ollendick, Vasey, & King, 2001). This reduction in anxiety due to exposure is thought to be a result of realizing that the fear and/or the cognitive error associated with that fear is unwarranted.

Lastly, a pathway to the maintenance of anxiety occurs when avoidance prevents mastery of normal developmental processes (Ollendick et al., 2001). That is, because anxious children tend to avoid a number of social and interpersonal contexts, they tend to show less competence in these areas. Accordingly, as described above, research shows that anxiety is associated with deficits in social interaction skills (Matson & Ollendick, 1988; Vernberg, Abwender, Ewell, & Beery, 1992). One such demonstrated pathway to this social incompetence can be seen in the case of anxious withdrawal. Rubin (1993), for example, showed that by mid- to late-childhood, social anxiety and withdrawal led to peer rejection and unpopularity. The rejection and social failure experienced by these children was hypothesized to at least partially be accounted for by their lack of practice in social situations because of their anxiety and withdrawal, resulting in social skills deficits.

The Role of Interpersonal and Social Factors in the Treatment of Childhood and Adolescent Anxiety Disorders

Thus far, we have focused on delineating the processes of normative interpersonal and social development and demonstrating how these factors may be related to the onset, maintenance, and persistence of anxiety disorders in children and adolescence. We now turn our attention to the role that interpersonal and social processes play in the treatment of anxiety disorders in youth. We should note from the onset, however, that most interventions have not attended very well to these interpersonal and social factors and that the treatments have largely conceptualized and treated the anxiety disorders as *intrapersonal* and not *interpersonal* in scope (Woody & Ollendick, 2006). That is, most interventions have viewed the anxiety disorder as being "in" the child, with little attention paid to the interpersonal or social context in which the anxiety is embedded and maintained.

Although various interventions have been used to treat childhood anxiety disorders, only cognitive behavioral therapy (CBT) has been recognized as an efficacious treatment (Ishikawa, Okajima, Matsuoka, & Sakano, 2007; Ollendick, King, & Chorpita, 2006; Silverman, Pina, & Viswesvaran, 2008). CBT is a psychosocial intervention that variably includes relaxation and anxiety management strategies, in vivo exposure, participant modeling, reinforcement, cognitive restructuring, social skills and problem-solving training, and homework. Recently, In-Albon and Schneider (2006) identified 24 randomized clinical trials (RCTs) examining the treatment of anxious children and *all* used a variant of CBT (e.g., individual/group, child/family). The vast majority of these trials examined the effects of CBT delivered individually to children between 7 and 14 years of age; both boys and girls were treated and the average age across studies was approximately 10 years of age. The children treated in these interventions presented with various anxiety disorders (e.g., SAD, OAD/GAD, Social Phobia/AD, and Specific Phobia). Parents and peers were minimally involved in these studies. Overall, about 67% of the treated children were diagnosis free at post-treatment, compared with less than 10% of those in waitlist control conditions. Maintenance of treatment gains was evidenced at 1, 3, and 7 year follow-ups (Kendall, 1994; Kendall, Flannery-Schroeder, Panichelli-Mindel, Southam-Gerow, Henin, & Waeman, 1997; Kendall, Safford, Flannery-Schroeder, & Webb, 2004; Kendall & Southam-Gerow, 1996).

Group CBT has also been found to be effective in treating anxious children (Barrett, 1998; Flannery-Schroeder & Kendall, 2000; Manassis, Mendlowitz, Scapillato et al., 2002; Silverman, Kurtines, Ginsburg et al., 1999a), with comparable improvement rates to those found with individual CBT at post-treatment (e.g., 64–69% versus 6–25% for those in waitlist control conditions) and follow-up at 3–12 months. In general, no differences have been found between individual and group CBT treatments for anxious children (Flannery-Schroeder & Kendall, 2000; In-Albon & Schneider, 2006; Manassis et al., 2002). Although a quasi-experimental trial, this tendency has also been replicated in Japan (Ishikawa, Motomura, Kawabata, Tanaka, Shimotsu, Sato, & Ollendick, 2012). These findings are somewhat surprising given the potential utility of peers as socialization agents for children and the opportunity for the treated children to acquire and use appropriate social and emotion regulation skills within the group setting. It may be the case, however, that the potential for utilization of peers has not been fully realized in these studies. That is, many of these group studies have simply treated individuals in groups and have not used the peer network to facilitate change.

In addition to these studies, a number of other studies have shown that individual or group CBT supplemented with family and/or parent anxiety management strategies produce greater outcomes than those observed in waitlist control conditions. Silverman, Kurtines, Gindburg et al. (1999b), for example, showed that group CBT supplemented with parent–child contingency management and behavioral contracting procedures produced outcomes superior to waitlist control conditions for 6- to 16-year-old children with an anxiety disorder. Moreover, other studies have shown that family-enhanced CBT might produce even greater outcomes than those obtained with individual or group CBT alone (Barrett, Dadds, & Rapee, 1996a; Cobham, Dadds, & Spence, 1998; Kendall, Hudson, & Gosch, 2008; Shortt, Barrett, & Fox, 2001), at least with younger children and children whose parents also have an anxiety disorder. To illustrate, Barrett et al. (1996a) showed that a parent-augmented treatment produced greater outcomes at post-treatment (84%) and 1 year follow-up (95%) than did individual CBT (57% at post-treatment and 70% at 1-year follow-up). However, the enhanced effects of this treatment were observed only for children between 7 and 11 years of age, and not for early adolescents between 12 and 14 years of age. For the young adolescents, no differences between individual and parent-augmented interventions were observed.

Similarly, Cobham et al. (1998) compared individual CBT to parent-enhanced CBT with anxious children between 7 and 14 years of age whose parents were either high or low in trait anxiety. They reported differences at both post treatment (77% versus 39%) and at 6-month follow-up (88% versus 44%), in favor of the parent-enhanced intervention. However, these effects were observed only for children whose parents were high in trait anxiety; for those whose parents were low in trait anxiety, no differences were detected. Finally, in a more recent study, Wood, Piacentini, Southam-Gerow, Chu, and Sigman (2006) showed that family-focused CBT produced superior outcomes to individual CBT with 6- to 13-year-old children who had an anxiety disorder. In this study, in contrast to earlier studies that focused on training parents to help their anxious child deal with anxiety in a more adaptive manner, individual CBT was supplemented with an intervention focused on parenting practices found to be directly related to the development and maintenance of childhood anxiety disorders; namely, parental intrusiveness and failure to grant autonomy to their children. For the enhanced group, 79% were diagnosis free at post-treatment compared to 53% in the individual CBT group.

However, in other studies, no differences between parent- or family-enhanced treatments and individual or group CBT have been found. For example, Spence, Donovan, and Brechman-Toussaint (2000) allocated 7- to 14-year-old children with social phobia to individual CBT, individual CBT supplemented with parent involvement, or a waitlist control condition. In this study, parents were taught specific coping skills to assist their children with exposure exercises and constructive ways to reinforce and encourage social behavior in their children. Although both active treatments were superior to the waitlist control condition, no differences were observed between the two treatment groups. In addition, Nauta, Scholing, Emmelkamp, and Minderaa (2003) reported similar findings with children who were diagnosed primarily with generalized anxiety disorder and separation anxiety disorder. It should be noted however that these latter studies did not use the procedures recommended by Wood et al. (2006), which targeted parental intrusiveness and failure to grant autonomy to their children.

Taken together, this emerging body of literature suggests that parents and families *may* have an impact on treatment outcome as we would expect based on an interpersonal perspective of childhood anxiety disorders. This is not surprising in as much as research supports the role of parents and families as interpersonal agents and contexts in which childhood anxiety disorders develop and flourish. Although some studies did not support the inclusion of parents and families, it may be the case that the parent-enhanced and family-enhanced strategies used in these studies were simply not the "right" ones and were not powerful enough to produce the anticipated effects. Still, as Barmish and Kendall (2005) assert, "alluring as it might be to include parents as co-clients for multiple theoretical reasons, the belief cannot be mistaken as evidence" (p. 578). They go on to recommend that "additional comparative research is needed and that the acceptance of either approach as superior is not yet justified" (p. 579). Although we agree, we maintain that if the programs involve the parents and families as facilitators of emotion regulation and emotion socialization, beneficial effects might more likely be obtained.

In addition to parent or family involvement, three RCTs have directly enlisted peers in the treatment of children with an anxiety disorder. From an interpersonal perspective, we might expect that treatments involving peers will be particularly effective. The first study examined the effects of peer involvement (along with parent involvement) in the treatment of children with a variety of anxiety disorders (GAD, SAD, social anxiety disorder) whereas the second explored the use of peers in the treatment of socially phobic children, without parental involvement. Shortt et al. (2001) evaluated the efficacy of the FRIENDS program, a family and peer group CBT intervention for anxious children. In addition to the standard individual CBT elements of intervention, the FRIENDS program instructs parents to reward children for coping with their fears and worries *and* encourages children to be their own friend and reward themselves when they try hard; *to make friends so that they can build their social support network;*

and *to talk to their friends when they are in difficult or worrying situations.* The group format encourages the development of parent support groups and provides considerable peer interchanges to practice what has been learned in treatment. In addition, systematic homework assignments with peers in the community are designed to reinforce social interaction skills acquired in the groups. In this study, 6- to10-year-old children and their parents were randomly assigned to the FRIENDS condition or a waitlist control condition. At post-treatment, 69% of children in the FRIENDS condition were diagnosis-free compared to 6% in the waitlist control condition. Quite obviously, this program shows considerable promise; however, at this time, it is unclear what components of the program are critical ones in as much as similar diagnostic outcomes have been achieved with individual CBT, group CBT, and individual or group CBT when augmented with parent or family involvement. The unique feature of this intervention – the role of peers and the training and reinforcement of friendship skills – needs to be evaluated systematically. Moreover, the effects of the program in improving interpersonal skills and in producing changes in sociometric networks and friendship patterns are yet to be determined.

In the second major RCT involving peers, Beidel and her colleagues evaluated the efficacy of Social Effectiveness Therapy for Children (SET-C) with 8- to 12-year-old children with social phobia (Beidel, Turner, & Morris, 2000). Based on considerable evidence that children with social phobia tend to have few friends, have limited involvement in outside activities and lack important interpersonal and social skills (Beidel, et al., 1999; Ollendick & Hirshfeld-Becker, 2002), this 12-week intervention consists primarily of group social skills intervention (90 minutes), *peer generalization activities* (90 minutes), and individualized in vivo exposure exercises (60–90 minutes). As is evident, each weekly session lasts about 3 hours, considerably longer than the other interventions described above (all consisting of 8–16 one-hour therapy sessions). Of importance, the intervention was designed to address the interpersonal and social skill deficits of the children, as well as their anxiety about social engagement. SET-C was compared to an active intervention designed to address test anxiety (Testbusters), a phenomenon frequently observed in socially phobic children. At post-treatment, SET-C children demonstrated enhanced social skills, reduced social anxiety, and increased overall social functioning; moreover, 67% no longer met diagnostic criteria for social phobia compared to 5% of children in the Testbusters control condition. At 3-year follow-up, 72% continued to be free of a social phobia diagnosis (Beidel, Turner, Young, & Paulson, 2005) and at 5-year follow-up 81% were diagnosis free (Beidel, Turner, & Young, 2006). Of additional importance, at the time of this 5-year follow-up, the children were mid-adolescents (13–17 year olds), the most common age of onset for social phobia and, because of the increased focus on peer relationships during this developmental period, an age at which relapse might likely occur. However, only one adolescent who was diagnosis-free at follow-up relapsed at the 5-year follow-up. In as much as social phobia tends not to remit without intervention, especially when onset is before age 11, these findings are particularly encouraging.

In the third study, Masia-Warner and her colleagues (2005) showed similar outcomes in a school-based, randomized waitlist control trial for adolescents who presented with social anxiety disorder. Adolescents in the intervention group demonstrated significantly greater reductions than those in the wail-list condition in social anxiety and avoidance, as well as significantly improved overall functioning. In addition, 67% of the treated adolescents were free of their disorder at post-treatment compared to only 6% of those in the control condition.

In contrast to these CBT interventions (whether delivered in an individual or group format, and with or without parent/family or peer components), other interventions have fared less well or have not been investigated at all. For example, given the salutatory effects of attachment-based and interpersonal psychotherapies with depressed children and adolescents (Diamond, Reiss, Diamond, Siqueland, & Isaacs, 2002; Mufson, Moreau, Weissman, & Klerman, 1993), and the role that attachment and interpersonal processes have in the development and expression of the anxiety disorders, it is surprising that only one small RCT has examined these interventions. In that trial, an attachment-based family therapy was compared to standard CBT. It was shown that 67% of the adolescents in the CBT condition were symptom-free following treatment compared to 40% of the adolescents in the attachment-based family therapy (Siqueland, Rynn, & Diamond, 2005). Moreover, although uncontrolled clinical trials (cf. Muratori, Picchi, Bruni, Patarnello, & Romagnoli, 2003) and retrospective chart reviews (cf., Target & Fonagy, 1994) illustrate the potential efficacy of psychodynamic-based psychotherapy, firm support is lacking for them and no RCT trials have been reported. In its most recent statement on practice parameters for the childhood anxiety disorders, the American Academy of Child and Adolescent Psychiatry indicates that "there is limited research on efficacy and effectiveness of psychodynamic psychotherapy alone, or in combined treatments, or compared with other modalities" (p. 274, 2007). Similarly there is little to no support for other commonly practiced interventions such as play therapy or family therapy (Ollendick et al., 2006). In its practice parameters statement, the American Academy of Child and Adolescent Psychiatry (2007) failed to include play therapy, attachment-based psychotherapy, or interpersonal psychotherapy in its recommendation of potentially useful interventions and commented on family therapy only as an adjunctive aide to CBT. Thus, considerably more research is needed before interventions other than CBT can be recommended.

Conclusion

The study of interpersonal and social factors in the development, expression, and treatment of the childhood and adolescent anxiety disorders is clearly in its own stage of early development (Ollendick et al., 2010). Although important interpersonal and social factors such as attachment, temperament, emotion regulation, parental socialization of emotion, and peer relationships have been identified and associated with the development and expression of anxiety disorders in childhood, they have been largely ignored in the development of treatment interventions with few notable exceptions (see Wood & McLeod, 2008, for the effects of parenting; Hannesdottir & Ollendick, 2007, for the effects of emotion regulation; and Beidel et al., 2000, for the effects of peer involvement). Moreover, even when such factors are included, it is not at all clear that they alone result in significant change or that they enhance treatment outcomes above and beyond those found in standard CBT trials. Still, it is evident that anxiety does not exist solely in the child and that interpersonal and social factors need to be examined in RCT trials as well as dismantling trials that isolate their individual and synergistic effects. Thus, much work remains to be done both in the conceptualization of meaningful interpersonal processes and in their utility in the treatment of children with anxiety disorders. Nonetheless, they show considerable promise and represent the next generation of studies that hopefully will result in even more successful outcomes for children with anxiety disorders and their families.

* * *

This chapter is based on Ollendick, T. H., Costa, N. M., & Benoit, K. E. (2010). Interpersonal processes and the anxiety disorders of childhood. In J. G. Beck (Ed.), *Interpersonal Processes in the Anxiety Disorders: Implications for Understanding Psychopathology and Treatment* (pp. 97–124). Washington, DC: American Psychological Association.

References

American Academy of Child and Adolescent Psychiatry (2007). Practice parameter of the assessment and treatment of children and adolescents with anxiety disorders. *Journal of the American Academy of Child and Adolescent Psychiatry, 46*, 267–282.

APA (1994). *Diagnostic and statistical manual of mental disorders*, 4th edn). Washington, DC: American Psychiatric Association.

Barber, B. K., & Harmon, E. L. (2001). Violating the self: Parental psychological control of children and adolescents. In B. K. Barber (Ed.), *Intrusive Parenting: How Psychological Control Affects Children and Adolescents* (pp. 125–159). Washington, DC: American Psychological Association.

Barmish, A. J., & Kendall, P. C. (2005). Should parents be co-clients in cognitive behavior therapy for anxious youth? *Journal of Clinical Child and Adolescent Psychology, 34*, 569–581.

Barrett, P. M. (1998). Evaluation of cognitive-behavioral group treatments for childhood anxiety disorders. *Journal of Clinical Child Psychology, 27*, 459–468.

Barrett, P. M., Dadds, M. R., & Rapee, R. M. (1996a). Family treatment of childhood anxiety: A controlled trial. *Journal of Consulting and Clinical Psychology, 64*, 333–342.

Barrett, P. M., Rapee, R. M., Dadds, M. M., & Ryan, S. M. (1996b). Family enhancement of cognitive style in anxious and aggressive children: Threat bias and the FEAR effect. *Journal of Abnormal Child Psychology, 24*, 187–203.

Beidel, D. C., & Turner, S. M. (1998). *Shy children, phobic adults: Nature and treatment of social phobia*. Washington DC: American Psychological Association.

Beidel, D. C., Turner, S. M., & Morris, T. L. (1999). Psychopathology of childhood social phobia. *Journal of the American Academy of Child and Adolescent Psychiatry, 38*, 643–650.

Beidel, D. C., Turner, S. M., & Morris, T. L. (2000). Behavioral treatment of childhood social phobia. *Journal of Consulting and Clinical Psychology, 68*, 1072–1080.

Beidel, D. C., Turner, S. M., & Young, B. J. (2006). Social Effectiveness Therapy for Children: Five years later. *Behavior Therapy, 37*, 416–425.

Beidel, D. C., Turner, S. M., Young, B. J., & Paulson, A. (2005). Social Effectiveness Therapy for Children: Three-year follow-up. *Journal of Consulting and Clinical Psychology, 73*, 721–725.

Biederman, J., Rosenbaum, J. E., Hirshfeld, D. N., Faraone, S. V., Bolduc, G., Gersten, M., Meminger, S. R., & Reznick, S. (1990). Psychiatric correlates of behavioral inhibition in young children of parents with and without psychiatric disorders. *Archives of General Psychiatry, 47*, 21–26.

Bowlby, J. (1973). *Attachment and Loss: Volume 2. Separation Anxiety and Anger*. NY: Basic Books.

Bowlby, J. (1987). *Attachment and the Therapeutic Process*. Madison, CT: International University Press.

Cartwright-Hatton, S., Hodges, L., & Porter, J. (2003). Social anxiety in childhood: The relationship with self and observer rated social skills. *Journal of Child Psychology and Psychiatry, 44,* 737–742.

Cartwright-Hatton, S., Tschernitz, N., & Gomersall, H. (2005). Social anxiety in children: Social skills deficit, or cognitive distortion? *Behaviour Research and Therapy, 43,* 131–141.

Cobham, V. E., Dadds, M. R., & Spence, S. H. (1998). The role of parental anxiety in the treatment of childhood anxiety. *Journal of Consulting and Clinical Psychology, 66,* 893–905.

Costa, N. M., & Weems, C. F. (2005). Maternal and child anxiety: Do attachment beliefs or children's perceptions of maternal control mediate their association? *Social Development. 14,* 574–590.

Costello, E. J., Egger, H. L., & Angold, A. (2005). The developmental epidemiology of anxiety disorders: phenomenology, prevalence, and comorbidity. *Child & Adolescent Psychiatric Clinics of North America, 14,* 631–648.

Dadds, M. R., & Barrett, P. M. (1996). Family processes in child and adolescent anxiety and depression. *Behaviour Change, 13,* 231–239.

Davila, J., La Greca, A. M., Starr, L. R., & Landoll, R. R. (2010). Anxiety disorders in adolescence. In J. G. Beck (Ed.), *Interpersonal processes in the anxiety disorders: Implications for understanding psychopathology and treatment* (pp. 97–124). Washington, DC: American Psychological Association.

Diamond, G. S., Reiss, B., Diamond, G. M., Siqueland, L., & Isaacs, L. (2002). Attachment-based family therapy for depressed adolescents: A treatment development study. *Journal of the American Academy of Child and Adolescent Psychiatry, 41,* 1190–1196.

Dumas, J. E., LaFreniere, P. J., & Serketich, W. J. (1995). "Balance of power": A transactional analysis of control in mother–child dyads involving socially competent, aggressive, and anxious children. *Journal of Abnormal Psychology, 104,* 104–113.

Eisenberg, N. (2002). Emotion-related regulation and its relation to quality of social functioning. In W. W. Hartup & R. A. Weinberg (Eds.), *Minnesota Symposia on Child Psychology: Vol. 32. Child Psychology in Retrospect and Prospect: In Celebration of the 75th Anniversary of the Institute of Child Development* (pp. 133–171). Mahwah, NJ: Erlbaum.

Eisenberg, N., Cumberland, A., Spinrad, T. L., Fabes, R. A., Shepard, S. A., Reiser, M., et al. (2001a). The relations of regulation and emotionality to children's externalizing and internalizing problem behavior. *Child Development, 72,* 1112–1134.

Eisenberg, N., & Fabes, R. A. (1992). Emotion, regulation, and the development of social competence. In M. S. Clark (Ed.), *Review of personality and social psychology: Emotion and social behavior* (Vol. 14, pp. 119–150). Newbury Park, CA: Sage.

Eisenberg, N., & Fabes, R. A. (1994). Emotion regulation and the development of social competence. In M. Clark (Ed.), *Review of Personality and Social Psychology* (pp. 119–150). Newbury Park, CA: Sage.

Eisenberg, N., & Fabes, R. A. (1998). Prosocial development. In W. Damon & N. Eisenberg (Eds.), *Handbook of Child Psychology, 5th edn: Social, Emotional, and Personality Development* (Vol. 3, pp. 701–778). New York: John Wiley & Sons, Inc.

Eisenberg, N., Losoya, S., Fabes, R., Guthrie, I., Reiser, M., Murphy, B., et al. (2001b). Parental socialization of children's dysregulated expression of emotion and externalizing problems. *Journal of Family Psychology, 15,* 183–205.

Essau, C., & Ollendick, T. H. (2009). Diagnosis and assessment of adolescent depression. In S. Nolen-Hoeksema & L. Hilt (Eds.), *Handbook of Aadolescent Depression* (pp. 33–52). New York: Routledge, Taylor & Francis Group.

Flannery-Schroeder, E. C., & Kendall, P. C. (2000). Group and individual cognitive-behavioral treatments for youth with anxiety disorders: A randomized clinical trial. *Cognitive Therapy and Research, 24,* 251–278.

Ginsburg, G. S., La Greca, A. M., & Silverman, W. K. (1998). Social anxiety in children with anxiety disorders: Relation with social and emotional functioning. *Journal of Abnormal Child Psychology, 26*, 175–185.

Hammen, C., & Goodman-Brown, T. (1990). Self-schemas and vulnerability to specific life stress in children at risk for depression. *Cognitive Therapy and Research, 14*, 215–227.

Hannesdottir, D. K., & Ollendick, T. H. (2007). The role of emotion regulation in the treatment of child anxiety disorders. *Clinical Child and Family Psychology Review, 10*, 275–293.

Hirshfeld, D. R., Rosenbaum, J. F., Biederman, J., Bolduc, E. A., Farapone, S. V., Snidman, N., et al. (1992). Stable behavioral inhibition and its association with anxiety disorder. *Journal of the American Academy of Child and Adolescent Psychiatry, 31*, 103–111.

Hudson, J., & Rapee, R. (2002). Parent–child interactions in clinically anxious children and their siblings. *Journal of Clinical Child and Adolescent Psychology, 31*, 548–555.

In-Albon, T., & Schneider, S. (2006). Psychotherapy of childhood anxiety disorders: A meta-analysis. *Psychotherapy and Psychosomatics, 14*, 1–10.

Ishikawa, S., Motomura, N., Kawabata, Y., Tanaka, H., Shimotsu, S., Sato, Y., & Ollendick, T. H. (2012). Cognitive behavioural therapy for Japanese children and adolescents with anxiety disorders: A pilot study. *Behavioural and Cognitive Psychotherapy, 40*, 271–285.

Ishikawa, S., Okajima, I., Matsuoka, H., & Sakano, Y. (2007). Cognitive-behavioural therapy for anxiety disorders in children and adolescents: A meta-analysis. *Child and Adolescent Mental Health, 12*, 164–172.

Ishikawa, S., Oota, R., & Sakano, Y. (2003). The relationship between anxiety disorders tendencies and subjective school maladjustment in childhood. *Japanese Journal of Counseling Science, 36*, 264–271.

Ishikawa, S., & Sakano, Y. (2005). The investigation on the relationship between anxiety symptoms and behavioral characteristics in childhood: Social skills in childhood from the teachers' points of view. *Japanese Journal of Counseling Sciences, 38*, 1–11.

Ishikawa, S., & Sakano, Y. (2006). The investigation on the relationship between social skills and anxiety symptoms in children by the self-report method. *Japanese Journal of Counseling Sciences, 39*, 202–211.

Jewell, J. D., Jordan, S. S., Hupp, S. D. A., Everett, G. E. (2009). Etiology and relationships to developmental disabilities and psychopathology. In J. L. Matson (Ed.), *Social Behavior and Skills in Children* (pp. 39–59). New York: Springer.

Kagan, J. (1994). Inhibited and uninhibited temperaments. In W. B. Carey & S. C. McDevitt (Eds.), *Prevention and Early Intervention: Individual Differences and Risk Factors for the Mental Health of Children* (pp. 35–41). New York: Brunner/Mazel.

Kagan, J., Reznick, J. S., & Gibbons, J. (1989). Inhibited and uninhibited types of children. *Child Development, 60*, 838–845.

Kagan, J., Reznick, J. S., & Snidman, N. (1987). The physiology and psychology of behavioral inhibition. *Child Development, 58*, 1459–1473.

Kagan, J., Reznick, J. S., & Snidman, N. (1988). Biological bases of childhood shyness. *Science, 240*, 167–171.

Kendall, P. C. (1994). Treating anxiety disorders in children: Results of a randomized clinical trial. *Journal of Consulting and Clinical Psychology, 62*, 100–110.

Kendall, P. C., Flannery-Schroeder, E., Panichelli-Mindel, S. M., Southam-Gerow, M., Henin, A., & Warman, M. (1997). Therapy for youths with anxiety disorders: A second randomized clinical trial. *Journal of Consulting and Clinical Psychology, 65*, 366–380.

Kendall, P. C., Hudson, J. L., & Gosch, E. (2008). Cognitive-behavioral therapy for anxiety disordered youth: A randomized clinical trial evaluating child and family modalities. *Journal of Consulting and Clinical Psychology, 76*, 282–297.

Kendall, P. C., Krain, A., & Treadwell, K. R. H. (1999). Generalized anxiety disorders. In Ammerman, R. T., Hersen, M., & Last, C. G. (Eds.), *Handbook of Prescriptive Treatments for Children and Adolescents*, 2nd edn. (pp. 155–171). Needham Heights, MA: Allyn & Bacon.

Kendall, P. C., Safford, S., Flannery-Schroeder, E., & Webb, A. (2004). Child anxiety treatment: Outcomes in adolescence and impact on substance use and depression at 7. 4-year follow-up. *Journal of Consulting and Clinical Psychology, 72,* 276–287.

Kendall, P. C., & Southam-Gerow, M. A. (1996). Long-term follow-up of a cognitive-behavioral therapy for anxiety-disordered youth. *Journal of Consulting and Clinical Psychology, 64,* 724–730.

Klimes-Dougan, B., & Zeman, J. (2007). Introduction to the special issue of social development: Emotion socialization in childhood and adolescence. *Social Development, 16,* 203–209.

La Greca, A. M., & Prinstein, M. J. (1999). Peer group. In W. K. Silverman & T. H. Ollendick (Eds.), *Developmental Issues in the Clinical Treatment of Children* (pp. 171–198). Needham Heights, MA: Allyn & Bacon.

Lemery, K. S., Essex, M., & Smider, N. (2002). Revealing the relationship between temperament and behavior problem symptoms by eliminating measurement confounding: Expert ratings and factor analyses. *Child Development, 73,* 867–882.

Manassis, K., & Bradley, S. (1994). The development of childhood anxiety disorders: Toward an integrated model. *Journal of Applied Developmental Psychology, 15,* 345–366.

Manassis, K., Bradley, S., Goldberg, S., Hood, J., & Swinson, L. (1994). Attachment in mothers with anxiety disorders and their children. *Journal of the American Academy of Child and Adolescent Psychiatry, 33,* 1106–1113.

Manassis, K., Bradley, S., Goldberg, S., Hood, J., & Swinson, R. P. (1995). Behavioural inhibition, attachment and anxiety in children of mothers with anxiety disorders. *Canadian Journal of Psychiatry, 40,* 87–92.

Manassis, K., Mendlowitz, S. L., Scapillato, D., Avery, D., Fiksenbaum, L., Freire, M., et al. (2002). Group and individual cognitive-behavioral therapy for childhood anxiety disorders. A randomized trial. *Journal of the American Academy of Child & Adolescent Psychiatry, 41,* 1423–1430.

Masia-Warner, C., Klein, R. G., Dent, H. C., Fisher, P. H., Alvir, J., Albano, A. M., & Guardino, M. (2005). School-based intervention for adolescents with social anxiety disorder: Results of a controlled study. *Journal of Abnormal Child Psychology, 33,* 707–722.

Mason, O., Platts, H., & Tyson, M. (2005). Early maladaptive schemas and adult attachment in a UK clinical population. *Psychology and Psychotherapy: Theory, Research, and Practice, 78,* 549–564.

Matson, J. L., & Ollendick, T. H. (1988). *Enhancing Children's Social Skills: Assessment and Training.* New York: Pergamon Press.

Mattis, S. G., & Ollendick, T. H. (1997). Panic in children and adolescents: A developmental analysis. *Advances in Clinical Child Psychology, 19,* 27–74.

Menzies, R., & Harris, L. (2001). Nonassociative factors in the development of phobias. In M. Vasey & M. Dadds (Eds.), *The Developmental Psychopathology of Anxiety* (pp. 183–204). New York, NY: Oxford University Press.

Miller, S. M., & Green, M. L. (1985). Coping with stress and frustration: Origins, nature, and development. In M. Lewis & C. Saarni (Eds.), *The Socialization of Emotions* (pp. 263–314). New York: Plenum.

Moore, P. S., Whaley, S. E., & Sigman, M. (2004). Interactions between mothers and children: Impact of maternal and child anxiety. *Journal of Abnormal Psychology, 113,* 471–476.

Mufson, L., Moreau, D., Weissman, M. M., & Klerman, G. L. (1993). *Interpersonal psychotherapy for depressed adolescents.* New York: The Guilford Press.

Muratori, F. Picchi, L., Bruni, G., Patarnello, M., & Romagnoli, G. (2003). A two-year follow-up of psychodynamic psychotherapy for internalizing disorders in children. *Journal of the American Academy of Child and Adolescent Psychiatry, 42,* 331–339.

Muris, P., & Meesters, C. (2002). Attachment, behavioral inhibition, and anxiety disorders symptoms in normal adolescents. *Journal of Psychopathology and Behavioral Assessment, 24,* 97–106.

Muris, P., & Ollendick, T. H. (2005). The role of temperament in the etiology of child psychopathology. *Clinical Child and Family Psychology Review, 8,* 271–289.

Nauta, M. H., Scholing, A., Emmelkamp, P. M. G., & Minderaa, R. B. (2003). Cognitive-behavioral therapy for children with anxiety disorders in a clinical setting: No additional effect of a cognitive parent training. *Journal of the American Academy of Child & Adolescent Psychiatry, 42,* 1270–1278.

Ollendick, T. H. (1998). Panic disorder in children and adolescents: New developments, new directions. *Journal of Clinical Child Psychology, 27,* 234–245.

Ollendick, T. H., Costa, N. M., & Benoit, K. E. (2010). Interpersonal processes and the anxiety disorders of childhood. In J. G. Beck (Ed.), *Interpersonal Processes in the Anxiety Disorders: Implications for Understanding Psychopathology and Treatment* (pp. 97–124). Washington, DC: American Psychological Association.

Ollendick, T., & Hirshfeld-Becker, D. (2002). The developmental and psychopathology of social anxiety disorder. *Biological Psychiatry, 51,* 44–58.

Ollendick, T., & Horsch, L. (2007). Fears in clinic-referred children: Relations with child anxiety sensitivity, maternal overcontrol, and maternal phobic anxiety. *Behavior Therapy, 38,* 402–411.

Ollendick, T. H., King, N. J., & Chorpita, B. F. (2006). Empirically supported treatments for children and adolescents. In P. C. Kendall (Ed.), *Child and Adolescent Therapy: Cognitive-behavioral Procedures,* 3rd edn. (pp. 492–520). New York: Guilford Press.

Ollendick, T. H., King, N. J., & Muris, P. (2002). Fears and phobias in children: Phenomenology, epidemiology, and aetiology. *Child and Adolescent Mental Health, 7,* 98–106.

Ollendick, T. H., & Seligman, L. D. (2006). Anxiety disorders in children and adolescents. In C. Gillberg, R. Harrington, & H. Steinhausen (Eds.), *Clinician's Desk Book of Child and Adolescent Psychiatry* (pp. 144–187). Cambridge: Cambridge University Press.

Ollendick, T. H., Vasey, M. W., & King, N. J. (2001). Operant conditioning influences in childhood anxiety. In M. Vasey & M. Dadds (Eds.), *The Developmental Psychopathology of Anxiety* (pp. 231–252). New York, NY: Oxford University Press.

Parke, R. D., Orstein, P. A., Rieser, J. J., & Zahn-Waxler, C. (1994). The past as prologue: An overview of a century of developmental psychology. In R. D. Parke, P. A. Orstein, J. J. Rieser, & C. Zahn-Waxler (Eds.), *A century of developmental psychology* (pp. 1–75). Washington, DC: American Psychological Association.

Rapee, R. M. (1997). Potential role of childrearing practices in the development of anxiety and depression. *Clinical Psychology Review, 17,* 47–67.

Rapee, R M., & Spence, S. H. (2004). The etiology of social phobia: Empirical evidence and an initial model. *Clinical Psychology Review, 24,* 737–767.

Roberts, W. (1994). *The socialization of emotional expression: Relation with competence in preschool.* Paper presented at the meetings of the Canadian Psychological Association, Penticton, British Columbia.

Rothbart, M. K., & Ahadi, S. A. (1994). Temperament and the development of personality. *Journal of Abnormal Psychology, 130,* 55–66.

Rothbart, M. K., & Bates, J. E. (1998). Temperament. In W. Damon (Series Ed.) and N. Eisenberg (Vol. Ed.), *Handbook of child psychology:. Social, emotional, and personality development* (Vol 3, pp. 105–176). New York: Wiley.

Rothbart, M. K., Posner, M. I., & Boylan (1990). Regulatory mechanisms in infant development. In J. Enns (Ed.), *The development of attention: Research and theory.* Dordrecht: Elsevier North-Holland.

Rubin, K. H. (1993). The Waterloo longitudinal project: Correlates and consequences of social withdrawal from childhood to adolescence. In K. H. Rubin & J. B. Asendorpf (Eds.), *Social withdrawal, inhibition, and shyness* (pp. 291–314). Hillsdale, NJ: Erlbaum.

Rubin, K., Both, L., Zahn-Waxer, C., Cummings, M., & Wilkinson, M. (1991). The dyadic play behaviors of children of well and depressed mothers. *Development and Psychopathology, 3,* 243–251.

Rubin, K. H., Bukowski, W., & Parker, J. G. (1998). Peer interactions, relationships, and groups. In N. Eisenberg (Ed.), *Handbook of child psychology (5th ed.); Vol. 3. Social, Emotional, and Personality Development* (pp. 619–700). New York: Wiley.

Seligman, L. D., & Ollendick, T. H. (2011). Cognitive behavior therapy for anxiety disorders in youth. *Psychiatric Clinics of North America, 20,* 217–238.

Selman, R., & Schultz, L. (1990). *Making a friend in youth: Developmental theory and pair therapy.* Chicago, IL: University of Chicago Press.

Shortt, A. L., Barrett, P. M., & Fox, T. L. (2001). Evaluating the FRIENDS Program: A cognitive-behavioral group treatment for anxious children and their parents. *Journal of Clinical Child Psychology, 30,* 525–535.

Silverman, W. K., & Ginsburg, G. S. (1998). Anxiety disorders. In T. Ollendick & M. Hersen (Eds.), *Handbook of Child Psychopathology*, 3rd edn. (pp. 239–268). New York, NY: Plenium Press.

Silverman, W. K., Kurtines, W. M., Ginsburg, G. S., Weems, C. F., Lumpkin, P. W., & Carmichael, D. H. (1999a). Treating anxiety disorders in children with group cognitive-behavioral therapy: A randomized clinical trial. *Journal of Consulting and Clinical Psychology, 67,* 995–1003.

Silverman, W. K., Kurtines, W. M., Ginsburg, G. S., Weems, C. F., Rabian, B., & Serafini, L. T. (1999b). Contingency management, self-control, and education support in the treatment of childhood phobic disorders: A randomized clinical trial. *Journal of Consulting and Clinical Psychology, 67,* 675–687.

Silverman, W. K., Pina, A. A., & Viswesvaran, C., (2008). Evidence-based psychosocial treatments for phobic and anxiety disorders in children and adolescents. *Journal of Clinical Child and Adolescent Psychology, 37,* 105–130.

Siqueland, L., Kendall, P. C., & Steinberg, L. (1996). Anxiety in children: Perceived family environments and observed family interaction. *Journal of Clinical Child Psychology, 25,* 225–237.

Siqueland, L., Rynn, M., & Diamond, G. S. (2005). Cognitive behavioral and attachment based family therapy for anxious adolescents: Phase I and II studies. *Journal of Anxiety Disorders, 19,* 361–381.

Spence, S. M., Donovan, C., & Brechman-Toussaint, M. (1999). Social skills, social outcomes, and cognitive features of childhood social phobia. *Journal of Abnormal Psychology, 108,* 211–221.

Spence, S. H., Donovan, C., & Brechman-Toussaint, M. (2000). The treatment of childhood social phobia: The effectiveness of a social skills training-based, cognitive-behavioural intervention, with and without parental involvement. *Journal of Child Psychology and Psychiatry, 41,* 713–726.

Strauss, C. C., Lahey, B. B., Frick, P., Frame, C. L., & Hynd, G. W. (1988). Peer social status of children with anxiety disorders. *Journal of Consulting and Clinical Psychology, 56,* 137–141.

Strauss, C. C., Lease, C. A., Kazdin, A. E., Dulcan, M. K., & Last, C. G. (1989). Multimethod assessment of the social competence of children with anxiety disorders. *Journal of Clinical Child Psychology, 18,* 184–189.

Target, M., & Fonagy, P. (1994). Efficacy of psychoanalysis for children with emotional disorders. *Journal of the American Academy of Child and Adolescent Psychiatry, 33,* 361–371.

Thompson, R. A. (1994). Emotion regulation: A theme in search of definition. In N. A. Fox (Ed.), *The Development of Emotion Regulation: Biological and Behavioral Considerations.* Monographs of the Society for Research in Child Development, 59 (2–3, Serial No. 240), 25–52.

Thompson, R. A. (2001). Childhood anxiety disorders from the perspective of emotion regulation and attachment. In M. Vasey & M. Dadds (Eds.), *The Developmental Psychopathology of Anxiety* (pp. 160–182). New York, NY: Oxford University Press.

Vasey, M. W., Daleiden, E. L., Williams, L. L., & Brown, L. (1995). Biased attention in childhood anxiety disorders: A preliminary study. *Journal of Abnormal Child Psychology, 23,* 267–279.

Verduin, T. L., & Kendall, P. C. (2008). Peer perception and liking of children with anxiety disorders. *Journal of Abnormal Child Psychology, 36,* 459–469.

Vernberg, E. M., Abwender, D. A., Ewell, K. K., & Beery, S. H. (1992). Social anxiety and peer relationships in early adolescence: A prospective analysis. *Journal of Clinical Child Psychology, 21,* 189–196.

Warren, S. L., Huston, L., Egeland, B., & Sroufe, L. A. (1997). Child and adolescent anxiety disorders and early attachment. *Journal of the American Academy of Child and Adolescent Psychiatry, 30,* 637–644.

Whaley, S. E., Pinto, A., & Sigman, M. (1999). Characterizing interactions between anxious mothers and their children. *Journal of Consulting and Clinical Psychology, 67,* 826–836.

Wood, J. J., & Mcleod, B. D. (2008). *Child Anxiety Disorders: a Family-Based Treatment Manual for Practitioners.* New York: W. W. Norton & Company, Inc.

Wood, J. J., McLeod, B. D., Sigman, M., Hwang, W., & Chu, B. C. (2003). Parenting and childhood anxiety: Theory, empirical findings, and future directions. *Journal of Child Psychology and Psychiatry, 44,* 134–151.

Wood, J. J., Piacentini, J. C., Southam-Gerow, M., Chu, B. C., & Sigman, M. (2006). Family cognitive behavioral therapy for child anxiety disorders. *Journal of the American Academy of Child and Adolescent Psychiatry, 45,* 314–321.

Woody, S. R., & Ollendick, T. H. (2006). Technique factors in treating anxiety disorders. In L. Castonguay & L. E. Beutler (Eds.), *Principles of Therapeutic Change that Work* (pp. 167–186). New York: Oxford University Press.

WHO (1992). *International Classification of Diseases, 10th Revision.* Geneva: World Health Organization.

Younger, A., & Boyko, K. (1987). Aggression and withdrawal as social schemas underlying children's peer perceptions. *Child Development, 58,* 1094–1100.

7

Information Processing Biases

Peter Muris[1] and Andy Field[2]

[1]Maastricht University, The Netherlands
[2]University of Sussex, UK

During the past decades, various theorists have emphasized the role of cognition in emotional problems such as anxiety disorders (e.g., Beck, Emery, & Greenberg, 1985; Eysenck, 1992; Harvey, Watkins, Mansell, & Shafran, 2004; Williams, Watts, MacLeod, & Mathews, 1997). Most of these authors assume that the primary pathology of an anxiety disorder is in the cognitive apparatus where information about the internal and external world is screened, encoded, organized, stored, and retrieved in a biased and dysfunctional way. In essence, anxious individuals' cognitions are centered on two themes, namely enhanced perception of physical and psychological threat and an exaggerated sense of vulnerability (see Eysenck, 1992). Research has originally focused on the investigation of such aberrant cognitive processes in anxious adults, but in the past 10 years considerable progress has been made with the study of biased cognition in children and adolescents with anxiety disorders (Hadwin & Field, 2010).

Kendall's (1985) cognitive theory provides a good starting point for discussing biased cognitive processes within the context of childhood anxiety disorders. According to this theory, pathological manifestations of anxiety result from the chronic activation of schemas organized around themes of danger and vulnerability. These overactive schemas are assumed to focus processing resources repeatedly on threat-relevant information and manifest themselves in so-called cognitive biases. These biases pertain to cognitive processes that are distorted and erroneous, and therefore yield dysfunctional and maladaptive thoughts and behaviors.

Information processing models represent a fruitful way to conceptualize the biased cognitive processes that typify anxiety disorders (see Williams et al., 1997). Briefly, such models describe the sequence of steps through which information is processed and modified as it progresses through the cognitive system (Massaro & Cowan, 1993). For example, the well-known model of Crick and Dodge (1994) proposes several subsequent information processing stages ranging from encoding (i.e., selecting information for further processing) and interpretation (i.e., attaching meaning to the information that is decoded), to response search and selection (i.e., retrieving and

The Wiley-Blackwell Handbook of The Treatment of Childhood and Adolescent Anxiety, First Edition.
Edited by Cecilia A. Essau and Thomas H. Ollendick.
© 2013 John Wiley & Sons, Ltd. Published 2013 by John Wiley & Sons, Ltd.

choosing an appropriate response), and eventually enactment (i.e., the production of the selected response). One advantage of such a step-wise approach is that researchers can identify the cognitive biases that occur during each of the stages, thereby providing a comprehensive framework for understanding the effects of distorted cognition in psychopathological anxiety. Another amenity is that this type of model not only considers conscious cognitive processes that occur during the later stages of information processing, but also has an eye for more automatic and non-conscious processes that take place during earlier stages. This has also methodological implications: while conscious cognition is usually open to self-report, experimental performance-based measures are commonly employed for uncovering automatic, unconscious processes (Harvey et al., 2004; Williams et al., 1997).

In the present chapter, a review will be provided on information processing biases in childhood anxiety. First, evidence for the occurrence of cognitive biases in anxious children and adolescents will be summarized and evaluated. Then, current views on the origins of cognitive biases in anxious youths will be discussed. Finally, the chapter will close with the presentation of a conceptual model and a discussion of the role of cognitive biases in the pathogenesis of childhood anxiety disorders and their relevance for the treatment of this type of psychopathology.

Anxiety-Related Cognitive Biases in Children

This section discusses various anxiety-related cognitive biases, and also provides a comprehensive overview of the evidence that has accumulated over the past years on their occurrence in children and adolescents. Not all the available research will be discussed in detail. Rather a number of studies will be highlighted to give the reader a good impression of the variety of methods that have been employed to examine information processing biases in youths.

Attention bias

One example of a cognitive distortion is attention bias, which refers to anxious people's tendency to display hyperattention towards potentially threatening material (e.g., Mathews & MacLeod, 1985). This phenomenon takes place during the encoding stage, and as such is considered to have a distorting effect on further information processing (Harvey et al., 2004). There are a number of experimental procedures that can be employed to investigate this bias, and these have also been used in research with children.

The first procedure for demonstrating attention bias is the modified Stroop task. In this task, people are required to name the colour in which words are printed while ignoring the meaning of these words. A consistent finding in Stroop studies is that anxiety disordered or phobic participants are slower in their colour-naming of fear-relevant words relative to that of neutral words. This would be because phobics automatically direct their attention to the content of the threatening words and this interferes with their main task of colour-naming (e.g., Watts, McKenna, Sharrock, & Trezise, 1986). Several studies have demonstrated the Stroop effect in the context of childhood fear and anxiety. For example, Martin, Horder, and Jones (1992) employed the Stroop task to test spider-fearful and non-fearful children. The results of their study showed that spider-fearful children exhibited retarded colour-naming times when confronted with spider-related words (e.g., "creepy", "hairy"), but not when confronted with neutral words (e.g., "table", "cars"). Research has also yielded some evidence for the presence of attention bias as indexed by the modified Stroop task in clinically referred youths. That is, children and adolescents with generalized anxiety disorder (GAD) showed significantly slower colour-naming latencies in response to negative-laden emotional information (Taghavi, Dalgleish, Moradi, Neshat-Doost, & Yule, 2003), whereas youths with post-traumatic stress disorder (PTSD) show greater interference when colour naming trauma-related words (Moradi, Taghavi, Neshat-Doost, Yule, & Dalgleish, 1999). Admittedly, not all studies that relied on the Stroop task have documented the expected attention bias effect in children and adolescents (e.g., Kindt, Brosschot, & Everaerd, 1997; Morren, Kindt, Van den Hout, & Van Kasteren, 2003), which makes that this paradigm is currently not considered as the most stable method for documenting attention bias effects in anxious youths.

More consistent findings have been documented with the dot probe detection task. During this task, two competing stimuli (words or pictures) are briefly presented on a computer screen: one stimulus is threat-relevant, whereas the other is emotionally neutral. Following the disappearance of the stimuli, a small probe appears on the location previously occupied by one of the stimuli. The latency to identify this probe provides an index of the extent to which a child's attention was directed towards the stimulus that has just disappeared. Thus, faster latencies to detect a probe following threatening stimuli relative to neutral stimuli would indicate an attention bias towards threat, whereas the opposite pattern would reflect a tendency to direct attention away from the threat (see Vasey & MacLeod, 2001). A number of studies have used the dot probe paradigm for assessing attention bias in relation to fear and anxiety in youths. For example, Vasey, Daleiden, Williams, and Brown (1995) administered the dot probe detection task to a group of 9- to 14-year-old children with anxiety disorders and a group of age-matched non-anxious control children. The results of this study demonstrated that anxiety-disordered children, relative to controls, were faster to react to a probe if it was preceded by a threatening rather than a neutral word. This finding is in keeping with the hypothesis that anxious youths allocate significantly more processing resources towards threat-related material. Other studies have reported similar effects in non-clinical children and adolescents with high anxiety levels (e.g., Vasey, El-Hag, & Daleiden, 1996) and clinically referred youths diagnosed with GAD and PTSD (Dalgleish, Moradi, Taghavi, Neshat-Doost, & Yule, 2001; Taghavi, Neshat-Doost, Moradi, Yule, & Dalgleish, 1999).

A final method that has been employed to document anxiety-related attention bias is the visual search paradigm. The basic paradigm asks participants to make a decision about the presence or absence of a specific target amongst distractors. Typically the response time is assessed, which is generally seen as an index of search efficiency. In anxiety research, participants are confronted with visual search tasks during which (a) a threat target has to be detected among a set of non-threat distractors, or (b) a non-threat target has to be searched among a set of threat distractors (e.g., Öhman, Flykt, & Esteves, 2001). For the former, one would expect faster response times whereas in the latter case one would predict slower response times in anxious or fearful participants, as a result of their attention bias for threat. Few studies have employed the visual search paradigm in anxious children. One exception is a study by Perez-Olivas, Stevenson, and Hadwin (2008) who indeed obtained some evidence to suggest that higher levels of separation anxiety in children were associated with an increased efficiency to detect angry faces relative to happy and neutral faces. Yet, it should also be noted that other researchers have documented quite different results using this paradigm (e.g., Waters & Lipp, 2008).

Based on the available data, it can be concluded that there is at least some empirical evidence for an attention bias in anxious youths. This type of cognitive distortion is typically assessed with reaction time paradigms (i.e., dot probe, Stroop, and visual search), which seem to be less reliable and thus also less valid in children due to (unwanted) differences in processing capacity, motor development, comprehension of the task, and so on. So far, the dot probe task has produced the most consistent results, and so it seems most fruitful to rely on this method for further exploring the attention bias phenomenon in youths. Much work needs to be done: refinements of the dot probe task have made it possible to investigate whether anxiety-related attention effects are due to the faster direction of attention towards threat or a difficulty in shifting attention away from threat (e.g., Koster, Crombez, Verschuere, & De Houwer, 2004), and this issue should certainly be examined in anxious and fearful children.

Interpretation bias

Another type of cognitive distortion is interpretation bias, which refers to the tendency to disproportionately impose threat upon ambiguous situations. This bias typically occurs during the interpretation stage of information processing, and is likely to fuel fear and anxiety, thereby prompting the individual to engage in flight (avoidance) and sometimes even fight behavior (Harvey et al., 2004).

The interpretation bias of anxious youths has been successfully documented in various ways. Most studies have relied on an ambiguous vignette task during which children are exposed to short descriptions of everyday situations and are invited to tell the experimenter how these situations will proceed. For example, in an investigation by Barrett, Rapee, Dadds, and Ryan (1996), children with anxiety disorders, children with oppositional defiant disorder, and normal controls (all aged between 7 and 14 years) were presented with brief stories of ambiguous situations and asked about what would happen in each situation. Then, youths were given two possible neutral outcomes and two possible negative outcomes and asked which outcome was most likely to occur. Results showed that both anxious and oppositional children more frequently interpreted ambiguous situations as threatening than normal controls. Interestingly, anxious youths more often chose avoidant negative outcomes, whereas oppositional youths more frequently chose aggressive negative outcomes. A different experimental approach was employed by Hadwin, Frost, French, and Richards (1997) who measured general anxiety levels in 7- to 9-year-old children, and then confronted them with ambiguous homophones that either had a neutral or a threatening interpretation (e.g., dye versus die). The results showed that children with higher anxiety levels were more likely to provide threatening interpretations of the homophones. Altogether, these and other studies (e.g., Bögels & Zigterman, 2000; Chorpita, Albano, & Barlow, 1996; Dineen & Hadwin, 2004; Taghavi, Moradi, Neshat-Doost, Yule, & Dalgleish, 2000) have demonstrated that interpretation bias is a cognitive distortion that consistently occurs in high-anxious and anxiety disordered youths.

Further experimental work has shown that anxious children's biased interpretations may even occur after perceiving very minor threat cues. That is, several research groups have demonstrated that anxious children only require very little information before deciding that a situation is dangerous, a phenomenon that is known as reduced evidence for danger (RED) bias. For example, Muris, Merckelbach, and Damsma (2000) exposed 8- to 13-year-old children, high and low on social anxiety, to vignettes of social situations which were presented to them in a stepwise manner (i.e., sentence by sentence). After hearing each sentence, children were asked to predict whether the pertinent story was going to be scary or not. The results showed that high socially anxious children needed to hear fewer sentences before deciding that a story was going to be threatening (i.e., displayed lower thresholds for threat perception) than their low, socially anxious counterparts (see also Lu, Daleiden, & Lu, 2007; Muris, Rapee, Meesters, Schouten, & Geers, 2003a).

Research has finally demonstrated that not only information about the external world may guide anxious children in making threat interpretations. Muris, Mayer, and Bervoets (2010a) asked 9- to 13-year-old children to complete a computerized ambiguous situations test for assessing their perception of threat under two conditions. In the experimental condition, children were attached to an apparatus that allegedly recorded their heart beat, the sound of which was presented to them via headphones. In the control condition, children listened to the sound of an African djembe drum while completing the ambiguous situations test. It was found that children in the experimental condition generally provided higher threat ratings than children in the control condition, and this difference remained significant when controlling for relevant anxiety parameters such as anxiety sensitivity and panic symptoms. These results lend support to the idea that children partially rely on internal physical sensations when evaluating the dangerousness of ambiguous events, a phenomenon which seems to be more prominent in high anxious youth (see Muris, Merckelbach, & Van Spauwen, 2003a).

Memory bias

Memory bias refers to a tendency to selectively recall memories congruent with an emotional state. In anxiety this would imply recall of memories referring to personal threat and vulnerability events, which are likely to have a negative influence on the interpretation of ambiguous situations. Only a few studies have examined this cognitive bias in children and adolescents, and the supportive evidence is thus far unconvincing. In an investigation by Moradi, Taghavi, Neshat-Doost, Yule, and Dalgleish (2000), 9- to 17-year-old youths with PTSD and a group of non-clinical controls were asked to memorize sets of negative (e.g., horror), positive (e.g., pleasant), and neutral (animal) words (e.g., lizard). After a 90-second distraction task, participants were given a free recall task followed by a recognition test in which they had to detect words of the original sets from an extended list of 120 words. During free recall, PTSD and control youths did not differ with regard to the recall of negative words, but the control participants recalled significantly more neutral and positive words. Hence one might conclude that youths with PTSD showed an inclination for recalling relatively more negative words relative to positive and neutral words as compared with control youths. There were no significant group differences during the recognition test. As such, this study provides rather weak evidence for a memory bias in anxious children.

Other studies have generally failed to demonstrate a memory bias in anxious children and adolescents (Dalgleish, Taghavi, Neshat-Doost, Moradi, Canterbury, & Yule, 2003; Watts & Weems, 2000), but there is one investigation suggesting that the picture of memory bias in youth is complicated by dissociations in memory effects in different memory systems. In that study, Daleiden (1998) asked 11- to 14-year-olds either high and low on trait anxiety to remember negative, positive, and neutral words. Then children were tested by means of a word fragment completion task (e.g., H_TE_ as cue for the word HATED) to measure perceptual memory processing, and a semantic cue task (e.g., DISLIKED as cue for the word HATED) to index conceptual memory processing. Results indicated that high anxious youths recalled more negative words relative to neutral words than their low anxious counterparts on the conceptual memory task, but there were no group differences on the perceptual memory task. These findings seem to suggest that memory bias only occurs in tasks that require processing of the meaning of stimuli.

Clearly, more research is needed to learn more about the boundary conditions under which this type of bias occurs in anxious youths.

Covariation bias

In anxiety syndromes, formation of judgment may also be affected and erroneous. For example, anxious individuals may display a covariation bias, which is concerned with a tendency to overestimate the association between fear- or anxiety-related stimuli and negative outcomes (Tomarken, Mineka, & Cook, 1989). In an experiment by Muris, Huijding, Mayer, Den Breejen, and Makkelie (2007a) evidence was obtained for the existence of this type of bias in 8- to 16-year-old youths. Children had to play a computer game during which they were exposed to a series of pictures containing spiders (i.e., negative fear-relevant stimulus), guns (i.e., negative fear-irrelevant stimulus), and flowers (i.e., neutral control stimulus). Immediately after each picture, a smiley was generated by the computer signaling the outcome of that trial: a happy smile indicated that the child had won three pieces of candy, a sad smiley indicated that the child had lost three pieces of candy, whereas a neutral smiley had no positive or negative consequences. The pictures were shown in a random order, and the computer game was programmed in such a way that each picture type was equally often followed by a happy, sad, or neutral smiley. After the computer game, children were asked to provide estimates on the observed contingencies between the three picture types and various outcomes. Results indicated that children in general displayed an inclination to link the negative outcome to negatively valenced pictures (i.e., they believed that they had more often lost candy following pictures of spiders and guns). Most importantly, the findings also demonstrated that this covariation bias was modulated by fear. That is, spider fearful youths showed a stronger tendency to associate the spider pictures with a negative outcome (i.e., losing candy). Further research has demonstrated that fearful children not only display covariation bias when retrospectively estimating the co-occurrence between fear-relevant stimuli and negative outcomes (i.e., *a posteriori* bias), but also when they are asked to prospectively predict such contingencies (i.e., *a priori* bias; Muris et al., 2007a; Muris, Rassin, Mayer, et al., 2009b; Muris & Van der Heiden, 2006).

Confirmation bias

Another prominent example of an anxiety-related cognitive bias is the confirmation bias, which refers to the inclination to selectively search for information that confirms danger, while ignoring information that disconfirms threat (De Jong et al., 1997). People often have convictions that boil down to conditional assumptions of the type "If P, then Q", with a certain stimulus (P) being predictive of a particular outcome (Q), for example, "If a dog barks, then he will bite" (e.g., Hawton, Salkovskis, Kirk, & Clark, 1989). In order to logically check the correctness of such an assumption, one should not only verify the rule (by ascertaining whether P is always followed by Q) but also falsify it (by assessing whether non-Q is never preceded by P). However, fearful and anxious individuals tend to rely on information that confirms the dangerousness of the dreaded stimulus or situation, and mainly ignore information that disconfirms threat (Smeets, De Jong, & Mayer, 2000).

Evidence for confirmation bias in children predominantly comes from experimental research in which mild fear is experimentally installed by providing children with negative information about an unknown animal. After fear induction children are confronted with a modified version of the Wason selection task in order to assess their reliance on verification and falsification strategies. Results have consistently shown that children who have learned to fear a novel animal, less frequently employ a falsification strategy (Muris et al., 2009b; Remmerswaal, Muris, Mayer, & Smeets, 2010). Another index that has been used to assess confirmation bias in children is the Search for Additional Information Scale, which simply asks what extra (i.e., threatening or non-threatening) information children would like to hear about a novel stimulus. Various studies have indicated that fearful children search for more threatening information about a potentially dangerous animal than their non-fearful counterparts who typically prefer to hear non-threatening formation (Muris et al., 2009b; Muris, Huijding, Mayer, Van As, & Van Alem, 2011a). Although the experimental findings on this type of cognitive distortions are quite convincing, it is also clear that more research is required to demonstrate the existence of confirmation bias outside the laboratory, in children with real phobias and other anxiety disorders.

Taken together, this abridged overview makes clear that information processing in youths with anxiety problems is often erroneous and biased in various ways. That is, anxious children selectively attend to threat-related stimuli (i.e., attention bias), interpret ambiguous stimuli and situations in a threatening way (i.e., interpretation bias), overestimate the co-occurrence between threat-related stimuli and negative outcomes (i.e., covariation bias), and search for information that confirms threat (i.e., confirmation bias). In addition, anxious children may also display enhanced recall for memories involving personal threat and vulnerability experiences, although the empirical evidence for this type of bias is at present unconvincing.

Origins of Information Processing Biases

Empirical data show that various types of cognitive biases occur in anxious children and adolescents, and there is emerging evidence indicating that the first spurs of these distortions in information processing already occur in children as young as 4 years (Muris,

Remmerswaal, Huijding, & El-Haloush, 2011b). One of the key questions remains: where do these distortions originate from? Part of the answer lies in genetically-based vulnerability factors. For example, Eysenck (1992) assumes that individuals high on neuroticism, which is a personality factor with a clear-cut genetic basis (Eysenck, 1967), are particularly vulnerable to display biased information processing. There are indeed cross-sectional data showing that neuroticism is positively associated with cognitive biases, and part of the evidence comes from child studies on attention bias (e.g., Hadwin et al., 1997) and interpretation bias (e.g., Muris, Meesters, & Rompelberg, 2007b). Yet, prospective research proving the actual involvement of neuroticism in the development of cognitive biases (and in its wake anxiety pathology) is currently lacking in the literature.

Meanwhile, there is also one study directly examining the genetic effect on cognitive biases in children. In that research, Eley, Gregory, Lau et al. (2008) studied symptom levels of anxiety and depression as well as interpretations of ambiguous scenarios and words in 8-year-old monozygotic and dizygotic twin pairs. Results indicated that 24% (ambiguous scenarios) and 30% (ambiguous words) of the interpretation bias scores were attributable to heritability. Interestingly, interpretation bias scores were found to be more convincingly associated with depression than with anxiety. The authors provide a number of explanations for this unexpected result (e.g., an attenuated range of anxiety symptoms, the interpretation bias indexes in this study may have been more relevant to depression), but at least the data indicate that future studies should at least include measures of depression in an attempt to distinguish anxiety-related biases from mood-related distortions.

The work by Eley et al. (2008) also points out that children's environment plays a dominant role in the origins of cognitive biases. These authors conclude that the majority of the variance (i.e., around 70%) in cognitive bias measures can be attributed to non-shared environment factors, which are indicative for child-specific learning experiences. Direct evidence for this notion comes from innovative research showing that cognitive biases can be experimentally installed (see Mathews & MacLeod, 2005, for a review). For example, Mathews and Mackintosh (2000) described an experimental paradigm during which participants were exposed to verbal descriptions of ambiguous events and positive or negative resolutions to these events were either provided in the text or were actively generated by participants through a fragment completion task. In this way, the researchers successfully installed interpretation biases that persisted beyond the training trials, which also produced increased levels of state anxiety. A parallel stream of research has shown that attention bias can also be learned during a dot probe detection task by consistently presenting the probes after threat words (thereby actively directing the participants' attention towards the threat stimuli; MacLeod, Rutherford, Campbell, Ebsworthy, & Holker, 2002). The implications of this body of work are clear: attention and interpretation biases to threat can be learned by non-anxious individuals, and the acquisition of such biases is likely to increase anxiety. In the recent literature, a number of studies have appeared on the training of cognitive biases in children, and these are mainly concerned with the modification of interpretation bias. For example, Muris, Huijding, Mayer, and Hameetman (2008) developed the "space odyssey" paradigm, a computer game during which children make an imaginary journey to an unknown planet. Children were presented with brief scenarios describing unknown situations on the planet. They were required to choose between a negative or positive outcome and then received feedback on the correctness of their choices. For half of the children, the negative outcome was consistently reinforced as correct (i.e., negative modification group), whereas for the other half the choice of positive outcomes was reinforced (i.e., positive modification group). After the modification procedure, children entered the crucial test phase during which they were confronted with ambiguous vignettes describing everyday situations that could occur on the new planet (e.g., going to school). Results indicated that children in the negative modification condition displayed higher interpretation bias and anxiety scores as compared to children in the positive modification condition. In addition, some evidence was obtained showing that these effects were more pronounced in children who already exhibited high levels of anxiety symptoms. These and other results (Lester, Field, & Muris, 2011; Muris, Huijding, Mayer, Remmerswaal, & Vreden, 2009a) demonstrate that interpretation bias in children can be acquired by feedback received from the environment.

Recently, more ecologically valid research has been carried out on the role of environmental influences in the origins of cognitive distortions. Based on the observation that there seem to be clear links between the cognitive biases of parents and their offspring (e.g., Creswell, Shildrick, & Field, 2011), researchers have begun to explore whether biases can be transferred from parents to children via the negative information pathway (see Muris & Field, 2010). The basic idea behind these studies is that children may develop a fear-related cognitive bias for a novel stimulus after hearing threat-related information from their parents (see Muris, Van Zwol, Huijding, & Mayer, 2010b). For example, Muris et al. (2011b) provided parents with ambiguous information about an unknown Australian marsupial (i.e., a cuscus) and then asked parents to engage in a computerized search task together with their child to obtain more information about the animal. The results clearly showed that fearful parents showed a confirmation bias in relation to the animal. Most importantly, these parents also encouraged their offspring to search for threat-related information during the joint computer task, thereby installing a fear-related confirmation bias in the children as well, which in turn also produced higher levels of fear. Thus, evidence is beginning to emerge indicating that cognitive biases and subsequently fear and anxiety reactions can be acquired via specific learning experiences that take place within the family environment.

Genetic and environmental factors do not operate independently (e.g., Rutter, Moffitt, & Caspi, 2006). For example, above we have identified parenting environments as a learning factor, but exposure to these environments will be affected by genes (i.e., gene–environment correlations). There are three types of gene–environment correlations (rGE's): the parenting environment that a given parent provides depends on their genes (i.e., passive rGE); also a child's genes determine the environments to which they expose themselves (i.e., active rGE); and finally, a child's genes influence their behaviors which in turn influence how others (including parents) behave towards them (i.e., evocative rGE). One important implication is that the environments to which youths are exposed will depend in part on their genetic make-up: a child with a genetically based tendency to interpret ambiguity in a threatening way, for example, may act in ways that evoke threat interpretations of ambiguous situations from their parents, leading to a self-perpetuating cycle of learning. The future of research into how cognitive biases in children develop depends on further examining these interactions, but also on identifying ways in which a child's behavior influences the environment around them to facilitate the development of cognitive biases.

Conceptual Framework

What role do these cognitive biases play in the pathogenesis of anxiety problems in youths? In an attempt to address this question, a conceptual framework is formulated, which essentially combines Kendall's (1985) cognitive theory of childhood anxiety and the information processing perspective of Crick and Dodge (1994). The model also includes current notions of the origins of cognitive biases as described above (see Muris & Field, 2008). As can be seen in the bottom part of Figure 7.1, children are confronted with all kinds of situations that require an appropriate response. To achieve this goal, the stimuli that comprise each situation are quickly scanned and encoded, thereby attending to relevant cues while ignoring irrelevant stimuli. During the next stage of interpretation, the encoded stimuli are evaluated and meaning is attached to them. If the situation is interpreted as dangerous and threatening, the fear/anxiety emotion will be elicited, which manifests itself in various types of physiological (e.g., increased heart rate, sweating), subjective (e.g., negative and catastrophic thoughts), and behavioral (i.e., avoidance, escape) symptoms.

As noted earlier, genetics and environment produce overactive schemas involving vulnerability and danger in some children. When confronted with potential threat, novelty, or ambiguity, the maladaptive schemas strongly guide the child's processing of information and chronically focus resources on threat-relevant information. The

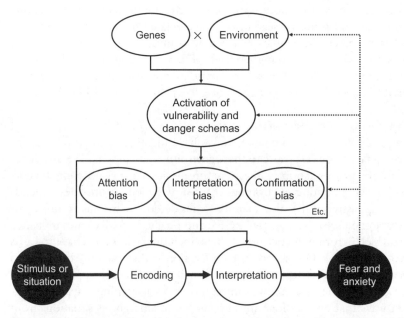

Figure 7.1 Conceptual model showing the origins of cognitive biases, and their impact on information processing and subsequent fear and anxiety in children.

enduring focus on threat manifests itself in various types of cognitive biases (attention bias, interpretation bias, memory bias, and so forth). For example, during the encoding stage, anxious children will shift their attention towards threatening stimuli (i.e., attention bias). Further, during the interpretation stage, they display enhanced memory for information about danger (i.e., memory bias) as well as a tendency to attach a threatening meaning to ambiguous stimuli (i.e., interpretation bias), which means that situations are readily evaluated as dangerous. Obviously, this biased information processing readily elicits feelings of fear and anxiety, which in turn enhances the occurrence of cognitive biases and may further strengthen the maladaptive vulnerability and danger schemas. In addition, it seems likely that anxious children will have an impact on their direct environment, and that this will prompt reinforcing reactions and feedback from parents, teachers, peers, and other persons, which in turn will further strengthen maladaptive schemas. Finally, anxious parents also display cognitive biases, which they are likely transfer to their offspring via modeling and negative information transmission. Altogether, it is likely that anxious children become trapped in a vicious circle of fear/anxiety and distorted information processing, and although it is still unclear to what extent cognitive biases play a causal role in the origins of anxiety problems in youths, it is plain to see their maintaining role.

Implications for Treatment

Assuming that information processing biases are involved in the maintenance of anxiety problems in children, it seems logical to assume that an undermining of such cognitive distortions results in marked reductions of fear and anxiety. Cognitive-behavioral therapy (CBT), which is currently viewed as the most effective and thus gold-standard intervention for children with phobias and anxiety disorders (In-Albon & Schneider, 2006), contains various elements that may help children to recognize cognitive biases and to combat them by means of exposure and cognitive restructuring (e.g., Barrett, 2001; Ollendick & King, 1998). There is evidence from intervention studies (Legerstee, Tulen, Dierckx, Treffers, Verhulst, & Utens, 2010; Waters, Wharton, Zimmer-Gembeck, & Craske, 2008) demonstrating that attention bias and interpretation bias are successfully reduced during CBT, although treatment outcome research examining whether change in biases acts as a formal mediator of such an intervention is currently lacking in the literature.

Interestingly, bias modification procedures can also be employed to correct cognitive biases, thereby reducing anxiety symptoms. For example, work in adults has demonstrated that a training designed to direct attention away from threat yields positive effects in patients with various types of anxiety disorders (e.g., Amir, Beard, Burns, & Bomyea, 2009; Amir, Weber, Beard, Bomyea, & Taylor, 2008). Recently, a number of studies have been conducted examining the effects of such an attention retraining procedure in anxious youths. Rozenman, Weersing, and Amir (2011) describe a case series of 16 10- to 17-year-old clinically referred youths with various types of anxiety disorders to evaluate a 4-week (12 sessions) attention modification program. Results indicated that youths in general experienced a significant decrease in anxiety symptoms, with 75% of them no longer fulfilling the diagnostic criteria of any anxiety disorder at post-treatment (see also Cowart & Ollendick, 2011). Comparable positive effects have been documented for an interpretation bias modification training in children with high levels of social anxiety (Vassilopoulos, Banerjee, & Prantzalou, 2009). Children who had received three sessions of the training were less likely to endorse threat interpretations of new ambiguous social situations, displayed lower levels of social anxiety, and less fear for an anticipated social encounter than children in the no-intervention control group. Altogether, these results indicate that direct modification of cognitive biases may be a promising approach of reducing anxiety in children.

Further, if it is indeed true that the family environment is important for the formation of cognitive biases in youths, it may also be important to reduce the vicarious and informational learning experiences that cause and maintain these biases. On the one hand, it may be sufficient to increase parents' awareness of these processes by means of psycho-education. On the other hand, if such modeling and information provision are strongly guided by parents' own anxiety-related cognitive biases, it may be fruitful to include parents in the CBT intervention as well. While the effects of the inclusion of parents in the treatment of children with anxiety disorders are mixed (Barmish & Kendall, 2005), no study has explicitly addressed the cognitive biases of parents, which might be a suitable target for an intervention.

As a final note, cognitive biases may also have value during the diagnostic assessment of children with anxiety problems. Some studies have obtained tentative evidence showing that cognitive biases have power to predict treatment outcome. For instance, a treatment outcome trial by Legerstee et al. (2010) has demonstrated that children who displayed a stronger tendency to attend toward severely threatening pictures required a more extensive CBT intervention to achieve treatment success. In addition, there are also indications that children who still display residual signs of cognitive biases after treatment may be more prone to develop new anxiety problems (Waters et al., 2008). Unfortunately, from a psychometric point of view, the measures employed to assess cognitive biases are certainly in need of improvement. This is particularly true for biases that occur during the encoding stage, such as attention bias, which are typically measured by means of reaction time paradigms (Broeren, Muris, Bouwmeester, Field, & Voerman, 2011). Only when reliable and valid assessment instruments are available, the chances will improve that clinicians adopt these constructs and measure them during their daily practice with anxiety disordered youths.

References

Amir, N., Beard, C., Burns, M., & Bomyea, J. (2009). Attention modification programs in individuals with generalized anxiety disorder. *Journal of Abnormal Psychology, 118,* 28–33.

Amir, N., Weber, G., Beard, C., Bomyea, J., & Taylor, C. T. (2008). The effect of a single-session attention modification program on the response to a public-speaking challenge in socially anxious individuals. *Journal of Abnormal Psychology, 117,* 860–868.

Barmish, A. J., & Kendall, P. C. (2005). Should parents be co-clients in cognitive-behavioral therapy for anxious youth? *Journal of Clinical Child and Adolescent Psychology, 34,* 569–581.

Barrett, P. M. (2001). Current issues in the treatment of childhood anxiety. In M. W. Vasey, & M. R. Dadds (Eds.), *The Developmental Psychopathology of Anxiety* (pp. 304–324). New York: Oxford University Press.

Barrett, P. M., Rapee, R. M., Dadds, M. R., & Ryan, S. M. (1996). Family enhancement of cognitive style in anxious and aggressive children. *Journal of Abnormal Child Psychology, 24,* 187–203.

Beck, A. T., Emery, G., & Greenberg, R. L. (1985). *Anxiety Disorders and Phobias: a Cognitive Perspective.* New York: Basic Books.

Bögels, S. M., & Zigterman, D. (2000). Dysfunctional cognitions in children with social phobia, separation anxiety disorder, and generalized anxiety disorder. *Journal of Abnormal Child Psychology, 28,* 205–211.

Broeren, S., Muris, P., Bouwmeester, S., Field, A. P., & Voerman, J. S. (2011). Processing biases for emotional faces in 4- to 12-year-old non-clinical children: An exploratory study of developmental patterns and relationships with social anxiety and behavioral inhibition. *Journal of Experimental Psychopathology, 2,* 454–474.

Chorpita, B. F., Albano, A. M., & Barlow, D. H. (1996). Cognitive processing in children: Relationship to anxiety and family influences. *Journal of Clinical Child Psychology, 25,* 170–176.

Cowart, M. J., & Ollendick, T. H. (2011). Attention training in socially anxious children: A multiple baseline design analysis. *Journal of Anxiety Disorders, 25,* 972–977.

Creswell, C., Shildrick, S., & Field, A. P. (2011). Interpretation of ambiguity in children: A prospective study of associations with anxiety and parental interpretations. *Journal of Child and Family Studies, 20,* 240–250.

Crick, N. R., & Dodge, K. A. (1994). A review and reformulation of social information-processing mechanisms in children's social adjustment. *Psychological Bulletin, 115,* 74–101.

Daleiden, E. L. (1998). Childhood anxiety and memory functioning: A comparison of systemic and processing accounts. *Journal of Experimental Child Psychology, 68,* 216–235.

Dalgleish, T., Moradi, A. R., Taghavi, M. R., Neshat-Doost, H., & Yule, W. (2001). An experimental investigation of hypervigilance for threat in children and adolescents with post-traumatic stress disorder. *Psychological Medicine, 31,* 541–547.

Dalgleish, T., Taghavi, M. R., Neshat-Doost, H., Moradi, A. R., Canterbury, R., & Yule, W. (2003). Patterns of processing bias for emotional information across clinical disorders: A comparison of attention, memory, and prospective cognition in children and adolescents with depression, generalized anxiety, and posttraumatic stress disorder. *Journal of Clinical Child and Adolescent Psychology, 32,* 10–21.

De Jong, P. J., Mayer, B., & Van den Hout, M. A. (1997). Conditional reasoning and phobic fear: Evidence for a fear-confirming reasoning pattern. *Behaviour Research and Therapy, 35,* 507–516.

Dineen, K. A., & Hadwin, J. A. (2004). Anxious and depressive symptoms and children's judgements of their own and others' interpretation of ambiguous social scenarios. *Journal of Anxiety Disorders, 18,* 499–513.

Eley, T. C., Gregory, A. M., Lau, J. Y. F., McGuffin, P., Napolitano, M., Rijsdijk, F. V., & Clark, D. M. (2008). In the face of uncertainty: A twin study of ambiguous information, anxiety, and depression in children. *Journal of Abnormal Child Psychology, 36,* 55–65.

Eysenck, H. J. (1967) *The Biological Basis of Personality.* Springfield, IL: Thomas.

Eysenck, M. W. (1992). *Anxiety: the Cognitive Perspective.* Hillsdale, NJ: Lawrence Erlbaum.

Hadwin, J. A., & Field, A. P. (2010). *Information Processing Biases and Anxiety. a Developmental Perspective.* Chichester: Wiley-Blackwell.

Hadwin, J., Frost, S., French, C. C., & Richards, A. (1997). Cognitive processing and trait anxiety in typically developing children: Evidence for interpretation bias. *Journal of Abnormal Psychology, 106,* 486–490.

Harvey, A., Watkins, E., Mansell, W., & Shafran, R. (2004). *Cognitive Behavioural Processes Across Psychological Disorders. A Transdiagnostic Approach to Research and Treatment.* Oxford: Oxford University Press.

Hawton, K., Salkovskis, P. M., Kirk, J., & Clark, D. M. (1989). *Cognitive Therapy for Psychiatric Problems.* Oxford: Oxford University Press.

In-Albon, T., & Schneider, S. (2006). Psychotherapy of childhood anxiety disorders: A meta-analysis. *Psychotherapy and Psychosomatics, 76,* 15–24.

Kendall, P. C. (1985). Toward a cognitive-behavioral model of child psychopathology and a critique of related interventions. *Journal of Abnormal Child Psychology, 13,* 357–372.

Kindt, M., Brosschot, J., & Everaerd, W. (1997). Cognitive processing bias of children in a real-life stress situation and a neutral situation. *Journal of Experimental Child Psychology, 64,* 79–97.

Koster, E., Crombez, G., Verschuere, B., & De Houwer, J. (2004). Selective attention to threat in the dot probe paradigm: Differentiating vigilance and difficulty to disengage. *Behaviour Research and Therapy, 42,* 1183–1192.

Legerstee, J. S., Tulen, J., Dierckx, B., Treffers, P., Verhulst, F. C., & Utens, E. (2010). CBT for childhood anxiety disorders: Differential changes in selective attention between treatment responders and non-responders. *Journal of Child Psychology and Psychiatry, 51,* 162–172.

Lester, K., Field, A. P., & Muris, P. (2011). Experimental modification of interpretation bias regarding social and animal fear in children. *Journal of Anxiety Disorders, 25,* 697–705.

Lu, W., Daleiden, E. L., & Lu, S. E. (2007). Threat perception bias and anxiety among Chinese school children and adolescents. *Journal of Clinical Child and Adolescent Psychology, 36,* 568–580.

MacLeod, C., Rutherford, E., Campbell, L., Ebsworthy, G., & Holker, L. (2002). Selective attention and emotional vulnerability: Assessing the causal basis of their association through the experimental manipulation of attentional bias. *Journal of Abnormal Psychology, 109,* 602–615.

Martin, M., Horder, P., & Jones, G. V. (1992). Integral bias in naming of phobia-related words. *Cognition and Emotion, 6,* 479–486.

Massaro, D. W., & Cowan, N. (1993). Information processing models: Microscopes of the mind. *Annual Review of Psychology, 44,* 382–425.

Mathews, A., & Mackintosh, B. (2000). Induced emotional interpretation bias and anxiety. *Journal of Abnormal Psychology, 109,* 602–615.

Mathews, A., & MacLeod, C. (1985). Selective processing of threat cues in anxiety states. *Behaviour Research and Therapy, 23,* 563–569.

Mathews, A., & MacLeod, C. (2005). Cognitive vulnerability to emotional disorders. *Annual Review of Clinical Psychology, 1,* 167–195.

Moradi, A. R., Taghavi, M. R., Neshat-Doost, H. T., Yule, W., & Dalgleish, T. (1999). Performance of children and adolescents with PTSD on the Stroop colour-naming task. *Psychological Medicine, 29,* 415–419.

Moradi, A. R., Taghavi, M. R., Neshat-Doost, H. T., Yule, W., & Dalgleish, T. (2000). Memory bias for emotional information in children and adolescents with posttraumatic stress disorder: A preliminary study. *Journal of Anxiety Disorders, 14,* 521–534

Morren, M., Kindt, M., Van den Hout, M. A., & Van Kasteren, H. (2003). Anxiety and the processing of threat in children: Further examination of the cognitive inhibition hypothesis. *Behaviour Change, 20,* 131–142.

Muris, P., & Field, A. (2008). Distorted cognition and pathological anxiety in children and adolescents. *Cognition and Emotion, 22,* 395–421.

Muris, P., & Field, A. P. (2010). The role of verbal threat information in the development of childhood fear. "Beware the Jabberwock!" *Clinical Child and Family Psychology Review, 13,* 129–150.

Muris, P., Huijding, J., Mayer, B., Den Breejen, E., & Makkelie, M. (2007). Spider fear and covariation bias in children and adolescents. *Behaviour Research and Therapy, 45,* 2604–2615.

Muris, P., Huijding, J., Mayer, B., & Hameetman, M. (2008). A space odyssey: Experimental manipulation of threat perception and anxiety-related interpretation bias in children. *Child Psychiatry and Human Development, 39,* 469–480.

Muris, P., Huijding, J., Mayer, B., Remmerswaal, D., & Vreden, S. (2009). Ground control to Major Tom: Experimental manipulation of anxiety-related interpretation bias by means of the "space odyssey" paradigm and effects on avoidance tendencies in children. *Journal of Anxiety Disorders, 23*, 333–340.

Muris, P., Huijding, J., Mayer, B., Van As, W., & Van Alem, S. (2011). Reduction of verbally learned fear in children: A comparison between positive information, imagery, and a control condition. *Journal of Behavior Therapy and Experimental Psychiatry, 42*, 139–144.

Muris, P., Mayer, B., & Bervoets, S. (2010). Listen to your heart beat and shiver! An experimental study of anxiety-related emotional reasoning in children. *Journal of Anxiety Disorders, 24*, 612–617.

Muris, P., Meesters, C., & Rompelberg, L. (2007). Attention control in middle childhood: Relations to psychopathological symptoms and threat perception distortions. *Behaviour Research and Therapy, 45*, 997–1010.

Muris, P., Merckelbach, H., & Damsma, E. (2000). Threat perception bias in nonreferred socially anxious children. *Journal of Clinical Child Psychology, 29*, 348–359.

Muris, P., Merckelbach, H., & Van Spauwen, I. (2003). The emotional reasoning heuristic in children. *Behaviour Research and Therapy, 41*, 261–272.

Muris, P., Rassin, E., Mayer, B., Smeets, G., Huijding, J., Remmerswaal, D., & Field, A. P. (2009). Effects of verbal information on fear-related reasoning biases in children. *Behaviour Research and Therapy, 47*, 206–214.

Muris, P., Rapee, R., Meesters, C., Schouten, E., & Geers, M. (2003). Threat perception abnormalities in children: the role of anxiety disorders symptoms, chronic anxiety, and state anxiety. *Journal of Anxiety Disorders, 17*, 271–287.

Muris, P., Remmerswaal, D., Huijding, J., & El-Haloush, N. (2011). Origins of anxiety-related reasoning biases in children. Paper presented at the 41st Annual Congress of the European Association for Behavioral and Cognitive Therapy. Reykjavik, Iceland.

Muris, P., & Van der Heiden, S. (2006). Anxiety, depression, and judgments about the probability of future negative and positive events in children. *Journal of Anxiety Disorders, 20*, 252–261.

Muris, P., Van Zwol, L., Huijding, J., & Mayer, B. (2010). Mom told me scary things about this animal! Parents installing fear beliefs in their children via the verbal information pathway. *Behaviour Research and Therapy, 48*, 341–346.

Öhman, A., Flykt, A., & Esteves, F. (2001). Emotion drives attention: Detecting the snake in the grass. *Journal of Experimental Psychology: General, 130*, 466–478.

Ollendick, T. H., & King, N. J. (1998). Empirically supported treatments for children with phobic and anxiety disorders: Current status. *Journal of Clinical Child Psychology, 27*, 156–167.

Perez-Olivas, G., Stevenson, J., & Hadwin, J. A. (2008). Do anxiety-related attentional biases mediate the link between maternal over-involvement and separation anxiety in children. *Cognition and Emotion, 22*, 509–521.

Remmerswaal, D., Muris, P., Mayer, B., & Smeets, G. (2010). "Will a Cuscus bite you, if he shows his teeth?" Inducing a fear-related confirmation bias in children by providing verbal threat information to their mothers. *Journal of Anxiety Disorders, 24*, 540–546.

Rozenman, M., Weersing, V. R., & Amir, N. (2011). A case series of attention modification in clinically anxious youths. *Behaviour Research and Therapy, 49*, 324–330.

Rutter, M., Moffitt, T. E., & Caspi, A. (2006). Gene-environment interplay and psychopathology: multiple varieties but real effects. *Journal of Child Psychology and Psychiatry, 47*, 226–261.

Smeets, G., De Jong, P. J., & Mayer, B. (2000). "If you suffer from a headache, then you have a brain tumour": Domain-specific reasoning 'bias' and hypochondriasis. *Behaviour Research and Therapy, 38*, 763–776.

Taghavi, M. R., Dalgleish, T., Moradi, A. R., Neshat-Doost, H. T., & Yule, W. (2003). Selective processing of negative emotional information in children and adolescents with generalized anxiety disorder. *British Journal of Clinical Psychology, 42,* 221–230.

Taghavi, M. R., Moradi, A. R., Neshat-Doost, H. T., Yule, W., & Dalgleish, T. (2000). Interpretation of ambiguous emotional information in clinically anxious children and adolescents. *Cognition and Emotion, 14,* 809–822.

Taghavi, M. R., Neshat-Doost, H. T., Moradi, A. R., Yule, W., & Dalgleish, T. (1999). Biases in visual attention in children and adolescents with clinical anxiety and mixed anxiety-depression. *Journal of Abnormal Child Psychology, 27,* 215–223.

Tomarken, A. J., Mineka, S., & Cook, M. (1989). Fear-relevant selective associations and covariation bias. *Journal of Abnormal Psychology, 98,* 381–394.

Vasey, M. W., Daleiden, E. L., Williams, L. L., & Brown, L. M. (1995). Biased attention in childhood anxiety disorders: A Preliminary-Study. *Journal of Abnormal Child Psychology, 23,* 267–279.

Vasey, M. W., El-Hag, N., & Daleiden, E. L. (1996). Anxiety and the processing of emotionally threatening stimuli: Distinctive patterns of selective attention among high- and low-test-anxious children. *Child Development, 67,* 1173–1185.

Vasey, M. W., & MacLeod, C. (2001). Information-processing factors in childhood anxiety: a review and developmental perspective. In M. W. Vasey, & M. R. Dadds (Eds.) *The Developmental Psychopathology of Anxiety* (pp. 253–277). New York: Oxford University Press.

Vassilopoulos, S. P., Banerjee, R., & Prantzalou, C. (2009). Experimental manipulation of interpretation bias in socially anxious children: Changes in interpretation, anticipated interpersonal anxiety, and social anxiety symptoms. *Behaviour Research and Therapy, 47,* 1085–1089.

Waters, A. M., & Lipp, O. V. (2008). Visual search for emotional faces in children. *Cognition and Emotion, 22,* 1306–1326.

Waters, A. M., Wharton, T. A., Zimmer-Gembeck, M. J., & Craske, M. (2008). Threat-based cognitive biases in anxious children: Comparison with non-anxious children before and after cognitive behavioural treatment. *Behaviour Research and Therapy, 46,* 358–374.

Watts, F. N., McKenna, F. P., Sharrock, R., & Trezise, L. (1986). Colour naming of phobia-related words. *British Journal of Psychology, 77,* 97–108.

Watts, S. E., & Weems, C. F. (2006). Associations among selective attention, memory bias, cognitive errors and symptoms of anxiety in youth. *Journal of Abnormal Child Psychology, 34,* 841–852.

Williams, J. M. G., Watts, F. N., MacLeod, C., & Mathews, A. (1997). *Cognitive psychology and emotional disorders.* New York: Wiley.

8

Cultural Factors and Anxiety in Children and Adolescents: Implications for Treatment

Cecilia A. Essau[1], Xenia Anastassiou-Hadjicharalambous[2], Constantina Demetriou[1], and Katere Pourseied[1]

[1]University of Roehampton, UK
[2]University of Nicosia, Cyprus

Most of our knowledge about anxiety in children and adolescents has come from studies conducted in Western countries (Muris, Merckelbach, Mayer et al., 1998). Findings of these studies have enhanced our understanding on the prevalence (Essau, Conradt, & Petermann, 2000; Lewinsohn, Gottlib, Lewinsohn, Seeley, & Allen, 1998; McGee, Feehan, Williams, Partridge, Silva, & Kelly, 1990), course (Wittchen & Essau, 1993), risk factors (Essau, Conradt, & Petermann, 2002; Ginsburg, La Greca, & Silverman, 1998), and treatment of anxiety in children and adolescents (Seligman & Ollendick, 2011). However, little is known about the extent to which these findings can be generalized to those who live in other cultures.

Although "culture" is a widely used term, its definition is still controversial. As early as 1952, Kroeber and Kluckhohn (1952) listed 160 definitions of culture found in anthropological literature. This is not surprising because culture is an abstract term covering various types of phenomena, and preferences regarding its definition are related to the investigator's theoretical orientation (Kroeber & Kluckhohn, 1952). We favor the definition of culture offered by Berry (1976), who defined the term as a "learned and shared pattern of behavior which is characteristic of a group living within fairly definite boundaries ... interacting socially among themselves" (p. 9). Culture may be explicit as shown by observable behavior or by the use of valued objects, and implicit as manifested through values, beliefs, and attitudes (Berry, 1976). Thus, individuals can be grouped into different cultures on the basis of shared norms (e.g., collectivistic or individualistic orientations), beliefs, and socialization practice (Varela & Hensley-Maloney, 2009). The term "cross-culture" refers to the systematic comparison of two or more cultures, explicitly or implicitly.

The Wiley-Blackwell Handbook of The Treatment of Childhood and Adolescent Anxiety, First Edition.
Edited by Cecilia A. Essau and Thomas H. Ollendick.
© 2013 John Wiley & Sons, Ltd. Published 2013 by John Wiley & Sons, Ltd.

The most prominent dichotomy in cross-cultural research is the individualism-collectivism distinction (Hofmann, Asnaani, & Hinton, 2010; Hofstede, 1980). This dichotomy is related to the individual's position in the society and their relation to its members. The person may feel an integral part of the world, of nature, of the family or the group, or as independent and as separate from the world and other people or even in conflict with them. In individualistic culture, high emphasis is placed on the individual self. An important goal in child-rearing is the promotion of independence, freedom, self-development, and autonomy (Trommsdorff & Essau, 1999). Social behavior is largely regulated by personal goals, likes and dislikes. Conflicts and confrontation within the group are acceptable and are seen as desirable because they "clear the air". By contrast, in collectivistic culture, high value is placed on conformity, submissiveness, and group orientation. Social behavior is largely determined by group norms; should a conflict between personal and group goals arise, it is socially desirable to give priority to the group goal over the personal goal for the sake of preserving group integrity and harmonious relationship among group members (Triandis, 1990). Harmony and face-saving are important attributes among individuals in collectivistic culture. The aim of socialization is the maintenance of harmony and cooperation (Triandis, 1995).

Another concept that is commonly used in cross-cultural research is self-construal, which refers to an individual's sense of self in relation to others. Markus and Kitayama (1991) differentiated between independent and interdependent self-construals. Independent self-construal is characterized by an autonomous sense of self that is separate from social context. Self-promotion, assertiveness, and uniqueness are highly valued. Interdependent self-construal is characterized by an emphasis on the inter-relatedness of the individual to others and to the social context. The self is seen as being intertwined with the social context, and that maintaining group harmony and fitting in are highly valued. It has been argued that an individual's dominant self-construal is determined by the cultural contexts of individualism and collectivism (Markus & Kitayama, 1991). Specifically, because individuals from collectivistic cultures are more likely to have been influenced by group-oriented cultural values, they tend to have a more interdependent self-construal; individuals from individualistic cultures are more likely to have been influenced by individual-focused cultural values, and as such they tend to have a more independent self-construal.

In this chapter, we examine the prevalence and expression of anxiety in children and adolescents in various cultures. On the basis of several studies, we suggest that cultural values and beliefs may occasion events which in turn may place the children at risk for or protect them against anxiety (Varela & Hensley-Maloney, 2009). Thus, it is important to examine how culture impacts anxiety for numerous reasons. First, cross-cultural studies could enable us to examine the universality of anxiety and the factors which elicit it. Second, they could help to examine cultural differences in help-seeking behavior among children and adolescents with anxiety. Third, they may help to explore the meaning and significance of anxiety symptoms, which according to Hinton, Park, Hsia et al. (2009) could produce certain culture-determined explanatory models; and, this in turn could influence the presentation, chronicity, and treatment of anxiety disorders. Fourth, cross-cultural research could help to determine the generalizability of theories on the development and maintenance of anxiety that have been developed in Western (individualistic) culture to other cultures. Fifth, cross-cultural studies will help to deter possible mismatches between the DSM criteria and the local phenomenology of anxiety disorders in specific cultures (Lewis-Fernandez, Hinton, Laria et al., 2010). Among adults, these mismatches are related to the definition of social anxiety and social reference groups in separation anxiety disorder, and the priority given to "difficult-to-control worry" in generalized anxiety disorder. In panic disorder, it is related to "unexpectedness" and the 10-minute crescendo criteria for associated panic attacks. Finally, knowledge of anxiety from different cultural backgrounds may enhance our broad understanding of anxiety in children and adolescents, which could provide useful information for the development of culturally sensitive treatment protocols for anxiety disorders in these different cultures.

Thus, culture is important in all aspects of anxiety research – from the design and translation of instruments, to the conceptual models that guide the research, to the interaction between researcher and research participants, to the definition and interpretation of anxiety symptom, and to the environment that surrounds a child's anxiety problems. Failure to take culture into account in the identification and treatment of anxiety disorders could potentially put children and adolescents and their families at jeopardy for misdiagnosis and inadequate treatment.

In terms of delivering care that is culturally sensitive, it is important to have a method that takes culture into account when doing a clinical assessment. One such method is the Cultural Formulation (CF) model (Lewis-Fernandez & Diaz, 2002). The model comprises:

(a) Individual's cultural identity (e.g., ethic or cultural reference group, language)
(b) Explanation of illness (e.g., perceived causes of illness, perceived severity of the symptoms, need for social support, idiom of distress through which symptoms are communicated)
(c) Psychosocial environment and level of functioning (e.g., social support, level of functioning and disability, interpretation of social stressors, role of religion and social networks in providing support), and
(d) Relationship between individual and clinician (e.g., difference in cultural and social status) which may cause difference in diagnosis and treatment.

Cross-Cultural Studies in Childhood Anxiety

Frequency

Despite the importance of understanding anxiety from a cross-cultural perspective, only a handful of studies (e.g., Dong, Yang, & Ollendick, 1994) have examined the frequency of anxiety symptoms in different cultures. In this section, we examine studies that compared the prevalence of anxiety among children and adolescents from various cultural backgrounds.

Studies based on the Revised Fear Survey Schedule
Most of the studies, conducted in the 1980s and early 1990s and based on the Revised Fear Survey Schedule (FSSC-R; Ollendick & King, 1991), have reported differences in the frequency and types of fears and anxiety reported by children and

adolescents in different cultures. For example, Nigerian children have been reported to show higher levels of fear than Chinese children, who in turn reported higher levels of fear than Australian and American children (Ollendick, Yang, King, Dong, & Akande, 1996). Furthermore, while some fears were common in all countries, some were specific to each culture; for example, a fear of looking foolish is most common in America, while a fear of snakes is common in Africa, and a fear of ghosts in China. Ollendick and colleagues (1996) argued that cultural differences and exposure to specific fear-provoking stimuli resulted in these differences in the content of fears across countries.

Among Turkish children, fears related to death and separation, and religious fears were very common (Erol & Sahin, 1995). It has been suggested that in order to achieve control and discipline over their children's behavior, parents often utilize the threat of religious punishment. In a study by Dong et al. (1994), social-evaluative fears were reported to be significantly higher among Chinese adolescents than adolescents in Western countries. This finding was explained in terms of Chinese child rearing practices which are generally restrictive, overly protective, and place considerable emphasis on other peoples' opinions, as well as in terms of Chinese educational practices.

In a study by Ginsburg and Silverman (1996), Latino parents reported their children as being more worried than did Caucasian parents. Specifically, Latino children had higher scores on fears of the unknown and danger and death. Varela and colleagues (Varela, Vernberg, Sanchez-Sosa, Riveros, Mitchell, & Mashunkashey, 2004; Varela, Sanchez-Sosa, Biggs, & Luis, 2008) conducted a series of studies comparing the prevalence of fear and anxiety among Latino and Caucasian children. Their results showed Latino to report more general worry symptoms compared to Caucasian children. Mothers of Mexican and Latino children (Varela et al., 2008) also reported more fears of the unknown and fears of danger and death for their children, compared to European American mothers reported for their children.

Studies based on the Spence Children's Anxiety Scale (SCAS; Spence, 1998)

Given the wide use of the DSM classification system, there has been a strong interest in using the Spence Children's Anxiety Scale (SCAS; Spence, 1998) to measure anxiety symptoms in children and adolescents in various countries around the world. The first cross-cultural study to have used SCAS was conducted by Muris and colleagues (2002) in which anxiety level of children in South Africa was compared to children in the Netherlands. South African children were found to have significantly higher levels of anxiety symptoms compared to Dutch children. This high level of anxiety symptoms was interpreted in terms of the child rearing practices in these two countries and to the stressful environment in South Africa after the apartheid regime. A study by Essau, Sakano, Ishikawa, and Sasagawa (2004) compared the frequency of anxiety symptoms among children in Germany and Japan. Japanese children were hypothesized to report higher numbers of anxiety symptoms because of Japanese child rearing practices which foster self-discipline, politeness, attentiveness to others, and a strong sense of personal and group identity (Weisz, Rothbaum, & Blackburn, 1984). In contrast to their expectation, Japanese compared to German children did not report significantly higher levels of anxiety. In fact, the overall levels of anxiety symptoms were equivalent across the two cultures.

A recent study by Essau and her colleagues (2011b) showed that adolescents in England reported significantly higher levels of anxiety symptoms than adolescents in Japan. The reason for this finding was unclear, although it seemed to be in line with previous surveys that showed higher prevalence of mental health problems among young people in England (Meltzer, Gatward, Goodman, & Ford, 2000). Furthermore, British parents reported less marital satisfaction and reported being a parent as more stressful than parents in Belgium, Denmark, and Sweden (Nekkebroeck, Barnes, Bonduelle et al., 2010). This, in turn, could have affected family life.

Essau, Sasagawa, Anastassiou-Hadjicharalambous et al. (2011c) recently compared the frequency of anxiety symptoms among adolescents in five European countries (i.e., Cyprus, Sweden, Italy, UK and Germany). Results showed that adolescents in the UK reported significantly more anxiety symptoms than adolescents in the other four European countries, with the lowest SCAS scores found in Germany. Adolescents in Cyprus were second highest in the self-report of anxiety symptoms, after the UK. Interestingly, OCD symptoms in Cyprus were significantly higher relative to all other countries. The higher level of OCD symptoms in Cypriot children was explained in terms of the use of over-controlling parental child-rearing practices found in this country (Yoshida, Taga, Matsumoto, & Fukui, 2005) and excessive fear of contamination, intertwined with individual characteristics (e.g., perfectionism; Moretz & McKay, 2009) and religious culture (Yoshida et al., 2005). For instance, previous studies have provided evidence for an association between religiosity and OCD even across monotheistic religions (Yorulmaz, Gençöz, & Woody, 2009). Further, OCD symptoms have been reported to be more prevalent in clinical populations from countries in which religion is at the core of society such as is the case in Cyprus (De Bilbao & Giannakopoulos, 2005). This finding was similar to our recent study (Essau, Anastassiou-Hadjicharalambous, & Muñoz, 2011a), which showed high levels of OCD symptoms among Cypriot children and adolescents. In addition to the above speculations, it could be that the items of the Greek translation of SCAS that tap OCD might have been viewed by the Greek Cypriot children as more socially acceptable relative to the items that tap the other scales. Evidence in favor of this possibility was provided by a study that involved a Greek sample in Greece (Mellon & Moutavelis, 2007). In this investigation (Mellon & Moutavelis, 2007) reported compulsive behavior in Greek children was also high, suggesting that Greek Cypriots raised in Cyprus and Greeks raised in Greece seem to share similar culture characteristics.

Another study by Essau, Leung, Conradt, Cheng, and Wong (2008) compared the frequency and correlates (i.e., learning experience) of anxiety symptoms among adolescents in Hong Kong and their counterparts in Germany. Results showed that adolescents in Hong Kong reported significantly higher levels of anxiety symptoms than adolescents in Germany. Anxiety symptoms showed different correlates in different cultures. Specifically, academic motivational goals to compete to get good grades and to be awarded for their performance correlated significantly with anxiety symptoms in Hong Kong. Another interesting finding was a significant correlation between anxiety symptoms and learning experience (i.e., instrumental, vicarious, and informational) among German adolescents. Interestingly, none of these findings were obtained in adolescents in Hong Kong. These findings were explained in terms of differences in socialization practices in dealing with anxious behavior, and in relation to the way in which family members interact in different cultures. Instead, anxiety in

Chinese adolescents is more related to high standards set for academic performance – an area much emphasized by Chinese parents. Indeed previous studies (Chao, 2001) have shown that Chinese parents, compared to parents in Western cultures, generally place more emphasis on educational achievement and set higher standards for their children; therefore, their controlling behavior is meant to push their children to reach educational success.

Studies based on the Screen for Child Anxiety Related Emotional Disorders

Muris and colleagues (2006) used the Screen for Child Anxiety Related Emotional Disorders (SCARED; Birmaher, Khetarpal, Brent et al., 1997) to compare anxiety levels among colored and black South African youths; the association of anxiety disorders symptoms and perceived parental rearing behavior was also examined. Colored and black South African children and adolescents reported significantly higher anxiety levels than White youths. The authors argued that following the apartheid regime, colored and black youths were still living in an environment characterized by deprivation, violence, and poverty. Similar to findings reported in studies conducted in Western countries (e.g., Grüner, Muris, & Merckelbach, 1999), perceived parental rearing behavior (i.e., anxious rearing, overprotection, and rejection) correlated significantly with anxiety symptoms.

In a recent study by Crocetti and colleagues (2009), adolescents in Italy reported significantly higher levels of anxiety symptoms than adolescents in the Netherlands. Differences between Italian and Dutch scores were large, with the largest difference found on generalized anxiety scores, followed by school anxiety scores. The authors interpreted Italian adolescent's higher anxiety scores as being in line with results of the Health Behavior in School-aged Children study (HBSC) of the World Health Organization (Currie, Nic Gabhainn, Godeau et al., 2008). Specifically, Dutch adolescents reported better communication with their mothers and fathers, a higher number of close friends, from whom they received higher support in dealing with school issues, and also less school pressure than Italian adolescents (Currie et al., 2008). Italian adolescents have also been found to exhibit a more unstable identity development than their Dutch peers, suggesting that Italian adolescents feel less confident about their lives and their future goals (Crocetti, Rubini, & Meeus, 2008).

Assessment

Assessment represents a fundamental step in understanding anxiety disorders in children and adolescents. Goals of assessment include diagnosis and prognosis, treatment planning, and treatment monitoring and evaluation (Essau & Ollendick, 2009). In clinical practice, assessment precedes treatment but is also an ongoing, fluid, and dynamic process. The success of the intervention often depends on the information obtained during the initial assessment process and the dynamic interplay between ongoing assessments throughout treatment (Essau & Ollendick, 2009). The assessment of anxiety has mostly been conducted using the same instruments that are developed and widely used in Western countries. While this approach enables the comparison of anxiety across cultural groups, there is a danger of making fallacious conclusions because of the potential for non-equivalence in assessment (Varela

& Hensley-Maloney, 2009). Another area of concern is related to the emic-etic distinction.

Equivalence. If comparisons are to be legitimately made across cultures, equivalent bases upon which to make such comparisons should be established (Lonner, 1979). Measurement equivalence has been defined as accurate assessment of a construct in diverse populations with the same instrument. There are four kinds of equivalence: (1) functional equivalence refers to the relationship between specific observations and the inferences made from these observations (Berry, 1976); (2) conceptual equivalence refers to the meanings individuals attach to specific stimuli or concepts (Lonner, 1979); (3) metric equivalence is related to establishing equivalent scores obtained with an instrument in one culture to those obtained in another culture; and (4) linguistic equivalence is related to the language used, and hence to translation.

The key to establishing linguistic equivalence includes the use of the bilingual approach, the committee approach, pretesting and back-translation techniques (Brislin, 1970). (1) In the bilingual approach, bilinguals complete both language versions of an instrument so that the discrepancies and non-equivalent meanings can be identified. (2) The committee approach involves having a committee of bilingual consultants evaluate the translated questionnaire. This approach, however, does not control for shared misconceptions and the fact that some consultants are hesitant to criticize the suggestions of other consultants. (3) In the pretesting technique, the investigators randomly select items from the translated instrument and ask probing questions about each of these items. This approach tends to be expensive when several language translations are used. (4) Back-translation technique (Brislin, 1970) is the most commonly used method for establishing linguistic equivalence. In this approach, an original version of the instrument is translated by a bilingual translator and then by another bilingual person who blindly translates it back into the original language. Both the original and back-translated versions of the instruments are then evaluated for equivalence to ensure that they are meaningful to target language monolinguals (Brislin, 1970). Differences in responses to the items of the original and back-translated versions of the instruments signal the need to examine the translated items.

Emic-etic distinction. The emic approach is "cultural specific" since it deals with the meanings and patterns of behavior within a single culture based on its own rules and values. The etic approach is "cross-cultural" because it focuses on behavior from a universal perspective by applying the same concepts and methods to different cultures. Some authors have suggested that both etic and emic items be included in the instruments used for cross-cultural research because investigators who use the etic approach may run the risk of using stereotypes of the dominant culture; other authors, however, do not consider the emic-etic distinction as important because the differences are often abstract and unclear (Jahoda, 1983).

One of the most commonly used approaches to provide evidence of measurement of equivalence is the confirmatory factor analysis (CFA) (Varela & Hensley-Maloney, 2009). In recent years, the Spence Children's Anxiety Scale (SCAS; Spence, 1998) and the Screen for Child Anxiety Related Emotional Disorders (SCARED; Birmaher et al., 1997) have been widely used in various countries, for which their factor structures have been analyzed using CFA.

Factor structures of the Spence Children's Anxiety Scale (SCAS)

The SCAS (Spence, 1998) taps anxiety symptoms that can be specifically linked to symptoms of DSM-IV anxiety disorders including generalized anxiety disorder, separation anxiety disorder, social phobia, panic disorder and agoraphobia, obsessive-compulsive disorder, and fears of physical injury. In the original studies (Spence, 1997, 1998), confirmatory factor analyses comparing four models (i.e., single-factor, six uncorrelated factors, six correlated factors, and six factors loading onto a single higher order factor) suggest that the six-factor, higher order model fits better than the other models. However, a subsequent study by Spence, Barrett, and Turner (2003), based on Australian adolescents, provided strong support for a six-correlated factor model which involved six factors related to generalized anxiety disorder, separation anxiety disorder, social phobia, panic disorder and agoraphobia, obsessive-compulsive disorder, and fears of physical injury. A recent study by Essau, Anastassiou-Hadjicharalambous, and Muñoz (2012a) among Cypriot children and adolescents gave further support to this model. The fit indices indicated that the same factor structure fit in Cyprus, and showed values in the same range as the original model. Although their finding was in accord of the original six-factor model, several items had low loadings.

With few exceptions (e.g., Essau, Sakano, Ishikawa, & Sasagawa, 2004; Muris, Merckelbach, Ollendick, King, & Bogie, 2002), most of the studies that explored the factor structure of the SCAS have been carried out in Western countries, with findings being inconsistent across studies. For example, among a Dutch sample (Muris et al., 2002), symptoms of generalized anxiety disorder and obsessive-compulsive disorder loaded on one and the same factor. Their findings also showed a four-factor structure which was different from any other country. These four factors were related to fears (i.e., fears of physical injury subscale and panic disorder and agoraphobia subscale, and a number of separation anxiety items), social phobia (i.e., the original five social phobia items and several general worry items), panic disorder (i.e., the physical symptom items from the original panic disorder and agoraphobia subscale), and worry and compulsion (i.e., items from the original generalized anxiety and separation anxiety subscales, and four items of the original obsessive-compulsive disorder subscale).

In a study by Essau and colleagues (2004), the factor structure of the SCAS was very similar when examined among adolescents in Germany and in Japan. In both countries, generalized anxiety and obsessive-compulsive disorder could not be extracted as a single factor. All items in the obsessive-compulsive disorder factor of the original SCAS (Spence, 1998) loaded onto a single factor. Separation anxiety disorder loaded onto two factors, with items in these two factors showing similar patterns in the two countries. In Germany, obsessive-compulsive disorder, generalized anxiety, and social phobia all loaded onto a single factor. In Japan, panic disorder was divided into two factors, and loaded on generalized anxiety and obsessive-compulsive disorder. These findings raise the question as to whether the SCAS is appropriate for measuring anxiety symptoms in non-Western countries.

This finding was replicated by Essau et al. (2008) when examining the psychometric properties of the Chinese SCAS among the 12- to 17-year-olds in Hong Kong. Further support for the five-factor model came from a study that used the Japanese SCAS (Ishikawa, Sato, & Sasagawa, 2009) in that the five-factor model with one higher order factor had a better fit for the Japanese data.

Factor structures of the Screen for Child Anxiety Related Emotional Disorders (SCARED)

The SCARED (Birmaher et al., 1997) is a self-report measure of anxiety symptoms for children and adolescents from 8 to 18 years old. Exploratory factor analysis of the SCARED revealed five factors, of which four measure anxiety disorder symptoms as conceptualized in the DSM-IV classification of anxiety disorders: panic/somatic, generalized anxiety, separation anxiety, and social phobia. The fifth subscale measures school phobia, which is a common type of childhood problem. Moreover, this finding has been replicated in numerous studies in different countries among children and adolescents in clinical and non-clinical settings. For example, in a study among adolescents in The Netherlands (Hale, Raaijmakers, Muris, & Meeus, 2005), the SCARED was found to have a five-factor structure, with each factor corresponding to the five anxiety disorders. This five-factor structure applied to various subgroups, such as males and females, early and middle adolescent groups, and for Dutch and ethnic minorities living in the Netherlands. A five-factor structure has similarly been reported among Italian adolescents from the general population (Crocetti, Hale, Fermani, Raaijmakers, & Meeus, 2009). The recent study by Essau and colleagues (2012b) among children and adolescents in Cyprus gave further support to the original five-factor model proposed by Birmaher et al. (1997, 1999). The fit indices indicated that the same factor structure fit adequately in Cyprus, and showed values in the same range as the original model.

Further support for a five-factor model resulted from a study that involved Chinese children and adolescents (Su, Wang, Fan, Su, & Gao, 2008). However, one of the items ("people tell me I look nervous") failed to load on any of the factors. This was explained in terms of the Chinese tendency to use indirect and indefinite comments. Another interesting finding was that only four somatic items loaded on the original somatic/panic factor. It was argued that somatic/panic symptoms in Chinese children may represent physical symptoms of several underlying anxiety factors such as generalized anxiety, separation anxiety, social phobia, and school phobia.

However, the five-factor solutions have not been replicated in all studies using the SCARED. For example, data from German adolescents (Essau et al., 2002) showed a six-factor model comprising generalized anxiety, school phobia, panic, social phobia, and two separation anxiety subscales. A study by Boyd, Ginsburg, Lambert, Cooley, and Campbell (2003) reported only a three-factor structure for African Americans, namely, somatic/panic, generalized anxiety, and social phobia. Separation anxiety and school phobia did not emerge as separate factors; this result was explained in terms of the composition of the samples. Because these adolescents had been recruited from a small parochial high school, they are presumed to come from a supportive and insular environment in comparison to those in inner-city high schools. The somatic/panic factor consisted of somatic/panic items and items related to worry and fears of being home alone and going to school. Wren, Berg, Heiden et al. (2007) found a four-factor solution similar to the original structure (Birmaher et al., 1997, 1999) except that school phobia did not emerge as a separate factor.

Culture-Bound Syndromes

DSM-IV provides a glossary of culture-bound syndromes that lists 25 recurring, culture-specific patterns of abnormal and distressing behavior (APA, 1994). The term culture-bound syndrome refers to a constellation of symptoms that are patterned and explainable through a cultural framework (Lewis-Fernandez, Guarnaccia, & Ruiz, 2009). Subsumed within the glossary of culture bound syndromes are local terms for describing distress that are referred to as idioms of distress. An idiom of distress refers to a broad range of expressions of negative feeling states that are commonly endorsed among members of a specific community.

One type of culture-bound syndrome and idioms of distress which have been reported in children and adolescents are Taijin Kyofusho and ataque de nervios, respectively.

Taikin-Kyuofu-Sho

Taijin Kyofusho is a culture-bound form of social phobia which is characterized by an intense fear that one's body parts or functions displease, embarrass, or are offensive to others (APA, 2000). The term taijin kyofusho literally means the disorder (sho) of fear (kyofu) of interpersonal relations (taijin) (Takahashi, 1989). It was first described by Masatake Morita in the 1920s as a manifestation of "shinkeishitsu", which was used to describe nervous character or temperament (Maeda & Nathan, 1999). Taijin Kyofusho is experienced when the individuals have a face-to-face contact with other people. Some common symptoms of taijin kyofusho include (a) fears of offending others by blushing, emitting offensive odors, staring inappropriately; (b) fears of offending others by presenting an improper facial expression, a blemish or physical defect; (c) strongly convinced of offending others; and (d) being obsessed with feeling of shame (Kirmayer, 1991; Maeda & Nathan, 1999). This fear of offending or bringing shame upon others often leads to social avoidance because it is believed that the individual's behavior will bring shame upon his or her social or familial group, or that he/she fears of disrupting group cohesiveness by making others uncomfortable.

Both taijin kyofusho and social phobia involve fear of negative evaluation from others and avoidance of social situations (Dinnel, Kleinknecht, & Tanaka-Matsumi, 2002). In DSM-IV-TR (APA, 2000), it is included under "Specific culture, age, and gender features" section of Social Phobia; in ICD-10 (WHO, 1992), taijin kyofusho is included under social phobia (anthropophobia). Taijin kyofusho symptoms tend to become the most exacerbated in social situations with acquaintances such as talking to colleagues, but less the case when interacting with strangers or intimate friends and family (Kirmayer, 1991; Maeda & Nathan, 1999). In social phobia, fear is related to being in social or performance situations in which the person is exposed to new or unfamiliar people, speaking to authorities, or to possible scrutiny by others. In taijin kyofusho, the symptoms are related to hypersensitivity to certain body parts, but not in social phobia. Specifically, individuals with taijin kyofusho fear that they will offend or embarrass others with their "inappropriate" behavior, which may thereby bring shame upon their social or familial group (Maeda & Nathan, 1999). Individuals with social phobia, fear that they will embarrass themselves (Kleinknecht, Dinnel, Kleinknecht, Hiruma, & Harada, 1997). These differences are explained from the scope of cultural background, child-rearing attitudes, norms of social interaction, and collectivistic values embedded in Asian families are believed to account for the high concern in others' thoughts and feelings (Kirmayer, Young, & Hayton, 1995). Nonetheless, there is little empirical evidence supporting such common views.

Essau and colleagues (2012b) compared the frequency of taijin kyofusho and its correlates among university students in England and in Japan. Results showed that young adults in Japan reported significantly higher levels of taijin kyofusho and social phobia symptoms than young adults in England. Family sociability had a consistent effect on both social phobia and taijin kyofusho symptoms across the two cultures, but parental rearing attitudes showed distinct patterns between the two countries. These researchers found no concrete evidence that taijin kyofusho has a distinct etiological background; rather, it seemed that taijin kyofusho may be a variant of social interaction anxiety. Parental rearing was found to have distinct effects on social phobia and taijin kyofusho symptoms in Japan and in the UK. Specifically, in the UK, parental care predicted fear of negative evaluation in performance situations, but failed to have an effect on anxiety in interaction situations and taijin kyofusho scores. On the other hand, parental overprotection predicted anxiety in interaction situations and taijin kyofusho scores, but not fear of negative evaluation in performance situations. These results can be interpreted that less parental care is associated with a harsher view of the world in terms of performance, whereas more parental overprotection leads to less experience and more fear of social interactions. In contrast, parental care had no effect on any of the scales in the Japanese data, but overprotection had an effect on all of the scales. Thus, the distinction between the different social anxiety situations was less evident in Japan. This may represent the fact that the Japanese participants were more sensitive to the observer's reaction in performance situations, thereby strengthening the interactional nature of the situation and diluting the distinction between performance and interaction situations. Within the Japanese culture, one needs to be sensitive and emphatic to the responses of others and to "read the atmosphere" in order for social performance to be successful, whereas in Western cultures, the emphasis is placed more on getting one's ideas across in a clear and effective way. The finding that parental overprotection was a main factor to increase fear in all of these situations suggests less exposure and possibly behavioral modeling plays an important role in the heightening of social anxiety regardless of situation.

Essau, Sasagawa, Ishikawa, Okajima, O'Callaghan, and Bray (in press) compared the frequency and correlates (i.e., social support and self-construal) of taijin kyofusho symptoms in Japanese adolescents and their parents. Their finding showed that adolescents reported significantly more taijin kyofusho symptoms than their parent/guardians. They suggested that the higher level of taijin kyofusho among adolescents could have been due to this developmental stage because social anxiety becomes more prevalent at or following puberty. As argued by some (e.g., Ollendick & Benoit, 2012; Ollendick & Hirshfeld-Becker, 2002), social anxiety might be part of normal development as children emerge into adolescence due to the increasing importance they place on how peers, friends, and adults perceive them and how they come across in their social interactions with them. Another suggestion was related to the amount of social support these participants received from their significant others. Indeed, this study also indicated that the adolescents, compared to their parents, received a significantly lower amount of social support than their parents. It is suggested that societal changes in the Japanese culture could have produced differences in social support across the same generation of a family, which may in turn influence the level of anxiety experienced. As argued by Takuma and Amau (1998), there have been significant changes in the social environment of the Japanese family; an example is the amendment of the Civil Law in 1948 which led to major social changes such as equalization of rights between the two genders. This in turn has influenced changes in the family environment of Japanese children, including an increasing number of women working outside the home and family members spending less time together. Along with these social changes, peer relationships among children and adolescents have also changed in recent years. Compared to their parents' generation, Japanese children and adolescents find it difficult to establish, maintain, and develop their relationships with their peers (Sato & Sato, 2006). Their findings also showed that in each generational sample, high taijin kyofusho symptoms were significantly associated with high levels of anxiety symptoms, with the strongest correlation with social phobia. The pattern of the relationship between self-construal and taijin kyofusho differed across the two generations. Among adolescents, independent self-construal was associated with lower taijin kyofusho whereas among parents, interdependent self-construal was associated with lower evaluative concerns from others.

Ataques de nervios

Ataque de nervios (literally "attack of nerves") is a cultural idiom of distress that is prominent among Latinos. A general feature of ataques de nervios is characterized by an intense episode of emotional distress, which is expressed through various symptoms that are similar to those of panic attack such as trembling, attacks of crying, numbness, difficulty breathing, screaming uncontrollably, and becoming verbally or physically aggressive. Although ataque de nervios has several symptoms that are similar to that of panic attacks, studies have shown that ataque de nervios and panic attack are phenomenologically distinct (Guarnaccia, Canino, Rubio-Stipec, & Bravo, 1993; Lewis-Fernandez et al., 2002).

Studies of ataque de nervios among children and adolescents are scant. Guarnaccia, Martinez, Ramirez, and Canino (2005) compared the prevalence of ataque de nervios and other disorders among 4–17 year olds in community and clinical settings in Puerto Rico. Their results showed that 9% and 26% of the children and adolescents in the community and clinical settings, respectively, were reported to have experienced an ataque de nervios. Older girls (11 years and older) had more than three times the rates of ataque de nervios than younger girls. Ataque de nervios was also associated with various types of mental disorder. Among community samples, ataque de nervios co-occurred frequently with dysthymia; among clinical samples, ataque de nervios most frequently comorbid with posttraumatic stress disorder and major depression. Lopez, Ramirez, Guarraccia, Canino, and Bird (2011) examined the association of ataque de nervios with somatic complaints among Puerto Rican children living in the South Bronx, New York, and in the San Juan metropolitan area in Puerto Rico. In both sites, children with ataque de nervios compared to those without ataque de nervios reported significantly more lifetime prevalence of asthma, headaches, stomach-aches, and a history of epilepsy or seizure. Although children in Puerto Rico had a worse somatic profile than those in New York, ataque de nervios was not related to a worse outcome in Puerto Rico. The pattern of association between ataque de nervios and physical complaints seemed to differ across context. That is, it was argued that ataque de nervios may be associated with more somatic concern among children in South Bronx because they were more exposed to stress and violence. In Puerto Rico, ataque de nervios was not related to an increase in physical distress because this condition is considered to be more culturally accepted (Lopez et al., 2011).

Conclusion and Future Directions

Studies comparing the frequency and correlates of anxiety in children and adolescents from different cultural backgrounds are scarce, despite suggestions of the need to consider the importance of cultural values in the development and maintenance of anxiety (Kitayama & Cohen, 2007; Kirmayer, Young, & Hayton, 1995; Varela & Hensley-Maloney, 2009). Based on our review, several limitations and recommendations for future research are offered.

First, in order to make a valid conclusion about cross-cultural comparison, normative patterns of anxiety among children and adolescents across cultures need to be established. Why children and adolescents in certain cultures (e.g., in England) have higher anxiety symptoms than those in other cultures is unclear. Possible lines of inquiry include examining the role of culture at a societal level, as well as the role of family interactions and the cognitive process in the expression of anxiety in children across cultures (Varela & Hensley-Maloney, 2009).

Second, the impact of high anxiety levels on psychosocial functioning among children and adolescents in different cultures is also unclear. Studies conducted in individualistic culture leave little room for debate on the impairing nature of excessive anxiety. Psychosocial impairments, such as underachievement and relationship difficulties (Beidel & Turner, 1998), were often found to be associated with excessive anxiety. However, a different picture was revealed in the Chinese culture. A study by Leung, Hung, Ho et al. (2008) showed that 77% of Chinese adolescents who, despite meeting symptom criteria of anxiety disorders, was not functioning in an impaired range. It was argued that consistent with the Confucian and Taoist philosophies, shy and inhibited behaviors are valued and encouraged in Chinese culture, and that shy-anxious children in China are regarded as socially competent and understanding (Chen, Rubin, & Li, 1995). It is unknown if Leung et al.'s (2008) finding on the lack of impact of excessive anxiety on psychosocial impairment could be replicated in other collectivistic cultures.

Third, all the self-report questionnaires that were used to compare anxiety symptoms among children and adolescents in different cultures were developed in Western countries. Beyond presenting internal consistency and factor structure, little attempt has been made to examine the equivalence of the constructs (anxiety, worry, fear) in different cultural groups. As argued by Varela and Hensley-Maloney (2009), in order for cross-cultural comparisons and generalizations of processes involved in the development of anxiety to be meaningful, it is paramount for the constructs to be equivalent across cultures. The use of simple translation–back translation processes in developing questionnaires for cross-cultural research has been criticized because it is considered not to be culturally sensitive (Van Widenfelt, Treffers, De Beurs, Siebelink, & Koudijs, 2005). To overcome common errors in assuming the equivalence of translated measures and the adequacy of the translation–back translation process for questionnaires to be used in different cultures, a complex translation method that combines various techniques should be used (Van Widenfelt et al., 2005). This includes the use of a team approach that involves the original author, a native translator, and piloting or pre-testing the questionnaire (Van Widenfelt et al., 2005). Another method is to explore the concept within the culture of interest using the emic approach by asking more open-ended questions in relation to the concept and issues that are relevant to it (Van Widenfelt et al., 2005).

Fourth, with very few exception (Guarnaccia et al., 2005), almost all studies that compared anxiety symptoms among children and adolescents in different cultures were conducted in community settings. The main advantage of using community samples is the ability to produce findings of greater generalizability than studies of clinical samples. Data from clinical settings are generally not representative of individuals with anxiety disorders because of the bias in service attendance through restrictions in evaluating, access, and selection processes in terms of help-seeking behavior, symptoms, and chronicity (Essau, Petermann, & Feehan, 1997). An additional problem with using clinical samples is that children's referrals to clinical settings may partly be related to parental characteristics (Shepherd, Oppenheim, & Mitchell, 1971). Samples from the community and clinical settings may differ in the risk factors, comorbidity, natural history, and response to treatment of their anxiety disorders (Dulcan, 1996). Therefore, to make further progress in this area, studies are needed to examine the extent to which cultural factors influence mechanisms of functioning among children and adolescents who suffer from anxiety disorders as well.

Finally, in order to provide evidence-based information for prevention and treatment effort, more studies are needed to examine factors which increase the children's risk to develop anxiety disorders. Such studies should use culturally sensitive approaches and include individual (e.g., temperament, cognitive functioning), interpersonal (e.g., family), and ecological factors (e.g., school system).

Overall, childhood anxiety – its development, expression, nature (frequency, comorbidity, course and outcome), and treatment – is an exciting area of research. However, much more needs to be done in helping us understand anxiety from a cross-cultural prospective. Still, we have learned much in recent years.

References

APA (1994). *Diagnostic and Statistical Manual of Mental Disorders*, 4th edn. Washington, DC: American Psychiatric Association.

APA (2000). *Diagnostic and Statistical Manual of Mental Disorders*, 4th edn. Washington, DC: American Psychiatric Association.

Beidel, D. C., & Turner, S. M. (1998). *Shy Children, Phobic Adults: Nature and Treatment of Social Phobia*. Washington, DC: American Psychological Association.

Berry, J. W. (1976). *Human Ecology and Cognitive Style: Comparative Studies in Cultural and Psychological Adaptation*. London: Sage.

Birmaher, B., Brent, D., Chiappetta, L., Bridge, J., Monga, S., & Baugher, M. (1999). Psychometric properties of the Screen for Child Anxiety Related Emotional Disorders (SCARED): A replication study. *Journal of the American Academy of Child and Adolescent Psychiatry*, *38*, 1230–1236.

Birmaher, B., Khetarpal, S., Brent, D., Cully, M., Balach, L., Kaufman, J., & McKenzie Neers, S. (1997). The Screen for Child Anxiety Related Emotional Disorders (SCARED): Scale construction and psychometric characteristics. *Journal of the American Academy of Child and Adolescent Psychiatry, 36,* 545–553.

Boyd, R. C., Ginsburg, G. S., Lambert, S. F., Cooley, M. R., & Campbell, K. D. (2003). Screen for Child Anxiety Related Emotional Disorders (SCARED): psychometric properties in an African-American parochial high school sample. *Journal of the American Academy of Child and Adolescent Psychiatry, 42,* 1188–1196.

Brislin, R. W. (1970). Back translation for cross-cultural research. *Journal of Cross Cultural Psychology, 1,* 185–216.

Chao, R. K. (2001). Extending research on the consequences of parenting style for Chinese Americans and European Americans. *Child Development, 72,* 1832–1843.

Chen, X., Rubin, K. H., & Li, Z. (1995). Social functioning and adjustment in Chinese children: A longitudinal study. *Developmental Psychology, 31,* 531–539.

Crocetti, E., Hale III, W. W., Fermani, A., Raaijmakers, Q., & Meeus, W. (2009). Psychometric properties of the Screen for Child Anxiety Related Emotional Disorders (SCARED) in the general Italian adolescent population: A validation and a comparison between Italy and the Netherlands. *Journal of Anxiety Disorders, 23,* 824–829.

Crocetti, E., Rubini, M., & Meeus, W. (2008). Capturing the dynamics of identity formation in various ethnic groups: Development and validation of a three-dimensional model. *Journal of Adolescence, 31,* 207–222.

Currie, C., Nic Gabhainn, S., Godeau, E., Roberts, C., Smith, R., Currie, D., et al. (Eds.) (2008) Inequalities in young people's health: HBSC international report from the 2005/06 Survey. Health Policy for Children and Adolescents, No. 5, WHO Regional Office for Europe, Copenhagen, Denmark. http://www.euro.who.int/en/what-we-do/health-topics/Life-stages/child-and-adolescent-health/publications2/2011/inequalities-in-young-peoples-health. -hbsc-international-report-from-the-20052006-survey

De Bilbao, F., & Giannakopoulos, P. (2005). Effect of religious culture on obsessive compulsive disorder symptomatology. *Revue médicale suisse, 1,* 2818–2821.

Dinnel, D. L, Kleinknecht, R. A., & Tanaka-Matsumi, J. (2002). A cross-cultural comparison of social phobia symptoms. *Journal of Psychopathology and Behavioral Assessment, 24,* 75–84.

Dong, Q., Yang, B., & Ollendick, T. H. (1994). Fears in Chinese children and adolescents and their relations to anxiety and depression. *Journal of Child Psychology and Psychiatry, 35,* 351–363.

Dulcan, M. K. (1996). Introduction: Epidemiology of child and adolescent mental disorders. *Journal of the American Academy of Child and Adolescent Psychiatry, 35,* 852–854.

Erol, N., & Sahin, N. (1995). Fears of children and the cultural context: the Turkish norms. *European Child & Adolescent Psychiatry, 4,* 85–93.

Essau, C. A., Anastassiou-Hadjicharalambous, X., & Muñoz, L. C. (2011a). Psychometric properties of the Spence Children's Anxiety Scale (SCAS) in Cypriot children and adolescents. *Child Psychiatry and Human Development, 42* (5), 557–568.

Essau, C. A., Anastassiou Hadjicharalambous, X., & Muñoz, L. C. (2012a). Psychometric properties of the Screen for Child Anxiety Related Emotional Disorders (SCARED) in Cypriot children and adolescents. *European Journal of Psychological Assessment, 1-9.* doi: 10.1027/1015-5759/a000116.

Essau, C. A., Conradt, J., & Petermann, F. (2000). Frequency, comorbidity, and psychosocial impairment of anxiety disorders in adolescents. *Journal of Anxiety Disorders, 14,* 263–279.

Essau, C. A., Conradt, J., & Petermann, F. (2002). Course and outcome of anxiety disorders in adolescents. *Journal of Anxiety Disorders, 16,* 67–81.

Essau, C. A., Ishikawa, S., Sasagawa, S., Sato, H., Okajima, I., Otsui, K., et al. (2011b). Anxiety symptoms among adolescents in Japan and England: Their relationship with self-construals and social support. *Depression and Anxiety, 28,* 509–518.

Essau, C. A., Leung, P. W. L., Conradt, J., Cheng, H., & Wong, T. (2008). Anxiety symptoms in Chinese and German adolescents: Their relationship with early learning experiences, perfectionism and learning motivation. *Depression and Anxiety, 25,* 801–810.

Essau, C. A., & Ollendick, T. H. (2009). Diagnosis and assessment of adolescent depression. In Nolen-Hoeksema, S. & L. M. Hilt (eds.), *Handbook of Depression in Adolescents.* New York: Routledge.

Essau, C. A., & Petermann, F. (1997). Introduction and general issues. In C. A. Essau & F. Petermann (Eds.), *Developmental Psychopathology: Epidemiology, Diagnostics, and Treatment* (pp. 1–18). London: Harwood Academic Publishers.

Essau, C. A., & Petermann, F. (Eds.) (2001), *Anxiety Disorders in Children and Adolescents: Epidemiology, Risk Factors, and Treatment.* London: Harwood Academic Publishers.

Essau, C. A., Petermann, F., & Feehan, M. (1997). Research methods and designs. In C. A. Essau & F. Petermann (Eds.), *Developmental Psychopathology: Epidemiology, Diagnostics, and Treatment* (pp. 63–95). London: Harwood Academic Publishers.

Essau, C. A., Sakano, Y., Ishikawa, S., & Sasagawa, S. (2004). Anxiety symptoms in Japanese and in German children. *Behaviour Research and Therapy, 42,* 601–612.

Essau, C. A., Sasagawa, S., Anastassiou-Hadjicharalambous, X., Olaya Guzmán, B., & Ollendick, T. M. (2011c). Psychometric properties of the Spence Child Anxiety Scale with adolescents from five European countries. *Journal of Anxiety Disorders, 25,* 19–27.

Essau, C. A., Sasagawa, S., Chen, J., & Sakano, Y. (2012b). Taijin kyofusho and social phobia symptoms in young adults in England and in Japan. *Journal of Cross-Cultural Psychology, 43,* 219–232.

Essau, C. A., Sasagawa, S., Ishikawa, S., OkajimaI., O'Callaghan, J., & Bray, D. (in press). A Japanese form of social anxiety (Taijin kyofusho): Frequency and correlates in two generations of the same family in Japan. *International Journal of Social Psychiatry.*

Ginsburg, G. S., La Greca, A. M., & Silverman, W. K. (1998). Social anxiety in children with anxiety disorders: Relation with social and emotional functioning. *Journal of Abnormal Child Psychology, 26,* 175–185.

Ginsburg, G. S., & Silverman, W. K. (1996). Phobic and anxiety disorders in Hispanic and European-American youth. *Journal of Anxiety Disorders, 10,* 517–528.

Gruner, K., Muris, P., & Merckelbach, H. (1999). The relationship between anxious rearing behaviors and anxiety disorders symptomatology in normal children. *Journal of Behavior Therapy, 30,* 27–35.

Guarnaccia, P. J., Canino, G., Rubio-Stipec, M., & Bravo, M. (1993). The prevalence of *ataques de nervios* in the Puerto Rico disaster study: The role of culture in psychiatric epidemiology. *The Journal of Nervous and Mental Disease, 181,* 157–165.

Guarnaccia, P. J., Martinez, I., Ramirez, R., & Canino, G. (2005). Are *ataques de nervios* in Puerto Rican children associated with psychiatric disorder? *Journal of the American Academy of Child and Adolescent Psychiatry, 44,* 1184–1192.

Hinton, D. E., Park, L., Hsia, C. et al. (2009). Anxiety disorder presentations in Asian populations: a review. *CNS Neuroscience & Therapeutics, 15,* 295–303.

Hofstede, G. (1980). *Culture's Consequences.* Beverly Hills, CA: Sage.

Hale III, W. W., Raaijmakers, Q., Muris, P., & Meeus, W. (2005). Psychometric properties of the Screen for Child Anxiety Related Emotional Disorders (SCARED) in the general adolescent population. *Journal of the American Academy of Child and Adolescent Psychiatry, 44,* 283–290.

Hofmann, S. G., Asnaani, A., & Hinton, D. E. (2010). Cultural aspects in social anxiety and social anxiety disorder. *Depression and Anxiety, 27,* 1117–1127.

Ishikawa, S., Sato, H., & Sasagawa, S. (2009). Anxiety disorder symptoms in Japanese children and adolescents. *Journal of Anxiety Disorders, 23,* 104–111.

Jahoda, G. (1983). The cross-cultural emperors' conceptual clothes: The emic-ethic issue revisted. In J. Deregowski, S. S. Dzuirawiec, & R. Annis (Eds.), *Explications in Cross-Cultural Psychology.* Lisse: Swets & Zeitlinger.

Kirmayer, L. J. (1991) The place of culture in psychiatric nosology: Taijin kyofusho and DSM-III-R. *Journal of Nervous and Mental Disease, 179,* 19 –28.

Kirmayer, L. J., Young, A., & Hayton, B. C. (1995). The cultural context of anxiety disorders. *The Psychiatric Clinics of North America, 18,* 503–521.

Kitayama, S., & Cohen, D. (Eds.) (2007). *Handbook of Cultural Psychology.* New York: Guilford Press.

Kleinknecht, R. A., Dinnel, D. L., Kleinknecht, E. E., Hiruma, N., & Harada, N. (1997). Cultural factors in social anxiety: A comparison of social phobia symptoms and Taijin Kyofusho. *Journal of Anxiety Disorders, 11,* 157–177.

Kroeber, A. L., & Kluckhohn, C. (1952). *Culture: A Critical Review of Concepts and Definitions* (Vol. 47). Harvard University Peabody Museum of American Archeology and Ethnology.

Leung, P. W. L., Hung, S. F., Ho, T. P., Lee, C. C., Liu, W. S., Tang, C. P., & Kwong, S. L. (2008). Prevalence of DSM-IV disorders in Chinese Adolescents and the effects of an impairment criterion: A pilot community study in Hong Kong. *European Child & Adolescent Psychiatry, 17,* 452–461.

Lewinsohn, P. M., Gottlib, I. H., Lewinsohn, M., Seeley, J. R., & Allen, N. B. (1998). Gender differences in anxiety disorders and anxiety symptoms in adolescents. *Journal of Abnormal Psychology, 107,* 109–117.

Lewis-Fernandez, R., & Diaz, N. (2002). The cultural formulation: A method for assessing cultural factors affecting the clinical encounter. *Psychiatric Quarterly, 73,* 271–295.

Lewis-Fernández, R., Guarnaccia, P. J., Martínez, I. E., Salmán, E., Schmidt, A., & Liebowitz, M. (2002). Comparative phenomenology of ataques de nervios, panic attacks, and panic disorder. *Culture, Medicine and Psychiatry, 26,* 199–223.

Lewis-Fernandez, R., Guarnaccia, P. J., & Ruiz, P. (2009). Culture-Bound Syndromes. In B. J. Sadock, V. A. Sadock, and P. Ruiz (Eds.), *Comprehensive Textbook of Psychiatry* (2519–2538). Baltimore, MD: Lippincot, Williams, & Wilkins.

Lewis-Fernandez, R., Hinton, D. E., Laria, A. J., et al. (2010). Culture and the anxiety disorders: recommendations for DSM-V. *Depression and Anxiety, 27,* 212–229.

Lonner, W. (1979). Issues in Cross-Cultural Psychology. In A. Marsella, A. Tharp, & T. Cibrowski (Eds.), *Perspectives in Cross-Cultural Psychology.* New York: Academic Press.

Lopez, I., Ramirez, R., Guarraccia, P., Canino, G., & Bird, H. (2011). *Ataques de Nervios* and Somatic Complaints Among Island and Mainland Puerto Rican Children. *CNS Neuroscience & Therapeutics, 17,* 158–166.

Maeda, F., & Nathan, J. H. (1999). Understanding taijin kyofusho through its treatment, Morita therapy. *Journal of Psychosomatic Research, 46,* 525–530.

Markus, H., & Kitayama, S. (1991). Culture and self: implications for cognition, emotion and motivation. *Psychological Review, 98,* 224–253.

McGee, R., Feehan, M., Williams, S., Partridge, F., Silva, P. A., & Kelly, J. (1990). DSM-III disorders in a large sample of adolescents. *Journal of the American Academy of Child and Adolescent Psychiatry, 29,* 611–619.

Mellon, R. C., & Moutavelis, A. G. (2007) Structure, developmental course, and correlates of children's anxiety disorder-related behaviour in a Hellenic community sample. *Journal of Anxiety Disorders, 21,* 1–21.

Meltzer, H., Gatward, R., Goodman, R., & Ford, T. (2000). *Mental Health of Children and Adolescents in Great Britain.* London: Stationery Office.

Moretz, M. W., & McKay, D. (2009). The role of perfectionism in obsessive-compulsive symptoms: "Not just right" experiences and checking compulsions. *Journal of Anxiety Disorders, 23,* 640–644.

Muris, P., Loxton, H., Neumann, A., DuPlessis, M., King, N. J., & Ollendick, T. H. (2006). DSM-defined anxiety disorders symptoms in South African youths: Their assessment and relationship with perceived parental rearing behaviors. *Behaviour Research and Therapy, 44,* 883–896.

Muris, P., Merckelbach, H., Mayer, B., van Brakel, A., Thissen, S., Moulaert, V., et al. (1998). The Screen for Child Anxiety Related Emotional Disorders (SCARED) and traditional childhood anxiety measures. *Journal of Behavior Therapy and Experimental Psychiatry, 29,* 327–339.

Muris, P., Merckelbach, H., Ollendick, T., King, N., & Bogie, N. (2002). Three traditional and three new childhood anxiety questionnaires: Their reliability and validity in a normal adolescent sample. *Behaviour Research and Therapy, 40,* 753–772.

Nekkebroeck, J., Barnes, J., Bonduelle, M. et al. (2010). International comparison of parenting styles in ICSI, IVF and natural conception families: results from a European study. *European Journal of Developmental Psychology, 3,* 329–349.

Ollendick, T. H., & Benoit, K. (2012). A parent-child interactional model of social anxiety disorder in youth. *Clinical Child and Family Psychology Review, 15,* 81–91.

Ollendick, T. H., & Hirshfeld-Becker, D. R. (2002). The developmental psychopathology of social anxiety disorder. *Biological Psychiatry, 51,* 44–58.

Ollendick, T. H., & King, N. J. (1991). Fears and phobias of childhood. In M. Herbert (Ed.), *Clinical Child Psychology: Social Learning, Development, and Behaviour* (pp. 309–329). Chichester: John Wiley & Sons, Ltd.

Ollendick, T. H., Yang, B., King, N. J., Dong, Q., & Akande, A. (1996). Fears in American, Australian, Chinese and Nigerian children and adolescents: a cross-cultural study. *Journal of Child Psychology and Psychiatry, 37,* 213–220.

Sato, S., & Sato, Y. (2006). Gakko ni okeru SST jissen gaido: Kodomo no taijin sukiru shido [*SST Practice Guide in School: Guidance of Social Skills Training for Children*]. Tokyo, Japan: Kongo Shuppan.

Seligman, L. D., & Ollendick, T. H. (2011). Cognitive behavior therapy for anxiety disorders in children and adolescents. *Psychiatric Clinics of North America, 20,* 217–238.

Shepherd, M., Oppenheim, B., & Mitchell, S. (1971). *Childhood Behaviour and Mental Health.* University of London Press.

Spence, S. H. (1997). Structure of anxiety symptoms among children: a confirmatory factor—analytic study. *Journal of Abnormal Psychology, 106,* 280–297.

Spence, S. H. (1998). A measure of anxiety symptoms among children. *Behaviour Research and Therapy, 36,* 545–566.

Spence, S. H., Barrett, P. M., & Turner, C. M. (2003). Psychometric properties of the Spence children's anxiety scale with young adolescents. *Journal of Anxiety Disorders, 17,* 605–625.

Su, L., Wang, K., Fan, F., Su, Y., & Gao, X. (2008). Reliability and validity of the Screen for Child Anxiety Related Emotional Disorders (SCARED) in Chinese children. *Journal of Anxiety Disorders, 22,* 612–621.

Takahashi, T. (1989). Social phobia syndrome in Japan. *Comprehensive Psychiatry, 30,* 45–52.

Takuma, T., & Amau, Y. (1998). The changing relations between twins in Japan. In G. Trommsdorff, W. Friedlmeier, & H.-J. Kornadt (Eds.), *Japan in Transition: Social and Psychological Aspects* (pp. 212–216). Lengerich, Germany: Pabst Science Publishers.

Triandis, H. C. (1990). Cross-cultural studies of individualism and collectivism. In J. Berman (Ed.), *Nebraska Symposium on Motivation, 1989* (pp. 41–133). Lincoln: University of Nebraska Press.

Triandis, H. C. (1995). *Individualism and Collectivism.* Boulder, CO: Westview Press.

Trommsdorff, G., & Essau, C. A. (1999). Japanese and German adolescents' control orientation: a cross-cultural study. In G. Trommsdorff, W. Friedlmeier, & H. J. Kornadt (Eds.), *Japan in Transition—A Comparative View on Social and Psychological Aspects* (198–211). Lengerich: Pabst Science Publishers.

Van Widenfelt, B. M., Treffers, P. D., De Beurs, E., Siebelink, B. M., & Koudijs, e. (2005). Translation and cross-cultural adaptation of assessment instruments used in psychological research with children and families. *Clinical Child and Family Psychology Review, 8,* 135–147.

Varela, R. E., & Hensley-Maloney, L. (2009). The influence of culture on anxiety in Latino youth: A review. *Clinical Child and Family Psychology Review, 12,* 217–233.

Varela, R. E., Sanchez-Sosa, J. J., Biggs, B. K., & Luis, T. M. (2008). Anxiety symptoms and fears in Latin American and European American children: *Cross-cultural measurement equivalence. Journal of Psychopathology and Behavioral Assessment, 30,* 132–145.

Varela, R. E., Vernberg, E. M., Sanchez-Sosa, J. J., Riveros, A., Mitchell, M., & Mashunkashey, J. (2004). Anxiety reporting and culturally associated interpretation biases and cognitive schemas: A comparison of Mexican, Mexican American, and European American families. *Journal of Clinical Child and Adolescent Psychology, 33,* 237–247.

Weisz, J. R., Rothbaum, F. M., & Blackburn, T. M. (1984). Standing out and standing in. The psychology of control in America and Japan. *American Psychologist, 39,* 955–969.

WHO (1992). *The ICD-10 Classification of Mental and Behavioural Disorders.* Geneva: World Health Organization.

Wittchen, H.-U., & Essau, C. A. (1993). Epidemiology of anxiety disorders. In A. M. Cooper (Ed.), *Psychiatry* (pp. 1–25). Philadelphia: J. B. Lippincott Company.

Wren, F. J., Berg, E. A., Heiden, L. A., Kinnamon, C. J., Ohlson, L. A., Bridge, J. A., et al. (2007). Childhood anxiety in a diverse primary care population: Parent–child reports, ethnicity and SCARED factor structure. *Journal of the American Academy of Child and Adolescent Psychiatry, 46,* 332–340.

Yorulmaz, O., Gençöz, T., & Woody, S. (2009). OCD cognitions and symptoms in different religious contexts. *Journal of Anxiety Disorders, 23,* 401–406.

Yoshida, T., Taga, C., Matsumoto, Y., & Fukui, K. (2005). Paternal overprotection in obsessive-compulsive disorder and depression with obsessive traits. *Psychiatry and Clinical Neurosciences, 59,* 533–538.

9

Evidence-Based Assessment and Case Formulation for Childhood Anxiety Disorders

Bryce D. McLeod[1], Amanda Jensen-Doss[2],
Emily Wheat[1], and Emily M. Becker[2]

[1]Virginia Commonwealth University, USA
[2]University of Miami, USA

Over the past two decades, the youth psychotherapy field has focused increased attention upon evidence-based practice (EBP). As the EBP movement has gained traction it has begun to shape practice and reimbursement patterns with professional organizations (e.g., APA Presidential Task Force on Evidence-Based Practice, 2006), state mental health agencies (e.g., Jensen-Doss, Hawley, Lopez, & Osterberg, 2009), and federal funders of mental health services and research (e.g., National Institute of Mental Health, 2010) endorsing increased use of EBP in clinical practice settings in order to improve the quality of mental health services. Looking forward, the EBP movement will likely increase its influence upon the field and widen its impact upon clinical practice in the coming years.

To date, the youth EBP movement has primarily focused upon promoting evidence-based treatments (EBTs) (Mash & Hunsley, 2005a). A number of comprehensive reviews document the advances made in developing and evaluating EBTs for a wide range of youth emotional and behavioral problems (see e.g., McLeod & Weisz, 2004; Weisz, Jensen, & McLeod, 2005). Recently, however, authors have noted that relatively little attention has focused upon evidence-based assessment (EBA; Mash & Hunsley, 2005a). In response to these calls, the EBA movement has started to gain momentum in recent years.

EBA is defined as an approach to clinical evaluation that utilizes science and theory to guide the assessment process (Hunsley & Mash, 2007). A goal of EBA is to develop and promote a set of assessment guidelines to direct research and inform clinical practice (Hunsley & Mash, 2007). Paralleling the earlier EBT efforts aimed at categorizing interventions according to level of empirical support, Hunsley and Mash (2008) recently proposed a set of criteria to classify assessment tools along psychometric dimensions such as reliability, validity, and clinical utility. This increased

The Wiley-Blackwell Handbook of The Treatment of Childhood and Adolescent Anxiety, First Edition.
Edited by Cecilia A. Essau and Thomas H. Ollendick.
© 2013 John Wiley & Sons, Ltd. Published 2013 by John Wiley & Sons, Ltd.

attention focused upon the quality of assessment tools represents a new chapter in the EBA movement. Though still taking shape, this move to categorize assessment instruments and dictate how assessment tools can, and perhaps should, inform clinical practice has real potential to shape the future of clinical practice.

Coinciding with the rise of the EBA movement is a focus upon case formulation. Broadly defined, case formulation is defined as generating a set of hypotheses about the causes, antecedents, and maintaining factors of a client's emotional, interpersonal, and behavior problems (Eells, 1997; Nezu, Nezu, Peacock, & Girdwood, 2004). Case formulation is recognized as an important psychotherapy skill that can help clinicians span the gap between science and practice, diagnosis and treatment. Indeed, case formulation is seen as a component of EBP that forms a bridge between assessment and treatment by providing a roadmap that helps a clinician select the constructs to be targeted for assessment and, ultimately, treatment (APA, 2006).

The scientific and theoretical underpinnings of a case formulation determine the nature and focus of assessment and treatment. In the current chapter, we argue that a case formulation for youth anxiety should be based upon the theory and empirical findings from the developmental psychopathology and cognitive-behavioral treatment literatures. Using these theories to select constructs for assessment informed by the principles of EBA can produce an accurate case formulation that can guide treatment of youth anxiety from the intake interview to termination.

The purpose of this chapter is to discuss how EBA and case formulation apply to the assessment and treatment of youth anxiety. We will review the principles of EBA and case formulation. Then, we offer an approach to developing a case formulation for youth anxiety informed by the principles of EBA to guide the treatment of youth anxiety.

Why Do We Assess?

Assessment is conceptualized as the process of gathering information and interpreting test results into a description of the assessed individual (Hunsley, 2002). Assessment serves several important roles in treatment. When a client presents for treatment, one of the first tasks of the therapist is to determine what the focus of treatment should be. Assessment tools can be used to briefly screen for a range of childhood disorders, identifying targets for more in-depth assessment. This more in-depth assessment often takes the form of generating a diagnosis, which can subsequently play several roles in treatment planning. Assessment at the beginning of treatment can also be used to quantify the severity of a client's problems, both to assist in treatment planning and to determine a baseline for outcome monitoring. A baseline assessment can also help identify factors that might be contributing to or maintaining the client's problems, such as family factors, and comorbid symptoms. Finally, once treatment begins, ongoing assessment of core symptoms and contributing factors can be used to monitor treatment response and to identify changes needed to the treatment plan.

At all of these stages, assessment can be used for either nomothetic or idiographic purposes. Nomothetic approaches seek to understand where an individual client falls relative to the larger population on a domain of interest. For example, a clinician seeking to make a decision about whether a child is in need of services might use an anxiety rating scale to determine whether that child falls above a clinical cut-off; this would indicate that the child's level of anxiety exceeds what is considered typical among similarly aged or gendered children. On the other hand, idiographic approaches seek to generate individualized information about a particular client. For example, a clinician seeking to design an exposure hierarchy for a given client might design a behavioral avoidance activity tailored to the client's specific fears to determine the exact type of situations most likely to elicit anxiety in that client.

As we note later in more detail, both nomothetic and idiographic approaches play important, and complimentary, roles in case formulation. A careful nomothetic approach helps a clinician determine caseness, which is an important first step in treatment selection. However, once a treatment is selected the clinician must tailor the treatment to the particular needs of an individual client. Idiographic approaches are particularly useful for this step because they are uniquely suited to gathering information about the topography of behavior that represent the targets of treatment.

What Is Evidence-Based Assessment?

Broadly defined, EBA refers to assessment practices that are empirically supported. However, efforts to incorporate EBA into clinical practice have been complicated by a lack of guidelines available to define exactly what constitutes EBA. Consequently, there is a need for more concrete definitions of this empirical support (Hunsley & Mash, 2007, 2008; Mash & Hunsley, 2005a), and the past few years have seen a movement to both define and provide EBA guidelines (e.g., see special sections of the *Journal of Clinical Child and Adolescent Psychology,* Mash & Hunsley, Eds., 2005a, and *Psychological Assessment,* Hunsley & Mash, Eds., 2005b). Hunsley and Mash (2007) define EBA as "an approach to clinical evaluation that uses research and theory to guide the selection of constructs to be assessed for a specific assessment purpose, the methods and measures to be used in the assessment, and the manner in which the assessment process unfolds" (Hunsley & Mash, 2007, p. 30).

More recently, Hunsley and Mash (2008) have developed a set of psychometric rating criteria to classify an evidence-based assessment tool's reliability, validity, and clinical utility as "adequate", "good", or "excellent". A reliable measure is one that is consistent and dependable. For an assessment tool to be considered reliable, Hunsley and Mash (2008) suggest that three measures of reliability be considered: inter-rater reliability, test–retest reliability, and internal consistency. Inter-rater reliability assesses the differences in obtained results among raters who are using the same instrument. For example, high inter-rater reliability would be obtained if separate clinicians reached the same conclusion following a diagnostic assessment. Test–retest reliability measures the concordance of scores on a measure completed multiple times by the same person. Internal consistency is a measurement of the consistency of items within a particular test. The internal consistency of a measure is used as an indicator of whether or not test items contribute to the measurement of the targeted construct, with higher levels indicating that items are contributing consistently to the same construct.

The validity of a measure refers to whether or not an assessment tool actually assesses what it purports to measure. There is no agreed upon single definition for validity (Kendell & Jablensky, 2003), but the *Standards for Educational and*

Psychological Testing (American Educational Research Association, American Psychological Association, & National Council on Measurement in Education, 1999) highlight convergent and discriminant validity (whether a measure converges or diverges with measures of similar and/or different constructs), test-criterion relationships (whether a measure relates to a present or future outcome that is theoretically related to the targeted construct), and validity generalization (whether or not the test-criterion relationships are generalizable to other settings) as particularly key concepts to consider. Hunsley and Mash's (2008) criteria include three validity ratings: content validity (whether a measure captures all aspects of the construct of interest), construct validity (which maps onto the Standards definitions of convergent and discriminant validity and test-criterion relationships), and validity generalization (whether or not a measure is generalizable to other settings and/or populations).

In addition to reliability and validity, Hunsley and Mash's (2008) criteria include two more psychometric ratings. The first captures the quality of a measure's norms, that is, whether there are measures of central tendency and distribution for the measure's scores from representative samples. The second rates the degree to which the measure is sensitive to change over a treatment period.

An additional factor to consider in determining evidence-based standards for assessments is some indicator of clinical utility (Hunsley & Mash, 2007; Nelson-Gray, 2003; Vasey & Lonigan, 2000). Clinical utility can include treatment utility (a measure's beneficial contribution to treatment outcome), diagnostic utility (a measure's ability to lead to a correct diagnostic conclusion), incremental utility (what information a particular measure can provide that cannot be provided by other instruments), and the feasibility of a measure. Essentially, determining the clinical utility of a given measure should assess whether there are improvements in the accuracy, outcome, or efficiency of clinical activities as a result of the assessment process (Hunsley & Mash, 2007). Hunsley and Mash's (2008) rating system includes one indicator of clinical utility, which is a global rating of the measure's clinical usefulness and also reflects practical considerations, such as the measure's cost and administration time.

It is important to note that a measure must possess respectable psychometric properties for its intended purpose. For example, if an assessment has been standardized on a sample of clinically anxious youth, it may not be appropriate for a sub-clinical population. For a more in-depth discussion of the suggested set of psychometric rating criteria that may guide evidence-based assessment (i.e., what specific numeric levels of reliability and validity may be considered "acceptable", "good", or "excellent"), see Hunsley and Mash (2008).

Finally, for an assessment to be considered evidence-based, there should be evidence suggesting that the entire assessment process (as opposed to the assessment tool itself) is empirically supported (Hunsley & Mash, 2007). This includes evidence supporting the selection of appropriate assessment tools, the proper score interpretation of the chosen assessment, and the methods used to integrate multiple sources of data.

Evidence-Based Assessment of Child and Adolescent Anxiety

Several excellent, thorough, reviews of EBA of child and adolescent anxiety have been conducted (Connolly & Bernstein, 2007; Silverman & Ollendick, 2005, 2008;

Southam-Gerow & Chorpita, 2007). The purpose of this section, therefore, is to describe the different methods that can be used in the EBA of youth anxiety, citing examples of these methods, to help the interested clinician think about the types of instruments that might be useful in a given stage of assessment. For a comprehensive review of the best-supported instruments falling into each of these categories, the interested reader is referred to the references listed here.

Unstructured interviews

The traditional method of gathering information at the beginning of treatment is the unstructured interview, in which a clinician interviews a child and/or parent, guided by his or her clinical expertise, to gather the information needed to determine a diagnosis. Unstructured interviews have many advantages that make them a useful assessment tool, including the flexibility to tailor the assessment to the client. Moreover, few standardized instruments include thorough assessment of the contextual factors that may be contributing to a child's symptoms, such as psychosocial stressors or family relationships (exceptions do exist, such as the Children's Interview of Psychiatric Syndromes; Weller, Weller, Fristad, Rooney, & Schecter, 2000), so unstructured interviews can be useful for gathering this information.

However, because the clinician does not follow a pre-determined set of questions, unstructured interviews are more susceptible to clinician bias than structured methods (Angold & Fisher, 1999; Garb, 1998, 2005), leading to questions about the validity of this method. When the results of unstructured interviews are compared to those of standardized research diagnostic interviews, agreement has been consistently found to be low (Rettew, Lynch, Achenbach, Dumenci, & Ivanova, 2009), and studies comparing the results of these two methods to external indicators of validity have found stronger support for the accuracy of the standardized interviews (e.g., Jewell, Handwerk, Almquist, & Lucas, 2004; Ramirez Basco, Bostic, Davies et al., 2000; Tenney, Schotte, Denys, van Megen, & Westenberg, 2003).

Standardized interviews

In an effort to create more reliable and valid ways to assess diagnoses, researchers have developed standardized interviews. These interviews are typically classified as "structured," wherein interviewers administer a standard set of questions guided by a strict set of rules for their administration, or "semi-structured," wherein interviewers can use clinical judgment to modify the interview by asking additional questions or clarifying the wording of interview questions[1]. Both types of standardized interviews are usually organized by diagnosis, with the interviewer administering a series of questions designed to assess the DSM criteria for given diagnoses. Most standardized interviews for youth psychopathology come in parallel parent-report and child-report versions that allow for comparison of data across reporters.

---

[1] These two types of interviews have also been referred to as "respondent-based," for interviews that follow a set script without the interviewer interpreting the respondent's answers, and "interviewer-based," for those with a standard set of questions, but in which the interviewer makes the final interpretation as to whether a symptom or diagnosis is present (Angold & Fisher, 1999).

Standardized interviews are most often used to assess for diagnoses at the beginning of treatment. However, they have also been recommended for use in treatment planning, case formulation, and treatment outcome monitoring, as the presence and types of anxiety disorder diagnoses are important pieces of information at these stages of assessment as well (Silverman & Ollendick, 2008; Southam-Gerow & Chorpita, 2007).

Silverman and Ollendick (2008) concluded that the Anxiety Disorders Interview Schedule for Children for DSM-IV: Child and Parent Versions (ADIS for DSM-IV: C/P; Silverman & Albano, 1996) is the strongest interview for childhood anxiety because it includes a more detailed assessment of the anxiety disorders than other interviews. They also rated its psychometric properties as stronger than other interviews. Southam-Gerow and Chorpita (2007) drew similar conclusions, pointing out that this is the only interview with reliability data for all of the anxiety disorders. However, Silverman and Ollendick also concluded that the Diagnostic Interview Schedule for Children (DISC-IV; Shaffer, Fisher, Lucas, Dulcan, & Schwab-Stone, 2000), the Diagnostic Interview for Children and Adolescents (DICA; Reich, 2000), and the Schedule for Affective Disorders and Schizophrenia in School-Age Children (K-SADS; Ambrosini, 2000) all had at least adequate psychometric properties for the assessment of youth anxiety disorders.

Rating scales

A rating scale is a "measure that provides relatively rapid assessment of a specific construct with an easily derived numerical score, which is readily interpreted, whether completed by the youth or someone else, regardless of the response format and irrespective of application." (Myers & Winters, 2002, p. 115). Numerous rating scales for youth anxiety exist, including questionnaires and checklists designed to assess anxiety alone and multidimensional scales that cover a wide range of problem areas. Many of these scales have parallel child-report and parent-report versions, and some – primarily the multidimensional scales – also have versions for other reporters, such as teachers and clinicians. Often, normative data are available for these measures to facilitate comparison of a given client to the broader population to determine whether that client's level of anxiety falls outside of what might be considered normal for a child of that age and/or gender.

Rating scales can serve a variety of assessment purposes. They can be used to efficiently screen for diagnoses that might warrant further assessment. They can also be used as part of the diagnostic process, although current EBA recommendations caution against using them as stand-alone diagnostic instruments, but instead be paired with standardized diagnostic interviews (Silverman & Ollendick, 2005, 2008). Some rating scales also have scales or items that can facilitate the treatment planning process by helping differentiate between subtypes of anxiety and a small number contain information about causal mechanisms that can also be useful in this regard (Southam-Gerow & Chorpita, 2007).

Most of the existing EBA reviews for child anxiety have focused primarily on reviewing anxiety-specific rating scales, rather than the anxiety subscales of multidimensional rating scales. Some examples of some well-reviewed anxiety specific scales include the Multidimensional Anxiety Scale for Children (MASC; March, Parker, Sullivan,

& Stallings, 1997), which Silverman and Ollendick (2008) recommend as useful at all stages in the assessment process, and the Revised Child Anxiety and Depression Scale (RCADS; Chorpita, Yim, Moffitt, Umemoto, & Francis, 2000), which Southam-Gerow and Chorpita (2007) recommend for screening, treatment planning, and post-treatment outcome measurement.

Direct observation

Although observational methods have been used in studies of childhood anxiety to measure sensitivity to social evaluation and the quality of parent–child relationships (Silverman & Ollendick, 2008), the most common form of direct observational measurement for youth anxiety is the behavioral avoidance task (BAT). A BAT typically involves exposing a child to a feared stimulus and asking him or her to engage in a series of increasingly anxiety-provoking tasks related to the stimulus (e.g., approaching it, touching it for increasing amounts of time, etc.). The child's avoidance is then coded and scored, using whatever metric is appropriate to the task (e.g., proximity to the object, amount of time the child can tolerate touching the object). Although the term "BAT" has been used by numerous researchers as if this were a single, standardized measure, several authors have pointed out that this is not a standardized instrument, as the tasks and the scoring are typically tailored to the type of anxiety being studied and sometimes to the specific child with which the task is being utilized (e.g., Langley, Bergman, & Piacentini, 2002; Mori & Armendariz, 2001). This makes it difficult to compare scores across research studies or clinical clients, decreasing their utility for nomothetic assessment purposes. Recently, however, authors have begun to use computer simulations to conduct BATs, which has the potential to standardize the presentation and scoring of BATs (e.g., Meng, Kirkby, Martin, Gilroy, & Daniels, 2004).

Due to their idiographic nature, observational methods are typically not recommended for screening or diagnostic purposes. Because BATs provide tailored information on what a child can "handle" in relation to their feared stimulus, they have been recommended for use in case formulation and treatment planning (Silverman & Ollendick, 2008; Southam-Gerow & Chorpita, 2007). For example, understanding how close a spider-phobic child can get to a spider at the beginning of treatment can help in planning exposure tasks for that child. Southam-Gerow and Chorpita (2007) also recommend these tasks for monitoring treatment progress, as they are tailored to a child's specific fears, potentially making them more sensitive to treatment changes than more general, nomothetic measures. However, given the lack of standardization for these measures, they also caution against relying on them alone and suggest combining them with other methods, such as questionnaires.

Self-monitoring

Self monitoring is defined as "the act of systematically observing and recording aspects of one's own behavior and internal and external environmental events thought to be functionally related to that behavior" (Cone, 1999, p. 411). For example, a child may be asked to fill out a sheet that records every time he or she experiences panic symptoms, detailing when and where the attack occurred, describing the physical symptoms, and recording the cognitions that were associated with those symptoms. Self-monitoring techniques are a common component of evidence-based treatments for youth anxiety (Chorpita & Daleiden, 2009), serving to help increase clients' awareness of their symptoms and to inform clinicians about treatment progress. Much of the available research on self-monitoring is about its use as an intervention tool (Shapiro & Cole, 1999), although this method may also be used as an assessment strategy. Craske and Tsao (1999) provide guidelines for setting up self-monitoring activities for individuals diagnosed with anxiety disorders and Shapiro and Cole (1999) provide guidelines for creating self-monitoring activities for children and adolescents.

As an assessment strategy, self-monitoring is subject to many of the same criticisms as direct observational methods. Because the behaviors being recorded are going to be specific to a client's anxiety, it is difficult to standardize this form of assessment across clients. In addition, questions have been raised about the ability of children, particularly young children, to accurately monitor and record their own behavior (Shapiro & Cole, 1999). Given that the act of self-monitoring is thought to hold the potential to change the behavior being monitored, it is also difficult to disentangle the assessment and intervention purposes of self-monitoring. Because of these limitations, like direct observation, self-monitoring is generally thought to be primarily useful for idiographic assessment. Noting the need for continued study of this assessment method, Silverman and Ollendick (2008) concluded that this method is probably useful for case formulation and treatment planning purposes.

What is Case Formulation?

Case formulation is defined as a set of hypotheses about the causes, antecedents, and maintaining factors of a client's emotional, interpersonal, and behavior problems (Eells, 1997; Nezu et al., 2004). Considered an important psychotherapy skill, the ability to develop a case formulation can help clinicians use findings from the scientific literature to inform the treatment for specific clients. This is because a case formulation generates a comprehensive picture of an individual, how his/her problems developed, and how the problems can be ameliorated. A case formulation therefore serves as a roadmap that guides assessment, identifies targets for treatment, and highlights potential markers for clinical change (Eells & Lombart, 2004).

Case formulation has its roots in the medical field. The core empirical principles embedded within most case formulation approaches can be traced to the medical diagnostic approaches developed by Hipprocrates in the fifth century BCE and Galen in the second century CE (cf. Eells & Lombart, 2004). The medical diagnostic traditions associated with Hipprocrates and Galen emphasized a rational, theory-driven approach to diagnosis guided by a comprehensive assessment. The Hippocratic approach stressed the importance of conducting a comprehensive assessment of the presenting medical problem guided by reason, logic, and observation to correctly diagnose the underlying cause of a disease (Eells & Lombart, 2004). The Galenic approach emphasized the importance of using empirical methods to test understanding of disease, human anatomy, and the accuracy of a medical diagnosis. The values of the Hippocractic and Galenic traditions are reflected in most case formulation approaches presently used to guide psychotherapy.

Case formulation has long been considered an important psychotherapy skill (Eells, 2006). However, the past decade has witnessed increased interest in case formulation, in part due to the EBP movement. A number of books focused upon case formulation have recently been written (e.g., Hersen & Porzelius, 2002; Horowitz, 2005), and books focused upon assessment have increasingly included chapters dedicated to case formulation (e.g., Nezu et al., 2004; Reitman, 2007; Rosqvist, 2008). Moreover, the APA considers case formulation to be a component of EBP stating that "The purpose of EBPP [Evidence Based Practice in Psychology] is to promote effective psychological practice and enhance public health by applying empirically supported principles of psychological assessment, *case formulation,* therapeutic relationship, and intervention" (APA, 2006; p. 273; italics added for emphasis). This increased attention has resulted in a number of unique case formulation approaches, though only a few approaches have been developed specifically for youth therapy. Some case formulation approaches do exist for youth therapy (e.g., Friedberg & McClure, 2002); however, these approaches do not focus specifically upon the treatment of child anxiety.

The empirical literature offers little guidance for those interested in selecting a particular case formulation approach to use for assessment and treatment. Little systematic research exists on the potential value of using different case formulations to guide assessment and treatment (Eells & Lombart, 2004; Nelson-Gray, 2003). However, existing data on correlates and contributors to child anxiety provide some guidance upon which to build an evidence-based approach to case formulation for the treatment of child anxiety. Below, we present a summary of such an approach.

Case formulation, assessment, and child anxiety

Next, we describe components of a case formulation approach for youth anxiety. This approach is designed to help clinicians apply the principles of EBA in a systematic way in order to generate a set of hypotheses about the factors that contribute to the development, maintenance, and amelioration of anxiety for individual clients. Based upon empirically supported theories, the approach is designed to help clinicians organize the complex information provided by youth and parents who present for treatment and translate it into a blueprint for treatment. As such, the approach guides the selection of constructs for assessment and treatment.

Our case formulation approach is guided by four principles. First, the assessment process should adhere to the principles of EBA (Hunsley & Mash, 2007). Second, the selection of constructs for assessment should be driven by empirically supported developmental and psychopathology theories (McFall, 2005; Hunsley & Mash, 2007). Third, the assessment process must be informed by an understanding of how developmental principles and cultural factors influence the expression of anxiety symptoms. Fourth, treatment selection and planning should be driven by the cognitive behavioral treatment literature. Above, we have described Principle 1, or the use of EBA. In the subsequent sections, we go into detail about the rest of these principles.

Principle 2: Developmental psychopathology

The developmental psychopathology perspective (e.g., Cicchetti & Cohen, 1995; Masten & Braswell, 1991) provides an organizational framework from which to understand the development, maintenance, and alleviation of childhood anxiety. Several concepts underlie developmental psychopathology theory and research that are relevant to case formulation. The first concept, called *multifinality,* states that the process (i.e., impact upon the individual) of a single factor (e.g., genetics, environment) is posited to vary depending upon the context (e.g., family system) in which the factor operates (Cicchetti & Cohen, 1995). For example, an inhibited temperament may lead to a variety of outcomes for a child depending upon her environment (e.g., parenting, school) and/or internal coping resources (Kagan, 1997; Kagan, Reznick, & Gibbons, 1989; Snidman, Kagan, Riordan, & Shannon, 1995). A related concept, called *equifinality,* states that any given outcome (i.e., a specific anxiety disorder) can have multiple causes. In other words, a single causal pathway does not universally account for the development of each specific anxiety disorder. For example, two distinct pathways to general versus specific social phobia likely exist (Stemberger, Turner, Beidel, & Calhoun, 1995). General social phobia seems to be linked to an inhibited temperament (i.e., genetic pathway) whereas specific social phobia seems to be linked to specific traumatic events (i.e., classical conditioning).

Factors that contribute to the development, maintenance, and alleviation of child anxiety include both protective and risk factors that are external (familial, social-environmental) and internal (biological, cognitive) to the individual (Cicchetti & Cohen, 1995). These factors interact to influence an individual's ability to successfully negotiate each stage of development (e.g., infancy, childhood, adolescence, etc.). Protective factors help foster competence by promoting adaptation to the new challenges faced at each stage of development. Competence (i.e., mastery of the skills associated with a specific stage of development), in turn, tends to promote later competence because the individual is better equipped to handle future developmental challenges. Risk factors decrease competence by promoting maladaptive efforts to resolve challenges associated with each successive developmental stage (Cicchetti & Cohen, 1995). Decreased competence (i.e., few internal and/or external resources) contributes to later incompetence. In fact, the longer an individual continues along a maladaptive developmental trajectory the more difficult it is to return to normalcy because the requisite skills associated with each new stage of development are not mastered. Outcomes are ultimately dependent upon the interplay of protective and risk factors, with the development of childhood anxiety more likely when risk factors outweigh protective factors (Vasey & Dadds, 2001).

Several developmental models have been proposed to explain the development of anxiety disorders (see e.g., Craske, 1999; Vasey & Dadds, 2001). In brief, most models assume that the majority of individuals affected by clinically significant anxiety possess certain inherited traits (i.e., trait anxiety) that predispose them to pathological anxiety (Craske, 1999). Trait anxiety is posited to arise from genetic risk factors (e.g., temperament, sympathetic nervous system [SNS] reactivity) and early individual life experiences (e.g., experiences with control; see Chorpita & Barlow, 1998) that contribute non-specifically to mood and anxiety disorders. Over time the cognitive and physiological features of trait anxiety are linked to specific classes of stimuli (e.g., social situations) through individual learning experiences (i.e., classical, operant, modeling). Negative experiences with particular stimuli can create vulnerabilities for specific anxiety disorders among individuals predisposed to develop anxiety (i.e., those with high trait anxiety). That is, specific anxiety disorders may develop when anxiety coalesces around a particular situation or theme (e.g., fear of public embarrassment following direct experiences with humiliation). This model explains how a general vulnerability can develop into a particular DSM-IV anxiety disorder. For more in-depth coverage of this topic please see Craske (1999) and Vasey and Dadds (2001).

Because the developmental psychopathology literature identifies the risk factors associated with the development and maintenance of each anxiety disorder, this literature represents the ideal starting source from which to select constructs for assessment. Moreover, the assessment process is guided by the understanding that (a) risk factors typically interact with one another to contribute to the development of a particular anxiety disorder, and (b) there is no single causal pathway to the development of particular anxiety disorders. Each child will therefore have a unique combination of factors implicated in the development of an anxiety disorder. Our approach to case formulation is to assess for the common risk factors associated with anxiety disorders in an effort to identify the unique combination of risk factors for each individual client.

Principle 3: Developmental and cultural factors

Developmental factors. Selecting constructs for assessment, determining a method for gathering assessment data, and interpreting the findings should be influenced by knowledge of the developmental norms associated with specific anxiety disorders and/or symptoms (Holmbeck, Thill, Bachanas et al., 2008; Silverman & Ollendick, 2005). Developmental factors can influence the expression of the cognitive, behavioral, and affective symptoms that represent the targets of CBT. Silverman and Ollendick (2005) suggest that cognitive and socioemotional developmental processes, normative guidelines for behaviors, age differences in behavior and symptom profiles, and an awareness of the stability and change of behavior over time all contribute to developmentally informed assessment. The following paragraphs provide general guidelines for how to take developmental factors into consideration when developing a case formulation. For more in-depth coverage of these factors, please see Warren and Sroufe (2004).

First, it is important to understand how symptoms manifest across developmental stages. Certain symptoms, such as fears, are appropriate at specific developmental periods. For example, it is typical for fear of separation to develop in infancy, for fear to move onto social situations in childhood, and for fear to become more generalized in adolescence (Gullone, 1996). So, an intense fear of separation from caregivers is typical in young children, but is not considered developmentally appropriate in school-aged children (Gullone, 1996; Warren & Sroufe, 2004). Thus, it is important to determine whether the expression of a particular symptom is congruent with a child's developmental level or likely to represent a symptom that is interfering with functioning (Silverman & Ollendick, 2005; Warren & Sroufe, 2004)

Second, cognitive factors can influence a child's experience of symptoms. Certain developmental milestones must be achieved before a child can manifest symptoms such as guilt, hopelessness, and worry. For example, worry requires insight, which may not fully develop until late childhood or early adolescence (e.g., Dadds, James, Barrett, & Verhulst, 2004). As another example, the ability to correctly identify and label emotions requires insight into one's internal states, and many children have not developed this ability (Sattler, 2001). As a result, children will often exhibit and/or report behavioral signs of emotional distress, such as headaches, but will be unaware of the semantic description of their affective state. Understanding the relation between cognitive development and the experience of certain symptoms can help clinicians avoid misattributing reports of child behavior to symptoms that are not consistent with the child's developmental level.

Third, a child's ability to report on his or her own symptoms can be influenced by developmental factors (Dadds et al., 2004; Schniering, Hudson, & Rapee, 2000). Language development and comprehension directly influence a child's ability to interpret and understand symptoms contained within clinical interviews and questionnaires (Schniering et al., 2000). For example, children have been found to interpret instructions about the experience of worry on a self-report form of anxiety differently than adolescents (cf. Dadds et al., 2004). Linguistic factors can therefore influence how children, adolescents, and adults understand different symptoms. So, it is important not to depend solely upon child self-report when assessing anxiety symptoms.

In sum, when working with children and adolescents it is important to take developmental factors into consideration when developing a case formulation. Developmental factors determine what assessment tools (e.g., interview, questionnaire, observation) will provide accurate and valid information and may increase the potential for miscommunication between clinicians, parents, and children.

Culture and diversity. Culture is defined as "an integrated pattern of human behavior that includes thought, language, action, and artifacts and depends on man's capacity for learning and transmitting knowledge to succeeding generations" (Frisby & Reynolds, 2005, p. 5). A person's nationality, ethnicity, acculturation level, poverty, and gender can all exert an influence upon the experience and expression of distress and thus need to be considered when conducting an assessment, developing a case formulation, and delivering treatment.

Failure to take culture and diversity into consideration when developing a case formulation can lead to (at least) two types of errors (Edwards, 1982; Ridley & Kelly, 2006). First, a clinician may conclude that a client's behavior is pathological when in fact the behavior can be explained by cultural factors. For example a clinician in the United States who hears about a 7-year-old who still sleeps with her parents might assume that child is experiencing separation anxiety, when there are many cultures in which co-sleeping at that age is considered normative. Second, a clinician may conclude that a client's behavior is due to cultural factors, when in fact the behavior is pathological. For example, a clinician might erroneously assume that a child's religious obsessions are normative for his culture, when in fact they are indicative of a diagnosis of OCD. Such errors result from the failure to thoughtfully take cultural factors into consideration and can result in a faulty case formulation.

Evidence suggests that the expression of symptoms and psychological distress may vary across cultures (Weisz, Sigman, Weiss, & Mosk, 1993). Some of this variation may be due to value differences. Cultures that place a high value on deference to authority appear to have lower rates of externalizing problems (Weisz, Suwanlert, Chaiyasit, & Walter, 1987). The acceptability of certain types of symptoms also varies across cultures and may influence symptom expression (Nguyen & Rosengren, 2004). Indeed, stigma attached to the expression of psychological symptoms in certain cultures may translate into higher rates of somatic symptoms (Weiss, Tram, Rescorla, &

Achenbach, 2009). For example, it has been hypothesized that the reason Latino children tend to report higher rates of somatic symptoms compared to Caucasian youth is the greater acceptability of medical symptoms over psychological symptoms in the Latino culture (see e.g., Pina & Silverman, 2004). As another example, families from inner city communities may see aggression as adaptive (Atkins, McKay, Talbott, & Arvanitis, 1996) and thus not report aggressive behaviors to a clinician. It therefore is important to understand the values and the acceptability of psychological symptoms within a particular culture so that an accurate case formulation can be developed.

Some guidelines exist for incorporating cultural and diversity factors into case formulation (see e.g., Friedberg & McClure, 2002; Ridley & Kelly, 2006). Suggested steps include: (a) awareness of culture and how it may influence the expression of symptoms and/or distress; (b) awareness of culture and how it may influence reporting practices; (c) knowledge of how to conduct a culturally sensitive assessment; and (d) the ability to distinguish between culture and psychopathology.

Principle 4: Cognitive behavioral conceptualization

In our case formulation approach, treament selection and planning is guided by cognitive-behavioral treatment (CBT) theory and research for two reasons. First, CBT is the best-supported treatment for youths with anxiety (Chorpita & Southam-Gerow, 2006; Silverman, Pina, & Viwesvaran, 2008), with support existing for child, parent, and group versions of CBT (Barmish & Kendall, 2005; Kendall, Hudson, Gosch, Flannery-Schroeder, & Suveg, 2008; Silverman, Kurtines, Jaccard, & Pina, 2009; Liber, Van Widenfelt, Utens et al., 2008). Second, CBT programs for child anxiety are based upon developmental psychopathology theories. The interventions contained within the programs were developed to target specific factors identified in the developmental psychopathology literature associated with the development, maintenance, and amelioration of youth anxiety. For example, physiological overarousal is a risk factor for anxiety that can be treated using relaxation techniques. Relying upon the CBT literature facilitates treatment selection and planning as well as helping to ensure that clients receive an efficacious treatment.

Steps for Developing a CBT Case Formulation for Child Anxiety

In this section we detail the process of developing a CBT case formulation for child anxiety. Developing a case formulation may be best viewed as a hypothesis-testing process designed to produce an understanding of a specific youth and the factors that contribute to his or her presenting problems. The steps for developing a case formulation for child anxiety parallel the goals of EBA (Mash & Hunsley, 2005a): (a) identifying and quantifying symptoms and behaviors; (b) diagnosing; (c) identifying and quantifying controlling/maintaining variables; (d) treatment selection and planning; and (e) evaluating and monitoring treatment outcomes. EBA strategies can therefore be applied at all stages of this process. However, it is important to note that any one step will not provide a definitive understanding of a youth. Information gathered at each step helps the clinician formulate hypotheses about the causes, antecedents, and maintaining factors of a youth's anxiety that need to be tested in subsequent steps. For example, hypotheses generated during an intake interview can be evaluated based upon the youth's response to treatment (Silverman & Ollendick, 2008). As treatment progresses, more information is gathered, hypotheses are tested and revised, and the resulting data used to inform treatment planning.

Step 1: Identifying and quantifying symptoms and behaviors

When a client initially presents for treatment, one of the first tasks of the therapist is to define the presenting problem(s). The topography (i.e., frequency, intensity, duration) of the presenting problem should be mapped out in terms of the cognitive, behavioral, and physiological features of anxiety. In essence, the description of the presenting problem serves as the dependent variable that the clinician seeks to change in treatment. It is important to generate a detailed and specific description of the presenting problem as this description provides the basis for setting treatment goals and serves as a baseline for outcome monitoring.

Assessment tools, such as a clinical interview, can be used to define the presenting problems and start the process of setting treatment goals (Nezu et al., 2004). An unstructured interview can help a clinician understand the presenting problem from the perspective of the client. The flexibility of the unstructured interview allows clinicians to tailor the assessment to the client, which, as noted above, is advantageous when trying to get a description of the reason for referral and establish a therapeutic relationship. A description of the presenting problem can usually be generated during an intake interview; however, it may take several sessions to map out the topography of the presenting problems. Self-monitoring assignments are particularly useful for this purpose as they can be tailored to fit the idiosyncratic needs of each client.

When conceptualizing the presenting problems of youth presenting with anxiety problems, it is important to understand how fear and anxiety are experienced in terms of cognitive, behavioral, and physiological symptoms. Youth experience fear and anxiety along a continuum of perceived threat imminence (Craske, 1999). This continuum ranges from the experience of the basic emotion of fear, the mood state of anxiety, to the experience of worry. Fear, anxiety, and worry are each defined by unique cognitive, behavioral, and physiological features that vary in their frequency, intensity, and duration. Understanding this progression is important when attempting to define the presenting problem of youth presenting with anxiety problems.

Fear operates at the extreme end of the continuum. Emotion theorists consider fear to be one of the four basic emotions. As such, fear is a hardwired biological, non-cognitive event that activates self-preserving behavior in the presence of perceived, imminent danger that manifests itself in a fight or flight response that helps promote survival (Craske, 1999; Izard, 1992). In humans, the fear response is accompanied by diminished cognitive functioning, the subjective experience of distress (e.g., fear of death), strong physiological activation – e.g., heart racing, sweaty palms – that serves to prepare an individual to respond to a perceived threat, and a strong desire to acquire a sense of safety from the perceived, imminent threat (Craske, 1999). Fear oftentimes leads youth to engage in fight/flight behavior designed to remove or avoid the feared stimuli. For example, a child who experiences severe separation anxiety may lash out at a parent, refuse to leave a situation, or cling to a parent when separation is occurring.

Avoidance of feared stimuli is, in fact, one of the most common behavioral symptoms of anxiety and is a key factor that contributes to the maintenance of pathological anxiety.

Anxiety is conceptualized as a negative mood state (Gunnar, 2001). The function of anxiety is to prepare the organism to counteract potential future threats. Anxiety occurs along the midpoint in the threat continuum and is characterized by a state of physiological arousal that results in mild to moderate physical symptoms (e.g., headaches, stomachaches), a narrowing focus of attention on perceived threat, ruminations about future potential dangers, and a general negative mood. Both cognitive (attentional biases) and physiological (e.g., autonomic arousal) features characterize anxiety. As the perceived danger nears, all of these symptoms build up to the basic emotion of fear. To manage anxiety symptoms, youth oftentimes avoid anxiety provoking stimuli. For example, children may resist starting homework (e.g., for fear of performing inadequately) and beg not to go to school in the morning to avoid the stress associated with class work.

Worry is considered the cognitive component of anxiety and is defined as thoughts and beliefs about possible problems that may occur in the future (Barlow, 1988). Primarily a cognitive phenomenon, worry is typified by SNS suppression. The function of worry is to prepare the individual to identify potential threats by focusing attention upon aspects of the environment that might represent dangers. Thus, worry is characterized by attentional and memory biases that predispose individuals to attend to threatening stimuli (Craske, 1999).

In sum, the first step in developing a case formulation is to define the cognitive, behavioral, and affective components of the presenting problem. Once the presenting problem has been identified, then the next step is to determine if the client meets DSM-IV criteria for one, or more, anxiety disorders.

Step 2: Diagnosis

The second step is to determine if a child meets criteria for one, or more, DSM-IV anxiety disorders. Generating a diagnosis plays several important purposes in case formulation. First, generating a diagnosis facilitates the process of identifying risk and protective factors that may play a role in causing and/or maintaining the presenting problem (Nezu et al., 2004). That is, generating a diagnosis allows a clinician to access the developmental psychopathology literature for each anxiety disorder that identifies potential controlling and maintaining variables that might represent targets for assessment and treatment. Second, diagnoses facilitate the treatment selection process. Although the assumption that treatments should be matched to diagnosis is largely untested (Nelson-Gray, 2003), diagnoses are currently the main avenue for clinicians to identify CBT therapies to use with their clients. For example, a recent review of EBTs for childhood phobic and anxiety disorders specified several treatments as effective for particular anxiety disorders (e.g., group CBT with parents was supported for social phobia only; Silverman et al., 2008), so a clinician interested in utilizing that list to inform treatment decisions would need to have conducted a good diagnostic assessment. In addition, given the important role of exposure in most EBTs for youth anxiety, an assessment specifying the nature of a client's fears and anxieties that can be used to generate an exposure hierarchy is an important step in treatment planning (Silverman & Ollendick, 2008). Lastly, diagnoses can be used to monitor treatment outcomes. Determining whether a child meets diagnostic criteria for an anxiety disorder at the end of treatment represents an important indicator of clinically significant change. Moreover, self-report measures have been developed for specific anxiety disorders (e.g., Revised Obsessive Compulsive Inventory; Foa, Huppert, Leiberg et al., 2002), which can be used to monitor treatment outcomes over the course of treatment.

The first two steps of case formulation will generally take place during the intake, so the clinician will likely need to employ several assessment methods to define the presenting problem and establish a diagnosis. Interviews are most often used to determine diagnostic status, with standardized interviews being the most psychometrically sound approach. As detailed above, the ADIS currently has the strongest level of support for this purpose (Silverman & Ollendick, 2008; Southam-Gerow & Chorpita, 2007). At this phase, self-report questionnaires can be used to supplement the interview data and quantify the severity of a client's problems. A broadband self-report measure, such as the CBCL (Achenbach & Rescorla, 2001), can help check for the presence of potential comorbid problems. More specific self-report measures, such as the RCADS (Chorpita et al., 2000) or the MASC (March et al., 1997), can help determine the severity of the anxiety disorder(s) and determine a baseline for outcome monitoring. The decision to use one, or more, assessment approach will be guided by the psychometric properties of the measures as well as the constraints of the setting in which the assessment will occur.

In sum, determining whether a child meets criteria for a DSM-IV anxiety disorder is the second step in developing a case formulation. This step facilitates treatment selection, outcome monitoring, and – perhaps most importantly – provides a way to access the developmental psychopathology literature that will help a clinician identify possible maintaining and/or controlling variables that will form the foundation of the case formulation.

Step 3: Identifying and quantifying controlling/maintaining variables

Next, developmental psychopathological theories are relied upon to identify risk and protective factors that may play a role in the development and maintenance of the DSM-IV anxiety disorder(s). Each anxiety disorder has unique risk factors associated with the development and maintenance of the disorder. It is beyond the scope of this chapter to review the risk factors associated with each specific anxiety disorder or more general risk factors that might contribute to emotional and behavioral problems in youth (e.g., family distress). So, here we will review the risk factors commonly implicated in the development and maintenance of youth anxiety disorders. We start with the biological bases of child anxiety – i.e., the inherited factors that contribute to anxiety disorders. We then progress onto the cognitive, environmental, and parental factors that contribute to the development and maintenance of child anxiety disorders. To develop an accurate case formulation each risk factor should be assessed for at the beginning of treatment.

Genetic factors. When developing a case formulation for child anxiety, it is important to establish whether there is a family history of anxiety disorders. Evidence suggests that genetic factors play a significant role in the development and maintenance of anxiety disorders. Behavioral inhibition, SNS reactivity, and the personality traits that are linked to anxiety (i.e., neuroticism and introversion) seem to be partially heritable (DiLalla, Kagan, & Reznick, 1994; Eley, 2001). Indeed, twin studies suggest that about 60–65% of the variance in trait anxiety is due to genetic factors (Eley, 2001; Hudziak, Rudiger, Neale, Heath, & Todd, 2000). The genetic makeup of an individual therefore plays a significant role in the development and maintenance of anxiety. Thus, when developing a case formulation, it is important to establish whether there is a family history of anxiety disorders.

Biological factors. Biological factors can play a role in maintaining anxiety, so an important component of developing a case formulation is determining whether physical and somatic symptoms help maintain anxiety. Many individuals with anxiety disorders experience frequent symptoms of SNS arousal such as increased heart rate, sweaty palms, and a flushed face. This tendency for physiological over-reactivity is marked by a "physiological prepared" set in which clinically anxious children tend to display elevated baseline physiological functioning marked by elevated heart rate, epinephrine, norepinephrine, and cortisol levels (Barlow, 1988). Physiological characteristics such as a strong startle response, strong gag reflex, or behavioral inhibition are markers of physiological over-reactivity that are linked to anxiety (Craske, 1999). The aversive physiological feelings that are elicited by SNS arousal are difficult for children to manage. Moreover, these aversive physiological feelings are believed to promote avoidance of feared objects and contribute to the maintenance of anxiety due to the sense of relief children experience from physiological discomfort stemming from such avoidance (Craske, 1999).

It is also important to determine whether a youth was behaviorally inhibited as a child (Dadds & Barrett, 2001). Research suggests that SNS reactivity (temperament) may represent an inherited risk factor that places children at increased risk for developing an anxiety disorder. Evidence for this association was produced in two longitudinal studies in which toddlers were grouped into "behaviorally inhibited" and "behaviorally uninhibited" groups based on their responses to novel stimuli in a laboratory setting during infancy. When presented with stressors, such as novel social interactions, the behaviorally inhibited group displayed signs of greater SNS reactivity (Kagan, 1997; Kagan et al., 1989; Snidman, et al., 1995). Importantly, the behaviorally inhibited children were more likely to develop anxiety disorders later in life. These findings provide evidence that SNS reactivity places children at greater risk for developing an anxiety disorder.

Learning processes. Once a particular fear is defined it is important to identify the pathway to fear acquisition and the associated learning process. Rachman (1977) proposed an influential three-pathway model of fear acquisition that is useful for understanding how particular fears might develop and/or become maintained. He stated that specific fears and anxiety could be acquired through direct or indirect learning experiences that included conditioning, vicarious learning, and transmission of information. Rachman associates more mild and common fears with indirect pathways (e.g., vicarious acquisition, transmission of information) and more intense fears with direct acquisition (e.g., conditioning).

Conditioning. Fears of specific stimuli can be acquired through classical conditioning. Classical conditioning involves the association of an unpleasant unconditioned stimulus (US) with a neutral conditioned stimulus (CS). For instance, a young child who gets lost in a shopping mall may come to associate fear (the US) with a shopping mall (the CS), leading to fear of large shopping malls. Classical conditioning can occur over multiple pairings of the CS and US as well as with only one pairing of the CS and US (Craske, 1999). When conditioning occurs during one pairing it is called traumatic conditioning.

Operant principles. Operant principles can play several different roles in anxiety formation. Some learning of fearful behavior may be mediated entirely through operant mechanisms, without classical conditioning. However, classical conditioning and operant conditioning typically work together to explain fear acquisition. Mowrer's two-factor theory (1939) explains how classical conditioning acts as the first "factor" that leads to the acquisition of fear. The second factor involves operant conditioning, specifically negative reinforcement. In negative reinforcement, removal of an unpleasant stimulus increases the chance that an antecedent behavior will be repeated in the future. CSs (e.g., feared stimuli) tend to be avoided, and this avoidance prevents the conditioned response (fear/anxiety) from occurring and thus becomes reinforced. The key point is that *avoidance* of specific stimuli or situations can reduce the unpleasant experience of fear and anxiety; as a result, avoidant behavior can become a habitual behavioral response to feared stimuli or situations—even when there is no real threat.

Vicarious learning. Albert Bandura (1997) illustrated how *modeling* can play a role in anxiety formation by increasing or reducing fear and anxiety. Modeling involves observing another person in a situation engage in a behavior or experience an emotion that increases the likelihood that the observer will engage in a similar behavior or experience a similar emotion in that situation. A simple example involves a child who observes her mother avoid public bathrooms and verbalize that such places are full of germs and disease. Through modeling, the child will have an increased chance of believing public bathrooms are dirty and perhaps avoid public bathrooms in the future. In short, various learning experiences, broadly defined, seem to contribute to the development of fear and anxiety in children.

To identify the pathway to fear acquisition when developing a case formulation, a number of questions should be asked (Dadds & Barrett, 2001). Does a specific event and/or stressor predate the onset of anxiety? Did direct and/or indirect learning experience influence fear acquisition? Direct learning experiences generally involve conditioning experiences in which previously neutral stimuli became associated with fear or loss of control. Indirect experiences typically involve operant and/or modeling that serve to reinforce avoidant behavior. Identifying the pathway(s) to fear acquisition for each client plays an important role in treatment planning as different CBT interventions are used to target the different learning processes.

Cognitive processes. Cognitive theories of anxiety emphasize the role of an individual's thoughts in the development and maintenance of anxiety and fear. The term cognition refers to the thoughts, attitudes, and beliefs an individual has regarding a specific situation. Cognitive theory generally differentiates between two levels of cognition: schemas and automatic thoughts (Sweeney & Pine, 2004). Schemas represent fundamental assumptions or beliefs about oneself and the world. These basic assumptions exert a profound impact upon how individuals interpret situations and events in their life. Automatic thoughts represent thoughts and images that occur in specific situations and influence how events are appraised and interpreted in that situation.

Automatic thoughts are posited to be linked to schemas, but are cued by specific situations.

Theoretical models hypothesize that when cognitions about the self, the world, or the future are inaccurate, mental health disorders may arise (Beck, Rush, Shaw, & Emery, 1979). Schema and automatic thoughts typical of anxiety disorders oftentimes include inaccurate information about the presence of threat and are shaped by learning experiences that focus attention upon certain stimuli (e.g., dogs, public speaking). Automatic thoughts make individuals more likely to interpret ambiguous situations as threatening, whereas inaccurate and sometimes catastrophic cognitions at the deeper levels of schemata are responsible for maladaptive emotional and behavioral responses (Beck et al., 1979). For example, a child possessing a catastrophic schema pertaining to being away from parents is liable to experience panic and fear when separation is imminent and thus engage in corresponding fight/flight behavior (e.g., refusing to leave; clinging; lashing out) designed to prevent the feared consequence (predicted by the schema) from coming to pass.

A final aspect of the cognitive model relevant to child anxiety is experience with self-efficacy (i.e., perceptions of agency and competence with regard to specific tasks; Bandura, 1997). Substantial research has illustrated an association between self-efficacy and anxiety regulation (e.g., Muris, 2002). Children who have few opportunities for mastery and control may not have opportunities to develop self-efficacy and thus be at increased risk for anxiety. Similarly, children's perceived control (i.e., perceptions that one can directly influence opportunities for positive and negative reinforcement) is another process that can influence the experience of anxiety in children (Chorpita, 2001; Chorpita & Barlow, 1998).

Identifying the role of cognitions in the development and maintenance of child anxiety represents a key step in developing a case formulation (Baldwin & Dadds, 2007). A number of questions related to cognitions can be asked. How does the child view his/her anxiety problems? What opportunities has the child had for mastery experiences; does he/she believe in his/her ability to effectively deal with the presenting problem? Are there any cognitive biases that may influence the child's perception of threat? This step has important implications for treatment planning as it will determine the extent to which cognitions are targeted in treatment.

Parental influences. Various parenting practices have been implicated in the development and maintenance of anxiety. However, parental control, particularly parental intrusiveness, and parental modeling of anxious behavior appear to be uniquely linked with child anxiety (McLeod, Wood, & Weisz, 2007; Wood, McLeod, Sigman, Hwang & Chu, 2003).

Parental intrusiveness. Parental intrusiveness is hypothesized to affect childhood anxiety through two processes: (a) influencing children's opportunities for habituation and extinction and (b) curtailing children's self-efficacy. Habituation and extinction play a key role in the amelioration of fear and anxiety wherein repeated exposure to a feared (but benign) stimulus leads to a reduction in the strength of the fear response (Rachman, 1990). Parents who act intrusively are posited to interfere with habituation by preventing the child from actually confronting feared stimuli (Fox, Henderson, Marshall, Nichols, & Ghera, 2005; Rapee, 2001). For example, the parents of a child who freezes when faced with unfamiliar peers in social situations (a common symptom of social anxiety in middle childhood) might remain close and interact for the child. Such parenting practices may unintentionally prevent the child from habituating to the setting by keeping him/her from experiencing the situation independently, learning there is nothing to be afraid of, and (eventually) experiencing a sense of mastery. Conversely, parents who refrain from intrusiveness may promote habituation at a rate that is comfortable to the child and thus contribute to the amelioration of child anxiety.

Children's self-efficacy (i.e., perceptions of agency and competence with regard to specific tasks; Bandura, 1997) is the second process hypothesized to be linked to intrusiveness. As discussed above, low self-efficacy is a risk factor for anxiety. It is hypothesized that parents who routinely take over tasks for children that they are likely able to do for themselves (i.e., act intrusively) may undermine children's self-efficacy and thus elevate their risk for anxiety (Krohne & Hock, 1991). In essence, the more that parents take over tasks for children, the greater their anxiety may become because they lack mastery experiences and presumably feel less efficacious.

Developmentally, the impact of intrusive parental behaviors may become more pronounced later in childhood. As children transition into early adolescence, autonomy becomes an increasingly important need (Allen, Hauser, Bell, & O'Connor, 1994; Soenens, Vansteenkiste, Lens et al., 2007; Steinberg, 1990) and parental behavior that restricts or limits autonomy might be particularly salient. Through the process of social comparison (see, e.g., Hedley & Young, 2006), early adolescents might perceive a difference between the level of autonomy granted by their parents and that granted to peers. The perceived discrepancy between expected and actual (experienced) levels of autonomy in specific situations could leave adolescents less self-confident, less efficacious, and more anxious (Hedley & Young, 2006; Irons & Gilbert, 2005). The impact of intrusive parenting on child anxiety may therefore increase during the transition into early adolescence.

Parental modeling of anxious behavior. As described above, there are several learning pathways through which anxiety may develop. For children, parents can play an important role in these processes. Parental modeling of anxious behavior refers to describing problems in a catastrophic manner and demonstrating avoidant behavior (Capps & Ochs, 1995; Whaley, Pinto, & Sigman, 1999). The mere presence of parental modeling of anxious behavior is not sufficient for anxiety development. However, children at elevated risk to developing an anxiety disorder may be susceptible to the influence of parental modeling of anxious behavior (Craske, 1999). Children of parents who model anxious behavior may come to believe that there is no way of coping effectively with problems (Barrett, Dadds, & Rapee, 1996; Capps & Ochs, 1995; Whaley et al., 1999). Thus, parental modeling of anxious behavior is believed to contribute to the development of cognitive biases that contribute to the development and maintenance of child anxiety.

In sum, defining the role that specific parental behaviors play in the development and maintenance of child anxiety represents an important step when building a case formulation. The following questions related to parenting can be asked. What opportunities do the parents provide for mastery experiences? Do the parents negatively influence a child's opportunities for habituation and extinction? Do the parents routinely take tasks over for youth that they could reasonably do for themselves? Do the parents model anxious or avoidant behavior? Answers to these questions aid treatment planning by helping to determine if the treatment plan should include parent-focused and/or family-focused CBT strategies.

Social skills. Peer social relations provide youth with an opportunity to learn valuable social skills. The social skills gained through peer relations cannot easily be learned from interactions with family members or adults. Moreover, the development of social skills evolves over time such that the acquisition of skills at younger ages impacts future skill acquisition (NICHD Early Child Care Research Network, 1995). So, youth who fail to learn social skills at an early age are at increased risk for poor social relations across childhood in adolescence.

Youth who fear social situations are at increased risk for poor social outcomes. Fearful and withdrawn youth are more likely to be rejected by peers as early as second grade (Rubin, 1993). For some youth, fear of social situations leads them to avoid peer interactions to alleviate the anxiety they experience when interacting with peers. Of course, avoiding social interactions limits opportunities to develop age-appropriate social skills. Deficits in social skills become increasingly pronounced when avoidance persists over a long time, which further increases the likelihood that socially anxious youth will be rejected. Repeated social rejection contributes to the formation of beliefs that serve to maintain social anxiety and reinforce the avoidance of social situations. For example, youth may begin to believe that they cannot say or do the right things in social situations, or come to expect to be bullied by their peers. Because social skills deficits can play such an important role in maintaining anxiety, it is important to assess whether an anxious child has developmentally appropriate social skills.

Summary. When developing a case formulation clinicians should assess for each of the domains previously reviewed. Assessments exist for some of the domains. For example, the Anxiety Sensitivity Index (Reiss, Peterson, Gursky, & McNally, 1986) assesses beliefs that anxiety related symptoms are harmful. As another example, behavioral avoidance tasks exist for evaluating social skills (e.g., social evaluative tasks; Beidel, Turner, & Morris, 2000). However, standardized assessments do not currently exist for most domains, and this information must therefore be gathered during an unstructured interview. An accurate and comprehensive picture of the risk factors is important, however, as this information shapes treatment selection and planning. As noted above, it is often the case that a full picture of the youth's causal and maintaining factors is not gathered during the initial interview. Rather, it is more often the case that specific hypotheses regarding the presence of certain risk factors are developed during the intake interview, which are then tested over subsequent therapy sessions. Two assessment approaches – self-monitoring and functional analyses – are particularly useful for this purpose.

Step 4: Treatment selection and planning

Treatment selection and planning generally occurs after the intake interview, when the clinician has generated a set of preliminary hypotheses about the nature and causes of the client's presenting problems. At this step, the formulation should include specific hypotheses that detail how a particular set of risk factors cause or maintain the child's anxiety. CBT interventions are then matched to the particular risk factors hypothesized to play a role in the child's anxiety. The sequencing and intensity of particular CBT interventions is also determined, in part, by the information gathered in the previous formulation steps. For example, if a child with severe social phobia has pronounced social skill deficits, then treatment would focus upon remediating the skill deficits prior to addressing the social anxiety. In this way, a detailed and specific treatment plan can be developed for each individual client.

Empirical findings support this type of prescriptive approach to the treatment of child anxiety. CBT for child anxiety has been shown to be maximally effective when CBT interventions are matched to the specific anxiety symptoms exhibited by individual youth (Eisen & Silverman, 1993, 1998; Ollendick, 1995; Ollendick, Hagopian, & Huntzinger, 1991). For example, Eisen and Silverman (1993) found that CBT was maximally effective when children presenting primarily with somatic complaints were provided relaxation training and children presenting primarily with worry were provided cognitive interventions. These findings provide support for the utility of the prescriptive approach to treatment planning advocated herein.

Because our approach advocates matching CBT interventions to particular risk factors, it is important to consider the type of treatment materials that are best suited for this purpose. A treatment manual that allows for the flexible application of CBT interventions based upon the case formulation is required. Flexibility is also important because data collected during treatment sometimes necessitates changes to the treatment plan. For example, a therapist treating a child for school refusal due to social phobia may become aware of parental behaviors that are facilitating school avoidance, requiring the addition of parent-focused treatment components. Thus, a manual that allows therapists to selectively target multiple risk factors throughout treatment is preferred.

To address these concerns, we suggest that therapists use a CBT intervention that adhere to a modular design, such as described by Chorpita (2007). Compared to traditional treatment manuals, which emphasize the serial application of sessions, modular treatments have a freestanding module for each core component of CBT for youth anxiety. Clinical algorithms provide decision rules about how and when to use each module, which allow therapists to adopt a patient-centered approach that matches the sequence and duration of interventions to the needs of each client. Modular treatment materials therefore allows therapists to address multiple risk factors throughout the course of treatment.

Step 5: Evaluating and monitoring treatment outcomes

Finally, once treatment begins ongoing assessment of core symptoms and contributing factors can be used to monitor treatment response and to identify changes needed to the treatment plan. This type of assessment is important during any type of treatment approach, but is particularly important when employing a modular approach, which is designed to be tailored to the individual, ongoing needs of each client. Research with adults also suggests that continuous assessment and feedback can improve therapy outcomes by identifying clients at risk for treatment failure and raising clinicians' awareness of a need to adjust their treatment approaches (Lambert, Whipple, Hawkins, Vermeersch, Nielsen & Smart, 2003). This link between assessment and outcomes has not yet been established in child samples, although retrospective data analyses have suggested that algorithms can be developed to predict treatment failures from symptom trajectories among children (Bishop, Bybee, Lambert, Burlingame, Wells, & Poppleton, 2005).

While ongoing outcome assessment is a common feature of EBA recommendations for child anxiety (Silverman & Ollendick, 2008; Southam-Gerow & Chorpita, 2007), very little systematic research exists on how to structure this process. Southam-Gerow and Chorpita (2007) differentiate between ongoing assessment during treatment, which serves the purpose of informing treatment planning, and post-treatment assessment, which serves to determine the overall impact of a completed course of treatment. While the latter form of assessment is commonly used in randomized controlled trials for child anxiety, the former is not (Silverman & Ollendick, 2008). Therefore, more empirical evidence exists regarding appropriate measures for post-treatment assessment than about measures appropriate for ongoing assessment.

For assessment during treatment, which can potentially become quite burdensome in terms of time, Southam-Gerow and Chorpita (2007) recommend focusing assessment on the specific symptoms being treated, rather than conducting broad assessment. They suggest utilizing brief checklists assessing the client's specific syndromes or utilizing idiographic measures, such as the number of panic attacks experienced in the past week. Idiographic measures can also be used to track contributing factors, given the lack of standardized measures for many of these variables. We are not aware of any research to inform decisions about how often to conduct this ongoing assessment. For some measures, particularly self-monitoring methods, daily or weekly assessment is likely most appropriate to help track client compliance and to ensure accurate recall of the behaviors under study. For some questionnaires, however, less frequent assessment may be more appropriate. For example, the State-Trait Anxiety Scale for Children (Spielberger, 1973) instructs informants to consider the presence of each symptom in the past 4 weeks, so administering it more frequently than every 4 weeks is not advised.

At the end of treatment, a more thorough assessment is warranted in order to understand the impact of treatment and to assess the need for further referrals or interventions. It is recommended that, if feasible, this assessment include measures of the syndrome that was the focus of treatment, broader anxiety measures, such as the RCADS or SCARED, a structured interview like the ADIS, and idiographic measures (Southam-Gerow & Chorpita, 2007). When selecting outcome measures for either form out outcome assessment, it is also important to select measures that have been demonstrated to be sensitive to change. Silverman and Ollendick (2008) conclude that the ADIS, the RCMAS, and the CBCL are the most widely used post-treatment outcome measures in the literature and all been found to be sensitive to change.

In sum, clinicians can use this five step process to develop a case formulation for youth seeking treatment for anxiety. This approach provides clinicians with a tool to help them develop hypotheses about the factors causing a client's problems that can be used to guide assessment and treatment from the intake interview to termination. By relying upon empirically validated theories and findings to guide assessment and treatment clinicians can produce treatment plans tailored to each individual client and thus help maximize the beneficial effects of cognitive-behavioral treatment for youth anxiety.

References

Achenbach, T. M., & Rescorla, L. A. (2001). *Manual for the ASEBA School-Age Forms and Profiles.* Burlington, VT: University of Vermont, Research Center for CHildren, Youth, & Families.

Allen, J. P., Hauser, S. T., Bell, K. L., & O'Connor, T. G. (1994). Longitudinal assessment of autonomy and relatedness in adolescent-family interactions as predictors of adolescent ego development and self-esteem. *Child Development, 65,* 179–194.

Ambrosini, P. J. (2000). Historical development and present status of the Schedule for Affective Disorders and Schizophrenia for School-Age Children (K-SADS). *Journal of the American Academy of Child & Adolescent Psychiatry, 39,* 49–58.

American Educational Research Association, American Psychological Association, & National Council on Measurement in Education. (1999). *Standards for Educational and Psychological Testing.* Washington, DC: American Educational Research Association.

Angold, A., & Fisher, P. W. (1999). Interviewer-based interviews. In D. Shaffer, C. P. Lucas & J. E. Richters (Eds.), *Diagnostic Assessment in Child and Adolescent Psychopathology* (pp. 34–64). New York, NY: Guilford Press.

APA Presidential Task Force on Evidence-Based Practice (2006). Evidence-based practice in psychology. *American Psychologist, 61,* 271–285.

Atkins, M. S., McKay, M. M., Talbot, E. & Arvanitis, P. (1996). DSM-IV diagnosis of conduct disorder and oppositional defiant disorder: Implications and guidelines for school mental health teams. *School Psychology Review, 25,* 274–283.

Baldwin, J. S., & Dadds, M. R. (2007). Anxiety disorders. In M. Hersen (Series Ed.) & D. Reitman (Ed.), *Handbook of Psychological Assessment, Case Conceptualization, and Treatment: Vol. 2 Children and Adolescents* (pp. 231–263). New Jersey: John Wiley & Sons, Ltd.

Bandura, A. (1997). *Self-efficacy: The Exercise of Control.* New York, NY: W. H. Freeman/ Times Books / Henry Hold & Co.

Barlow, D. H. (1988). *Anxiety and Its Disorders: The Nature and Treatment of Anxiety and Panic.* New York: Guilford Press.

Barmish, A., & Kendall, P. C. (2005). Should parents be co-clients in cognitive-behavioral therapy for anxious youth? *Journal of Clinical and Child Adolescent Psychology, 34,* 569–581.

Barrett, P. M., Dadds, M. R., & Rapee, R. M. (1996). Family treatment of childhood anxiety: A controlled trial. *Journal of Consulting & Clinical Psychology, 64,* 333–342.

Beck, A. T., Rush, A. J., Shaw, B. F., & Emery, G. (1979). *Cognitive Therapy for Depression.* Hoboken, NJ: John Wiley & Sons, Ltd.

Beidel, D. C., Turner, S. M., & Morris, T. L. (2000). Behavioral treatment of childhood social phobia. *Journal of Consulting and Clinical Psychology, 68,* 1072–1080.

Bishop, M. J., Bybee, T. S., Lambert, M. J., Burlingame, G. M., Wells, M. G., & Poppleton, L. E. (2005). Accuracy of a rationally derived method for identifying treatment failure in children and adolescents. *Journal of Child and Family Studies, 14,* 207–222.

Capps, L., & Ochs, E. (1995). *Constructing Panic: the Discourse of Agoraphobia.* Cambridge, MA: Harvard University Press.

Chorpita, B. F. (2007). *Modular Cognitive-Behavioral Therapy for Childhood Anxiety Disorders.* New York: Guilford.

Chorpita, B. F. (2001). Control and the development of negative emotion. In M. W. Vasey & M. R. Dadds (Eds.) *The Developmental Psychopathology of Anxiety* (pp. 112–142). Oxford: Oxford University Press.

Chorpita, B. F., & Barlow, D. H. (1998). The development of anxiety: The role of control in the early environment. *Psychological Bulletin, 124,* 3–21.

Chorpita, B. F., & Daleiden, E. L. (2009). Mapping evidence-based treatments for children and adolescents: Application of the distillation and matching model to 615 treatments from 322 randomized trials. *Journal of Consulting and Clinical Psychology, 77*, 566–579.

Chorpita, B. F., & Southam-Gerow, M. A. (2006). Fears and Anxieties. In E. J. Mash & R. A. Barkley (Eds.), *Treatment of Childhood Disorders*, 3rd edn (pp. 271–335). New York, NY: Guilford Press.

Chorpita, B. F., Yim, L., Moffitt, C., Umemoto, L. A., & Francis, S. E. (2000). Assessment of symptoms of DSM-IV anxiety and depression in children: A revised child anxiety and depression scale. *Behaviour Research and Therapy, 38*, 835–855.

Ciccheti, D., & Cohen, D. J. (1995). *Developmental Psychopathology, Volume 1: Theory and Methods*. Oxford, England: John Wiley & Sons.

Cone, J. D. (1999). Introduction to the special section on self-monitoring: A major assessment method in clinical psychology. *Psychological Assessment, 11*, 411–414.

Connolly, S. D., & Bernstein, G. A. (2007). Practice parameter for the assessment and treatment of children and adolescents with anxiety disorders. *Journal of the American Academy of Child & Adolescent Psychiatry, 46*, 267–283.

Craske, M. G. (1999). *Anxiety Disorders: Psychological Approaches to Theory and Treatment*. Boulder, CO: Westview Press.

Craske, M. G., & Tsao, J. C. I. (1999). Self-monitoring with panic and anxiety disorders. *Psychological Assessment, 11*, 466–479.

Dadds, M. R., & Barrett, P. M. (2001). Psychological management of anxiety disorders in childhood. *Journal of Child Psychology and Psychiatry, 42*, 999–1011.

Dadds, M. R., James, R. C., Barrett, P. M., & Verhulst, F. C. (2004). Diagnostic issues. In T. H. Ollendick & J. S. March (Eds.), *Phobic and Anxiety Disorders in Children and Adolescents: A Clinician's Guide to Effective Psychosocial and Pharmacological Interventions* (pp. 3–33). New York: Oxford University Press.

DiLalla, L. F., Kagan, J., & Reznick, J. S. (1994). Genetic etiology of behavioral inhibition among 2-year-old children. *Infant Behavior & Development, 17*, 405–412.

Edwards, A. W. (1982). The consequences of error in selecting treatment for blacks. *Social Casework, 63*, 429–433.

Eells, T. D. (1997). *Handbook of Psychotherapy Case Formulation*. New York: Guilford Press.

Eells, T. D. (2006). *Handbook of Psychotherapy Case Formulation*, 2nd edn. New York: Guilford Press.

Eells, T. D., & Lombart, K. G. (2004). Case formulation: Determining the focus in brief dynamic psychotherapy. In D. P. Charman (Ed.), *Core Processes in Brief Psychodynamic Psychotherapy: Advancing Effective Practice*, (pp.119–144). Mahwah, NJ: Lawrence Erlbaum Associates.

Eisen, A. R., & Silverman, W. K. (1993). Should I relax or change my thoughts? A preliminary study of the treatment of Overanxious Disorder in children. *Journal of Cognitive Psychotherapy, 7*, 265–280.

Eisen, A. R., & Silverman, W. K. (1998). Prescriptive treatment for generalized anxiety disorder in children. *Behavior Therapy, 29*, 105–121.

Eley, T. C. (2001). Contributions of behavioral genetics research: Quantifying genetic, shared environmental and nonshared environmental influences. In M. W. Vasey & M. R. Dadds (Eds.), *The Developmental Psychopathology of Anxiety* (pp. 45–59). New York: Oxford University Press.

Foa, E. B., Huppert, J. D., Leiberg, S., Langner, R., Kichic, R., Hajcak, G. et al. (2002). The Obsessive-Compulsive Inventory: Development and validation of a short version. *Psychological Assessment, 10*, 206–214.

Fox, N. A., Henderson, H. A., Marshall, P. J., Nichols, K. E., & Ghera, M. M. (2005). Behavioral inhibition: Linking biology and behavior within a developmental framework. *Annual Review of Psychology, 56*, 235–262.

Friedberg, R., & McClure, J. (2002). Review of clinical practice of cognitive therapy with children and adolescents. *Journal of Developmental and Behavioral Pediatrics, 23,* 457–458.

Frisby, C. L., & Reynolds, C. R. (2005). *Comprehensive Handbook of Multicultural School Psychology.* Hoboken, NJ: John Wiley & Sons, Inc.

Garb, H. N. (1998). *Studying the Clinician: Judgment Research and Psychological Assessment.* Washington, DC: American Psychological Association.

Garb, H. N. (2005). Clinical judgment and decision making. *Annual Review of Clinical Psychology, 1,* 67–89.

Gullone, E. (1996). Normal fear in people with a physical or intellectual disability. *Clinical Psychology Review, 16,* 689–706.

Gunnar, M. R. (2001). The role of glucocorticoids in anxiety disorders: A critical analysis. In M. W. Vasey & M. R. Dadds (Eds.), *The Developmental Psychopathology of Anxiety* (pp. 143–159). New York: Oxford University Press.

Hedley, D., & Young, R. (2006). Social comparison processes and depressive symptoms in children and adolescents with Asperger syndrome. *Autism, 10,* 139–153.

Hersen, M., & Porzelius, L. K. (2002). *Diagnosis, conceptualization, and treatment planning for adults: A step-by-step guide.* Mahwah, NJ: Lawrence Erlbaum Associates.

Holmbeck, G. N., Thill, A. W., Bachanas, P., Garber, J., Miller, K. B., Abad, M., et al. (2008). Evidence-based assessment in pediatric psychology: Measures of psychosocial adjustment and psychopathology. *Journal of Pediatric Psychology, 33,* 958–980.

Horowitz, M. (2005). *Understanding Psychotherapy Change: a Practical Guide to Configurational Analysis.* Washington, DC: American Psychologaical Association.

Hudziak, J. J., Rudiger, L. P., Neale, M. C., Heath, A. C., & Todd, R. D. (2000). A twin study of inattentive, aggressive, and anxious/depressed behaviors. *Journal of the American Academy of Child & Adolescent Psychiatry, 39,* 469–476.

Hunsley, J. (2002). Psychological testing and psychological assessment: A closer examination. *American Psychologist, 57,* 139–140.

Hunsley, J., & Mash, E. J. (2007). Evidence-based assessment. *Annual Review of Clinical Psychology, 3,* 29–51.

Hunsley, J., & Mash, E. J. (2008). *A Guide to Assessments That Work.* New York: Oxford University Press.

Irons, C., & Gilbert, P. (2005). Evolved mechanisms in adolescent anxiety and depression symptoms: The role of the attachment and social rank systems. *Journal of Adolescence, 28,* 325–341.

Izard, C. E. (1992). Basic emotions, relations among emotions, and emotion-cognition relations. *Psychological Review, 99,* 561–565.

Jensen-Doss, A., Hawley, K. M., Lopez, M., & Osterberg, L. D. (2009). Using evidence-based treatments: The experiences of youth providers working under a mandate. *Professional Psychology: Research and Practice, 40,* 417–424.

Jewell, J., Handwerk, M., Almquist, J., & Lucas, C. (2004). Comparing the validity of clinician-generated diagnosis of conduct disorder to the Diagnostic Interview Schedule for Children. *Journal of Clinical Child and Adolescent Psychology, 33,* 536–546.

Kagan, J. (1997). Temperament and the reactions to unfamiliarity. *Child Development, 68,* 139–143.

Kagan, J., Reznick, J. S., & Gibbons, J. (1989). Inhibited and uninhibited types of children. *Child Development, 60,* 838–845.

Kendell, R., & Jablensky, A. (2003). Distinguishing between the validity and utility of psychiatric diagnoses. *The American Journal of Psychiatry, 160,* 4–12.

Kendall, P. C., Hudson, J. L., Gosch, E., Flannery-Schroeder, E., & Suveg, C. (2008). Cognitive-behavioral therapy for anxiety disordered youth: A randomized clinical trial evaluating child and family modalities. *Journal of Consulting and Clinical Psychology, 76,* 282–297.

Krohne, H. W., & Hock, M. (1991). Relationships between restrictive mother-child interactions and anxiety of the child. *Anxiety Research, 4,* 109–124.

Lambert, M. J., Whipple, J. L., Hawkins, E. J., Vermeersch, D. A., Nielsen, S. L., & Smart, D. W. (2003). Is it time for clinicians to routinely track patient outcome? A meta-analysis. *Clinical Psychology, Science and Practice, 10,* 288–301.

Langley, A. K., Bergman, R. L., & Piacentini, J. C. (2002). Assessment of childhood anxiety. *International Review of Psychiatry, 14,* 102–113.

Liber, J. M., Van Widenfelt, B. M., Utens, E. M. W. J., Ferdinand, R. F., Van der Leeden, A. J. M., Van Gastel, W., etal. (2008). No difference between group versus individual treatment of childhood anxiety disorders in a randomised clinical trial. *Journal of Child Psychology and Psychiatry, 49,* 886–893.

March, J. S., Parker, J. D. A., Sullivan, K., & Stallings, P. (1997). The Multidimensional Anxiety Scale for Children (MASC): Factor structure, reliability, and validity. *Journal of the American Academy of Child & Adolescent Psychiatry, 36,* 554–565.

Mash, E. J., & Hunsley, J. (2005a). Developing guildelines for the evidence-based assessment of child and adolescent disorders [Special Section]. *Journal of Clinical Child & Adolescent Psychology, 34,* 362–558.

Mash, E. J., & Hunsley, J. (2005b). Introduction to the special section on developing guidelines for the evidence-based assessment (EBA) of adult disorders. *Psychological Assessment, 17,* 251–255.

Masten, A. S., & Braswell, L. (1991). Developmental psychopathology: An integrative framework. In P. R. Martin (Ed.), *Handbook of behavior therapy and psychological science: An integrative approach, Pergamon general psychology series,* Vol. 164 (pp. 35–56). Elmsford, NY, US: Pergamon Press.

McFall, R. M. (2005). Theory and utility-Key themes in evidence-based assessment: Comment on the special section. *Psychological Assessment, 17,* 312–323.

McLeod, B. D., & Weisz, J. R. (2004). Using dissertations to examine potential bias and child and adolescent clinical trials. *Journal of Consulting and Clinical Psychology, 72,* 235–251.

McLeod, B. D., Wood, J. J., & Weisz, J. R. (2007). Examining the association between parenting and childhood anxiety: A meta-analysis. *Clinical Psychology Review, 27,* 155–172.

Meng, C. T. T., Kirkby, K. C., Martin, F., Gilroy, L. J., & Daniels, B. A. (2004). Computer-delivered behavioural avoidance tests for spider phobia. *Behaviour Change, 21,* 173–185.

Mori, L. T., & Armendariz, G. M. (2001). Analogue assessment of child behavior problems. *Psychological Assessment, 13,* 36–45.

Mowrer, O. H. (1939). A stimulus-response analysis of anxiety and its role as a reinforcing agent. *Psychological Review, 46,* 553–565.

Muris, P. (2002). Relationships between self-efficacy and symptoms of anxiety disorders and depression in a normal adolescent sample. *Personality & Individual Differences, 32,* 337–348.

Myers, K., & Winters, N. C. (2002). Ten-year review of rating scales. I: Overview of scale functioning, psychometric properties and selection. *Journal of the American Academy of Child & Adolescent Psychiatry, 41,* 114–122.

National Institute of Mental Health. (2010). The National Institute of Mental Health Strategic Plan. Retrieved February 17, 2010, from http://www. nimh. nih. gov/about/strategic-planning-reports/index. shtml

Nelson-Gray, R. O. (2003). Treatment utility of psychological assessment. *Psychological Assessment, 15,* 521–531.

Nezu, A. M., Nezu, C. M., Peacock, M. A., & Girdwood, C. P. (2004). Case formulation in cognitive-behavior therapy. In S. N. Haynes (Ed.), E. M. Heiby (Ed.), & M. Hersen (Series Ed.), *Comprehensive Handbook of Psychological Assessment: Vol. 3. Behavioral Assessment* (pp. 402–426). New York: Wiley.

Nichd Early Child Care Research Network. (1995). Child Care and Child Development: Results from the Nichd Study of Early Child Care and Youth Development (Pp. 281–296). New York: Guilford Press.

Nguyen, S. P., & Rosengren, K. S. (2004). Causal reasoning about illness: A comparison between European and Vietnamese-American children. *Journal of Cognition and Culture, 4,* 51–78.

Ollendick, T. H. (1995). Cognitive behavioral treatment of panic disorder with agoraphobia in adolescents: A multiple baseline study. *Behavior Therapy, 26,* 395–399.

Ollendick, T. H., Hagopian, L. P., & Huntzinger, R. M. (1991). Cognitive-behavior therapy with nighttime fearful children. *Journal of Behavior Therapy and Experimental Psychiatry, 22,* 113–121.

Pina, A. A., & Silverman, W. K. (2004). Clinical phenomenology, somatic symptoms, and distress in Hispanic/Latino and European American youths with anxiety disorders. *Journal of Clinical Child and Adolescent Psychology, 33,* 227–236.

Rachman, S. (1977). Conditioning theory of fear-acquisition—critical-examination. *Behaviour Research and Therapy, 15,* 375–387.

Rachman, S. (1990). *Fear and Courage,* 2nd edn. New York: W. H. Freeman.

Ramirez Basco, M., Bostic, J. Q., Davies, D., Rush, A. J., Witte, B., Hendrickse, W., et al. (2000). Methods to improve diagnostic accuracy in a community mental health setting. *The American Journal Of Psychiatry, 157,* 1599–1605.

Rapee, R. M. (2001). The development of generalized anxiety. In M. W. Vasey & M. R. Dadds (Eds.), *The Developmental Psychopathology of Anxiety* (pp. 481–503). Oxford: Oxford University Press.

Reich, W. (2000). Diagnostic Interview for Children and Adolescents (DICA). *Journal of the American Academy of Child & Adolescent Psychiatry, 39,* 59–66.

Reiss., S., Peterson, R. A., Gursky, D. M., & McNally, R. J. (1986). Anxiety sensitivity, anxiety frequency and the prediction of fearfulness. *Behavioral Research and Therapy, 24,* 1–8.

Reitman, D. (Ed.) (2007). Volume 2: Children and Adolescents. In M. Hersen (Series Ed.), *Handbook of Psychological Assessment, Case Conceptualization, and Treatment.* New Jersey: John Wiley & Sons, Ltd.

Rettew, D. C., Lynch, A. D., Achenbach, T. M., Dumenci, L., & Ivanova, M. Y. (2009). Meta-analyses of agreement between diagnoses made from clinical evaluations and standardized diagnostic interviews. *International Journal of Methods in Psychiatric Research, 18,* 169–184.

Ridley, C. R., & Kelly, S. M. (2006). Multicultural considerations in case formulation. In. T. D. Eells (Ed.), *Handbook of psychotherapy case formulation (2nd Edition).* New York, NY: The Guilford Press.

Rosqvist, J. (Ed.) (2008). Volume 1: Adults. In M. Hersen (Series Ed.), *Handbook of Psychological Assessment, Case Conceptualization, and Treatment.* New Jersey: John Wiley & Sons, Ltd.

Rubin, K. H. (1993). The Watterloo Longitudinal Project: Correlates and consequences of social withdrawal from childhood to adolescence. In K. H. Rubin & J. B. Asendorph (Eds.), *Social Withdrawal, Inhibition, and Shyness in Childhood* (pp. 291–314). Hillsdale, NJ: Erlbaum.

Sattler, J. M. (2001). *Assessment of Children: Cognitive Applications,* 4th edn. La Mesa, CA: Jerome M. Sattler.

Schniering, C. A., Hudson, J. L., & Rapee, R. M. (2000). Issues in the diagnosis and assessment of anxiety disorders in children and adolescents. *Clinical Psychology Review, 20,* 453–478.

Shaffer, D., Fisher, P., Lucas, C. P., Dulcan, M. K., & Schwab-Stone, M. E. (2000). NIMH Diagnostic Interview Schedule for Children Version IV (NIMH DISC-IV): Description, differences from previous versions, and reliability of some common diagnoses. *Journal of the American Academy of Child & Adolescent Psychiatry, 39,* 28–38.

Shapiro, E. S., & Cole, C. L. (1999). Self-monitoring in assessing children's problems. *Psychological Assessment, 11,* 448–457.

Silverman, W. K., & Albano, A. M. (1996). *Anxiety Disorders Interview Schedule for Children for DSM-IV: (Child and Parent Versions)*. San Antonio, TX: Psychological Corporation/Graywind Publications Incorporated.

Silverman, W. K., Kurtines, W. M., Jaccard, J., & Pina, A. A. (2009). Directionality of change in youth anxiety treatment involving parents: An initial examination. *Journal of Consulting and Clinical Psychology, 77,* 474–485.

Silverman, W. K., & Ollendick, T. H. (2005). Evidence-based assessment of anxiety and its disorders in children and adolescents. *Journal of Clinical Child and Adolescent Psychology, 34,* 380–411.

Silverman, W. K., & Ollendick, T. H. (2008). Child and adolescent anxiety disorders. In J. Hunsley & E. J. Mash (Eds.), *A Guide to Assessments that Work*. New York: Oxford University Press.

Silverman, W. K., Pina, A. A., & Viwesvaran, C. (2008). Evidence-based psychosocial treatments for phobic and anxiety disorders in children and adolescents. *Journal of Clinical Child and Adolescent Psychology, 37,* 105–130.

Snidman, N., Kagan, J., Riordan, L., & Shannon, D. C. (1995). Cardiac function and behavioral reactivity during infancy. *Psychophysiology, 32,* 199–207.

Soenens, B., Vansteenkiste, M., Lens, W., Luyckx, K., Goossens, L., Beyers, W., & Ryan, R. M. (2007). Conceptualizing parental autonomy support: Adolescent perceptions of promotion of independence versus promotion of volitional functioning. *Developmental Psychology, 43,* 633–646.

Southam-Gerow, M. A., & Chorpita, B. F. (2007). Anxiety in children and adolescents. In E. J. Mash & R. A. Barkley (Eds.), *Assessment of childhood disorders*, 4th edn (pp. 347–397). New York: Guilford Press.

Spielberger, C. (1973). *Manual for the State-Trait Anxiety Inventory for Children*. Palo Alto, CA: Consulting Psychologists Press.

Steinberg, L. (1990). Autonomy, conflict, and harmony in the family relationship. In S. S. Feldman & G. R. Elliott (Eds.), *At the Threshold: the Developing Adolescent* (pp. 255–276). Cambridge, MA: Harvard University Press.

Stemberger, R. T., Turner, S. M., Beidel, D. C., & Calhoun, K. S. (1995). Social phobia: An analysis of possible developmental factors. *Journal of Abnormal Psychology, 104,* 526–531.

Sweeney, M., & Pine, D. (2004). Etiology of fear and anxiety. In. T. H. Ollendick (Ed.): *Phobic and Anxiety Disorders in Children and Adolescents: A Clinician's Guide to Effective Psychosocial and Pharmacological Interventions* (pp. 34–60). New York: Oxford University Press.

Tenney, N. H., Schotte, C. K. W., Denys, D. A. J. P., van Megen, H. J. G. M., & Westenberg, H. G. M. (2003). Assessment of DSM-IV personality disorders in obsessive-compulsive disorder: Comparison of clinical diagnosis, self-report questionnaire, and semi-structured interview. *Journal of Personality Disorders, 17,* 550–561.

Vasey, M. W., & Dadds, M. R. (2001). *The Developmental Psychopathology of Anxiety*. New York: Oxford University Press.

Vasey, M. W., & Lonigan, C. J. (2000). Considering the clinical utility of performance-based measures of childhood anxiety. *Journal of Clinical Child Psychology, 29,* 493–508.

Warren, S. L., & Sroufe, L. A. (2004). Developmental issues. In T. H. Ollendick & J. S. March (Eds.), *Phobic and Anxiety Disorders in Children and Adolescents: A Clinician's Guide to Effective Psychosocial and Pharmacological Interventions* (pp. 92–115). New York: Oxford University Press.

Weiss, B., Tram, J. M., , Rescorla, L. & Achenbach, T. M. (2009). Differential symptom expression and somatization in Thai versus U. S. children. *Journal of Consulting and Clinical Psychology, 77* (5), 987–992.

Weisz, J. R., Jensen, A. L., & McLeod, B. D. (2005). Milestones and methods in the development and dissemination of child and adolescent psychotherapies: Review, commentary, and a new deployment-focused model. In E. D. Hibbs & P. S. Jenson (Eds.), *Psychosocial Treatments for Child and Adolescent Disorders: Empirically Based Strategies for Clinical Practice*, 2nd edn (pp. 9–39). Washington, DC: American Psychological Association.

Weisz, J. R., Jensen-Doss, A. J., & Hawley, K. M. (2005). Youth psychotherapy outcome research: a review and critique of the evidence base. *Annual Review of Psychology, 56,* 337–363.

Weisz, J. R., Sigman, M., Weiss, B., & Mosk, J. (1993). Behavioral and emotional problems among Embu Children in Kenya: Comparisons with African-American, Caucasian, and Thai children. *Child Development, 64,* 98–109.

Weisz, J. R., Suwanlert, S., Chaiyasit, W. & Walter, B. R. (1987). Over- and undercontrolled referral problems among children and adolescents from Thailand and the United States: The wat and wai of cultural differences. *Journal of Consulting & Clinical Psychology, 55,* 719–726.

Weller, E. B., Weller, R. A., Fristad, M. A., Rooney, M. T., & Schecter, J. (2000). Children's Interview for Psychiatric Syndromes (ChIPS). *Journal of the American Academy of Child & Adolescent Psychiatry, 39,* 76–84.

Whaley, S. E., Pinto, A., & Sigman, M. (1999). Characterizing interactions between anxious mothers and their children. *Journal of Consulting & Clinical Psychology, 67,* 826–836.

Wood, J. J., McLeod, B. D., Sigman, M., Hwang, W. C., & Chu, B. C. (2003). Parenting and childhood anxiety: Theory, empirical findings, and future directions. *Journal of Child Psychology & Psychiatry & Allied Disciplines, 44,* 134–151.

10

Empirically Supported Psychosocial Treatments

Katharina Manassis

The Hospital for Sick Children, Toronto, Canada

When students ask me to summarize empirically supported treatments for childhood anxiety disorders, I often answer with a simplistic formula: CBT ± SSRI. In other words: cognitive behavioral therapy (CBT) with or without concurrent use of a medication targeting serotonin (selective serotonin reuptake inhibitor or SSRI). There is some truth to this rather facetious answer, but it obscures some of the complexities of the literature. While it is true that there is more empirical support for CBT than for any other psychosocial treatment in this population, not all children respond to it, the strength of the evidence varies among disorders, mechanisms of action for CBT in children are poorly understood, and CBT's optimal integration with other treatments has received only limited study. Therefore, there is a role for a critical examination of *all* psychosocial treatments that may benefit anxious children. A further clinical challenge is presented by the inconsistent availability of CBT in community settings, so optimal means of CBT dissemination and community-based prevention approaches also merit further study.

These issues encompass a vast literature which is rapidly expanding, so this chapter is designed to merely provide an overview. It emphasizes the empirical findings that are (in the author's opinion) of greatest relevance to the clinicians working with these children. Although this emphasis may result in reduced attention to specific methodological issues (e.g., sampling biases in various studies; variation in outcome measures across studies), it is hoped that it will serve to highlight ideas that are most clinically applicable. The chapter begins with the area with the largest evidence-base: CBT for children with various anxiety disorders. It then reviews other psychosocial treatments studied in this population, and disorder-specific treatments. It concludes with some considerations for clinicians using empirically supported treatments in community settings, and a summary of key points.

The Wiley-Blackwell Handbook of The Treatment of Childhood and Adolescent Anxiety, First Edition.
Edited by Cecilia A. Essau and Thomas H. Ollendick.
© 2013 John Wiley & Sons, Ltd. Published 2013 by John Wiley & Sons, Ltd.

Where the Evidence is Strong: "Coping Cat" and its Derivatives

In the early 1990s, an individual, manualized cognitive behavioral treatment for children with generalized anxiety disorder (termed "overanxious disorder" at the time), social phobia (termed "avoidant disorder" at the time) and separation anxiety disorder was developed by Philip Kendall and called "Coping Cat" as the program's mascot was a cat. Key treatment elements included emotion recognition, relaxation, cognitive restructuring, and practicing exposure to feared situations. These elements were combined into a child-friendly acronym termed "FEAR" (Feeling Frightened, Expecting bad things to happen, Attitudes and Actions that help, Results and Rewards) to help children remember their coping strategies and more readily apply them both within and outside sessions. The first randomized controlled trial of Coping Cat in 9- to 13-year-old children was published in 1994 (Kendall, 1994). In this trial, 64% of treated children showed remission of their primary disorder compared to 5% of children in a waitlist control condition.

These encouraging results have since been replicated not only by Kendall (Kendall, Flannery-Schroeder, Panichelli-Mindel, Southam-Gerow, Henin, & Warman, 1997) but by numerous other research groups internationally (see Compton, March, Brent, Albano, Weersing, & Curry, 2004). Many groups have adapted Coping Cat to better suit the local culture, to treat children in groups and vary the degree of parental involvement (e.g., Mendlowitz, Manassis, Bradley, Scapillato, Miezitis, & Shaw, 1999), and to allow transportability to school settings (see "Preventative approaches"). Nevertheless, they have retained the key treatment elements of the original program.

Several large systematic reviews and meta-analyses of this literature have been published (Cartwright-Hatton, Roberts, Chitsabesan, Fothergill, & Harrington, 2004; Compton et al., 2004; Hudson, 2005; In-Albon & Schneider, 2007; Ishikawa, Okajima, Matsuoka, & Sakano, 2007; James, Soler, & Weatherall, 2005; Rapee, Schniering, & Hudson, 2009; Seligman & Ollendick, 2011). They have concluded that this form of CBT is probably efficacious; however, a substantial number of children do not remit. Effect sizes from pre- to post-treatment were large (0.86 in In-Albon & Schneider, 2007; 0.94 in Ishikawa et al., 2007), and still quite robust when compared to control group (0.61 in Ishikawa et al., 2007). However, Cartwright-Hatton and colleagues (2004) reported an overall remission rate of 56.5% post-treatment and 34.8% post-control condition; James and colleagues (2005) reported remission rates of 56% for CBT and 28.2% for controls. These reviews suggest that approximately 40% of treated children continue to meet criteria for anxiety disorders after CBT.

Providing the program in a group format seems to be equally efficacious to individual treatment in most cases (In-Albon & Schneider, 2007), and allows for the treatment of large numbers of anxious children in a cost-effective manner. Flannery-Schroeder and Kendall (2000) found non-significant differences between individual and group treatment (slightly higher remission for individual treatment). Manassis, Mendlowitz, Scapillato, and colleagues (2002) found equivalent symptomatic improvements for group and individual treatment, with the exception of children with high social anxiety who made greater gains in individual treatment. Reasons for this finding are not clear, but one could speculate that the group format may have been overwhelming for these children, reducing their treatment involvement in this format. Several other research groups have shown efficacy of group CBT for anxious children relative to non-intervention (see Hudson, 2005).

To increase rates of remission for this treatment, a number of further avenues of research have been pursued. These include: increasing family or parental involvement, integration of CBT with other treatments, and examining moderators and mediators of treatment response. Each will now be briefly reviewed, but each will likely require additional study before definitive conclusions can be drawn.

Family/parental involvement in CBT

CBT for children with anxiety disorders generally includes a few sessions focused on parental psychoeducation (Kendall, 1994). More extensive parent or family involvement, however, has been advocated by some researchers for the following reasons. Without therapeutic guidance, parents who are anxious themselves may have difficulty supporting their children's use of adaptive, non-anxious coping (Cobham, Dadds, & Spence, 1998). Overprotective or controlling parenting styles are common in families of children with anxiety disorders (Rapee et al., 2009), and may contribute to the maintenance of anxiety over time. Furthermore, parents of anxious children have been found to inadvertently reinforce use of avoidant coping, which is likely to exacerbate anxiety (Barrett, Rapee, Dadds, & Ryan, 1996). Constructive parental involvement in treatment, however, could facilitate generalization of the child's gains to real-world situations and improve the maintenance of gains over time (Manassis, 2007). This may be especially likely if therapists gradually transfer control of child management to the parents through contingency management training (i.e., training parents in how to consistently reinforce "brave" behaviors) (Barmish & Kendall, 2005).

Unfortunately, there are discrepant findings as to the merits of extensive parent or family involvement in child CBT. Some reviews have concluded that there is no difference between child-focused and family-focused treatments (In-Albon & Schneider, 2007), and others that family treatment is superior for some outcome measures, especially for children of anxious parents (Cresswell & Cartwright-Hatton, 2007). Some trials found that extensive parental involvement in CBT confers no added benefit to the anxious child (e.g., Nauta, Scholing, Emmelkamp, & Minderaa, 2003), others that children show greater gains or more adaptive coping strategies when parents are extensively involved (e.g., Mendlowitz et al., 1999), others that extensive parental involvement is only beneficial in the context of parental anxiety (Cobham et al.,1998) or is beneficial by parent report but not by child report (Wood, McLeod, Piacentini, & Sigman, 2009b). It has also been suggested that the reported benefits of extensive parental involvement may be non-specific, and are reflective of added therapeutic contact time with the family.

Examining the literature more closely, though, it is evident that the nature of parental or family involvement in CBT for childhood anxiety disorders varies widely across studies. Optimal parental involvement may also differ depending on the child's age or developmental level. Developmental influences await further study. Overall, it may therefore not be possible to draw definitive conclusions at this time.

In a thoughtful review, Barmish and Kendall (2005) have reported study variability in: content of parent sessions (e.g., behavior management focus versus parental anxiety focus), number and format of parent and child sessions, participants in parent sessions, outcome measures, extent to which treatment attrition is considered, and the age and principal diagnosis of treated children. They suggest that future research should code studies for the extent of parental involvement both within and between sessions, and the content of that involvement.

Although the above may be confusing for clinicians, it is worth noting (a) the theoretical reasons above outlining why parents of anxious children may struggle to be helpful to their children; (b) the need for psychoeducation as part of any cognitive behavioral program; and (c) the increasing availability of resources for parents who want to contribute to their anxious child's recovery (e.g., Manassis, 2007; Rapee, 2009).

Integration of CBT with other treatments

The largest systematic study involving integration of CBT with other treatments in childhood anxiety disorders has been the multi-site CAMS trial (Child/Adolescent Anxiety Multimodal Study; Compton, Walkup, Albano et al., 2010). This randomized controlled trial compared outcomes for 488 children and adolescents randomly assigned to CBT alone, sertraline (an SSRI) alone, pill placebo, or CBT and sertraline in combination. There were numerous cross-site quality controls to ensure high treatment fidelity, safety, and methodological rigor. All treatments were well-tolerated, and all treated groups (that is, those *not* receiving pill placebo) showed significantly decreased anxiety symptoms and improved functioning. However, gains were somewhat greater for children receiving both CBT and sertraline than for those receiving either treatment alone. Mediators and moderators of response as well as long-term outcomes are currently being evaluated.

Although the results are impressive, they do not eliminate the need for clinical judgment in deciding whether or not a particular anxious child should receive CBT, medication, or both. Many children with mild to moderate impairment, for example, can benefit from CBT alone and one may question whether the modest additional benefit of adding a medication is worth the risk of medication-related side effects. In severely impaired children, this risk is usually offset by the potential benefit of medication and the potential difficulty of doing CBT when a child exhibits overwhelming anxiety during therapy sessions. Children with anxiety disorders and significant cognitive limitations, on the other hand, may benefit from medication but not from CBT. Therefore, it is advisable to discuss the potential risks and benefits of all treatment options with the child and family.

Combinations of CBT with other psychotherapies have received little study in childhood anxiety disorders. Common sense suggests one avoid overburdening the child with multiple concurrent therapies, especially if these have different treatment foci (e.g., a psychodynamic therapy and CBT concurrently) (Manassis, 2009a), but concurrent therapy for other family members is less likely to be problematic and may even be helpful. Children with complex presentations may benefit from sequential treatment of several problems, either with modular CBT (Chorpita, 2007) or with another psychotherapy being offered prior to or following CBT.

Moderators and mediators of treatment response

Moderators are factors that are associated with better or worse treatment outcomes. Hudson (2005) summarized the predictors of less favorable outcome in CBT for childhood anxiety disorders. Although there are some inconsistent findings, these factors may include older age, male gender, greater severity of symptoms, comorbid depressive symptoms, family stress, family dysfunction, parental psychopathology, and low child involvement in the latter stages of therapy. A more recent meta-analysis (Bennett, Manassis, Cheung, Schachter, & Walter, 2008) has found that age may not moderate treatment effect. As most of these findings have come from academic settings, however, there may be additional or different moderators in community settings (see later). Clinicians may need to tailor treatment to better suit children with these adverse predictors.

Mediators are treatment elements that are thought to be most closely linked to change. Mediators explain how a treatment works and therefore also what has gone wrong if the treatment fails. Knowledge of these factors will be crucial to improving remission rates for CBT of childhood anxiety disorders and may also allow simplification of existing protocols, resulting in more potent and/or more cost effective treatment. Unfortunately, this area has received limited study. A few authors have linked improvements in CBT to changes in automatic thoughts (e.g., Muris, Mayer, den Adel, Roos, & van Wamelen, 2009) or to exposure to feared stimuli (e.g., Kendall et al., 1997), consistent with cognitive-behavioral theory. However, a meta- analysis by Spielmans, Pasek and McFall (2007) found that CBT was no more efficacious than bona fide non-CBT treatments, suggesting that therapeutic benefits may not be specific to treatment elements considered essential to CBT. Broader outcome assessments that elucidate potential mechanisms of change are clearly needed.

Follow-up results and new directions

Short-term follow-up results (1 year or less) are included in many studies, and generally show maintenance of treatment gains at that time (Compton et al., 2004). Few authors have examined children several years post-CBT, likely due to the challenges of recruiting subjects after that length of time and the difficulty of disentangling developmental changes from treatment effects when subjects, for example, move from childhood to adolescence. Existing studies reported maintenance of gains over 2–7 years, but with 30–50% of treated children eventually seeking further treatment for anxiety-related problems (Hudson, 2005). Notably, long-term follow-ups to date have been uncontrolled, so one cannot conclude that CBT in childhood necessarily alters the natural history of anxiety disorders or is superior to other forms of intervention in ameliorating the developmental impact of anxiety disorders.

Other formats for providing CBT are being evaluated in childhood anxiety disorders, although to date these have received limited study. Computer-based or computer-assisted models for CBT may be appealing for some children or adolescents, may reduce demands on therapist time (thus allowing more children to be seen), and may aid in exporting CBT to distant or rural areas. Bibliotherapy, where CBT is conducted via written materials provided to parents, has also shown encouraging early results relative to non-intervention (Rapee, Abbott, & Lyneham, 2006), but not relative to standard treatment.

Other Psychosocial Treatments for "Emotional Disorders" of Childhood

Psychodynamic approaches

Empirical support for psychodynamic psychotherapy and psychoanalysis in the treatment of childhood anxiety disorders has been limited for several reasons. The nature of these therapies (longer than CBT and less specifically described) makes them difficult to study, especially in a randomized controlled fashion. Funding agencies and governments are often reluctant to support studies of these therapies, as they appear less cost-effective than CBT. Further, the tendency for psychodynamic therapists to group all internalizing problems as "emotional disorders" rather than using specific diagnoses and to evaluate outcomes that are not always symptom-focused makes this literature difficult to interpret.

Nevertheless, a group at the Anna Freud Centre in London has reported several large retrospective chart reviews in which independent raters evaluated outcomes of children treated with psychodynamic therapy. They acknowledge the limitations of this method, but advocate considering a psychodynamic approach for children considered the most disadvantaged, either for constitutional or environmental reasons, and those unresponsive to other therapies (Fonagy & Target, 2002). Their largest report specific to anxiety or depressive disorders (Target & Fonagy, 1994) included 352 charts of children treated with either psychodynamic therapy (1–3 times per week) or psychoanalysis (4–5 times per week). They concluded that longer treatment and more frequent sessions were associated with greater improvements, especially in the most severely impaired children. Absence of depression, young age (under age 11), high IQ, good peer relations, concurrent treatment of the mother, and absence of maternal antisocial behavior were further positive predictors of outcome.

Lifestyle modification

Even though the evidence for using lifestyle modifications to reduce childhood anxiety is limited, clinicians often recommend these in addition to other treatments in the hope of enhancing gains.

Physical exercise has received limited study in general groups of children that were not being treated for any specific psychiatric disorder. Six small trials, described in a Cochrane database review (Larun, Nordheim, Ekeland, Hagen, & Heian, 2006), found a trend towards reduced anxiety symptoms in children who did vigorous exercise in comparison to no intervention. Further study is needed to determine whether this modest effect could contribute towards prevention of anxiety disorders or enhance the effect of other anxiety-focused treatments.

From the medical literature, it is also clear that sympathomimetic substances including caffeine products and sympathomimetic medications (e.g., asthma inhalers) can increase anxiety (Nardi, Lopes, Freire et al., 2009), so there may be some merit in encouraging anxious children to limit their use.

Families of anxious children often enquire about practices such as yoga and meditation, as these are gaining in popularity. Although not specifically evaluated in childhood anxiety disorders, they can sometimes provide an alternative to other relaxation techniques offered as part of a CBT program. Families' enquiries about dietary modifications or about herbal remedies can be honestly answered with "they haven't been studied in childhood anxiety", and encouragement to ascertain potential risks as well as potential benefits.

Preventative approaches

Most attempts to prevent childhood anxiety disorders have focused on offering CBT-based interventions in school settings. Schools are thought to offer access to larger numbers of potentially affected children than clinics, and to avoid the stigma sometimes associated with visiting a children's mental health centre.

Neil and Christensen (2009) reviewed 27 trials of school-based CBT for childhood anxiety and identified universal, selective (selecting participants based on risk factors for disorder), and indicated (selecting participants based on mild symptoms of disorder) trials. Most were based on the Coping Cat principles and were found to reduce symptoms, but with a wide range of effect sizes (0.11–1.37) and with few studies targeting adolescents. Research involving long-term follow-up, attention control conditions, and teacher delivery was advocated.

The FRIENDS program for childhood anxiety (Barrett, Lock, & Farrell, 2005; Lock & Barrett, 2003; Stallard, Simpson, Anderson, Hibbert, & Osborn, 2007), is a universal school-based intervention that has been widely evaluated in comparison to waitlist (non-intervention) conditions when administered by psychologists, graduate students, school nurses, and teachers. Decreased anxiety symptoms are reported regardless of leader type relative to non-intervention (Stallard et al., 2007), with some evidence for greater benefit in primary school children than in teens and of greater gains at 12-month follow-up than immediately post-intervention (Barrett et al., 2005; Lock and Barrett, 2003). A 2- and 3-year follow-up (Barrett, Farrell, Ollendick, & Dadds, 2006) found that the frequency of highly symptomatic students in the intervention condition remained relatively stable over time whereas there was substantial increase in the frequency of highly symptomatic students in the control condition over time.

Selective interventions have received limited study to date. One study examined child anxiety and adaptive behavior following parental divorce (Stolberg & Mahler, 1994), with children randomized to non-intervention, support, or CBT skills plus support. Behavioral gains were more evident in the skill-building conditions than in the non-intervention or support groups. Intervention studies targeting developmental antecedents of childhood anxiety disorders are currently being done. Behavioral inhibition – the tendency for young children to avoid novelty and to limit exploration – is thought to be a particularly salient antecedent of childhood anxiety, especially social anxiety (Hirshfeld-Becker, Micco, Henin, Bloomfield, Biederman, & Rosenbaum, 2008). Preliminary evidence suggests that children with this characteristic can benefit from early cognitive-behavioral intervention (Hirshfeld-Becker et al., 2008). Perceptual biases result in some anxious children focusing excessively on threatening stimuli, and are also considered to be a developmental risk factor for anxiety disorders.

Treatments designed to modify these biases are currently being developed (Bar-Haim, 2010; Cowart & Ollendick, 2010).

Several indicated programs have been evaluated. For example, the Penn Resiliency Program uses CBT principles to reduce symptoms of anxiety and depression in children, and has included teachers and graduate students as group leaders (Gilham, Reivich, Freres et al., 2007). It was compared with an intervention that controlled for non-specific intervention ingredients, and found to be superior in reducing depressive (but not anxiety) symptoms in two of three schools (Gilham et al., 2007). Our own group randomized 148 Grade 3–6 children with elevated anxious or depressive symptoms ($t > 60$ on standardized inventories) to a 12-session CBT program provided by mental health professionals in schools or a structured activity control condition of similar length (Manassis, Wilansky-Traynor, Farzan, Kleiman, Parker, & Sanford, 2010). We found that self-reported anxious and depressive symptoms decreased significantly over time, but with no group by time interaction. There was a trend towards fewer children meeting diagnostic criteria for an anxiety disorder at 1-year post-CBT than post-control. Positive reinforcement of child behavior (regardless of condition) was associated with change in anxiety symptoms.

Findings for indicated programs that used waitlist (non-intervention) controls are generally more robust. For example, Bernstein, Bernat, Victor, and Layne (2008) studied anxious children ages 7–11 randomized to group CBT, group CBT with parent training, and non-intervention. The CBT conditions consistently resulted in greater reduction of anxiety severity and impairment than non-intervention. Dadds, Holland, Spence, Laurens, Mullins, and Barrett (1999) studied 7–14 year olds anxious either by self-report or teacher nomination, randomized to a school-based child- and parent-focused psychosocial intervention administered by psychology graduate students or a monitoring (non-intervention) group. Both groups improved post-intervention, with lower rates of anxiety disorders for the active intervention at 6-months and 2 years but not 1 year. Misfud and Rapee (2005) randomized children with anxiety symptoms to either 'Cool Kids', an 8-session CBT program provided by mental health professionals, or waitlist control. They found significant group differences in anxiety symptoms at 4 months post-intervention.

Further research directions

This section has reviewed interventions outside traditional, office-based CBT for childhood anxiety disorders for which at least limited evidence exists. All merit further evaluation. Psychodynamic studies may benefit anxious children who fail to respond to interventions with the largest evidence base (i.e., CBT and serotonergic medication), although such is untested at this time. Physical exercise and lifestyle modifications could be studied to determine their potential for augmenting the benefits of CBT or serotonergic medication. Studies of interventions that target developmental antecedents of childhood anxiety disorders hold the promise of primary prevention.

Further clarity is needed in the field of school-based interventions, where children in active comparison groups seem to do almost as well as those receiving CBT. The mixed results likely reflect our poor understanding of the mechanisms of action of CBT in childhood anxiety, particularly in subclinical populations. Dismantling studies are needed to elucidate key mediators of change and to determine whether mildly anxious children really need CBT or (as our study suggested) could benefit from simpler interventions.

Interventions for Individual Disorders or Conditions

Obsessive-compulsive disorder

Perhaps because of the distinct and sometimes bizarre rituals associated with OCD, children who have this disorder are usually treated separately from those with other forms of anxiety. Since John March's original description of CBT for childhood OCD (March, 1995), numerous randomized controlled trials have focused on this population. Drawing on experience with adults, CBT for childhood OCD has emphasized exposure and response prevention, where children gradually face situations where they normally perform rituals and learn to tolerate *not* performing them. Anxiety management and cognitive strategies are also considered important treatment elements, as they facilitate children's ability to tolerate the exposure. Family involvement in treatment varies in degree, but almost all programs include some parental psychoeducation and encouragement that parents refrain from accommodating the child's rituals. Parental accommodation (e.g., washing many loads of towels for a frequent hand-washer), can contribute to the maintenance of rituals.

Several systematic reviews and meta-analyses have been published on the use of CBT in this population (Barrett, Farrell, Pina, Peris, & Piacentini, 2008; O'Kearney, 2007; O'Kearney, Anstey, & von Sanden, 2006; Turner, 2006; Watson & Rees, 2008). Results are encouraging, with the majority of children showing symptomatic improvement on the Yale-Brown Obsessive Compulsive Scale for Children, the most common outcome measure used. It is currently considered a probably efficacious treatment (Barrett et al., 2008; O'Kearney et al., 2006), and effect sizes appear greater than for pharmacotherapy (Watson & Rees, 2008). Family-focused CBT offered individually or in group format is considered possibly efficacious (Barrett et al., 2008). Remission rates reported vary widely though, from 37% (O'Kearney, 2007) to 40–85% (Barrett et al., 2008). Some authors have also questioned whether a better cognitive understanding of childhood OCD (compared to adult OCD) should inform CBT with children (Turner, 2006) to optimize treatment response.

The combined use of CBT and serotonin-specific medication has received greater attention in the literature on childhood OCD than that on other anxiety disorders. A large, multi-site trial, the Pediatric OCD Treatment Study (POTS, 2004) addressed the question of whether combined treatment (CBT and sertraline) was superior to either treatment alone or to pill placebo. Interestingly, the remission rate for combined treatment (53.6%) did not differ significantly from that for CBT alone (39.3%), but did exceed those for pharmacotherapy (21.4%) and pill placebo (3.6%) suggesting that either combined CBT and serotonin-specific medication or CBT alone is an acceptable first-line treatment. For children with comorbid tics, CBT seemed particularly important, as their medication response rates did not differ from placebo (March, Franklin, Leonard et al., 2007). Subsequent meta-analyses that included this study and others (O'Kearney et al., 2006; Watson & Rees, 2008) have been consistent with the above findings.

Enhancing treatment response has been the focus of much recent research, given that "response" is currently defined as a 25% symptom reduction (Storch, Lewin, De Nadai, & Murphy, 2010), suggesting that a substantial number of children with OCD continue to suffer many symptoms despite being considered treatment responders. Predictors of poor response include: purely obsessional symptoms, more severe obsessions and compulsions, poor insight, cognitive deficits, poorer social and academic functioning, greater family dysfunction, comorbid aggression, oppositionality or anxiety, and rigid religious beliefs (Turner, 2006). Treatment may need to be tailored to address these factors if they are present. On the other hand, Krebs and Heyman (2010) have summarized literature on treatment resistance and conclude that poor response may reflect inadequate CBT, rather than child or family characteristics. They advocate checking that CBT included an adequate number of sessions (at least six of 40 minutes or more), exposure during sessions, consistent homework between sessions, and a clear focus on OCD rather than other issues during sessions. If these criteria have been met, motivation enhancement strategies, intensive CBT, or home-based CBT may be considered.

Mediators of change in CBT for childhood OCD have received little study, although most reviews conclude that exposure is essential for successful treatment. Studies of such mediators will be important to enhance treatment response and increase rates of remission.

Limited access to CBT in non-academic centers is clearly a problem for children with OCD, and also needs further study. Recent open trials in community settings have been encouraging (Farrell, Schlup, & Boschen, 2010; Valderhaug, Larsson, Gatestam, & Piacentini, 2007), suggesting that CBT should be transportable to such settings. One small, waitlist-controlled randomized trial in Britain also showed effectiveness of CBT for children and adolescents with OCD treated in typical outpatient settings (Williams, Salkovskis, Forrester, Turner, White, & Allsopp, 2010).

Post-traumatic stress disorder

Unlike most anxiety disorders of childhood whose origin is thought to be multifactorial, post-traumatic stress disorder (PTSD) can be linked clearly to a single cause: exposure to one or more traumatic events. Because the nature of those events is variable, children's reactions also vary. Man-made traumas such as abuse or interpersonal violence may elicit different reactions than natural disasters or accidents. Childhood PTSD following a single traumatic event (often termed "Type 1 PTSD") often differs from PTSD that follows multiple, repeated traumas (often termed "Type 2 PTSD") (Terr, 1981). The child's proximity to the trauma, his or her developmental level at the time, and the parents' reaction to the event can further influence the nature of the child's reaction. Treatment studies have therefore focused on particular types of traumas and particular age groups, with variable involvement of parents.

The largest number of controlled trials have evaluated trauma-focused CBT (TF-CBT) in children and adolescents aged 8 years and above (with narrower age groups in each trial) who have experienced sexual abuse. TF-CBT is an individual treatment involving psychoeducation, parenting skills, relaxation skills, affect modulation skills, cognitive coping skills, trauma narrative and cognitive processing of the traumatic event(s), in vivo mastery of trauma reminders, conjoint child–parent sessions, and discussions of enhancing safety and of the child's future developmental trajectory (Cohen & Mannarino, 2008). Learning stress management skills precedes the imaginal exposure and discussion of traumatic events, ensuring that children and parents tolerate the treatment emotionally and are likely to complete it.

A recent meta-analysis concluded that TF-CBT can be considered a well-established treatment for sexually abused children and adolescents (Silverman, Ortiz, Viswesvaran et al., 2008). Strengths of this literature include frequent use of active comparison conditions, inclusion of follow-up data, use of community samples (implying high effectiveness), and use of narrow age groups resulting in greater confidence in its benefit for a given age group (Silverman et al., 2008). Interestingly, much of this literature has emerged from the same research group, although some findings have been independently replicated.

TF-CBT has also been applied successfully with other traumatized populations including children and adolescents with exposure to single-incident traumas (Smith, Yule, Perrin, Tranah, Dalgleish, & Clark, 2007), traumatic grief (Cohen, Mannarino, & Staron, 2006), and multiply traumatized children (i.e. those experiencing sexual abuse and additional traumas) (Cohen, Deblinger, Mannarino, & Steer, 2004). Similar CBT interventions in group format have also been evaluated and found beneficial in children exposed to community violence (Stein, Jaycox, Katacka et al., 2003) and those exposed to natural disasters (Giannopoulou, Dikaiakou, & Yule, 2006). TF-CBT has also been adapted for and evaluated in sexually abused preschoolers (Cohen & Mannarino, 1996). There are case reports of preschoolers exposed to single-incident traumas who have also been treated successfully with CBT adapted to their age group, with emphasis on trauma-related exposure exercises, relaxation techniques, and parental support of progress (Scheeringa, Salloum, Arnberger, Weems, Amaya-Jackson, & Cohen, 2007).

In a small randomized trial of psychosocial and medical intervention in sexually abused girls, 24 girls and their primary caretakers were assigned to either TF-CBT with sertraline or TF-CBT with placebo. TF-CBT with sertraline was superior on only one outcome measure, suggesting an initial trial of TF-CBT may be indicated before adding medication (Cohen, Mannarino, Perel, & Staron, 2007), but larger trials are indicated.

Parental emotional reaction to sexual abuse consistently predicts the child's response to TF-CBT, with poorer response when the parent is more distressed. However, the impact of parental distress seems to decrease over time (Cohen & Mannarino, 1998). Parents can support the child's therapeutic progress in many ways, but few studies have examined the impact of parental involvement in treatment. Existing studies have produced inconsistent results (reviewed in Dalgleish, Meiser-Stedman, & Smith, 2005). Other moderators and mediators of CBT response await further evaluation.

Several therapies are considered possibly efficacious in child PTSD (reviewed in Silverman et al., 2008). Eye-movement desensitization retraining (EMDR) involves graduated imaginal exposures at the same time that the child tracks therapist hand movements with his or her eyes. In two small trials it was found superior to waitlist but not to CBT. It is not clear whether the addition of the eye movements impacts child PTSD beyond the benefits of imaginal exposure. There is also limited evidence for child–parent psychotherapy, resilient peer treatment, and various cognitively based therapies other than TF-CBT.

One final point worth noting with respect to traumatized children is that, left untreated, the majority do not develop PTSD, especially following single-event traumas. Attempts to "debrief" large groups of children by urging them to talk about a recent traumatic event may do more harm than good, as they can interfere with children's natural coping abilities for mastering traumatic experiences (reviewed in Szumilas, Yifeng, & Kutcher, 2010). CBT may, however, be helpful for those children still experiencing post-traumatic symptoms several weeks after the traumatic event.

Selective mutism

Although not officially classified as an anxiety disorder, selective mutism is a condition closely linked to social anxiety and is often seen in clinics specializing in anxiety disorders (Manassis, 2009b). Children with this condition fail to speak in situations where speech is expected, most typically at school. The following summary of evidence for psychosocial treatments is adapted from a recent review by the author (Manassis, 2009b).

Research on psychosocial treatments for selective mutism is limited to numerous open trials and case reports. There have also been a few small, randomized controlled trials on the use of serotonin-specific medication, with favorable results. One pilot study reported improved outcomes when selectively mute children received medication in addition to psychosocial intervention (Manassis & Tannock, 2008). Psychosocial interventions for selective mutism are often multidisciplinary, and focus on decreasing anxiety, increasing social speech, and ameliorating impairment. Symptomatic improvement has been demonstrated most consistently with behavioral or cognitive-behavioral interventions and with multimodal treatments that include school and family participation as well as behavioral methods. Reports of successful therapy also exist for group therapy, psychodynamic psychotherapy, and family systems therapy. Persistence of some selective mutism or anxiety symptoms despite treatment is common.

Behavioral treatments often include one or more of: shaping (reinforcing speech approximations such as gestures or whispers), positive reinforcement of speech, self-modeling (exposure to edited audio- or videotapes which make it seem that the child is speaking in settings where he or she is currently mute), desensitization (speaking in increasingly challenging situations), and stimulus fading (gradually increasing the number of people present when the child speaks). Social skills training may be needed in some children, as these skills may be underdeveloped or have deteriorated with lack of use due to selective mutism. The need to decrease the child's self-consciousness during all psychosocial interventions has been emphasized. For example, overly effusive praise can sometimes result in treatment setbacks, as it increases the child's self-consciousness.

CBT can be considered for older children with selective mutism (age 8 years and above). This therapy focuses on decreasing the social anxiety often present in children with selective mutism. Multimodal interventions include family or school interventions in addition to behavior therapy. Coordinating a treatment plan between home and school can be challenging, and is described in detail in a practical book by McHolm, Cunningham, and Vanier (2005). Parental psychoeducation is an important component of these interventions.

In summary, although existing evidence favors behavioral, cognitive behavioral, and multimodal interventions, there is no single "gold standard" treatment for selective mutism. Family psychopathology has been found to be associated with less favorable outcomes for behavior therapy (Sluckin, Foreman, & Herbert, 1991). Studies of mediators or mechanisms of change are lacking. Further development of treatments targeting specific etiological factors, controlled treatment studies, and studies of optimal involvement of families and schools in treatment are needed to improve outcomes for children with selective mutism.

Additional applications of CBT in anxiety disorders and anxiety-related conditions

At this point, the reader familiar with all anxiety diagnoses of childhood may wonder why panic disorder and specific phobias have not been discussed. The reason is simply that the literature on psychosocial interventions for these disorders in children is less extensive than for other anxiety disorders; however, promising advances are being made (Seligman & Ollendick, 2011). There are also anxiety-related conditions that are not considered disorders but have been the subject of empirical study. School refusal and anxiety in children with autism spectrum disorders are two examples. Some studies specific to social phobia have also been done in adolescents, and some specific to anxiety disorders in young children (age 7 years or younger). These topics will now be briefly reviewed. Additional CBT applications for children with test anxiety or with Williams syndrome are reviewed in other chapters in this volume.

Panic disorder is uncommon prior to adolescence, and few studies have been done that are specific to adolescents. More often, adolescent subjects are included in studies of adults with panic disorder. Reviews of this literature find that CBT is an efficacious, well-tolerated, and cost-effective treatment even in the presence of comorbidity (Landon & Barlow, 2004; Schmidt & Keough, 2010). Dissemination of CBT to community settings is lagging, and greater understanding of risk factors that may moderate outcome is advocated (Schmidt & Keough, 2010). Anxiety sensitivity – the tendency to become anxious in response to bodily sensations – has been studied in children and is thought to be one important risk factor for panic (Bernstein, Zvolensky, Stewart, & Comeau, 2007).

Specific phobias may be neglected because they are perceived to be less serious than other anxiety disorders, but if severe they can result in substantial impairment. Moreover, repeated exposure (the treatment of choice) is not always easy to design, depending on what is feared. Virtual reality simulations have recently been used for phobias related to infrequent events (for example, fear of air travel), and intensive but brief (single-session) exposure treatments have been designed and studied. Outcomes for the latter treatments were found superior to an education support intervention as well as to waitlist control (Ollendick, Ost, Reuterskiald et al., 2009). The presence of comorbid phobias or anxiety disorders did not moderate results, and the clinical severity of these co-occurring conditions decreased with treatment of the specific phobia (Ollendick, Ost, Reuterskiald, & Costa, 2010).

Children with chronic school refusal (also termed school avoidance or school pho-bia) often meet criteria for one or more anxiety disorders, although the condition itself is not classified as an anxiety disorder. A recent review of psychosocial interventions concluded that BT and CBT most consistently resulted in improvements in attendance and anxiety symptom levels, but much of the literature consists of single-case designs and small open trials (Pina, Zerr, Gonzales, & Ortiz, 2009). The largest comparative trial to date evaluated the of response school-refusing adolescents to 8 weeks of CBT with or without concurrent treatment with imipramine (a tricyclic antidepressant med-ication) (Layne, Bernstein, Egan, & Kushner, 2003). A higher rate of attendance at baseline, male gender, and receiving imipramine predicted better outcomes. The pres-ence of separation anxiety disorder or avoidant disorder (an older term, similar to the current diagnosis of generalized social anxiety disorder) predicted worse outcomes. The need for individualized treatment planning was highlighted. Usually, such treat-ment plans require active and coordinated participation by the family and the school, with an emphasis on behavioral measures that foster gradual re-integration of the stu-dent into a school program. Cognitive strategies may ease the anxiety associated with this process, but exposure to the school environment is essential to treatment success.

Several authors have recently adapted anxiety-focused CBT for use with children who have autism spectrum disorders (Sofronoff, Attwood, & Hinton, 2005; White, Ollendick, Scahill, Oswald, & Albano, 2009; Wood, Drahota, Sze, Har, Chiu, & Langer, 2009a). Initial results are encouraging, with most children showing decreased anxiety symptoms relative to untreated children (Sofronoff et al., 2005; Wood et al., 2009a). In some cases, social skills training has been added to CBT as this is a particular area of difficulty in this population (White et al., 2009). Parental involvement has been found to be helpful (Sofronoff et al., 2005). Importantly, children included in these studies have all been at the high-functioning end of the autistic spectrum. Lower functioning autistic individuals usually lack the cognitive and verbal ability to benefit from CBT.

A small number of trials support the efficacy of CBT for generalized social anxiety in adolescents (reviewed in Herbert, Gaudiano, Rheingold et al., 2009). Group and individual modalities have been developed and recently compared. CBT treated adolescents showed reduced symptoms and gains in behavioral measures regardless of modality (Herbert et al., 2009). Recall that, by contrast, social anxiety predicted preferential response to individual treatment in a study of children with various anxiety disorders (Manassis et al., 2002). Perhaps having all members of the group suffering from the same condition reduces the anxiety normally associated with social/group situations in this population, allowing them to benefit from CBT.

Given their limited cognitive ability, children below age eight have often been considered too young for CBT (a few researchers have included 7-year-olds in trials of older children). Some authors, however, have adapted CBT for child-hood anxiety to allow treatment of younger children. Consistent parental involve-ment is important in this age group, and children typically learn to identify anx-ious states, practice relaxation techniques, and learn rudimentary cognitive strategies with the aid of stories and puppets. A recent evaluation of such a program found reduced anxiety symptoms afterwards relative to waitlist control (Monga, Young, & Owens, 2009).

Using Empirically Supported Treatments in Community Settings

Empirically supported treatments such as CBT do not always achieve the same results in community settings as they do in academic research centers. For example, a recent meta-analysis by Ishikawa and colleagues (2007) found that effect sizes for CBT for anxious children conducted in university clinics were substantially higher than those for other clinics. Success in community settings (termed "treatment effectiveness") can be more difficult to achieve than success in academic settings (termed "treatment efficacy") for several reasons. These include differences in the client population seen, differences in the training and supervision of the therapists, and organizational factors (see Manassis, 2009a for details).

Complex presentations where both the child and the family struggle with multiple problems are more common in community practice than in academic practice. Providing successful CBT in this context may require careful assessment and treatment planning, including prioritizing presenting problems; modifying CBT to better address cognitive limitations, comorbid conditions, or client's cultural background; modifying treatment expectations (i.e. that one brief course of CBT may not resolve all emotional and behavioral issues, but specific goals can be achieved); deferring CBT until other aspects of the treatment plan are in place (e.g., if family circumstances must be stabilized first or the child must be stabilized on medication first); use of a modular CBT approach (see Chorpita, 2007 for details); and regular communication among all members of the treatment team.

Therapists typically receive less intensive training and supervision in community settings than in academic settings. On the other hand, familiarity of the community therapists with their clients' particular background and culture may contribute to effective care. Few studies have evaluated training of community therapists in child CBT. Those that have, suggest that training which includes ongoing supervision of one or more cases is more helpful than didactic training alone (Manassis, Ickowicz, Picard et al., 2009). The need to adapt CBT to better meet the needs of clients in the community may also pose challenges. Although flexibility can be helpful in child CBT, it can result in lack of treatment fidelity if it is excessive. Thus, families may report that their child has received CBT, but the child has really received an eclectic form of therapy that may not be optimal. Optimal child CBT for anxiety usually includes psychoeducation of children and parents about the goals of therapy and how these will be achieved; structured sessions where specific, anxiety-focused skills are taught; homework between sessions to practice skills; regular, planned exposures to anxious situations; and a manual or other written record of what has been learned.

Finally, organizational factors in community settings can sometimes present obstacles to the successful provision of child CBT. Addressing these factors can improve the chances of effective community-based child CBT. Some common problematic factors may include lack of diagnostic screening questions at intake; lack of commitment to evidence-based practice at any level of the organization; lack of communication among clinicians; therapists must provide CBT, regardless of child and family's treatment suitability; payment structures resulting in an inadequate number of sessions; and community stigma associated with the child and family being seen at that setting.

Conclusions

Overall, there is a large body of evidence in favor of CBT in the treatment of childhood anxiety disorders, but the degree of treatment response varies so not all children achieve remission. To maximize gains, we should encourage children and families to persevere with CBT, practice their strategies consistently, and focus on signs of progress, even if this is incremental. Other psychosocial interventions may need to be added in some cases. Furthermore, we must stay abreast of new developments in the treatment of childhood anxiety disorders, as this is a rapidly expanding field. Understanding the mechanisms that mediate therapeutic change, adapting CBT to different populations and settings of practice, optimizing the role of parents and families in treatment, and learning how to best integrate CBT with other treatment modalities are just some of the challenges for the coming years. Evaluating disorder-specific treatments, preventative approaches, and treatments based on knowledge of children's specific developmental risks are further promising areas of research.

Summary of Key Points

- CBT for generalized anxiety disorder, social phobia, and separation anxiety disorder has been shown efficacious in either individual or group format in numerous trials internationally, but remission occurs in only about 60% of children.
- Psychoeducation for parents of anxious children is essential, and parent or family involvement in CBT may be helpful.
- Combining CBT with serotonin-specific medication appears to be safe and may be more efficacious than either treatment alone.
- Mechanisms of change are poorly understood in CBT for childhood anxiety disorders, and require further study to improve remission rates.
- Long-term outcomes for CBT appear favorable, but are uncontrolled so it is not clear if CBT alters the developmental trajectory of anxious youth.
- Physical exercise may have a positive effect on children's anxiety symptoms, but should be combined with other treatments.
- There may be a role for psychodynamic therapies in children unresponsive to CBT, but such remains to be clearly demonstrated.
- School-based prevention programs have been evaluated, and so far CBT seems superior to non-intervention but not necessarily to other active interventions.
- Prevention approaches focused on developmental antecedents of anxiety (e.g. behavioral inhibition, threat-perception biases) are currently being evaluated.
- CBT is probably efficacious for childhood OCD, but response rates are variable and combination treatment with CBT and serotonin-specific medication may need to be considered in severe cases.
- Trauma-focused CBT seems effective for PTSD due to childhood sexual abuse, with some evidence for effectiveness following other forms of trauma as well.
- Limited but increasing evidence exists for BT and CBT for children and adolescents with panic disorder, specific phobias, school refusal, anxiety related to autism spectrum disorders, generalized social anxiety in adolescents, and CBT for young anxious children.

- Careful treatment planning and adequate training of therapists is important to ensure effective child CBT in community settings of practice.

References

Bar-Haim, Y. (2010). Modifying emotional processing biases: a novel application of the dot probe task. Oral presentation: Anxiety Disorders Association of America Annual Meeting, Baltimore, MD.

Barmish, A. J., & Kendall, P. C. (2005). Should parents be co-clients in cognitive-behavioral therapy for anxious youth? *Journal of Clinical Child and Adolescent Psychology, 34,* 569–581.

Barrett, P. M., Rapee, R. M., Dadds, M. M., & Ryan, S. M. (1996). Family enhancement of cognitive style in anxious and aggressive children. *Journal of Abnormal Child Psychology, 24,* 187–203.

Barrett, P. M., Lock, S., & Farrell, L. J. (2005). Developmental differences in universal preventive intervention for child anxiety. *Clinical Child Psychology and Psychiatry, 10,* 539–555.

Barrett, P. M., Farrell, L. J., Ollendick, T. H., & Dadds, M. (2006). Long-term outcomes of an Australian universal prevention trial of anxiety and depression symptoms in children and youth: an evaluation of the friends program. *Journal of Clinical Child and Adolescent Psychology, 35,* 403–411.

Barrett, P. M., Farrell, L., Pina, A. A., Peris, T. S., & Piacentini, J. (2008). Evidence-based psychosocial treatments for child and adolescent obsessive-compulsive disorder. *Journal of Clinical Child and Adolescent Psychology, 37,* 131–155.

Bennett, K., Manassis, K., Cheung, A., Schachter, H., & Walter, S. (2008). Does age moderate treatment effect for cognitive behavioural therapy in child and adolescent anxiety? Poster presented at the Canadian Cochrane Symposium, Edmonton, March, 2008.

Bernstein, A., Zvolensky, M. J., Stewart, S., & Comeau, N. (2007). Taxometric and factor analytic models of anxiety sensitivity among youth: exploring the latent structure of anxiety psychopathology vulnerability. *Behavior Therapy, 38,* 269–283.

Bernstein, G. A., Bernat, D. H., Victor, A. M., & Layne, A. E. (2008). School-based interventions for anxious children: 3-, 6-, and 12-month follow-ups. *Journal of the American Academy of Child and Adolescent Psychiatry, 47,* 1039–1047.

Cartwright-Hatton, S., Roberts, C., Chitsabesan, P., Fothergill, C., & Harrington, R. (2004). Systematic review of the efficacy of cognitive behavior therapies for childhood and adolescent anxiety disorders. *British Journal of Clinical Psychology, 43,* 421–436.

Chorpita, B. F. (2007). *Modular Cognitive Behavioral Therapy for Childhood Anxiety Disorders.* New York: Guilford Press.

Cobham, V. E., Dadds, M. R., & Spence, S. H. (1998). The role of parental anxiety in the treatment of childhood anxiety. *Journal of Consulting and Clinical Psychology, 66,* 893–905.

Cohen, J. A., & Mannarino, A. P. (2008). Trauma-focused cognitive behavioural therapy for children and parents. *Child and Adolescent Mental Health, 13,* 158–162.

Cohen, J. A., Mannarino, A. P., Perel, J. M., & Staron, V. (2007). A pilot randomized controlled trial of combined trauma-focused CBT and sertraline for childhood PTSD symptoms. *Journal of the American Academy of Child and Adolescent Psychiatry, 46,* 811–819.

Cohen, J. A., Mannarino, A. P., & Staron, V. R. (2006). A pilot study of modified cognitive behavioral therapy for childhood traumatic grief (CBT-CTG). *Journal of the American Academy of Child and Adolescent Psychiatry, 45,* 1465–1473.

Cohen, J. A., Deblinger, E., Mannarino, A. P., & Steer, R. A. (2004). A multisite, randomized controlled trial for children with sexual abuse-related PTSD symptoms. *Journal of the American Academy of Child and Adolescent Psychiatry, 43,* 393–402.

Cohen, J. A., & Mannarino, A. P. (1998). Interventions for sexually abused children: Initial treatment findings. *Child Maltreatment, 3,* 17–26.

Cohen, J. A., & Mannarino, A. P. (1996). A treatment outcome study for sexually abused preschool children: initial findings. *Journal of the American Academy of Child and Adolescent Psychiatry, 35,* 42–50.

Compton, S. N., March, J. S., Brent, D., Albano, A. M., Weersing, V. R., & Curry, J. (2004). Cognitive behavioral psychotherapy for anxiety and depressive disorders in children and adolescents: An evidence-based medicine review. *Journal of the American Academy of Child and Adolescent Psychiatry, 43,* 930–959.

Compton, S. N., Walkup, J. T., Albano, A. M., Piacentini, J. C., Birmaher, B., Sherrill, J. T., et al. (2010). Child/Adolescent Anxiety Multimodal Study (CAMS): rationale, design, and methods. *Child and Adolescent Psychiatry and Mental Health, 4,* 1.

Cowart, M. J. W., & Ollendick, T. H., (2010). Attentional biases in children: Implication for treatment. In J. A. Hadwin, & A. P. Field (Eds.), *Information Processing Biases and Anxiety: A Developmental Perspective* (pp. 297–319). Oxford: Oxford University Press.

Cresswell, C., & Cartwright-Hatton, S. (2007). Family treatment of child anxiety: Outcomes, limitations and future directions. *Clinical Child and Family Pyschology, 10,* 232–252.

Dadds, M. R., Holland, D. E., Spence, S. H., Laurens, K. R., Mullins, M., & Barrett, P. M. (1999). Early intervention and prevention of anxiety disorders in children: Results at 2-year follow-up. *Journal of Consulting and Clinical Psychology, 67,* 627–635.

Dalgleish, T., Meiser-Stedman, R., & Smith, P. (2005). Cognitive aspects of post-traumatic reactions and their treatment in children and adolescents: An empirical review and some recommendations. *Behavioural and Cognitive Psychotherapy, 33,* 459–486.

Farrell, L. J., Schlup, B., & Boschen, M. J. (2010). Cognitive behavioral treatment of childhood obsessive compulsive disorder in community-based clinical practice: clinical significance and benchmarking against efficacy. *Behavioral Research and Therapy, 48,* 409–417.

Flannery-Schroeder, E., & Kendall, P. C. (2000). Group and individual cognitive-behavioural treatments for youth with anxiety disorders: A randomized clinical trial. *Cognitive Therapy and Research, 24,* 251–278.

Fonagy, P., & Target, M. (2002). The history and current status of outcome research at the Anna Freud Centre. *The Psychoanalytic Study of the Child, 57,* 27–60.

Giannopoulou, I., Dikaiakou, A., & Yule, W. (2006). Cognitive-behavioural group intervention for PTSD symptoms in children following the Athens 1999 earthquake: a pilot study. *Clinical Child Psychology and Psychiatry, 11,* 543–553.

Gilham, J. E., Reivich, K. J., Freres, D. R., Chaplin, T. M., Shatte, A. J., Samuels, B., et al. (2007). School-based prevention of depressive symptoms: A randomized controlled study of the effectiveness and specificity of the Penn Resiliency Program. *Journal of Consulting and Clinical Psychology, 75,* 9–19.

Herbert, J. D., Gaudiano, B. A., Rheingold, A. A., Moitra, E., Myers, V. H., Dalrymple, K. L., et al. (2009). Cognitive behavior therapy for generalized anxiety disorder in adolescents: a randomized controlled trial. *Journal of Anxiety Disorders, 23,* 167–177.

Hirshfeld-Becker, D. R., Micco, J., Henin, A., Bloomfield, A., Biederman, J., & Rosenbaum, J. (2008). Behavioral inhibition. *Depression and Anxiety, 25,* 357–367.

Hudson, J. L. (2005). Efficacy of cognitive-behavioral therapy for children and adolescents with anxiety disorders. *Behaviour Change, 22,* 55–70.

In-Albon, T., & Schneider, S. (2007). Psychotherapy of childhood anxiety disorders: a meta-analysis. *Psychotherapy and Psychosomatics, 76,* 15–24.

Ishikawa, S., Okajima, I., Matsuoka, H., & Sakano, Y. (2007). Cognitive behavioural therapy for anxiety disorders in children and adolescents: A meta-analysis. *Child and Adolescent Mental Health, 12,* 164–172.

James, A., Soler, A., & Weatherall, R. (2005). Cognitive behavioural therapy for anxiety disorders in children and adolescents. *Cochrane Database of Systematic Reviews,* Issue 4, Art. No. : CD004690.

Kendall, P. C. (1994). Treating anxiety disorders in children: Results of a randomized clinical trial. *Journal of Consulting and Clinical Psychology, 62,* 100–110.

Kendall, P. C., Flannery-Schroeder, E., Panichelli-Mindel, S. M., Southam-Gerow, M., Henin, A., & Warman, M. (1997). Therapy for youths with anxiety disorders: A second randomized clinical trial. *Journal of Consulting and Clinical Psychology, 65,* 366–380.

Krebs, G., & Heyman, I. (2010). Treatment-resistant obsessive-compulsive disorder in young people: assessment and treatment strategies. *Child and Adolescent Mental Health, 15,* 2–11.

Landon, T. M., & Barlow, D. H. (2004). Cognitive behavioral treatment for panic disorder: current status. *Journal of Psychiatric Practice, 10,* 211–226.

Larun, L., Nordheim, L. V., Ekeland, E., Hagen, K. B., & Heian, F. (2006). Exercise in prevention and treatment of anxiety and depression among children and young people. *Cochrane Database of Systematic Reviews,* Issue 3, Art. No. : CD004691.

Layne, A. E., Bernstein, G. A., Egan, E. A., & Kushner, M. G. (2003). Predictors of treatment response in anxious-depressed adolescents with school refusal. *Journal of the American Academy of Child and Adolescent Psychiatry, 42,* 319–326.

Lock, S., & Barrett, P. M. (2003). A longitudinal study of developmental differences in universal preventive intervention for child anxiety. *Behaviour Change, 20,* 183–199.

Lyneham, H. J., & Rapee, R. M. (2006). Evaluation of therapist-supported parent-implemented CBT for anxiety disorders in rural children. *Behavioral Research and Therapy, 44,* 1287–1300.

Manassis, K. (2009). *Cognitive Behavioral Therapy with Children: A Guide for the Community Practitioner.* New York: Routledge.

Manassis, K. (2009b). Silent suffering: understanding and treating children with selective mutism. *Expert Review in Neurotherapeutics, 9,* 235–243.

Manassis, K., & Tannock, R. (2008). Comparing interventions for selective mutism: A pilot study. *Canadian Journal of Psychiatry, 53,* 700–703.

Manassis, K. (2007). *Keys to Parenting Your Anxious Child,* 2nd edn. Hauppauge, NY: Barron's Educational Series, Inc.

Manassis, K., Mendlowitz, S. L., Scapillato, D., Avery, D., Fiksenbaum, L., Freire, M., et al. (2002). Group and individual cognitive behavioral therapy for childhood anxiety disorders: A randomized trial. *Journal of the American Academy of Child and Adolescent Psychiatry, 41,* 1423–1430.

Manassis, K., Ickowicz, A., Picard, E., Antle, B., McNeill, T., Chahauver, A., et al. (2009). Coping Communities: An innovative child CBT teaching program for community practitioners in Ontario. *Academic Psychiatry, 33,* 394–399.

Manassis, K., Wilansky-Traynor, P., Farzan, N., Kleiman, V., Parker, K., & Sanford, M. (2010). The Feelings Club: A randomized controlled trial of school-based intervention for anxious and depressed children. *Depression and Anxiety, 27,* 945–952.

March, J. S. (1995). Cognitive-behavioral psychotherapy for children and adolescents with OCD: A review and recommendations for treatment. *Journal of the American Academy of Child and Adolescent Psychiatry, 34,* 7–18.

March, J. S., Franklin, M. E., Leonard, H., Garcia, A., Moore, P., Freeman, J., et al. (2007). Tics moderate treatment outcome with sertraline but not cognitive-behavior therapy in pediatric obsessive compulsive disorder. *Biological Psychiatry, 61,* 344–347.

McHolm, A., Cunningham, C., & Vanier, M. (2005). *Helping Your Child with Selective Mutism: Practical Steps to Overcome a Fear of Speaking.* California: New Harbinger Publications Inc.

Mendlowitz, S. L., Manassis, K., Bradley, S., Scapillato, D., Miezitis, S., & Shaw, B. F. (1999). Cognitive behavioral group treatments in childhood anxiety disorders: the role of parental involvement. *Journal of the American Academy of Child and Adolescent Psychiatry, 38,* 1223–1229.

Misfud, C., & Rapee, R. M. (2005). Early intervention for childhood anxiety in a school setting: Outcomes for an economically disadvantaged population. *Journal of the American Academy of Child and Adolescent Psychiatry, 44,* 996–1004.

Monga, S., Young, A., & Owens, M. (2009). Evaluating a cognitive behavioral therapy group program for anxious five to seven year old children: A pilot study. *Depression and Anxiety, 26,* 243–250.

Muris, P., Mayer, B., den Adel, M., Roos, T., & van Wamelen, J. (2009). Predictors of change following cognitive-behavioral treatment of children with anxiety problems: A preliminary investigation on negative automatic thoughts and anxiety control. *Child Psychiatry and Human Development, 40,* 139–151.

Nardi, A. E., Lopes, F. L., Freire, R. C., Veras, A. B., Nascimento, I., Valenasa, A. M., et al. (2009). Panic disorder and social anxiety disorder subtypes in caffeine challenge test. *Psychiatry Research, 169,* 149–153.

Nauta, M. H., Scholing, A., Emmelkamp, P. M., & Minderaa, R. B. (2003). Cognitive-behavioral therapy for children with anxiety disorders in a clinical setting: no additional effect of a cognitive parent training. *Journal of the American Academy of Child and Adolescent Psychiatry, 42,* 1270–1278.

Neil, A. L., & Christensen, H. (2009). Efficacy and effectiveness of school-based prevention and early intervention programs for anxiety. *Clinical Psychology Review, 29,* 208–215.

O'Kearney, R. (2007). Benefits of cognitive behavioral therapy for children and youth with obsessive-compulsive disorder: re-examination of the evidence. *Australia and New Zealand Journal of Psychiatry, 41,* 199–212.

O'Kearney, R. T., Anstey, K. J., & von Sanden, C. (2006). Behavioral and cognitive behavioral therapy or obsessive compulsive disorder in children and adolescents. *Cochrane Database Systematic Reviews,* Issue 4, Art. No. CD004856.

Ollendick, T. H., Ost, L. G., Reuterskiald, L., Costa, N., Cederlund, R., Sirbu, C., et al. (2009). One-session treatment of specific phobias in youth: a randomized clinical trial in the United States and Sweden. *Journal of Consulting and Clinical Psychology, 77,* 504–516.

Ollendick, T. H., Ost, L. G., Reuterskiald, L., & Costa, N. (2010). Comorbidity in youth with specific phobias: Impact of comorbidity on treatment outcome and the impact of treatment on comorbid disorders. *Behavioral Research, & Therapy, 48,* 827–831.

Pina, A. A., Zerr, A. A., Gonzales, N. A., & Ortiz, C. D. (2009). Psychosocial interventions for school refusal behavior in children and adolescents. *Child Development Perspectives, 3,* 11–20.

POTS (2004). Cognitive behavior therapy, sertraline, and their combination for children and adolescents with obsessive-compulsive disorder: the Pediatric OCD Treatment Study (POTS) randomized controlled trial. *Journal of the American Medical Association, 292,* 1969–1976.

Rapee, R. M. (2009). *Helping Your Anxious Child: A Step by Step Guide for Parents, Revised.* California: New Harbinger.

Rapee, R. M., Schniering, C. A., & Hudson, J. L. (2009). Anxiety disorders during childhood and adolescence: origins and treatment. *Annual Review of Clinical Psychology, 5,* 311–341.

Rapee, R. M., Abbott, M., & Lyneham, H. (2006). Bibliotherapy for children with anxiety disorders using written materials for parents: a randomized controlled trial. *Journal of Consulting and Clinical Psychology, 74,* 436–444.

Scheeringa, M. S., Salloum, A., Arnberger, R. A., Weems, C. F., Amaya-Jackson, L., & Cohen, J. A. (2007). Feasibility and effectiveness of cognitive-behavioural therapy for posttraumatic stress disorder in preschool children: two case reports. *Journal of Traumatic Stress, 20,* 631–636.

Schmidt, N. B., & Keough, M. E. (2010). Treatment of panic. *Annual Review of Clinical Psychology, 6,* 241–256.

Seligman, L. D., & Ollendick, T. H. (2011). Cognitive Behavior Therapy for anxiety disorders in children and adolescents. *Psychiatric Clinics of North America, 20,* 217–238.

Silverman, W. K., Ortiz, C. D., Viswesvaran, C., Burns, B. J., Kolko, D. J., Putnam, F. W., et al. (2008). Evidence-based psychosocial treatments for children and adolescents exposed to traumatic events. *Journal of Clinical Child and Adolescent Psychology, 37,* 156–183.

Sluckin, A., Foreman, N., & Herbert, N. (1991). Behavioural treatment programs and selectivity of speaking at follow-up in a sample of 25 selective mutes. *Australian Psychologist, 26*, 132–137.

Smith, P., Yule, W., Perrin, S., Tranah, T., Dalgleish, T., & Clark, D. M. (2007). Cognitive-behavioral therapy for PTSD in children and adolescents: a preliminary randomized controlled trial. *Journal of the American Academy of Child and Adolescent Psychiatry, 46*, 1051–1061.

Sofronoff, K., Attwood, T., & Hinton, S. (2005). A randomized controlled trial of a CBT intervention for anxiety in children with Asperger syndrome. *Journal of Child Psychology and Psychiatry, 46*, 1152–1160.

Spielmans, G. I., Pasek, L. F., & McFall, J. P. (2007). What are the active ingredients in cognitive and behavioral psychotherapy for anxious and depressed children? A meta-analytic review. *Clinical Psychology Review, 27*, 642–654.

Stallard, P., Simpson, N., Anderson, S., Hibbert, S., & Osborn, C. (2007). The FRIENDS emotional health programme: Initial findings from a school-based project. *Child and Adolescent Mental Health, 12*, 32–37.

Stein, B. D., Jaycox, L. H., Katacka, S. H., Wong, M., Tu, W., Elliott, M. N., et al. (2003). A mental health intervention for school children exposed to violence: A randomized controlled trial. *Journal of the American Medical Association, 290*, 603–611.

Stolberg, A. L., & Mahler, J. (1994). Enhancing treatment gains in a school-based intervention for children of divorce through skill training, parental involvement, and transfer procedures. *Journal of Consulting and Clinical Psychology, 62*, 147–156.

Storch, E. A., Lewin, A. B., DeNadal, A. S., & Murphy, T. K. (2010). Defining treatment response and remission in obsessive-compulsive disorder: A signal detection analysis of the Children's Yale-Brown Obsessive Compulsive Scale. *Journal of the American Academy of Child and Adolescent Psychiatry, 49*, 708–717.

Szumilas, M., Yifeng, W., & Kutcher, S. (2010). Psychological debriefing in schools. *Canadian Medical Association Journal, 182*, 883–884.

Target, M., & Fonagy, P. (1994). The efficacy of psychoanalysis for children with emotional disorders. *Journal of the American Academy of Child and Adolescent Psychiatry, 33*, 361–371.

Terr, L. C. (1981). Psychic trauma in children: observations following the Chowchilla school-bus kidnapping. *American Journal of Psychiatry, 138*, 14–19.

Turner, C. M. (2006). Cognitive-behavioral theory and theapy for obsessive compulsive disorder in children and adolescents: current status and future directions. *Clinical Psychology Review, 26*, 912–938.

Valderhaug, R., Larsson, B., Gatestam, K. G., & Piacentini, J. (2007). An open clinical trial of cognitive-behavioral therapy in children and adolescents with obsessive-compulsive disorder administered in regular outpatient clinics. *Behavioral Research and Therapy, 45*, 577–589.

Watson, H. J., & Rees, C. S. (2008). Meta-analysis of randomized, controlled treatment trials for pediatric obsessive-compulsive disorder. *Journal of Child Psychology and Psychiatry, 49*, 489–498.

Weersing, V. R., & Weisz, J. R. (2002). Community clinic treatment of depressed youth: benchmarking usual care against CBT clinical trials. *Journal of Consulting and Clinical Psychology, 70*, 299–310.

White, S. W., Ollendick, T., Scahill, L., Oswald, D., & Albano, A. M. (2009). Preliminary efficacy of a cognitive behavioral treatment program for anxious youth with autism spectrum disorders. *Journal of Autism and Developmental Disorders, 39*, 1652–1662.

Williams, T. I., Salkovskis, P. M., Forrester, L., Turner, S., White, H., & Allsopp, M. A. (2010). A randomized controlled trial of cognitive behavioural treatment for obsessive compulsive disorder in children and adolescents. *European Child and Adolescent Psychiatry, 19*, 449–456.

Wood, J. J., Drahota, A., Sze, K., Har, K., Chiu, A., & Langer, D. A. (2009). Cognitive behavioral therapy for anxiety in children with autism spectrum disorders: a randomized controlled trial. *Journal of Child Psychology and Psychiatry, 50,* 224–234.

Wood, J. J., McLeod, B. D., Piacentini, J. C., & Sigman, M. (2009). One-year follow-up of family versus child CBT for anxiety disorders: Exploring the roles of child age and parental intrusiveness. *Child Psychiatry and Human Development, 40,* 301–316.

Chapter 11

Pharmacological Treatment of Anxiety Disorders in Children and Adolescents

Boris Birmaher and Dara Sakolsky
University of Pittsburgh Medical Center, USA

Anxiety disorders are one of the most common pediatric psychiatric disorders affecting up to 20% of children and adolescents (Costello & Angold, 2004; Costello, Egger, & Angold, 2005; Merikangas, He, Brody, Fisher, Bourdon, & Koretz, 2010). These disorders are usually comorbid with other disorders (e.g. depression) and among themselves are associated with significant psychosocial impairment (Langley, Bergman, McCracken, & Piacentini, 2004; Wood, 2006) and increased risk of adult anxiety disorders. In addition, they increase the risk for major depressive disorder, suicide attempts, and substance use disorders (Beesdo, Bittner, Pine et al., 2007; Bittner, Egger, Erkanli, Costello, Foley, & Angold, 2007; Bolton, Cox, Afifi, Enns, Bienvenu, & Sareen, 2008; Buckner, Schmidt, Lang, Small, Schlauch, & Lewinsohn, 2008). Thus, there is a need for their early identification and successful treatment.

The aim of this chapter is to review the existing literature regarding the pharmacological treatment of youths with anxiety disorders including general anxiety disorder (GAD), social phobia (SP), separation anxiety disorder (SAD), obsessive compulsive disorder (OCD), and post-traumatic stress disorder (PTSD). Since selective serotonin reuptake inhibitors (SSRIs) have become the first choice medication for these disorders, this chapter will mainly discuss these compounds (Table 11.1). Other types of medications such as selective serotonin and norepinephrine reuptake inhibitors (SNRIs), tricyclic antidepressants (TCAs), and benzodiazepines will be discussed briefly. Psychotherapies, particularly cognitive behavioral therapy (CBT), have also been found to be efficacious for the treatment of anxiety disorders in youths (see Chapters 12–25).

For this chapter, unless specified, youths indicates children and adolescents.

The Wiley-Blackwell Handbook of The Treatment of Childhood and Adolescent Anxiety, First Edition. Edited by Cecilia A. Essau and Thomas H. Ollendick.
© 2013 John Wiley & Sons, Ltd. Published 2013 by John Wiley & Sons, Ltd.

Table 11.1 Acute RCTs of medication for youths with generalized anxiety disorder, social phobia, or separation anxiety disorder.

Study	Subjects	Active treatment	Response rate drug vs placebo[a]	NNT[b] (95% CI)
RUPP Anxiety Study Group (2001)	GAD, SoP, or SAD Ages 6–17 $n = 128$	Fluoxamine (50–250 mg/day child, 50–300 mg/day adolescents	76% vs 29%	3 (2–4)
Rynn et al. (2001)	GAD Ages 5–17 $n = 22$	Sertraline (50 mg/day)	91% vs 9%	2 (1–2)
Birmaher et al. (2003)	GAD, SoP, or SAD Ages 7–17 $n = 74$	Fluoxetine (20 mg/day)	61% vs 35%	4 (3–27)
Wagner et al. (2004)	SoP Ages 8–17 $n = 322$	Paroxetine (10–50 mg/day)	78% vs 38%	3 (3–4)
Beidel et al. (2007)	SoP Ages 7–17 $n = 139$	Fluoxetine (40 mg/day) or social effectiveness therapy	36% vs 6%	Not calculated
March et al. (2007)	SoP Ages 8–17 $n = 293$	Venlafaxine extended-release (37.5–225 mg/day)	56% vs 37%	6 (4–14)
Rynn et al. (2007)	GAD Ages 6–17 $n = 320$	Venlafaxine extended-release (37.5–225 mg/day)	69% vs 48%	5 (4–11)
Walkup et al. (2008)	GAD, SoP, or SAD Ages 7–17 $n = 488$	Sertraline (25–200 mg/day), CBT, or their combination	55% vs 24%	3 (3.2–3.5)

[a]CGI-I response rates for medication versus placebo. All studies defined response as CGI-I $\leq$ 2, except RUPP Anxiety Study which defined response as CGI-I $\leq$ 3.
[b]Number needed to treat (NNT) for medication versus placebo (Bridge, Iyengar, Salary et al., 2007; Walkup, Albano, Piacentini et al., 2008).

General Anxiety Disorder, Social Phobia, and Separation Anxiety Disorder

The largest and most comprehensive existing randomized controlled trial (RCT) for the treatment of youths with GAD, SAD, and/or SP is the National Institute Mental Health funded multicenter study, The Child/Adolescent Anxiety Multimodal Treatment Study (CAMS) (Walkup, Albano, Piacentini et al., 2008). This study compared the 12-week efficacy of CBT, a flexible dose of sertraline (25–200 mg/day, mean dose

134 mg/day), the combination of sertraline and CBT, and placebo in 488 youths with the above noted anxiety disorders. Patients were assessed by independent interviewers blind to treatment condition. In all primary outcomes, anxiety self-reports, and measurements of functioning, the combination of CBT and sertraline were more effective than either treatment alone, and all were significantly better than placebo. There were no differences between CBT and sertraline. Using the Clinical Global Improvement (CGI) Scale ≤ 2, the response rates were 80.7% for the combination treatment, 54.9% for sertraline, 59.7% for CBT, and 23.7% for placebo. The number needed to treat (NNT) for the combination treatment, sertraline, and CBT, were 1.7, 3.2, and 2.8, respectively.

Depending on the definition of remission, rates of remission after 12 weeks of treatment ranged from 46 to 68% for the combination treatment, 34–46% for sertraline, 20–46% for CBT, and 15–27% for placebo (Ginsburg, Kendall, Sakolsky et al., 2011). Therefore, most children remained symptomatic suggesting a need to augment or extend current treatments for some children. The most consistent predictors of remission were younger age, lower baseline anxiety severity, the absence of a comorbid internalizing disorder, and the absence of social phobia.

Four other RCTs using the SSRIs have also shown the benefit of these medications compared to placebo (Table 11.1). The Research Unit of Pediatric Psychopharmacology (RUPP) Anxiety Study Group (2001) administered a flexible dose fluvoxamine (25–250 mg/day children in 6–12 years old, 25–300 mg/day for adolescents 13–17 years old) or placebo to 128 youths with GAD, SP, and/or SAD for 8 weeks. Youths treated with fluvoxamine showed significantly better response than those with placebo (76% vs 29%, using a CGI-I ≤ 3). After the acute RCT of fluvoxamine, youths were offered 6 months of open treatment; fluvoxamine responders were continued on fluvoxamine ($n = 35$); placebo non-responders were treated with fluvoxamine ($n = 14$); and fluvoxamine non-responders were switched to fluoxetine ($n = 48$) (RUPP Anxiety Study Group, Walkup, Labellarte et al., 2002). During the 6 months of open treatment, anxiety symptoms remained low in youths who had initially responded to fluvoxamine, and anxiety symptoms improved when placebo non-responders were treated with fluvoxamine or when fluvoxamine non-responders were switched to fluoxetine.

Rynn and colleagues (2001) showed that 9 weeks of sertraline (50 mg/day maximum) was significantly better than placebo for 22 children (5–17 years old) with GAD (91% vs 9%, using a CGI-I ≤ 2). Birmaher and colleagues (2003) reported that 12 weeks of fixed dose fluoxetine (20 mg/day) was significantly better than placebo for 74 youths (7–17 years old) with GAD, SP, or SAD (61% vs 35%, using a CGI-I ≤ 2). Most of the improvement was accounted for by youths with SP. After the acute RCT of fluoxetine, youths were offered 1 year of open treatment with fluoxetine, alternative medication, and/or CBT following the RCT of fluoxetine and placebo (Clark, Birmaher, Axelson et al., 2005). Youths taking fluoxetine ($n = 42$) showed superior outcomes on most outcome measures compared to those taking no medication ($n = 10$). Wagner and colleagues (2004) in a multicenter study showed that 16-week flexible dose paroxetine (10–50 mg/day, mean dose 27 mg/day for children and 35 mg/day for adolescents) for 322 youths with SP was significantly better than placebo (78% vs 38%, using a CGI ≤ 2).

Finally, Beidel and colleagues (2007) compared fluoxetine (40 mg/day), Social Effectiveness Therapy for Children (SET-C), and placebo for 12 weeks in 122 youths (7–17 years of age) with social phobia. Both SET-C and fluoxetine were more efficacious than placebo in reducing anxiety symptoms and increasing general functioning (response rates using CGI-I $\leq$ 2: SET-C: 79% vs fluoxetine: 36.4% vs placebo: 6.3%). Prior to the publication of the CAMS (Walkup et al., 2008) and Beidel and colleagues' (2007) study, a meta-analyses that included all the existing SSRIs RCTs for youths with GAD, SP, and/or SAD reported that the overall response to the SSRIs was 63% and placebo 43% (Bridge, Iyengar, Salary et al., 2007). These results translated to an overall NNT of 3 (range 2–5). Similar results to the ones reported in the meta-analysis were obtained in the CAMS and Beidel and colleagues' study.

Panic Disorder

While cued panic attacks are common in youths, panic disorder – which is characterized by recurrent, *unexpected* panic attacks – occurs at a much lower rate in adolescents, and is almost nonexistent in children. The National Comorbidity Survey Replication-Adolescent Supplement (NCS-A) found that 2.3% of adolescents have panic disorder (Merikangas et al., 2010). The prevalence of this disorder showed a modest increase with age across adolescence. In the NCS-A, all adolescents with panic disorder endorsed "a lot" or "extreme" impairment in daily activities and "severe" or "very severe" distress from their anxiety symptoms.

Despite the impairment and severity of symptoms for youths with panic disorder, no RCTs have evaluated the efficacy of SSRIs for panic disorder in youths. Renaud and colleagues (1999) openly treated 12 youths with panic disorder. Nine youths received fluoxetine (20–60 mg/day, mean 34 mg/day), two were prescribed paroxetine (20 mg/day) and one was treated with sertraline (125 mg/day). In this open trial, SSRIs were effective for panic disorder in youths. Similarly, a chart review of 18 youths (7–16 years of age) with panic disorder showed flexible dose paroxetine (10–40 mg/day, mean 24 mg/day) to be effective for panic disorder in children and adolescents (Masi, Toni, Mucci, Millepiedi, Mata, & Perugi, 2001). In summary, limited data supports the use of SSRIs in the treatment of panic disorder in children and adolescents. Large RCTs are needed to confirm effective treatment options for panic disorder in youths.

Obsessive-Compulsive Disorder

OCD was once thought to be a rare condition, but is now recognized as a severe condition that affects 1–3% of the world's population (Rasmussen & Eisen, 1994). As many as 80% of all cases of OCD have their onset in childhood and adolescence (Nestadt, Samuels, Riddle et al., 2000; Pauls, Alsobrook, Goodman, Rasmussen, & Leckman, 1995). Therefore, the development of effective treatments for the condition during childhood and adolescence is critical.

Numerous RCTs have established the acute efficacy of SSRIs in the treatment of pediatric OCD (Mancuso, Faro, Joshi, & Geller, 2010). Three SSRIs (fluvoxamine, fluoxetine, and sertraline) have FDA indications for the treatment of OCD in youths (Table 11.2). A meta-analysis of RCTs of SSRIs for pediatric OCD (Bridge et al., 2007) found that overall, 52% of youths with OCD responded to SSRIs and 32% responded to placebo. The overall NNT to benefit from an SSRI was 6 (range 4–8) with comparable efficacy for children and adolescents. It is important to mention that not all the studies used the same criteria for response. For example some studies used the CGI-I scale and others a ≥ 40% or 25% reduction in the Children's Yale-Brown Obsessive Compulsive Scale (CY-BOCS) (Bridge et al., 2007).

Fluvoxamine was the first SSRI to be FDA approved for use in children and adolescents with OCD. A large RCT of fluvoxamine ($n = 120$) compared medication (50–200 mg/day, mean 157 mg/day in children and 170 mg/day in adolescents) and placebo in youths (8–17 years of age) for 10 weeks. Fluvoxamine was superior to placebo in reducing OCD symptom severity (≥ 25% reduction in the CY-BOCS: 42% vs 27%) (Riddle, Reeve, Yaryura-Tobias et al., 2001). Subsequent investigation to determine the long-term (12-month) efficacy of fluvoxamine in 99 youths (8–17 years of age) with OCD was conducted (Walkup, Reeve, Yaryura-Tobias et al., 1998). After the first 3 weeks of treatment, fluvoxamine dose was increased in all patients to 200 mg/day. A significant reduction in OCD symptom severity was seen initially and this improvement was maintained during the follow-up period. Youths with OCD who improved after acute treatment during the RCT demonstrated additional benefit during long-term treatment (mean additional reduction in OCD symptom severity of 31%). Thus, additional improvement with longer-term SSRI treatment may be achieved in pediatric OCD patients.

Two large RCTs have assessed the efficacy of fluoxetine in the treatment of OCD in youths. The first large RCT compared flexible dose fluoxetine (20–60 mg/day, mean 25 mg/day) and placebo for 13 weeks in 103 youths (7–17 years of age) with OCD (Geller, Hoog, Heiligenstein, et al., 2001). Fluoxetine showed significantly greater improvement in OCD symptoms compared to placebo (≥ 40% reduction in the CY-BOCS: 49% vs 25%). The second RCT compared fluoxetine (20–80 mg/day, mean 65 mg/day) and placebo for 8 weeks in 43 youths (6–18 years of age) with OCD (Liebowitz, Turner, Piacentini et al., 2002). Both groups had lower OCD symptoms at week 8, but there was no difference between fluoxetine and placebo on the primary outcome measure or most secondary measures (for the CGI-I ≤ 2: 57% vs 32%). Treatment responders ($n = 18$) were continued on fluoxetine or placebo for an additional 8 weeks. After 16 weeks, youths receiving fluoxetine had significantly lower OCD symptoms than youths taking placebo on the primary outcome measure and some secondary measures. Thus, fluoxetine has been shown to be efficacious in the treatment of pediatric OCD, but its effectiveness may take longer than 8 weeks to manifest.

The effectiveness of paroxetine for pediatric OCD has been evaluated in one large RCT (Geller, Wagner, Emslie et al., 2004). In this study, flexible dose paroxetine (10–50 mg/day, mean dose of 25 mg/day for children and 37 mg/day for adolescents) was compared to placebo in 207 youths (aged 7–17 years) with OCD for 10 weeks. Paroxetine showed significantly greater improvement in symptoms compared to the

Table 11.2 Acute RCTs of medication for youths with obsessive compulsive disorder.

Study	Subjects	Active treatment	Response criteria	Response rate drug vs placebo	NNT[a] (95% CI)
March et al. (1998)	Ages 6–17 $n = 128$	Sertraline (25–200 mg/day for children, 50–200 mg/day for adolescents)	≥25% reduction in CY-BOCS	53% vs 37%	7 (4–44)
Geller et al. (2001)	Ages 7–17 $n = 103$	Fluoxetine (20–60 mg/day)	≥40% reduction in CY-BOCS	49% vs 25%	5 (3–19)
Riddle et al. (2001)	Ages 8–17 $n = 120$	Fluvoxamine (50–200 mg/day)	≥25% reduction in CY-BOCS	42% vs 27%	—
Liebowitz et al. (2002)	Ages 8–17 $n = 43$	Fluoxetine (20–80 mg/day)	CGI ≤ 2	57% vs 32%	—
Geller et al. (2004)	Ages 7–17 $n = 203$	Paroxetine (10–50 mg/day)	≥25% reduction in CY-BOCS	65% vs 41%	5 (3–10)
POTS study team (2004)	Ages 7–17 $n = 112$	Sertraline (25–200 mg/day), CBT, or their combination	CY-BOCS Total score ≤ 10	21% vs 4%	6 (3–84)

[a]Number needed to treat for medication versus placebo (Bridge et al., 2007). Values are presented only when a significant treatment effect was observed.

placebo group on the primary outcome measure (adjusted mean change in CY-BOCS total score from baseline to week 10) and several secondary measures.

Two large RCTs have evaluated the efficacy of sertraline in the treatment of pediatric OCD. The first RCT compared sertraline (maximum 200 mg/day, mean dose 167 mg/day in children and 180 mg/day in adolescents) and placebo for 12 weeks in 187 youths (6–17 years of age) with OCD (March, Biederman, Wolkow et al., 1998). Youths treated with sertraline showed significantly greater improvement in OCD symptoms compared to placebo ($\geq$ 25% reduction in the CY-BOCS: 53% vs 37%). To evaluate the long-term effectiveness of sertraline for pediatric OCD, youths who participated in the RCT were offered open treatment with sertraline 50–200 mg/day (mean dose 108 mg/day in children and 132 mg/day in adolescents) for 12 months. Continued sertraline treatment resulted in additional improvement in OCD symptom severity.

The acute efficacy of sertraline for pediatric OCD was also evaluated in the Pediatric OCD Treatment Study (POTS) which compared CBT, flexible dose sertraline (25–200 mg/day, mean dose 170 mg/day), their combination (sertraline mean dose 133 mg/day), and pill placebo in 112 youths (7–17 years of age) for 12 weeks (POTS Team, 2004). The combination treatment was significantly greater than each monotherapy and placebo. There were no differences between the sertraline and CBT and both were significantly better than placebo (CY-BOCS total score $\leq$ 10: 53.6% for combination treatment, 39.3% for CBT, 21.4% for sertraline and 3.6% for placebo). Although, in general, several RCTs have established the short-term efficacy of SSRIs in the treatment of pediatric OCD, controlled studies are needed to determine the optimal length of continuation or maintenance treatment.

Post-Traumatic Stress Disorder

Most individuals who experience life-threat events develop post-traumatic symptoms immediately; however, only about 30% report enduring symptoms beyond the first month (Kessler, Sonnega, Bromet, Hughes, & Nelson, 1995). The NCS-A found 5.0% of adolescents (13–18 years of age) endorsed symptoms of post-traumatic stress disorder (Merikangas et al., 2010). PTSD was more frequent in females and its prevalence increased modestly with age. In the NCS-A, 30% of adolescents with PTSD reported severe anxiety symptoms and significant daily impairment.

Practice guidelines for the treatment of PTSD in children and adolescents recommend trauma-focused psychotherapies as first-line treatments (Cohen, Bukstein, Walter et al., 2010). Two recent RCTs have assessed the efficacy of SSRIs in the treatment of PTSD (Cohen, Mannarino, Perel, & Staron, 2007; Robb, Cueva, Sporn, Yang, & Vanderburgh, 2008) (Table 11.3). Both studies failed to find a difference between SSRI and placebo. The first RCT compared trauma-focused CBT plus flexible dose sertraline (50–200 mg/day, mean 150 mg/day) and trauma-focused CBT plus placebo for 12 weeks in 24 females (10–17 years of age) with PTSD (Cohen et al., 2007). Significant improvement was seen in both groups from pre- to post-treatment, but no group-by-time differences were observed for PTSD symptoms. The second RCT compared flexible dose sertraline (50–200 mg/day) and placebo for 10 weeks in 129 youths (6–17 years of age) with PTSD (Robb et al., 2008). As in the previous

Table 11.3 Acute RCTs of medication for youths with post-traumatic stress disorder.

Study	Subjects	Treatment	Results
Cohen et al. (2007)	Ages 10–17 $n = 24$	Sertraline (50–200 mg/d) + trauma focused CBT vs placebo + trauma focused CBT	No difference between treatments
Robb et al. (2008)	Ages 6–17 $n = 129$	Sertraline (50–200 mg/d) vs placebo	No difference between treatments

study, both groups experienced a significant improvement in PTSD symptoms from pre- to post-treatment, but no difference between the sertraline and placebo group was found.

In summary, current data is lacking to support the use of SSRIs in the treatment of childhood PTSD. However, SSRIs can be considered for youths with PTSD who have comorbid disorders known to be responsive to SSRI treatment (e.g., major depressive disorder (MDD), OCD, GAD, or SP) or those who do not respond to psychotherapy alone (Cohen et al., 2010).

Pharmacokinetics

As youths differ from adults in many ways, pharmacokinetic studies in children and adolescents can provide useful information regarding how to prescribe these medications most effectively for pediatric populations (Table 11.4). This is important because medication dosing strategies in several RCTs may have contributed not only to the failure of these trials to show a difference in efficacy between medication and placebo, but also to our understanding of the safety and tolerability of these medications (Findling, McNamara, Stansbrey et al., 2006). Comprehending the pharmacokinetics of SSRIs is of great clinical importance because withdrawal effects (e.g., irritability) caused by SSRIs with a short half-life can not only interfere with a child's daily functioning, but also may be confused with symptoms of psychiatric illness. For example, if a youths becomes more irritable as a consequence of withdrawal effects, the clinician may think that the symptoms are due to the primary psychiatric illness (e.g., GAD) and modify treatment without taking into account that the symptoms may be due to the short half-life of the medication (see section on withdrawal).

Pharmacokinetic properties for fluoxetine were described in a population pharmacokinetic study of children and adolescents (Wilens, Cohen, Biederman et al., 2002). Mean steady-state levels of fluoxetine (127 ng/ml) and its primary metabolite, norfluoxetine (151 ng/ml), were achieved after 4 weeks of treatment. High inter-subject variability was reported. Concentrations of fluoxetine and norfluoxetine were approximately two times higher in children than adolescents. When normalized to body weight, fluoxetine and norfluoxetine concentrations were comparable for both

Table 11.4 Clinical use of SSRI in youths with pediatric anxiety disorders.

Generic name (brand name)	Typical starting dose[a]	Clinical dose range	FDA dose range[b]	Formulations
Citalopram (Celexa)	10 mg daily	10–80 mg		Tablets: 10, 20, 40 mg Solution: 10 mg/5 ml
Escitalopram (Lexapro)	5 mg daily	10–40 mg	10–20 mg	Tablets: 5, 10, 20 mg Solution: 5 mg/5 ml
Fluoxetine (Prozac)	10 mg daily	10–80 mg	20–60 mg	Tablets: 10, 20 mg Capsules: 10, 20, 40 mg Delayed release capsule: 90 mg Solution: 20 mg/5 ml
Fluvoxamine (Luvox)	25 mg daily	50–300 mg	50–200 mg (children) 50–300 mg (adolescents)	Tablets: 25, 50, 100 mg Extended release capsule: 100, 150 mg
Paroxetine (Paxil)	10 mg daily	10–60mg	10–60 mg	Tablets: 10, 20, 30, 40 mg Extended release capsule: 12.5, 25, 37.5 mg Suspension: 10 mg/5 ml
Sertraline (Zoloft)	25 mg daily	50–300 mg	25–200 mg	Tablets: 25, 50, 100 mg Solution: 20 mg/ml

[a]Starting doses for children maybe lower (e.g., 5 mg daily for fluoxetine or paroxetine).
[b]Escitalopram has an FDA indication for major depressive disorder in adolescents (12 years and older); fluoxetine has an FDA indication for major depressive disorder in youths (8 years and older) and for OCD in youths (7 years and older); fluvoxamine has an FDA indication for OCD in youths (8 years and older); paroxetine has an FDA indication for OCD in youths (7 years and older); sertraline has an FDA indication for OCD in youths (6 years and older).

groups. Time to steady state concentration, plasma level at steady state, and ratio of drug to metabolite were analogous in adolescents when compared to adult studies. Based on these findings, Wilens and colleagues (2002) suggested that children begin fluoxetine at 10 mg/day whereas adolescents may start at 20 mg/day.

Pharmacokinetic studies of citalopram, escitalopram, and sertraline in youths suggest that these medications have shorter half-lives at low doses, but their half-life becomes equivalent to the half-life in adults at a higher dose range. S-citalopram, marketed as escitalopram, is the therapeutically active isomer of racemic citalopram (Hyttel, Bogeso, Perregaard, & Sanchez, 1992). A pharmacokinetic study of adolescents examined the half-life of R-citalopram and S-citalopram after a single 20 mg dose and after 2 weeks of 20 mg/day (Perel, Axelson, Rudolph, & Birmaher, 2001). The single dose and steady state half-life of S-citalopram was found to be significantly shorter than previously reported in adults. Based on these findings, the authors recommended twice daily dosing when prescribing citalopram 20 mg/day. Likewise, a pharmacokinetic study of a single 10 mg dose of escitalopram found the half-life of escitalopram was shorter in adolescents (19.0 hours) than adults (28.9 hours). A pharmacokinetic study of steady state citalopram (40 mg/day) found pharmacokinetic parameters were similar in adolescents (e.g., half-life 38 hours) and adults (e.g., half-life 44 hours). This same pattern is also observed in pharmacokinetic studies of sertraline. Pharmacokinetic studies of sertraline in adolescents have reported the mean steady state half-life is 15.3 hours at 50 mg/day, 20.4 hours at 100–150 mg/day, and 27.1 hours at 200 mg/day (Alderman, Wolkow, Chung, & Johnston, 1998; Axelson, Perel, Birmaher et al., 2002). The steady state half-life of sertraline at 200 mg/day was similar to that previously observed in adults. Based on these findings, Axelson and colleagues (2002) suggested an optimal dosing strategy of twice per day at doses of 50 mg/day and once daily at 200 mg/day. In summary, when prescribing citalopram, escitalopram, or sertraline in the low dose range, twice daily dosing should be considered.

The pharmacokinetic properties of fluvoxamine have been investigated in one study with youths. This study evaluated the steady state pharmacokinetic properties of fluvoxamine at 50, 100, and 200 mg/day in children and 50, 100, 200, and 300 mg/day in adolescents (Labellarte, Biederman, Emslie et al., 2006). Children demonstrated higher mean peak plasma concentration, higher means area under the curve, and lower apparent clearance compared to adolescents. No pharmacokinetic differences were observed between adolescents and adults prescribed 150 mg twice daily. Nonlinear kinetics of fluvoxamine was observed over the dose range studied. Based on these findings, the authors concluded that children have a higher exposure to fluvoxamine than adolescents, while adolescents and adults seem to have similar drug exposure.

The pharmacokinetic properties of paroxetine have been reported in two studies with youths. The first study reported that the half-life of paroxetine, after a single 10 mg dose (11.1 hours), was significantly shorter than the half-life previously observed in adult studies (Findling, Reed, Myers et al., 1999). Other pharmacokinetic parameters (e.g., time to maximum concentration, intersubject variability, and nonlinear kinetics) were similar to those found in adult studies. For youths who were maintained on 10 mg/day, paroxetine concentrations generally remained stable during treatment; however, an almost 7-fold increase in drug concentration was reported in participants whose dose was raised to 20 mg/day. Based on these findings, Findling and colleagues (1999) concluded that once daily administration of paroxetine was adequate. The second study assessed steady state pharmacokinetic properties after 2 weeks of 10 mg/day, 20 mg/day, and 30 mg/day (Findling, Nucci, Piergies et al., 2006). Nonlinear kinetics of paroxetine was established as supra-proportional increases in drug concentration were seen with each dose increase. Drug concentration at steady state was higher in children than adolescents at each dose studied. Based on these findings, the authors suggested that when paroxetine is prescribed to prepubertal children, clinicians start at 5 mg/day or use an extended titration schedule such as 10 mg/day for at least 4 weeks.

In summary, pharmacokinetics studies with SSRIs suggest optimal dosing strategies may be different for children compared to adolescents and, in particular, for children with low weight. First, fluoxetine, fluvoxamine, and paroxetine need to be initiated at lower doses in low-weight youths. Second, clinicians may start citalopram, escitalopram, or sertraline at once daily dosing and observe closely for withdrawal effects. If withdrawal effects are noted (see section on withdrawal), then the dosing regimen should be changed to twice daily dosing.

Adverse effects

Common

In acute RCTs, SSRIs are generally well tolerated. Most side effects seem to be dose-dependent and often decrease with time (Cheung, Emslie, & Mayes, 2006; Emslie, Kratochvil, Vitiello et al., 2006; Safer & Zito, 2006). The most common adverse effects include gastrointestinal symptoms (e.g., nausea, abdominal pain, and diarrhea), appetite disturbance (increase or decrease), headache, dizziness, sleep changes (e.g., insomnia or somnolence, vivid dreams or nightmares), dry mouth, restlessness, akathisia, and sexual dysfunction.

Impulsivity, silliness, irritability, disinhibition or "behavioral activation" can be seen in 3–8% of youths, especially in children, taking SSRIs. This adverse reaction is characterized by goofiness, silliness, increased activity, and is usually mild to moderate in severity and has an abrupt onset after starting or changing a medication dose (Wilens, Wyatt, & Spencer, 1998). It can occur with many types of medication (e.g., benzodiazepines, antihistamines, or tricyclic antidepressants). We recommend discussing this side effect with the parents and child being treated beforehand as this side effect is transient. Symptoms resolve quickly when the medication dose is lowered or discontinued. Careful differentiation between this phenomena and hypomania or mania is critical. It is also worth pointing out that many patients treated with SSRIs including patients with anxiety disorders, OCD, and severe depression may be remarkably inhibited at baseline and it is important not to confuse healthy childhood behavior with a medication side effect. For example, if parents are concerned about behavior that is not typical of their child, but is common in their child's peers, this may suggest a decrease in anxiety and not an adverse medication reaction.

SSRIs have been associated with hypomania and mania in children and adolescents. This may be a particular concern in youths with depression who may have a higher risk of ultimately developing bipolar disorder. However, it is not clear at present how to discriminate depressed youths who will develop bipolar disorder from those who will not. A family history of bipolar disorder and depression with psychosis carry an increased risk for bipolar disorder in youths, so that caution is indicated when prescribing SSRIs to these youths. Any patient being treated with an antidepressant should be monitored for symptoms of mania/hypomania. As described by Wilens and colleagues (1998), the unmasking of a primary psychiatric disorder (e.g., bipolar disorder with a hypmomanic/manic episode) can be distinguished from disinhibition by the onset of symptoms, the offset of symptoms, the severity of symptoms, and the nature of the symptoms. In comparison to disinhibition, a hypomanic or manic episode has a delayed onset; a prolonged offset; and moderate to severe symptomatology including elated mood, grandiosity, decreased need for sleep, talkativeness, flight of ideas, distractibility, and excessive involvement in pleasurable activities that have a high potential for painful consequences. The reader is strongly encouraged to read the brief review by Wilens and colleagues (1998) which includes very helpful advice in differentiating disinhibition from the unmasking of a primary psychiatric disorder, such as bipolar disorder.

Uncommon and serious

Less common but more severe side effects include serotonin syndrome (Boyer & Shannon, 2005) and increased risk of bleeding (e.g., easy bruising, epistaxis, gastrointestinal bleeding, and perioperative bleeding) (Lake, Birmaher, Wassick, Mathos, & Yelovich, 2000; Weinrieb, Auriacombe, Lynch, & Lewis, 2005). The most publicized and controversial is the increased spontaneous reports of suicidal ideation and behavior.

Given the serious concerns about suicidal ideation and behavior with SSRIs, two meta-analyses have evaluated the risk of suicidal ideation and behavior in children and adolescents taking antidepressants (Bridge et al., 2007; Hammad, Laughren, & Racoosin, 2006). In collaboration with researchers at Columbia University, the US Food and Drug Administration (FDA) evaluated the effect of nine antidepressants on suicidality in 24 RCTs of pediatric depression, anxiety disorders or attention deficit hyperactivity disorder (Hammad et al., 2006). The primary outcome measures were *spontaneous* reports of suicidal ideation and suicidal behavior termed "suicidal adverse events." The overall risk ratio (RR) for suicidality for all the trials and indications was 1.95 (95% CI, 1.28–2.98). When analyses were limited to depression trials with SSRIs, the overall RR was 1.66 (95% CI, 1.02–2.68). These results suggest that 1–3 spontaneously reported suicide adverse events occur for every 100 children or adolescents treated with an antidepressant. This meta-analysis (Hammad et al., 2006) also examined worsening or emergence of suicidality using the suicide item scores of depression rating scales from 17 RCTs. These analyses did not reveal any significant RR for worsening of suicidality (0.92; 95% CI, 0.76–1.1) or for emergence of suicidality (0.93; 95% CI, 0.75–1.15).

A second meta-analysis examined the effect of antidepressants on suicidality in 27 published and unpublished RCTs of pediatric depression and anxiety disorders (Bridge et al., 2007). When using similar statistical methods as the previous study, this meta-analysis found comparable results, a small but significant increase in overall RR for suicidality for all disorders (1.9; 95% CI, 1.3–3.0) and for depression (1.9; 95% CI 1.2–2.9). Since RR analysis is limited to trials with at least one event, and several trials had no events, Bridge and colleagues (2007) also assessed risk difference (RD), which permits inclusion of trials with no events. When using random-effects analysis of RD instead of RR, there was a small but significant overall RD for drug compared with placebo (0.7%; 95% CI, 0.1–1.3). No significant difference was found when analyses were limited to studies with depression (0.9%; 95% CI, −0.1 to 1.9%), OCD (0.5%; 95% CI, −0.4 to 1.8%), or other anxiety disorders (0.7%; 95% CI, −0.4 to 1.8%). Bridge et al. (2007) analyzed the NNH for the spontaneous report of suicidal ideation and suicide attempt. The NNH for GAD, SP, and SAD was 143 and for OCD 200. In comparison with the NNT results noted earlier, these numbers suggest a very favorable risk–benefit profile for SSRIs in the treatment of childhood and adolescent anxiety disorders.

The interpretation of these findings and their implications for clinical practice are not clear since there has been a dramatic decline in the rate of suicide for youths in the USA during the time of increased usage of SSRIs (Olfson, Shaffer, Marcus, & Greenberg, 2003). Prior to the FDA black box warning on SSRIs, epidemiological studies suggested a positive relationship between the reduction in adolescent suicide rate and use of SSRIs (Gibbons, Hur, Bhaumik, & Mann, 2006; Olfson et al., 2003;

Valuck, Libby, Sills, Giese, & Allen, 2004). Since US and European regulators issued warnings on SSRIs, there has been a reduction in the rate of SSRI prescriptions to children and adolescents and an increase in completed suicides rates in the USA and the Netherlands (Gibbons, Brown, Hur et al., 2007). Thus, epidemiological studies show not only a correlation between increased usage of SSRIs and reduction in suicide rates, but also an association between reduced SSRI usage and increased suicide rates in youths.

In summary, spontaneous reports of suicidal ideation or behavior are more common in adolescents treated with SSRIs than placebo. Although this event is rare, some youths experience a new onset or worsening in suicidal ideation or behavior after starting treatment with an SSRI. Thus, it is important to evaluate for the presence of suicidal risk before treatment and carefully after starting treatment with an SSRI (see section below on Monitoring for Adverse Effects).

However, the long-term impact of SSRIs is unknown. The effect on brain development and function are often a concern of the child and family for whom SSRI treatment is being considered. It should be noted that the illnesses for which SSRIs are prescribed can be quite serious and can result in substantial morbidity and mortality, so a risk/benefit analysis is indicated. Long-term study of SSRIs is clearly warranted to address concerns about the medication's effect on brain development and other potentially unknown side effects.

Withdrawal

Withdrawal and flu-like syndromes can occur when the SSRIs are abruptly discontinued, when SSRIs are taken inconsistently, or when a patient rapidly metabolizes a medication. Somatic symptoms can include: gastrointestinal (e.g., nausea or emesis), disequilibrium (e.g., dizziness, vertigo, or ataxia), sleep disturbance (e.g., insomnia or vivid dreams), flu-like symptoms (e.g., fatigue, sedation, myalgia, or chills), and sensory disturbances (e.g., paresthesia) (Schatzberg, Haddad, Kaplan et al., 1997). Given the similarity between adverse effects and withdrawal symptoms, it is important to inquire about medication adherence when problems with medication are reported. In studies with adults (Baldwin, Montgomery, Nil, & Lader, 2007; Tint, Haddad, & Anderson, 2008), discontinuation symptoms have been shown to differ among the SSRIs. For example, Baldwin and colleagues (2007) observed significantly fewer discontinuation symptoms with escitalopram compared to paroxetine. Tint and colleagues (2008) reported fewer discontinuation symptoms with fluoxetine compared to short half-life antidepressants (i.e., citalopram, fluvoxamine, paroxetine, and venlafaxine) and found a similar frequency of discontinuation symptoms with a short taper (3 days) compared to longer taper (14 days). Thus, tapering an SSRI is preferable and some youths may require especially gradual tapering over 4–6 weeks to minimize withdrawal and/or symptom recurrence.

Other pharmacological treatments

Venlafaxine. A large multicenter RCT evaluated the efficacy of venlafaxine extended release (ER) in 293 children and adolescents ages 8 to 17 with generalized social anxiety disorder.[62] Overall venlafaxine ER was well tolerated and there were no suicidal attempts. Venlafaxine ER or placebo was titrated from a starting dose of

37.5 mg to a maximum dose of 225 mg over 16 weeks. Venlafaxine was significantly better than placebo (56% vs 37%). A polled analysis of two large multicenter 8-week RCTs in 220 children and adolescents with GAD showed that overall the flexible dosage of extended-release venlafaxine was significantly better than placebo (69% versus 48%). Common adverse events were asthenia, anorexia, pain, and somnolence.

TCAs. Except for clomipramine for OCD, the few existing RCTs comparing TCAs and placebo for youths with anxiety disorders have yielded inconsistent results. These studies have several methodological problems including small samples, inclusion of children with significant depression and children with school phobia (which is not always accounted by an anxiety disorder) (Birmaher, Yelovich, & Renaud, 1998). The results of these studies, combined with the fact that the TCAs are associated with significant cardiovascular and other side effects and that they may be lethal after an overdose, have precluded their use for a variety of childhood psychiatric disorders.

Benzodiazepines. Two very small RCTs comparing a clonazepam for SAD and alprazolam for general anxiety disorders did not show differences with placebo (Birmaher et al., 1998). However, some open reports have suggested that the benzodiazepines may be temporarily used for some youths with severe anxiety disorders before the SSRIs exert their effect or to lower the anxiety levels and gain the cooperation before starting CBT. In any case, due to the abuse risk and potential cognitive side effects, the use of benzodiazepines in youths remains controversial.

Other medications have been used alone or more often in combination with the SSRIs, especially for resistant cases including the atypical antipsychotics, buspirone, buproprion, and propanolol, but currently, except for sporadic case reports, there is no evidence supporting their use in anxious youths.

Novel pharmacological treatments

Several novel compounds that directly or indirectly affect the glutamatergic and GABA systems appear useful for the treatment of anxiety disorders. For example, small RCTs using a partial receptor agonist of the N-methyl-D-aspartame system, D-cycloserine (DCS) in adults, appear to indicate that this compound helps to consolidate the emotional learning that occurs during exposure to anxiety-provoking situations (Norberg, Krystal, & Tolin, 2008; Rynn, Riddle, Yeung, & Kunz, 2007). Riluzole, an antiglutamatergic medication; memantine, an NMDA receptor antagonist; and some anticonvulsivant medications with effects on the glutamate and GABA systems (e.g., gabapentin and pregabalin), seem to be useful for the treatment of anxiety disorders. However, with the exception of DCS, current studies have been case studies or open trials and their efficacy and safety have not been well studied in youths.

Practical Recommendations and Summary

Currently there is strong evidence supporting the combination of CBT and SSRIs as well as each of these treatments alone for the acute treatment of most, but not all, pediatric anxiety disorders. Athough more research is needed regarding the factors associated with treatment response, the choice of treatment should be based on a variety factors including anxiety severity, duration of illness, type of anxiety disorder, prior response to intervention, familial and environmental factors, availability of treatment, comorbid disorders, patient and family preference.

When deciding among the available treatments options, benefits and risks should be discussed to help families make an educated decision. In general, for youths with mild to moderate disorders and mild to moderate psychosocial impairment, CBT is usually the first line treatment. Pharmacological treatment alone, or in combination with CBT, is recommended when a child's symptoms are in the moderate-to-severe range, when the child has severe impairment, CBT or another form of psychotherapy is not available, or the child and/or family are not able to cooperate with the therapy.

If pharmacological treatment will be used, the SSRIs are considered first-line treatment, as these medications have been consistently shown to be efficacious, well tolerated, and, in general, no blood tests are needed. For youths who do not respond or tolerate a specific SSRI, a trial with another SSRI is indicated. If the youths still do not respond, a trial with venlafaxine ER may be appropriate. Since venlafaxine may reduce weight, blood pressure and pulse, monitoring of weight and vital signs is indicated.

Although there are some differences in pharmacokinetics between youths and adults, dosing regimens of SSRIs for youths are quite similar to adults. It is advisable to start with a low dose, but increase weekly until a minimum effective dosage is reached. If persistent side effects develop during titration, the medication dose should be lowered to the highest tolerable amount. Children and adolescents should receive an adequate and tolerable dosage for a minimum of 6–8 weeks. If a youth has tolerated the SSRI, but remains symptomatic after 6–8 weeks, a dose increase should be considered. When a youth shows only partial improvement or fails to show significant improvement after 10–12 weeks, alternative strategies should be considered (see Practice Parameters for the treatment of obsessive-compulsive disorder, anxiety disorders and post-traumatic stress disorder from the American Academy of Child and Adolescent Psychiatry).

Prior to starting medication, children and families should be told what to expect in terms of side effects, including the small but clinically significant increase in suicidal ideation with the SSRIs. Families should understand what to do when side effects occur, how to communicate medication concerns with the child's clinician, or if necessary the child's pediatrician or the emergency room.

Although SSRI and venlafaxine have demonstrated efficacy for the acute treatment of most pediatric anxiety disorders, 20–35% of youths do not respond; even those who respond usually remain symptomatic. In cases of partial or no response, it is important to first evaluate why the child has not responded and evaluate for factors such as poor adherence to treatment, inadequate dose or length of time for the medication to work, presence of comorbid disorders (e.g., depression, bipolar disorder, ADHD, substance abuse), and environmental factors or stressors that may be worsening the child's anxiety (e.g., ongoing conflicts, parental psychopathology, abuse, problems at school or with peers). When the above factors have been ruled out, some have suggested augmentation with buspirone, benzodiazepines, stimulants, atypical antipsychotics, and TCAs. However, at least for children and adolescents, there is currently little to no empirical evidence to support these options. Thus, there continues to be a need for developing new, more efficacious, acute and long-term treatments, as well as strategies to manage resistant cases.

While RCTs have confirmed the short-term efficacy of SSRIs in treatment of child-hood anxiety disorders, few continuation studies have been conducted and those that have are limited (e.g., lack of a randomized control design). Clearly, controlled studies are needed to establish the long-term efficacy and safety of the SSRIs in the treatment of childhood anxiety disorders. Until such studies are preformed, it is recommended following the same clinical practice as continuation treatment for depression in youths (i.e., SSRI are continued at the same dose that resulted in response during acute treatment for 6–12 months). The SSRI dose may be increased during continuation treatment to diminish residual anxiety symptoms provided that side effects are not problematic. In fact, several studies have shown that after the acute RCTs, children maintained on the medications continue to show incremental improvement. After 6–12 months with minimal anxiety symptoms, if clinically indicated, a gradual trial off medication (e.g., 10–25% every 3–6 weeks) during a low-stress period (e.g., summer vacation) should be considered. The SSRI should be restarted if anxiety symptoms reoccur.

Finally, it is important to evaluate and address other psychiatric disorders that require a different type of treatment (e.g., ADHD), manage the ongoing school, family and peer problems, and importantly treat parents and siblings own psychiatric problems.

References

Alderman, J., Wolkow, R., Chung, M., & Johnston, H. F. (1998). Sertraline treatment of children and adolescents with obsessive-compulsive disorder or depression: pharmacokinetics, tolerability, and efficacy. *Journal of the American Academy of Child and Adolescent Psychiatry, 37* (4), 386–394.

Axelson, D. A., Perel, J. M., Birmaher, B., Rudolph, G. R., Nuss, S., Bridge, J., et al. (2002). Sertraline pharmacokinetics and dynamics in adolescents. *Journal of the American Academy of Child and Adolescent Psychiatry, 41* (9), 1037–1044.

Baldwin, D. S., Montgomery, S. A., Nil, R. (2007). Lader M. Discontinuation symptoms in depression and anxiety disorders. *International Journal of Neuropsychopharmacology, 10* (1), 73–84.

Beidel, D. C., Turner, S. M., Sallee, F. R., Ammerman, R. T., Crosby, L. A., & Pathak, S. (2007). SET-C versus fluoxetine in the treatment of childhood social phobia. *Journal of the American Academy of Child and Adolescent Psychiatry, 46* (12), 1622–1632.

Beesdo, K., Bittner, A., Pine, D. S., Stein, M. B., Hofler, M., Lieb, R., et al. (2007). Incidence of social anxiety disorder and the consistent risk for secondary depression in the first three decades of life. *Archives of General Psychiatry, 64* (8), 903–912.

Birmaher, B., Axelson, D. A., Monk, K., Kalas, C., Clark, D., Ehmann, M., et al. (2003). Fluoxetine for the treatment of childhood anxiety disorders. *Journal of the American Academy of Child and Adolescent Psychiatry, 42* (4), 415–423.

Birmaher, B., Yelovich, A. K., & Renaud, J. (1998). Pharmacologic treatment for children and adolescents with anxiety disorders. *Pediatric Clinics of North America, 45* (5), 1187–1204.

Bittner, A., Egger, H. L., Erkanli, A., Costello, E., Foley, D. L., & Angold, A. (2007). What do childhood anxiety disorders predict? *Journal of Child Psychology & Psychiatry & Allied Disciplines, 48* (12), 1174–1183.

Bolton, J. M., Cox, B. J., Afifi, T. O., Enns, M. W., Bienvenu, O. J., & Sareen, J. (2008). Anxiety disorders and risk for suicide attempts: findings from the Baltimore Epidemiologic Catchment area follow-up study. *Depression and Anxiety, 25* (6), 477–481.

Boyer, E. W., & Shannon, M. (2005). The serotonin syndrome. *New England Journal of Medicine, 352* (11), 1112–1120.

Bridge, J. A., Iyengar, S., Salary, C. B., Barbe, R. P., Birmaher, B., Pincus, H. A., et al. (2007). Clinical response and risk for reported suicidal ideation and suicide attempts in pediatric antidepressant treatment: a meta-analysis of randomized controlled trials. [see comment]. *Jama, 297* (15), 1683–1696.

Buckner, J. D., Schmidt, N. B., Lang, A. R., Small, J. W., Schlauch, R. C., & Lewinsohn, P. M. (2008). Specificity of social anxiety disorder as a risk factor for alcohol and cannabis dependence. *Journal of Psychiatric Research, 42* (3), 230–239.

Cheung, A. H., Emslie, G. J., & Mayes, T. L. (2006). The use of antidepressants to treat depression in children and adolescents. *Canadian Medical Association Journal, 174* (2), 193–200.

Clark, D. B., Birmaher, B., Axelson, D., Monk, K., Kalas, C., Ehmann, M., et al. (2005). Fluoxetine for the treatment of childhood anxiety disorders: open-label, long-term extension to a controlled trial. *Journal of the American Academy of Child and Adolescent Psychiatry, 44* (12), 1263–1270.

Cohen, J. A., Bukstein, O., Walter, H., Benson, S. R., Chrisman, A., Farchione, T. R., et al. (2010). Practice parameter for the assessment and treatment of children and adolescents with posttraumatic stress disorder. *Journal of the American Academy of Child and Adolescent Psychiatry, 49* (4), 414–430.

Cohen, J. A., Mannarino, A. P., Perel, J. M., & Staron, V. (2007). A pilot randomized controlled trial of combined trauma-focused CBT and sertraline for childhood PTSD symptoms. *Journal of the American Academy of Child and Adolescent Psychiatry, 46* (7), 811–819.

Costello, E. J. & Angold, A. (2004). Developmental epidemiology of anxiety disorders. In Thomas H. Ollendick Jsm (Ed.): *Phobic and Anxiety Disorders in Children and Adolescents: a Clinician's Guide to Effective Psychosocial and Pharmacological Interventions*. New York Oxford University Press.

Costello, E. J., Egger, H., & Angold, A. (2005). 10-year research update review: the epidemiology of child and adolescent psychiatric disorders: I. Methods and public health burden. *Journal of the American Academy of Child and Adolescent Psychiatry, 44* (10), 972–986.

Emslie, G., Kratochvil, C., Vitiello, B., Silva, S., Mayes, T., McNulty, S., et al. (2006). Treatment for Adolescents with Depression Study (TADS): safety results. *Journal of the American Academy of Child and Adolescent Psychiatry, 45* (12), 1440–1455.

Findling, R. L., McNamara, N. K., Stansbrey, R. J., Feeny, N. C., Young, C. M., Peric, F. V., et al. (2006). The relevance of pharmacokinetic studies in designing efficacy trials in juvenile major depression. *Journal of Child & Adolescent Psychopharmacology, 16* (1–2), 131–145.

Findling, R. L., Nucci, G., Piergies, A. A., Gomeni, R., Bartolic, E. I., Fong, R., et al. (2006). Multiple dose pharmacokinetics of paroxetine in children and adolescents with major depressive disorder or obsessive-compulsive disorder. *Neuropsychopharmacology, 31* (6), 1274–1285.

Findling, R. L., Reed, M. D., Myers, C., O'Riordan, M. A., Fiala, S., Branicky, L., et al. (1999). Paroxetine pharmacokinetics in depressed children and adolescents. *Journal of the American Academy of Child and Adolescent Psychiatry, 38* (8), 952–959.

Geller, D. A., Hoog, S. L., Heiligenstein, J. H., Ricardi, R. K., Tamura, R., Kluszynski, S., et al. (2001). Fluoxetine treatment for obsessive-compulsive disorder in children and adolescents: a placebo-controlled clinical trial. *Journal of the American Academy of Child and Adolescent Psychiatry, 40* (7), 773–779.

Geller, D. A., Wagner, K. D., Emslie, G., Murphy, T., Carpenter, D. J., Wetherhold, E., et al. (2004). Paroxetine treatment in children and adolescents with obsessive-compulsive disorder: a randomized, multicenter, double-blind, placebo-controlled trial. *Journal of the American Academy of Child and Adolescent Psychiatry, 43* (11), 1387–1396.

Gibbons, R. D., Brown, C. H., Hur, K., Marcus, S. M., Bhaumik, D. K., Erkens, J. A., et al. (2007). Early evidence on the effects of regulators' suicidality warnings on SSRI prescriptions and suicide in children and adolescents. *American Journal of Psychiatry, 164* (9), 1356–1363.

Gibbons, R. D., Hur, K., Bhaumik, D. K., & Mann, J. J. (2006). The relationship between antidepressant prescription rates and rate of early adolescent suicide. *American Journal of Psychiatry, 163* (11), 1898–1904.

Ginsburg, G. S., Kendall, P. C., Sakolsky, D., Compton, S. N., Piacentini, J., Albano, A. M., et al. (2011). Remission after acute treatment in children and adolescents with anxiety disoders: Findings from the CAMS. *Journal of Consulting and Clinical Psychology, 79* (6), 806–813.

Hammad, T. A., Laughren, T., & Racoosin, J. (2006). Suicidality in pediatric patients treated with antidepressant drugs. *Archives of General Psychiatry, 63* (3), 332–339.

Hyttel, J., Bogeso, K. P., Perregaard, J., & Sanchez, C. (1992). The pharmacological effect of citalopram residues in the (S)-(+)-enantiomer. *Journal of Neural Transmission, 88* (2), 157–160.

Kessler, R. C., Sonnega, A., Bromet, E., Hughes, M., & Nelson, C. B. (1995). Posttraumatic stress disorder in the National Comorbidity Survey. *Archives of General Psychiatry, 52* (12), 1048–1060.

Labellarte, M., Biederman, J., Emslie, G., Ferguson, J., Khan, A., Ruckle, J., et al. (2006). Multiple-dose pharmacokinetics of fluvoxamine in children and adolescents. *Journal of the American Academy of Child and Adolescent Psychiatry, 43* (12), 1497–1505.

Lake, M. B., Birmaher, B., Wassick, S., Mathos, K., & Yelovich, A. K. (2000). Bleeding and selective serotonin reuptake inhibitors in childhood and adolescence. *Journal of Child & Adolescent Psychopharmacology, 10* (1), 35–38.

Langley, A. K., Bergman, R. L., McCracken, J., & Piacentini, J. C. (2004). Impairment in childhood anxiety disorders: preliminary examination of the child anxiety impact scale-parent version. *Journal of Child & Adolescent Psychopharmacology, 14* (1), 105–114.

Liebowitz, M. R., Turner, S. M., Piacentini, J., Beidel, D. C., Clarvit, S. R., Davies, S. O., et al. (2002). Fluoxetine in children and adolescents with OCD: a placebo-controlled trial. *Journal of the American Academy of Child and Adolescent Psychiatry, 41* (12), 1431–1438.

Mancuso, E., Faro, A., Joshi, G., & Geller, D. A. (2010). Treatment of pediatric obsessive-compulsive disorder: a review. *Journal of Child & Adolescent Psychopharmacology, 20* (4), 299–308.

March, J. S., Biederman, J., Wolkow, R., Safferman, A., Mardekian, J., Cook, E. H., et al. (1998). Sertraline in children and adolescents with obsessive-compulsive disorder: a multicenter randomized controlled trial. [Erratum appears in JAMA 2000 Mar 8;283(10):1293]. *Jama, 280* (20), 1752–1756.

March, J. S., Entusah, A. R., Rynn, M., Albano, A. M., & Tourian, K. A. (2007). A Randomized controlled trial of venlafaxine ER versus placebo in pediatric social anxiety disorder. *Biol Psychiatry, 62* (10), 1149–1154.

Masi, G., Toni, C., Mucci, M., Millepiedi, S., Mata, B., & Perugi, G. (2001). Paroxetine in child and adolescent outpatients with panic disorder. *Journal of Child & Adolescent Psychopharmacology, 11* (2), 151–157.

Merikangas, K. R., He, J. -P., Brody, D., Fisher, P. W., Bourdon, K., & Koretz, D. S. (2010). Prevalence and Treatment of Mental Disorders Among US Children in the 2001–2004 NHANES. *Pediatrics, 125* (1), 75–81.

Nestadt, G., Samuels, J., Riddle, M., Bienvenu, O. J., 3rd, Liang, K. Y., LaBuda, M., et al. (2000). A family study of obsessive-compulsive disorder. *Archives of General Psychiatry, 57* (4), 358–363.

Norberg, M. M., Krystal, J. H., & Tolin, D. F. (2008). A meta-analysis of D-cycloserine and the facilitation of fear extinction and exposure therapy. *Biological Psychiatry, 63* (12), 1118–1126.

Olfson, M., Shaffer, D., Marcus, S. C., & Greenberg, T. (2003). Relationship between antidepressant medication treatment and suicide in adolescents. *Archives of General Psychiatry, 60* (10), 978–982.

Pauls, D. L., Alsobrook, J. P., Goodman, W., Rasmussen, S., & Leckman, J. F. (1995). A family study of obsessive-compulsive disorder. *American Journal of Psychiatry, 152* (1), 76–84.

Pediatric OCD Treatment Study (POTS) Team (2004). Cognitive-behavior therapy, sertraline, and their combination for children and adolescents with obsessive-compulsive disorder: the Pediatric OCD Treatment Study (POTS) randomized controlled trial. *Jama, 292* (16), 1969–1976.

Perel, J. M., Axelson, D. A., Rudolph, G., & Birmaher, B. (2001). Steroselective pharmacokinetic/ pharmacodynamic (PK/PD) of ± citalopram in adolescents, comparisons with adult findings. *Clinincal Pharmacology and Therapeutics, 69.*

Rasmussen, S. A., & Eisen, J. L. (1994). The epidemiology and differential diagnosis of obsessive compulsive disorder. [Review] [35 refs]. *Journal of Clinical Psychiatry, 55,* 5–10.

Renaud, J., Birmaher, B., Wassick, S. C., & Bridge, J. (1999). Use of selective serotonin reuptake inhibitors for the treatment of childhood panic disorder: a pilot study. *Journal of Child & Adolescent Psychopharmacology, 9* (2), 73–83.

Riddle, M. A., Reeve, E. A., Yaryura-Tobias, J. A., Yang, H. M., Claghorn, J. L., Gaffney, G., et al. (2001). Fluvoxamine for children and adolescents with obsessive-compulsive disorder: a randomized, controlled, multicenter trial. *Journal of the American Academy of Child and Adolescent Psychiatry, 40* (2), 222–229.

Robb, A., Cueva, J., Sporn, J., Yang, R., & Vanderburgh, D. (2008). Efficacy of sertraline in childhood posttraumatic stress disorder. *The Scientific Proceedings of the 2008 Annual Meeting of the American Academy of Child & Adolescent Psychiatry.*

RUPP (Research Unit on Pediatric Psychopharmacology) Anxiety Study Group, Walkup, J., Labellarte, M., Riddle, M. A., Pine, D. S., Greenhill, L., et al. (2002). Treatment of pediatric anxiety disorders: an open-label extension of the research units on pediatric psychopharmacology anxiety study. *Journal of Child & Adolescent Psychopharmacology, 12* (3), 175–188.

RUPP (Research Unit on Pediatric Psychopharmacology) Anxiety Study Group (2001). Fluvoxamine for the treatment of anxiety disorders in children and adolescents. The Research Unit on Pediatric Psychopharmacology Anxiety Study Group. *New England Journal of Medicne, 344* (17), 1279–1285.

Rynn, M. A., Riddle, M. A., Yeung, P. P., & Kunz N. R. (2007). Efficacy and safety of extended-release venlafaxine in the treatment of generalized anxiety disorder in children and adolescents: two placebo-controlled trials. *American Journal of Psychiatry, 164* (2), 290–300.

Rynn, M. A., Siqueland, L., & Rickels, K. (2001). Placebo-Controlled Trial of Sertraline in the Treatment of Children With Generalized Anxiety Disorder. *American Journal of Psychiatry, 158* (12), 2008–2014.

Safer, D. J. & Zito, J. M. (2006). Treatment-emergent adverse events from selective serotonin reuptake inhibitors by age group: children versus adolescents. *Journal of Child & Adolescent Psychopharmacology, 16* (1–2), 159–169.

Schatzberg, A. F., Haddad, P., Kaplan, E. M., Lejoyeux, M., Rosenbaum, J. F., Young, A. H., et al. (1997). Serotonin reuptake inhibitor discontinuation syndrome: a hypothetical definition. Discontinuation Consensus panel. *Journal of Clinical Psychiatry, 7,* 5–10.

Tint, A., Haddad, P. M., & Anderson, I. M. (2008). The effect of rate of antidepressant tapering on the incidence of discontinuation symptoms: a randomised study. *Journal of Psychopharmacology, 22* (3), 330–332.

Valuck, R. J., Libby, A. M., Sills, M. R., Giese, A. A., & Allen, R. R. (2004). Antidepressant treatment and risk of suicide attempt by adolescents with major depressive disorder: a propensity-adjusted retrospective cohort study. *CNS Drugs, 18* (15), 1119–1132.

Wagner, K. D., Berard, R., Stein, M. B., Wetherhold, E., Carpenter, D. J., Perera, P., et al. (2004). A Multicenter, Randomized, Double-blind, Placebo-Controlled Trial of Paroxetine in Children and Adolescents With Social Anxiety Disorder. *Archives of General Psychiatry, 61* (11), 1153–1162.

Walkup, J. T., Albano, A. M., Piacentini, J., Birmaher, B., Compton, S. N., Sherrill, J. T., et al. (2008). Cognitive Behavioral Therapy, Sertraline, or a Combination in Childhood Anxiety. *New England Journal of Medicine, 359* (26), 2753–2766.

Walkup, J., Reeve, E., Yaryura-Tobias, J., Wong, L., Claghorn, J., Gaffney, G., et al. (1998). Fluvoxamine for childhood obsessive compulsive disorder: long-term treatment. New Clinical Drug Evaluation Unit Program (NCDEU) Abstracts, 38th Annual Meeting, Boca Raton, Florida.

Weinrieb, R. M., Auriacombe, M., Lynch, K. G., & Lewis, J. D. (2005). Selective serotonin re-uptake inhibitors and the risk of bleeding. *Expert Opinion on Drug Safety, 4* (2), 337–344.

Wilens, T. E., Cohen, L., Biederman, J., Abrams, A., Neft, D., Faird, N., et al. (2002). Fluoxetine pharmacokinetics in pediatric patients. *Journal of Clinical Psychopharmacology, 22* (6), 568–575.

Wilens, T. E., Wyatt, D., & Spencer, T. J. (1998). Disentangling disinhibition. *Journal of the American Academy of Child and Adolescent Psychiatry, 37* (11), 1225–1227.

Wood, J. J. (2006). Effect of anxiety reduction on children's school performance and social adjustment. [erratum appears in *Developmental Psychology* 2007 March, *43* (2), 416. Note: Wood, Jeffrey [corrected to Wood, Jeffrey J.].] *Developmental Psychology, 42* (2), 345–349.

12

Cool Teens: A Computerized Intervention for Anxious Adolescents

Viviana M. Wuthrich, Michael J. Cunningham, and Ronald M. Rapee

Macquarie University, Sydney, Australia

Effective computerized treatment programs are increasingly being used in adult populations, but are less available for adolescents and children. This chapter describes the development and evaluation of the *Cool Teens* computerized CD-ROM for anxious adolescents. *Cool Teens* is an eight-module computerized program that teaches adolescents cognitive behavioral skills to manage anxiety. Although they are under self control, modules are completed – preferably weekly – over a 12-week period by the adolescent on their home computer. The computerized format allows the addition of multimedia components such as video and audio to make the learning and application of cognitive behavioral skills more appealing to adolescents. In addition, its portability helps to increase access to this program for populations who are unable or unwilling to reach traditional forms of therapy. This chapter describes the development of the program and provides a summary of the results from two randomized controlled trials evaluating the intervention with clinically anxious adolescents. The first trial assesses the program in a self-help format supplemented with email support. The second trial assesses the program when delivered with additional parental involvement and therapist supported telephone calls. Future directions of computerized programs for children and adolescents are discussed.

Theoretical Background and Development of the Intervention Program

Anxiety disorders are among the most common mental health conditions in young people and can cause tremendous suffering and predisposition to further health problems. By interfering with the personal and academic life of a young person, they cause significant illness and cost to society (Andlin-Sobocki & Wittchen, 2005; NYMHF, 2005). Despite the high burden of illness caused by anxiety disorders and the demand and economic burden they place on mental healthcare resources, they often do not

The Wiley-Blackwell Handbook of The Treatment of Childhood and Adolescent Anxiety, First Edition. Edited by Cecilia A. Essau and Thomas H. Ollendick.
© 2013 John Wiley & Sons, Ltd. Published 2013 by John Wiley & Sons, Ltd.

receive as much attention as other problems in the teenage years, such as depression, substance abuse, or conduct problems.

Up to 5% of young people meet diagnostic criteria for an anxiety disorder at any point in time (Rapee, Schniering, & Hudson, 2009). Many types of anxiety disorders may be present in the teenage years including social phobia, generalized anxiety disorder (GAD), specific (or simple) phobia, obsessive-compulsive disorder (OCD), separation anxiety, panic disorder with or without agoraphobia, and post-traumatic stress disorder (PTSD). A wide variety of symptoms are associated with anxiety disorders, including fear or anxiety; excessive worrying; panic attacks; loss of control, irritability or uneasiness; being "highly strung"; difficulty relaxing, concentrating or sleeping; avoidance, ritualizing; and physical symptoms such as palpitations, sweating, and trembling.

Several models of the development of anxiety disorders have identified the combined influence of a genetic/temperamental diathesis, modified by environmental factors including parent anxiety, childrearing styles, and specific life experiences (e.g., Chorpita & Barlow, 1998; Hudson & Rapee, 2004; Manassis & Bradley, 1994; Rapee, 2001). Females have higher prevalence for most forms of anxiety. Anxiety disorders can cause personal suffering, academic underperformance, interference with relationships and socializing, and predisposition to depression, substance abuse, and future anxiety (Brady & Kendall, 1992; Hofstra, van der Ende, & Verhulst, 2002; Woodward & Fergusson, 2001).

Cognitive behavioural therapy (CBT) is the most commonly used and best supported treatment for child anxiety (Rapee et al., 2009) and is a "probably efficacious treatment" for anxiety (Kendall & Ollendick, 2004, p. 65). Since the early 1990s, CBT programs for anxious adolescents have been researched extensively. Studies show that by teaching young people skills to deal with their anxiety and by providing exposure to feared cues, the use of these programs results in marked improvements in anxiety levels and symptoms (Rapee et al., 2009). Long-term follow-up has shown that these gains are maintained for up to 8 years (Barrett, Duffy, Dadds, & Rapee, 2001; Kendall, Safford, Flannery-Schroeder, & Webb, 2004).

Many empirically supported CBT programs have now been developed and evaluated (see reviews by Cartwright-Hatton, Roberts, Chitsabesan, Fothergill, & Harrington, 2004; James, Soler, & Weatherall, 2005; Rapee et al., 2009). Examining intention-to-treat analyses of 13 studies involving 498 children and adolescents with mild to moderate anxiety, James et al. (2005) reported an overall remission rate of 56% for CBT programs versus 28.2% for controls. There was no evidence of differences between individual, group, or parental/family formats. With some overlap of the studies in the James et al. (2005) review, Cartwright-Hatton et al. (2004) evaluated 10 randomised controlled trials of CBT for young people up to 19 years of age with anxiety. They also reported a higher remission rate in treatment groups (56.5%) than in control groups (34.8%).

The global results reported in these reviews imply that positive treatment effects can be demonstrated right across the developmental spectrum. Consistent with this impression, several studies have failed to demonstrate that age is a significant moderator of treatment effects for anxiety in youth (Rapee et al., 2009). However, the majority of evaluations restrict their samples to less than 15 years and older adolescents, especially at the older levels, are heavily under-represented in the empirical literature on treatment of child anxiety.

To date, no large, well-conducted studies have specifically focused on treatment of anxious older teenagers. In a pilot study involving 35 socially phobic female adolescents with a mean age of 15.8 years, 12 adolescents were allocated to 16 weeks of clinic-based group CBT while the remaining 23 remained on waitlist (Hayward, Varady, Albano, Thieneman, Henderson, & Schatzberg, 2000). At the end of treatment, 45% of participants in active treatment no longer met criteria for social phobia compared with 4% on waitlist. However, there was continued improvement in both groups over the following period and the groups did not differ significantly at 1-year follow-up.

Another pilot study involving 12 African-American adolescents aged 14–17 years (mean 15.6 years) with primary anxiety compared a 10-session, school-based group CBT program with a group attention-support control condition (Ginsburg & Drake, 2002). Among those who attended more than one treatment session, three of the four adolescents in the CBT group no longer met diagnostic criteria compared with one of the five adolescents in the control group.

Some other research involving older teenagers with social phobia has been reported (Albano, Marten, Holt, Heimberg, & Barlow, 1995). A preliminary study involving five teenage participants (including three who were aged 15 or 16 years) evaluated a 16-session CBT group program with parental involvement in selected sessions. Structured diagnostic interviews administered 1 year after treatment showed full remission of social phobia for four participants and partial remission for the other participant. More recently, a pilot study of a simplified, community-based CBT group program (Baer & Garland, 2005) was evaluated with 12 adolescents aged 13–18 years. Compared to a waitlist group, treated participants showed greater improvement in both examiner-evaluated interviews (Anxiety Disorders Interview Schedule for Children: ADIS-C-IV; Silverman & Albano, 1996) and self-reported symptoms of social anxiety (effect sizes [d], 1.63 and 0.85, respectively).

Even fewer reports of studies examining GAD in this age group could be found in the literature. One case series, involving seven adolescents aged 16–18 years, has been reported (Léger, Ladouceur, Dugas, & Freeston, 2003). A CBT program consisting of weekly 1-hour sessions (mean treatment length of 13.2 hours) produced clinically significant improvement for three participants, while some positive change was observed for other participants. Gains were maintained at both 6- and 12-month follow-up assessments.

Current Treatment Gaps

In summary, there is some evidence to support the value of CBT for anxious older adolescents but this age group remains relatively under-represented in empirical evaluations of the treatment of anxiety in young people. Clinical experience suggests that there may be reasons to believe that this group will be less responsive to standard treatment packages for anxiety. Older adolescents are a notoriously difficult group to engage. Traditional treatment services, involving face-to-face contact with an older professional are generally not appealing to teens. Similarly, most referral for child services comes from parents and parents usually report that they have less control over the lives of their teenagers. Middle to older adolescence is also a time of emotional development and change and is the time when major depressive episodes become markedly more common (Hankin, Abramson, Silva, McGee, & Moffitt, 1998; Roza, Hofstra, van der Ende, & Verhulst, 2003). In turn, the existence of depression may reduce efficacy of anxiety treatment programs (Rapee et al., 2009).

Adolescents are a group for whom there are relatively few services, especially outside major cities. There is a significant treatment gap for this age group. Many young people do not readily access mental health services for anxiety and, when they do, they commonly encounter barriers to ongoing contact (Andlin-Sobocki & Wittchen, 2005; Department of Health and Ageing, 2004; WHO Child Mental Health Atlas, 2005). Overall, only one in four young people receives professional help (NYMHF, 2005; Sawyer & Patton, 2000).

Many common barriers to young people's access to healthcare services in general, and to mental healthcare services in particular, have been proposed (Booth, Bernard, Quine et al., 2004; NSWAAH, 2005; WHO Child Mental Health Atlas, 2005). These include geographical distance from services, the potential stigma of receiving therapy, a perceived lack of privacy and confidentiality, the cost of services and accessing them, the format or environment in which face-to-face therapy is carried out, waiting times due to therapist availability, and comfort with therapists and their communication styles.

Overall, it seems that the needs of this age group are often poorly met by existing treatment delivery systems and therefore young people may benefit from more "youth-specific responses" (NYMHF, 2005) and "creative and innovative treatment approaches" (Department of Health and Ageing, 2004, p. III).

Computer-based Cognitive Behavioural Therapy (CCBT)

One alternative to traditional therapy that has been shown to be efficacious and to increase access for anxious adults is computer-delivered, or computerized, CBT (CCBT). Proudfoot (2004, p. 356) reports that the most recent CCBT programs feature "state-of-the-art interactive, multimedia functionality, and incorporate both specific active therapeutic techniques and non-specific features of the therapeutic relationship." This review also highlights two major reasons why CBT lends itself to computerization. First, CBT teaches patients a combination of techniques and activities (e.g., recognition of connections between thoughts and behaviors, identification of problem areas, collection of evidence, experiment planning) that can be delivered using multimedia to partly reflect the way a therapist would present this information (see also Proudfoot, Swain, Widmer et al., 2003). Second, CBT is a structured therapy with well-delineated procedures and clear concepts to guide their selection and use.

Many authors have listed potential benefits and advantages, dangers and disadvantages, and legal and ethical issues associated with therapies delivered through new media such as the Internet (summarized in Table 12.1). While individual pros and cons can be proposed, every CCBT project needs to be assessed by weighing up the combined effects of several components on the overall goal of providing high levels of program accessibility, user-friendliness, and content engagement.

Christensen, Griffiths, & Evans (2002) highlight some major potential advantages of the Internet in mental health and many of these are applicable to CCBT in any format. These benefits include improved access, cost reduction, innovative services,

Table 12.1   Potential Advantages and Disadvantages of CCBT Programs.

Advantages	*Disadvantages*
Wider access	Large development cost
Standardized program content	Loss of "therapeutic alliance"
Cheaper delivery cost	Lack of live group exposure
Promotes self monitoring	Reduced supervision
Built in feedback and outcome measures for patient and clinician	Potential for insecure data storage and collection
Anonymity/increased privacy	Requires equipment
Reduction or even removal of stigma	Reduced support for problem solving
No need for travel	Avoidance of social contact
Ease of data collection	Language and cultural barriers
Can be used any day and anytime	Requires computer literacy
Can be re-used at a later date	Varying functional literacy of users
Potential for personalized content	Lack of actual customized solutions
No deficiencies due to lack of therapist training or expertise	Skepticism from patients, clinicians and organizations providing services
Address shortage of trained therapists	Can be somewhat research focused
Can shorten therapy waiting times	Some products are poorly designed
Less therapist time involvement	Can lack non-specific therapy factors
	Reduced individual tailoring

and democratization of health care and facilitation of consumer empowerment. An Australian Senate Select Committee on Mental Health (2006) report encourages using this "new way of targeting problems" and stresses the added benefit of anonymity, which would likely lead to reduction of stigma for many users. Kaltenthaler, Shackley, Stevens, Beverley, Parry, and Chilcott (2002) point out that these programs are convenient in that users can work through them using a rate and timing to suit themselves. CCBT may be a particularly suitable delivery format for self-help. Many people already use the Internet to access a wide variety of self-help information (Christensen et al., 2002). The National Institute for Mental Health in England (Lewis, Anderson, Araya et al., 2003) proposes that computers are another way of providing access to self-help materials, especially for people who are not keen on working through books or manuals.

Many of the potential advantages of CCBT are for the patient. However, as Wright & Wright (1997) remind us, there are also several potential advantages for therapy practitioners: freeing up time from some of the repetitive parts of treatment, systematic feedback to the clinician, increased client numbers and practice revenues due to having time, and even additional revenues from charging for integrated access to software.

However, there are also many concerns and potential disadvantages with using CCBT (Pier, Klein, Austin, Mitchell, Kiropoulos, & Ryan, 2006). These stem mainly from the independent or minimal-support format of many of these programs, which may raise fears about lack of compliance and effectiveness. Highlighted areas of concern include the erosion of the relationship between therapist and patient (or client–therapist alliance) and the associated potential reduction in client engagement, the ability (or inability) of some youth to learn new techniques or skills on their own or with reduced parental or professional help, and the likelihood of compliance for program and "homework" completion. In addition, the legal and ethical aspects of technology-delivered therapy raise new privacy and duty-of-care challenges that require program safeguards to ensure secure data access, storage, and transmission. One final possible problem that will be assessed as CCBT programs are studied more is the question of potentially providing therapy options that suit clients whose avoidance of face-to-face therapy is actually a part of their anxiety problem.

Clinical outcomes with adult CCBT programs

A systematic review of 15 randomized controlled trials evaluating several self-help CCBT Internet sites for depression, anxiety, stress, insomnia, headache, eating disorder, and encopresis (Griffiths & Christensen, 2006) reports that most of these interventions have been shown to be effective for reducing risk factors or improving symptoms. In addition to several positive clinical outcomes, seven of the studies reported positive user satisfaction data and feedback to these programs. This is a key finding for program design and development teams.

Computer programs have been widely proposed for the self-help and minimal-support treatment of a variety of anxiety disorders in adults (Andersson, Bergstrom, Carlbring, & Lindefors, 2005; Newman, 2004). Many programs have now been designed, developed, and evaluated for several types of anxiety disorder in adults including panic disorder (Kenardy, McCafferty, & Rosa, 2006; Klein, Richards, & Austin, 2006), GAD (Robinson, Titov, Andrews, McIntyre, Schwenke, & Solley, 2010), specific phobias (Botella, Hofmann, & Moscovitch, 2004; Gilroy, Kirkby, Daniels, Menzies, & Montgomery, 2000), social phobia (Carlbring, Nordgren, Furmark, & Andersson, 2009; Przeworski & Newman, 2004), OCD (Greist, Marks, Baer et al., 2002), and PTSD (Lange, van de Ven, & Schrieken, 2003).

When compared with face-to-face therapy, many of these programs have individually been demonstrated to have equal or similar efficacy (e.g., Kenwright, Marks, Gega, & Mataix, 2004). While research involving these interventions varies greatly in terms of the types of anxiety studied, the control groups used, and the duration of therapy and follow-up, meta-analyses are now being performed with encouraging findings. Two reviews of the literature have shown that internet treatments for anxiety in adults can produce large effect size changes (around 1) (Cuijpers, Marks, van Straten, Cavanagh, Gega, & Andersson, 2009; Spek, Cuijpers, Nyklicek, Riper, Keyzer, & Pop, 2007). Importantly, interventions that include therapist support tend to show larger effects than interventions without therapist support.

Opportunity: CCBT for Anxious Teenagers

Although CCBT has been shown to be of value for anxious adults for some years now, programs for an adolescent target audience have only more recently become a research interest (Chu, Choudhury, Shortt, Pincus, Creed, & Kendall, 2004).

At the time when the *Cool Teens* program was being developed (2005), no such programs specifically for anxious adolescents had yet been evaluated. One existing computer-based anxiety intervention study involving adolescents had been reported up to this point. A computer game for treating spider phobia – the computer-aided vicarious exposure (CAVE) – had been evaluated in a randomized controlled trial of 28 10- to 17-year-olds (Dewis, Kirkby, Martin, Daniels, Gilroy, & Menzies, 2001). While this study involved adolescents, the computer game was not designed specifically for young people and was adapted from an earlier adult treatment protocol. Nevertheless, the results of this study showed that three 45-min sessions with CAVE lead to clinically significant improvements in spider phobia on a number of measures compared with a waitlist. Live graded exposure achieved superior results to the CAVE computer game. These early results highlighted the promise of CCBT for broader based anxiety disorders in older adolescents.

The opportunity to use CCBT in adolescents is underpinned by the fact that increasing numbers of adolescents have access to computers and use the Internet to seek help for mental health problems. Many young people could be considered likely to embrace a computer-based therapy option. Further encouragement that CCBT programs might be appropriate for young people comes from earlier research findings that showed computer programs to be an acceptable way of delivering educational content on various medical health conditions to this age group. For example, health education was found to be more effective when presented to children in computerized formats than in paper formats in studies involving children with leukemia (Dragone, Bush, Jones, Bearison, & Kamani, 2002) and cystic fibrosis (Davis et al., 2004) and in drug abuse prevention in schools (Di Noia, Schwinn, Dastur, & Schinke, 2003).

Due to this promise, several research teams have been working on developing computerized interventions for anxious adolescents. A systematic review of the literature on internet interventions for child and adolescent anxiety and depression by Calear and Christensen (2010) identified four internet-based programs that have been developed and evaluated (BRAVE-ONLINE, Project CATCH-IT, MoodGYM and Grip op je dip online). All these programs use CBT and are delivered over 5–14 sessions (mean 8), and six of the eight evaluation studies on these programs reported post-intervention reductions in symptoms of anxiety and/or depression and three reported improvement at follow-up. Also, recent results demonstrate the effectiveness of the CAMP COPE-A-LOT: The coping cat CD computerized program for children (Khanna & Kendall, 2010) with the program being found to be as effective as face to face individual CBT. There are other anxiety management CCBT programs under further evaluation such as: the climate schools series (http://www.climateschools.tv). The next few years are likely to be an exciting time for child CCBT programs. See Table 12.2 for a description of the main anxiety CCBT programs.

Aims of the "*Cool Teens*" Program

At the outset of this research, a clear need to improve the provision of mental healthcare services for anxiety in young people was identified. Recent research from the Centre for Emotional Health and other centers had developed excellent treatment programs to reduce the impact of this problem. However, these programs mostly required individuals to present for face-to-face therapy. Our team has had good results using bibliotherapy with both anxious adults (Rapee, Abbott, Baillie, & Gaston, 2007) and

Table 12.2   Description of CCBT anxiety programs for adolescents.

BRAVE for Teenagers – ONLINE is a CBT program for anxious adolescents aged 13–17 years delivered on the Internet (Spence et al., 2008). This program involves ten 1-hour youth sessions, 5–6 parent sessions, and two booster sessions. The program includes text, colorful graphics, animation, quizzes, games, and interactive forms. The young person completes a variety of exercises and home tasks online that are accessible to a therapist, who provides help or reinforcement as appropriate. Two case studies have recently been published to describe early experiences with the program. An earlier version of BRAVE for younger children was successfully delivered using a combination of Internet sessions and clinic visits (Spence, Holmes, March, & Lipp, 2006).

CLIMATE for Schools is a project delivering online health education courses for alcohol, stress, and other problems (including anxiety), to empower students by learning about ways to avoid illness and to optimise their mental health. It uses cartoon-style illustrations with speech and thought bubbles. Assessment quizzes, work samples, and suggested homework activities are included in each module. Preliminary results show that the alcohol and stress modules are effective, with the other modules currently being evaluated in randomised controlled trials (Andrews, Van Vliet, & Wuthrich, 2007).

Camp Cope-A-Lot: The Coping Cat CD is a new 12-session interactive CD-ROM-based program providing CBT for 7 to 13-year old anxious youth (Khanna & Kendall, 2008). The program consists of 6 sessions for the child alone, followed by 6 sessions with therapist guidance. Initial responses to a prototype from youth and therapists are favorable. The project includes CBT4CBT, the first computer-based clinician training program in CBT for anxiety in youth.

---

children (Rapee, Abbott, & Lyneham, 2006), so delivery of an anxiety program using a computerized format was considered appropriate.

We set about developing and evaluating *Cool Teens,* a multimedia computer-based CBT program for 14–18 year-olds with anxiety. The goal of the program was to provide an alternative treatment modality for anxious adolescents that did not require the young person to present to a traditional clinical facility. Additional goals were that the program could be delivered in a self-help or minimal therapist contact format with adolescents undertaking treatment largely on their own or with minimal involvement from parents and that the program could be delivered in regional and rural settings, thereby improving access to therapy for many adolescents. Based on research indicating the success of CCBT interventions for anxious adults and research indicating that adolescents consider computerized interventions as engaging and desirable, the design of an effective computerized treatment for anxiety in this age group was undertaken. It was anticipated that a computerized version would be effective and accessible to adolescents. It was further hoped that multimedia delivery of treatment components might lead to better engagement of adolescents in treatment compared with face-to-face interventions.

As we aimed to make the intervention as appealing and engaging to adolescents as possible, the program was designed to include videos of interviews with professionals, adolescents describing their anxiety and experiences with treatment, and adolescent hosts. In addition, the program was designed to use cartoons, pictures, and graphics to present information and to present worksheets in a format that allowed them to be completed on the computer and printed for future reference as needed. It was an additional aim that the program could be used with minimal support from parents and others.

One major issue in the development of the program was whether to make it Internet-based or CD-ROM based. For a discussion of the pros and cons of both methods see Cunningham, Donovan, and March (2007). In the end, we decided on a CD-ROM format particularly so that we could include higher-quality live video and to create a "product" rather than a website-delivered offering that would require continued monitoring. This decision resulted in lack of exploration of some components that could be implemented in a centralized online setting. The CD-ROM software was programmed using Macromedia Flash MX 2004 Professional (2004) and the resulting application is an auto-run CD-ROM for both Windows and Mac operating systems. The program could also be packaged as an Internet download (set of files) for installation on a local computer.

Initial Feedback to a Prototype

The development of the program was extensive and included scripting and recording videos, scripting text, and designing exercise worksheets. The CD-ROM includes six video case studies of young people who role-play different anxiety problems and skill use throughout the program, homework tables that are completed on the computer, and self-report questionnaires that graph changes in anxiety symptoms over time. Modules are accessed through a homepage menu and are completed in a recommended order, although adolescents can move freely in and out of modules as they choose.

The program was initially developed in a prototype version and issued to adolescents (individuals and focus groups) to gather feedback. The prototype version contained one full module (Realistic Thinking) and components from two other modules (see Figure 12.1). The prototype version was administered to a group of non-clinical participants recruited from local advertising and a group of previous clients from the Centre for Emotional Health. Participants were aged between 14 and 18 years. They were asked to evaluate the program's content and multimedia format and to identify delivery issues that might affect user satisfaction with using CCBT. Finally, in order to compare the use of the CD-ROM to group therapy, participants who had previous experience with group therapy for anxiety were asked to list the perceived advantages and disadvantages of the CD-ROM and to compare its hypothetical use either as a replacement for, or in combination with, group therapy. It was expected that these questions would elicit some information about how a computer-based approach might help overcome some of the access and treatment barriers that have been proposed as reasons for the low rates of mental health help seeking from traditional professional psychological services by young people.

Thirteen non-clinical participants (seven female) and nine adolescents who had previously attended group therapy for an anxiety disorder (six female) returned feedback. The majority of participants in both groups rated all of the multimedia components and general aspects of the program favorably, and the data showed a strong preference for live video over cartoons, audio, and text options. Generally, participants thought that the program was "interesting and fun to learn from". In answering the various

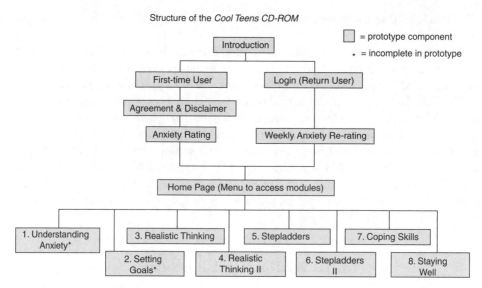

Figure 12.1   Components of the prototype CD-ROM.

questions in the evaluation, they reported several perceived advantages of the CD-ROM that could be explored to help address some of today's barriers to adolescent treatment. These include convenience, privacy, comfort, ability to focus on your own areas of interest, and better recording/tracking of your progress.

While most participants reported that the CD-ROM was easy to use, the navigation system was rated as "poor" or "very poor" by three people. This feedback was used to make several modifications to the program to ensure that the various navigation options were more user-friendly. More detailed information about the feedback given to the prototype version is available (Cunningham, Rapee, & Lyneham, 2006).

Session-By-Session Delivery of the Program

Initial set-up

Privacy

The *Cool Teens* CD was designed so that the information that adolescents enter into the program is kept private. Therefore, on first use, new users create a username and password for themselves. The program creates a local, unique password-protected file that is used to store all data entered during their subsequent program use. User data is saved as a local Flash file using password-protected encryption implemented by this software. When users reuse the CD, they must enter their username and private password when prompted.

Anxiety progress chart

On first using the program, adolescents are asked to answer six questions about how anxiety interferes with their life each week. This short assessment measure reappears weekly and enables the user to view a Progress Chart of their total anxiety level score and their progress over time.

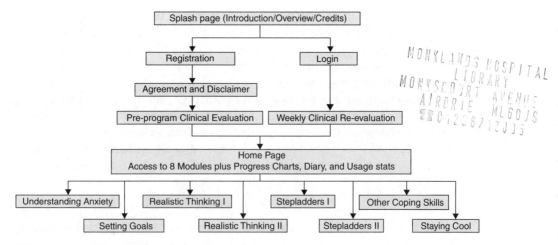

Figure 12.2   Flow diagram of *Cool Teens* components.

Homepage

From the homepage, users can navigate to any of the eight therapy modules, as well as select icons to access the background music options and volume controls, program credits, Progress Chart, diary, program menu (Home Zone), and exit button (see Figures 12.2 and 12.3).

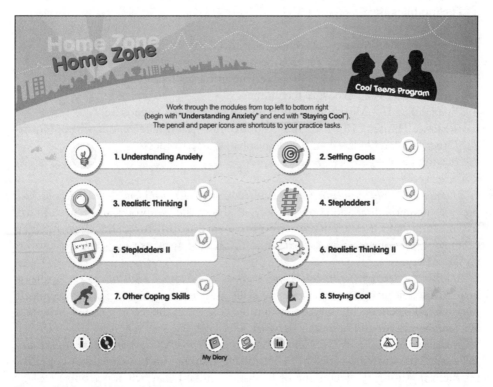

Figure 12.3   *Cool Teens* home zone.

The open format menu on the homepage allows users to move through the modules and return to any module as needed. One of the interesting considerations we made was to weigh up a traditional structure for CBT (which typically requires a systematic order to sessions) against a common use of the Internet by adolescents, which often involves jumping from link to link. Ultimately we decided on a compromise by allowing the user to jump around through the homepage, but strongly recommending an order of completion through the layout and the verbal instructions by the hosts. In addition to linking to the modules, direct access links are provided to a summary page of practice tasks for each technique. This is especially important for the many return visits a user will make to access the forms they use to plan and record progress.

Therapy modules

Cool Teens includes eight modules with each module taking an adolescent between 15 and 30 minutes to complete. The time taken to complete practice tasks is in addition to this time, and the amount of time needed for practice varies from week to week and from individual to individual. Each program module includes information, interactive exercises, hypothetical scenarios, and case studies. The program also features practice tasks that the adolescent will engage in outside of the time they spend on the computer program.

Cool Teens is based on the *Cool Kids* anxiety management program (Rapee et al., 2006) and teaches CBT techniques for managing anxiety in eight therapy modules with a strong focus on cognitive restructuring and graded exposure.

The modules are:

1. Understanding Anxiety – Psychoeducation
2. Setting Goals – Preparing to use the program
3. Realistic Thinking I – A cognitive restructuring technique
4. Stepladders I – An exposure technique
5. Stepladders II – More information on the technique of exposure
6. Realistic Thinking II – Using the cognitive restructuring technique without forms
7. Other Coping Skills – e.g., problem solving, assertiveness
8. Staying Cool – Relapse prevention

Module 1 – Understanding Anxiety: "All about anxiety and how it can affect people" provides psycho-education about anxiety. It shows the symptoms and types of anxiety disorders and uses animated cartoon sequences and high-quality video to show examples of various fears and worries and to provide answers to common questions about anxiety.

Module 2 – Setting Goals: "Helps you to focus on what you want to achieve" explains how to use the program to learn new skills and to work on specific problems. It highlights the benefits of moving through the content in the recommended order and at a suitable speed, and of practicing what is learned.

Module 3 – Realistic Thinking I: "A technique to replace worried thoughts with calm ones" presents the problem of unrealistic thinking and explains that cognitive restructuring using the technique of Realistic Thinking can help a person to replace worried thoughts with calmer ones. Animations and a flowchart are used to explain how thoughts, feelings, and behaviors are related. Practice activities help users to analyze their problems.

Module 4 – Stepladders I: "Helps you to fight your fears by facing them" introduces the key CBT technique of exposure that will allow the user to face their fears in a step-by-step manner. A cartoon example is used to show that a fear won't go away unless the person stands up to it and faces the situation that anxiety is telling them to avoid. The seven steps to creating and using an exposure stepladder are presented.

Module 5 – Stepladders II: "Helps you to tackle all of your fears and worries" continues with the technique of exposure and stresses that the user must develop a stepladder for each of their fears and worries. It suggests ways to get the maximum value out of their stepladders.

Module 6 – Realistic Thinking II: "Shows you how to easily use Realistic Thinking" returns to the technique of Realistic Thinking and explains that this skill can be simplified so that it can be used "in your mind" at the time when a person has an anxious thought. It proposes the idea that since most people tend to have patterns to their negative thoughts, it can be helpful to make a list of questions that often help them.

Module 7 – Other Coping Skills: "Helps you find strategies for dealing with anxiety" introduces a selection of complementary skills for the user to try in order to reduce the overall level of anxiety in their life. The technique of Problem Solving is shown in six steps and is illustrated using a video example from one of the program characters.

Module 8 – Staying Cool: "Helps you deal with problems and face future challenges" encourages the user to review their progress by comparing where they were when they started to where they are now. It explains that they may still have goals to achieve and that they can continue to work on problems and to practice and further develop all the skills learned. The program then suggests several approaches if the user has ongoing problems.

Empirical Evaluation of *Cool Teens*

Pilot study

In our first test of the efficacy and suitability of the full *Cool Teens* program we used a case series design (Cunningham, Wuthrich, Rapee, Lyneham, Schniering, & Hudson, 2008) with five adolescents (four female, one male) who met diagnostic criteria for a primary anxiety disorder. Participants used the *Cool Teens* CD-ROM program on their home computer for 12 weeks supported by fortnightly telephone calls by a therapist.

Method

Participants   Participants were five adolescents (four females, one male) who consecutively contacted the clinic for treatment of a primary anxiety disorder and had access to a home computer (age range 14–16 years). Participants were required to stabilize current medication and to not engage in other active therapy during the study period. Four participants had a primary diagnosis of DSM-IV GAD and the other had separation anxiety disorder (SAD). Of the five participants, three were from the Sydney region, one from rural New South Wales, and one from interstate (Australian Capital Territory). Two additional males (one from Sydney and one from rural NSW), aged 13 and 15 years, diagnosed with social phobia during clinical interview were offered the CD-ROM but did not return the signed consent form and self-report measures and therefore did not participate in the trial.

Assessment Assessments were conducted immediately prior to treatment and repeated immediately following treatment (12 weeks) and again 3 months later. Assessment was based on both a structured diagnostic interview (ADIS-IV-C and P) as well as self-reported and parent-reported symptoms using the Spence Children's Anxiety Scale (SCAS: Spence, 1998) and the Children's Automatic Thoughts Scale (CATS: Schniering & Rapee, 2002). During a therapist contact telephone call every 2 weeks, a shortened version of the child SCAS, using only the subscale relevant to each participant's principal anxiety diagnosis, was administered along with an Anxiety Symptom Tracking Measure. This measure was used to re-assess the participant's main fears and worries over time. It assessed progress based on the person's reported anxiety ratings from 0 (not at all anxious) to 8 (extremely anxious) in response to two questions regarding how anxious they would feel facing the situation today and to what extent they would want to avoid the situation.

Procedure Adolescents or their parents contacted the clinic and received information about the trial. Following pre-treatment assessment, suitable participants were sent their copy of the *Cool Teens* CD-ROM and a clinical psychologist made a telephone call to each participant every 2 weeks to ask a set of questions regarding progress and understanding of material. The purposes of the contact calls were to provide motivation, to keep participants moving through the modules at a reasonable pace, and, if needed, to provide a way for them to seek additional help or clarification around the skills they learned. Participants were asked questions such as: Which module are you up to now? Is there anything you need clarification around? Which skills are you finding most helpful? Therapists also encouraged each adolescent to keep using the CD-ROM. If a participant was moving through the program too slowly, they were reminded that they had a total of 12 weeks to complete it and that they should aim to finish a given module before the next call. Although the telephone call was not designed to provide actual therapy, minimal therapy assistance was included in some of the calls. As an example, one participant reported that she did not know how to break down her fear of sleeping away from home into gradual steps and the therapist spent a few minutes helping her to brainstorm a hierarchy of steps.

Results

Participant 1, was a 15-year-old female with GAD and comorbid separation anxiety, social phobia (situational type), and specific phobia (blood-injection-injury type). She completed all eight modules within the initial treatment period. Her most positive gain was a large improvement in her anxiety rating for one main fear (crowded places, reduced from 6 to 2) as measured by the Anxiety Symptom Tracking Measure administered during the therapist support calls. Her parent SCAS score demonstrated some reduction in anxiety but no changes in ADIS diagnosis or severity were observed.

Participant 2, a 16-year-old female with GAD and a comorbid specific phobia completed six modules during the 12-week treatment period and improved greatly in the anxiety rating for her main fear of meeting new people (from 8 to 1). She left school to start a new job during this time and reported that the CD-ROM gave her confidence to deal with this challenge. At post-treatment, her ADIS-C rating was reduced from 6 to 4 for GAD. However, this improvement was not supported by ADIS-P and self-report measures data. In addition, she was also diagnosed with social phobia at this time. At follow-up, her ADIS-C rating was slightly reduced from the pre-treatment level. Some gains were made in her SCAS and CATS scores.

Participant 3, a 14-year-old female with SAD along with secondary GAD and a specific phobia, completed seven of the modules during the 12-week period. At post-treatment her separation anxiety rating showed a slight improvement and she reported that she was "just getting to" the major steps in her exposure hierarchy – to sleep over at a friend's house. Severity ratings for her secondary diagnoses had both reduced to subclinical levels based on combined ADIS-C and ADIS-P data (from 5 to 2 for GAD and from 5 to 3 for specific phobia). At follow-up, her ADIS-C rating for separation anxiety was 1 (she'd now slept away from home and successfully combated her fear) and the ADIS-P and combined ratings for all three of her anxiety disorders were at subclinical levels.

Participant 4, a 15-year-old female with GAD and four comorbid specific phobias, completed only two modules before discontinuing treatment after week 4 because she reported she no longer had anxiety and required no further therapy. While a dropout to treatment, this participant and her mother both reported that the early CD-ROM content, especially the psychoeducation module, had helped her discuss her problems more with her family. Her post-treatment ratings (ADIS-C and ADIS-P) were reduced to subclinical levels for GAD and all but one specific phobia.

Participant 5, a 16-year-old male with GAD, was the only participant without a secondary anxiety diagnosis. He completed all modules and showed an improvement in GAD to a subclinical level as shown by an ADIS-C anxiety rating reduction from 6 to 2. This finding was supported by some gains in SCAS and CATS scores and by the paternal SCAS-P scores. At follow-up, this participant's ADIS-C anxiety rating remained at a subclinical level and was even further reduced (to 0).

Conclusion

Post-treatment assessment showed two participants (40%) had anxiety severity ratings that were reduced to a subclinical level for at least one clinical anxiety disorder. At 3-month follow-up, these two participants no longer met diagnostic criteria for any clinical anxiety disorder. Two other participants failed to make gains based on diagnostic criteria but showed improvement in anxiety symptoms for one main fear. The adolescent who had the greatest overall improvement was the only one who had no secondary diagnoses. The participant who had the next best overall gains had two secondary diagnoses but her primary problem was SAD rather than a broader disorder. In contrast, the participants who had a larger number of secondary diagnoses and more complex clinical presentations made the least overall improvements. Not all measures indicated improvements. Indeed, participant scores on some scales increased from pre- to post-treatment. One possibility is that the program increased some individual adolescents' awareness of their anxiety. The overall level of effectiveness from this pilot evaluation of the *Cool Teens* CD-ROM, with its mixed findings for various participants, may suggest two broad possibilities. First, there may be ways to improve the program by enhancing the CD-ROM's various components with the goal of increasing user compliance, motivation, and benefit. Second, this self-help format may never be expected to do as well as therapist-led treatment in terms of clinical efficacy.

The next step was to examine the effectiveness of the *Cool Teens* program in a randomized controlled trial. We now report on the effectiveness of the program delivered with varying levels of support given to the adolescent. In the first trial we examined the program's effectiveness when adolescents used it in a self-help format (with minimal therapist contact and no parental involvement). In a second randomized controlled trial we added more structured therapist support and parental involvement. The details of these two trials and a summary of the results are presented here.

Randomised controlled trial 1: Self-help format of the *Cool Teens* program

In this trial, we examined the efficacy of using the *Cool Teens* program in a mostly self-help format with adolescents who met criteria for a primary anxiety disorder. Since the study involved limited therapist contact, several duty-of-care issues needed to be addressed as part of the trial design. First, consent for participation was obtained from adolescents only and for this reason the minimum entry age into the trial was 14 years (this is the minimum age at which adolescents are allowed by law to seek independent and confidential medical advice in Australia). Second, it was decided that although adolescents did not need to involve a parent or guardian in the treatment component, they were required to provide emergency contact details of a parent or guardian. In order to keep the amount of therapist contact to a minimum, contact with the clinical psychologist involved in the trial was restricted to weekly emails. However, for reasons of duty of care, if an adolescent failed to respond to their weekly email, they were called by the therapist to check on their welfare.

Method

Participants   Participants were recruited using a variety of methods including workshops to professionals involved with providing healthcare support to youth, flyers on display at schools, youth groups, information provided in GP surgeries, information listed on various youth and mental health websites, and through direct referrals from school counselors, GPs, psychiatrists, and psychologists.

Participants were included in the trial if they met DSM-IV criteria for a primary anxiety disorder diagnosis based on a structured interview with the adolescent over the telephone. Adolescents were required to provide details of an emergency contact and to have regular access to a home computer and email address. Participants reporting self-harm, suicidal ideation, psychosis, bipolar disorder, or who were in a sexually or physically abusive environment, were excluded from the trial. Adolescents who reported being more than one grade behind in their schooling were also excluded.

A total of 28 adolescents participated in the trial (males = 11, females = 15, missing = 2, age range 14–17, mean age = 15.32, SD = 1.12), with primary diagnoses of social phobia (31%), GAD (38%), specific phobia (7%), SAD (10%), panic disorder (7%), and OCD (7%).

Assessment   Diagnostic criteria were determined on the basis of a structured clinical interview (ADIS-IV-C: Silverman & Albano, 1996) conducted with the adolescent only and completed either in person or over the telephone if they were not local. Participants also completed questionnaire measures of symptoms of anxiety: Spence Child Anxiety Scale (SCAS: Spence, 1998), negative automatic thoughts: Children's Automatic Thoughts Scale (CATS: Schniering & Rapee, 2002), depression: Centre for Epidemiological Studies Depression Scale for Children (CES-D: Weissman, Orvaschel, & Padian, 1980), and life interference: Adolescent Life Interference Scale (LIM: Schniering & Rapee, unpublished). At the conclusion of the program, adolescents also completed scales measuring barriers to treatment and user preferences specific to the CD-ROM treatment format.

Procedure   Adolescents contacted the clinic via telephone or email, or their parents contacted the clinic on their behalf. Each adolescent then completed the pre-treatment assessment and were randomly allocated to either the active condition ($n = 15$) or waitlist ($n = 13$). Adolescents in the active-treatment group were immediately sent their copy of the program, and a follow-up call was made to them a week later to make sure that they had received the CD-ROM and that it was working without fault on their computer.

Adolescents were then sent reminder and motivational emails each week asking them about their progress using the program. The email consisted of a semi-standardized message that could be flexibly modified by clinicians to make each email more personalized. If an adolescent did not respond to two emails in a row, they were contacted by phone to check in on them. No adolescent ever asked to be contacted by phone for a follow-up to the email. A sample of the weekly email is shown here.

Hi, This is your regular email to check-in on how you are going with the Cool Teens program. I hope that you are still using your program regularly and finding the skills helpful.:-) I would really love to hear how you are going with it. Please email me back replies to the questions below as soon as you can. If I don't hear from you, I will give you a call to check that everything is still okay.

Q1: Last time you said you were working on the ***** module. Please give me some idea of the (delete irrelevant) types of goals you set/unhelpful thoughts you have and what challenges you have come up with/steps you have planned and attempted/coping skills you have tried.

Q2: Which module are you working on at the moment?

Q3: Is there anything in this module that you don't understand or would like some clarification on?

Q4: Which skills are you finding helpful?

Q5: Would you like me to give you a call?

Remember regular practice is the best way! By about this stage in the program you should be aiming to be around the *** module.

Please call me on 02 9850 **** or email me at *************** if you have any questions at any stage. Looking forward to hearing from you.

Post-treatment assessment for both groups was conducted 12 weeks after pre-treatment, following which participants in the waitlist condition were sent a copy of the CD and received equivalent calls and emails.

Results

The results of changes on the diagnostic interviews are shown in Figure 12.4. As can be seen, participants who completed the *Cool Teens* program showed a marked drop in diagnostic severity from pre-treatment (moderate clinical severity) to post-treatment (minimal clinical severity) and this improvement continued at follow-up (average sub-clinical severity). However, adolescents on the waitlist showed an equivalent decrease from pre- to post-treatment and there was little difference between groups. Similar effects were shown on the questionnaire measures. There were significant main effects of time for the SCAS total score, CATS physical threat score, CATS total score, CES-DC, and LIM measures, but there were no significant group by time interactions on any of these measures.

Conclusion

Adolescents in both the treatment and waitlist groups reported similar improvements in their anxiety at the 12-week assessment. Despite the impressive improvements shown by adolescents in the active treatment, it was surprising that those on waitlist reported as much improvement in anxiety. These results might indicate that the *Cool Teens* program produces effects that are no better than the effects of time. However, the changes seen among the waitlist participants are not consistent with the often reported stability of childhood anxiety (Costello, Mustillo, Erkanli, Keeler, & Angold, 2003; Pine, Cohen, Gurley, Brook, & Ma, 1998). Thus, it is also possible that the reliance in this study entirely on self-reports from adolescents might have provided unreliable assessments. It is not uncommon among treatment trials for childhood anxiety to find self-reported reductions in anxious symptoms by children that

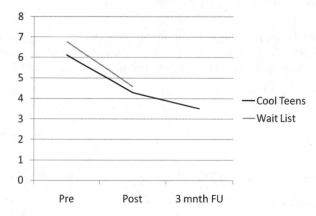

Figure 12.4   Mean ADIS severity ratings for primary anxiety disorder trial 1.

are not reflected in parent or clinician measures (Rapee et al., 2009). This is consistent with the commonly reported desynchrony between parent and child measures of emotional distress (De Los Reyes & Kazdin, 2005) and anxious children in particular have been shown to "fake good" (Kendall & Chansky, 1991). Thus, in a second randomized control trial (discussed later) we decided to include parents in the assessment of outcome.

The nature of the study design also resulted in a number of significant problems. (1) Adolescents in the active treatment group often provided very brief responses to emails from the therapists and therefore it was unclear how successfully and how thoroughly skill practice was occurring. Adolescents often responded to emails late, with very little information and with many of the therapist questions unanswered, and sometimes in text shorthand (which made them difficult to read). (2) When adolescents failed to reply to their regular email, they were called by therapists to check on their safety. However, in all cases of phone calls made by the clinical psychologist, no issues of safety were encountered. Rather, adolescents reported minor reasons such as they had been away on holidays, that they had been busy with exams, or that they hadn't had time to work on the program or answer the email. Phone calls from therapists usually resulted in improvements with treatment compliance in future weeks. (3) Adolescents were slow to return pre- and post-treatment questionnaires and had to be followed up a number of times. We had thought that direct reimbursement of time (with Aus $30 payments) would have increased motivation, but the adolescents were not motivated by money. These difficulties resulted in significant challenges in trial implementation for the therapists and researchers.

Randomised controlled trial 2: Parent- and therapist-supported format of the *Cool Teens program*

Given the findings and complications identified in trial 1, the design of the subsequent randomized controlled trial was modified to include pre-, post- and follow-up parental assessment of adolescent anxiety. Parental involvement was also encouraged in the treatment intervention, and therapist phone calls took the place of email contact to monitor progress and assist with the application of skills to each individual's circumstances. The aim was to encourage adolescents to still take primary responsibility for their own treatment, but to provide added parental and therapist involvement so that adolescent responsibility could be encouraged and monitored.

Method

Participants   Participants were recruited and accepted into the trial based on the same inclusion and exclusion criteria as described for trial 1. Intake into the trial was conducted in 2006–2007 and was supported by a grant from Australian Rotary Health. Forty-three anxious adolescents participated in the trial (males = 16, females = 27, age range from 14–17 years, mean age = 15.17, SD = 1.11,) with primary diagnoses of social phobia (40%), GAD (37%), specific phobia (6%), SAD (4%), panic disorder (4%), OCD (4%), and anxiety disorder not otherwise specified (2%).

Assessment   Assessment was the same as for trial 1 with adolescents completing the SCAS, CATS, and ALIS, except that parents also provided diagnostic information to the structured interview and also completed parent versions of the SCAS, and the Strengths and Difficulties Questionnaire (Goodman, Meltzer, & Bailey, 1998).

Procedure   After intake, families were sent the information and consent form and the questionnaire measures. If the adolescent met the inclusion criteria, they were randomly allocated to either the active condition ($n = 24$) or the waitlist condition ($n = 19$).

Families in the active condition were immediately sent the adolescent *Cool Teens* computerized program and parent handouts, and a follow-up call was made to them a week later to make sure that they had received the CD-ROM and that it was working without fault.

Parent handout. To encourage parental involvement in the program, a brief handout was designed for parents to provide them with basic information about the computerized program and the core skills taught. The parent handouts provided psychoeducation about anxiety, goal setting, rationale and key principles of graded exposure, and how to support graded exposure. Adolescents were encouraged to work through the computerized modules on their own, and the parents were encouraged to ask their adolescent how they could assist them to implement the skills taught in the modules.

Telephone sessions. Brief telephone sessions between the therapist and adolescent occurred after weeks 1, 2, 3, 4, 5, and 7, 9, and 11. The purpose of the therapist calls was to problem solve any difficulties that had arisen and to assist in the application of the skills to the adolescent's life. Each telephone call lasted an average of 16 minutes. The telephone calls between the therapist and the adolescent's parent occurred after weeks 1, 4, and 7. The purpose of these calls was to assist the parent to help their adolescent to complete the program, to encourage parents to allow adolescents time to work on the homework exercises, and to provide the adolescent with parental support to complete exposure exercises. The average duration of each phone call to parents was 17.3 minutes. Thus, therapists spent an average of less than 3 hours with each family over the entire program.

Results

The results of changes on the diagnostic interviews are shown in Figure 12.5. Participants who completed the *Cool Teens* program showed a marked drop in diagnostic

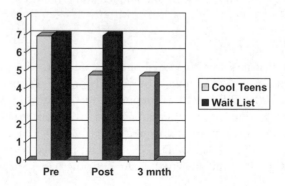

Figure 12.5   Mean ADIS severity ratings for primary anxiety disorder trial 2.

severity from pre-treatment (moderate clinical severity) to post-treatment (minimal clinical severity) and this improvement was significantly better than changes shown in the waitlist condition over the twelve week period (subclinical on average). Similar effects were found on most questionnaire measures with adolescents using the *Cool Teens* program demonstrating significantly greater reductions compared to the waitlist group. All improvements were maintained at three month follow up. See Wuthrich et al. (2012) for more detailed results.

Conclusions

Compared to waitlist, adolescents using the *Cool Teens* program with support from their mother and therapist phone calls demonstrated significant and lasting improvements in their anxiety symptoms both in terms of clinician reported clinical severity and self-report measures from the adolescents and their mothers independently. These results indicate that the *Cool Teens* program is an effective computerized intervention for adolescent anxiety.

These results mirror the latest findings from two other computerized programs for anxious children and adolescents. Published case studies (Spence, Donovan, March et al., 2008) and the full trial of the BRAVE online anxiety program for teenagers (Spence, Donovan, March et al., 2011) report good clinical outcomes for adolescents with anxiety using the internet program that are comparable to face-to-face CBT and are similar to our findings. Also recent results demonstrate the effectiveness of the CAMP COPE-A-LOT: The coping cat CD computerized program for children (Khanna & Kendall, 2010) with the program being found to be as effective as face to face individual CBT. These results together indicate that there are exciting times ahead for the use of computerized treatment for child and adolescent anxiety as well as for other disorders.

Interestingly, the amount of improvement in anxiety reported by the adolescents in the *Cool Teens* program is similar to those improvements reported by the adolescents using the *Cool Teens* in trial 1 (reported above). The striking difference here, is the adolescents in the waitlist condition in trial 2, did not report significant improvements during the waitlist period, and therefore, the differences between these groups is significant over time (unlike in trial 1 where similar "improvements" were reported by both groups of adolescents). If the reason for the lack of significant results in trial 1 was because the waitlist adolescents "faked good" or provided unreliable reports of their own anxiety, then this suggests that even email support from a therapist might still be enough to bring about clinically significant change. This is of course only speculation that will need to be addressed in a carefully controlled trial with parent report added at pre and post intervention.

Summary and Future Directions

With increasing research demonstrating the effectiveness of computerized treatments for child and adolescent anxiety, in the future we are likely to see greater use of the Internet and computers in therapy, especially with skills-based interventions such as CBT. Given initial findings indicating that computer-based CBT is effective in children with anxiety and other disorders, in the future research needs to focus on what is the best use of the computer delivery format. For example, it is unclear what differences there are in the effectiveness of different delivery formats such as using online programs, CD-ROM programs, online chat, forums, and web cameras and differences in their ability to engage the adolescent in therapy.

Further, it is unclear what level of therapist support and parent support is needed in order to detect reliable change in anxiety symptoms using these types of interventions. No studies have examined this issue systematically. The results from our own *Cool Teens* program delivered in different formats highlights the differences in effectiveness and robustness that might come with different levels of therapist and parent support for adolescent samples. In trial 1, minimal assistance was provided while in trial 2 more therapist assistance was provided and parents were encouraged to be involved (although still to a small amount in comparison to face-to-face interventions). It is unknown whether a minimal support intervention, such as the email support provided in trial 1, would provide a sufficient level of support if parents had either been encouraged to be involved in their adolescent's treatment or if parent report of symptoms pre- and post-trial had been included in the assessment. Obviously, the less support needed from therapists, the more cost effective and accessible computerized treatments will be. These are interesting issues that need to be established in future research.

Finally, one of the great attractions of computerized delivery is the potential for quickly and easily delivering up-to-date and evidence-based treatment to vast numbers of sufferers who possibly would not have presented to traditional, face-to-face therapy for a host of reasons such as financial, distance, shyness, and stigma. Continued research and implementation of these programs into health services in this area has the potential to be of great benefit to the international community.

References

Albano, A. M., Marten, P. A., Holt, C. S., Heimberg, R. G., & Barlow, D. H. (1995). Cognitive-behavioral group treatment for social phobia in adolescents: A preliminary study. *Journal of Nervous and Mental Disease, 183,* 649–656.

Andersson, G., Bergstrom, J., Carlbring, P., & Lindefors, N. (2005). The use of the Internet in the treatment of anxiety disorders. *Current Opinions in Psychiatry, 18,* 73–77.

Andlin-Sobocki, P., & Wittchen, H.-U. (2005). Cost of anxiety disorders in Europe. *European Journal of Neurology, 12* (Suppl 1), 39–44.

Andrews, G., Van Vliet, H., & Wuthrich, V. M. (2007). The reduction of anxiety in school children: preliminary results with www.climateschools.tv. In D. Castle, S. Hood & M. Kyrios (Eds.), *Anxiety Disorders: Current Controversies, Future Directions* (pp. 149–159). Australia: Australian Postgraduate Medicine.

Baer, S., & Garland, E. J. (2005). Pilot study of community-based cognitive behavioral group therapy for adolescents with social phobia. *Journal of the American Academy of Child & Adolescent Psychiatry, 44,* 258–264.

Barrett, P. M., Duffy, A., Dadds, M. R., & Rapee, R. M. (2001). Cognitive-behavioral treatment of anxiety disorders in children: Long-term (6-year) follow-up. *Journal of Consulting and Clinical Psychology, 69,* 135–141.

Booth, M. L., Bernard, D., Quine, S., Kang, M. S., Usherwood, T., Alperstein, G., et al. (2004). Access to health care among Australian adolescents—young people's perspectives and their sociodemographic distribution. *Journal of Adolescent Health, 34,* 97–103.

Botella, C., Hofmann, S. G., & Moscovitch, D. A. (2004). A self-applied, Internet-based intervention for fear of public speaking. *Journal of Clinical Psychology, 60,* 821–830.

Brady, E. U., & Kendall, P. C. (1992). Comorbidity of anxiety and depression in children and adolescents. *Psychological Bulletin, 111,* 244–255.

Calear, A. L., & Christensen, H. (2010). Review of internet-based prevention and treatment programs for anxiety and depression in children and adolescents. *Medical Journal of Australia, 192* (11), S12–S14.

Carlbring, P., Nordgren, L. B., Furmark, T., & Andersson, G. (2009). Long-term outcome of internet-delivered cognitive-behavioural therapy for social phobia: A 30-month follow-up. *Behaviour Research and Therapy, 47* (10), 848–850.

Cartwright-Hatton, S., Roberts, C., Chitsabesan, P., Fothergill, C., & Harrington, R. (2004). Systematic review of the efficacy of cognitive behaviour therapies for childhood and adolescent anxiety disorders. *British Journal of Clinical Psychology, 43,* 421–436.

Chorpita, B. F., & Barlow, D. H. (1998). The development of anxiety: The role of control in the early environment. *Psychological Bulletin, 124,* 3–21.

Christensen, H., Griffiths, K. M., & Evans, K. (2002). *e-Mental Health in Australia: Implications of the Internet and Related Technologies for Policy.* ISC Discussion Paper No 3. Commonwealth Department of Health and Ageing, Canberra.

Chu, B. C., Choudhury, M. S., Shortt, A. L., Pincus, D. B., Creed, T. A., & Kendall, P. C. (2004). Alliance, Technology, and Outcome in the Treatment of Anxious Youth. *Cognitive and Behavior Practice, 11,* 44–55.

Costello, E., Mustillo, S., Erkanli, A., Keeler, G., & Angold, A. (2003). Prevalence and development of psychiatric disorders in childhood and adolescence. *Archives of General Psychiatry, 60*(8), 837–844.

Cuijpers, P., Marks, I. M., van Straten, A., Cavanagh, K., Gega, L., & Andersson, G. (2009). Computer-aided psychotherapy for anxiety disorders: A meta-analytic review. *Cognitive Behaviour Therapy, 38*(2), 66–82.

Cunningham, M. J., Donovan, C. L., & March, S. (Eds.). (2007). *Developing and Delivering Computer-based CBT for Anxiety Disorders in Young People.* Sydney: Australian Academic Press.

Cunningham, M. J., Rapee, R. M., & Lyneham, H. J. (2006). Feedback to a prototype self-help computer program for anxiety disorders in adolescents. *Australian e-Journal for the Advancement of Mental Health, 5* (3), 216–224.

Cunningham, M. J., Wuthrich, V. M., Rapee, R. M., Lyneham, H. J., Schniering, C. A., & Hudson, J. L. (2008). The Cool Teens CD-ROM for anxiety disorders in adolescents: A pilot case series. *European Journal of Child and Adolescent Psychiatry, 18* (2), 125–129.

Davis, R. (2004). the Use of Interactive Multimedia in the Promotion of Mental Health in Schools. Retrieved Feb. 1, 2007 (not available at this URL now.)

De Los Reyes, A., & Kazdin, A. E. (2005). Informant discrepancies in the assessment of childhood psychopathology: A critical review, theoretical framework, and recommendations for further study. *Psychological Bulletin, 131*(4), 483–509.

Department of Health and Ageing (2004). *Responding to the Mental Health Needs of Young People in Australia. Discussion Paper: Principles and Strategies.* Retrieved Jan 16, 2006 (not available at this URL now).

Dewis, L. M., Kirkby, K. C., Martin, F., Daniels, B. A., Gilroy. L. J., & Menzies, R. G. (2001). Computer-aided vicarious exposure versus live graded exposure for spider phobia in children. *Journal of Behavior Therapy & Experimental Psychiatry, 32,* 17–27.

Di Noia, J., Schwinn, T. M., Dastur, Z. A., & Schinke, S. P. (2003). The relative efficacy of pamphlets, CD-ROM, and the Internet for disseminating adolescent drug abuse prevention programs: an exploratory study. *Preventive Medicine, 37,* 646–653.

Dragone, M. A., Bush, P. J., Jones, J. K, Bearison, D. J., & Kamani, S. (2002). Development and evaluation of an interactive CD-ROM for children with leukemia and their families. *Patient Educ Couns, 46,* 297–307.

Gilroy, L., Kirkby, K. C., Daniels, B. A., Menzies, R. G., & Montgomery, I. M. (2000). A controlled comparison of computer-aided vicarious exposure versus in vivo exposure in the treatment of spider phobia. *Behavior Therapy, 31,* 733–744.

Ginsburg, G. S., & Drake, K. L. (2002). School-based treatment for anxious African American adolescents: A controlled pilot study. *Journal of the American Academy of Child and Adolescent Psychiatry, 41,* 1–8.

Goodman, R., Meltzer, H., & Bailey, V. (1998). The Strengths and Difficulties questionnaire: A pilot study on the validity of the self-report version. *European Child & Adolescent Psychiatry, 7,* 125–130.

Greist, J. H., Marks, I. M., Baer, L., Kobak, K. A., Wenzel, K. W., Hirsch, M. J., et al. (2002). Behaviour therapy for obsessive compulsive disorder guided by a computer or by a clinician compared with relaxation as a control. *Journal of Clinical Psychiatry, 63,* 138–145.

Griffiths, K. M., & Christensen, H. (2006). Review of randomised controlled trials of Internet interventions for mental disorders and related conditions. *Clinical Psychologist, 10,* 16–29.

Hankin, B. L., Abramson, L. Y., Silva, P. A., McGee, R., & Moffitt, T. E. (1998). Development of depression from preadolescence to young adulthood: Emerging gender differences in a 10-year longitudinal study. *Journal of Abnormal Psychology, 107*(1), 128–140.

Hayward, C., Varady, S., Albano, A. M., Thieneman, M., Henderson, L., & Schatzberg, A. F. (2000). Cognitive behavioral group therapy for female socially phobic adolescents: Results of a pilot study. *Journal of the American Academy of Child and Adolescent Psychiatry, 39,* 721–726.

Hofstra, M. B., van der Ende, J., & Verhulst, F. C. (2002). Child and adolescent problems predict DSM-IV disorders in adulthood: A 14-year follow-up of a Dutch epidemiological sample. *Journal of the American Academy of Child and Adolescent Psychiatry, 41,* 182–189.

Hudson, J. L., & Rapee, R. M. (2004). From anxious temperament to disorder: An etiological model of generalized anxiety disorder. In R. G. Heimberg, C. L. Turk & D. S. Mennin (Eds.), *Generalized Anxiety Disorder: Advances in Research and Practice* (pp. 51–76). New York: Guilford.

James, A., Soler, A., & Weatherall, R. (2005). Cognitive behavioural therapy for anxiety disorders in children and adolescents. *The Cochrane Database of Systematic Reviews,* Issue 4.

Kaltenthaler, E., Shackley, P., Stevens, K., Beverley, C., Parry, G., & Chilcott, J. (2002). A systematic review and economic evaluation of computerized cognitive behavioural therapy for depression and anxiety. *Health Technology and Assessment, 6*(22).

Kenardy, J., McCafferty, K. & Rosa, V. (2006). Internet-delivered indicated prevention for anxiety disorders: Six-month follow up. *Clinical Psychologist, 10*(1), 39–42.

Kendall, P. C., & Chansky, T. E. (1991). Considering cognition in anxiety-disordered children. *Journal of Anxiety Disorders, 5,* 167–185.

Kendall, P. C., & Ollendick, T. H. (2004). Setting the research and practice agenda for anxiety in children and adolescence: A topic comes of age. *Cognitive and Behavioral Practice, 11,* 65–74.

Kendall, P. C., Safford, S., Flannery-Schroeder, E., & Webb, A. (2004). Child anxiety treatment: Outcomes in adolescence and impact on substance use and depression at 7.4 year follow-up. *Journal of Consulting and Clinical Psychology, 72*(2), 276–287.

Kenwright, M., Marks, I. M., Gega, L., & Mataix, D. (2004). Computer-aided self-help for phobia/panic via internet at home: A pilot study. *British Journal of Psychiatry, 184,* 448–449.

Khanna, M. S., & Kendall, P. C. (2008). Computer-assisted CBT for child anxiety: The Coping Cat CD-ROM. *Cognitive and Behavioral Practice, 15,* 159–165.

Khanna, M. S., & Kendall, P. C. (2010). Computer-assisted cognitive behavioral therapy for child anxiety: Results from a randomised control trial. *Journal of Consulting and Clinical Psychology, 78*(5), 737–745.

Klein, B., Richards, J. C., & Austin, D. W. (2006). Efficacy of internet therapy for panic disorder. *Journal of Behavior Therapy and Experimental Psychiatry, 37,* 213–238.

Lange, A., van de Ven, J. P., & Schrieken, B. (2003). Interapy: Treatment of post-traumatic stress through the Internet. *Cognitive Behaviour Therapy, 32,* 110–124.

Léger, E., Ladouceur, R., Dugas, M. J., & Freeston, M. H. (2003) Cognitive-Behavioral Treatment of Generalized Anxiety Disorder Among Adolescents: A Case Series. *Journal of the American Academy of Child & Adolescent Psychiatry, 42,* 327–330.

Lewis, G., Anderson, L., Araya, R., Elgie, R., Harrison, G., Proudfoot, J., et al. (2003). *Self-help interventions for mental health problems.* Report to the Department of Health R&D Programme.

Manassis, K., & Bradley, S. J. (1994). The development of childhood anxiety disorders: Toward an integrated model. *Journal of Applied Developmental Psychology, 15,* 345–366.

NYMHF (2005). Media Alert. The Importance of Youth Mental Health. Retrieved Feb. 1, 2007, from www. orygen. org. au/docs/RESEARCH/NYMHF_summary. pdf

Newman, M. G. (2004). Technology in psychotherapy: An introduction. *Journal of Clinical Psychology, 60,* 141–145.

NSWAAH (NSW Centre for the Advancement of Adolescent Health) (2005). *Understanding Adolescents.* Retrieved 1 Feb 2007, from http://www.caah.chw.edu.au/resources/gp-section1.pdf.

Pier, C., Klein, B., Austin, D., Mitchell, J., Kiropoulos, L., & Ryan, P. (2006). Reflections on internet therapy: Past, present and beyond. *InPsych Highlights.*

Pine, D. S., Cohen, P., Gurley, D., Brook, J., & Ma, Y. (1998). The risk for early-adulthood anxiety and depressive disorders in adolescents with anxiety and depressive disorders. *Archives of General Psychiatry, 55,* 56–64.

Proudfoot, J. (2004). Computer-based treatment for anxiety and depression: is it feasible? Is it effective? *Neuroscience and Biobehavioural Reviews, 28,* 353–363.

Proudfoot, J., Swain, S., Widmer, S., Watkins, E., Goldberg, D., Marks, I., et al. (2003). The development and beta-test of a computer-therapy program for anxiety and depression: Hurdles and lessons. *Computers in Human Behavior, 19,* 277–289.

Przeworski, A., & Newman, M. G. (2004). Palmtop computer-assisted group therapy for social phobia. *Journal of Clinical Psychology, 60,* 179–88.

Rapee, R. M. (2001). The development of generalised anxiety. In M. W. Vasey & M. R. Dadds (Eds.), *The Developmental Psychopathology of Anxiety* (pp. 481–504). New York: Oxford University Press.

Rapee, R. M., Abbott, M. J., Baillie, A. J., & Gaston, J. E. (2007). Treatment of social phobia through pure self help and therapist-augmented self help. *British Journal of Psychiatry, 191,* 246–252.

Rapee, R. M., Abbott, M. J., & Lyneham, H. J. (2006). Bibliotherapy for children with anxiety disorders using written materials for parents: A randomized controlled trial. *Journal of Consulting and Clinical Psychology, 74* (3), 436–444.

Rapee, R. M., Schniering, C. A., & Hudson, J. L. (2009). Anxiety disorders during childhood and adolescence: Origins and treatment. *Annual Review of Clinical Psychology, 5,* 311–341.

Robinson, E., Titov, N., Andrews, G., McIntyre, K., Schwencke, G., & Solley, K. (2010). Internet treatment for generalized anxiety disorder: A randomized controlled trial comparing clinician vs. technician assistance. *PLoS ONE, 5* (6).

Roza, S. J., Hofstra, M. B., van der Ende, J., & Verhulst, F. C. (2003). Stable prediction of mood and anxiety disorders based on behavioral and emotional problems in childhood: A 14-year follow-up during childhood, adolescence, and young adulthood. *American Journal of Psychiatry, 160* (12), 2116–2121.

Sawyer, M. G., & Patton, G. C. (2000). Unmet need in mental health service delivery: Children and adolescents. In G. Andrews & S. Henderson (Eds.), *Unmet need in psychiatry: Problems, resources, responses* (pp. 330–344). New York: Cambridge University Press.

Schniering, C. A., & Rapee, R. M. (2002). Development and validation of a measure of children's automatic thoughts: the children's automatic thoughts scale. *Behaviour, Research and Therapy 40,* 1091–1109.

Senate Select Committee on Mental Health (2006). *A national approach to mental health— from crisis to community – A first report.* Commonwealth of Australia. ISBN 0 642 71636 6.

Silverman, W. K., & Albano, A. M. (1996). *The Anxiety Disorders Interview Schedule for Children – IV (child and parent versions).* San Antonio: Texas: Psychological Corporation.

Spek, V., Cuijpers, P., Nyklicek, I., Riper, H., Keyzer, J., & Pop, V. (2007). Internet-based cognitive behaviour therapy for symptoms of depression and anxiety: a meta-analysis. *Psychological Medicine, 37,* 319–328.

Spence, S. H. (1998). A measure of anxiety symptoms among children. *Behaviour, Research and Therapy, 36,* 545–566.

Spence, S. H., Donovan, C. L., March, S., Gamble, A., Anderson, R., Prosser, S., et al. (2008). Online CBT in the treatment of child and adolescent anxiety disorders: Issues in the development of BRAVE-ONLINE and two case illustrations. *Behavioural and Cognitive Psychotherapy, 36,* 411–430.

Spence, S. H., Donovan, C. L., March, S., Gamble, A., Anderson, R.E., Prosser, S., & Kenardy, J. (2011). A randomized controlled trial of online versus clinic-based CBT for adolescent anxiety. *Journal of Consulting and Clinical Psychology, 79,* 629–642.

Spence, S. H., Holmes, J. M., March, S., & Lipp, O. V. (2006). The feasibility and outcome of clinic plus internet delivery of cognitive-behavior therapy for childhood anxiety. *Journal of Consulting and Clinical Psychology, 74* (3), 614–621.

Weissman, M. M., Orvaschel, H., & Padian, N. (1980). Children's symptom and social functioning self report scales: Comparison of mothers' and children's reports. *Journal of Nervous Mental Disorders, 168* (12), 736–740.

WHO Child Mental Health Atlas (2005). *Child and Adolescent Mental health Resources Global Concerns: Implications for the future. Barriers to Care.* Retrieved Nov. 20, 2010, from http://www.who.int/mental_health/resources/Child_ado_atlas.pdf

Woodward, L. J., & Fergusson, D. M. (2001). Life course outcomes of young people with anxiety disorders in adolescence. *Journal of the American Academy of Child & Adolescent Psychiatry, 40,* 1086–1093.

Wright, J. H., & Wright, A. S. (1997). Computer-assisted psychotherapy. *Journal of Psychotherapy Practice and Research, 6,* 315–329.

Wuthrich, V. M., Rapee, R. M., Cunningham, M. J., Lyneham, H. J., Hudson, J. L., & Schniering, C. A. (2012). A randomized controlled trial of the Cool Teens CD-ROM computerized program for adolesent anxiety. *Journal of the American Academy of Child and Adolescent Psychiatry, 51* (3), 261–270.

13

Bibliotherapy for Anxious and Phobic Youth

Mary Coffman[1], Frank Andrasik[2], and Thomas H. Ollendick[3]

[1]Independent Practice, West Union, South Carolina, USA
[2]University of Memphis, Memphis, USA
[3]Virginia Polytechnic Institute and State University, Blacksburg, USA

Books serve many functions. They can inform, educate, enlighten, entertain, soothe, and, potentially, heal. An inscription above a Grecian library in Thebes several thousand years ago labeled the library "... healing place of the soul" (Carner, 1966, p. 76). Almost a century ago, Oliver (1928) suggested that "the right kind of a book may be applied to a mental illness, just as a definite drug is applied to some bodily need" (p. 291). More recently, the United Kingdom has endorsed this philosophy by making use of self-help books through their various health programs. Books on Prescription, a program that allows general practicioners and mental health workers to "prescribe" specific books that can be checked out at the local library (Chamberlain, Heaps, & Robert, 2008; Richardson, Richards, & Barkham, 2010), is but one example. Although bibliotherapy can come in many forms (e.g., book, audio, DVD, computer software), the focus of this chapter is on written materials (i.e., books).

Albert Ellis (1999), author of many self-help books, stated that through his correspondence with "thousands" of readers he was convinced that a "large number" of people benefited from reading. Researchers (Elgar & McGrath, 2008; Gould & Clum, 1993; Hirai & Clum, 2006) have pointed out that self-help treatments are often as effective as traditional therapy, though the evidence base for self-help for childhood disorders is not as strong as for adults (Elgar & McGrath, 2008). In a rather large study of 267 children, Rapee, Abbott, and Lyneham (2006) compared a commerically available parent book, *Helping Your Anxious Child: A Step-by-Step Guide* (Rapee, Spence, Cobham, & Wignall, 2000), to a 12-week, evidence-based group therapy program based on the Cool Kids Program, and to a waiting list group. Although results from this study were mixed, children in the bibliotherapy group improved compared to those in the waiting list group but not as much as those in the therapy group. This led the authors to point out the usefulness of bibliotherapy as an interim or intermediate approach, with the option of eventually using a therapist for those for whom the bibliotherapy approach was not successful. Despite limitations in research on self-help books for children, self-help therapies are potentially a powerful

The Wiley-Blackwell Handbook of The Treatment of Childhood and Adolescent Anxiety, First Edition.
Edited by Cecilia A. Essau and Thomas H. Ollendick.

option because of cost effectiveness, convenience, flexibility, lack of stigma, and the ability of self-help materials to fulfill many of the functions normally associated with individual therapy (Elgar & McGrath, 2008; Mains & Scogin, 2003; Watkins, 2008).

One may question whether the severity of a child's problem is a mitigating factor in the decision to use children's book. Theoretically, it is possible that for some problems, such caution may be warranted. However, as some researchers have noted (Otto, Pollack, & Maki, 2001) in relation to panic disorders, factors such as comorbidity and severity are potential issues even when the approach involves well-established treatments (e.g., pharmacotherapy or CBT) because these factors are often "inconsistent" predictors of outcome. In a review of evidence-based treatments of childhood disorders that included anxiety disorders, Ollendick, Jarrett, Grills-Taquechel, Hovey, and Wolff (2008) found that co-morbidity was not as much of a problem as one might expect. However, for the two studies in the review that involved bibliotherapy treatment co-morbidity analyses were not available. Although the impact of severity and co-morbidity on the use of juvenile bibliotherapy is not clear, it is possible that for some childhood problems, a bibliotherapy approach has the potential for superior outcome, even for severe problems, because of factors such as ease of administration, potential to inspire motivation, and ability to incorporate a number of therapeutic components into a format that is intrinsically appealing to many children.

One of the most important advantages of bibliotherapy for children is that it can be conducted in the home, which makes it particularly helpful to parents. As Starker (1989) points out, in its use of bibliotherapy, the home can serve as a clinic. Bibiotherapy is potentially a tool that can empower parents to handle a number of problems without outside assistance, either independent of, or prior to, the use of more intensive services through an individual therapist. Economic barriers often reduce access to mental health services (Mains & Scogin, 2003), with some treatments being described as "punitively costly" (Elgar & McGrath, 2008). Childhood anxiety is an area that could greatly benefit from the availability of a cost-effective bibliotherapy approach because of its prevalence (Vande Voort, Svecova, Jacobsen, & Whiteside, 2010) and persistence (Podell, Mychailyszyn, Edmunds, Puleo, & Kendall, 2010). Effective cognitive behavioral therapies exist for many anxiety problems, and these principles have been extended to children. *Coping Cat* (as cited in Kendall, Hudson, Gosch, Flannery-Schoeder, & Suveg, 2008) is an example of a well-researched, effective CBT bibliotherapy approach in the sense that it utilizes written materials for children (i.e., a workbook) and a therapist manual. However, it is also therapist-directed, not self-directed or parent-directed because it involves a number of individual or group therapy sessions as part of the program. Hirshfeld-Baker, Masek, Henin et al. (2010) compared a cognitive behavioral treatment group (i.e., adaptation of the Coping Program to include additional "parent only" sessions) to a waiting-list group of children aged 4–7 years. Results suggested that even very young children could benefit from cognitive behavioral treatment (e.g., significant decrease in anxiety disorders with an effect size of 0.55; significant decrease in specific phobias with an effect size of 0.78).

Within the framework of self-help bibliotherapy programs for children (i.e., those programs meant to be used by child and parent in the home), there are basically two forms. One is a directive, informational, non-fiction, how-to approach. Dawn Huebner's series, published by Magination Press, is an excellent example of such books. In her book that addresses anxiety, *What to Do When You Worry Too Much* (2006), the author directly addresses the child as "you" and provides reassuring comments about what worry is and how the child can handle it. Huebner gives specific therapeutic suggestions (e.g., use logical thinking, establish a specific "worry time," use relaxation techniques). The book is illustrated and has a workbook format with spaces for the child to write down things such as a list of the " . . . active and fun things you can do to reset your system" (p. 61). Another book in the series, *What to Do When You Dread Your Bed* (Heubner, 2008), addresses insomnia and nighttime fears in a similar format.

James Christ's 121 page book, *What to Do When You're Scared and Worried: A Guide for Kids* (2004), is another informational approach to help children cope with fears and anxieties. Chapters are education-oriented and address such things as "where do fears and worries come from" as well as specific disorders, such as separation anxiety, generalized anxiety disorder, obsessive-compulsive disorder, and even post-traumatic stress disorders. It includes suggestions and coping skills (e.g., relaxing, journaling). In the final chapter the author explains how therapists can be helpful and also includes information for adults. Like the Huebner books mentioned earlier, *What to Do When You're Scared and Worried: A Guide for Kids* addresses the child as "you."

The other type of self-help bibliotherapy approach uses a story format, that may be either fiction or non-fiction. Non-fiction includes the genre of biographical or autobiographical stories. Often these non-fiction stories are written about celebrities or historical figures, although with the advent of publish-on-demand resources, less renown people are also contributing their stories. Many adults have read the book, *A Brilliant Madness* (Duke & Hochman, 1992), about Patty Duke's struggles with bipolar disorder. Similarly, Kay Jamison, a prominent psychologist and researcher in the area of bipolar illness, authored *An Unquiet Mind* (1996) that sheds light on her illness. The assumption underlying such books is that they potentially provide inspiration, encouragement, and modeling of helpful behaviors which have helped the authors learn to cope with their problems. As early as 1847, John Frost released a book that contained hundreds of biographical vignettes. In the preface it is clear that he hopes the book will have an effect on the behavior of the young through the power of imitation learning:

> In proposing Historical Examples to the young, the author of this work hopes to incite them to the study and practice of those active duties and virtuous habits which form the basis, not less of success in life and private happiness than of distinction and honour among men. Example is said to be better than precept. It certainly is more effective, inasmuch as it leads the pupil gently along that difficult path where precept seeks to drive, or merely to point the way. Precept says, "Go on!" Example says, "Come on! follow me!" The greater efficiency of the latter exhortation, especially with the young, who are naturally more imitative than obedient, must be obvious to every one. (p. 3)

Although there are many testimonials about the effects of biographical books on the reader's life (e.g., Canfield & Hendricks, 2006; Internet testimonials), formal research in this area is sparse. However, some of the testimonials about the effect of such books can be impressive. President Theodore Roosevelt is an example of someone who has written about the powerful effect of books, both fiction and non-fiction, on his thoughts and behaviors. In his autobiography, President Roosevelt (1920) described himself when a child as "nervous and timid" (p. 27). It is difficult to imagine how such a self-described "timid and nervous" child could become what George Grant in his preface (2000) to the book *Hero Tales* (Roosevelt & Lodge, 1891) described as "one of the most accomplished men of the twentieth century" (p. 10). Nevertheless, it is Roosevelt himself (1920) who explains how the process of reading contributed so much to his development:

> Yet from reading of the people I admired,—ranging from the soldiers of Valley Forge, and Morgan's riflemen, to the heroes of my favorite stories ... I felt a great admiration for men who were fearless and could hold their own in the world, and I had a great desire to be like them. (p. 27)

The potential impact of the fictional type of story on cognitions and behaviors is also illustrated by the comments of Theodore Roosevelt (1920). It is interesting that Roosevelt, whose behavior was so often characterized by courage in the face of danger (e.g., leading the charge at San Juan Hill, heading off a cattle stampede, facing a grizzly bear), attributes learning how to act fearless from the advice given in one of Frederick Marryat's fictional adventure books. Marryat, a writer during the mid to late 1800s, was himself a captain in the English Royal Navy. Part of the advice of the heroic boat captain in the fictional story was to "act" fearless even when one does not feel fearless, the type of advice that might well be given by a cognitive behavioral therapist today! According to Roosevelt,

> This was the theory upon which I went. There were all kinds of things of which I was afraid at first, ranging from grizzly bears to 'mean' horses and gun-fighters; but by acting as if I was not afraid I gradually ceased to be afraid. (pp. 52–53)

Fictional bibliotherapy has the potential of being particularly useful for children. First, reading stories to young children is ubiquitous, an activity familiar to most families. Second, listening to a story and looking at illustrations is generally perceived to be fun, pleasant, and enjoyable by most of the target audience: the child. Third, by its very nature, a fictional story can embody therapeutic techniques, such as modeling and cognitive restructuring. Behavior, thoughts, and emotions can all be modeled in the story. Behavioral descriptions embedded in the plot and through pictures provide numerous modeling opportunities. Thoughts can be described and are easily presented in the form of a monologue or a "self-dialogue." Fourth, a story about another child can serve as a motivational stimulus because the child can explore the advantages of overcoming the problem despite the issues that may have to be addressed to overcome it.

Hundreds of fictional books have been written on the topics of childhood anxiety and fears. Because fear of the dark is so prevalent in children (Muris, Merckelbach, Ollendick, King, & Bogie, 2001), many books have been written on this topic. Most of these books are relatively short (e.g., *Franklin in the Dark,* Bourgeosis, 1987; *Don't Be Afraid of the Dark: Bear in the Big Blue House,* Henson, 2001), and few have ever been evaluated to determine if they are indeed helpful in reducing fear of the dark.

Some fictional stories are more deliberate than others in their attempts to entwine therapeutic components within the plot and characters involved in the story. *Uncle Lightfoot* (Coffman, 1980–1983, 1987), which in a subsequent version, became *Uncle Lightfoot, Flip That Switch: Overcoming Fear of the Dark* (2012) was a deliberate effort to incorporate therapeutic elements (e.g., modeling, graduated exposure, relaxation) into a story to address this pervasive fear in children and efforts were made to determine the book's effectiveness (Mikulas & Coffman, 1989). The main character is a severely dark-phobic child who learns to overcome his fear of the dark while visiting an elderly Creek-Indian retired teacher and family friend, Uncle Lightfoot. Through a series of cognitive-behavioral secrets and numerous exposure games, the child gradually overcomes his fear of the dark. Currently there are two versions. The shorter version, *Uncle Lightfoot, Flip That Switch* (Coffman, 2012), for ages 4–7 focuses almost entirely on exposure games. The longer version, *Uncle Lightfoot, The Path to Bravery* (Coffman, in press), includes not only additional exposure games but also focuses on specific cognitive-behavioral coping techniques. Parent instructions are included with both versions.

As early as 1948, Josette Frank had pointed out that an uncharted area of research was the effect of children's literature on emotional health. Despite the need for self-help bibliotherapy research specific to childhood problems, there appears to be little research available to us. To illustrate this issue, in the recent 446-page book, entitled *Handbook of Self-Help Therapies* (Watkins & Clum, 2008), there was only a single, 32-page chapter that specifically addressed self-help materials for childhood disorders. One would hope that by the twenty-first century that clinicians proclaiming the values of such a bibliotherapeutic process would have systematically researched the principles underlying such a potentially life-enhancing medium. Unfortunately, that has not happened. As Clum and Watkins (2008) have pointed out, even though hundreds of studies have been conducted since the early 1970s, the field of self-help media (of which bibliotherapy is a part) is merely in its initial stages, an opinion that is understandable because most self-help programs that are on the market have not been tested (Rosen, Barrera, & Glasgow, 2008). According to Clum and Watkins (2008), although some general guidelines have been established, "In one real sense we have no better idea today how to write a self-help book than we did 30 years ago" (p. 421).

In addition, much of the current research that is being conducted is designed to answer cause–effect questions, which are important questions in themselves, but the questions do not necessarily explore principles underlying the practice of bibliotherapy, particularly as it applies to children. Although recognizing the need for both types of research, the focus of this chapter is on underlying issues and principles regarding fictional bibliotherapy, a much neglected area of study (Campbell & Smith, 2003).

Thus, the primary purpose of this chapter is to use the development of one book, *Uncle Lightfoot*, as a prototype to provide suggestions that might contribute to our understanding of how to create evidence-based fictional therapeutic bibliotherapy materials, particularly for childhood phobic and anxiety disorders. Both qualitative and quantitative research was conducted during the development of *Uncle Lightfoot*, a methodological combination recommended by Clum and Watkins (2008). As Gordon, King, Gullone, Muris, and Ollendick (2007b) have pointed out, *Uncle Lightfoot* is one of only two stories for nighttime fears that have actually been researched over the years. In addition to the research (i.e., Mikulas, Coffman, Dayton, Frayne, &

Maier, 1985; Mikulas & Coffman, 1989) conducted by the developers and referred to in Gordon et al. (2007b), independent researchers, Santacruz, Mendez, and Sanchez-Meca (2006), reported that an earlier version of *Uncle Lightfoot* was effective in reducing fear of the dark compared to a waiting list group, with an effect size of 1.13 for Bed Time Recording and 2.53 for Dark Behavior Recording-Modified (behavioral approach tasks), producing large effect sizes. The research represented an independent study that suggested the potential usefulness of a bibliotherapeutic approach to fear of the dark.

Based on our experience, we provide a list of suggestions that might be useful in the development of fictional bibliotherapy materials, along with a discussion of the relevant issues. What will become obvious, as with most research, is that more questions are raised than answered at this nascent stage.

1. Use a feedback-driven approach during the development of the book. The first author gained her initial experience in bibliotherapy in the early 1970s when she wrote a very simple 41-page book for dark-fearful children entitled *Lightfoot* (1973), which incorporated desensitization and modeling techniques. Coffman (1975) compared the materials to a group receiving a published book (i.e., *Boo Who Used to Be Afraid of the Dark* by Munro Leaf, 1949), and a no treatment group. Although there was no significant difference on the primary dependent measure (i.e., Fear Behavior Checklist), comments from the parents and children suggested that bibliotherapy held promise for dark-fearful children. More importantly, it suggested a feedback-driven approach to bibliotherapy:

> Another implication of this research is that it suggests a method of approaching the writing of children's books that deal with psychological problems or books intended to be therapeutically beneficial. For example, in dealing with fears, it appears to be helpful to first find out what the hierarchy actually is for a number of children for a particular fear. Then a story can be written around the hierarchy. After initial testing the book can be revised and then tested on larger populations. Such an approach gives the writer much needed feedback. This research has shown the usefulness of obtaining such feedback in the writing of a book because it enables changes to be made on the basis of empirical data rather than intuition alone. (Coffman, 1975, pp. 64–65)

It often takes therapists years to hone the techniques they use with clients in individual therapy or group therapy, becoming more skilled as they gain expertise in applying the techniques. Therefore, when clinicians switch from delivering face-to-face therapy to writing materials, should they not expect that there will be a similar learning curve when developing bibliotherapeutic materials? While the therapist may be the teacher or facilitator of change during face-to-face therapy, in some ways it is the client who becomes the teacher or change agent when the therapist submits the materials to scientific evaluation, provided the therapist gives the client ample opportunity for feedback, both in the form of formal quantitative assessment and also informal qualitative formats (e.g., logs, diaries). It is important to identify and understand both the successes and failures of participants in our studies (Hayes, Barlow, & Nelson-Gray, 1999). The best "research-subject" teachers are often the ones who failed to succeed in the program. If the therapist is a very careful "listener," the failures may well provide clues as to why the program failed for a particular client, clues that will ultimately lead to a better program.

Coffman later created *Uncle Lightfoot* (1980), a much longer book than *Lightfoot*, with a more involved story that included the use of games, which was tested through a series of four experiments. What was learned from the next four studies (using the 1980–1983 versions) as well as a few single subject studies (using the 1987 version) was how much was *not* known in terms of the science of bibliotherapy. The first issue had to do with which methodological approach is most useful to the feedback process.

The methodology used in the initial *Lightfoot* study and the four subsequent *Uncle Lightfoot* studies consisted of group comparisons. Using group comparisons for the development of a bibliotherapuetic intervention was a mistake. Not only was the use of group comparisons an inappropriate approach in the *initial* development of a bibliotherapy approach for darkness phobia, it was, in fact, an inefficient expenditure of a researcher's greatest asset: subjects. During the mid 1980s, the authors of *The Scientist Practitioner* (Barlow, Hayes, & Nelson, 1984) pointed out that during the development stage for a therapeutic intervention, the most advantageous approach is to use a single subject design until the intervention has been fairly well developed and *then* switch over to a group design to determine whether the intervention works when compared to waiting list, control, or other therapeutic groups. A single subject methodology allows one to catch and correct mistakes early.

2. **Make sure that the assessment instruments being used can adequately measure the identified problem behavior that is being addressed in the story.** Assessment was a recurrent problem in the previous darkness studies, and some measures were more useful than others in developing the materials. One mistake in the earlier studies was the failure to incorporate a standardized structured interview such as the Anxiety Disorders Interview Schedule (Silverman & Albano, 1996) in selecting participants, a mistake common to many earlier studies. Although most of the children were very fearful and thus approximated a clinical sample, failure to include a structured diagnostic interview led to the inclusion of some children who were not truly phobic and likely confounded the findings. For example, a few years after the earlier *Uncle Lightfoot* studies (Mikulas et al., 1985; Mikulas & Coffman, 1989) were completed, the current authors realized during extended discussions that some parents may have mistaken the behavior of children with attention deficits for that of children with darkness phobia because of failure to remain in bed. This revelation led to a reanalysis of the fourth group study wherein seven children identified by parents on an intake form as being "easily distracted" were removed. This reanalysis indicated significant improvement ($p < 0.002$) for the Book/Game group on the Dark Tolerance Test, though not for the Parental Attention group, the Games Only group, or the Book Only group. Children with very poor attention spans may find it difficult to benefit from a treatment that requires them to attend to the reading of a story. Therefore, a more structured interview, including diagnostic items, would have been helpful during the development of the bibliotherapy materials.

The 5- and 7-point Likert scales that we used in our early evaluation studies did not seem to be very helpful as a pre-post assessment tool, although they were useful for addressing questions such as "Did the treatment help?" On the other hand, the Fear Survey Scale for Children – Revised (FSSC-R; Ollendick, 1983) was useful in identifying children who were not only afraid of the dark but who also had other nighttime fears (e.g., monsters, burglars) or other fears in general. Still, the FSSC-R failed to provide specific information about fear of the dark itself. What did prove to be very useful in the development of the materials was incorporating behavioral instruments, such as the Behavior Approach Tasks (BAT) as well as the Dark Tolerance Test (DTT). Coffman later turned the Dark Tolerance Test, which required the child to lie in bed in the dark for a certain number of minutes without calling out, into a series of behavior approach tasks and used it with several individual cases. Santacruz et al. (2006) used a similar but somewhat modified approach. They modified the behavior tolerance/approach tests used in our earlier *Uncle Lightfoot* studies and reported father–mother agreement of 0.90 on the Dark Behavior Recording-Modified (DBR-M). In addition, Santacruz et al. (2006) found the Bed Time Recording they used had a father-mother agreement of 0.97, yielding a reliable measure of nighttime behaviors.

Unfortunately, while behavior approach tasks or behavior recordings are a useful component of pre- and post-assessment, they too are inconvenient to use as repeated measures from the parent's perspective, particularly if the materials are being used on an almost daily basis. To address this issue, when single subject methodology was used with the 1987 version of Uncle Lightfoot, a self-efficacy scale for fear of the dark, "What I Think I Can Do at Night" (WICDAN) was developed for children who could read. Figures 13.1 and 13.2 illustrate the usefulness of this measure in providing feedback on the child's feelings of self-efficacy during the use of the materials. The WICDAN (1987) contained 12 items, with three possible responses: "Yes, easily" (2 points), "Yes, but it would be hard" (1 point), or "No, it would be too hard to do" (0 points). The range of scores on the WICDAN was from 0 to 24. Although the instrument was used with only a few children, a reasonably high inter-rater reliability (i.e., child–parent agreement ranged from 87 to 93%) was found. For the parents of very young children, the first author developed a modified version of the WICDAN along with a Nighttime Behaviors Survey for parents to complete. Ideally, researchers will someday develop an easy-to-administer test that has been

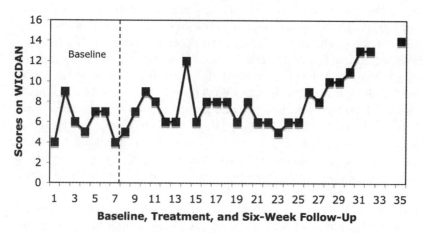

Figure 13.1 Performance of dark-phobic 7-year-old on What I Think I Can Do (WICDAN) self-efficacy scale during baseline and during the use of Uncle Lightfoot materials (possible range of score on WICDAN: 0-24)

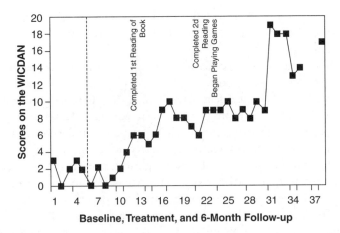

Figure 13.2 Performance by 10-year-old dark-phobic child on self-efficacy scale, What I Think I Can Do at Night (WICDAN), when using the Uncle Lightfoot materials.

standardized on a number of dark-fearful children, which could then be included with the bibliotherapy materials. Readers may find the comprehensive review of numerous types of instruments developed by researchers over the years for fear of the dark, completed by Orgiles, Espada, and Mendez (2008), of interest.

3. If the objective is to better understand the underlying principles of bibliotherapy, select a relatively simple problem (e.g., dog phobia) to address. The very first children's book the first author wrote was for snake phobia. It was in response to a class assignment to complete a project for a graduate behavior modification class in 1971. She initially considered testing the snake book with young children because snake phobia was so common and would entail a simple approach behavior test. However, in the author's geographical location (i.e., panhandle of Florida), there were four highly poisonous species. The first author was concerned that parents would be reluctant to participate in the study with their children because many of them had either deliberately taught their children to be afraid or were afraid of snakes themselves and felt the fear was normal. As a result, Coffman chose another fear that she thought was a simple, common childhood fear: fear of the dark.

The assumption that fear of the dark was "common" was correct. For example, researchers (Hvolby, Jorgensen, & Bilenberg, 2008) found that in terms of sleep issues with children, fear of going to bed in the dark was the most common (i.e., 19.4%). When fear of the dark is expanded to include things that might be present in the dark (e.g., closets, shadows, burglars), the problem is even more pervasive, with 58.8% of ages 4–6, 84.7% of ages 7–9, and 79.6% of ages 8–12 in one study (Muris et al., 2001) reporting nighttime fears.

The assumption that fear of the dark was a "simple" fear, however, was not borne out. Fear of the dark is one of 34 nighttime fears (Gordon, King, Gullone, Muris, & Ollendick, 2007a). A number of the children in the studies had other associated issues, such as fear of being alone, fear of nightmares, or fear of burglars as well as fear of the dark, complicating the clinical picture. Additionally, fear of the dark proved to be difficult from the perspective of assessment. Laboratory dark tolerance or laboratory behavior approach tests do not necessarily correlate with performance in the familiar home setting. If a home version of the DTT or BAT is used, comparison may be difficult across children because of issues related to intensity of lightning and variation in distances between rooms.

Animal phobias (e.g., dogs, reptiles) or other specific phobias would likely be more suitable and less complex to initially explore the principles of bibliotherapy than a more complicated phobia such as fear of the dark, unless there are excellent assessment tools readily available for the more complex problem. That said, the very complexity of nighttime problems provides opportunities to better understand the capacity of bibliotherapy to alleviate phobic and other anxiety driven responses.

4. Insure the child is successful by making incremental or "hierarchical" steps towards the target goal in the story. The behavioral technique of shaping, or successive approximation, is a simple procedure but potentially a very powerful one. An old behavioral axiom is that success begets success. Self-efficacy is often cited (e.g., Bandura, 1997) as the means through which behavioral change occurs, and competencies in particular skills are one of the major contributors to increased feelings of self-efficacy and possibly one of the quickest routes to success.

Part of the original systematic desensitization technique involved establishment of a fear hierarchy (Wolpe, 1958). Sometimes the hierarchy is intuitive and easy to set up. At other times it may be counterintuitive, which points out the importance of conducting careful, thoughtful assessments. Because the children in the study on the precursor to *Uncle Lightfoot* (Coffman, 1975) were very young (i.e., 3–7), parents, not children, were asked to rate items on a fear of dark hierarchy based on the child's behavioral responses. For children, a hierarchy order is very desirable, particularly when dealing with anxiety issues (Bouchard, Mendlowitz, Coles, & Franklin, 2004). For example, it would seem to be counterproductive to ask a child to remain in the dark for 5 minutes if the child is terrified when the light is off for 30 seconds.

If one is working on a phobia, for instance, one would want to envision a range that starts where the child is already comfortable and extends upward to an almost "off the scale" response in terms of intensity of the problem. If one is attempting to reach a broad range of children, then one can start very low on the hierarchy and then make small incremental steps towards the targeted end goal. Having stated this, it should be noted that the issue of the size of the step is one that needs to be explored further.

Two of the four group studies conducted on *Uncle Lightfoot* (Mikulas et. al., 1985; Mikulas & Coffman, 1989) by graduate students, Debra Costello (1981) (Dayton) and Cynthia Frayne (1981), illustrate the importance of step-wise progression. First, it should be noted that there are two main target goals for fear of the dark: (1) to approach, and remain for several minutes, in darkened rooms/situations, and (2) to be able to sleep in the dark alone in one's own bed. In addition to a Dark Tolerance Test that required the child to lie in bed in the dark, the two studies used behavior approach tasks for approaching dark situations.

The BAT percentages in Table 13.1 illustrate how the progression in success occurred. The percentage of children who improved varied from item to item. Children who made the least improvement on the BAT proved informative, as their results suggested the need to revise or add to the *Uncle Lightfoot* materials. Although Costello and Frayne used slightly different instructions for their respective BATs that may have affected participant responses and neither used control groups, Table 13.1 nevertheless

Table 13.1 Percentage of Children Successful in Completing Behavior Approach Tasks

Experiment 1 Costello (Dayton) BAT	Pretest	Posttest	Experiment 2 Frayne BAT	Pretest	Posttest
Child and Parent Together	85%	100%	Find Object with Hint	45%	100%
Child at Entrance	75%	95%	Turn Lights Off 1×1	45%	91%
Parent at Door	70%	95%	Errand Outside	36%	82%
Find Object with Hint	35%	75%	Parent Hides	27%	91%
Find Object without Hint	0%	60%			

Note. The data presented here were taken from unpublished data from studies reported in Mikulas, Coffman, Dayton, Frayne, & Maier (1985). The book used was the 1980 edition of *Uncle Lightfoot*. Also, the first experiment includes four different types of groups: Coping Book Only Group (no parent instructions with suggestion to play games described in the book); Coping Book with Games Group (parent instructions with suggestion to play games described in the book); Mastery Book Only Group; Mastery Book with Games Group. The second experiment used two groups (both had parent instructions in the book): Coping Book with Games Group and Coping Book with Games and with Tangible Reward Group.

illustrates the potential helpfulness of including a BAT for feedback when developing bibliotherapy materials.

5. If possible, provide dosage recommendations for the use of the bibliotherapy materials. Some of the questions that need to be asked when a book is being used as the treatment vehicle are how often, for how long, and under what conditions should the book be read to the child to ensure maximal success. These questions suggest that the concept of "dosage" may have application to the field of bibliotherapy. Hahlweg, Heinrichs, Kuschel, and Feldmann (2008) found a dosing effect while using a therapist-assisted CBT bibliotherapy program to teach parenting skills. Improvements in parenting skill correlated significantly with the number of chapters the parents read. For children, an additional question would be what dosage is appropriate for what age range? For example, is it possible that a 10-year-old should read the story through twice before playing the games whereas a 4-year-old may need to play the games immediately after reading each chapter or that a 6-year-old should read through the book once before playing the games – or perhaps the opposite is true? This is uncharted territory in the field of bibliotherapy.

One of the most intriguing questions about the *Uncle Lightfoot* materials is which approach should be used in terms of how much material should be read prior to attempting the games. The options range from a major focus on mental rehearsal (e.g., read the book several times) to a major focus on behavioral rehearsal (play the games as soon as the chapter is read). Below is a list of some possible approaches or methods that can be used with the book as well as potential issues with such methods. A second question is whether to use a massed or spaced practice in terms of reading the book itself.

To explore the first question, a number of approaches were used in *Uncle Lightfoot* research. It is not appropriate to limit the materials to just one approach because it may be that the book is beneficial but only when a different approach is used, or it may be that one approach is more effective than another. Without testing a series of approaches, one could easily overlook the most effective approach. For example, following are the therapeutic approaches or "dosages" that were used with *Uncle Lightfoot* during its development.

Approach 1: Begin playing the games immediately as soon as a particular chapter is completed – and do not read further in the book or play any more games until the child can successfully play the game (i.e., succeed at the task required to play the game). This approach is actually the one closest to Wolpe's original desensitization technique. Many children were successful using this approach in the early studies (Mikulas & Coffman, 1989). However, a potential problem with this approach is that it may actually increase the child's frustration if the child does not succeed, and the child may become "stuck" and unable to complete the remainder of the tasks.

This seemed to be what happened in a case with a severely fearful child who used the 1987 version of *Uncle Lightfoot* as seen in Figure 13.1 (Coffman & Huebner, 1993). During the initial interview the mother stated that her goal was for her child to be able to sleep in the child's own bed. Although there were a number of disruptive behaviors (average of 13 per night during pre-treatment phase), the behavior of most concern and frustration to the 7-year-old's mother was the child's unwillingness to sleep alone, even with the overhead light on. Our earlier research found that fear of being alone often accompanied fear of the dark, with about 41% children in two of our combined studies (Mikulas & Coffman, 1989) identified by their parents as being afraid of being alone in addition to being afraid of the dark.

The goal of sleeping alone was achieved by the time the child had made it less than one-half of the way through the book. The mother reported that she was "thrilled" by her child's success and the child enjoyed the book, even though mother and child did not complete the entire book/games. In addition to an improvement on the WICDAN, there was also a decrease in disruptive behaviors and a decrease in the number of minutes it took to get to bed and to fall asleep based over a 7-night period (i.e., took 19 minutes less at the end).

The family of the child in Figure 13.1 did not complete the reading of the book, possibly because the parent used the "traditional desensitization" approach that had been used in one of our earlier studies (i.e., the child does not go further until the child can succeed at the game at the end of the chapter). Using this method, it seems that this particular child became "stuck" and could not go further. It is possible that it would have been more therapeutic to have the child read further in the book, even though the child could not play the game initially since the child may have success with a different game later in the book. Nevertheless, this treatment was successful in the sense of meeting the mother's original goal, and as Ost and Ollendick (1999) have pointed out, " . . . treatment outcome can be very good even if the ultimate goal of the therapist has not been fully reached during the session" (p. 7).

In the 2012 parent guidebook that accompanies *Uncle Lightfoot, Flip That Switch,* the author recommended against the use of this approach because of the potential for "getting stuck." However, the recommendation was based on a short-term clinical decision to enhance the low-demand nature of the materials in the interest of promoting safety and child engagement. The validity of this clinical decision needs to be determined through future research. It should also be noted that in the previous example, the parent did not record any major negative interactions, such as crying as a result of this "stop and do not go further" approach. On the contrary, the child seemed very pleased with the limited success. However, the authors suggest that because the program is being carried out by the parent in the home setting, in the short term at least, it is preferable to reduce the likelihood of frustration for the family. Again, this is an area that needs further exploration.

Approach 2: Begin playing the games immediately as soon as a particular chapter is completed. If the child does not succeed at the game (or does not wish to play it), skip it and go on to the next chapter and game. The advantage of this approach is that it may prevent the child from getting stuck. Also, because the games start out very simple, the child may experience immediate success, thus increasing feelings of self efficacy. Additionally, because the child is playing the game immediately and does not know what will be expected of him or her "eventually," it is possible that the child may not be as likely to ruminate on thoughts about what frightening possibilities may await him or her, thoughts that might be more prevalent if the child reads through the entire story (i.e., pictures of the child sleeping all night in the bed). Ost and Ollendick (1999) recommend in one-session treatment that:

> Our clinical experience suggests that disclosing the ultimate goal that the therapist might have in mind for the last step will only lead to the child's ruminating about how anxiety arousing and impossible this will be; such ruminations prevent him/her from carrying out the current step in the treatment and making satisfactory progress (p. 9).

Clum and Watkins (2008) point out one of the problems with self-help materials is that readers have control over the "sequence" and can skip sections, discarding whatever sections they choose. They express concern that current evidence suggests that it is best to apply the most elements in the order that the self-help author considers critical. However, without research to define what is critical, such a concern, though understandable, may not have a solid basis, particularly if the therapist has included an "abundance" of steps. The case of the 7-year-old described in the previous section who got stuck is an example that suggests that there may be an advantage to allowing the child to skip sections. Also, if giving the child a sense of control over choice of the timing of the exposure reduces one of the demand factors, it may be advantageous from a safety standpoint. If a child is not allowed to go further, it may increase the child's frustration and sense of failure and lead to crying and negative emotions, which potentially adds stress to the parent–child interaction. In fact, Clum and Watkins (2008) point out that the less structured approach could ultimately be determined to have the best outcome and that such an approach will likely need to be determined on a case by case basis.

Approach 3: Read through the entire book once and then begin playing the games as you are reading through the book the second time. This approach allows for a greater impact of modeling on the child, but it may create the situation described above in which the child has more opportunity to think about (and possibly fear) the end task of sleeping alone in the dark. With this approach one still has to address the issue of whether to skip games or not to go further until one has successfully played a particular game.

Approach 4: Read through the entire book twice and then begin playing the games as you are reading through the book for the third time. This approach allows for the greatest impact of modeling because the child is able to experience the story several times before being asked to perform, possibly increasing the child's sense of "I can do that, too!" Also, in theory it is possible this approach may actually heighten motivation. Because most children want to play the games immediately, requiring the child to delay playing the games may build up suspense, excitement, and motivation. On the other hand, if Ost and Ollendick (1999) are correct in their belief related to one-session treatment that discussion of the end goal produces too much anxiety, one might expect that this would not be the most advantageous method of using the book. Currently, we have no such data on *Uncle Lightfoot* to suggest that reading to the end of the story is a problem. It may be that a child can better tolerate reading about someone else approaching the end goal (or quickly turn the page to control the exposure) in a book rather than facing it in real life. With this approach one must also decide whether to skip games that the child is not yet ready to play.

The 1987 edition was used with a severely fearful 10-year-old child (Figure 13.2) who had been afraid of the dark for 5 years. She had other nighttime fears as well. In fact, much of the child's nighttime fear appeared to center around other nighttime fears that often accompany fear of the dark (e.g., burglars, murderers, and kidnappers) that were not directly addressed in the 1987 edition of the book. On the BAT pre-test, the child scored 1, and on the BAT post-test the child scored 11 (out of a possible 12 items). In addition to an improvement on the self-efficacy scale (see Figure 13.2), the child went from an average of 13 disruptive behaviors per night to 3 behaviors per night. It took the child 22 fewer minutes to go to bed and to sleep on post-test than on pre-test. At pre-test the child rated her fear as 10 on a 1–10 scale, with 10 being a very severe problem. At post-test, the child rated the problem as a 5, suggesting that she was still fearful despite her improved ability to perform the exposure tasks, though not at the debilitating level she was at prior to the use of the book. As mentioned earlier, the child's fear of the dark was complicated by the presence of other nighttime fears.

Parents read the book through twice in its entirety before playing any of the games. Figure 3.3 suggests that well before in vivo exposure began the child had begun to feel more capable (and likely less anxious about) going into dark situations. Although the family moved to another house just prior to completing the second reading of the book, the move did not seem to impact the fear very much. A 6-month follow-up indicated that the child had made some additional gains over post-test scores on the WICDAN (i.e., score of 17).

Massed versus spaced. A separate dosage-related issue is whether to use spaced or massed practice. In other words, should the parent "administer" the book in 20 minutes sessions, 3 days a week or 5 days a week? Or, would it be more effective for the parent to spend as much time as the child's attention might allow (e.g., an hour or even longer reading and playing the games if the child's attention permits because the chapters are short and most chapters include a game for the child). Is it better to have the parent read one chapter a night, or would it be better for the parent to read as many chapters at one time as the child's developmental level and attention span will allow? Several researchers (e.g., Davis III, Ollendick, & Ost, 2009) have indicated that in terms of one-session-treatment with adults "180 minutes of OST has been found to be comparable in treatment gains to 300 minutes of spaced sessions

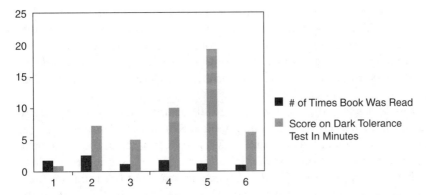

Figure 13.3   Improvement & Group Type. 1 = Coping Book Only-D; 2 = Mastery Book Only-D; 3 = Mastery with Games-D; 4 = Coping + Games-D; 5 = Coping + Games & Tangible Rewards-F; 6 = Coping + Games-F. Unpublished data from Mikulas et al., 1985, D = Daylon; F = Frayne.

of exposure or cognitive therapy (e.g., Ost, Alm, Brandberg, & Breitholtz, 2001)" (p. 19). Does this hold true for children using a bibliotherapy approach?

Length of children's book. One issue that impacts dosage is the length of the book, and this should be determined by therapeutic need, not by marketing need. Many publishers seem to have rigid ideas about the length of books for younger children. The number "32" seems almost magical when it comes to book length. Does this mean that a child's attention automatically turns off when they arrive at the 32nd page? Or, is it that 32-pages have been found to be a financially rewarding number of pages (along with fitting the previous demands of an offset-press printing world) for the publisher? *Lightfoot*, the precursor to *Uncle Lightfoot*, almost met this demand, as it was 41 pages long. Unfortunately, it was not sufficiently therapeutic, at least not the way it was written. It certainly may be possible to write a 32-page book that will help children overcome a phobia, but it is highly unlikely that all phobias can be dealt with in such an expedited or lock-step manner, particularly when addressing complex phobias such as fear of the dark.

Of course, while book length should not be written in stone by publishers, it is important for authors to understand age differences and the need for the book to be developmentally appropriate. While it is true that the attention span of a 5-year-old limits the child's ability to listen to a lengthy book, it is possible to divide the book into chapters as long as each chapter has a satisfactory emotional ending that keeps the child wanting to continue reading on another night. Also, children often listen to parents reading to them from books that are several years above their own reading level. The identified problem and the bibliotherapeutic solution should be used to determine the number of pages in the books.

6. Maintain an appreciation for the potential complexities of modeling factors in the story. For fictional bibliotherapy, the main characters can model specific behaviors under a variety of circumstances. As the story plot develops in books written for children by regular child authors, failure stories are often followed by success stories. Such failure is often very important to the development of the character in the story. It seems intuitive that such portrayal of a struggle (combination of effort success and effort failure) would be very beneficial. In fact, there is no doubt that thousands of adults and children have benefited from models who struggle. However, one of the first things the first author learned from children during the *Uncle Lightfoot* research was the need to be careful about the portrayal of failure, at least with children ages 4–7.

Mastery versus coping. Two *Uncle Lightfoot* (1980) versions were originally created: a coping version and a mastery version. The coping version was similar to what earlier research (e.g., Kazdin, 1973; Meichenbaum, 1971) had suggested was the best model. The *Uncle Lightfoot* coping model was initially fearful, had an experience of failure, but eventually overcame the fear. The *Uncle Lightfoot* mastery model did not focus on descriptions of fearful emotions the child was having but rather focused on the difficulty of the task, which required some effort, but did not lead to failure.

Although early research suggested that coping models had advantages over mastery models, Bandura (1997) and others (Ginther & Roberts, 1983; Schunk & Hanson, 1985) have questioned assumptions regarding the superiority of coping models over mastery models. Also, when clinicians (e.g., Ost and Ollendick, 1999) use a therapist to model approach behaviors, the approach "model" or "therapist" does not act afraid or talk about being afraid. There is certainly the possibility that a non-fearful model could create cognitive-dissonance within a child (e.g., "the child in the story says this is not scary but I think it is scary"), which may lead to their rejection of the mastery model or a possible lessening of self-efficacy feelings.

In the 1980 coping and mastery versions there was a game that involved the child lying in bed in the dark on three separate occasions in the book. The second episode with the game involved the child in the story experiencing failure in the coping book, and some of the children seemed to have an immediate decrease in length of time they would remain in the dark after this section of the book was read to them. However, because of the severity of the children's problems, in essentially all of the cases the amount of time spent in the dark did not go below the baseline level, but for a number of the children affected by the scene, the time did not return to the level it had reached previously. Although as a group, children receiving the coping book along with parental instructions to play the games scored a little higher on dark tolerance than the mastery group, when instructions were not provided, children using the mastery model both with and without instructions scored higher than children using the coping without instructions book.

Knowing that some parents may not read instructions or that the child may read the book alone, does this mean it is safer to use a mastery model? Because of the small number of fearful children examined in these two experiments it is unclear how to interpret these clinical results (e.g., Figure 13.3). However, some researchers (Field, Lawson, & Banerjee, 2008), following the work of earlier theoreticians (e.g., Rachman, 1991), have suggested a possible mechanism for modeling by pointing out that modeling (or vicarious learning) can be considered associative learning. As such, it is understandable that one must exercise caution in the use of failure scenes.

On the other hand, perhaps the failure scene was helpful to children whose parents did not report a problem with the game after reading about the failure scene. In fact, according to the theoretical underpinnings of intensive one-session treatment (Ost & Ollendick, 1999), it is desirable to have the child's fear level heightened so that the fear response can be fully activated and extinction can take place during the exposure. If that is true, it is possible that the coping version may be the most optimal version. It should be noted that we do not recall that parents in any of the groups reported crying episodes during any of the previous studies on *Uncle Lightfoot*, even with the use of the coping version. Although crying and other signs of visible distress are often considered a "normal" part of exposure therapy for children (Ost & Ollendick, 1999), the guiding approach taken in *Uncle Lightfoot* is for the bibliotherapy experience to be as positive as possible.

Addressing the coping versus mastery issue is complicated by the fact that there were insufficient approach skills taught by the games. Now that additional safety features as well as a number of intermediate behavior approach tasks have been added, it would be important to compare the 2012 edition (a blended approach, with an emphasis on mastery) with the 1980 coping edition (with updated pictures and additional games added to the older coping version). It may well be that a coping model would yield superior results without the negative effects given that the games themselves have been modified and the number of games increased, providing a slower, step-wise progression through a series of graded behavior approach tasks. This would also provide a useful test of whether, as one-session therapy suggests, that it is beneficial for the child to experience anxiety in the presence of the stimuli so that extinction can occur.

The issue of personality characteristics, fearfulness, as well as failure experiences by the main character are among the most interesting, necessary, and potentially fruitful issues in the development of fictional bibliotherapy for children. The following questions need consideration:

- How fearful should the model be?
- How much should the model "struggle" with the problem being addressed?
- Should the focus be on the fearfulness of the child or on the difficulty of the task?
- What personality characteristics are better for the child model in the story?
- Is failure useful? If so, how much failure?
- How often should the model experience difficulty or failure?
- How are children of different ages affected by failure scenes?
- How do personality factors (e.g., extroversion, introversion) impact or mitigate failure scenes?

Other issues relevant to modeling. There are a number of other issues related to the child model portrayed in the story, with some research addressing model characteristics (Schunk, 1985). However, the research needs to be specific to the medium used. Much of the previous research on model characteristics has focused on videotaped models, not models in the printed material of a children's book. Also, although some research (e.g., Ramsey, 1989) has suggested a preference for realistic artwork over cartoons as children grow older, the effect of specific styles of artwork on children is an area of bibliotherapy that beckons much more research.

In several of our earlier studies (Mikulas & Coffman, 1989) effects related to demographic variables were not apparent. However, with larger sample sizes, such differences may become evident. When Coffman revised the book in 1987, she tried to expand the book's application to a wider age range. There are currently two versions, one for ages 4–7 and one for ages 7–10. The books overlap for the age of 7 as this seems to be a transitional age that could utilize either edition, depending on such factors as attention span and cognitive ability. Comparisons need to be made between the two age groups using the two different versions to better define age recommendations (e.g., in Santacruz et al.'s (2006) study, children as old as 8 years successfully used a version originally designed for ages 4–7). In terms of the 1980–1983 versions, the two children in the story were white males, although parental feedback indicated that females in the study enjoyed the story and benefited as well. In 1987, the story included two males, with the addition of a female Creek Indian girl who was severely sight impaired. The reason for adding a blind child to the plot was simply because blind children are "experts" on coping with darkness. During the 1987 rewrite of *Uncle Lightfoot*, the author visited a school for the blind to observe these experts who so effectively cope with darkness on a daily basis. For the most recent version, the friend of the main character was drawn as an African-American male in the hopes of enhancing modeling effects for non-white children. The success of the earlier *Uncle Lightfoot* book with an Hispanic population (Santacruz et al., 2006) suggests that the book may have cross-cultural application, but further research is needed in this area as well.

   7. **Maximize the use of the principles of reinforcement, which include vicarious reinforcement, social reinforcement, and tangible reinforcement in the development of bibliotherapy materials.** There are several ways of using rewards in a fictional bibliotherapy approach. The main characters in the story can be praised by other characters in the story when they succeed as they seek to overcome a problem – or can receive tangible rewards during the story, thus providing vicarious reinforcement for the child listening to the story. The original *Uncle Lightfoot* (1980) provided opportunities for children to observe the main character being rewarded verbally (i.e., praise) during the story and in one place the child in the story received a toy. Another component of the current edition (as well as the 1987 version) is that the child in the story earns rewards for lying in bed for increasing amounts of time. In addition, the *Parent Guidebook* encourages the parent, when possible, to use tangible rewards as modeled in the book to optimize the chances of success. Tangible rewards in the book as well as the parent's use of rewards with the child can function as powerful motivators for many children. However, it is not known whether or not this is actually necessary for most children. Tangible rewards (in which the parents were asked to use beads to reinforce specific approach behaviors) were only used with one of our previous groups in the earlier studies (Mikulas & Coffman, 1989), and while the rewards seemed to contribute to greater clinical success compared to using the materials without the rewards, a number of other children did, in fact, improve without such rewards when using the earlier versions.

   The later group studies (Mikulas & Coffman, 1989) did not use tangible rewards because it was (a) likely that some parents would not use rewards even if they were recommended and (b) because we wanted to make sure the use of rewards did not camouflage the need to improve on items for the story's hierarchy. The 1987 edition added another reward for bravery in the storyline itself. One of the advantages of the use of tangible rewards is that it helps provide additional motivation, while still allowing the child to make the decision as to whether or not they want to engage in an approach behavior. The use of tangible rewards may help the parent focus on positive approach behaviors rather than on fearful behaviors and thus may decrease the likelihood the parent will reward the child with attention for fearful behavior. One option is to use a character in which more "courageous" actions are modeled, without any reinforcement given. Self-reinforcement for courageous actions may actually be more desirable, but for younger children the use of tangible rewards may be more beneficial.

8. Include instructions for using bibliotherapy materials that are parent-friendly and address the issues and concerns that the parent may have. The early studies compared the use of the materials with and without parent instructions. Although the sample size was too small to reach statistical conclusions, clinically it appeared that parents were more likely to play the games when they were given specific instructions to do so. Providing instructions to parents, in addition to informing them "how to" accomplish desired behaviors, allows the clinician to address safety issues to the extent possible. The authors have immense respect for the common sense and wisdom of the majority of parents. However, parents, like therapists, are human and make mistakes. During the early research it became clear that once in a while a parent could simply misunderstand a written instruction or could make an error in judgment, despite the well-intentioned instructions included with the book. One example is the case of a parent who kept insisting that a child play one of the approach games despite the specific written instructions "do not force your child" (Mikulas & Coffman, 1989). It would be difficult, if not impossible, to create a totally fail-proof system in which no errors are made in carrying out a therapeutic program. However, this holds true for therapist-directed programs, just as it does for parent-driven self-help materials.

It is also true that therapy, even under the direction of a trained, highly experienced therapist, is a fluid, evolving and at times unpredictable process. Each child and each parent is unique, and it is not possible to totally anticipate each person's reactions to instructions. Nevertheless, the bibliotherapy writer should attempt to make the therapeutic process as clear as possible in the parent instructions so that understanding will be enhanced.

Santacruz et al. (2006) supplemented the *Uncle Lightfoot* group and their own play therapy group with therapist-directed group education training sessions, but it is unclear how this impacted the two groups. However, all of the other group experiments with *Uncle Lightfoot* used the materials alone, without additional parent training. The early versions contained only a few pages of directions whereas the 2012 version contains a much more detailed parent guidebook. A future edition could include a CD/DVD with clips demonstrating techniques, should further research suggest the need. During the revision process for the 1987 edition changes were made to make the book as parent-friendly as possible. For example, several safety concerns were briefly addressed in the text of the story to make sure parents did not overlook them in the parent manual.

9. As has been pointed out in reference to the development of therapy pro-grams (e.g., Hayes et al., 1999), once the initial development work is completed for the specific bibliotherapy materials, then it is important to facilitate an understanding of the relative effects of the individual components and also to encourage comparisons with other treatment approaches. The primary initial effort is to create a book that is maximally effective for a particular problem with a particular group of children, even though the book may contain some "unnecessary" components. Once one has indications of success in enhancing efficacy and approach behaviors, the next question is why or how the bibliotherapy works? It would be as helpful to understand the relative contribution of the various components in bibliotherapy as it is in traditional therapy. In fact, bibliotherapy is potentially a useful vehicle for testing theories about which components work and why, because the material can be easily deleted from the book for comparisons. In traditional therapy, the client– therapist interaction is often so fluid that it is difficult at times to isolate variables. Bibliotherapy is inherently a cognitive approach, and because of this, it provides a vehicle through which one can test a variety of theoretical positions. For example, would it be possible to clarify some of the issues in the debate as to whether CBT is as effective as behavior therapy alone by trying to operationalize some of the differences between these two theoretical camps and incorporating them into a story (e.g., Uncle Lightfoot) for comparisons?

Of course, "more" is not always "better" in terms of components. An older study (Ollendick, Hagopian, & Huntzinger, 1991) as well as one recent study (Vande Voort, Svecova, Jacobsen, & Whiteside, 2010) found that exposure alone was superior to exposure combined with such components as cognitive restructuring with young children. For that reason, it would be useful to compare *Uncle Lightfoot, The Path to Bravery: Overcoming Fear of the Dark* (in press), which has a strong focus on cognitive restructuring and cognitive training in addition to exposure, with the shorter version, *Uncle Lightfoot, Flip That Switch: Overcoming Fear of the Dark* (2012), that is primarily focused on exposure.

In addition to component studies, there are several other studies that would contribute to our understanding of fiction as bibliotherapy as it relates to childhood anxieties in general and childhood phobias in particular. First, it would be useful to compare the fictional to non-fictional bibliotherapy approach (e.g., a fictitious book such as *Uncle Lightfoot: Overcoming Fear of the Dark* compared to a non-fiction book such as *What to Do When You Dread Your Bed*). How do these two different book approaches affect a child's nighttime behaviors, from fear of the dark to behavioral problems or sleep problems? What long-term effects does a particular approach have? In addition to randomized studies, it would be helpful to incorporate a single subject reversal ABAC design with multiple subjects (e.g., Read a general story for first three weeks; institute *Dread the Bed*, reinstitute the baseline story, and then switch to *Uncle Lightfoot* and vice versa) to determine whether there might be a facilitory effect or an additive effect if a clinician were to use first one book approach and then the other. The more knowledge a clinician has about which bibliotherapy tools are available and how they might interact, the more likely the clinician is to engage in successful intervention with children.

Secondly, it would be important to compare the same children's story in written form to those packaged in other forms, such as animated versions, audio-only, DVDs, and computer software. Clum and Watkins (2008) point out that at the current time, no study has been conducted that actually examines different approaches to presenting the same self-help materials. This is a much needed area of research.

Thirdly, since individual treatment and group treatment are generally considered the "gold standard" for treatment, it would be useful to compare a fictional approach such as *Uncle Lightfoot* with effective therapist-directed treatments for anxiety and phobia disorders (e.g., one-session intensive treatment or Coping Cat).

10. Be aware of the potential for generalization and innoculation effects in developing bibliotherapy materials. In terms of fiction, can a book such as *Uncle Lightfoot*, designed for fear of the dark, inoculate the child against other fears or problems through a process of generalization? As a result of reading the book, will the child be able to address other fears or problems, using the cognitive-behavioral techniques contained in the book? Graziano and Mooney (1982) completed a follow-up of therapist-treated nighttime phobic children, ages 6–13, and found that 59% of the 34 parents felt that the "child's successful experience of having solved or significantly decreased their long and severe nighttime fear problems seemed to have helped them become generally more 'confident' in facing problems" (p. 598). This effect was also found in a recent trial of one session treatment (Ollendick, Ost, Reuterskiold et al., 2009) and was attributed to a sense of self-efficacy and mastery over the fear. The issue of generalization has some support in the use of *Uncle Lightfoot* with a 10-year-old whose major presenting problem was separation anxiety (Figure 13.4).

Six months earlier the child's step-father had died, and the child had extreme anxiety about being separated from his mother when at school. Over a 2-month period, he cried so frequently at school that he was spending most of the day in the counselor's office. The school counselor reported having unsuccessfully attempted a "cognitive approach." Because a separation issue is often involved in fear of the dark (i.e., child learning to sleep in own bed instead of with parent), and because the child also had a mild fear of the dark, the clinician asked the child to read *Uncle Lightfoot* (1987), the precursor to *Uncle Lightfoot, The Path to Bravery*, and to identify ways in which the child could apply the techniques in the book to the school separation anxiety problem. The child was seen for four sessions. Within 8 weeks of his first session, the child's crying episodes had ceased totally and he was able to spend the entire day in his classroom. A follow-up was conducted a year later and the problem had not reoccurred. Although no baseline data were collected (and other variables may have influenced the outcome as well), clinically it seemed that the adjunct use of the book was helpful, and it suggests the possibility that the materials may be used

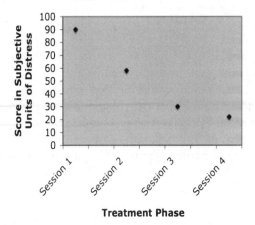

Figure 13.4 Performance of 10-year-old child with separation anxiety after receiving Uncle Lightfoot materials with instructions to use approach for separation issues. The higher the score, the more the distress or anxiety. Range: 0-100.

as an adjunct to the treatment of problems other than nighttime fears and within a traditional therapeutic context.

There are other ways in which stories, both fiction and non-fiction, might provide inoculation. Consider the case of an elementary school student who is an avid reader of biographies. Will reading a variety of biographies of people such as the Mayo brothers, Dwight Eisenhower, Madame Curie, and George Washington Carver – or even sports heroes like Willie Mays or Jackie Robinson – contribute to persistence in the child's own personality and character when the child faces major obstacles? This would be an interesting area for longitudinal research.

Can bibliotherapeutic interventions create self-efficacy feelings similar to immune system antibodies circulating in the system, generating an "I can do it" attitude that will be available when dealing with other problems or a reoccurrence of the targeted problem? Or, by allowing the child to read about a particular problem, will it prevent a potentially more difficult problem from developing, as suggested early on by Darling (1947):

> The obvious analogy here is with the inoculation to prevent the contagious disease. A little vicarious injection of experience with a problem in a book is to prevent a hard case of this same kind of experience in the young reader's development. (p. 293)

It should be noted that when a component analysis is completed, it may be possible to shorten the bibliotherapy book by removing some components. However, although component analysis is important, one must be careful not to prematurely "throw the baby out with the bath water" for several reasons. First, in some cases, components may be inert when used alone, but make a significant contribution when used in conjunction with another or several other components. Secondly, components that do not benefit the child immediately may, in fact, prove to be "active" ingredients when viewed longitudinally, at least for future problems the child may encounter. For example, the 1980–1983 editions contained relaxation techniques taught through the puppet game. Feedback from those studies as well as from Santacruz and colleagues (2006) indicated that this was the least liked game. In fact, Santacruz et al. suggested that relaxation "does not seem to be an especially suitable procedure for specific phobias in young children" (p. 31).

Although the author of *Uncle Lightfoot* considered removing the puppet game, she decided to modify the game instead of removing the relaxation techniques totally for several reasons. First, component testing had not been performed to determine its usefulness. Secondly, the fact that the children did not like the game as much as other games did not mean that relaxation techniques were not useful or that they did not contribute in some way. The inclusion of the game, even if it did not contribute immediately, might, as information, be useful in an inoculation sense and be used later on in anxiety-producing situations, especially given that some children did in fact like the game. Fourth, researchers (e.g., Ollendick & Cerny, 1981; Powers & Andrasik, 2005) have found relaxation techniques to be useful in addressing a number of problems experienced by children. Because of these issues, instead of deleting the puppet game, the author modified it (e.g., the puppet game became the droopy dog game) to make it potentially more appealing to children. Also, added instructions encouraged parents of younger children (or those who do not like the game) to simply skip this game if the child did not want to play it. This allows the child to hear and learn about the techniques, which could be potentially useful later on in terms of innoculation, without having to use the techniques as part of the program. Also, it is possible to remove this game from either or both versions of the book should future research confirm its lack of effectiveness. It is important not to prematurely delete components.

Conclusion

Stories, both fiction and non-fiction, are potential vehicles to provide therapeutic interventions in a cost-effective and more accessible manner. Longer than there have been books, there have been stories. In fact, one author has described humans as the "story species" (Gold, 2002). Fictional bibliotherapy may prove to be a very enjoyable and effective way for children to learn cognitive-behavioral skills, particularly those children with phobic and anxiety issues. Although hundreds of fictional books have been written with the goal of helping children with specific problems, there is much work to be done to develop the artistic and scientific principles underlying such a genre.

References

Bandura, A. (1997). *Self-Efficacy: the Exercise of Control*. New York: W. H. Freeman and Company.

Barlow, D. H., Hayes, S. C., & Nelson, R. O. (1984). *The Scientist Practitioner*. New York: Pergamon Press.

Bouchard, S., Mendlowitz, S. L., Coles, M. E., & Franklin, M. (2004). Considerations in the use of exposure with children. *Cognitive and Behavioral Practice, 11,* 56–65.

Bourgeosis, P. (1987). *Franklin in the Dark*. New York: Scholastic Paperbacks.

Campbell, L. F., & Smith, T. P. (2003). Integrating self-help books into psychother-apy. *Journal of Clinical Psychology/In Session: Psychotherapy in Practice, 59,* 177–186. doi/10.1001/jclp.10140

Canfield, J., & Hendricks, G. (with Kline, C.) (2006). *You've Got to Read This Book!; 55 People Tell the Story of the Book That Changed Their Life*. New York: Harpercollins.

Carner, C. (1966, December). Reaching troubled minds through reading. *Today's Health,* 75–76.

Chamberlain, D., Heaps, D., & Robert, I. (2008). Bibliotherapy and information prescriptions: a summary of the published evidence base and recommendations from past and ongoing Books on Prescription projects. *Journal of Psychiatric and Mental Health Nursing, 15,* 24–36. doi/10.1111/j.1365-2850.2007.01201.x

Christ, J. J. (2004). *What to Do When You're Scared and Worried: A Guide for Kids*. Minneapolis, MN: Free Spirit Publishing Inc.

Clum, G. A., & Watkins, P. L. (2008). Self-help therapies: Retrospect and prospsect. In P. L. Watkins, & G. A. Clum (Eds.), *Handbook of Self-Help Therapies* (pp. 419–436). New York: Routledge.

Coffman, M. F. (1973). *Lightfoot*. Unpublished manuscript.

Coffman, M. F. (1975). The use of desensitization, modeling, and emotive imagery in children's books for the reduction of fears. Master's Thesis. Pensacola, Florida: University of West Florida.

Coffman, M. F. (1980–1983). *Uncle Lightfoot*. Unpublished manuscript.

Coffman, M. F. (1987). *Uncle Lightfoot*. Unpublished manuscript.

Coffman, M.F. (1987). What I think I can do at night. Unpublished instrument.

Coffman, M. F. (2012). *Uncle Lightfoot, Flip That Switch: Overcoming Fear of the Dark*. Charleston, SC: Footpath Press.

Coffman, M. F. (in press). *Uncle Lightfoot, the Path to Bravery: Overcoming Fear of the Dark*. Charleston, SC: Footpath Press.

Coffman, M. F., & Huebner, D. (1993). *Data on response of 7-year-old dark-phobic child to Uncle Lightfoot materials*. Unpublished data.

Costello, D. (1981). Behavioral bibliotherapy and the treatment of childhood fear of the dark. Master's Thesis. Pensacola: University of West Florida.

Darling, R. L. (1947). Mental hygiene and books. *Wilson Library Bulletin, 32*, 293–296.

Davis III, T. E., Ollendick, T. H., & Ost, L.-G. (2009). Intensive treatment of specific phobias in children and adolescents. *Cognitive and Behavioral Practice, 16*, 294–303.

Duke, P., & Hochman, G. (1992). *A Brilliant Madness: Living with Manic Depressive Illness*. New York: Bantam Books.

Elgar, F. J., & McGrath, P. J. (2008). Self-help therapies for childhood disorders. In P. L. Watkins, & G. A. Clum (Eds.), *Handbook of Self-Help Therapies*. New York: Routledge.

Ellis, A. (1999). *How to Make Yourself Happy and Remarkably Less Disturbable*. Atascadero, CA: Impact Publishers, Inc.

Field, A. P., Lawson, J., & Banerjee, R. (2008). The verbal threat information pathway to fear in children: The longitudinal effects on fear cognitions and the immediate effects on avoidance behavior. *Journal of Abnormal Psychology, 117*, 214–224.

Frank, J. (1948). Books and children's emotions. *Child Study, 26*, 24–26.

Frayne, C. (1981). Reinforced practice of in vivo desensitization skills in conjunction with the use of a children's book to reduce fears. Master's Thesis. Pensacola, Florida: University of West Florida.

Frost, J. (1847). *The Book of Good Examples; Drawn from Authentic History and Biography; Designed to Illustrate the Benefits of Virtuous Conduct*. New York: D. Appleton & Co. Retrieved from http://books.google.com

Ginther, L. J., & Roberts, M. C. (1983). A test of mastery versus coping models in the reduction of children's dental fears. *Child and Family Behavior Therapy, 4*, 41–52.

Gold, J. (2002). *The Story Species: Our Life-Literature Connection*. Allston, MA: Fitzhenry & Whiteside.

Gordon, J., King, N. J., Gullone, E., Muris, P., & Ollendick, T. (2007a). Nighttime fears of children and adolescents: Frequency, content severity, harm expectations, disclosure, and coping behaviours. *Behaviour Research and Therapy, 45*, 2464–2472.

Gordon, J., King, N. J., Gullone, E., Muris, P., & Ollendick, T. H. (2007b). Treatment of children's nighttime fears: The need for a modern randomised controlled trial. *Clinical Psychology Review, 27*, 98–113.

Gould, R. A., & Clum, G. A. (1993). A meta-analysis of self-help treatment approaches. *Clinical Psychology Review, 13*, 169–186.

Grant, G. (2000). Preface. In T. Roosevelt, & H. C. Lodge, (Eds.), *Hero Tales: How Common Lives Reveal the Heroic Spirit of America*. Nashville: Cumberland House Publishing, Inc.

Graziano, A. M., & Mooney, K. C. (1982). Behavioral Treatment of "nightfears" in children: Maintenance of improvement at $2^{1}/_{2}$- to 3-year follow-up. *Journal of Consulting and Clinical Psychology, 50*, 598–599.

Hahlweg, K., Heinrichs, N., Kuschel, A., & Feldmann, M. (2008). Therapist-assisted, self-administered bibliotherapy to enhance parental competence: Short-and long-term effects. *Behavior Modification, 32*, 659–681. doi: 10.1177/0145445508317131

Hayes, S. C., Barlow, D. H., & Nelson-Gray, R. O. (1999). *The Scientist-Practitioner: Research and Accountability in the Age of Managed Care*. Boston: Allyn & Bacon.

Henson, J. (2001). *Don't Be Afraid of the Dark: Bear in the Big Blue House*. New York: Simon & Schuster Children's Publishing Division.

Hirai, M., & Clum, G. A. (2006). A meta-analytic study of self-help interventions for anxiety problems. *Behavior Therapy, 37,* 99–111.

Hirshfeld-Baker, D. R., Masek, B., Henin, A., Blakely, L. R., Pollock-Wurman, R. A., McQuade, J., Biederman, J. (2010). Cognitive behavioral therapy for 4- to 7-year-old children with anxiety disorders: A randomized clinical trial. *Journal of Consulting and Clinical Psychology, 78,* 498–510.

Hvolby, A., Jorgensen, J., & Bilenberg, N. (2008). Sleep and sleep difficulties in Danish children aged 6–11 years]. *Ugeskr Laeger, 170,* 448–51. Abstract retrieved from http://www.ncbi.nlm.nih.gov./pubmed/18252179

Huebner, D. (2006). *What to Do When You Worry Too Much*. Washington, DC: Magination Press.

Huebner, D. (2008). *What to Do When You Dread Your Bed*. Washington, DC: Magination Press.

Jamison, K. R. (1996). *An Unquiet Mind*. New York: Vintage Books.

Kazdin, A. E. (1973). Covert modeling and the reduction of avoidance behavior. *Journal of Abnormal Psychology, 81,* 87–95.

Kendall, P. C., Hudson, J. L., Gosch, E., Flannery-Schoeder, E., & Suveg, C. (2008). Cognitive-behavioral therapy for anxiety disordered youth: A randomized clinical trial evaluating child and family modalities. *Journal of Consulting and Clinical Psychology, 76,* 282–297.

Leaf, M. (1949). *Boo Who Used to Be Afraid of the Dark*. New York: Random House.

Mains, J. A., & Scogin, F. R. (2003). The effectiveness of self-administered treatments: A practice-friendly review of the research. *Journal of Clinical Psychology, 59,* 237–246.

Meichenbaum, D. H. (1971). Examination of model characteristics in reducing avoidance behavior. *Journal of Personality and Social Psychology, 17,* 298–307.

Mikulas, W. L., & Coffman, M. F. (1989). Home-based treatment of children's fear of the dark. In S. E. Schaefer, & J. M. Briesmeister (Eds.), *Handbook of Parent Training: Parents as Co-therapists for Children's Behavior Problems* (pp. 179–202). New York: John Wiley & Sons, Ltd.

Mikulas, W. L., Coffman, M. F., Dayton, D. C., Frayne, C., & Maier, P. L. (1985). Behavioral bibliotherapy and games for treating fear of the dark. *Child and Family Behavior Therapy, 7,* 1–7.

Muris, P., Merckelbach, H., Ollendick, T. H., King, N. J., & Bogie, N. (2001). Children's nighttime fears: Parent–child ratings of frequency, content, origins, coping behaviors and severity. *Behavior Research and Therapy, 39,* 13–28.

Oliver, J. R. (1928). *Fear: The Autobiography of James Edwards*. New York: The MacMillan Co.

Ollendick, T. H. (1983). Reliability and validity of the Revised Fear Survey Schedule for Children (FSSC-R), *Behaviour Research and Therapy, 21,* 685–692.

Ollendick, T. H., & Cerny, J. A. (1981). *Clinical Behavior Therapy with Children*. New York: Plenum Press.

Ollendick, T. H., Hagopian, L. P., & Huntzinger, R. M. (1991). Cognitive-behavior therapy with nighttime fearful children. *Journal of Behavior Therapy and Experimental Psychiatry, 22,* 113–121.

Ollendick, T. H., Jarrett, M. A., Grills-Taquechel, A. E., Hovey, L. D., & Wolff, J. C. (2008). Comorbidity as a predictor and moderator of treatment outcome in youth with anxiety, affective, attention deficit/hyperactivity disorder, and oppositional/conduct disorder. *Clinical Psychology Review, 28,* 1447–1471.

Ollendick, T. H., Ost, L.-G., Reuterskiold, L., Costa, N., Cederlund, R., Sirbu, C., Thompson, T. E. III., & Jarrett, M. A. (2009). One-session treatment of specific phobias in youth: A randomized clinical trial in the United States and Sweden. *Journal of Consulting and Clinical Psychology, 77,* 504–516.

Orgiles, M., Espada, J. P., & Mendez, X. (2008). Assessment instruments of darkness phobia in children and adolescents: A descriptive review. *International Journal of Clinical and Health Psychology, 8,* 315–333. http://redalyc.uaemex.mx/pdf/337/33780120/pdf

Ost, L.-G., & Ollendick, T. H. (1999). *Manual for the One Session Treatment (OST) of Specific Phobias in Children and Adolescents.*

Otto, M., Pollack, M. H., & Maki, K. M. (2001). Empirically supported treatments for panic disorder. *Journal of Consulting and Clinical Psychology, 68,* 556–563.

Podell, J. L., Mychailyszyn, M., Edmunds, J., Puleo, C. M., & Kendall, P. C. (2010). The coping cat program for anxious youth: The FEAR plan comes to life. *Cognitive and Behavioral Practice, 17,* 132–141.

Powers, S. W., & Andrasik, F. (2005). Biobehavioral treatment, disability, and psychological effects of pediatric headaches. *Pediatric Annals, 34,* 461–481.

Rachman, S. (1991). Neo-conditioning and the classical theory of fear acquisition. *Clinical Psychology Review, 11,* 155–173.

Ramsey, I. L. (1989). An investigation of children's verbal response to selected art styles. *Journal of Educational Research, 83,* 46–51.

Rapee, R. M., Abbott, M. J., Lyneham, H. J. (2006). Bibliotherapy materials for children with anxiety disorders using written materials for parents: A randomized controlled trial. *Journal of Consulting and Clinical Psychology, 74,* 436–444.

Rapee, R. M. Spence, S. H., Cobham, V., & Wignall, A. M. (2000). *Helping Your Anxious Child: a Step-By-Step Guide for Parents.* Oakland, CA: New Harbinger Publications.

Richardson, R., Richards, D. A., & Barkham, M. (2010). Self-help books for people with depression: the role of the therapeutic relationship. *Behavioural and Cognitive Psychotherapy, 38,* 67–81.

Roosevelt, T. (1920). *Theodore Roosevelt: An Autobiography.* New York: Charles Scribner's Sons.

Roosevelt, T., & Lodge, H. C. (1891). *Hero Tales: How Common Lives Reveal the Heroic Spirit of America.* Nashville, TN: Cumberland House Publishing.

Rosen, G. M., Barrera, J. M., & Glasgow, R. E. (2008). Good intentions are not enough: Reflections on past and future efforts to advance self-help. In P. L. Watkins, & G. A. Clum (Eds.), *Handbook of Self-Help Therapies* (pp. 25–39). New York: Routledge.

Santacruz, I., Mendez, F. J., & Sanchez-Meca, J. (2006). Play therapy applied by parents for children with darkness phobia: Comparison of two programmes. *Child & Family Behavior Therapy, 28,* 19–34. http://dx.doi.org/10.1300/J019v28n01_02

Schunk, D. H. (1987). Peer models and children's behavioral change. *Review of Educational Research, 57,* 149–174.

Schunk, D. H., & Hanson, A. R. (1985). Peer models: Influence on children's self-efficacy and achievement. *Journal of Educational Psychology, 77,* 313–322. doi: 10.1037/0022-0663.77.3.313

Silverman, W. K., & Albano, A. M. (1996). *Anxiety Disorders Interview Schedule – Child Parent Interview Schedule.* Graywind Publications.

Starker, S. (1989). *Oracle at the Supermarket.* New Brunswick, NJ: Transaction Publishers.

Vande Voort, J. L., Svecova, J., Jacobson, A. B., & Whiteside, S. P. (2010). A retrospective examination of the s imilarity between clinical practice and manualized treatment for childhood anxiety disorders. *Cognitive and Behavioral Practice, 17,* 322–328.

Watkins, P. L. (2008). Self-help therapies: Past and present. In P. L. Watkins, & G. A. Clum (Eds.), *Handbook of Self-Help Therapies* (pp. 1–24). New York: Routledge, Taylor & Francis Group.

Watkins, P. L., & Clum, G. A. (Eds.). (2008). *Handbook of Self-Help Therapies.* New York: Routledge.

Wolpe, J. (1958). *Psychotherapy by Reciprocal Inhibition.* Stanford: Stanford University Press.

14

Separation Anxiety Disorder

Silvia Schneider[1] and Kristen L. Lavallee[2]

[1]University of Bochum, Germany
[2]University of Basel, Switzerland

Separation anxiety is a developmentally typical social phenomenon, emerging in healthy attachment relationships between babies and their caregivers between 7 and 12 months, peaking at 15–18 months, and serving the adaptive purpose of protecting the child from danger (Sroufe, 1997). The atypical continuation of strong and prolonged separation anxiety into the preschool and school years, however, is an indicator that the child–parent dyad has not successfully facilitated the developmental task of mastering the child's early fear and moving toward individuation (Havighurst, 1952). In cases of separation anxiety disorder (SAD), extreme anxiety can cause significant impairment in daily living (children with SAD are often not able to attend kindergarten or school, have trouble sleeping alone, staying with a babysitter, or even being in a room alone in the house), as well as continue to disrupt and delay the developmental process of individuation.

The central feature of SAD is unrealistic and excessive anxiety upon separation or anticipation of separation from major attachment figures. This anxiety is often characterized by worries that harm will befall the self (e.g., getting kidnapped, becoming ill at school, etc.) and/or major attachment figures (e.g. parents will not come back, will be involved in a car accident, etc.) upon separation. When separated from major attachment figures, the child with SAD often feels a need to know his or her whereabouts and to stay in touch with them via frequent telephone calls or other modes of communication. Physical symptoms are also reported in approximately 30–50% of cases, depending on informant (Allen, Lavallee, Herren, Ruhe, & Schneider, 2010), and include headaches, stomachaches, nausea, or even vomiting when separation from major attachment figures occurs or is anticipated. Repeated complaints about physical symptoms may necessitate medical clarification. Children may display oppositional behavior when separation avoidance is not possible (e.g. screaming, temper tantrums). Younger children may be unable to stay in a room by themselves and may display "clinging" behavior, staying close to or "shadowing" the parent around the house. Further, although less common, repeated nightmares involving the theme of

The Wiley-Blackwell Handbook of The Treatment of Childhood and Adolescent Anxiety, First Edition.
Edited by Cecilia A. Essau and Thomas H. Ollendick.
© 2013 John Wiley & Sons, Ltd. Published 2013 by John Wiley & Sons, Ltd.

separation may be present. Diagnosis of SAD using the *Diagnostic and Statistical Manual* (DSM-IV) currently requires at least three out of eight separation-related symptoms, causing both (1) significant interference in social and academic functioning and (2) continuous disturbance for at least 1 month.

Studies of children with school refusal and comorbid SAD indicate that dysfunctional family patterns are present in the families of these children (King & Bernstein, 2001). These families seem to have a low degree of cohesion (i.e., members are often disengaged from one another) and adaptability, presenting as highly rigid and inflexible (Bernstein, Warren, Massie, & Thuras, 1999), with extremity related to increased child pathology and somatization. Further research indicates that children with anxiety disorders tend to have families which are less accepting and autonomy-granting (Siqueland, Kendall, & Steinberg, 1996), less sociable and supportive, and more conflictual and enmeshed (Stark, Humphrey, Crook, & Lewis, 1990) than families of children without anxiety disorders. The existing literature provides considerable evidence that in general, parental over-control, and to lesser extent a rejecting family environment, is associated with elevated child anxiety levels (Bogels & Brechman-Toussaint, 2006; Rapee, 1997). In addition, parents' own dysfunctional cognitions are elevated and parenting self-efficacy and satisfaction diminished in parents of children with SAD as compared with parents of healthy children. Parents of children with SAD also have lower self-efficacy than parents of children with social phobia (Herren, In-Albon, & Schneider, 2013).

Etiology and Maintenance

To date, no specific model for the development and maintenance of SAD has been published. However, general models of the etiology and maintenance of anxiety disorders in childhood shed light on SAD and point to directions for intervention. The behavioral inhibition–attachment and cognitive models both provide direction in understanding SAD, complement each other, and may be combined, as in the general anxiety model presented by Murray, Creswell and Cooper (2009) or in disorder specific models for other childhood anxiety disorders such as social anxiety disorder (Ollendick & Hirshfeld-Becker, 2002), to provide a more comprehensive and complete picture of SAD, which serves as the basis for intervention.

Early Vulnerability Models

Manassis and Bradley (1994), in their Behavioral Inhibition–Attachment Model, propose a set of factors contributing to anxiety disorders that includes an interplay between innate temperament, (encompassing genetic predispositions and behavioral inhibition) and insecure parent–child attachment stemming from the caregiver's own vulnerability, including his or her non-autonomous state of mind and attachment relationship with the child. They posit that extremes in either behaviorally-inhibited child temperament (Kagan, Snidman, & Arcus, 1998) or insecure attachment (Bowlby, 1973) can directly result in the development of childhood anxiety disorders. That is, children born with temperamental vulnerability to sympathetic arousal, and/or raised by an abusive, seriously depressed, or highly unpredictable parent, without access to effective emotion-coping strategies for managing situations that elicit attachment behavior (i.e. threatening situations such as separation), may develop chronic anxiety. In addition, both behavioral inhibition and the attachment relationship impact the child's internal working model, and result in dysfunctional cognitions, diminished coping skills, and subsequent interpersonal experiences, which, over time, can also result in an anxiety disorder. Contributing to this process over time are cognitive maturation, developmental events, and traumatic events. Tempering the effects of attachment, are relationships with others.

In a separate model of the development and maintenance of generalized anxiety disorder (GAD), which may also provide direction in understanding SAD, Rapee (2001) outlines an unfolding of similar factors in the etiology of anxiety, asserting that parental pathology – specifically parental anxiety – influences both the child's genetic tendencies (temperament in Manassas & Bradley, 1994) and parental reactions or style (which would result in attachment in Manassas & Bradley, 1994). Further, Rapee (2001) acknowledges the role of non-specific stressors in addition to specific traumatic events in contributing to the development of anxiety.

Empirical evidence lends support to these models (Murray et al., 2009). Support for the link between parental pathology and SAD comes from several studies indicating that parents with panic disorder (Unnewehr, Schneider, Florin, & Margraf, 1998; Warner, Mufson, & Weissman, 1995) and major depressive disorder both separately (Warner et al., 1995) and comorbidly (Biederman, Faraone, Hirshfeld-Becker, Friedman, Robin, & Rosenbaum, 2001), as well as parents with agoraphobia (Capps, Sigman, Sena, Henker, & Whalen, 1996), are more likely to have offspring with SAD. Further, a longitudinal study with over 900 New Zealand children found that mothers' fear at child age 9 predicted child separation anxiety at age 11 (Poulton, Milne, Craske, & Menzies, 2001). Both the Rapee (2001) and the Manassis and Bradley (1994) models indicate that the link between parental pathology and child anxiety may flow through two pathways: via innate child temperament, or via parental reactions and attachment. Behavioral inhibition is indeed associated with different types of anxiety disorders in childhood and adolescence (Biederman, Rosenbaum, Bolduc-Murphy et al., 1993; Hirshfeld, Rosenbaum, Biederman et al., 1992), as is insecure attachment, which may be an even stronger predictor of anxiety disorders than child temperament or parental anxiety (Manassis, 2001; Warren, Huston, Egeland, & Sroufe, 1997). Further, parental verbal behavior and conveyance of information about potentially threatening situations is also associated with higher anxiety in children (Barrett, Rapee, Dadds, & Ryan, 1996), presumably through the mechanism of influencing child cognitions (Prins, 2001; see next section on cognition). While the strength of the role of parenting and problematic family functioning in developing and maintaining SAD specifically remains an area for further investigation, evidence suggests that parental factors (such as behavior stemming from dysfunctional cognitions) are indeed factors in child SAD (Herren, In-Albon, & Schneider, 2013).

Cognitive Models

The cognitive processes underlying anxiety have received much attention (Prins, 2001; Williams, Kinney, Harap, & Liebmann, 1997) and multiple influential psychological models of anxiety disorders (Beck, Emery, & Greenberg, 1985; Foa & Kozak, 1986) have postulated the importance of cognitive processes in the maintenance of these disorders. One such model of the development and maintenance of anxiety disorders in childhood and adolescence, posed by Kendall and colleagues (Kendall, 2000; Kendall & Ronan, 1990), consists of two central elements: (1) chronic activity of threat schemas and (2) cognitive distortions (biased or erroneous cognitive process). The theory postulates that anxiety disorders result from the chronic overactivity of schemas organized around themes of threat or danger, resulting in a disproportionate focus of processing resources on threat-relevant information. Further, cognitive distortions refer to biased or erroneous cognitive operations (interpretation, attentional, and memory bias) and products (conscious images and thoughts, such as self-talk), which therefore result in further dysfunctional and maladaptive processing (Prins, 2001).

Empirical evidence for the assumptions of the cognitive model comes from research with children high on trait anxiety and children with anxiety disorders (for reviews see Daleiden & Vasey, 1997; Hadwin, Garner, & Perez-Olivas, 2006; Muris & Field, 2008; Murray et al., 2009), though disorder-specific research is still underdeveloped in the area of SAD. Interpretation bias, attentional bias and anxiety sensitivity have all been linked to childhood anxiety disorders, with findings supporting the existence of an overall biased information-processing style in anxious children (Barrett et al., 1996; Bögels & Zigterman, 2000; Chorpita, Albano, & Barlow, 1996) and predictive prospective effects (Warren, Emde, & Sroufe, 2000). One recent study has investigated cognitive processes in children with SAD, with results indicating attentional bias in children with separation anxiety disorder when exposed to disorder specific stimuli. Children with SAD gaze more at threatening stimuli (pictures of separations) after the first instant of presentation, and then decrease their gaze thereafter in a "vigilance-avoidance" pattern as compared to non-anxious children (In-Albon, Kossowsky, & Schneider, 2010).

An Integrative SAD Model

The most relevant and empirically supported elements from the general models are combined here in a working model of the development and maintenance of SAD (Figure 14.1), which serves as the foundation for treatment as outlined in this chapter. In the present model, parental vulnerability is the cornerstone of the model, impacting child emotional vulnerability as well as parental cognitions and subsequent parenting behaviors. These factors impact early experiences including the attachment relationship, and conditioning. Both child vulnerability and early learning may result in child SAD, if extreme. However, over time, continued parental behaviors and the parent–child relationship have a prolonged and profound impact on child cognitions, and the information processing cycle feedback loop among cognition, emotional coping skill use, and experiences of avoidance and non-success in separation situations. This feedback loop, when untempered by positive strategies, experiences, and cognitions, can also result in disorder.

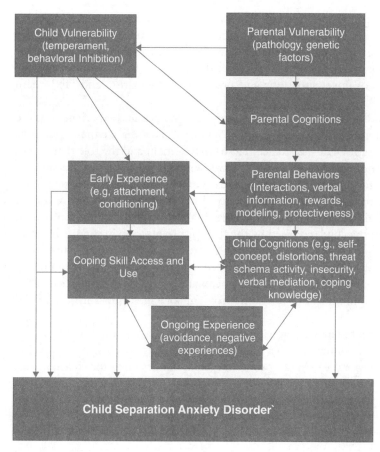

Figure 14.1   Model of the development and maintenance of SAD.

Therapy Overview

Therapeutic Targets

Behavioral therapy for childhood anxiety disorders has undergone major development in recent years. The first treatment approaches, based closely on the tenets of learning theory, focused on reversing the conditioning to fear triggering stimuli, and extinguishing the fear response. The addition of cognitive change approaches have, of course, revolutionized treatment for internalizing disorders, and are based solidly in findings from basic research on the development and maintenance of anxiety disorders in childhood and adolescence (see Schneider, 2004). Current treatment programs such as "Coping Cat" (Kendall, 1994) or "FRIENDS," a modified version of the "Coping Cat" program (Barrett, Sonderegger, & Sonderegger, 2001; Shortt, Barrett, & Fox, 2001), contain, in addition to the "classical" aspects of behavioral interventions, aspects that go well beyond conditioning. In addressing the cognitive aspects of anxiety, the child's worries and beliefs regarding the fear-triggering situation, as well as his or her knowledge of various coping strategies for managing these situations are considered in detail and with new replacement skills and cognitions taught in an age-appropriate manner. In addition to anxiety reduction in the strictest sense, the goal of cognitive-behavioral therapy is to strengthen the child's autonomy and sense of self-efficacy. Children in therapy learn to be "strong" so they can tackle a variety of novel situations and problems as they arise, and "fix" them themselves.

In addition to addressing child cognitions, coping strategies, and experiences, as the traditional CBT programs do, some therapy programs also emphasize the importance of family issues (Barrett, Dadds, & Rapee, 1996) in treatment and the role that parent concerns and behaviors play in the positive treatment outcome and maintenance of gains. In addition to child change, parents are guided and coached to reflect on aspects of their parenting, including dysfunctional beliefs, their own fears, and their behaviors, and to make changes if necessary. Parents are also included in role-plays and in vivo practice with the child, coached by the therapist to respond in ways that better support the child in anxiety-producing situations. Further, parents are instructed, often through a process of guided discovery, to reduce overprotective behavior, granting the child more autonomy. The overall family climate is improved through practice with more effective communication and joint problem-solving, facilitating better child outcomes.

The program presented in the following sections of this chapter combines the aforementioned therapy components into a comprehensive theory-based and empirically-based cognitive-behavioral treatment program specifically designed for children with SAD, incorporating both training for the child as well as the parents. The TAFF (*TrennungsAngstprogramm Für Familien*; English: Separation Anxiety Family Therapy) program (Schneider, Blatter-Meunier, Herren, Adornetto, In-Albon, & Lavallee, 2011), was developed at the University of Basel, Switzerland, with support from the Swiss National Science Foundation.

Therapeutic Methods

Materials

Great emphasis has been placed on developing child-friendly therapy materials for TAFF that can be used without child reading skills, and thus the program be used with children as young as age 4. The upper age range of the therapy materials is approximately age 13, allowing for flexible use of the program across the typical age spectrum of children who suffer from SAD. Materials, including a therapist's handbook, reproducible parent and child color handouts, illustrations, and games, and the daily diary are available from the authors, and are expected to be available in the English language and in published form in the future.

Program structure and specific goals

The TAFF program consists of four weekly psychoeducational sessions with the child alone, alternating with four psychoeducational sessions with the parents alone. These eight sessions are followed by eight exposure and practice sessions with child and parents together. Figure 14.2 provides an overview of the contents of the sessions. The content of the first four child and four parent sessions is similar in focus, but age- and role-tailored to meet the specific needs of the child and parents. Table 14.1 provides an overview of the program goals.

<table>
<tr><td>

4 Child Sessions:
- Psychoeducation
- Cognitive restructuring
- Exposure preparation

</td><td>

4 Parent Sessions:
- Psychoeducation
- Cognitive restructuring
- Exposure preparation

</td></tr>
</table>

8 Parent -Child Sessions:
- Intensive exposure in vivo
- Intensive parent coaching
- Improving parenting skills
- Improving family climate
- Relapse prevention

Figure 14.2   Program structure.

Table 14.1   Program goals.

Child	Parent
1. Identify the three components of anxiety (physical symptoms, thoughts, and actions).	1. Understand separation as a developmental task
2. Explain the process of the development and maintenance of separation anxiety	2. Understand the process of the development and maintenance of separation anxiety
3. Identify dysfunctional panic thoughts, and replace them with more realistic thoughts	3. Identify dysfunctional panic thoughts, and replace them with more realistic thoughts
4. Face the fears in graduated exposure	4. Learn and practice behaviors to help and support the child before, during, and after separation
5. Use new techniques outside of therapy to successfully cope with separation fears	5. Support child in coping with separation fears after therapy has ended

---

TIP

It is easy for the psychotherapist to fall into a lead role in therapy. However, it is important to convey new information using the "guided discovery" process in a child-friendly manner and "dose," providing the child with frequent "recognition points" compatible with his or her own experiences.

Case example of guided discovery: What is fear?

"Let's think about what fear is for a moment. How do you know when you are scared? ... (child responds) ... Yes, so you notice that you feel scared in your belly and your body, and you have a lot of silly but scary thoughts in your head, such as "my mom is never coming back.""

Session structure

Each session follows a structured format, as outlined in Table 14.2. The structure stays the same across sessions, with the content and activities changing. Session-specific content is provided in the program delivery section, which follows.

Table 14.2   Session structure.

I. Agenda	Provide session overview. Ask for family's discussion points.
II. Review of the week	Solicit information about the past week, and review the daily diary and homework, if there was any.
III. Session-specific content	Psychoeducation and/or exposure exercises. In parent-child sessions, content is first discussed with the parents and child together, and/or exercises are carried out with both parent and child present. Then the child is allowed to play nearby or in an adjoining room while the therapist and parent discuss any additional parent-specific content.
IV. Review of the session and homework	Relevant family members to review the content of the session, with the therapist filling in or eliciting important missing points. The family receives any relevant homework tasks (detailed in the manual), including completing the daily diary.

Program Delivery: Session-Specific Content

Session 1 (parents): Separation anxiety as a developmental task

1. TAFF daily diary

The therapist explains how to record daily separation experiences using the TAFF diary (an example is provided in Figure 14.3), and completes an example with the parents using the previous day's events. The parents and child are expected to complete

---

Today's date:_____

How many separation situations did you have today that made you feel **afraid?**_____

Pick one situation:

What happened?_____

What did I do?:_____

How many separation situations did you have today where you were **not afraid?**_____

Pick one situation:

What happened?_____

What did I do?:_____

Today's feelings: How afraid did you feel today overall?

○ Really afraid ○ afraid ○ calm ○ really calm

Figure 14.3   Daily diary.

the diary each day in between sessions, and to summarize the week's events on a separate summary sheet.

2. Separation anxiety as a developmental task

2a: Communicating the diagnosis and definition of separation anxiety The therapist provides the parents with the diagnosis, based on the diagnostic interview process, prevalence rates (3%), and definition of separation anxiety including key symptoms.

2b: Definition of fear, functions of fear, fear of strangers, healthy and pathological anxiety The therapist provides introductory information about anxiety using guided discovery. Ensure positive interaction with the parents, asking for their personal experiences, relating them to the material and asking additional questions. Lectures and long therapist monologues should be avoided.

> ## Therapist dialogue with parent
>
> How do you explain what fear is to your child? Fear is a normal emotion that everyone experiences, and is not always bad. Fear is the body's reaction to threat, and is a survival mechanism that helps us to recognize dangers early and act quickly. It is also part of normal human development. Children have to learn to cope with different fears at certain ages. At what point do you think a child is first able to feel fear; when did you notice it in your own child? . . . Fear of strangers is typically the first fear, emerging around 6–8 months. Was it like that with your child? . . . In addition to these normal, age-typical fears, some children experience fear so intensely and frequently that it becomes a major restrictive burden in everyday life. Very problematic fears constitute anxiety disorders.

2c: Components of anxiety Lastly, the therapist introduces the three components of anxiety: thoughts, physical reactions, and actions.

> Fear affects us in three different areas: thoughts, physical reactions, and behaviors. Regarding thoughts, anxiety can show up as a vicious cycle of fearful thoughts about perceived dangers or threats. Can you tell me a typical fearful thought that your child might have? . . . Exactly, children with separation anxiety often think their parent will have a car accident or that something bad will happen to themselves. A second area is physical. Typical physical reactions include rapid heartbeat, stomach pain, nausea, sweating, headache, or fatigue. Which physical complaints have you observed in your child? . . . The most easily observable effect of anxiety is on your child's actions or behavior. Children may cry when they are afraid. You might find that you change your own behavior to avoid situations that might upset your child. What does your child do when s/he is

anxious? ... That is very typical of children with separation anxiety. They may also try to avoid staying over at a friend's house, going to school, or staying at home with a babysitter. By avoiding these situations, however, children don't get to see whether their fear is justified or not. They don't realize that the situation isn't dangerous, or that they can cope and should trust themselves. Which of these three areas are of most concern to you?

3. Homework: Completion of the daily diary, and readings on SAD

Session 2 (child): What is separation anxiety?

1. Brief introduction and getting to know each other

As sensitivity to separation from parents is symptomatic of children with SAD, they should not be hurried or pushed at the beginning of the program. The relationship between the therapist and child is critical to the success of the program, and sufficient time should be allowed for building a trusting relationship. Connect with the child to help him or her feel more comfortable, possibly through the use of a stuffed animal or puppet interview with younger children.

2. What is separation anxiety?

The therapist uses guided discovery to engage the child in understanding separation anxiety. The interaction should be upbeat, and the child should be asked for his or her own experiences. Eye contact, active listening, and asking follow-up questions in response to the child's statement are important.

2a. What is fear?   Engage in a discussion with the child surrounding anxiety in general using the following questions as discussion starters. What is fear? Which different kinds of fear exist? What is separation anxiety? The therapist may introduce the topic via a children's book. Let the child know that everyone experiences fear, and that there are different kinds of fear.

Many children are afraid of some things. But what exactly is fear? ... Fear is a feeling that everyone has. All children and adults are afraid once in a while. That's normal. There are many things that people can feel afraid of. Do you know any other children or adults who are afraid of something? What are they afraid of? ... Let's write the things down (or draw them) on this sheet. Are you afraid of any of these things too? ... Hey, you're doing great. As you can see, fears can be different for everyone. For example, Max is afraid of big kids, while Lara's afraid to sleep alone at night.

2b. What is separation anxiety?   The therapist explains what is separation anxiety is, and talks with the child about the diagnosis of separation anxiety disorder. Storybooks that address separation fears may be used to supplement the lesson and serve to start a discussion about separation anxiety.

Do you know what separation anxiety means? Children who have separation anxiety are afraid to be alone without mom or dad. Sometimes they … (list some of the symptoms that the child has, based on the diagnostic interview, such as fear of having an accident, sleeping along, being kidnapped, having nightmares, not wanting to go to school or friends' houses, etc.). Some of these things sound familiar to you, right?

2c. Healthy versus unhealthy fear   The therapist clarifies the difference between healthy and unhealthy fear, clarifies the function of fear, and provides examples of different anxiety disorders.

Why does everyone feel afraid once in a while? … Fear is a very old feeling. When someone in the Stone Age saw a tiger coming, fear helped him or her to fight back, or to run away as fast as possible. Body reactions, such as faster breathing or a fast heartbeat tell you that your body is ready to try its best. Fear also makes sense for people living today. For example, if you are crossing a road, and a car is about to hit you, fear makes you get out of the way quickly, and can save your life.

On the other hand, fear can make some children very sick. When do you think fear can be unhealthy? Some children have such strong anxiety that they don't go to school or do many things that they would like to. The things they are afraid though of are not even really dangerous. That is the biggest difference between healthy and unhealthy fear. If a car is about to hit you, it's really dangerous and it's good if you get scared. Then you can quickly run away and save yourself, and the fear helps you do this by getting your body ready. But if you are really afraid of a Daddy Long Legs spider, the fear isn't really necessary and actually makes things harder for you, because Daddy Long Legs aren't even dangerous. Children with unhealthy anxiety think things are dangerous when they are actually really safe, and have fears that last a long time. Luckily, there are things that children with separation anxiety can do to help them deal with being afraid of being away from their parents. We are going to talk about and try out some of these helpful ideas in our therapy sessions together and figure out how you can conquer your separation anxiety.

2d. The frequency of anxiety disorders and separation anxiety   The therapist now works with TAFF (Figure 14.4): The frequency of anxiety disorders in children, to illustrate the frequency of anxiety disorders.

How many children do you think suffer from unhealthy anxiety? … Out of every 100 children, 10 have such strong fears that the fears can be called an illness. Could you please pick a crayon and circle 10 children? … Out of every 100 children, 2–3 have separation anxiety. Could you please pick a different crayon and recircle three children? ... That's a lot! What do you think?

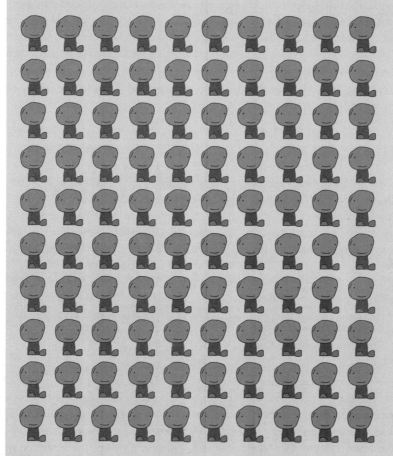

Figure 14.4   How many children have anxiety disorders?

Session 3 (parents): Model of disorder development and maintenance

1. Maintenance: "Components of separation anxiety"

The therapist uses guided discovery to help the parents explore the components of anxiety including body sensations, thoughts, feelings, and behaviors. The therapist works through and discusses each of the child's symptoms, pointing out that while some children report more physical symptoms (e.g., stomachaches), other children report more on thoughts about threats to self or parents. The therapist explains that the components of fear are all interconnected. Thoughts can influence emotions, which have an effect on the body, which can trigger behaviors.

Let's think about an example of how thoughts, feelings, and physical reactions are connected: A child sees that her parents are on their way to the theater and thinks hopefully they will come back soon. This thought makes the child feel nervous. Then she gets a stomachache. Her thoughts get worse and she thinks they will have a car accident. The child becomes anxious and her heart starts pounding. The child starts crying, clinging to her mother, and asking her to stay home with her. Does this type of situation sound familiar? Can you imagine another situation that might play out like this?

It is important for the parents to understand that certain feelings are connected with certain ideas. Separation anxiety is often accompanied by thoughts about possible dangers. These thoughts, like a command center, influence feelings and behavior. However, people can direct this command center, and decide whether to think in a helpful way, and thus feel better, or in a less helpful way, resulting in feeling worse. Imagine this in your own life. For example, when your partner is not home on time, what thoughts go through your head? . . . If you think catastrophic thoughts, such as that he had a car accident, you have emotional response, which is worry or fear.

2. Development

The therapist interactively explains the origins of separation anxiety, noting how factors from both the parent and child play a role in anxiety development. It is important during this discussion that the parents are not made to feel guilty, but rather simply learn to identify factors that may be changed. The following factors should be discussed, including individual examples from the child at appropriate points, and may be written down by the therapist: child temperament, learning history (models, instruction, traumatic experience), cognitive characteristics of parents (dysfunctional thoughts regarding separation and personality of the child), psychological characteristics of parents, parenting style, and behaviors.

At some point, you may have asked yourselves how this anxiety developed in your child. . . . What are your theories? . . . Temperament is one factor. From birth, some children are more sensitive in certain situations than others. Child temperament also has an impact on how you behave towards your child. Another factor that influences separation anxiety is your child's individual learning history. Your child has had many experiences over the years that have influenced him or her. Your child might learn from what you tell him or from what you do. There are also parent characteristics that can influence the development of separation anxiety. For example, parents of fearful children may have a lot of anxiety themselves. These parents may have to make an extra effort to support their child's courageous behavior. Less helpful thoughts on the part of the parents can cause the child to become more anxious.

3. Homework: Completing the diary and reading handouts with additional information.

Session 4 (child): A closer look at separation anxiety and TAFF thoughts

1. Components of anxiety: thoughts, body, and behavior

The therapist explains the components of anxiety, highlighting how anxiety affects thoughts, feelings, the body, and behavior, and illustrates the concepts with pictures, such as the one in Figure 14.5, which demonstrates how anxiety can be felt in the body (in the heart, and via sweating).

Figure 14.5   Sample illustrations of anxiety manifesting in the body (i.e., heart racing, sweating).

> How do you know when you're afraid? ... Fear can be felt all over the body. This happens in animals too. Can you tell when a cat is scared? Right, their fur stands up. Something like that happens to you too. When you are scared, you notice that certain things happen in your body. It might be that your heart starts to race or you get a stomachache. Many children also say that they notice a lot of thoughts running through their heads. They think things like "I can't do it," and "I want to go home." Other children sometimes feel like running away to get rid of their fear. So, as you can see, you can notice fear in different places in your body, in different thoughts, and in different things that you do.

2. Understanding individual components of anxiety and how they influence each other   The therapist uses an outline of the human body (therapist draws) and thought bubbles (Figure 14.6) to illustrate the three components: drawing the body reactions, writing ideas in the balloons, and drawing the behaviors. If the child has difficulty, the therapist can provide examples of typical anxiety thoughts other children give. The therapist and child should do this exercise for multiple situations: general anxiety situations, specific situations chosen from the daily diary, and positive situations.

Figure 14.6 Thought bubbles.

What do you feel when you're scared?.. (Draw red arrows pointing to the places on the human figure where the child feels anxiety). Now write what goes through your head when you're scared here in the first thought bubble. ... Now let's draw or write what you do in situations where you feel afraid on this blank sheet.

3. Defeat separation anxiety: TAFF-thoughts

The therapist helps the child to change anxiety thoughts into more positive thoughts, and to develop strategies to better cope with separation anxiety situations. First, discuss how to change the child's fear thoughts into "TAFF" thoughts. Make cards or posters with pictures or sentences.

We saw in the "anxiety circle" how thoughts and feelings affect each other. In certain situations, unhelpful thoughts go through our head that can bother us. These are panic thoughts, and they make our fears worse. On the other hand, TAFF thoughts help us through the situation, and make us braver. Which anxiety thoughts do you have when you are scared?.. Let's write them down on this sheet. Do you also have any TAFF thoughts that help you in these situations?..

Next, come up with very concrete strategies that the child can use in separation situations. The aim of these strategies should be to promote self-efficacy, and facilitate the belief that the child can overcome separation situations by himself/herself. Distinguish between strategies that should be used before and during separation situations, and list them on paper. Note whether each strategy is to be used when the parents are leaving or when it is the child who has to go somewhere, and ensure that all strategies can be easily implemented.

SAMPLE STRATEGIES

Before the separation situation (strategies in this category should be ones that help at the moment of separation): Communicating how I feel (sad, scared, etc.), telling my parents that I'll try and be brave, hug mom and dad one more time and then do something else, say goodbye clearly and then go off and do an activity, don't hesitate, just go right away.

DURING THE SEPARATION

(a) Child is going away: lucky rock/stuffed toy, TAFF-thought or say-aloud (according to prompt), look at TAFF thought on a card, go to school/kindergarten with friends, set goals: (1) go to school, (2) first hour/class, (3) second hour/class.
(b) The child stays, parents go away: read a favorite story, make a surprise for mother/father for when they get back, play a favorite game, cuddle/play with pets, play with the babysitter, listen to or make music.

We talked about how your fear can give you certain thoughts and make you feel upset. (Discuss example from diary). Now we are going to think of what you can do to get the fear to leave you alone. Do you know any things you can do that help when you feel really scared?

4. Homework: review or complete the TAFF thought and strategy cards

Session 5 (parents): Reframe dysfunctional thoughts about separation anxiety

1. Reframe dysfunctional thoughts about separation anxiety

Define the concept of dysfunctional and functional thoughts using the terms anxiety thoughts and TAFF thoughts, as in the child session. Use this concept to lead into the idea that parents also have helpful and not-so-helpful thoughts. Dysfunctional thoughts of the parents regarding the child (e.g., "I am a bad parent if I leave my child alone in this situation") in feared situations (e.g., going to school) should be explored in the context of conversation, systematically checked for their realistic content, and corrected/reframed.

First, choose a dysfunctional negative thought ("It is already dark and Melanie is not home yet. She must have had a bicycle accident!"). The parents then rate their conviction that the thought is true on a scale of 0–100% (they may be at 80% at this point). Third, the parents come up with points for and against the thought's validity ("Melanie knows the way, she has a light on her bike, there is usually not much traffic in this residential area, Melanie is a careful cyclist, accidents do happen, Melanie is usually on time"). The parents then provide an alternative thought to the prior dysfunctional thought ("her practice lasted longer because they are having a game on Sunday") and rate how convinced they are of the old thought's truth again (perhaps 50% now). Finally, the parents are asked to rate how likely they think the new alternative thought is (perhaps 60%).

Typical dysfunctional thoughts: My child will be traumatized and harmed for life by this separation; My child has always been sensitive and needs a lot of attention; My relationship with my child will be destroyed if I push my child to separate; If my child cannot do something, it's better if I do it.

In the child's therapy sessions, we call the thoughts that help kids to deal with certain situations TAFF thoughts. We call the thoughts that can make situations worse, panic thoughts. Throughout therapy, we are going to learn how to replace less helpful thoughts with more helpful ones. Your child is not the only person who might have less helpful anxiety thoughts that hinder progress in a separation situation. As parents, you also have more- and less-helpful thoughts. Many parents of children with SAD report having thoughts such as "my child is not capable of tolerating separation," or "I am a bad mother/father if I leave my child alone in this situation," or "it is my fault if my child is scared." Have you had thoughts like these? There is a very easy way to do a reality check on these thoughts and figure out how likely they really are to be true. Lets take a look at this idea. First, a panic thought gets into your head. Then, think about how convinced you are that this thought is true (conviction rating 1). You then think about the arguments for and against this thought. Then ask yourself: what could be an alterative thought to the panic thought? Then rate the anxiety thought again. Finally, rate how convinced you now are of the new alternative thought? Let's work through an example from your own life.

2. Homework: Practice reframing panic thoughts

Session 6 (child): Conquer separation anxiety: TAFF thoughts review

1. Repetition of the components of anxiety

As in session 4 (second session with the child), using an example situation from the past week (from the diary entries), discuss the experience of separation anxiety, highlighting the various components including thoughts, feelings, behaviors, and body reactions).

2. Defeat separation anxiety using TAFF-thoughts and additional coping strategies

As in session 4, explain that you will now work together to think of ways that the child can stop the fear cycle by stopping fearful thoughts for the selected situation from step 1. Work together on further coping strategies that can help the child in the selected separation situation, which should be made into a poster or noted (in writing or drawings) on a card that the child can take home.

4. Homework: review or complete (write or draw) his or her TAFF thoughts and coping strategies on provided index cards

Optional: Reality check (8 years and up). For older children, the therapist may teach the child the process of the reality check that was taught to the parents in session 5, teaching the child the method of identifying the realism of thought content, and using the terms anxiety thoughts and TAFF thoughts.

1. Blank chart for client
to draw on

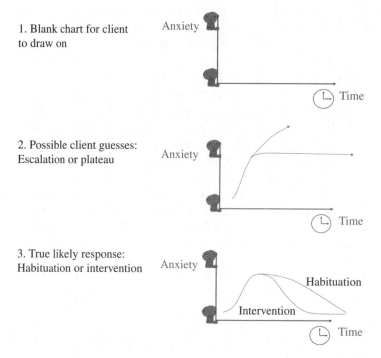

2. Possible client guesses:
Escalation or plateau

3. True likely response:
Habituation or intervention

Figure 14.7   Anxiety habituation curve.

Session 7 (parents): Preparation for the confrontation

1. Preparation for the confrontation

The therapist presents the rationale for exposure. Using guided discovery, work with the parents on understanding the anxiety habituation curve (Figure 14.7) and the learning process that takes place during exposure, using a selected separation situation from the past few weeks. The therapist points out that due to experiencing intense fear in separation situations, the child has developed anticipatory anxiety, so that he or she becomes scared before such situations even happen. Therefore, the child tries to escape earlier every time from these situations, or tries to generally avoid situations in which fear is involved. The child then feels like the anxiety gets better or even goes away when the situations are avoided or escaped from. However, the anxiety is not stabilized in the long term by this behavior.

2a. Graphical representation of past experiences in separation anxiety situations

The therapist talks with the parents about a typical separation situation, and what the child does and experiences when it is time to separate from the parents. The therapist asks the parent to graph their estimations of the course of the anxiety in a sample situation on the worksheet "Anxiety habituation curve" (Figure 14.7, number 1). It is important that the therapist records the time points of the most important events during the situation on the sheet (e.g., the parents ask the child to go to school, allow the child to stay home, etc.).

2b. Explanation of child's previous learning experience

Using guided discovery, the therapist guides the parents to the understanding that avoidance behavior can be effective against fear in the short-term, but that in the long term, it actually reinforces and stabilizes fear. The therapist points out that even though the fear disappears very quickly through avoidance, it is actually expanding, and over time it will occur earlier and earlier with respect to upcoming situations.

2c. Thought experiment: What if . . . ?

The therapist asks the parents to imagine what would happen if the child were in an anxiety-producing situation and was not able to leave. The therapist encourages the parents to think the situation through until the very end. The goal is for the parents to discover on their own that the child's anxiety is not likely to get worse or go on forever (Figure 14.7, number 2), but would eventually diminish on its own (Figure 14.7, number 3), without any of the parent's feared catastrophes occurring (e.g., the fear never disappears, my child stops trusting me, my child is traumatized for life).

2d. Explanation of the therapeutic goal

The therapist clarifies that it is very important for the child to now face his or her fears in order to break the cycle of association between the situation and fear. This can be achieved by providing the child with new experiences with the feared situation. The child must experience that the anxiety in the situation decreases when the child simply stays in the situation for a longer period of time. The child should not try to suppress the fear, but rather to face it, using his or her new strategies for dealing with fear.

2e. Create a fear hierarchy

Work with the parent on creating a hierarchy of fear-triggering situations that the parents want to work on (you may use index cards to order them if that is helpful). It is important here to differentiate between mild, moderate, and strong anxiety provoking situations.

2f. Supportive parenting behavior

Finally, the therapist works with the parents on techniques that they can use to help support their child in separation situations. The starting point of these strategies is for the parents to clearly set their expectations for the child's behavior. The therapist asks the parents for their expectations, and explores the strategies that the parents have already tried to help their child meet the expectations. Using these as a springboard, the therapist explains how brave behavior can be increased, and fearful behavior decreased.

> What are your goals and expectations for your child's behavior (e.g., "for my child to be more courageous, and not afraid to be alone anymore")? . . . What have you already tried? What are your current strategies? . . . There is no standard parenting practice that helps every child. Each child and each family are unique. You know your child best. I would now like to introduce you to some practices that we have found to be particularly helpful for many children in reducing anxiety.

2f.1. Use reinforcement to promote desired, courageous (i.e., not anxious) behavior   In this section the therapist explains the concept of positive and negative reinforcement.

In general, desired behaviors, including courageous behavior, can be increased through rewards. Children can learn that when they do specific things or behave in certain ways, they can get more positive attention, perhaps in the form of a shared game, praise, or an activity. Along with praise, parents should provide a clear reason for why the child is being praised. Rewards can also be relief from an undesired activity, such as chores. Rewards should be fun for the child, should match the size of the success, and should be given at the same time as the behavior. It works well if the child can make a choice. It is important to always follow through on promised rewards.

2f.2. Use ignoring to stop unwanted anxious behavior   In this section, the therapist explains the principle of extinction.

Anxious behavior can also be reduced by not paying attention to it. Concretely, this means that if your child shows unwanted anxious behavior, you pause the activity with him or her, or decline to engage in conversation about it, until he or she stops the behavior. It is important to tell your child why you ignore these types of behaviors: not because you don't care about him or her, but that you want to help your child to overcome anxiety. You should also tell your child what he or she could do to overcome anxiety, and praise him or her once brave and courageous behavior has been shown (e.g., "you have not tried to avoid the situation, great").

3. Homework: conduct daily exercises in practicing supportive parental behaviors as discussed during the session, recording the date, what the child did, how the parent reacted, and how the child responded

Session 8 (child): Conquer separation anxiety – prepare for TAFF training

1. Practice makes perfect

The therapist explains the concept of exposure. First asking the child to identify a situation that he or she was initially nervous in, but then over time could better cope with because he or she kept trying it. Then repeat the exercise with a separation example. Help the child to understand that fear can be conquered, even when it is uncomfortable or looks scary at first. Older children (over 7) can plot the course of the fear as the parents did in the previous session (Figure 14.7). Ideally, the child's curve should match the shape of the sample curve (Figure 14.7, number 3).

Now I would like to talk to you about your experiences with learning to ride a bike using this worksheet. Here you see a vertical line with faces on the side. At the bottom, we have a very happy and relaxed looking face (the therapist points to the face at the bottom). The face up here looks very scared, and in the middle, the face looks a bit nervous, but not completely afraid. People can use this like a thermometer to say how scared they are at different times. How would you use this line to say how scared you are right at this moment? ... And, how scared were you the last time you had to be away from your parents? ... Now, on this horizontal line, you see a clock. This line shows the time. The farther you go toward the right-hand side, the more time has passed. Now let's think about how you felt when you learned how to ride a bike ...

2. Presenting avoidance behavior as a fear strengthener

Using guided discovery, guide the child to an understanding that avoidance of situations can actually make anxiety stronger instead of weaker.

Please describe exactly what usually happens when you are supposed to go to school in the morning. ... OK, you cry and scream until your mom lets you stay home? ... and then how do you usually feel afterwards? Your stomachache goes away and you don't feel as scared? Now let's think about what happens the next morning when you have to go to school again. Is the fear still gone? ... Oh OK, so it comes back and it is just as strong as it was the day before. Does that mean that the day before, you didn't really defeat your fear after all? What do you think? ... So, staying home seems like it is helping on that particular day, but actually, it isn't really a good, permanent cure, because the fear keeps coming back.

3. Face your fear in order to permanently overcome it

Now the experiences from the separation situation are compared with the experiences with first fear (i.e., riding a bike). The therapist asks the child to describe the differences between these two situations. The therapist points out that the most important difference between these situations is that in one situation, the child seeks out the uncomfortable activity and stays in the situation, but with the separation situation, the child tries to avoid it. Through guided discovery, the child is guided toward the knowledge that avoiding situations makes the fear worse, while facing the feared situation reduces anxiety.

When you learned how to ride a bike, you didn't just give up, but kept trying, and your fear got smaller over time. What do you think? ... Did you know that if you practice again and again, just like you did with learning to ride a bike, that

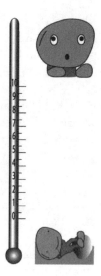

Figure 14.8   Fear thermometer.

your fear of being away from your parents can also be defeated? ... Instead of running away from the fear, look it in the face and stand up to it. The TAFF training that we are going to do together is a way to practice defeating the fear. The more often you do this, the faster the fear will go away. Then, you would be able to go to school in the morning and to stay there without being scared.

4. Fear hierarchy and rewards

The therapist introduces the graduated plan for overcoming fear, using the metaphor of a mountain. The child may use the Fear Thermometer (Figure 14.8) to rate various situations, and order them from easiest to hardest in creating a fear hierarchy that resembles that of the parents.

Defeating anxiety is like climbing a mountain. You can't get to the top right away, but instead have to follow the trail and go in steps. So we will start out our training with something that's not too hard. It should be a situation that is not completely easy, but that you can do. Then we will try a situation that is just a little bit harder for the next step. We will keep going like this until you reach the goal. Since these are tricky situations to overcome for you, we will also pick out a reward that you can earn after you have completed each step. Think about the situations that you would like to be braver in (guide the child using the situations picked by the parents). Now we will use the thermometer to see how much anxiety you have in each situation, and put them in order of difficulty.

Session 9 (parents and child): Preparing for the exposure exercises

1. Preparation for exposure (parents and child)

1a. Review of the exposure rationale by the child Ask the child to explain the rationale for the confrontation to the parents as a review of the last meeting. Ensure that the child can repeat the most important points, and that the parents do not speak for him or her.

1b. Create a joint fear hierarchy First, discuss the fear hierarchies that the parents and child created separately in their last sessions. Together, the family then decides which anxiety situations they want to work on, and records these on paper.

1c. Discuss the first practice situation The therapist chooses the first situation to practice. Planning the exposure exercises requires the therapist's organizational skills, and a good understanding of the child's environment and individual symptoms. Start with mild to moderately strong fear-triggering situations, which allow for a moderate fear increase and a marked habituation experience. It is important that the first exercises are carefully planned and carried out, because the experiences in these first exercises are crucial to determining the further course of the treatment. A poorly planned or carried out exposure exercise can reduce motivation, or lead to the parents ending further exercises. The first practice should preferably take place in a secure place, where there is no danger that the exercise will be interrupted.

Guidelines for the exposure exercises

1. The therapist should attend the first exercises to ensure that the child is moved into the practice quickly (without long discussions with the child beforehand), and stays in the situation long enough for habituation to occur.
2. The parent should accompany the child from the beginning (except in rare circumstances where the child is extremely aggressive toward the parent, or the parent is debilitated by his or her own anxiety), and should gradually conduct the exercises themselves. The parents should observe how the therapist prepares and instructs the child during the first exercise. After two to three successful exposure practices, the parents are asked to take turns performing the exercises themselves, with the therapist observing and coaching if necessary.
3. The exercise situations should be started quickly. The most difficult moment of the exposure for the child is the moment in which he or she must confront her/his fear and overcome his or her anticipatory anxiety. It is therefore critical for the success of the exposure that it takes place quickly and without long discussions with the child before the situation.

4. The objective of the exposure exercises is a significant increase in anxiety and then a decline while still in the situation. The therapist should allow sufficient time for the child to experience a reduction of fear in the situation, even if it means several hours for the first exposure practice. No increase in anxiety is problematic because it does not allow the child a new learning experience, and means the exercise was too easy.

5. The child receives rewards for coping with anxiety (rather than for being fearless).

6. The experience is documented in writing, using the worksheet "Practice Makes Perfect" (Figure 14.9). Documentation illustrates the learning experience, and looking back at successes can help to motivate the child during more difficult exercises.

7. Exposure exercises must follow each other closely. The most common mistake is that the exercises are not conducted systematically and close together in time. It is important to ensure that after the first exposure, the child receives practice every day, performing several exercises in a row in a block. The family should commit to daily exposure exercises before consenting to exposure therapy.

Situation	Fear at the beginning of practice (0–10)	Strongest fear during practice (0–10)	Fear at the end of practice (0–10)	Notes

Figure 14.9 Practice Makes Perfect.

8. Depending on the situation and exercise, it may be useful to systematically and continuously to extend the duration of exposure. If the child should learn, for example, to be at home with a sitter, the parents can first leave the house for 10 minutes, and then come back shortly after, but to again leave the house (regardless of whether the child is anxious or not), gradually extending the time to 15, 20, and 25 minutes. The exposure would end when the child has a significant reduction in anxiety.

9. A plan should be set in place for every exercise block. The family should consider what they would like to work on and formulate a goal (e.g., "stay home with a sitter"). The family then works on accomplishing smaller steps towards the goal, beginning with a moderately fear-triggering situation. Details should be discussed for each step, including what the child will do, what the parents will do, which coping strategies are available to the child, what the child can think, and which rewards will earned. The exact date and time that the confrontation will take place should be confirmed by the therapist.

1d. Develop a reinforcement plan   In developing the reinforcement plan, describe the expected behavior as accurately as possible in writing, and document the rewards to be earned (stars, points, etc.), reminding the parents to deliver rewards with praise and immediately after the behavior. If the child does not reach the objective, it is important not to criticize him or her, or to take any previously earned rewards away. Slowly taper off the reinforcement plan. The therapist explains to the family that the child can only gain from the exercises (it is a win–win situation). If the child has no fear of going to sports practice during the exercise, then there should be no reason to avoid this situation in the future. If the child is afraid, he or she gains an opportunity to use new strategies learned in therapy, and would become less and less anxious.

2. Supportive behavior during exposure exercises (parents-only, if the child is younger than 8 years old)

The therapist and the family (including the child if he or she is 8 or older) discuss the plan for the first therapist-led exposure exercise, as well as daily home exercises, as specifically as possible, using role-play or rehearsing their roles. The therapist should provide information (verbally and in the form of handouts) on handing specific situations relevant to the family (i.e., avoiding school, sleeping alone, etc.).

Sessions 10–15 (parents and child): Parent-guided exposure exercises

General content

1. Discuss the events of the last week and the parent-guided exposure exercises (parents and child)

Using the worksheet "Practice makes perfect" (Figure 14.9), the therapist discusses the family's experiences with the home exposure exercises (they may not have conducted home exercises yet at session 10, but should have home exercises to report on at sessions 11–15). The therapist can ask an older child to plot the course of anxiety during the exposure (if it was a new experience) on the "Anxiety habituation curve." This part may be omitted if the therapist has personally attended the exercises, and if the child has already plotted fear right after the exercise. In either case, the therapist praises the child for bravery in trying the exercises. The therapist checks to make sure that the exercises were well-chosen, and not too easy or too hard, and asks whether the child received the agreed-upon rewards for successful completion of the exercises.

2. Exposure exercises accompanied by the therapist if appropriate (parent and child)

The first exposure exercises in session 10 should be accompanied by the therapist. Further therapist accompaniment is on an as-needed basis and may take place in the office or another location. During the exposure, the therapist follows the guidelines for the exposure exercises (see box), and asks the child from time to time to rate his or her anxiety. After the child reports a decrease in anxiety, the exercise is completed, and the child is praised for his or her successful mastery of the anxiety. The situation should be practiced multiple times (2–4) in a block. After two to three successful exposure practices, the parents should be asked to perform the exercise themselves in the presence of the therapist. Once the parents are confident that they are able to conduct the exposure exercises, the exposure session block can be ended, and the child rewarded. The therapist and family discuss the child's experience with the first exposure exercises, and the therapist determines whether the exercises were appropriate.

3. Preparation for further exposure exercises (parents and child)

Using the information from the fear hierarchy, completed in a prior session, further practice situations are discussed, and concrete implementation steps agreed upon. The therapist emphasizes the guidelines (i.e., that practice be conducted daily, for long enough, documented, rewarded, etc.). If necessary, these exercises can be accompanied by the therapist. Toward the end of therapy (i.e., session 13), it is important to create an overview detailing which situations the child is to practice by the end of the therapy, in order to ensure that the most difficult situations are planned for practice by no later than the seventh parent–child session. If necessary, and especially toward the end of the therapy, the therapist points out that it is important to continue to practice even those situations which have been successfully completed. The exercises should only be stopped when the child naturally seeks out situations involving separation.

4. Concrete parental guidance for upcoming exposure exercises (parents only)

While the child plays nearby or in an adjoining room, upcoming exposure exercises should be discussed with the parents as concretely as possible, using role-play, strategy review, informational handouts, etc.

5. Session specific content (parents and/or child)

The parents and/or child and therapist address session-specific content (see next section).

Session-specific content

Session 10 (child and parents): First therapist-guided exposure exercise

This session should be devoted to the first exposure exercises, which are to be accompanied by the therapist as described in the general content above. There is no further session-specific content.

Session 11. Parental overprotection, meta-messages, and the development of autonomy: Part I

Many parents of children with anxiety disorders try to spare their children from fear, stress, and responsibility. However well-intentioned, excessive help and overprotection (such as bringing the child to school every morning, although all the other children walk alone), send the message that the child is not capable of doing such things without the parents. It also teaches children that fear, stress, or responsibility are dangerous and should be avoided at any cost. Parents do not always realize that through successfully overcoming stressful situations and frustration, the child may become more self-confident and mentally healthier.

The goal in this session is to work on an understanding of this cause-and-effect relationship with the parents. The therapist clarifies that parents' behavior in both stressful, unpleasant situations – as well as in everyday situations – always contains messages that the child takes to heart. The therapist allows the parents to think about what the child learns when the parents relieve them of responsibility. As the parents recognize the meta-messages that overprotective parenting sends, they can work with the therapist to develop new behaviors that show the child the parent is confident that he or she can cope with stressful or unpleasant situations. One or two specific areas for change should be discussed in more depth (e.g., the child calling a friend on his or her own; riding the school bus to school, or riding the bike to a neighbor's house) and practiced as homework.

Session 12. Parental overprotection, meta-messages, and the development of autonomy: Part II

The therapist asks how the parents did with giving the child more autonomy in the last week, as discussed in the last meeting. The therapist encourages the parents to be consistent and firm with the child, and discusses further autonomy-building exercises. Furthermore, the therapist reviews information from the fourth parents-only meeting on encouraging and strengthening brave behavior and reducing or eliminating anxious behavior in the child. The parents should be encouraged to praise coping behavior, to prevent avoidance of situations, and to sensitively empathize with the child, but not to strengthen fear through overprotection. Parents should be encouraged not to over-identify with the child's anxiety, to excessively reassure the child, to be overly directive ("You go into the elevator!"), and not to become impatient or show frustration.

Session 13. Mid-training evaluation and work on changing the child's dysfunctional thinking

Using the "Practice makes perfect" worksheets as a guide, the therapist speaks with the parents and child about all exposure exercises conducted up to this point. The therapist evaluates progress, emphasizes the habituation process since the first parent-child session, and highlights the child's achievements.

The therapist also reviews the topic of dysfunctional beliefs, and discusses with the child whether or not his or her fears have been confirmed. The therapist reviews all dysfunctional thoughts with the child again, and asks the child how convinced s/he is at the moment that those fears will be confirmed.

While the child plays nearby or in an adjoining room, the therapist reviews the parents' prior dysfunctional thoughts, and asks the parents to what extent their fears have or have not been confirmed. The therapist reviews the schema of checking dysfunctional beliefs with the parents.

Session 14. General parent-education

The parents are given the opportunity to discuss individual concerns related to parenting in general or specific issues in the home. The therapist should be familiar with fundamental positive and authoritative parenting principles (e.g., Triple P positive parenting program; Sanders, Turner, & Markie-Dadds, 2003) in order to provide the parents with appropriate feedback and relevant strategies based on their questions or concerns.

Session 15. Relapse prevention

1. Remaining dysfunctional thoughts of the child   The risk of relapse depends on the tendency of the child and parents to harbor persistent dysfunctional thoughts. The therapist must therefore address all remaining dysfunctional thoughts of the child, and help the child to reframe or correct them if necessary, based on the child's new experiences during the exposure exercises.

2. Addressing fear of relapse   It is possible that the family fears the anxiety could return after therapy, and wipe out all of the successes and achievements experienced thus far. Often underlying this fear, lies a belief that relapse means the therapy didn't work. Such thoughts are normal and understandable. Sometimes the fears will go away completely, but sometimes there will be setbacks, and some reoccurrence of the fear is normal. The therapist should point out that the family now has many strategies it can use to overcome new fears. Setbacks can even be a useful way for the family to check that they can still implement what they learned in therapy. Thus, it is not important to perfectly prevent every tiny feeling of anxiety, but rather to learn to deal with the anxiety. The ultimate goal of the therapy is not "no fear," but rather to achieve a normal level of anxiety or fear in the child and for the child to learn to cope with anxiety.

In order to prepare the family for possible setbacks, the therapist can work through a hypothetical scenario with them: the parents and child should imagine that the child is going to school on the first day back after the summer break, and the night before the first day, the child has a stomachache and complains that he or she is afraid to go to school. What would they do? This is an opportunity to ensure that the family has all of the important coping strategies in place in case of a relapse situation. If the parents and child have difficulty identifying the right solutions to this task, the therapist can support them using guided discovery. The therapist should stress that a setback is not a catastrophe, and that they should stay calm and try to figure out what it is that the child is afraid of through rational discussion. The parents and child should decide on strategies together and face the situation as quickly as possible. If avoidance behavior does occur, it should not be rewarded (e.g., by letting the child watch television during school days). If necessary, facing the feared situation can be encouraged through reward as in the exposure exercises.

3. Remaining dysfunctional thoughts of the parents; "devil's advocate" While the child plays nearby or in an adjoining room, the therapist explores the parents' remaining dysfunctional thoughts with them, playing "devil's advocate" in a role-play where the therapist argues for the dysfunctional thoughts identified in session 5, and the parents argue against them and convince the therapist of the irrationality of these thoughts. The therapist raises as many objections as possible for the parent to contest.

Session 16 (parents and child): Reflection on the course of therapy and closing

The therapist provides an overview of the child's progress in therapy, discussing any final questions the family might have. The therapist encourages the parents and the child to continue to practice applying the strategies in new situations, pointing out that the best protection against setbacks is to apply the skills to all possible situations, allowing the family to gain more and more control over the child's anxiety. The therapist informs the family that they may contact the therapist anytime questions or problems arise. To conclude, the child receives a certificate of achievement and praise from the therapist for such great cooperation and hard work!

Empirical Support

Cognitive-behavioral therapy for childhood anxiety disorders. Research on psychotherapy for childhood anxiety disorders has advanced considerably in recent years. Evidence for the efficacy of cognitive-behavioral therapy (CBT) comes from case reports, single case experimental studies (for an overview see Morris & Kratochwill, 1998), and randomized controlled trials (RCTs). Meta-analyses and reviews indicate that cognitive-behavioral therapy can be considered an evidence-based psychotherapeutic technique for the treatment of anxiety disorders, with 68.9% of children completing CBT no longer meeting diagnostic criteria for their principal pre-treatment anxiety disorder, on average, compared to only 12.9% of children assigned to a waitlist (In-Albon & Schneider, 2007; Silverman, Pina, & Viswesvaran, 2008). Intention-to-treat analyses indicate an average remission rate for anxiety disorders of 56% after receiving CBT, versus 28.2% for controls (In-Albon & Schneider, 2007; James, Soler, & Weatherall, 2005). Overall, across studies examining the effects of CBT on anxiety, results indicate large effects, with a mean pre-post treatment effect size of 0.86 for treatment completers and moderate effects of 0.58 in intention-to treat analyses, with waitlist effects at 0.13 (In-Albon & Schneider, 2007; James, et al., 2005). No differences in outcome were found between individual and group treatments or child-based and family-based treatments. The fail-safe number (24 studies) in the In-Albon & Schneider (2007) meta-analysis suggests that 79 file drawer studies with effect sizes of zero are necessary to reduce the effect size of 0.86 to a mean effect size of 0.20. Further, the mean pre-follow-up effect size was 1.36, and 72% of the children did not meet the criteria for their principal pre-treatment diagnosis at follow-up, suggesting that treatment gains were well maintained. Indeed, other studies have indicated that CBT gains can be maintained up to several years post-treatment (Kendall, Safford, Flannery-Schroeder, & Webb, 2004).

Although these findings provide evidence that anxiety disorders in children can be treated efficaciously, there are still about 30% of children with anxiety disorders for whom treatment is not efficacious. Thus, the present intervention was designed with the aim of improving outcomes through disorder-specific content and materials, materials designed for use with younger children, and content addressing family factors, including parent cognitions, which impact child cognitions (Bogels & Siqueland, 2006), family functioning, and parenting.

Disorder-specific treatment. Research on adults indicates effectiveness for disorder-specific treatments for adult anxiety disorders (Stewart & Chambless, 2009), producing higher effect sizes than those indicated in the In-Albon and Schneider (2007) meta-analysis of disorder-general childhood treatment programs for anxiety disorders. While it is possible that psychotherapy simply works better for adults than for children, an alternative possibility is that the effect sizes are lower in children because child treatments have not been tailored to address specific anxiety disorders as they have for adults. Some evidence in favor of disorder-specific approaches for children comes from a meta-analysis on treatment studies for social phobia, indicating large pre-post treatment effect sizes of $d = 1.02$ for trait anxiety and $d = 1.06$ for social phobia symptoms (Kremberg & Mitte, 2005).

Cognitive-behavioral family therapy. The role of parental involvement in the treatment of childhood anxiety disorders has been a major issue in current literature. In a recent review, Barmish and Kendall (2005) postulated that the successful treatment of anxiety disorders in youth does not require the inclusion of the parent. However, there are data suggesting that younger children and children with parents who have an anxiety disorder themselves may benefit more from a combined child and parent treatment than from a child-alone therapy (Cobham, Dadds, & Spence, 1998). Studies directly comparing child alone vs a combined parent and child treatment are rare. In one comparison using a sample of diverse anxiety disorders in children aged 7 and older, no additional effect of parent training was found above the effect of child-only treatment, although this sample had sufficient power only to detect large, and not medium or small effect sizes (Nauta, Scholing, Emmelkamp, & Minderaa, 2003). In a separate study with children aged 7–14, adding a family component was indeed beneficial above the effect of child-alone cognitive behavioral therapy (Barrett et al., 1996). As SAD is an anxiety disorder of young childhood and because the anxiety of the SAD child is related to the parent, it seems very plausible that SAD children may benefit more from a family-based treatment than from a child-only treatment. Very recent evidence indicates efficacy for family-based cognitive behavioral therapy with very young children (aged 4–7) with diverse anxiety disorders as compared to a waitlist condition (Hirshfeld-Becker, Masek, Henin et al., 2010), and awaits direct comparison with a child-only therapy.

Program-Specific Support

Research on the present program is in the early stages. In a sample of young children aged 5–7, the TAFF program demonstrated efficacy in comparison to a waitlist comparison condition (Schneider et al., 2011). Intention-to-treat analyses indicated that 76.19% of children allocated to the treatment group definitively no longer fulfilled DSM-IV criteria for SAD at follow-up, compared with 13.64% in the waitlist condition. Global success ratings from therapists, mothers, fathers, and the children themselves were in the "very much improved" or "much improved" ranges for 91–100% of children post-reatment. Results also indicated large pre-post by treatment condition interaction effect sizes ($d = 0.98$–1.41) across informants (parents and children) on rating scales assessing distress/avoidance in separation situations on the Separation Anxiety Inventory, and in parent rating of impairment and distress at the post-test for the treatment condition. Significant medium effects ($d = 0.62$ and 0.66) were observed in parent-rated quality of life (IQL). Further, all improvements were maintained at the 4-week follow-up assessment. Further, parents reported significant improvements in child's life quality, with medium effect sizes of $d = 0.62$ to 0.66. Notably, effect sizes were larger than those reported in prior meta-analyses and reviews on the effectiveness of general and child-only CBT for children with anxiety disorders (In-Albon & Schneider, 2007; James, et al., 2005; Silverman, et al., 2008). Finally, treatment gains were maintained at the 4-week follow-up assessment, indicating positive results so far that disorder-specific CBT can work with very young children. Research comparing the present treatment to a child-only therapy condition is currently underway, with initial results in older children aged 8–13 indicating that the TAFF program is as effective as a well-established general child-only program (Kendall, 1994).

References

Allen, J. L., Lavallee, K. L., Herren, C., Ruhe, K., & Schneider, S. (2010). DSM-IV criteria for childhood separation anxiety disorder: Informant, age, and sex differences. *Journal of Anxiety Disorders, 24*, 946–952.

Barmish, A. J., & Kendall, P. C. (2005). Should parents be co-clients in cognitive-behavioral therapy for anxious youth? *Journal of Clinical Child and Adolescent Psychology, 34* (3), 569–581.

Barrett, P. M., Dadds, M. R., & Rapee, R. M. (1996). Family treatment of childhood anxiety: A controlled trial. *Journal of Consulting and Clinical Psychology, 64*, 333–342.

Barrett, P. M., Rapee, R. M., Dadds, M. M., & Ryan, S. M. (1996). Family enhancement of cognitive style in anxious and aggressive children. *Journal of Abnormal Child Psychology, 24*, 187–203.

Barrett, P. M., Sonderegger, R., & Sonderegger, N. L. (2001). Evaluation of an anxiety-prevention and positive-coping program (FRIENDS) for children and adolescents of non-English-speaking background. *Behaviour Change, 18* (2), 78–91.

Beck, A. T., Emery, G., & Greenberg, R. (1985). *Anxiety Disorders and Phobias*. New York: Basic Books.

Bernstein, G. A., Warren, S. L., Massie, E. D., & Thuras, P. D. (1999). Family dimensions in anxious-depressed school refusers. *Journal of Anxiety Disorders, 13* (5), 513–528.

Biederman, J., Faraone, S. V., Hirshfeld-Becker, D. R., Friedman, D., Robin, J. A., & Rosenbaum, J. F. (2001). Patterns of psychopathology and dysfunction in high-risk children of parents with panic disorder and major depression. *American Journal of Psychiatry, 158*, 49–57.

Biederman, J., Rosenbaum, J. F., Bolduc-Murphy, E. A., Faraone, S. V., Chaloff, J., Hirshfeld, D. R., et al. (1993). A 3-year follow-up of children with and without behavioral inhibition. *Journal of the American Academy of Child and Adolescent Psychiatry, 32*, 814–821.

Bögels, S., & Zigterman, D. (2000). Dysfunctional cognitions in children with social phobia, separation anxiety disorder, and generalized anxiety disorder. *Journal of Abnormal child Psychology, 28,* 205–211.

Bogels, S. M., & Brechman-Toussaint, M. L. (2006). Family issues in child anxiety: Attachment, family functioning, parental rearing and beliefs. *Clinical Psychology Review, 26* (7), 834–856.

Bogels, S. M., & Siqueland, L. (2006). Family cognitive behavioral therapy for children and adolescents with clinical anxiety disorders. *Journal of the American Academy of Child and Adolescent Psychiatry, 45* (2), 134–141.

Bowlby, J. (1973). *Attachment and Loss: Separation Anxiety and Anger* (Vol. 2). New York: Basic Books.

Capps, L., Sigman, M., Sena, R., Henker, B., & Whalen, C. (1996). Fear, anxiety and perceived control in children of agoraphobic parents. *Journal of Child Psychology and Psychiatry, 37,* 445–452.

Chorpita, B. F., Albano, A. M., & Barlow, D. H. (1996). Cognitive processing in children: relation to anxiety and family influences. *Journal of Clinical Child Psychology, 25,* 170–176.

Cobham, V. E., Dadds, M. R., & Spence, S. H. (1998). The role of parental anxiety in the treatment of childhood anxiety. *Journal of Consulting and Clinical Psychology, 66,* 893–905.

Daleiden, E. L., & Vasey, M. W. (1997). An information-processing perspective on childhood anxiety. *Clinical Psychology Review, 17* (4), 407–429.

Foa, E. B., & Kozak, M. J. (1986). Emotional processing of fear: Exposure to corrective information. *Psychological Bulletin, 99,* 20–35.

Hadwin, J. A., Garner, M., & Perez-Olivas, G. (2006). The developmental of information processing biases in childhood anxiety: A review and exploration of its origins in parenting. *Clinical Psychology Review, 26,* 876–894.

Havighurst, R. J. (1952). *Developmental Tasks and Education.* New York: David Mckay.

Herren, C., In-Albon, T., & Schneider, S. (2013). Beliefs regarding child anxiety and parenting competence in parents of children with separation anxiety disorder. *Journal of Behavior Therapy and Experimental Psychiatry, 44,* 53–60.

Hirshfeld, D. R., Rosenbaum, J. F., Biederman, J., Bolduc, E. A., Faraone, S. V., Snidman, N., et al. (1992). Stable behavioral inhibition and its association with anxiety disorder. *Journal of the American Academy of Child and Adolescent Psychiatry, 31,* 103–111.

Hirshfeld-Becker, D. R., Masek, B., Henin, A., Blakely, L. R., Pollock-Wurman, R. A., McQuade, J., et al. (2010). Cognitive behavioral therapy for 4- to 7-year-old children with anxiety disorders: A randomized clinical trial. *Journal of Consulting and Clinical Psychology, 4,* 498–510.

In-Albon, T., Kossowsky, J., & Schneider, S. (2010). Vigilance and avoidance of threat in the eye movements of children with separation anxiety disorder. *Journal of Abnormal Child Psychology, 38,* 225–235.

In-Albon, T., & Schneider, S. (2007). Psychotherapy of childhood anxiety disorders: A meta-analysis. *Psychotherapy and Psychosomatics, 76,* 15–24.

James, A., Soler, A., & Weatherall, R. (2005). Cognitive behavioural therapy for anxiety disorders in children and adolescents (Review). *The Cochrane Database of Systematic Reviews,* Issue 4, 1–25.

Kagan, J., Snidman, N., & Arcus, D. (1998). Childhood derivates of high and low reactivity in infancy. *Child Development, 6,* 1483–1493.

Kendall, P. C. (1994). Treating anxiety disorders in children: Results of a randomized clinical trial. *Journal of Consulting and Clinical Psychology, 62,* 100–110.

Kendall, P. C. (Ed.). (2000). *Child & Adolescent Therapy–Cognitive-Behavioral Procedures.* New York: Guilford Press.

Kendall, P. C., & Ronan, K. R. (1990). Assessment of children's anxieties, fears, and phobias: Cognitive-behavioral models and methods. In C. R. Reynolds & R. W. Kamphaus (Eds.), *Handbook of Psychological and Educational Assessment of Children*. New York: The Guilford Press.

Kendall, P. C., Safford, S., Flannery-Schroeder, E., & Webb, A. (2004). Child anxiety treatment: outcomes in adolescence and impact on substance use and depression at 7.4-year follow-up. *Journal of Consulting and Clinical Psychology, 72* (2), 276–287.

King, N. J., & Bernstein, G. A. (2001). School refusal in children and adolescents: a review of the past 10 years. *Journal of the American Academy of Child and Adolescent Psychiatry, 40,* 197–205.

Kremberg, E., & Mitte, K. (2005). Kognitiv-behaviorale und behaviorale Interventionen der Sozialen Phobie im Kindes- und Jugendalter. *Zeitschrift für Klinische Psychologie und Psychotehrapie, 34* (3), 196–204.

Manassis, K. (2001). Child-parent relations: attachment and anxiety disorders. In W. K. Silverman & P. D. A. Treffers (Eds.), *Anxiety Disorders in Children and Adolescents* (pp. 255–272). New York: Cambridge University Press.

Manassis, K., & Bradley, S. J. (1994). The development of childhood anxiety disorders: Toward an integrated model. *Journal of Applied Developmental Psychology, 15,* 345–366.

Morris, R. J., & Kratochwill, T. R. (1998). *The Practice of Child Therapy*. Boston: Allyn and Bacon.

Muris, P., & Field, A. P. (2008). Distorted cognition and pathological anxiety in children and adolescents. *Cognition and Emotion, 22* (3), 395–421.

Murray, L., Creswell, C., & Cooper, P. J. (2009). The development of anxiety disorders in childhood: an integrative review. *Psychological Medicine, 39,* 1413–1423.

Nauta, M. H., Scholing, A., Emmelkamp, P. M., & Minderaa, R. B. (2003). Cognitive-behavioral therapy for children with anxiety disorders in a clinical setting: no additional effect of a cognitive parent training. *Journal of the American Academy of Child and Adolescent Psychiatry, 42* (11), 1270–1278.

Ollendick, T. H., & Hirshfeld-Becker, D. R. (2002). The developmental psychopathology of social anxiety disorder. *Biological Psychiatry, 51,* 44–58.

Poulton, R., Milne, B. J., Craske, M. G., & Menzies, R. G. (2001). A longitudinal study of the etiology of separation anxiety. *Behaviour Research Therapy, 39* (12), 1395–1410.

Prins, P. J. M. (2001). Affective and cognitive processes and the development and maintenance of anxiety and its disorders. In W. K. Silverman & P. D. A. Treffers (Eds.), *Anxiety disorders in children and adolescents*. Cambridge: Cambridge University Press.

Rapee, R. M. (1997). Potential role of childrearing practices in the development of anxiety and depression. *Clinical Psychology Review, 17,* 47–67.

Rapee, R. M. (2001). *The development of generalized anxiety. In: Vasey MW, Dadds MR, eds. The developmental psychopathology of anxiety.* New York: Oxford Press.

Sanders, M. R., Turner, K. M., & Markie-Dadds, C. (2003). The development and dissemination of the Triple P-Positive Parenting Program: A multilevel, evidence-based system of parenting and family support. *Prevention Science, 3,* 173–189.

Schneider, S., Blatter-Meunier, J., Herren, C., Adornetto, C., In-Albon, T., & Lavallee, K. (2011). Disorder-specific cognitive-behavioral treatment for separation anxiety disorder in young children: A randomized waitlist-controlled trial. *Psychotherapy and Psychosomatics, 80,* 206–215.

Shortt, A. L., Barrett, P. M., & Fox, T. L. (2001). Evaluating the FRIENDS programm: A cognitive-behavioral group treatment for anxious children and thei parents. *Journal of Clinical Child Psychology, 30,* 525–535.

Silverman, W. K., Pina, A. A., & Viswesvaran, C. (2008). Evidence-based psychosocial treatments for phobic and anxiety disorders in children and adolescents. *Journal of Clinical Child Adolescent Psychology, 37* (1), 105–130.

Siqueland, L., Kendall, P. C., & Steinberg, L. (1996). Anxiety in children: perceived family environments and observed family interaction. *Journal of Clinical Child Psychology, 25,* 225–237.

Sroufe, L. A. (1997). Psychopathology as an outcome of development. *Development and Psychopathology, 9,* 251–268.

Stark, K. D., Humphrey, L. L., Crook, K., & Lewis, K. (1990). Perceived family environments of depressed and anxious children: Child's and maternal figure's perspectives. *Journal of Abnormal Child Psychology, 18* (5), 527–547.

Stewart, R. E., & Chambless, D. L. (2009). Cognitive–Behavioral Therapy for Adult Anxiety Disorders in Clinical Practice: A Meta-Analysis of Effectiveness Studies. *Journal of Consulting and Clinical Psychology, 77,* 595–606.

Unnewehr, S., Schneider, S., Florin, I., & Margraf, J. (1998). Psychopathology in children of patients with panic disorder or animal phobia. *Psychopathology, 31,* 69–84.

Warner, V., Mufson, L., & Weissman, M. M. (1995). Offspring at high and low risk for depression and anxiety: mechanisms of psychiatric disorder. *Journal of the American Academy Child & Adolescent Psychiatry, 34* (6), 786–797.

Warren, S. L., Emde, R. N., & Sroufe, L. A. (2000). Internal representations: Predicting anxiety from children's play narratives. *Journal of the American Academy of Child and Adolescent Psychiatry, 39,* 100–107.

Warren, S. L., Huston, L., Egeland, B., & Sroufe, L. A. (1997). Child and adolescent anxiety disorders and early attachment. *Journal of the American Academy of Child and Adolescent Psychiatry, 36* (5), 637–644.

Williams, S. L., Kinney, P. J., Harap, S. T., & Liebmann, M. (1997). Thoughts of agoraphobic people during scary tasks. *Journal of Abnormal Psychology, 106,* 511–520.

15

Social Anxiety Disorder

Deborah C. Beidel[1], Candice A. Alfano[2],
and Brian E. Bunnell[1]

[1]University of Central Florida, USA
[2]University of Houston, USA

Descriptions of childhood anxiety disorders date back to the early 1900s. In particular, shy or inhibited temperaments were considered a personality style rather than a distinct disorder. With the publication of the third edition of the *Diagnostic and Statistical Manual of Mental Disorders* (DSM-III; APA, 1980), the ability to assign children and adolescents a diagnosis of social phobia was possible. Yet, during the 1980s, few researchers were examining this disorder (Beidel, 1991; Francis, Last, & Strauss, 1992), most likely due to diagnostic overlap with other DSM-III disorders of overanxious disorder and avoidant disorder of childhood. With the publication of the DSM-IV (APA, 1994), avoidant disorder was removed from the diagnostic schema and overanxious disorder was revised, removing many of the criteria that overlapped with social phobia. Since that time, there has been an explosion of research in the area, including 27 randomized controlled trials examining behavioral or cognitive-behavioral treatments, either alone or as part of a larger group of children with various anxiety disorder diagnoses (this does not include pharmacological treatment trials). Overall, the results of these investigations indicate that these interventions are effective for childhood anxiety disorders, and in some cases, for social anxiety disorder in particular. In this chapter we examine one empirically supported treatment for social anxiety disorder in youth – Social Effectiveness Therapy for Children.

Theoretical Background of SET-C

Social Effectiveness Therapy for Children (SET-C) is a comprehensive behavioral treatment program developed to address the social anxiety and avoidance that is characteristic of children and adolescents with a diagnosis of social phobia, now more commonly called social anxiety disorder (SAD). The efficacy of SET-C has been established in several clinical trials and is one of only two treatments listed as probably efficacious for the treatment of SAD in youth (Silverman, Pina, & Viswesvaran, 2008).

The Wiley-Blackwell Handbook of The Treatment of Childhood and Adolescent Anxiety, First Edition.
Edited by Cecilia A. Essau and Thomas H. Ollendick.
© 2013 John Wiley & Sons, Ltd. Published 2013 by John Wiley & Sons, Ltd.

Below we present the theoretical background for SET-C, its therapeutic goals and methods, the major elements, session by session program delivery, and recent empirical outcome.

The theoretical basis of SET-C derives from a large empirical literature examining the prevalence, development, features and course of SAD across the lifespan. Further, in line with extensive research demonstrating the efficacy of behavioral and cognitive-behavioral strategies (e.g., Feske & Chambless, 1995; Heimberg, Dodge, Hope, Kennedy, Zollo, & Becker, 1990; Turner, Beidel, Cooley, Woody, & Messenger, 1994a), SET-C builds on the success of Social Effectiveness Therapy (SET); a comprehensive treatment program developed for adults with SAD (Turner, Beidel, & Jacob, 1994b; Turner, Beidel & Cooley-Quille, 1995, 1997). Initial efforts to treat adults with SAD utilizing exposure therapy demonstrated differential efficacy for individuals with the generalized and non-generalized subtypes. Specifically, exposure therapy was efficacious for individuals with the non-generalized subtype, whereas patients with the generalized subtype had a much lower rate of response (Turner, Beidel, & Jacob, 1994b). When attempting to determine possible rate-limiting factors for the generalized subtype, it became evident that this subtype was lacking in the basic social skills necessary for effective social interactions. Thus, SET was designed not only to target individual and impairing symptoms of social anxiety, but also to improve the long-term functioning of patients through the use of psychoeducation, skill building, and programmed practice exercises. In particular, initial comprehensive assessment of each patient's specific symptoms and behaviors allows for the development of targeted in-session exposure tasks and out-of-session practice exercises aimed at optimizing treatment outcomes.

Extant data reveal that SAD occurring during childhood is very similar to the adult disorder (Beidel & Turner, 1998). However, some important differences also exist. First, while shyness and social fears are common during the childhood years, SAD can be differentiated from developmentally appropriate social anxiety based on its prevalence, chronicity, and imposed impairments (Heiser, Turner, Beidel & Roberson-Nay, 2009; Turner, Beidel & Townsley, 1990). Among adults, SAD affects up to 15% of the general population (Essau, Conradt, & Petermann, 1999; Lewinsohn, Hops, Roberts, Seeley, & Andrews, 1993; Wittchen, Stein, & Kessler, 1999) with mid-adolescence designated as the developmental period with the greatest likelihood of onset (Liebowitz, Gorman, Fyer, & Klein, 1985; Turner, Beidel, Dancu, & Keys, 1986). Nonetheless, SAD is commonly diagnosed in children as young as 7 years of age and an early age of onset is prognostic for a more severe disorder and associated impairments (Dalrymple, Herbert, & Gaudiano, 2007; Stemberger, Turner, Beidel, & Calhoun, 1995). Paradoxically, individuals with the most severe symptoms and impairments may also be the least likely to receive effective treatment (Ruscio et al., 2008). Early identification and treatment are therefore considered critical for long-term recovery.

Although SAD is characterized by a chronic and unremitting course, specific fears and forms of social avoidance change over the course of development and with greater chronicity. For both children and adolescents with SAD, school is the most commonly feared social setting (Beidel, Turner, & Morris, 1999a; Strauss & Last, 1993) where speaking to unfamiliar people and reading aloud/giving an oral report are the most frequent anxiety-producing social situations (Beidel, Turner, & Taylor-Ferreira, 1999b;

Rao et al., 2007). Other commonly-feared situations include taking tests, performing in front of others, and speaking to adults. Yet, despite these age-based similarities, adolescents with SAD endorse an overall broader pattern of fears compared to children (Rao et al., 2007) which include attending parties/dances, inviting a friend to get together, talking on the phone and dating. While certainly reflective of the normative physical, cognitive and social changes that characterize this period, these developmental differences also indicate a need for effective intervention strategies to target a child's unique social fears. SET-C therefore uses developmentally-appropriate, individual exposure tasks to target specific social fears based on the process of habituation (i.e., a decrease in arousal due to repeated presentations of a feared stimulus).

Behavioral signs of distress and avoidance also differ in children versus adolescents (see Beidel & Alfano, 2011). For example, younger children may express social fears in the form of crying, freezing/refusing to talk, or hiding behind others. Although children with SAD may physically enter anxiety-provoking social situations (e.g., Girl Scout meetings, group performances) they may agree to do so only with the support of a parent or sibling. Further, due to their more limited cognitive abilities, children may not necessarily identify these behaviors as avoidance or believe that they are unreasonable (DSM-IV-TR; APA, 2000). By comparison, social avoidance during the adolescent years is often more apparent and pervasive, and in severe cases of SAD, complete refusal to attend school may be present. Regardless of age or the manner in which social 'escape' presents, avoidance serves to negatively reinforce social anxiety via withdrawal from or removal of the feared stimulus (Lang, 1968). Other negative consequences of continued social avoidance include fewer friendships, feelings of loneliness, and decreased social competence. Child-reported loneliness, in particular, may be a critical mediator of treatment outcome for youth with SAD (Alfano, Pina, Villalta, Beidel, Ammerman, & Crosby, 2009). It is therefore critical that pre-treatment assessment procedures identify specific forms and consequences of socially-avoidant child behaviors.

Consistent with research among adult with SAD, empirical evidence for social skills deficits in youth with SAD of all ages is considerable (Alfano, Beidel, & Turner, 2006; Beidel et al., 1999a; Spence, Donovan, & Brechman-Toussaint, 1999; Rao et al., 2007). Parents, clinicians and observers blind to children's diagnostic status rate youth with SAD as less skilled in social situations as compared to their non-anxious peers (Alfano et al., 2006; Beidel et al., 1999a; Rao et al., 2007). Identified skill deficits include poor eye contact or facial gaze, long speech latencies, mumbled speech, difficulty initiating/maintaining conversations, and an inability to identify social cues/facial affect in others. The presence of such deficits suggests that even in the face of reduced social anxiety and avoidance, youth with SAD may be at continued risk for negative social encounters and difficulty developing friendships. Efficacious intervention should therefore focus on helping these youth acquire appropriate and effective social skills, in addition to decreasing social anxiety and distress, through the use of group-based social skills training sessions.

Finally, although social skills training programs may improve social competence and skillfulness within the therapeutic group setting, previous research indicates that generalization of these skills to 'real-world' social settings does not occur spontaneously (see Beidel & Turner, 1998). Thus, mere acquisition of a set of skills in the clinic (e.g., for interacting with others, making/keeping friends, being assertive, etc.) does not necessarily ensure their continued use outside of the clinic setting or after treatment had ended. In light of the importance of skill generalization, SET-C includes peer generalization activities that follow each social skills training session. These activities are uniquely aimed at providing increased opportunities for practicing newly-acquired social skills with unfamiliar peers in community settings where children often engage in social interactions.

Therapeutic Goals and Methods

SET-C begins with a session focused on educating children and parents about child-hood SAD and the specifics of the treatment program, and provides families with an opportunity to ask questions (though they are encouraged to ask questions through-out the program). In addition, the introductory session provides an opportunity to become acquainted with the SET-C group leaders (therapists) and the other children in the group. The overview of SAD provided to families includes topics such as var-ious etiologies, presentations, and individual differences of the disorder. Parents also learn effective ways to reinforce their children's appropriate behaviors. Following this initial session, there are 12 weekly individual sessions (an average of 60 minutes in length), 12 60-minute group social skills training sessions followed immediately by 90-minute peer generalization sessions. In research protocols, treatment is provided twice weekly—one individual session and one group session—over a 12-week period of time. However, in clinical practice, where it may not be possible for youth to be seen more than once per week, the components could be sequenced, such that either the group or individual sessions occur first, followed by the other component.

Systematic (graduated) exposure

Exposure is the cornerstone of successful behavioral interventions for SAD in patients of all ages (Beidel, Turner & Morris, 2000; Feske & Chambless, 1995; Scholing & Emmelkamp, 1993; Turner et al., 1994a). SET-C includes 12 individual sessions ded-icated to exposure, where children face anxiety-provoking situations/stimuli with the help of the therapist. Exposure sessions are developed based on the child's unique fears and therefore, actual exposure targets will vary for different children. The primary goal of exposure is for the child to habituate to the feared situation/stimulus. Habituation is evaluated during exposure tasks using the subjective units of distress scale (SUDS) which includes Likert-type ratings. However, therapist observation of the child may also be critical, particularly for younger children who sometimes have difficulty accu-rately rating their anxiety. As a rule of thumb, the child's distress should decrease within a single exposure task by at least 50% (Beidel & Turner, 1998). Thus, when conducting exposure sessions, therapists must commit to continuing exposure tasks until anxiety has decreased significantly. Overall, individual sessions average about 60 minutes in length.

Although exposure can be conducted in several formats, SET-C uses gradu-ated in-vivo exposure, beginning with less anxiety-provoking tasks and progressing toward more challenging ones over time. This format helps ensure initial success and gradually teaches the child that anxiety symptoms, though uncomfortable, will eventually diminish if the situation is not avoided. A "fear hierarchy" created by the patient and therapist together during the first individual session is used to guide the order of exposure tasks. Nonetheless, the need to revise a child's fear hierarchy as treatment progresses is not uncommon, either because anxiety associated with certain tasks may be over or underestimated or because other important avoidance behaviors to be targeted are identified.

Social skills training

Based on substantial evidence of impaired social performance among children and adolescents with SAD (Alfano et al., 2006; Beidel et al., 1999a; Spence et al., 1999), SET-C also includes sessions specifically focused on the acquisition of social skills. Social skills training is conducted in small groups of 4 to 6 children with weekly sessions lasting approximately 60–90 minutes, depending on group size. Each group session begins by focusing on a specific topic, followed by instruction and therapist modeling of specific skills. Youth are then provided opportunities to practice these new skills and receive feedback on their performance. In-session role-plays and feedback are the crux of the social skills training group and are particularly important in shaping new skill development in that they allow for repeated practice in a structured, supportive environment prior to use in real-world settings.

The SET-C social skills training includes two areas of focus, Social Environment Awareness and Interpersonal Skill Enhancement, which when combined address common problems associated with SAD (Beidel et al., 2000). Social environment awareness instructs children when, where, and why to initiate and terminate interpersonal interactions. Interpersonal skill enhancement teaches verbal and nonverbal mechanics of successful social encounters while focusing on problematic areas that are distinctive of children with SAD (e.g., joining a group of children, establishing and maintaining friendships, being assertive). As noted, the teaching of these components is delivered through *instruction, modeling, behavior rehearsal, corrective feedback, and positive reinforcement,* all of which are elements of traditional social skills training. *Instruction* presents the framework for the identified skill. Group leaders and group members discuss the parameters (verbal and nonverbal) required for the correct use of the social skill. The skill is then *modeled* by the group leader, followed by a discussion. It is sometimes beneficial to model correct and incorrect use of the social skill in order to provide a better understanding of the skill. The most critical component of social skills training, *behavior rehearsal,* involves practicing the recently learned skill in a controlled environment. The majority of each training session is devoted to this behavioral practice, as it is crucial for the acquisition of new skills. The skill is practiced with the group leader along with the other children in the group (at least twice per instructional component). *Corrective feedback* is given if children practice skills incorrectly, and is followed by additional practice. Further modeling may be required at this point. *Positive reinforcement* also plays an essential role in the acquisition of new skills, and is given throughout the session. Practicing these new skills in front of the group leaders and group members is a form of social performance—the specific type of situation that youth with SAD fear. Thus, group participants will need encouragement and reinforcement in order to participate in the group.

Social skills training sessions need to be tailored to the specific social challenges of participants in order to be most effective. That is, developmental differences exist in the skills required to make friends and gain social acceptance at different stages of development. Thus, although young children with SAD may require help in learning how to invite a school mate over to play, adolescents with SAD frequently struggle with negotiating their way into an established group of friends or asking a romantic interest out on a date. Clearly, different skills and behaviors are required for success in each of these situations. For all youth, each group session is concluded with an assigned homework task that requires practice of the specific skills covered that week.

Peer generalization activities

As described above, the inclusion of peers as part of treatment for children and adolescents with SAD helps ensure generalization of newly acquired social skills to real-world settings. Since the social networks of socially-anxious children and adolescents are relatively limited, peer experiences provide these youth with naturalistic opportunities for practicing social skills among a small group of outgoing, friendly peers. Thus, each social skills training session is followed by a peer generalization activity where youth with SAD are joined by same-aged, non-anxious peers for a 90-minute, age-appropriate activity such as bowling, board games, laser tag, craft making or pizza parties. Children with SAD frequently report anxiety related to eating in social situations, therefore the activity always includes lunch or a snack. Finding and selecting appropriate peers for the peer generalization component is critical, as inappropriate peer selection could lead to more rejection experiences. Peers should be within the group's age range, exhibit outgoing (but not excessive) social behavior, and be able to model appropriate social behavior. Peers should also include both males and females if possible.

Structured and unstructured tasks are purposely used to mimic children's usual social interactions and peers are not provided with specific instructions on what to say or how behavior in the interaction, except to engage the children in social interaction and in the activity. Similarly, therapists oversee peer activities but only intervene as needed (e.g., if a child with SAD is avoiding participation). Peer generalization sessions purposely include a different activity each week as well as different peers to ensure opportunities to interact with a variety of children in a number of different settings.

Although SET-C outcome data indicate that peer generalization experiences are associated with significant increases in social skill/competence compared to other treatments for SAD (e.g., Beidel, Turner, Sallee, Ammerman, Crosby, & Pathak, 2007), some challenges exist in successfully implementing this specific treatment component in typical practice settings. For example, recruiting and securing peers to help with weekly generalization activities can be time consuming and requires ensuring that youth are appropriate for this task. Additionally, protection of confidentiality needs to be considered as disclosure of patient-status is a typical and inevitable aspect of peer-based treatment activities. Involving additional therapists/clinical assistants in the treatment process and arranging real-world social activities also involves added costs and logistical considerations.

Homework assignments

The therapist provides homework assignments for both the social skills training and in vivo exposure sessions. Each assignment is specific to that day's session and allows the child to practice recently learned skills. Thus, if the social skill training session focused on initiating and maintaining conversations, a possible homework assignment could be for the child to initiate a conversation with both a stranger and familiar person and report back to the therapist the following week. Additionally, if the in vivo exposure session was focused on speaking in front of groups of people, a possible homework assignment might be to read aloud to the family in the evening.

While the task of completing homework assignments is given to the child, parents play a large role in homework compliance. They facilitate completion of the homework both by helping the child complete the assignment and reinforcing them for their accomplishment (e.g., providing praise, treats, stickers).

Session-By-Session Delivery of the Program

The social skills training groups that are part of the SET-C program are closed groups with a defined beginning and ending. The program is designed to be 12 weeks in length but can be expanded or contracted to fit the needs of the group. A detailed overview of the social skills training phase of the program is depicted in Table 15.1. As illustrated, the social skills program has several integrated components: group training, peer generalization, and homework. The content of the social skills training program is cumulative – it begins with very elemental skills and builds to more complex behaviors. Therefore, attendance at the group is critical – if children miss the initial sessions, they will not be able to catch up with the rest of the group.

One skill is taught each week, to assure that the youth have adequate opportunity to practice and acquire the behavior. The structure of a typical social skills training group is depicted in Table 15.2. As illustrated, the core procedures for acquisition of the skill include instruction, modeling, behavior rehearsal, feedback and positive reinforcement. The manner in which the therapists structured the group and use the allotted time most effectively is depicted in Figure 15.1. As indicated, this group is planned for 90 minutes and time is allocated to the various activities including review of last week's session, review of homework, introduction and acquisition of new skill, and homework assignment. A perusal of this figure indicates that the majority of the group session is devoted to behavior rehearsal, positive reinforcement and feedback. Reinforcement is in the form of tokens or points for adolescents and in the form of "fun money" (similar to Monopoly money) for younger children. As the end of each group, youth are allowed a few minutes to trade in points/money for small rewards or prizes or to bank their points for a larger reward at the next session.

Following the 90 minute social skills training group, children are transported by their parents to the weekly peer generalization activity. Prior to the start of each 12 week group, we organize an activity calendar that is distributed to the parents at the first session. The calendar includes the date and places of the activity, driving directions from the clinic to the activity, an exact meeting spot for the start of the activity, and any special needs for the activity (bring a lunch if food is not available or

Table 15.1 Overview of SET-C program.

Session number	Social skills training topic	Generalization activity/assignment	Homework assignment
Psychoeducation	—	—	—
Session 1	Conversation Skills I: Recognition of social cues, greetings and introductions	Bowling: Before beginning the activity, all children will introduce themselves	Greet five people before the next session Describe one greeting at the next session
Session 2	Conversation Skills II: Initiating conversations and appropriate conversation topics	Kite flying: Children should practice initiating conversations	Start a conversation with both a familiar and unfamiliar child
Session 3	Conversation Skills III: Maintaining conversations and topic transitions	Kickball: Children should practice maintaining conversations with at least two peer facilitators	Practice conversation skills with friends
Session 4	Listening and remembering	Billiards: Children should practice listening and remembering new information with at least one peer facilitator	Use newly acquired listening and remembering skills to obtain and remember at least one new piece of information about another child/adolescent
Session 5	Skills for joining groups	Mini golf: Children should attempt to enter an ongoing conversation between peers and group members	Identify potential situations to meet new children who are a source for new friendships

Session 6	Establishing and maintaining friendships	Pizza party: Children should attempt to enter an ongoing conversation between peers and group members	Invite at least one person to join in an activity
Session 7	Giving and receiving compliments	Scavenger hunt: Children will practice use of compliments with peer facilitators	Give compliments
Session 8	Appropriate Assertiveness I: Refusing unreasonable requests	Zoo/Animal Park: Children should practice appropriate assertiveness	Make a list of situations where it is difficult to say no
Session 9	Appropriate Assertiveness II: Asking for a change in behavior	Dinner at a restaurant: Children should practice appropriate assertiveness	Practice eye contact and appropriate assertiveness
Session 10	Appropriate Assertiveness III: Assertion with authority figures	Video arcade: Children should practice appropriate assertiveness	Practice appropriate assertiveness with authority figures
Session 11	Telephone skills	Nature walk: Children should role-play requesting phone numbers, initiating calls, and maintaining phone conversations	Make at least one phone call and take at least one phone message
Session 12	Review and wrap-up	Frisbee golf: Children should be joined by the groups of peer facilitators to socialize	

Table 15.2   Typical group social skills training session outline.

Components
Review of last week's session
Homework review and reinforcement
Introduction to new topic
Instruction – Why is it important? What is the right way to do it?
Modeling – "right" and "wrong" way
Behavior rehearsal (role-play) – using a scenario specifically developed for the group
Feedback and *positive reinforcement* – after each rehearsal
Repeat behavior rehearsal procedure with a different scene and keep repeating until all children have acquired the skill
Assign homework
Begin peer generalization

child has dietary restrictions; wear sunscreen if the activity will be outside). We also give an exact start and stop time for the activity. There are several rules regarding child safety – all children must be picked up by a parent or other responsible adult known to us in advance and no child is ever left at an activity if a parent is late. Staff remains thee until parents arrive. Furthermore, if activities are outside or in crowded places such as pizza video arcades, we have all the children wear the same color t-shirt so it is easier to keep track of them at the activity. Although there is no exact rule regarding the number of adults to the number of children (this may vary with the particular activity), we do not exceed a 4 child to 1 adult ratio.

The goal behind the peer generalization activity is that the child is provided with an opportunity to engage in activities in places where they are often not invited and to engage with peers without the interference of adults. Before ending the formal skills group, children are given an assignment to complete at the event. For example, if the skill taught in group is introductions, the assignment might be "learn the name of three children who join us for bowling." We do not closely monitor the children to assure that they complete the activity as a properly executed generalization session is one in which the activity is quickly organized by the group leader and then the youth interact on their own. If the activity occurs at the bowling alley, adult assistance will be required to pay for the bowling, make sure everyone has bowling shoes and bowling balls, and is assigned to one of the lanes. Peers should be given instructions concerning which child in the social skills group with whom he/she is assigned to interact (I want you to spend time talking to Chris today, even if she does not talk back). The therapist should then distance himself/herself and just observe, intervening only if one of the children becomes moderately distressed or if there is a need to give further instructions to the peers regarding social engagement.

Peers are recruited from the community through newspaper advertisements, announcements in church or school newsletters, or through groups such as Boy Scouts or Girl Scouts. Many school districts now require students to perform community service and "assisting in a program to help shy children" has always fulfilled this requirement. Peers are not compensated for their time but their admission to any activity is paid and they receive a free lunch. Parents are required to drop off and pick

5:15 – 5:20 Review and Homework

- Review last week (Recognition of Social Cues and Greeting Skills)
- Homework review

5:20 – 5:35 Initiating Conversations

- When to start a conversation
  - When you are introduced to someone
  - When you run into neighbors
  - Before or after activities (dance practice, class)
  - Sitting next to classmate and allowed to talk
  - When another person appears to be receptive (How do we know?)
    - Do they look busy?
    - Do they look at you encouragingly? (smiling, eye contact)
    - Do they say something first?
- Model and have children decide if receptive

How to start a conversation

- With strangers and those you know
  - Smile, introduce yourself
  - Comment on something you have in common (Ask if unsure, try to observe things)

Choosing Appropriate Conversational Topics

- What are some things to talk about with people we know? Write on board
  - School, where you live, how many brothers and sisters, favorite (foods, subject in school. . .)
- What to talk about with people we don't know
  - Where do you go to school, where do you live, have you seen any good movies lately
- Group Leaders Model "How to start a conversation"

5:35 – 6:30 Behavioral Rehearsal (Role Play)

- For each scene below, each child first rehearses with the group leader and then with other group members
- With a stranger
  - It is your first day in a new school year. There is a new boy or girl and the teacher says to you "_____ is new here at school. Will you show him/her around our school?" You say. . .
  - You are in the cafeteria sitting next to a person you don't know, they smile at you and make eye contact with you, you say. . .
- With someone you know
  - It is the first day of soccer practice
  - You are in the cafeteria sitting next to a person that is in your class, they smile at you and make eye contact with you, you say. . .
- Have group initiate conversation with each other

6:30 – 6:45 Wrap-up

- Go over homework assignment—Start a conversation with a child you know and someone you do not know
- Allow children to redeem "fun money" earned for group participation for prizes.

Figure 5.1 Group social skills training example.

up their children. Peers are screened for their ability to engage others in social interaction and for an absence of externalizing disorders so as to minimize the possibility of negative events during the generalization sessions.

It is not necessary to have twelve different activities (one for each week of the group). A variety of activities is valuable as it prevents boredom and allows more opportunities for generalization. In some instances because of their extensive social avoidance, children with social phobia may have no prior experience with activities such as roller skating or bowling. Therefore, it may be necessary to teach the child the mechanics of the activity before they can be expected to both engage in the activity and interact socially. Although originally structured as a social skills generalization opportunity, it is clear that this activity may also serve as an exposure session.

The final aspect of the social skills component of SET-C is the homework assignment. Children are given a written homework sheet containing an assignment that is directly related to what was taught in the group (see Table 15.1). Children are reinforced at the following group session for completion of homework assignments. Consistent with the proper implementation of behavior therapy, assignments should be reasonable but within the child's ability to complete successfully without the aid of the therapist. Furthermore, each child does not need the exact same assignment. The key is that each child should be engaging in homework as frequently as possible during the week in order to assure skill acquisition. If children do not complete their homework assignments during the week, they must complete them during the individual in vivo exposure session.

As noted, in addition to weekly group social skills training and peer generalization sessions, SET-C includes weekly in vivo exposure sessions. Many therapists, particularly those in clinical settings, question whether in vivo exposure is possible for children with SAD as arranging for others to observe the children is considered difficult if not impossible. However, it is possible to use public settings where people naturally congregate. These places could include video game arcades, dog parks, basketball courts/playgrounds, and shopping malls, among other places. Of course, the child's safety is of the utmost concern and children should never be left unsupervised during the exposure sessions. Examples of exposure settings used in the SET-C program are presented in Table 15.3.

In the SET-C program, exposure therapy is conducted in a hierarchical fashion – to a certain degree. Because exposure sessions are therapist-accompanied, we begin with a task that elicits moderate distress, in order to be sure that we will have sufficient time to complete the items on the top of the hierarchy within the 12 allocated sessions. Each item is presented and the child remains in the situation until any distress that is elicited has dissipated (i.e., until habituation is achieved. Although the specific length of the session will vary with the child and the severity of the disorder, typically exposure therapy sessions average 60 minutes.

One of the challenges of conducting exposure therapy for social phobia is ensuring the presence of other people in order to observe the child engaging in the feared behavior. Given that social phobia is an extreme fear of negative evaluation, engaging in exposure requires that other people be there to interact with or observe the behavior. Taking advantage of settings/situations where other children congregate (video arcades, parks, playgrounds) provides an audience at no cost and minimal effort for the therapist.

Table 15.3 Examples of in vivo exposure tasks.

Anxiety-provoking situation	Potential exposure sessions
Taking tests	Child takes an oral arithmetic or spelling test with some problems or words that are above grade level (so the child will make errors).
Eating in front of others	In a fast food restaurant or food court at the mall, child sits in view of others and eats.
Speaking to adults	Child asks a store clerk to help find an item in the store.
Answering or talking on the telephone	Child calls pet stores and ask questions such as "Do you sell yellow parakeets?"
Musical or athletic performances	Child plays a musical instrument in a (quiet or crowded) public place.
	Child plays basketball or another sport in a public place where others will watch.
Writing on the whiteboard	Child draws or illustrates points of a presentation on a whiteboard or overhead projector.
Starting or joining in on a conversation	Child plays a game such as Monopoly with a peer (child must engage in social conversation at the same time).
	In a "child-friendly place" (e.g., pizza parlors, children's museums), child invites another child to engage in an activity (e.g., play a video game, participate in a "hands-on" exhibit.
Other tasks designed to call attention to the child in public places	Child walks backwards in public.
	Child stands on one leg in public.
	Child wears a silly hat or wig in public.
	Child drops a jar of coins on a tile floor where others will hear the noise.

Recent Empirical Findings

In the initial randomized controlled trial of SET-C (Beidel et al., 2000), 50 children diagnosed with SAD were assigned to either SET-C or Testbusters, which served as a non-specific active control intervention. Testbusters is a study-skills and test-taking strategy program designed specifically for children between the ages of 8 and 12 (Beidel et al., 1999b). Testbusters addresses common study and test taking skills including establishing good study habits, the development of a study contract, instruction in the Survey, Question, Read, Review, and Recite (SQ3R; Carmen & Adams, 1972) method of study skills, test-taking preparation, and specific instructions in how to answer multiple-choice, matching, and fill-in-the-blank questions (Beidel, et al., 1999b). Testbusters was an appropriate non-specific control intervention for two reasons: 1) it mimicked many crucial elements of the SET-C program (skill-building, minimal opportunities to read aloud in group); and 2) over 80% of children in the study reported test-taking anxiety. At post-treatment, 67% of children treated with SET-C no longer met criteria for a SAD diagnosis in comparison to 5% treated with

Testbusters. Of particular significance is that 53% of the SET-C children met the more stringent 'treatment responder' criteria in comparison to 5% in the Testbusters condition. A Behavioral Assessment Test (BAT), using role-play scenarios requiring interaction with a same age peer, was also conducted at post-treatment. In comparison to Testbusters, children treated with SET-C had significant improvement on self-ratings of subjective anxiety, and independent evaluator's rating of anxiety and social effectiveness. A 6-month follow-up revealed that treatment gains in the SET-C group were maintained. Scores on the Social Phobia and Anxiety Inventory for Children (SPAI-C; Beidel, Turner & Morris, 1995) were also within the normal range, suggesting that the children were not just improved but were improved to such an extent that their scores fell below the cut-off indicative of the presence of SAD.

Additional follow-up studies of the children treated with SET-C were conducted three (Beidel, Turner, Young, & Paulson, 2005) and five (Beidel, Turner & Young, 2006) years subsequent to this initial study. At the three year follow-up, the sample included 27 of the original 30 children that participated in the SET-C study plus 2 adolescents who had participated in a pilot version of SET-C for adolescents. The children (now adolescents) were assessed using self-report and parental inventories, clinician ratings, treatment responder status, and behavioral assessment by independent evaluators. Results indicated that children treated with SET-C maintained their treatment gains three years later, including gains in actual skill and anxiety in social interactions as assess by independent evaluators and self-report (Beidel et al., 2005). The second follow-up study examined the same sample (now consisting of 26 adolescents and young adults) using the same assessment strategy (self-report, parental report, clinician ratings, and behavioral assessments at three, four, and five years following treatment). Five years later, and with no intervening treatment, 21 (80.8%) of the 26 participants still did not meet criteria for SAD, and 16 adolescents (61.5%) were considered treatment responders. Hierarchical linear modeling revealed that anxiety during role play and read aloud tasks (BATs) significantly decreased as a function of time following SET-C treatment (Beidel et al., 2006). Overall it is apparent that SET-C treatment outcome is stable and maintained over time.

In a second randomized controlled trial (Beidel et al., 2007) SET-C was compared to fluoxetine, and pill placebo. Fluoxetine, a selective serotonin reuptake inhibitor, was selected for the active drug condition as it is a commonly used pharmacological treatment for youths with anxiety disorders, including SAD. Of the 122 children who participated in this study, 57 youths were assigned the SET-C group, 33 to the fluoxetine group, and 32 received pill placebo. Children were assessed using diagnostic interviews, independent evaluator ratings, self-report inventories, parent reports, behavioral assessment, and treatment responder criteria. Results indicated that although both SET-C and fluoxetine were efficacious in the reduction of symptoms in social situations, more children treated with SET-C did not have a diagnosis of SAD at post-treatment, when compared to the fluoxetine and pill placebo groups. Moreover, only SET-C resulted in improved social skills, confirming that the intervention teaches skill as well as reducing anxiety.

Examining possible mediators and moderators of SET-C outcome (Alfano et al., 2009), a number of possible variables were analyzed using 88 participants treated with SET-C who participated in one of the two treatment trials discussed above. There were no moderator effects, but scores on the Loneliness Scale (LS; Asher &

Wheeler, 1985) and degree of social skill significantly predicted treatment outcome. Self-reported loneliness was also found to partially mediate post-treatment changes in social anxiety symptoms. Important to this study was the additional finding that neither age nor depressive symptoms moderated treatment outcomes, suggesting that SET-C is efficacious for children and adolescents and even for children with some depressive symptoms.

Summary

SET-C is a comprehensive intervention to address the unique needs of children and adolescents with SAD. In addition to anxiety reduction strategies such as exposure, it includes social skills training to address existing deficits in social behavior that are most likely the result of an extensive pattern of prior social avoidance. Additionally, SET-C includes planned peer generalization activities, designed to promote generalization of social skills to non-clinic, 'real world' settings. Although designing and implementing peer generalization sessions requires additional effort, control of this element by the clinician assures proper implementation and eliminates the need to rely on parents for completing what we believe is a critical aspect of treatment efficacy.

References

Alfano, C. A., Beidel, D. C., & Turner, S. M. (2006). Cognitive correlates of social phobia among children and adolescents. *Journal of Abnormal Psychology, 34,* 189–201.

Alfano, C. A., Pina, A. A., Villalta, I. K., Beidel, D. C., Ammerman, R. T., & Crosby, L. E. (2009). Mediators and moderators of outcome in the behavioral treatment of childhood social phobia. *Journal of the American Academy of Child and Adolescent Psychiatry, 48,* 945–953.

APA (1980). *Diagnostic and Statistical Manual of Mental Disorders,* 3rd edn *(DSM-III).* Washington, DC: American Psychiatric Association.

APA (1994). *Diagnostic and Statistical Manual of Mental Disorders,* 4th edn *(DSM-IV).* Washington, DC: American Psychiatric Association.

APA (2000). *Diagnostic and Statistical Manual of Mental Disorders,* 4th edn, *Text Revision.* Washington, DC: American Psychiatric Association.

Asher, S. R., & Wheeler, V. A. (1985). Children's loneliness: a comparison of rejected and neglected peer status. *Journal of Consulting and Clinical Psychology, 53,* 500–505.

Beidel, D. C. (1991). Social phobia and overanxious disorder in school-age children. *Journal of the American Academy of Child and Adolescent Psychiatry, 30,* 545–552.

Beidel, D. C., & Alfano, C. A. (2011). *Childhood Anxiety Disorders: A Guide to Research and Treatment* (2nd edition). Taylor & Francis/Routledge Mental Health; New York, NY.

Beidel, D. C., & Turner, S. M. (1998). *Shy Children, Phobic Adults: Nature and Treatment of Social Phobia.* Washington, DC: American Psychological Association.

Beidel, D. C., Turner, S. M., & Morris, T. L. (1995). A new inventory to assess childhood social anxiety and phobia: the Social Phobia and Anxiety Inventory for Children. *Psychological Assessment, 7,* 73–79.

Beidel, D. C., Turner, S. M., & Morris, T. L. (1999). Psychopathology of childhood social phobia. *Journal of the American Academy of Child and Adolescent Psychiatry, 38,* 643–650.

Beidel, D. C., Turner, S. M., & Morris, T. L. (2000). Behavioral treatment of childhood social phobia. *Journal of Consulting and Clinical Psychology, 68,* 1072–1080.

Beidel, D. C., Turner, S. M., Sallee, F. R., Ammerman, R. T., Crosby, L. A., & Pathak, S. (2007). SET-C vs. fluoxetine in the treatment of childhood social phobia. *Journal of the American Academy of Child and Adolescent Psychiatry, 46,* 1622–1632.

Beidel, D. C., Turner, S. M., & Taylor-Ferreira, J. C. (1999). Teaching study-skills and test-taking strategies to elementary school children: The Testbusters program. *Behavior Modification, 23,* 630–646.

Beidel, D. C., Turner, S. M., & Young, B. J. (2006). Social effectiveness therapy for children: five years later. *Behavior Therapy, 37,* 416–425.

Beidel, D. C., Turner, S. M., Young, B., & Paulson, A. (2005). Social Effectiveness Therapy for Children: Three-year follow-up. *Journal of Consulting and Clinical Psychology, 17,* 721–725.

Carmen, R. A., & Adams, R. W. J. (1972). *Study skills: A student's guide for survival.* New York: Wiley.

Dalrymple, K. L., Herbert, J. D., & Gaudiano, B. A. (2007). Onset of illness and developmental factors in social anxiety disorder: Preliminary findings from a retrospective interview. *Journal of Psychopathology and Behavioral Assessment, 29,* 101–110.

Essau, C. A., Conradt, J., & Petermann, F. (1999). Frequency and comorbidity of social phobia fears in adolescents. *Behaviour Research and Therapy, 37,* 831–843.

Feske, U., & Chambless, D. L. (1995) Cognitive behavioral versus exposure only treatment for social phobia: a meta-analysis. *Behavior Therapy, 26,* 695–720.

Francis G., Last C. G., & Strauss C. C. (1992). Avoidant disorder and social phobia in children and adolescents. *Journal of the American Academy of Child and Adolescent Psychiatry, 31,* 1086–1094.

Heimberg, R. G., Dodge, C. S., Hope, D. A., Kennedy, C. R. Zollo, L., & Becker, R. E. (1990). Cognitive behavioral group treatment of social phobia: comparison to a credible placebo control. *Cognitive Therapy and Research, 14,* 1–23.

Heiser, N. A., Turner, S. M., Beidel, D. C., & Roberson-Nay, R. (2009). Differentiating social phobia from shyness. *Journal of Anxiety Disorders, 23,* 469–476.

Lang, P. (1968). Fear reduction and fear behavior: Problems in treating a construct. *Research in psychotherapy,* vol I (pp. 90–102). Washington, DC: American Psychological Association.

Lewinsohn, P., Hops, H., Roberts, R., Seeley, J., & Andrew, J. (1993). Adolescent psychopathology: I. Prevalence and incidence of depression and other DSM-III-R disorders in high school students. *Journal of Abnormal Psychology, 10,* 133–144.

Liebowitz, M. R., Gorman, J. M., Fyer, A. J., & Klein, D. F. (1985). Social phobia: Review of a neglected anxiety disorder. *Archives of General Psychiatry, 42,* 729–736.

Rao, P. A., Beidel, D. C., Turner, S. M., Ammerman, R. T., Crosby, L. E., & Sallee, F. R. (2007). Social anxiety disorder in childhood and adolescence: Descriptive psychopathology. *Behavior Research and Therapy, 45,* 1181–1191.

Ruscio, A. M., Brown, T. A., Chiu, W. T., Sareen, J., Stein, M. B., & Kessler, R. C. (2008). Social fears and social phobia in the USA: Results from the national comorbidity survey replication. *Psychological Medicine, 38,* 15–28.

Scholing, A., & Emmelkamp, P. M. G. (1993b). Exposure with and without cognitive therapy for generalized social phobia: Effects of individual and group therapy. *Behaviour Research and Therapy, 31,* 667–681.

Silverman, W. K., Pina, A. A., & Viswesvaran, C. (2008). Evidence-based psychosocial treatments for phobic and anxiety disorders in children and adolescents: A review and meta-analyses. *Journal of Clinical Child & Adolescent Psychology, 37,* 105–130.

Spence, S. H., Donovan, C., & Brechman-Toussaint, M. (1999). Social skills, social outcomes, and cognitive features of childhood social phobia. *Journal of Abnormal Psychology, 108,* 211–221.

Stemberger, R. T., Turner, S. M., Beidel, D. C., & Calhoun, K. S. (1995). Social phobia: An analysis of possible developmental factors. *Journal of Abnormal Psychology, 104,* 526–531.

Strauss, C. C., & Last, C. G. (1993). Social and simple phobias in children. *Journal of Anxiety Disorders, 2*, 141–152.

Turner, S. M., Beidel, D. C., Cooley, M. R., Woody, S., & Messer, S. C. (1994). A multicomponent behavioral treatment for social phobia: Social effectiveness therapy. *Behaviour Research and Therapy, 32*, 381–390.

Turner, S. M., Beidel, D. C., & Cooley-Quille, M. R. (1995). Two-year follow-up of social phobics treated with Social Effectiveness Therapy. *Behaviour Research and Therapy, 33*, 553–555.

Turner, S. M., Beidel, D. C., & Cooley-Quille, M. R. (1997). *Social effectiveness therapy: A program for overcoming social anxiety and social phobia*. Toronto, Ontario, Canada: Multi-Health Systems.

Turner, S. M., Beidel, D. C., Dancu, C. V., & Keys, D. J. (1986). Psychopathology of social phobia and comparison to avoidant personality disorder. *Journal of Abnormal Psychology, 95*, 389–394.

Turner, S. M., Beidel, D. C., & Jacob, R. G. (1994). Social phobia: a comparison of behavior therapy and atenolol. *Journal of Consulting and Clinical Psychology, 102*, 350–358.

Turner, S. M., Beidel, D. C., & Townsley, R. M. (1990). Social phobia: Relationship to shyness. *Behaviour Research & Therapy, 28*, 497–505.

Wittchen H. U., Stein, M. B., & Kessler, R. C. (1999). Social fears and social phobia in a community sample of adolescents and young adults: prevalence, risk factors and comorbidity. *Psychological Medicine, 29*, 309–3.

16

Specific Phobias

Maria J. W. Cowart and Thomas H. Ollendick
Virginia Polytechnic Institute and State University, USA

A specific phobia is defined as a persistent, excessive, and unreasonable fear that is cued by certain specific objects or situations (APA, 2000). The *Diagnostic and Statistical Manual of Mental Disorders* (DSM-IV) classifies specific phobias into five distinct types as follows: animal (e.g., dogs, insects, snakes), natural environment (e.g., thunderstorms, heights, darkness), situational (e.g., elevators, flying), blood-injection-injury (e.g., seeing blood, injections), and other (e.g., loud noises, costumed characters). Specific phobia is one of the most common psychological disorders experienced by children and adolescents, affecting approximately 5–10% of youth in community samples (Kessler, Berglund, Demler, Jin, Merikangas, & Walters, 2005). The most commonly occurring phobia types in children include animal and natural environment types (Last, Perrin, Hersen, & Kazdin, 1992; Milne, Garrison, Addy et al., 1995; Silverman, Kurtines, Ginsburg, Weems, Rabian, & Serafini, 1999). Youth diagnosed with specific phobias frequently experience significant interference in their daily lives (Essau, Conradt, & Petermann, 2000; Ollendick, Hagopian, & King, 1997; Ollendick, King, & Muris, 2004; Silverman et al., 1999), and are at increased risk for academic difficulties (Dweck & Wortman, 1982; Ialongo, Edelsohn, Werthamer-Larsson, Crockett, & Keellam, 1995; Klein & Last, 1989) and social distress (Ollendick & King, 1994; Ollendick, King, & Muris, 2002; Strauss, Lease, Kazdin, Dulcan, & Last, 1989). Moreover, phobias may persist throughout the lifetime (Ollendick et al, 1997) and lead to other psychological difficulties in adulthood (Kendall, Safford, Flannery-Schroeder, & Webb, 2004; Ollendick & March, 2004; Pine, Cohen, & Brook, 2001).

When discussing specific phobias in children, it is important to consider the developmental psychopathology of fear. Fear is a normative part of development, which serves an adaptive function throughout life (Barlow, 2002; Ollendick et al., 2004). The content of normative fears follows a predictable course, which has been called the "ontogenetic parade of normal fears" (Marks, 1987, p. 109). Specifically, children's fears coincide with cognitive development, such that more concrete fears emerge early in childhood (e.g., fears of strangers, animals, etc.) while more abstract fears (e.g.,

The Wiley-Blackwell Handbook of The Treatment of Childhood and Adolescent Anxiety, First Edition. Edited by Cecilia A. Essau and Thomas H. Ollendick.

social fears, agoraphobia) tend to develop in adolescence (Gullone, 2000; Muris, Merckelbach, Gadet, & Moulaert, 2000; Ollendick et al., 2004). Further, specific fears become less common over the course of childhood, being most common in early childhood, peaking between the ages of 7 to 9 years, and declining in children 10 and older (Muris et al., 2000). While fears tend to be a transient part of normal development, a subset of children will see their "normal" fears become more intense and long-lasting, eventually developing into a phobia (Ollendick et al., 2004).

Etiology

Genetics

Several etiological pathways have been identified as leading to specific phobias. Family and twin studies have demonstrated a genetic component to specific phobias. Some studies, in fact, suggest that specific phobias "breed true"; that is, offspring of a phobic individual are most likely to develop the same phobia as their parent. For example, in a review of current literature in anticipation of DSM-V, LeBeau and colleagues (2010) reported evidence of familial aggregation such that offspring of phobic individuals were at increased risk only for the phobia displayed by their parent. In contrast, some studies indicate a common genetic vulnerability for animal, natural environment, and situational phobia, with a separate genetic risk for phobia of blood-injection-injury type (Hettema, Prescott, Myers, Neale, & Kendler, 2005). Still other studies have indicated that a general genetic factor puts individuals at risk for a wide range of anxiety disorders, with other factors determining the more specific presentation of the anxiety (Taylor, 1998). Thus, there seems to be a genetic component to the etiology of specific phobia, but the specificity of the vulnerability remains unclear at this time.

Learning

Rachman (1976, 1977) has proposed three etiological pathways to specific phobias which are based in learning theory. These include classical conditioning, vicarious conditioning (modeling), and negative information about the phobic object. A phobia developed as a result of classical conditioning must involve a direct negative experience with the phobic object. For example, a child who is bitten by a dog and then develops a phobia of dogs would be said to have developed the phobia through classical conditioning. In contrast, children may develop fears and phobias through modeling by observing and imitating the behaviors of those around them. An example of this type of conditioning would include the child who becomes afraid of snakes after observing other people behaving in a fearful manner around snakes, despite a lack of direct experiences by the child. The third learning pathway proposed by Rachman is the negative information pathway. Children may develop phobias through the negative information pathway by hearing negative information about a particular phobic object. For example, a child may become fearful of heights following a news report about someone experiencing injury or death due to a fall from a high place.

Parenting

In addition to general learning pathways, phobias in children may be developed and/or maintained through parenting factors. The parents of anxious children have been described as intrusive and "overprotective" (Barrett, Rapee, Dadds, & Ryan, 1996; Chorpita, Albano, & Barlow, 1996; Dadds, Barrett, Rapee, & Ryan, 1996; Siqueland, Kendall, & Steinberg, 1996; Whaley, Pinto, & Sigman, 1999). Such parents tend to shield their children from potential negative experiences such as injury, failure, or misfortune. In observational studies of parent–child interactions in ambiguous or stressful situations, such parents have been shown to intrude on their children in efforts to protect and insulate them from potential stress or harm (Barrett et al., 1996; Dadds et al., 1996). Such a pattern has been labeled the FEAR effect, or Family Enhancement of Avoidant Responses (Barrett et al., 1996; Dadds et al., 1996). With regard to specific phobias, parents may reinforce avoidance of the phobic object in order to prevent the child from having a potentially negative experience. These patterns prevent the child from gaining positive information about their phobic object, which could counteract fear-related information. Therefore, the child does not have the opportunity to learn that the fearful events that they are anticipating will not, in fact, occur.

Non-associative

The etiological pathways listed above may not account for all possible causes of specific phobias. The non-associative model of fear acquisition suggests that some fears may be biologically prepared through evolution (Poulton, Waldie, Craske, Menzies, & McGee, 2000). That is, fears of some stimuli (e.g., heights, snakes) may have represented significantly life-threatening dangers in early times, and therefore may not require any aversive conditioning experience to arise. In contrast, some individuals experience negative events but do not develop a phobia. In such cases, past positive experiences with the stimulus or other factors may serve a protective function against developing a phobia. Specific phobia etiology is complex, and all potential factors must be taken into account. That is, an individual's biological and genetic make-up, in addition to learning history and family environment will interact with exposure, information, and modeling to produce a phobia. The levels required for any determinant to produce a phobia will likely vary for each individual (Marks, 2002; Ollendick et al., 1997).

Phenomenology

As noted above, fear is a normative experience for children. However, for some children, fears persist and become interfering. When fears become abnormal with regard to frequency or the intensity of distress and avoidance experienced, a child may be diagnosed with a specific phobia. According to DSM-IV (APA, 2000), a diagnosis of specific phobia requires the presence of a fear for at least 6 months which is accompanied by avoidance or distress, including an immediate anxiety response when faced with the feared object or situation. The anxiety response in specific phobias is frequently accompanied by physiological symptoms in the presence of the feared object or situation, including increased heart rate and/or breathing, sweating, shaking, and others. Behaviorally, children may have tantrums or cry, freeze up, or cling to an available caregiver.

Lang (1967, 1979; Lang, Cuthbert, & Bradley, 1998) has described a tripartite model of fear and phobias, such that fears comprise a neural network of three components: behavior, physiology, and cognition. As noted above, when children are exposed to the object or situation they fear, they may think catastrophic thoughts (cognitive component), experience activation of the autonomic nervous system (physiological component), and engage in avoidance behavior such as running away (behavioral component). The responses are considered concordant when all are activated together, although discordant responding is also possible. Hodgson and Rachman (1974) suggested that concordance should be greater with higher levels of fear. Indeed, recent research suggests that phobic children tend to exhibit concordant responding when faced with their feared stimuli, although there is variability with regard to the concordance of responding (Ollendick, Allen, Benoit, & Cowart, 2011). Specifically, some children can be characterized as responding primarily along one dimension and not the others. For example, primarily behavioral responders may show avoidant behavior (running away, clinging) in the absence of negative cognitions or physiological arousal.

Another significant concern with regard to specific phobias in children is comorbidity. In both clinical and community samples, specific phobias co-occur with at least one other phobia in 50% or more of cases (Costello, Egger, & Angold, 2004). Comorbidity with other disorders is also common, occurring in 25% of community samples, and more commonly in clinical samples (Costello et al., 2004; Ollendick et al., 2002). In clinical samples, comorbidity rates with disorders other than specific phobias range from 30 to 72% (Last et al., 1992; Ollendick, Raishevich, Davis, Sirbu, & Öst, 2010b; Silverman et al., 1999). Most commonly, specific phobias are comorbid with other anxiety disorders such as generalized anxiety disorder, separation anxiety disorder, and social anxiety disorder. However, comorbidity with major depressive disorder and externalizing disorder is also observed (Last et al., 1992). It is interesting to note that recent research suggests that comorbidity does not seem to adversely affect phobia treatment outcomes. Further, successful treatment of specific phobias has been shown to produce reductions in the clinical severity of comorbid anxiety disorders (Ollendick, Öst, Reuterskiöld, & Costa, 2010a).

Assessment

Given the complexity of etiology, phenomenology, and comorbidity of specific phobias, a thorough, evidence-based assessment is critical before beginning treatment. Multi-method (e.g., clinical interview, questionnaires, observation) and multi-informant (e.g., child, parent, teachers, etc.) assessment is ideal (King, Muris, & Ollendick, 2005; Silverman & Ollendick, 2005). Further, assessment of all aspects of the phobic response (i.e., cognitive, behavioral, physical) allows for the fullest understanding of the phobia. Specific phobias, as noted earlier, are frequently comorbid. Therefore, a broad assessment of psychopathology is important to understand the full psychological profile of a given child and to rule out other disorders which may be mistaken for a phobia (e.g., separation anxiety disorder versus phobia of dark). Clinicians should also consider the developmental trajectory of fear, taking into account what is normative for a given developmental level.

A variety of tools are available for the assessment of phobias, including diagnostic interviews, questionnaires, and observational methods. The use of a combination of these measures will provide a broad understanding of a child's phobia and allow for selection of the most appropriate treatment approach.

Diagnostic interviews

Diagnostic interviews allow clinicians to assess for the presence and severity of a range of psychopathology. For childhood anxiety disorders, the most well-established interview is the Anxiety Disorders Interview Schedule for DSM-IV, Child and Parent Versions (ADIS-IV-C/P; Silverman & Albano, 1996). The ADIS-IV-C/P is designed to assess childhood anxiety disorders, mood disorders, and externalizing disorders, with modules for each specific disorder. Additional screening questions are included for assessing additional disorders (e.g., pervasive developmental disorders, eating disorders, learning disorders). For the most part, the parent and child interviews are similar. However, the parent interview contains modules for several additional disorders (e.g., conduct disorder, oppositional defiant disorder, enuresis), as well as requesting additional information with regard to history and interference of specific problems. The child version requests additional information regarding symptoms and phenomenology of disorders, and uses simpler language. The structure of the ADIS modules allows the clinician to administer the entire interview, or just the specific phobia module. Further, the ADIS-C/P can be administered in a structured or semi-structured manner, which allows clinician flexibility with regard to reliability and validity. Following the interview, clinicians assign severity ratings for each disorder on a 9-point scale, ranging from 0 (not present) to 8 (very severe). Ratings of 4 or above are considered to represent clinically significant diagnoses.

In addition to the ADIS-C/P, several other diagnostic interviews are available for assessing specific phobias and other disorders. These include the NIMH Diagnostic Interview Schedule for Children, Version IV (DISC-IV; Shaffer, Fisher, Lucas, Dulcan, & Schwab-Stone, 2000), the Schedule for Affective Disorders and Schizophrenia for School-Aged Children (K-SADS; Ambrosini, 2000), and the Diagnostic Interview for Children and Adolescents (DICA; Reich, 2000). However, these interviews have been used less frequently with children and adolescents with phobic and anxiety disorders and their psychometric properties are less well-established at this time (Silverman & Ollendick, 2005).

Questionnaires

In addition to diagnostic interviews, comprehensive assessment of specific phobias should include the administration of questionnaire measures to a variety of reporters (e.g., the child, parent, and teacher). As with the diagnostic interview, questionnaires should assess not only the specific phobia, but also other anxiety disorders and forms of psychopathology. Several broad questionnaire measures of psychopathology, including the Child Behavior Checklist (CBCL; Achenbach, 1991) and the Behavior Assessment Scale (BASC; Reynolds & Kamphaus, 2000), assess a wide range of potential psychopathology. These two measures also include versions designed for parent, teacher, and child report.

These broad measures should be accompanied by more specific measures of anxiety and fear. Overall anxiety can be assessed through self-report measures such as the Multidimensional Anxiety Scale for Children (MASC; March, Parker, Sullivan, Stallings, & Conners, 1997) or the Revised Children's Manifest Anxiety Scale, Version 2 (RCMAS-2; Reynolds & Richmond, 2008). The MASC and RCMAS-2 comprise subscales describing different types of anxiety difficulties (e.g., anxiety in social situations or due to separation from caregivers, physiological symptoms), as well as validity scales. Both measures have been normed against a nationally representative sample, and provide guidelines for identifying clinical versus normative levels of anxiety.

For more specific measurement of fears and phobias, the Fear Survey Schedule for Children, Revised (FSSC-R; Ollendick, 1983), is considered the gold-standard questionnaire measure. The FSSC-R is a self-report measure administered to children or adolescents to assess overall fearfulness. The measure requires youths to report their level of fear of 80 specific objects or situations. Higher scores indicate greater overall fearfulness and may indicate a specific phobia. Examination of phobia-specific items can also be helpful with regard to determining the presence and severity of any one specific phobia.

Behavioral approach test

The Behavioral Approach Test (BAT) is the ideal measure for allowing direct observation of a child's phobic behavior. The test consists of a number of increasingly difficult steps in which individuals are asked to approach a phobic object or situation, but are told that they can stop the test at any time. BATs can be designed flexibly for all possible phobia types, and therefore allow for some variation in the specifics of the task for a given fear. For example, a child who is afraid of dogs may be brought to a door and told that a dog is leashed inside the room. The child would be instructed to enter the room and pet the dog for a short period of time (e.g., 20 seconds). However, as noted, the child would be told that they only need to complete as much of the task as they are comfortable doing, and that they can stop the task at any time. The clinician can inquire about the child's subjective fear throughout the task, and may choose to collect physiological data (e.g., with a heart rate monitor). This allows the clinician to observe all three components of the child's phobic response (behavior, cognition, and physiology) in a controlled and standardized fashion (Ollendick et al., 2004, 2011). The administration of the BAT allows a clinician to directly observe the child's avoidance behavior in the presence of the feared stimulus, providing crucial confirmatory evidence related to diagnostic interviews and questionnaire measures. The BAT can also be an important tool with regard to treatment planning. Specifically, it serves as a brief exposure exercise for building a foundation to begin graduated exposure hierarchy for use in treatment. The child's behavior during the BAT allows the clinician to determine what the child is and is not able to do before beginning treatment. In addition, the BAT may provide information about the child's motivation to overcome his or her fear and/or the child's willingness to engage in therapy. That is, a child's willingness to engage in the BAT and attempt the exposure activity is a metric by which to measure how the child may engage in treatment.

Treatment

Treatment planning to address childhood phobias should be theoretically driven, be informed by current research, and be evidence based. Several procedures have empirical support for the treatment of childhood phobia (King et al., 2005; Ollendick, Davis, & Sirbu, 2009a). The most commonly used strategies, and those with the most empirical support, are those derived from a behavioral or cognitive-behavioral perspective. Exposure-based therapies have been found to be particularly efficacious (Wolitzky-Taylor, Horowitz, Powers, & Telch, 2008). More specifically, techniques such as systematic desensitization, contingency management, and participant modeling have been shown to be effective for the treatment of specific phobias (King et al., 2005).

Systematic desensitization

Systematic desensitization (SD) is not considered an evidence-based treatment for the treatment of childhood phobias because large-scale randomized control trials with carefully diagnosed youths have not yet been conducted (Davis, 2009; Davis & Ollendick, 2005). However, the approach, designed by Wolpe in 1958, represents one of the earliest treatments developed and is used widely in the treatment of specific phobias in children. The technique is based on the theory of reciprocal inhibition, specifically that one cannot experience two incompatible emotions simultaneously. Systematic desensitization typically proceeds through training in progressive muscle relaxation (PMR) and the development of a graduated fear hierarchy with the child. PMR involves training the child to briefly tense and relax their muscles in sequence (e.g., Ollendick & Cerny, 1981). Using the graduated fear hierarchy, imaginal and in vivo exposures are implemented while the child is coached to use PMR throughout the exposure activities. The combination of exposure and PMR is designed to provide a counterconditioning experience, such that the child "unlearns" the fear response. The goal, therefore, of SD is to have the child *not* experience a high level of fear in the presence of the phobic stimulus. Because of the physical and cognitive demands of SD, the technique tends to be used more frequently with adolescents and older children as opposed to younger children (King et al., 2005).

Contingency management

Another behaviorally based treatment strategy for use with childhood specific phobias is contingency management, also referred to as reinforced practice (RP). RP has received considerable support over the years and is considered to be an evidence-based treatment (Davis & Ollendick, 2005), and is based on an operant conditioning approach. Like SD, RP requires the development and implementation of a fear hierarchy in partnership with the child. However, RP does not include induction of a competing response. Rather, the goal of RP is to alter avoidant behavior through the

manipulation of consequences for such behavior. Specifically, when using RP, therapists work with the child to develop a list of palatable reinforcers (e.g., praise, stickers,
food items, etc.). Therapists then deliver the identified reinforcers contingent upon
the completion of increasingly difficult steps in the hierarchy. Using this approach,
behavior can be chained or shaped over time, and reinforcers can eventually be phased
out. To further shape behavior, the therapist may also incorporate ignoring techniques
to address negative (i.e., avoidant) behaviors.

Modeling

Modeling is based on social learning theory, and has its roots in the work of
Bandura and colleagues (Bandura, 1969). When implementing modeling, the therapist demonstrates approach behavior toward the phobic stimulus, as well as appropriate methods for interacting with the feared stimulus. In this way, the child gains
skills and experiences reduced anxiety. With regard to the effectiveness of modeling,
multiple controlled studies have confirmed that participant modeling is most effective, followed by live modeling and finally, film modeling (see King & Ollendick,
1997; Ollendick & King, 1998). Indeed, participant modeling (PM) is considered an
evidence-based treatment for childhood fears (Davis & Ollendick, 2005). PM consists
of the therapist modeling appropriate behavior while engaging in physical contact with
the child to draw the child closer to the feared stimulus. For example, when treating
a dog phobia, PM could be utilized such that the therapist models petting the dog
then uses hand-over-hand assistance to encourage the child to pet the dog as well. PM
is also useful for graduating steps in an exposure task, and for teaching and building
skills in the child. In the dog phobia example here, for instance, the child might be
instructed to first touch the therapist's shoulder while the therapist pets the dog. The
child's hand can then be gradually moved down the therapist's arm until, as stated
above, the therapist uses hand-over-hand assistance to encourage the child to pet the
dog. The ultimate goal of PM is to have the child gain the ability to independently
engage in each step of their fear hierarchy.

One-session treatment

The techniques described earlier, along with some other techniques, have been incorporated into what has come to be called One-Session Treatment (OST), a more
recently developed treatment package that has demonstrated empirical support for
the treatment of specific phobia in children and adults (Ollendick, Öst, Reuterskiöld
et al., 2009b; Öst, 1987, 1989; Zlomke & Davis, 2008). OST comprises a single,
3-hour session of massed exposure which incorporates aspects of psychoeducation
and skills training, cognitive restructuring, graduated hierarchical exposure, PM, and
RP. The single session is typically preceded by a 45-minute functional assessment session, in which the therapist meets with the child and parent(s) to identify the child's
fear-related cognitions, to construct a graduated fear hierarchy, and to provide information about the OST session. During the functional assessment session, the therapist
attempts to build rapport and motivation for treatment in the child. The therapist provides a rationale for treatment that identifies the child and therapist as a "team" who
are working together to overcome the child's fear. Treatment is described as a series

of behavioral "experiments," and the child is encouraged to think of himself or herself as a "scientist" or "detective" who is testing out their phobic cognitions. Children are told that treatment will proceed at their pace, and that they will not have to do anything that they are not prepared to do. However, the therapist also indicates that the child will need to experience some fear during the session in order to overcome their phobia.

The OST session proceeds much as described to the child. Ideally, at least three phobic stimuli are made available (approximately one per hour), and exposure exercises are planned around the child's fear hierarchy. The treatment details can vary widely from child to child, as the therapist works at the pace of the child and in direct response to the child's initial hierarchy and response to various exposure activities. In order to engage the child in the treatment activities, efforts should be made to make the exposure exercises as fun and engaging as possible. For example, when treating a fear of the dark, the therapist may consider playing hide and seek with the child and with glow-in-the-dark toys to reinforce the idea that positive experiences can occur in the dark. The therapist should also engage in frequent praise and encouragement for engagement in exposure activities, and reinforce approach behavior to make the experience more positive for the child.

Throughout treatment, behavioral "experiments" should be proposed based on the child's identified cognitions about their phobic object (e.g., "You said that you think a dog will bite you if you pet it on the head. Let's try it and see what happens"). While there is some variation, behavioral experiments generally proceed through several steps: modeling by the therapist (including PM), attempt by the child, and discussion and feedback regarding the attempt (PR). In concert with these behavioral experiments, the therapist provides psychoeducation regarding the phobic stimulus, highlighting positive information (e.g., storms help to clean the air) and training in appropriate methods for interacting with the phobic stimulus (e.g., how to read a dog's body language to determine if it is friendly). The session should proceed as directed with repetition across multiple exemplars to encourage generalization. At the close of treatment, children are reminded that they should continue to practice exposures to their phobic stimulus in order to continue to make progress.

While OST has been shown to be effective for approximately 60% of children (Ollendick et al., 2009b), some children continue to experience clinically significant levels of fear following treatment. Given the evidence that parents may inadvertently reinforce and maintain their children's fears (Barrett et al., 1996), treatment which incorporates parents into child treatment may prove advantageous as compared to individual treatment (see Cobham, Dadds, Rapee, & Spence, 1998; Nauta, Scholing, Emmelkamp,& Minderaa, 2003). Ollendick and colleagues are currently evaluating an augmented form of one-session treatment for children which incorporates parents. The intervention is identical to standard OST with the addition of training for the parent. Parents are provided with psychoeducation regarding fears and phobias, and are given the opportunity to observe their child's OST treatment to learn methods for engaging their child in exposure activities outside of treatment. At the close of the OST treatment session, parents are invited into the therapy session to give them an opportunity to practice implementing exposure activities with their child. Control of the activities is gradually transferred from the therapist to the parent. In addition to these in-session activities, parents are trained in the use of a contingency management program. They are encouraged to implement such a program at home to reward their children for engaging in exposure activities. Data is still being collected at this time, but it is expected that this augmentation may provide better treatment success as compared to standard OST.

Emerging treatment techniques

Virtual reality and computer-based treatments. In addition to the empirically supported treatment strategies described above, researchers are continuing to explore new tools and techniques for use in the treatment of specific phobias. Recent research has incorporated the use of computer and virtual reality technologies to assist in exposure-based therapy. Computer-aided vicarious exposure (CAVE) involves the use of a computer program which guides clients through vicarious exposure activities on a computer. For example, Gilroy and colleagues (2000) used a CAVE program for treatment of adults with spider phobia. The program allowed participants to guide an avatar (on-screen character) through the "house." Inside the virtual "house" were a variety of available spider images (e.g., still picture, plastic spider, "live" spider). Participants were able to decide their level of exposure to each scenario. Results suggested that CAVE produced treatment outcomes similar to live exposure, with the exception of change on the behavioral test (BAT). Participants receiving live exposure treatment were able to perform more steps on the BAT and reported less distress during the task as compared to those in the CAVE condition.

Virtual reality treatment is similar to CAVE, but involves more advanced technology. It allows participants to interact with computer-generated simulations of their phobic stimulus using real-time computer graphics, sensory inputs, and body tracking technologies. VR allows a greater "sense of presence" than does CAVE; that is, the technology feels more realistic to participants and therefore, allows them to better process their exposure experience emotionally (Rothbaum, Hodges, Smith, Lee, & Price, 2000). To date, controlled studies of VR have demonstrated its effectiveness for the treatment of adults with fears such as flying (Krijn, Emmelkamp, Olafsson et al., 2007; Maltby, Kirsch, Mayers, & Allen, 2002; Rothbaum et al., 2000; Rothbaum, Anderson, Zimand, Hodges, & Lang, 2006), spiders (Garcia-Palacios, Hoffman, Carlin, Furness, & Botella, 2002), and heights (Emmelkamp, Krijn, Hulsbosch, de Vries, Schuemie, & van der Mast, 2002; Krijn, Emmelkamp, Biemond et al., 2004; Rothbaum, Hodges, Kooper, Opdyke, Williford, & North, 1995) in adult samples. Specifically, recent meta-analyses have indicated that VR treatment is equipotent when compared to exposure treatment with regard to effects on anxiety symptom reduction, cognition, psychophysiology, and behavior (Parsons & Rizzo, 2008; Powers & Emmelkamp, 2008). In addition to their demonstrated effects on phobia symptoms and related outcomes, CAVE and VR approaches are appealing in their potential for ease of dissemination. In one survey, 90% of individuals with a spider phobia indicated that they would prefer VR exposure to in vivo exposure (Garcia-Palacios, Hoffman, See, Tsai, & Botella, 2001). Unfortunately, despite these promising outcomes in adult samples, no studies have yet been published regarding the use of VR in phobic children. Therefore, the utility of this approach is unclear in youth samples.

D-cycloserine. Another new development with regard to the treatment of specific phobias that has received recent attention is the facilitation of exposure treatment with D-cycloserine (DCS). There is currently no clear evidence that the combination of anxiolytic medication and exposure therapy is superior to exposure therapy alone for the treatment of specific phobias (Foa, Franklin, & Moser, 2002). However, recent evidence suggests that the use of DCS may enhance the effects of exposure therapy. DCS is thought to operate through its effects on the formation and consolidation of fear learning and extinction. DCS may strengthen extinction memories such that they are easier to retrieve during future exposures to the phobic stimulus (see Hofmann, 2007 for review). A recent meta-analysis regarding the use of DCS to facilitate exposure therapy indicated that DSC augments exposure therapy, perhaps by increasing its speed or efficiency (Norberg, Krystal, & Tolin, 2008). Further, DCS was found to be most effective when administered either directly before or after exposure therapy, supporting the theory that DCS operates through its effects on memory consolidation.

The first study of DCS in the treatment of specific phobia examined its effectiveness in a sample of adults with acrophobia (fear of heights; Ressler, Rothbaum, Anderson et al., 2004). In this study, participants received either DCS or placebo 2–4 hours before exposure-based VR treatment. Those receiving DCS displayed greater reductions in skin conductance fluctuations during exposures, and reduced phobia symptoms at post-treatment and 3-month follow-up. Since this initial study, DCS has been successfully utilized with other adult specific phobia populations, including spider phobia (e.g., Guastella, Dadds, Lovibond, Mitchell, & Richardson, 2007).

Despite some indication that DCS effectively facilitates exposure therapy for fear reduction, there remain a number of unanswered questions related to the approach. At this time, the optimal dosage and timing of DCS are unclear (Hoffman, 2007; Norberg et al., 2008), as are the long-term consequences of DCS exposure. Further, possible differential effects of DCS have not been tested across subpopulations. For example, the effects of gender, ethnicity, or age have not been explored for DCS (Hoffman, 2007). Most importantly for the purposes of the current chapter, DCS has not yet been utilized in child populations.

Thus, both computer-based exposure treatments and D-cycloserine augmentation remain experimental for the treatment of specific phobias in children. The use of these approaches in research regarding adult samples is promising, and indicates the need for such research with children. Obviously, future research is needed to determine if either computer-based exposure treatments or D-cycloserine are efficacious for use with children with specific phobias.

Summary

Specific phobias represent one of the most common psychological disorders affecting children. Phobias are frequently comorbid, may cause significant interference and distress, and put children at risk for academic and social difficulties, as well as adult psychopathology. While some fear is developmentally appropriate among children, some childhood fears persist and increase in frequency, intensity, and duration such that they become specific phobias. Specific phobias have a complex etiology, arising from a multiplicity of factors including genetics or evolutionary preparedness, learning history, modeling, and parenting. Due to the complex nature of specific phobias in children, multi-method, multi-informant assessment is crucial before beginning treatment. A variety of evidence-based assessment tools are available for assessing specific phobias and associated symptoms, including diagnostic interviews, questionnaire measures, and behavioral approach tasks. Once a thorough assessment has been completed, the information can be utilized to determine the most appropriate treatment strategy. Exposure-based treatments have been shown to be most effective with specific phobias. When used alone, therapy approaches such as systematic desensitization, contingency management, and modeling have been shown to be somewhat efficacious for the treatment of childhood specific phobias. One-Session Treatment (OST) is a somewhat newer treatment package which incorporates all of the strategies mentioned above in a brief (3-hour) treatment. The approach has demonstrated effectiveness in the treatment of specific phobias in children. New strategies for specific phobia treatment continue to be identified in the literature. A parent-augmented form of OST is currently being evaluated in a child sample. Further, computer-based approaches have been shown to produce positive results in adult phobia samples, as has the use of D-cycloserine to facilitate exposure treatment. These latter two approaches have not yet been tested in child samples, but more research is encouraged with regard to these promising techniques.

References

Achenbach, T. M. (1991). *Manual for the Child Behaviour Checklist 14–18 and 1991 Profile*, Burlington, VT: University of Vermont Department of Psychiatry.

Ambrosini, P. J. (2000). Historical development and present status of the Schedule for Affective Disorders and Schizophrenia for School-Age Children (K-SADS). *Journal of the American Academy of Child and Adolescent Psychiatry, 39*, 49–58.

APA (2000). *Diagnostic and Statistical Manual of Mental Disorders*, 4th edn, *Text Revision*. Washington, DC: American Psychiatric Association.

Bandura, A. (1969). *Principles of Behavior Modification*. New York: Holt.

Barlow, D. H. (2002). *Anxiety and Its Disorders: the Nature and Treatment of Anxiety and Panic*, 2nd edn. New York: Guilford Press.

Barrett, P. M., Rapee, R. M., Dadds, M. R., & Ryan, P. (1996). Family enhancement of cognitive style in anxious and aggressive children: Threat bias and the FEAR effect. *Journal of Abnormal Child Psychology, 24*, 187–203.

Chorpita, B. F., Albano, A. M., & Barlow, D. H. (1996). Child anxiety sensitivity index: Considerations for children with anxiety disorders. *Journal of Clinical Child Psychology, 25*, 77–82.

Cobham, V. E., Dadds, M. R., Rapee, R. M., & Spence, S. (1998). The role of parental anxiety in the treatment of childhood anxiety. *Journal of Consulting and Clinical Psychology, 66* (6), 893–905.

Costello, E. J., Egger, H. L., & Angold, A. (2004). Developmental epidemiology of anxiety disorders. In T. H. Ollendick & J. S. March (Eds.), *Phobic and Anxiety Disorders in Children and Adolescents: a Clinician's Guide to Effective Psychosocial and Pharmacological Interventions* (pp. 61–91). New York: Oxford University Press.

Dadds, M. R., Barrett, P. M., Rapee, R. M., & Ryan, S. M. (1996). Family process and child psychopathology: An observational analysis of the FEAR effect. *Journal of Abnormal Child Psychology, 24* (6), 715–734.

Davis III, T. E. (2009). PTSD, anxiety, and phobias. In J. Matson, F. Andrasik, & M. Matson (Eds.). *Treating Childhood Psychopathology and Developmental Disorders* (pp. 183–220). New York: Springer Science and Business Media, LLC.

Davis III, T. E., & Ollendick, T. H. (2005). A critical review of empirically supported treatments for specific phobia in children: Do efficacious treatments address the components of a phobic response? *Clinical Psychology: Science and Practice, 12,* 144–160.

Dweck, C. S., & Wortman, C. B. (1982). Learned helplessness, anxiety, and achievement motivation: Neglected parallels in cognitive, affective, and coping responses. *Series in Clinical and Community Psychology: Achievement, Stress, and Anxiety,* 93–125.

Emmelkamp, P. M. G., Krijn, M., Hulsbosch, A. M., de Vries, S., Schuemie, M. J., & van der Mast, C. A. P. G. (2002). Virtual reality treatment versus exposure in vivo: A comparative evaluation in acrophobia. *Behaviour Research & Therapy, 40* (5), 509–516.

Essau, C. A., Conradt, J., & Petermann, F. (2000). Frequency, comorbidity, and psychosocial impairment of specific phobia in adolescents. *Journal of Clinical Child Psychology, 29* (2), 221–231.

Foa, E. B., Franklin, M. E., & Moser, J. (2002). Context in the clinic: How well do cognitive-behavioral therapies and medications work in combination? *Biological Psychiatry, 10,* 987–997.

Garcia-Palacios, A., Hoffman, H. G., Carlin, A., Furness, T. A. III, & Botella, C. (2002). Virtual reality in the treatment of spider phobia: A controlled study. *Behaviour Research and Therapy, 40* (9), 983–993.

Garcia-Palacios, A., Hoffman, H. G., See, S. K., Tsai, A., & Botella, C. (2001). Redefining therapeutic success with virtual reality exposure therapy. *Cyber Psychology & Behavior, 4* (3), 341–348.

Gilroy, L. J., Kirkby, K. C., Daniels, B. A., Menzies, R. G., & Montgomery, I. M. (2000). Controlled comparison of computer-aided vicarious exposure versus live exposure in the treatment of spider phobia. *Behavior Therapy, 31,* 733–744.

Guastella, A. J., Dadds, M. R., Lovibond, P. F., Mitchell, P., & Richardson, R. (2007). A randomized controlled trial of the effect of D-cycloserine on exposure therapy for spider fear. *Journal of Psychiatric Research, 41,* 466–471.

Gullone, E. (2000). The development of normal fear: A century of research. *Clinical Psychology Review, 20,* 429–451.

Hettema, J. M., Prescott, C. A., Myers, J. M., Neale, M. C., & Kendler, K. S. (2005). The structure of genetic and environmental risk factors for anxiety disorders in men and women. *Archives of General Psychiatry, 62,* 182–189.

Hodgson, R., & Rachman, S. (1974). II. Desynchrony in measures of fear. *Behaviour Research and Therapy, 12,* 319–326.

Hoffman, S. G. (2007). Enhancing exposure-based therapy from a translational research perspective. *Behaviour Research and Therapy, 45,* 1987–2000.

Ialongo, N., Edelsohn, G., Werthamer-Larsson, L., Crockett, L., & Kellam, S. (1995). The significance of self-reported anxious symptoms in first-grade children: Prediction to anxious symptoms and adaptive functioning in fifth grade. *Journal of Child Psychology and Psychiatry, 36* (3), 427–437.

Kendall, P. C., Safford, S., Flannery-Schroeder, E., & Webb, A. (2004). Child anxiety treatment: Outcomes in adolescence and impact on substance use and depression at 7.4 year follow-up. *Journal of Consulting and Clinical Psychology, 72* (2), 276–287.

Kessler, R. C., Berglund, P., Demler, O., Jin, R., Merikangas, K. R., & Walters, E. (2005). Lifetime prevalence and age-of-onset distributions of DSM-IV disorders in the National Comorbidity Survey Replication. *Archives of General Psychiatry, 62,* 593–603.

King, N. J., Muris, P., & Ollendick, T. H. (2005). Childhood fears and phobias: Assessment and treatment. *Child and Adolescent Mental Health, 10* (2), 50–56.

King, N. J., & Ollendick, T. H. (1997). Annotation: Treatment of childhood phobias. *Journal of Child Psychology and Psychiatry, 38,* 389–400.

Klein, R. G., & Last, C. G. (1989). Anxiety disorders in children. *Developmental Clinical Psychology and Psychiatry Series, 20.* Thousand Oaks, CA: Sage.

Krijn, M., Emmelkamp, P. M. G., Biemond, R., de Wilde de Ligny, C., Schuemie, M. J., & Van der Mast, C. A. P. G. (2004). Treatment of acrophobia in virtual reality: The role of immersion and presence. *Behavior Research and Therapy, 42* (2), 229–239.

Krijn, M., Emmelkamp, P. M., Olafsson, R. P., Bouwman, L. J., Van Gerwen, L. J., Spinhoven, P. H., et al. (2007). Fear of flying treatment methods: Virtual reality exposure vs. cognitive behavioral therapy. *Aviation, Space, and Environmental Medicine, 78,* 121–128.

Lang, P. J. (1967). Fear reduction and fear behavior: Problems in treating a construct. In J. M. Shlien (Ed.), *Research in Psychotherapy* (pp. 332–368). Washington, DC: American Psychological Association.

Lang, P. J. (1979). A bio-informational theory of emotional imagery. *Psychophysiology, 16,* 495–512.

Lang, P. J., Cuthbert, B. N., & Bradley, M. M. (1998). Measuring emotions in therapy: Imagery, activation, and feeling. *Behavior Therapy, 29,* 655–674.

Last, C. G., Perrin, S., Hersen, M., & Kazdin, A. (1992). DSM-III-R anxiety disorders in children: Sociodemographic and clinical characteristics. *Journal of the American Academy of Child and Adolescent Psychiatry, 31,* 1070–1076.

LeBeau, R. T., Glenn, D., Liao, B., Wittchen, H., Beesdo-Baum, K., et al. (2010). Specific phobia: A review of DSM-IV specific phobia and preliminary recommendations for DSM-V. *Depression and Anxiety, 27,* 148–167.

Maltby, N., Kirsch, I., Mayers, M., & Allen, G. J. (2002). Virtual reality exposure therapy for the treatment of fear of flying: A controlled investigation. *Journal of Consulting and Clinical Psychology, 70* (5), 1112–1118.

March, J. S., Parker, J. D. A., Sullivan, K., Stallings, P., & Conners, K. (1997). The Multidimensional Anxiety Scale for Children (MASC): Factor structure, reliability, and validity. *Journal of the American Academy of Child and Adolescent Psychiatry, 36,* 554–565.

Marks, I. M. (1987). *Fears, Phobias, and Rituals: Panic, Anxiety, and Their Disorders.* New York: Oxford University Press.

Marks, I. (2002). Innate and learned fears are at opposite ends of a continuum of associability. *Behaviour Research and Therapy, 40* (2), 165–167.

Milne, J. M., Garrison, C. Z., Addy, C. L., McKeown, R. E., Jackson, K. L., Cuffe, S., et al. (1995). Frequency of phobic disorder in a community sample of young adolescents. *Journal of the American Academy of Child and Adolescent Psychiatry, 34,* 1202–1211.

Muris, P., Merckelbach, H., Gadet, B., & Moulaert, V. (2000). Fears, worries, and scary dreams in 4- to 12-year-old children: Their content, developmental pattern, and origins. *Journal of Clinical Child Psychology, 29,* 43–52.

Nauta, M. H., Scholing, A., Emmelkamp, P. M. G., & Minderaa, R. B. (2003). Cognitive-behavioral therapy for children with anxiety disorders in a clinical setting: No additional effect of a cognitive parent training. *Journal of the American Academy of Child and Adolescent Psychiatry, 42* (11), 1270–1278.

Norberg, M. M., Krystal, J. H., & Tolin, D. F. (2008). A meta-analysis of d-cycloserine and the facilitation of fear extinction and exposure therapy. *Biological Psychiatry, 63,* 1118–1126.

Ollendick, T. H. (1983). Reliability and validity of the Revised Fear Survey Schedule for Children (FSSC-R). *Behaviour Research and Therapy, 21,* 685–692.

Ollendick, T., Allen, B., Benoit, K., & Cowart, M. (2011). The tripartite model of fear in phobic children: Assessing concordance and discordance using the behavioral approach test. *Behavior Research and Therapy, 49,* 459–465.

Ollendick, T. H., & Cerny, J. A. (1981). *Clinical Behavior Therapy with Children.* New York: Plenum.

Ollendick, T. H., Davis, T. E., III, & Sirbu, C. (2009). Specific phobias. In D. Mckay & E. A. Storch (Eds.). *Cognitive Behavior Therapy for Children: Treating Complex and Refractory Cases.* New York: Springer.

Ollendick, T. H., Hagopian, L. P., & King, N. J. (1997). Specific phobias in children. In G. C. L. Davey (Ed.), *Phobias: a Handbook of Theory, Research, and Treatment* (pp. 201–223). London: John Wiley & Sons, Ltd.

Ollendick, T. H., & King, N. (1994). Fears and their level of interference in adolescents. *Behaviour Research and Therapy, 32* (6), 635–638.

Ollendick, T. H., & King, (1998). Empirically supported treatments for children with phobic and anxiety disorders. *Journal of Clinical Child Psychology, 27,* 156–167.

Ollendick, T. H., King, N. J., & Muris, P. (2002). Fears and phobias in children: Phenomenology, epidemiology, and aetiology. *Child and Adolescent Mental Health, 7,* 98–106.

Ollendick, T. H., King, N. J., & Muris, P. (2004). Phobias in children and adolescents. In M. Maj, H. S. Akiskal, J. J. Lopez-Ibor, & Okasha, A. (Eds.), *Phobias* (pp. 245–279). London: John Wiley & Sons, Inc.

Ollendick, T. H., & March, J. S. (2004). *Phobic and Anxiety Disorders in Children and Adolescents: a Clinician's Guide to Effective Psychosocial and Pharmacological Interventions.* New York: Oxford University Press.

Ollendick, T. H., Öst, L., Reuterskiöld, L., & Costa, N. (2010). Comorbidity in youth with specific phobias: Impact of comorbidity on treatment outcome and the impact of treatment on comorbid disorders. *Behaviour Research and Therapy, 48,* 827–831.

Ollendick, T. H., Öst, L. G., Reuterskiöld, L., Costa, N., Cedurlund, R., Sirbu, C., et al. (2009). One-session treatment of specific phobias in youth: A randomized clinical trial in the USA and Sweden. *Journal of Consulting and Clinical Psychology, 77,* 504–516.

Ollendick, T. H., Raishevich, N., Davis, T. E., Sirbu, C., & Öst, L. (2010). Specific phobia in youth: Phenomenology and psychological characteristics. *Behavior Therapy, 41,* 133–141.

Öst, L. G. (1987). One-session treatments for a case of multiple simple phobias. *Scandinavian Journal of Behavior Therapy, 16,* 175–184.

Öst, L. G. (1989). One-session treatment of specific phobias. *Behaviour Research and Therapy, 27,* 1–7.

Parsons, T. D., & Rizzo, A. A. (2008). Affective outcomes of virtual reality exposure therapy for anxiety and specific phobias: A meta-analysis. *Journal of Behavior Therapy and Experimental Psychiatry, 39,* 250–261.

Pine, D. S., Cohen, P., & Brook, J. (2001). Adolescent fears as predictors of depression. *Biological Psychiatry, 50* (9), 721–724.

Poulton, R., Waldie, K. E., Craske, M. G., Menzies, R. G., & McGee, R. (2000). Dishabituation process in height fear and dental fear: An indirect test of the non-associative model of fear acquisition. *Behaviour Research and Therapy, 38,* 909–919.

Powers, M. B., & Emmelkamp, P. M. G. (2008). Virtual reality exposure therapy for anxiety disorders: A meta-analysis. *Journal of Anxiety Disorders, 22,* 561–569.

Rachman, S. J. (1976). The passing of the two-stage theory of fear and avoidance: Fresh possibilities. *Behaviour Research and Therapy, 14,* 125–131.

Rachman, S. J. (1977). The conditioning theory of fear acquisition: A critical examination. *Behaviour Research and Therapy, 15,* 375–387.

Reich, W. (2000). Diagnostic interview for children and adolescents (DICA). *Journal of the American Academy of Child and Adolescent Psychiatry, 39,* 59–66.

Ressler, K. J., Rothbaum, B. O., Anderson, P., Zimand, E., Tannenbaum, L., Hodges, L., & Davis, M. (2004). D-cycloserine, a putative cognitive enhancer, accelerates extinction of fear in humans. *Archives of General Psychiatry, 61,* 1136–1144.

Reynolds, C. R., & Kamphaus, R. W. (2000). *Behavior Assessment System for Children,* 2nd edn. Circle Pines, MN: AGS Publishing.

Reynolds, C. R., & Richmond, B. O. (2008). *The Revised Children's Manifest Anxiety Scale,* 2nd edn. *RCMAS-2.* Los Angeles: Western Psychological Services.

Rothbaum, B. O., Anderson, P., Zimand, E., Hodges, L., & Lang, D. (2006). Virtual reality exposure therapy and standard (in vivo) exposure therapy in the treatment of fear of flying. *Behavior Therapy, 37,* 80–90.

Rothbaum, B. O., Hodges, L., Smith, S., Lee, J. H., & Price, L. (2000). A controlled study of virtual reality exposure for fear of flying. *Journal of Consulting and Clinical Psychology, 68,* 1020–1026.

Rothbaum, B. O., Hodges, L. F., Kooper, R., Opdyke, D., Williford, J. S., & North, S. (1995). Effectiveness of computer-generated (virtual reality) graded exposure in the treatment of crophobia. *American Journal of Psychiatry, 152,* 626–628.

Shaffer, D., Fisher, P., Lucas, C., Dulcan, M. K., & Schwab-Stone, M. E. (2000). NIMH Diagnostic Interview Schedule for Children, Version IV (NIMH DISC-IV): Description, differences from previous versions, and reliability of some common diagnoses. *Journal of the American Academy of Child and Adolescent Psychiatry, 39,* 28–38.

Silverman, W. K., & Albano, A. M. (1996). *Anxiety Disorders Interview Schedule for DSM-IV, Child and Parent Versions.* San Antonio, TX: Psychological Corporation.

Silverman, W. K., Kurtines, W. M., Ginsburg, G. S., Weems, C. F., Rabian, B., & Serafini, L. T. (1999). Contingency management, self-control, and education support in the treatment of childhood phobia: A randomized clinical trial. *Journal of Consulting and Clinical Psychology, 67,* 675–687.

Silverman, W. K., & Ollendick, T. H. (2005). Evidence-based assessment of anxiety and its disorders in children and adolescents. *Journal of Clinical Child and Adolescent Psychology, 34,* 380–411.

Siqueland, L., Kendall, P. C., & Steinberg, L. (1996). Anxiety in children's perceived family environments and observed family interaction. *Journal of Clinical Child Psychology, 25* (2), 225–237.

Strauss, C. C., Lease, C. A., Kazdin, A. E., Dulcan, M. K., & Last, C. G. (1989). Multimethod assessment of the social competence of children with anxiety disorders. *Journal of Clinical Child Psychology, 18* (2), 184–189.

Taylor, S. (1998). The hierarchic structure of fears. *Behaviour Research and Therapy, 36,* 205–214.

Whaley, S. E., Pinto, A., & Sigman, M. (1999). Characterizing interactions between anxious mothers and their children. *Journal of Consulting and Clinical Psychology, 67,* 826–836.

Wolitzky-Taylor, K. B., Horowitz, J. D., Powers, M. B., & Telch, M. J. (2008). Psychological approaches in the treatment of specific phobias: A meta-analysis. *Clinical Psychology Review, 28,* 1021–1037.

Wolpe, J. (1958). *Psychotherapy by Reciprocal Inhibition.* Stanford, CA: Stanford University Press.

Zlomke, K., & Davis III, T. E. (2008). One-session treatment of specific phobias: A detailed description and review of treatment efficacy. *Behaviour Therapy, 39,* 207–223.

17

Generalized Anxiety Disorder

Kendra L. Read, Chiaying Wei,
Courtney L. Benjamin[*], Matthew P. Mychailyszyn[**],
and Philip C. Kendall
Temple University, Philadelphia, USA

Generalized anxiety disorder (GAD), for both youth and adults, is characterized by the presence of excessive, uncontrollable, and persistent worry about a number of events or activities. To meet diagnostic criteria for GAD, youth must worry more days than not for a period of at least 6 months, and have associated somatic symptoms (APA, 2000). Worry has been characterized as "a chain of thoughts and images, negatively affect-laden and relatively uncontrollable" (Borkovec, Robinson, Pruzinsky, & DePree, 1983, p. 10). Children with GAD tend to worry uncontrollably across such domains as personal health and safety, the health and safety of loved ones, family matters, community or world events, perfectionism, and school or academic performance (Kendall, Krain, & Treadwell, 1999; Silverman, La Greca, & Wasserstein, 1995). Children with GAD frequently seek reassurance from others to lessen their anxiety (Flannery-Schroeder, 2004). Sometimes, the frequency of worrying may seem comparable to that experienced by non-anxious children; however, children with GAD worry with greater intensity (Weems, Silverman, & La Greca, 2000). The overall prevalence of GAD in youth has been estimated between 2.4% and 10.8% in the community (Bell-Dolan & Brazeal, 1993; Bowen, Offord, & Boyle, 1990; Costello, Stouthamer-Loeber, & DeRosier, 1993) and between 2.8% and 15% in youth referred to general mental health facilities (Last, Strauss, & Francis, 1987b; Silverman & Nelles, 1988). GAD has been associated with social problems, poor academic achievement, substance abuse, and suicidal ideation (Albano & Hack, 2004); if untreated it may be a precursor to other anxiety and mood disorders (Cantwell & Baker, 1989; Last, Hersen, Kazdin, Finkelstein, & Strauss, 1987a; Last, Perrin, Hersen, & Kazdin, 1992).

Models of treatment for GAD in youth (e.g., Kendall, Gosch, Furr, & Sood, 2008; Walkup, Albano, Piacentini et al., 2008) generally follow the same conceptual approach as that used with other anxiety disorders, such as social phobia (SP) and separation anxiety disorder (SAD). The development of efficacious treatments for GAD has been shaped by cognitive, behavioral, and social learning theories.

[*]Courtney L. Benjamin is currently affiliated with the University of Pennsylvania.
[**]Matthew P. Mychailyszyn is currently affiliated with Towson University, Department of Psychology.

The Wiley-Blackwell Handbook of The Treatment of Childhood and Adolescent Anxiety, First Edition.
Edited by Cecilia A. Essau and Thomas H. Ollendick.
© 2013 John Wiley & Sons, Ltd. Published 2013 by John Wiley & Sons, Ltd.

Behavioral Perspectives

Initial treatment models for anxiety originated from early classical and operant behavioral paradigms (Gosch, Flannery-Schroeder, Mauro, & Compton, 2006). Respondent conditioning theories hold that the development and maintenance of anxiety disorders rest on repeated pairings of an unconditioned fear- or anxiety-provoking stimulus (i.e., unconditioned stimulus; UCS) with a neutral stimulus (i.e., conditioned stimulus; CS). Over time, the neutral stimulus elicits the fear response (i.e. conditioned response, CR; Watson & Rayner, 1920). Although this explanation has merit, not all anxiety disorders are marked by a US-CS pairing (Menzies & Clarke, 1995). Additionally, some fear responses (e.g., panic) persist in the absence of a particular situation (Forsyth & Eifert, 1998).

Central to behavioral theories is the emphasis on avoidance in the face of perceived fear or threat from a stimulus (Mowrer, 1960). According to approach-avoidance perspectives, anxious children avoid fearful situations and approach only those that are viewed as safe. This behavior (avoidance) is reinforced by the experience of relief, which serves to maintain the avoidance behavior (Barrios & O'Dell, 1998; Delprato & McGlynn, 1984; Kendall, 2011). Operant learning paradigms emphasize the environmental consequences or contingencies that reward (reinforce) avoidant, anxious behavior (e.g. Skinner, 1969). Parents and other important individuals in the child's life (i.e. peers, teachers) may reinforce anxious behavior through their attention or actions (e.g. reducing demands or helping the child avoid situations). At the same time, the environment may fail to reward brave (non-anxious) behavior, especially when parents or others in the environment are fearful themselves (Gosch et al., 2006). These contingencies can lead to hypervigilance toward threat and a lowered sense of one's ability to cope with feared situations. Consistent with these behavioral models, treatment provides the child with skills that allow him or her to choose adaptive (non-avoidant) behavior in the face of feared situations. Changing one's behavior in the face of a feared stimulus (approach instead of avoidance) will have successive positive effects on related behaviors and anxiety symptoms (e.g., Gosch et al., 2006; Vittimberga, Scotti, & Weigle, 1999).

Treatment from a behavioral perspective emphasizes the prevention of avoidance and the provision of opportunities to learn new behaviors. Repeated exposure to the feared situation, without the experience of harm, results in a decrease in fear or anxiety, and an increase in one's ability to cope with the situation (habituation). In addition to exposure tasks, behavioral approaches include anxiety-reduction strategies such as deep breathing and relaxation exercises. However, in controlled exposure tasks (exposure to feared stimuli) research indicates that anxious individuals may report decreased levels of anxiety even without use of these relaxation techniques (Gillan & Rachman, 1974). Exposure to once-feared situations is central within the behavioral perspective.

Cognitive Components

Models of treatment for GAD include a focus on the cognitive processing of the anxious individual. Research suggests that although behavioral avoidance is important in understanding anxiety and its disorders, cognitive processing factors are needed for a more complete understanding (Gosch et al., 2006).

A cognitive understanding of GAD emphasizes the role of cognitive dysfunction and distortion. Children with GAD often engage in maladaptive cognitive processes, such as catastrophizing, overestimating the probability of negative events and consequences, and underestimating their ability to cope with imminent threat (Albano, Chorpita, & Barlow, 2003; Ingram & Kendall, 1987). Treatment from the cognitive perspective draws from social learning theory (Bandura, 1986) in its emphasis on children's sense of their personal ability, or self-efficacy, to cope with feared situations. Anxious children have lower self-efficacy in the face of anxiety (Southam-Gerow & Kendall, 2002), but confidence with feared situations rises through first-hand experience, and also through observation or vicarious interaction. (Bandura, 1986; Rachman, 1991). Accordingly, parental and peer reactions serve as models for these children.

Individuals with anxiety disorders also exhibit distortions and biases in information processing (Kendall, 2011), including perception, encoding, interpretation, and retrieval. Schemas, or organizational approaches to the world, greatly impact their anxiety symptomotology, given that they guide attention and memory for particular stimuli. Anxious individuals often exhibit a bias toward, and a heightened memory for, threatening stimuli (Beck, Emery, & Greenberg, 1985; Vasey & MacLeod, 2001). They are more likely to interpret ambiguous stimuli as threatening (e.g., Barrett, Rappee, Dadds, & Ryan, 1996). Importantly, anxious youth make significantly fewer interpretive biases when in a positive emotional state (Hughes & Kendall, 2008), which can be targeted and encouraged in therapy.

Not only do anxious children attend to and remember more fear-provoking material, but they fail to recognize their ability to control and change emotions (Southam-Gerow & Kendall, 2002). This can lead to decreased confidence in the ability to cope with their heightened arousal in the face of danger, resulting in persistent avoidance of potentially anxiety-inducing situations (Bogels & Zigterman, 2000). Anxious children experience a diminished sense of control and capability to deal with anxious feelings, which may be linked to highly reactive physiological arousal systems, and unpredictable or inconsistent environments (Chorpita & Barlow, 1998). Beck indentified particular self-schemas in anxious children, including low evaluations of self-efficacy and an overestimation of negative outcomes or threat within the environment (Beck, 1976). These schemas are thought to result from faulty information processing systems that lead to cognitive distortions such as polarized thinking, catastrophization, and overestimation of negative events (Albano & Hack, 2004; Beck 1976).

Treatment from this perspective retains behavioral strategies while including cognitive components, and focuses on challenging, changing, or providing alternative possibilities to the maladaptive thinking patterns that anxious children bring to situations. Treatment goals include changing the child's perception of his/her ability to cope with his/her anxiety when confronted with a feared situation. In-vivo, imaginal, and vicarious exposure to the feared stimulus allow the child to use coping skills learned in therapy and build confidence in his/her self-efficacy to cope with the anxious feelings that arise (Barrios & O'Dell, 1998). Given this strategy, targeting the distorted interpretation of threat in the environment during treatment assists in boosting self-efficacy and alleviating anxiety, subsequently reducing avoidance. Teaching the child to identify anxious physiological arousal and understand its relationship to the feared stimulus (as well as other factors that interfere with adaptive behavior) leads the child toward more adaptive responses (Barrios & O'Dell, 1998; Lang, 1977).

Tripartite Model

The tripartite model views the development of anxiety from the perspective of three specific vulnerabilities: a genetic component, a psychological propensity toward the assessment of threat, and early learning of anxious responses through experiences of threat or anxiety (Barlow, 2000). The development of anxiety from this perspective is greatly influenced by a diminished sense of personal control. According to the tripartite perspective, this perceived loss of control may arise from an uncontrollable or highly reactive arousal system, early stressful experiences, or early socialization, modeling, or learning that emphasizes impending threat and subsequent anxious responses (Chorpita & Barlow, 1998; Gosch et al., 2006). A lowered sense of control has been shown to mediate the relationship between the development of anxiety and stressful early experiences, and may further contribute to the development of anxiety in the face of stress later in development (Chorpita & Barlow, 1998). Treatment from this perspective targets the particular vulnerabilities by teaching coping skills, and providing opportunities to practice them in the face of anxiety-provoking situations – all in the service of building a greater sense of control for the child. Treatment may also provide opportunities to train and educate parents in modeling adaptive coping and improving consistency and responsiveness in parenting an anxious child (transfer of control; Ginsburg, Silverman, & Kurtines, 1995).

Summary

The conceptualization and treatment of GAD in youth has roots in behavioral models that include the cognitive components of anxiety (cognitive distortions; overestimation of threat). Most models of CBT for anxiety emphasize the use of exposure tasks that allow the child to practice adaptive coping strategies, increase self-efficacy, and acquire more realistic expectancies. The goals, methods, and basic structure of these empirically supported cognitive-behavioral strategies are outlined in the following sections.

Treatment Goals and Methods

The behavior of anxious youth is characterized by avoidance, which leads to distress for the children themselves, as well as their caregivers. Anxious youth frequently avoid age-appropriate situations and interactions that would otherwise contribute to and foster healthy development. CBT programs for childhood anxiety disorders, including GAD, are designed to teach youth to recognize signs of anxious arousal and to apply anxiety management strategies in response to these signals. The overarching goal is to help children learn to identify, regulate, and cope with their anxiety and to approach, rather than avoid, anxiety-provoking situations. The aim is not to eliminate anxiety altogether, but to "turn down the volume" of the child's anxiety.

CBT for childhood anxiety disorders has demonstrated efficacy, and reviews of the literature endorse its utility (Kazdin & Weisz, 2003; Silverman, Pina, & Viswesvaran, 2008). Variations exist in the treatments of anxiety disorders in children, though these various interventions share similar underlying goals and treatment components. Six components are found within the majority of CBT programs for youth with GAD. These include psychoeducation, relaxation/somatic management, changing self-talk (cognitive coping/restructuring), problem-solving, exposure to anxiety-provoking situations, and relapse prevention. As encouraged in Kendall (2006), the therapist serves as a "coach," teaching the child skills and leading the child to practice the skills they have learned. Rather than modeling mastery, an approach that illustrates successful coping, therapists serve as a "coping model," by identifying the difficulty of the situation and then demonstrating active efforts to cope.

Psychoeducation

The psychoeducational components set the stage for later cognitive and behavioral elements of treatment. Broadly, psychoeducation involves sharing facts about anxiety (e.g., anxiety can adaptive, anxiety can be normal) with the child. Learning these facts helps to build rapport and facilitates greater awareness and acceptance for the child. The new knowledge can guide the child's expectations about, and involvement in, treatment. Children also learn to recognize early physical signs or signals of their anxiety – a crucial step in knowing when to apply the coping strategies that will be learned and practiced throughout treatment.

CBT differs from some other therapies in that it does not place an emphasis on trying to uncover the cause of a child's anxiety. Rather, the adaptive and normative nature of anxiety (i.e., to alert and protect us from danger) is explained. The child may be encouraged to think of anxiety as a continuous and evolutionarily beneficial trait that, for some, is "turned up" too high or is too sensitive. It is helpful to explain the importance of anxiety (e.g., "What would happen if your safety alarm never went off?") and the child's need to dial down an overly sensitive alarm system. By reframing anxiety as a useful instinct to be managed, the therapist communicates that the treatment's aim is to help children cope with, rather than totally eliminate, anxiety. In addition to education about anxiety in general, learning the somatic manifestations of anxiety can also normalize the child's experience and facilitate involvement in treatment.

Although some children may be painfully aware of their anxious arousal, they often do not initially possess the vocabulary to articulate their experiences or recognize the malleability of these states (Southam-Gerow & Kendall, 2000). During the initial psychoeducation, youth are given the terminology and skills to identify a variety of affective states not only within themselves, but also in others. Youth with anxiety may misattribute anxious symptoms, such as muscle tension, stomachaches, or a racing heart, to physical causes, rather than emotional distress. The intensity and instability of emotional experiences can be distressing to youth, especially when these feelings are believed to be unmanageable. CBT therapists sort through this confusion by helping the child generate various reactions to anxiety. Because youth may be wary about sharing their experiences with these anxious symptoms (e.g., blushing, sweating, shaking), CBT therapists use self-disclosure and model their own anxious reactions with the child and discuss common somatic symptoms of anxiety.

Many anxious youth are unaware of the connection between their thoughts, feelings, and behavior or the potential to modify one's emotional reaction through changes in self-talk and repeated experience. Psychoeducation provides an expanded awareness and vocabulary about emotional experiences so that youth can begin to draw these connections. Thoughts can be used to help the child sort through different emotional states with overlapping physical cues (i.e. laughing can result from both amusement and nervousness). Once attuned to somatic cues and able to distinguish them from other reactions, youth can begin to implement the coping skills they will learn in treatment more easily and effectively. Psychoeducation can also help alert the child to the disorganizing effects of anxiety. When faced with an anxious situation, children may struggle to think clearly. The therapist may explain to the child that they will practice facing his/her fears again and again, moving from low level to highly anxiety-provoking situations. By doing so, the skills become more automatic and less susceptible to anxious arousal.

The beneficial nature of affective education has been supported in CBT prevention and treatment programs (Suveg, Southam-Gerow, Goodman, & Kendall, 2007). Learning to recognize the somatic antecedents of anxiety helps youth intervene while their level of arousal is low and malleable. This increases the likelihood of successful intervention and builds a sense of efficacy over time. Building a greater awareness of different somatic and emotional states facilitates rapport, normalizes the child's experience, and facilitates coping.

Relaxation/somatic management

Relaxation training is often part of CBT for childhood internalizing difficulties, including GAD (Compton, March, Brent, Albano, Weersing, & Curry, 2004). In some studies, relaxation alone has been shown to be effective (Borkovec & Costello, 1993; Ost & Breitholtz, 2000), highlighting its merits within a broader CBT program. Relaxation may be viewed as reciprocal inhibition (Borkovec & Costello, 1993), but within CBT it is often presented as a coping skill that can be developed and used as needed.

The rationale for relaxation training may not be obvious to youth (Stark, 1990) and some children may be intimidated or embarrassed by relaxation procedures, which often entail moving in ways that are different from what the child is used to. Because of this, CBT therapists spend time explaining the rationale for relaxation in a developmentally appropriate and engaging manner. CBT therapists may describe a variety of relaxation strategies and encourage the child to choose which is preferred. Depending on the child's age, the therapist may actively participate in relaxation practice with the child (i.e., for younger clients) or face away from the client so that the youth can practice without feeling self-conscious (i.e., for a teenager).

Relaxation can be varied based on the child's age, and versions of relaxation training scripts are available (some take the form of games or imaginative play for young children). Ollendick and Cerny (1981) developed a modification of deep muscle relaxation training with children that has been recommended and integrated into CBT protocols

(Kendall, Chansky, Kane et al., 1992; Stark, 1990). Children are taught to sequentially tighten and relax various muscle groups, while becoming increasingly aware of their physiological indictors of tension. Repeated muscle tension and release help children identify early signs of stress they may have previously overlooked. Such exercise also helps refute the notion that anxious somatic reactions are entirely automatic and outside the youth's control. The use of scripts to help youth target, tense, and relax core muscle groups associated with anxiety can be helpful with young children (e.g. practicing muscle relaxation by pretending to squeeze the juice out of a lemon). Pre-recorded relaxation scripts are used to allow the therapist to participate in exercises with youth and may facilitate the child's engagement in the relaxation process. For young children, relaxation may be delivered through games (e.g., the Robot-Rag doll comparison; Kendall & Braswell, 1993).

Deep breathing can also be taught through games and interactive exercises. For example, the therapist and child may practice taking many short, quick breaths in succession and then notice how their bodies feel. The therapist may then coach the child in how to take several deep, relaxing breaths in which the child breathes deeply into his/her belly, blowing it up like a balloon. To demonstrate this with young children, the therapist may place a small toy, pillow, or stuffed animal on the child's stomach and watch it move up and down with each breath. For older children or adolescents, this can be practiced by asking the youth to place a hand on his/her stomach. After several minutes of successful deep breathing, the therapist and child can notice how their bodies feel and contrast this with the experience of taking many quick, shallow breaths. Relaxation exercises allow the child to build upon his/her recognition of various affective states by increasing awareness of one's body and encouraging experimentation with his/her somatic experience. To facilitate competence with relaxation and increase the likelihood that the child will use relaxation in his/her daily life, relaxation strategies should be reviewed and practiced across sessions and assigned as homework.

Cognitive change

An integral feature of CBT for GAD youth is helping the child understand the connection between thoughts, feelings, and behavior. Youth are introduced to the concept of "self-talk," and the fact that everyone engages in self-talk. Self-talk, often introduced as and discussed with reference to "thought bubbles," can motivate us to cope in stressful situations or it can make us more nervous. Anxious youth come to recognize that self-talk can be helpful or unhelpful. For youth who struggle with anxiety, their self-talk is frequently negative and laden with themes of evaluative threat. Anxious self-talk is a target of treatment that has been found to mediate a favorable outcome; less engagement in anxious negative self-talk is associated with a reduction in anxiety (Kendall & Treadwell, 2007).

Many anxious youth interpret situations to be more dangerous than they really are and consequently have many negative and anxious thoughts. The therapist helps the child recognize that anxious thoughts can promote anxiety. Identifying anxious self-talk with youth can be challenging, but it can be helpful for the therapist to introduce the concept of self-talk through the use of cartoon thought bubbles. The therapist and child look at the pictures and provide examples of thoughts that might accompany the events depicted, progressing from concrete to more abstract or ambiguous scenarios. Once the child has achieved a level of mastery identifying the self-talk of characters in cartoons or pictures, the child is asked about his/her own thoughts. This process is done prior to targeting the thoughts for discussion (acceptance, change). The concept of self-talk is expanded from pleasant or neutral situations to anxiety-provoking situations, progressing from low to high levels of anxiety.

By addressing anxious self-talk, the therapist (1) helps youth recognize their individual thinking patterns and (2) helps them understand that self-talk can be modified (restructured). Youth with GAD often fall into a pattern of thinking characterized by negative expectations about a situation's outcome, which may be labeled as "thinking traps." These include a variety of cognitive distortions such as all-or-nothing thinking, focusing only on the negative possibilities, making faulty attributions, and predicting catastrophic outcomes.

Following the child's recognition of his/her anxious self-talk, the therapist can begin implementing strategies to challenge the accuracy or value of the anxious self-talk. The goal is to foster more adaptive "coping" self-talk as a response to the child's anxious self-talk. By modifying distorted interpretations and generating rational alternatives to unhelpful thoughts, the child engages in an active coping process. This coping process involves reflection, decatastrophizing, examining the evidence in support of and against a thought, and reframing (Friedberg & McClure, 2002; Kearney, 2005). Behavioral experiments (e.g., exposure tasks; see later in this chapter) provide opportunities to challenge one's cognitive appraisals.

Problem solving

For youth with GAD, the somatic distress and anxious self-talk they experience hinders their ability to be confident and to cope with stress. Education and practice in problem-solving strategies helps the child see things differently: "issues" are just problems to be solved.

Problem solving is a multistep process. First, the problem must be identified. While this may seem like a straightforward task, anxious youth have a history of becoming overwhelmed in anxiety-provoking situations and they may lack experience moving beyond their feelings of distress and accurately identifying the problem. For many anxious youth, this first step facilitates a transition from the abstract notion that "something" is wrong to a more concrete identification of the problem. Accurate identification can make a problem seem more manageable and increase the opportunity for eventual success.

Following problem identification, the next step is to brainstorm possible solutions or coping strategies. Anxious youth may "get stuck" trying to think of the perfect solution or may be willing to only consider particular actions. An important feature of this step is to delay judgment of each possibility's merit. The therapist helps the child to think "outside the box" by offering suggestions (including silly or exaggerated ones) to facilitate creative problem solving.

The next problem-solving step is to evaluate the possible solutions that were generated. Each alternative is discussed and the pros and cons of each considered. Once these assessments have been made, the child is asked to choose a preferred option (one that is likely to be successful) and to rank the others in the order in which they could be tried if the first is not successful. Because many problems may require two or more attempts before they are solved, it is important to have several viable solutions available upfront. This decreases the chance that the child will become overwhelmed if his/her first attempt to solve the problem is unsuccessful.

The final step involves trying out the potential solutions, beginning with the option that was rated as having the greatest probability of success, while being ready to implement the alternatives should the first prove unsuccessful. The successful learning of a step-by-step problem-solving process is important. It demonstrates thinking through an issue and addressing the challenges in daily life by generating a list of possible solutions.

When teaching problem solving to youth, start with a situation that would not be particularly anxiety provoking for the child, such as, "What could you do if you couldn't find your shoes when it was time to leave the house?" (as in the *Coping Cat Workbook*, Kendall & Hedtke, 2006b) or, "What if you didn't like what was being served for lunch at school?" Teaching problem solving in such a manner decreases the likelihood that the child will be overwhelmed by his/her own anxiety, allowing them to be more focused on and comfortable with the task at hand. Once problem solving has been mastered, the therapist can move on to practicing problem solving in anxiety-provoking situations via exposure tasks.

Exposure tasks

Engagement in hierarchy-based exposure tasks is common in CBT. Exposure is often considered the critical component of the treatment of anxiety disorders (Antony & Swinson, 2000; Barlow, Gorman, Shear, & Woods, 2000; Bouchard, Mendlowitz, Coles, & Franklin, 2004; Kendall, Robin, Hedtke, Gosch, Flannery-Schroeder, & Suveg, 2005; Rapee, Wignall, Hudson, & Schniering, 2000). Anxiety disorders are characterized by avoidance, and feared situations are often avoided due to excessive responses to *perceived* (as opposed to actual) threat. Exposure tasks are systematic experiences with anxiety-provoking situations in which youth engage the situation, and are presented with the opportunity to practice coping skills. Exposure tasks allow youth to "face their fears" (do not permit avoidance), develop adaptive responses to the feared situation, and distinguish real from perceived danger through direct experience.

It is common for youth to have routinely engaged in avoidance of anxiety-provoking situations by the time they present for treatment. After the initial psychoeducation sessions and practice in coping skills needed to manage anxiety-provoking situations, the therapist collaborates with the youth to actively plan and conduct exposure tasks. The therapist's role is that of a coach (Kendall, 2006) whose goal is to help the youth engage with (i.e., not avoid) the exposure task and test predictions regarding negative outcomes. Over time, participation in exposure tasks helps instill a sense of mastery and success in situations where the youth would not have confidence previously.

Recently, Bouchard et al. (2004), Kendall et al. (2005), and Rapee et al. (2000) have independently published guidelines for conducting exposures including examples of specific exposure tasks that they recommend for use with anxious youth. Exposure tasks may be maximally effective when they are prolonged and carried out in the real situation. There is consensus that the feared situation should be endured until some decrease in anxiety is experienced, often measured using Subjective Units of Distress/Discomfort Scale (SUDS; Wolpe & Lazarus, 1966) ratings. With youth, SUDS scales can range from 0 to 8 (Kendall & Hedtke, 2006a, 2006b), with 0 indicating "no distress" and 8 indicating the "highest level of distress." Therapists collaborate with youth on how to report SUDS ratings and both therapist and child can rate the child's SUDS.

Repetition of exposure tasks is often valuable. SUDS ratings can be helpful, with the therapist and youth comparing and even charting the SUDS ratings at the beginning of an exposure task across several repetitions. The exposure task can be repeated until these initial ratings decrease sufficiently (Kendall et al., 2005). Similarly, Rapee and colleagues (2000) suggest that exposure tasks be repeated until they become "boring" (i.e., the child has achieved mastery). The repeated practice allows the youth to build a history of successful experiences in anxiety-provoking situations, making it easier to generate helpful coping thoughts (e.g., "I've done it before; I can do it again!"), making it more difficult to discount successful experiences in the future, and allowing him/her to collect information to help defuse negative predictions. Practice across settings, such as at home, school, or with peers is also encouraged to produce generalization effects (Bouchard et al., 2004) and can be useful when the ideal exposure cannot feasibly be conducted within the clinic setting (Kendall et al., 2005).

Two types of exposure tasks are used: imaginal and *in vivo* exposure. Imaginal exposure tasks may involve the youth "role-playing" the feared situation with the therapist, considering different obstacles that may arise. Imaginal exposure can be used as preparation for *in vivo* exposure tasks, or as lower level experiences on the child's hierarchy (Kendall et al., 2005). Imaginal exposure tasks can also be helpful for youth with more abstract worries, such as those commonly reported by youth with GAD (e.g., health-related issues, death). Imaginal exposures can involve having the youth discuss and explain the specifics of their feared catastrophe (e.g., getting sick, death of a parent), how the situation will progress, and how it might end (e.g., "Who would take care of you if something did happen to your parents?"). The therapist can have the youth write a story about the feared event, describing in detail what would happen, and then have the youth read the story out loud or listen to a recording of it until his/her anxiety is reduced.

In vivo exposure involves actually being confronted with a feared situation or stimulus and enduring the distress that it creates until a level of anxiety reduction is achieved. *In vivo* exposure tasks vary in content depending on the nature of the youth's anxiety and are tailored to address the youth's individual fears and worries. For example, an *in vivo* exposure task for a youth with perfectionism worries could have him or her take a test, in-session, without being allowed to erase any answers or go back to check his/her work. Consider the severity of the disorder when planning exposure tasks: attend to the youth's expectations, prepare him/her for possible outcomes, and help the child problem-solve how to cope with possible occurrences. Exposure tasks may take place in- or out-of-session, and in- or out-of-the-office. Consequently, the therapist may need to consult with adults in the youth's life (parents, teachers) to plan out-of-session exposure tasks and aid their successful completion. Sometimes it may be helpful or necessary for the therapist to model leading an exposure task for the parents or teachers. Research suggests that, with the exception of safety-seeking behavior, variations in child behavior and several characteristics of the exposure tasks themselves (e.g., length of exposure task) are not related to treatment outcomes (e.g., Hedtke, Kendall, & Tiwari, 2009; Tiwari, Kendall, Hoff, Harrison, & Fizur, in press).

CBT for youth with GAD follow a format with exposure tasks consisting of collaborative selection of the exposure task to be practiced during the session, preparation for the task, execution of the task, evaluating performance during the task, and providing rewards for effort. Preparation involves discussing the upcoming situation, anticipating possible reactions (e.g., somatic, cognitive), and developing ways in which the youth can manage his or her anxiety during the situation (e.g., see Kendall & Hedtke, 2006a, 2006b). The therapist and youth can role-play, through imaginal exposure, to allow the youth to practice coping before the actual *in vivo* exposure task (Kendall et al., 2005).

During the actual exposure task, several factors must be considered. SUDS may be used to determine the length of an exposure, or, if this is not possible (e.g., it interferes with the task), the therapist can use clinical judgment to determine when the exposure task be terminated. It is very important for the therapist to tolerate the youth's distress during the exposure task and to not support or reinforce the youth's potential desire to avoid the situation. Short-term discomfort (the youth, parent, or therapist's) should not outweigh the long-term benefits associated with exposure treatment (Kendall et al., 2005). Despite the uncomfortable nature of exposure tasks, research indicates that they do not negatively affect the alliance between therapist and child, and promote, rather than damage the child's therapeutic gains (Kendall, Comer, Marker et al., 2009).

Following the exposure task, it is recommended that the youth and therapist evaluate the outcome and that the child is praised for his/her effort to cope, and not the ultimate outcome of the task. When processing an exposure task, the youth and therapist might discuss how the child was feeling, what he/she was thinking, and how the youth chose to manage his/her anxiety. Any obstacles that were encountered can be discussed, as well as what aspects of the task made it easy or difficult, and what, if anything, could be done differently in the future. Feedback and rewards are presented immediately after the completion of an exposure task (Kendall et al., 2005).

Relapse prevention

CBT programs for GAD youth vary in length; however, youth generally "graduate" from treatment when they have successfully engaged in a number of exposure tasks and demonstrated the ability to cope with anxiety-provoking situations in their life. The end of treatment is exciting, and potentially anxiety-provoking, for youth and their families. It is important to discuss strategies to maintain treatment gains and prevent relapse.

The therapist encourages continued engagement in post-treatment "challenges" (exposure tasks) rather than a return to the child or family's old routine. The old routines likely facilitated avoidance, which will only allow unwanted anxiety to return and escalate. Chorpita (2007) talks about having youth embrace an "exposure lifestyle" in which they continually approach, rather than avoid, anxiety-provoking situations. An "exercise metaphor" may be used with families to help them understand the importance of continued exposure (non-avoidance): When a person begins exercising, he or she often engages in an intensive phase to become physically fit – but it is continued exercise that is necessary to stay in shape. Parents and caregivers can assist youth with maintenance of gains by encouraging approach, bravery, and providing frequent praise when youth use their coping skills. Those who complete CBT will predictably encounter stressful situations (e.g., tests, graduations) after treatment. Efforts are made to communicate that although the nature of the situation may change, the newly-acquired coping skills will likely be similar.

Part of relapse prevention is explaining what to do when anxiety re-emerges. Youth who have successfully completed treatment can have modest setbacks. Minor lapses are to be expected. These lapses can serve as an indication that it is time to practice the skills learned in treatment again. A relapse, as opposed to a lapse, is the return of a larger problem. Relapses can occur when youth stop practicing their coping skills or when someone overreacts during a lapse. If a relapse occurs it does not mean that the youth cannot recover and it does not constitute a full-blown collapse. The youth may need to return to the clinic for booster sessions and, in many cases, a few visits help the youth feel in control again. It is our experience that youth who have participated in CBT programs for anxiety often recover from setbacks more quickly than they did prior to treatment.

Session-by-Session Program Delivery

One CBT treatment program for anxious youth, including youth with GAD, is the *Coping Cat* program (Kendall & Hedtke, 2006a, 2006b). The *Coping Cat* is a 16-session manual-based treatment with an accompanying child workbook; there is also an adolescent version, known as the *C.A.T. Project,* with an accompanying workbook and therapist manual (Kendall, Choudhury, Hudson, & Webb, 2002a, 2002b). Additionally, there is a computerized version, *Camp Cope-A-Lot* (Kendall & Khanna, 2008), as well as translations which allow implementation of the program in a manner that is compatible with the languages and customs of other countries (e.g., Argentina; Kendall & Kosovsky, 2010a, 2010b: Norway: Kendall, Martinsen, & Neumer, 2006a, 2006b). The majority of sessions are conducted individually with the child, incorporating parents as needed. There are two dedicated parent sessions included in the program. Over the course of treatment youth learn the *FEAR* plan (described later), an acronym representing steps to follow for engaging in effective coping with anxiety. The *Coping Cat* program encourages active and collaborative involvement in therapy; opportunities to demonstrate participation are offered by completing "Show-That-I-Can" (STIC) tasks – brief take-home exercises that foster practice of learned skills between sessions. However, although CBT is work-focused, there are also ample opportunities to engage the child and build rapport through play (Podell, Martin, & Kendall, 2009).

CBT for child anxiety has undergone numerous research evaluations and is considered an empirically-supported treatment. The *Coping Cat,* similarly, has undergone multiple empirical validations and has been found to produce beneficial gains when applied alone (Kendall, 1994; Kendall, Flannery-Schroeder, Panichelli-Mindel, Sotham-Gerow, Henin, & Warman, 1997; Kendall, Hudson, Gosch, Flannery-Schroeder, & Suveg, 2008), when applied in combination with medications (Walkup et al., 2008), and when implemented in a computer-assisted format (Khanna & Kendall, 2010). The following section provides a brief overview of the overarching goals to be accomplished across each session of the *Coping Cat* program. However, it is crucial to remember that manualized therapy approaches are not intended to be delivered in a mechanistic, "cookbook," fashion. Rather, implementation must be flexible, specifically adapted to the particular needs – developmentally as well as emotionally – of each unique client while also remaining adherent to the treatment (Beidas, Benjamin, Puleo, Edmunds, & Kendall, 2010; Kendall & Beidas, 2007; Kendall, Gosch et al., 2008).

Session 1

Youth with GAD commonly worry about situations that are novel and uncertain, and the start of treatment can be one such situation. The first session of the *Coping Cat* program focuses on providing the child with a brief introduction to the treatment and explaining the collaboration that the child can expect in the weeks to come. The therapist works to build rapport with the child, establish trust, and begin forming a strong therapeutic alliance, which has been found to be associated with positive outcomes for clients – especially when CBT is delivered in a one-on-one format (Liber et al., 2010). Because youth with GAD frequently worry about their performance and making mistakes, the therapy space is clearly distinguished from school; there are no "wrong" answers and "giving it a try" (effort) is important. A playful end-of-session activity helps to strengthen rapport and ensure that the child feels comfortable and has fun: The primary goal of Session 1 is to ensure that the child is willing – and ideally even looking forward – to coming back for the next session. Don't focus too much on anxiety. Work collaboratively and have some fun!

Session 2

The focus of Session 2 is an exploration of feelings and their outward manifestations. The therapist introduces the concept that various emotions are associated with different physical expressions; the therapist then builds on this notion, helping the child learn to distinguish anxious or worried feelings from other types of feelings. Another goal is to normalize anxiety: anxiety is a normal part of the human experience, and the goal of treatment will not be to eliminate anxiety, but rather to learn strategies to easily recognize its signs and cope/manage the experience more effectively. Finally, the therapist begins gathering information about what situations are anxiety provoking for the child, organizing these into an individualized hierarchy that will guide later exposure tasks.

Session 3

The third session is intended to educate the client about somatic responses to anxiety. Session 2 concepts are expanded upon as the therapist and child learn about the experience of a variety of internal bodily sensations in response to emotional states. The goal of this session is to help the child learn to identify his or her own unique somatic reactions to anxiety. Once this has been accomplished, the therapist introduces the "F" step of the *FEAR* Plan, "Feeling Frightened?" The F step encourages the child to use his or her newly gained knowledge about bodily feelings to recognize these as possible cues to the presence of anxiety, and to ask himself/herself, "Am I Feeling Frightened?" In this way, the client begins to link distressing somatic responses with the presence of negative emotional states; such knowledge can help to reduce the potential to be overwhelmed by such unpleasant bodily reactions as well as cue the child to use subsequent steps of the *FEAR* plan, which are introduced in later sessions.

Session 4

The fourth session of the *Coping Cat* program involves an individual meeting with the client's parent(s) or primary caregivers, with the chief purpose being to encourage parental engagement in treatment and to provide guidance on how this can be optimally achieved. The therapist provides parent(s) with information about the concepts being taught to the child and the progression of therapy (e.g. Kendall, Podell, & Gosch, 2010). Another important goal is to allay any existing parental apprehensions by offering answers to any questions or concerns raised. A third objective is to gather information from parents about the situations in which their child becomes anxious. Finally, the therapist offers ways for parents to be involved, and briefly introduces topics to consider in preparation for the next parent session (i.e., Session 9).

Session 5

Session 5 deals with relaxation strategies for some of the somatic discomfort associated with feeling anxious. Expanding on Session 3's discussion of bodily responses to anxiety, the therapist points out that anxiety can also lead to muscle tension. The child is encouraged to use the somatic symptoms identified in the F step as signals to cue the use of progressive muscle relaxation and diaphragmatic breathing. The therapist helps the client understand when it might be useful to implement these techniques, and collaborates in practicing them with the child in session to ensure that he or she knows how to do them properly.

Session 6

The sixth session of the program helps youth understand the role that their thoughts play in the experience of anxiety. The first goal of this session is to introduce the concept of self-talk, assisting the child in recognizing the content of his or her own self-talk, especially in anxiety-provoking scenarios. This leads into the introduction of the "E" step, "Expecting bad things to happen?" in which the client asks him- or herself, "Am I Expecting bad things to happen?" The therapist inquires about the child's anxious predictions, and explores with the child how likely they are to happen, what is the worst that could happen, and how helpful the thoughts are. From there, the therapist emphasizes the distinction between anxious self-talk, and more positive, coping-focused self-talk. The therapist emphasizes that by knowing the F and E steps, the child is now equipped to fully identify when he or she is feeling anxious, as well as the feelings and thoughts underlying that anxiety.

Session 7

The main purpose of Session 7 is to develop problem-solving strategies to manage anxiety. Problem-solving is introduced as a multi-step process that can be beneficial to individuals of all ages for dealing with a variety of challenges. The components of problem-solving (described earlier) are taught to the child, and the therapist practices working through this process under relatively benign and then more anxiety-provoking circumstances. At this point, the "A" step is introduced, "Attitudes and Actions that can help." The therapist emphasizes that the client has now learned a variety of strategies (e.g. relaxation, cognitive restructuring, problem-solving) that can allow him or her to more effectively approach, rather than avoid, anxiety-provoking situations.

Session 8

Session 8 of the *Coping Cat* program is focused on learning how to evaluate one's attempts to face anxious situations and preparing the client for the upcoming "challenges" (exposure tasks). The first goal of the session is to introduce the concepts of self-rating and reward. To this end, the "R" step is established as the last piece of the *FEAR* plan, in which the client is encouraged to consider the "Results and Rewards" of/for giving one's best effort to deal with anxiety. Highlighting that the client has now learned the whole *FEAR* plan for effectively coping with anxiety, the therapist then reviews and collaboratively completes the exposure hierarchy with the child, while discussing the upcoming activities. The therapist emphasizes that the hierarchy situations are likely to induce anxiety, but that they will be faced in a gradual and repeated manner that will allow the practicing of formerly learned skills until a significant reduction in distress is experienced. Be sure that there are items on the hierarchy that are goals for the youth: the hierarchy should not only be things that others want!

Session 9

The ninth session marks the second parent meeting, during which the therapist provides an update on the course of therapy and discusses with parents the upcoming exposure tasks. The exposure hierarchy is reviewed to obtain parents' feedback and ensure that planned exposures target the child's anxieties. Additional psychoeducation about the mechanisms of anxiety is provided to parents in order to prepare them to assist their child in completing exposures out of session. Specifically, the manner in which avoidance maintains and heightens anxiety is underscored and the importance of using coping skills while remaining in contact with the anxiety-inducing stimulus is emphasized.

Sessions 10–15

These sessions of the *Coping Cat* program are generally similar in their purpose and format. Intended to provide opportunities to practice coping in anxiety-provoking situations, the sessions include the collaborative engagement in exposure tasks ("challenges"). Sessions begin with the collaborative design and selection of the exposure task(s) to be completed, the development of a specific *FEAR* plan for that particular exposure task, and the implementation of that plan while being in contact with/engaging in the feared situation/activity. The therapist is encouraging and expresses confidence in the child's ability to effectively face the situation, while also making sure not to provide disingenuous promises that nothing bad will happen or that everything will be "just fine." Rather, the therapist recognizes that the situation is likely to be difficult and acknowledges that the client may experience some distress, but that overall he or she is confident that the child can make it through by using the *FEAR* plan. The difficulty of the exposure tasks increases over these sessions, allowing the client to experience a sense of mastery and draw upon prior successes to promote bravery for future challenges. Quality exposure tasks are creative and genuinely challenging for the youngster.

Session 16

The last session in the program involves a final exposure task, often reflecting an anxiety-provoking situation near the top of the youth's hierarchy that allows the child to finish with a sense of mastery and success. Following the final exposure, the therapist and client review what has been accomplished by having the child create a "commercial" during which he or she is provided with the opportunity to "show off" the knowledge and skills that have been acquired throughout therapy. These treatment termination activities are often done in the context of a "graduation" from the program in which the client's progress is celebrated.

Recent Empirical Findings

The majority of randomized clinical trials (RCTs) of CBT for childhood anxiety have included youth with GAD, SAD, and/or SP because these disorders commonly co-occur in youth and share some overlapping symptoms (Barrett, Dadds, & Rapee, 1996; Kendall, 1994; Kendall et al., 1997). A few studies have examined the psychosocial treatment of GAD in particular, but these reports are limited by small sample sizes (e.g., Eisen & Silverman, 1993, 1998; Kane & Kendall, 1989). Nevertheless, RCTs that included youth with a principal diagnosis of GAD have demonstrated efficacy for three treatment options: CBT (Kazdin & Weisz, 1998; Ollendick, King, & Chorpita, 2006), selective serotonin-reuptake inhibitors (SSRIs; Birmaher , Axelson, Monk et al., 2003; RUPP Anxiety Study Group, 2001; Walkup et al., 2008), as well as the combination of the *Coping Cat* CBT protocol and medication (Walkup et al., 2008).

Among existing treatments for anxious youth, CBT has undergone the most empirical scrutiny and is considered the psychosocial treatment of choice (Keeton, Kolos, & Walkup, 2009; Silverman et al., 2008). A 2007 meta-analysis examined 20 RCTs and found a large mean effect size of $d = 0.94$ for CBT in the treatment of children and adolescents with anxiety disorders (Ishikawa, Okajima, Matsuoka, & Sakano, 2007). The treatment gains were maintained from 3 to 24 months post-treatment. Individual clinical trials have also reported efficacy for individual CBT (Eisen & Silverman, 1993, 1998; Kendall, 1994; Kendall et al., 1997), group CBT (Barrett, 1998; Flannery-Schroeder & Kendall, 2000; Silverman, Kurtines, Ginsburg, Weems,

Lumpkin, & Carmichael, 1999), and family-focused CBT (Barrett et al., 1996; Cobham, Dadds, & Spence, 1998; Kendall, Hudson et al., 2008; Shortt, Barrett, & Fox, 2001).

In one recent RCT, Kendall, Hudson et al. (2008) compared the relative efficacy of individual CBT (ICBT), family CBT (FCBT), and a family-based education/support/ attention (FESA) active control. Study participants included parents and children aged 7–14 with a principal diagnosis of SAD, SP, and/or GAD. Outcome was evaluated at post-treatment and 1-year follow-up using measures of diagnostic severity, child self-report, parent report, and teacher report. FCBT and ICBT were superior to FESA in reducing the presence and severity of the principal anxiety disorder, and ICBT was superior to FCBT as well as FESA on teacher reported child anxiety. These treatment gains were maintained at 1-year follow-up.

Another clinical trial compared group CBT and a group support and attention (GSA) control condition in 120 children, aged 7–16 years, with a principal anxiety disorder diagnosis (approximately 50% of youth met diagnostic criteria for GAD; Hudson, Rapee, Deveney, Schniering, Lyneham, & Bovopoulos, 2009). At 6-month follow-up, 68.6% of children in the CBT condition no longer met diagnostic criteria for their principal anxiety diagnosis, compared with 45.5% of the children in the GSA condition. Here, CBT was significantly more efficacious than the control treatment.

A smaller clinical trial compared group CBT (GCBT) with parent and child (aged 4–8 years; $n = 24$), GCBT with parent only ($n = 25$), and a wait-list control group ($n = 11$; Waters, Ford, Wharton, & Cobham, 2009). Consisting of 10 sessions of GCBT, both active treatment groups were found to be superior to the control condition, with 55.3% of children in the parent only condition and 54.8% of children in the parent and child condition no longer meeting criteria for their principal diagnosis at post-treatment. These treatment gains were maintained at both 6- and 12-month follow-ups.

Parents often prefer CBT to other treatment strategies (Brown, Deacon, Abramowitz, Dammann, & Whiteside, 2007), but medication may also be effective. Indeed, for the full range of cases, including severe cases, CBT and medications were each effective, with the combination of the two being especially helpful (Walkup et al., 2008). With regard to medications, SSRIs (e.g., sertraline) are the most widely recommended medication for the treatment of anxiety disorders in youth (Sakolsky & Birmaher, 2008). Though the literature on pharmacological treatments of GAD in youth (for a review see Walkup, Labellarte, & Ginsburg, 2002; Stein & Seedat, 2004) is more sparse than the research on psychosocial approaches (see also Kendall, Pimentel, Rynn, Angelosante & Webb, 2004a), open-label trials and RCTs of SSRIs have provided useful information on the efficacy, safety, and tolerability of this class of medication for anxious youth (Keeton et al., 2009; Seidel & Walkup, 2006).

The Child/Adolescent Anxiety Multimodal Treatment Study (CAMS) was a randomized, placebo-controlled study that compared the relative efficacy of an SSRI (sertraline), CBT (*Coping cat* and *C.A.T. Project*, depending on client age), and a combined CBT and SSRI condition in youths with SAD, SP, and GAD of a moderate to severe nature (Walkup et al., 2008). The study included 488 children and adolescents aged 7–17 years. After 12 weeks (14 sessions) of treatment, the response rate was 80.7% for combined therapy, 59.7% for CBT, and 54.9% for sertraline, all of which were significantly superior to the placebo response rate. Combination therapy was superior to either SSRI or CBT alone. Overall, this study documents that both sertraline and the *Coping Cat* program are effective treatments for anxiety, and the combination of both demonstrated additional benefit.

Studies also reveal promising long-term outcomes for CBT (Kendall & Southam-Gerow, 1996; Kendall, Safford, Flannery-Schroeder, & Webb, 2004b; Puleo, Conner, Benjamin, & Kendall, 2011). One treatment study, which consisted of 16–20 sessions of CBT for avoidant, overanxious, and/or separation anxious disorder, observed maintenance of treatment gains in children 3 years post-treatment (Kendall & Southam-Gerow, 1996). Another study found that a meaningful percentage of participants maintained significant improvements in anxiety 7.4 years following a 16-week CBT course (Kendall et al., 2004b). The same study also found that successful CBT with anxious youth was associated with fewer substance use problems at the time of follow-up (Puleo et al., 2011).

Despite the progress in developing and evaluating efficacious treatments for children with GAD, additional research is needed. Not all youth have a favorable response to treatment, and work needs to be done to determine optimal treatments for the non-responders. More needs to be known about the optimal "dose" (Southam-Gerow, Kendall, & Weersing, 2001) and the potential mediators and moderators of a favorable treatment outcome. Additionally, although the CAMS study demonstrated an advantage of combination therapy (Walkup et al., 2008), more needs to be known about the sequencing, combining, and integrating of CBT and pharmacological interventions (Keeton & Ginsburg, 2008).

References

Albano, A. M., Chorpita, B. F., & Barlow, D. H. (2003). Childhood anxiety disorders, In E. J. Mash & R. A. Barkley (Eds.), *Child Psychopathology*, 2nd edn (pp. 279–329). New York: Guilford Press.

Albano, A. M., & Hack, S. (2004). Children and adolescents. In R. Heimberg, C. L. Turk, D. S. Mennin (Eds.), *Generalized Anxiety Disorder: Advances in Research and Practice* (pp. 383–408). New York: Guilford Press.

APA (2000). *Diagnostic and statistical manual of mental disorders*, 4th edn, *Text revision*. Washington, DC: American Psychiatric Association.

Antony, M. M., & Swinson, R. P. (2000). *Phobic Disorders and Panic in Adults*. New York: American Psychological Association.

Bandura, A. (1986). Fearful expectations and avoidant actions as co-effects of perceived self-inefficacy. *American Psychologist, 41,* 1389–1391.

Barlow, D. (2000). Unraveling the mysteries of anxiety and its disorders from the perspective of emotion theory. *American Psychologist, 55,* 1245–1263.

Barlow, D. H., Gorman, J. M., Shear, M. K., & Woods, S. W. (2000). Cognitive-behavioral therapy, imipramine, or their combination for panic disorder: A randomized controlled trial. *Journal of the American Medical Association, 283,* 2529–2574.

Barrett, P. M. (1998). Evaluation of cognitive-behavioral group treatments for childhood anxiety disorders. *Journal of Clinical Child Psychology, 27,* 459–468.

Barrett, P. M., Dadds, M. M., & Rapee, R. M. (1996). Family treatment of childhood anxiety: A controlled trial. *Journal of Consulting and Clinical Psychology, 64,* 333–342.

Barrett, P. M., Rapee, R. M., Dadds, M. M., & Ryan, S. M. (1996). Family enhancement of cognitive style in anxious and aggressive children. *Journal of Abnormal Child Psychology, 24,* 187–203.

Barrios, B. A., & O'Dell, S. L (1998). Fears and anxieties. In E. J. Mash & R. A. Barkley (Eds.), *Treatment of Childhood Disorders*, 2nd edn. New York: Guilford.

Beck, A. (1976). *Cognitive Therapy and the Emotional Disorders*. New York: International Universities Press.

Beck, A. T., Emery, G., & Greenberg, R. L. (1985). *Anxiety Disorders and Phobias: a Cognitive Perspective*. New York: Basic Books.

Beidas, R., Benjamin, C., Puleo, C., Edmunds, J., & Kendall, P. C. (2010). Flexible applications of The Coping Cat Program for anxious youth. *Cognitive and Behavioral Practice, 17*, 142–153.

Bell-Dolan, D., & Brazeal, T. J. (1993). Separation anxiety disorder, overanxious disorder, and school refusal. *Child and Adolescent Psychiatric Clinics of North America, 2*, 563–580.

Birmaher, B., Axelson, D. A., Monk, K., Kalas, C., Clark, D. B., Ehmann, M., et al. (2003). Fluoxetine for the treatment of childhood anxiety disorders. *Journal of the American Academy of Child and Adolescent Psychiatry, 42*, 415–423.

Bogels, S. M., & Zigterman, D. (2000). Dysfunctional cognitions in children with social phobia, separation anxiety disorder, and generalized anxiety disorder. *Journal of Abnormal Child Psychology, 28*, 205–211.

Bouchard, S., Mendlowitz, S. L., Coles, M. E., & Franklin, M. (2004). Considerations in the use of exposure with children, *Cognitive and Behavioral Practice, 11*, 56–65.

Borkovec, T. D., & Costello, E. (1993). Efficacy of applied relaxation and cognitive-behavioral therapy in the treatment of generalized anxiety disorder. *Journal of Consulting and Clinical Psychology, 61*, 611–619.

Borkovec, T. D., Robinson, E., Pruzinsky, T., & DePree, J. A. (1983). Preliminary exploration of worry: Some characteristics and processes. *Behaviour Research and Therapy, 21*, 9–16.

Bowen, R. C., Offord, D. R., & Boyle, M. H. (1990). The prevalence of overanxious disorder and separation anxiety disorder: Results from the Ontario Child Health Study. *Journal of the American Academy of Child & Adolescent Psychiatry, 29*, 753–758.

Brown, A. M., Deacon, B. J., Abramowitz, J. S., Dammann, J., & Whiteside, S. P. (2007). Parents' perceptions of pharmacological and cognitive-behavioral treatments for childhood anxiety disorders. *Behaviour Research and Therapy, 45*, 819–828.

Cantwell, D. P., & Baker, L. (1989). Stability and natural history of *DSM-III* childhood diagnoses. *Journal of the American Academy of Child & Adolescent Psychiatry, 29*, 691–700.

Chorpita, B. F. (2007). *Modular Cognitive-Behavioral Therapy for Childhood Anxiety Disorders*. New York: Guilford.

Chorpita, B. F., & Barlow, D. H. (1998). The development of anxiety: The role of control in the early environment. *Psychological Bulletin, 124*, 3–21.

Cobham, V. E., Dadds, M. R., & Spence, S. H. (1998). The role of parental anxiety in treatment of childhood anxiety. *Journal of Consulting and Clinical Psychology, 66*, 893–905.

Compton, S. N , March, J. S., Brent, D., Albano, A. M., Weersing, R., & Curry, J. (2004). Cognitive-behavioral psychotherapy for anxiety and depressive disorders in children and adolescents: An evidence-based medicine review. *Journal of the American Academy of Child & Adolescent Psychiatry, 43*, 930–959.

Costello, E. J., Stouthamer-Loeber, M., & DeRosier, M. (1993). Continuity and change in psychopathology from childhood to adolescence. Paper presented at the annual meeting of the society for research in child and adolescent psychopathology; Santa Fe, NM.

Delprato, D. J., & McGlynn, F. D. (1984). Behavioral theories of anxiety disorders. In S. M. Turner (Ed.), *Behavioral Treatment of Anxiety Disorders* (pp. 63–122). New York: Plenum.

Eisen, A. R., & Silverman, W. K. (1993). Should I relax or change my thoughts? A preliminary examination of cognitive therapy, relaxation training, and their combination with overanxious children. *Journal of Cognitive Psychotherapy, 7*, 265–279.

Eisen, A. R., & Silverman, W. K. (1998). Prescriptive treatment for generalized anxiety disorder in children. *Behavior Therapy, 29,* 105–121.

Flannery-Schroder, E. (2004). Generalized anxiety disorder. In T. L. Morris & J. S. March, *Anxiety Disorders in Children and Adolescents,* 2nd edn) pp. 125–140. New York: Guilford.

Flannery-Schroder, E. C., & Kendall, P. C. (2000). Group and individual cognitive-behavioral treatments for youth with anxiety disorders: A randomized clinical trial. *Cognitive Therapy and Research, 24,* 251–278.

Forsyth, J. P., & Eifert, G. H. (1998). Phobic anxiety and panic: An integrative behavioral account of their origin and treatment. In J. J. Plaud & G. H. Eifert (Eds.), *From Behavior Theory to Behavior Therapy* (pp. 38–67). Needham Heights, MA: Allyn & Bacon.

Friedberg, R. D., & Mcclure, J. M. (2002). *Clinical Practice of Cognitive Therapy with Children and Adolescents: The Nuts and Bolts.* New York: Guilford.

Gillan, P., & Rachman, S. (1974). An experimental investigation of desensitization in phobic patients. *British Journal of Psychiatry, 112,* 392–401.

Ginsburg, G. S., Silverman, W. K., & Kurtines, W. K. (1995). Family involvement in treating children with phobic and anxiety disorders: A look ahead. *Clinical Psychology Review, 15,* 457–473.

Gosch, E. A., Flannery-Schroeder, E., Mauro, C. F., & Compton, S. N. (2006). Principles of cognitive-behavioral therapy for anxiety disorders in children. *Journal of Cognitive Psychotherapy: An International Quarterly, 20,* 247–262.

Hedtke, K. A., Kendall, P. C., & Tiwari, S. (2009). Safety-seeking and coping behavior during exposure tasks with anxious youth. *Journal of Clinical Child and Adolescent Psychology, 38,* 1–15.

Hudson, J. L., Rapee, R. M., Deveney, C., Schniering, C. A., Lyneham, H. J., & Bovopoulos, N. (2009). Cognitive-behavioral treatment versus an active control for children and adolescents with anxiety disorders: a randomized trial. *Journal of the American Academy of Child & Adolescent Psychiatry, 48,* 533–544.

Hughes, A., & Kendall, P. C. (2008). Effect of a positive emotional state on interpretation bias for threat in children with anxiety disorders. *Emotion, 8,* 414–418.

Ingram, R. E., & Kendall, P. C. (1987). The cognitive side of anxiety. *Cognitive Therapy and Research, 11,* 523–536.

Ishikawa, S., Okajima, I., Matsuoka, H., & Sakano, Y. (2007). Cognitive behavioural therapy for anxiety disorders in chiidren and adolescents: a meta-analysis. *Child Adolescent Mental Health, 12* (4), 164–172.

Kane, M. T., & Kendall, P. C. (1989) Anxiety disorders in children: A multiple-baseline evaluation of a cognitive-behavioral treatment. *Behavior Therapy, 20,* 499–508.

Kazdin, A. E., & Weisz, J. R. (1998). Identifying and developing empirically supported child and adolescent treatments. *Journal of Consulting and Clinical Psychology, 66,* 19–36.

Kazdin, A. E., & Weisz, J. R. (2003). *Evidence-Based Psychotherapies for Children and Adults.* New York: Guilford.

Kearney, C. A. (2005). *Social anxiety and social phobia in youth: Characteristics, assessment, and psychological treatment.* New York: Springer Publishing Co.

Keeton, C. P., & Ginsburg, G. S. (2008). Combining and sequencing medication and cognitive-behaviour therapy for childhood anxiety disorders. *International Review of Psychiatry, 20,* 159–164.

Keeton, C. P., Kolos, A. C., & Walkup, J. T. (2009). Pediatric generalized anxiety disorder: epidemiology, diagnosis, and management. *Paediatric Drugs, 11,* 171–183.

Kendall, P. C. (1994). Treating anxiety disorders in children: results of a randomized clinical trial. *Journal of Consulting and Clinical Psychology, 62,* 100–110.

Kendall, P. C. (Ed.). (2006). *Child and adolescent therapy: cognitive-behavioral procedures.* New York: Guilford.

Kendall, P. C. (2011). Treating anxiety disorders in youth. In P. C. Kendall (Ed.), *Child and adolescent therapy: Cognitive-behavioral procedures (4ᵗʰ ed.)* New York: Guilford Press.

Kendall, P. C., & Beidas, R. (2007). Smoothing the trail for dissemination of evidence-based practices for youth: Flexibility within fidelity. *Professional Psychology: Research and Practice,* *38*, 13–20.

Kendall, P. C., & Braswell, L. (1993). *Cognitive Behavioral Therapy for Impulsive Children*, 2nd edn. New York: Guilford Press.

Kendall, P. C., Chansky, T. E., Kane, M., Kane, R., Kortlander, E., Ronan, K., Et Al. (1992). *Anxiety Disorders in Youth: Cognitive-Behavioral Interventions.* Needham Heights, MA: Allyn & Bacon.

Kendall, P. C., Choudhury (Khanna), M., Hudson, J., & Webb, A. (2002a). *The C.A.T. Project Workbook for the Cognitive-Behavioral Treatment of Anxious Adolescents.* Ardmore, PA: Workbook Publishing. www.workbookpublishing.com

Kendall, P. C., Choudhury (Khanna), M., Hudson, J., & Webb, A. (2002b). *The C.A.T. Project Therapist Manual.* Ardmore, PA: Workbook Publishing. www.workbookpublishing.com

Kendall, P. C., Comer, J., Marker, C., Creed, T., Puliafico, A., Hughes, A., et al. (2009). In-session exposure tasks and therapeutic alliance across the treatment of childhood anxiety disorders. *Journal of Consulting and Clinical Psychology, 77,* 517–525.

Kendall, P. C., Flannery-Schroeder, E., Panichelli-Mindel, S. M., Southam-Gerow, M., Henin, A., & Warman, M. (1997). Therapy for youths with anxiety disorders: a second randomized clinical trial. *Journal of Consulting and Clinical Psychology, 65* (3), 366–380.

Kendall, P. C., Gosch, E., Furr, J., & Sood, E. (2008). Flexibility within fidelity. *Journal of the American Academy of Child and Adolescent Psychiatry, 47,* 987–993.

Kendall, P. C., & Hedtke, K. A. (2006a). *Cognitive-Behavioral Therapy for Anxious Children: Therapist Manual*, 3rd edn. Ardmore, PA: Workbook Publishing. www.workbookpublishing.com

Kendall, P. C., & Hedtke, K. A. (2006b). *The Coping Cat Workbook*, 2nd edn. Ardmore, PA: Workbook Publishing. www.workbookpublishing.com

Kendall, P. C., Hudson, J. L., Gosch, E., Flannery-Schroeder, E., & Suveg, C. (2008). Cognitive-behavioral therapy for anxiety disordered youth: A randomized clinical trial evaluating child and family modalities. *Journal of Consulting and Clinical Psychology, 76,* 282–297.

Kendall, P. C., & Khanna, M. (2008). *Camp Cope-A-Lot: The Coping Cat DVD.* Ardmore, PA: Workbook Publishing.

Kendall, P. C., Krain, A., & Treadwell, K. R. (1999). Generalized anxiety disorders. In R. T. Ammerman, M. Hernsen, & C. G. Lasdt (Eds.), *Handbook of Prescriptive Treatments for Children and Adolescents*, 2nd edn (pp. 155–171). Needham Heights, MA: Allyn & Bacon.

Kendall, P. C., & Kosovsky, R. (2010a). *Tratamiento Cognitivo-Conductual Para Trastornos De Ansiedad En Ninos: Manual Para El Terapeuta.* Buenos Aires, Argentina: Libreria Akadia Editorial.

Kendall, P. C., & Kosovsky, R. (2010b). *El Gato Valiente: Cuaderno De Activdades.* Buenos Aires, Argentina: Libreria Akadia Editorial.

Kendall, P. C., Martinsen, K. D., & Neumer, S.-P. (2006a). *Mestringskatten: Kognitiv Atferd-sterapi for Barn Med Angst Terapeutmanual.* Oslo: Universitetsforlaget.

Kendall, P. C., Martinsen, K. D., & Neumer, S.-P. (2006b). *Mestringskatten: Kognitiv Atferd-sterapi for Barn Med Angst. Arbeidsbok.* Oslo: Universitetsforlaget.

Kendall, P. C., Pimentel, S., Rynn, M. A., Angelosante, A., & Webb, A. (2004). Generalized anxiety disorder. In T. H. Ollendick & J. S. March (Eds.), *Phobic and Anxiety Disorders in Children and Adolescents: a Clinician's Guide to Effective Psychosocial and Pharmacological Interventions* (Pp. 334–380). New York: Oxford University Press.

Kendall, P. C., Podell, J., & Gosch, E. (2010). *The Coping Cat: Parent Companion.* Ardmore, Pa: Workbook Publishing. www.workbookpublishing.com

Kendall, P. C., Robin, J. A., Hedtke, K. A., Gosch, E., Flannery-Schroeder, E., & Suveg, C. (2005). Conducting CBT with anxious youth? Think exposures. *Cognitive and Behavioral Practice, 12,* 136–150.

Kendall, P. C., Safford, S., Flannery-Schroeder, E., & Webb, A. (2004). Child anxiety treatment: Outcomes in adolescence and impact on substance use and depression at 7.4-year follow-up. *Journal of Consulting and Clinical Psychology, 72,* 276–287.

Kendall, P. C., & Southam-Gerow, M. A. (1996). Long-term follow-up of a cognitive-behavioral therapy for anxiety-disordered youth. *Journal of Consulting and Clinical Psychology, 64,* 724–730.

Kendall, P. C., & Treadwell, K. (2007). The role of self-statements as a mediator in treatment for anxiety-disordered youth. *Journal of Consulting and Clinical Psychology, 75,* 380–389.

Khanna, M., & Kendall, P. C. (2010). Computer-assisted cognitive-behavioral therapy for child anxiety: Results of a randomized clinical trial. *Journal of Consulting and Clinical Psychology, 78,* 737–745.

Lang, P. J. (1977). Fear imagery: An information processing analysis. *Behavior Therapy, 8,* 862–886.

Last, C. G., Hersen, M., Kazdin, A. E., Finkelstein, R., & Strauss, C. (1987) Comparison of *DSM-III* separation anxiety and overanxious disorders: Demographic characteristics and patterns of comorbidity. *Journal of the American Academy of Child and Adolescent Psychiatry, 26,* 527–31.

Last, C. G., Perrin, S., Hersen, M., & Kazdin, A. E. (1992). *DSM-III-R* anxiety disorders in children: Sociodemographic and clinical characteristics. *Journal of the American Academy of Child and Adolescent Psychiatry, 31,* 1070–1076.

Last, C. G., Strauss, C. C., & Francis, G. (1987). Comorbidity among childhood anxiety disorders. *The Journal of Nervous and Mental Disease, 175,* 726–730.

Liber, J. M., McLeod, B. D., Van Widenfelt, B. M., Goedhart, A. W., van der Leeden, A. J. M., Utens, E. M. W. J., et al. (2010). Examining the relation between therapeutic alliance, treatment adherence, and outcome of cognitive behavioral therapy for children with anxiety disorders. *Behavior Therapy, 41,* 172–186.

Menzies, R. G., & Clarke, J. C. (1995). The etiology of phobias: A nonassociative account. *Clinical Psychology Review, 15,* 23–48.

Mowrer, O. H. (1960). *Learning Theory and Behavior.* Oxford: Wiley.

Ollendick, T. H., & Cerny, J. A. (1981). *Clinical Behavior Therapy with Children.* New York: Plenum.

Ollendick, T. H., King, N. J., & Chorpita, B. F. (2006). Empirically supported treatments for children and adolescents. In P. C. Kendall (Ed.), *Child and Adolescent Therapy.* New York: Guilford Press.

Ost, L. G., & Breitholtz, E. (2000). Applied relaxation versus cognitive therapy in the treatment of generalized anxiety disorder. *Behavior Research and Therapy, 38,* 777–790.

Podell, J., Martin, E., & Kendall, P. C. (2009). Incorporating play in a manual-based treatment for children and adolescents with anxiety disorders. In A. Drewes (Ed.) *Blending play therapy with cognitive behavior therapy: Evidence-based and other effective treatments and techniques.* New York: Wiley and Sons.

Puleo, C. M., Conner, B. T., Benjamin, C. L., & Kendall, P. C. (2011). CBT for childhood anxiety and substance use at 7.4-year follow-up: A reassessment controlling for known predictors. *Journal of Anxiety Disorders, 25,* 690–696.

Rachman, S. J. (1991). Neoconditioning and the classical theory of fear acquisition. *Clinical Psychology Review, 11,* 115–173.

Rapee, R. M., Wignall, A., Hudson, J. L., & Schneiring, C. A. (2000). *Treating Anxious Children and Adolescents: an Evidence-Based Approach.* Oakland, CA: New Harbinger Publications.

RUPP (Research Unit on Pediatric Psychopharmacology) Anxiety Study Group. (2001). Fluvoxamine for the treatment of anxiety disorders in children and adolescents. *New England Journal of Medicine, 344,* 1279–1285.

Sakolsky, D., & Birmaher, B. (2008). Pediatric anxiety disorders: management in primary care. *Current Opinion in Pediatrics, 20,* 538–543.

Seidel, L., & Walkup, J. T. (2006). Selective serotonin reuptake inhibitor use in the treatment of the pediatric non-obsessive-compulsive disorder anxiety disorders. *Journal of Child and Adolescent Psychopharmacology, 16,* 171–179.

Shortt, A. L., Barrett, P. M., & Fox, T. L. (2001). Evaluating the FRIENDS program: A cognitive-behavioral group treatment for anxious children and their parents. *Journal of Clinical Child Psychology, 30,* 525–535.

Silverman, W. K., Kurtines, W. M., Ginsburg, G. S., Weems, C. F., Lumpkin, P. W., & Carmichael, D. H. (1999). Treating anxiety disorders in children with group cognitive-behavioral therapy: A randomized clinical trial. *Journal of Consulting and Clinical Psychology, 67,* 995–1003.

Silverman, W. K., La Greca, A. M., & Wasserstein, S. (1995). What do children worry about?: Worries and their relationship to anxiety. *Child Development, 66,* 671–686.

Silverman, W. K., & Nelles, W. B. (1988). The anxiety disorders interview schedule for children. *Journal of the American Academy of Child and Adolescent Psychiatry, 27,* 772–778.

Silverman, W., Pina, A. A., & Viswesvaran, C. (2008). Evidence-based psychosocial treatments for phobic and anxiety disorders in children and adolescents. *Journal of Clinical Child and Adolescent Psychology, 37,* 105–130.

Skinner, B. F. (1969). *Contingencies of Reinforcement: A Theoretical Analysis.* New York: Appleton.

Southam-Gerow, M. A., & Kendall, P. C. (2000). Emotion understanding in youth referred for treatment of anxiety disorders. *Journal of Clinical Child Psychology, 36,* 77–85.

Southam-Gerow, M. A., & Kendall, P. C. (2002). A preliminary study of the emotion understanding of youths referred for treatment of anxiety disorders. *Journal of Clinical Child Psychology, 29,* 319–327.

Southam-Gerow, M. A., Kendall, P. C., & Weersing, V. R. (2001). Examining outcome variability: correlates of treatment response in a child and adolescent anxiety clinic. *Journal of Clinical Child Psychology, 30,* 422–436.

Stark, K. D. (1990). *The Treatment of Depression During Childhood: A School-Based Program.* New York: Guilford Press.

Stein, M. B., & Seedat, S. (2004). Pharmacotherapy. in T. L. Morris & J. S. March (Eds.), *Anxiety Disorders in Children and Adolescents* (pp. 329–354). New York: Guilford.

Suveg, C., Southam-Gerow, M., Goodman, K., & Kendall, P. C. (2007). The role of emotion theory and research in child therapy development. *Clinical Psychology: Science and Practice, 14,* 358–372.

Tiwari, S., Kendall, P. C., Hoff, A. L., Harrison, J. P., & Fizur, P. (in press). Characteristics of Exposure Sessions as Predictors of Treatment Response in Anxious Youth. *Journal of Clinical Child and Adolescent Psychology,* in press.

Vasey, M. W., & MacLeod, C. (2001). Information-processing factors in childhood anxiety: A review and developmental perspective. In M. W. Vasey & M. R. Dadds (Eds.), *The Developmental Psychopathology of Anxiety* (pp. 253–277). New York: Oxford University Press.

Vittimberga, G. L., Scotti, J. R., & Weigle, K. L. (1999). Standards of practice and critical elements in an educative approach to behavioral intervention. In J. R. Scotti & L. H. Meyer (Eds.), *Behavioral Intervention: Principles, Models, and Practices* (pp. 25–46). Baltimore: Brookes.

Walkup, J. T., Albano, A. M., Piacentini, J., Birmaher, B., Compton, S. N., Sherrill, J. T., Ginsberg, G., Rynn, M., McCracken, J., Waslick, B., Iyengar, S., March, & J., Kendall., P.

(2008). Cognitive behavioral therapy, sertraline, or a combination in childhood anxiety. *New England Journal of Medicine, 359,* 2753–2766.

Walkup, J. T., Labellarte, M. J., & Ginsburg, G. S. (2002). The pharmacological treatment of childhood anxiety disorders. *International Review of Psychiatry, 14,* 135–142.

Waters, A. M., Ford, L. A., Wharton, T. A., & Cobham, V. E. (2009). Cognitive-behavioural therapy for young children with anxiety disorders: Comparison of a Child + Parent condition versus a Parent Only condition. *Behaviour Research and Therapies, 47,* 654–662.

Watson, J. B., & Rayner, R. (1920). Conditioned emotional reactions. *Journal of Experimental Psychology, 3,* 1–14.

Weems, C. F., Silverman, W. K., & La Greca, A. M. (2000). What do youth referred for anxiety problems worry about? Worry and its relation to anxiety and anxiety disorders in children and adolescents. *Journal of Abnormal Child Psychology, 28,* 63–7

Wolpe, J., & Lazarus, A. A. (1966). *Behavior Therapy Techniques.* New York: Pergamon.

18

Obsessive-Compulsive Disorder

Phoebe S. Moore[1], Martin E. Franklin[2],
Jennifer Freeman[3], and John March[4]

[1]University of Massachusetts Medical School, USA
[2]University of Pennsylvania School of Medicine, USA
[3]Alpert Medical School of Brown University & Rhode Island Hospital, USA
[4]Duke University Medical Center, USA

This chapter focuses on the treatment of pediatric obsessive-compulsive disorder (OCD), with an emphasis on the best-supported psychosocial treatment for the disorder – cognitive-behavioral therapy (CBT) utilizing exposure with ritual prevention (EX/RP). We begin with a brief overview of the problem of OCD in youth and the importance of studying, refining, and disseminating the most effective treatments possible for this debilitating disorder. We then follow with a discussion of the fundamental principles that guide our understanding of OCD and form the theoretical basis for CBT treatment; a review of the goals and methods used in this protocol; and a detailed session-by-session review, with example dialogue. The chapter continues with a review of the recent efficacy and effectiveness evidence for this treatment model. We conclude with recommendations for future research.

As a general rule, pediatric OCD is a prevalent, distressing, and functionally impairing anxiety disorder. By late adolescence, the lifetime prevalence of childhood OCD is estimated to fall between 2 and 3% (Rapoport, Inoff-Germain, Weissman et al., 2000), while point prevalence estimates indicate that, at any given moment, between 0.5 and 1% of the pediatric population suffers from OCD (Flament, Whitaker, Rapoport et al., 1988). The disorder is highly disruptive to the normal developmental trajectory, causing impairment in school performance, friendships, family relationships, and vocational functioning (Piacentini, Bergman, Keller & McCracken, 2003; Adams, Waas, March, & Smith, 1994). In many to most cases, it tends to persist in a waxing and waning course through adolescence and into adulthood, indicating a need for early intervention (Stewart, Geller, Jenike et al., 2005).

OCD is characterized by two main symptoms: obsessions and compulsions. Obsessions are recurrent and persistent thoughts, images, or impulses that are ego-dystonic, intrusive, and usually acknowledged as senseless by the patient. Obsessions are generally accompanied by negative affects, such as fear, disgust, doubt, or a feeling of incompleteness, and are therefore distressing to the affected individual. To alleviate obsession-related discomfort, young persons with OCD typically attempt to ignore,

The Wiley-Blackwell Handbook of The Treatment of Childhood and Adolescent Anxiety, First Edition.
Edited by Cecilia A. Essau and Thomas H. Ollendick.
© 2013 John Wiley & Sons, Ltd. Published 2013 by John Wiley & Sons, Ltd.

suppress, or neutralize obsessive thoughts and associated uncomfortable feelings by performing compulsions, which are repetitive, purposeful behaviors performed in response to an obsession, often according to certain rules or in a stereotyped fashion. Compulsions can be observable repetitive behaviors, such as washing, or covert mental acts, such as counting. These compulsive behaviors relieve, at least in the short term, the anxiety or sense of discomfort caused by the obsessions, and thus the compulsions are strengthened through a process of negative reinforcement. In children and adolescents with OCD, it is common for compulsions to include family members. Examples of this can include direct participation in the ritual, such as reassurance seeking (a parent provides reassurance to child as part of compulsive checking ritual) or indirect support such as supplying the child with cleaning supplies.

One prominent concern with OCD that onsets during childhood, is its harmful effect on the child's developmental course. OCD can affect everything from academics to friendships to family relationships, undermining role functioning. Due to the impact of compulsive rituals or avoidance behavior, children and adolescents with OCD may drop out of activities they used to enjoy, avoid social contact, experience academic problems, or lose sleep. Thus, in addition to the risk of OCD symptoms persisting into adulthood and causing impairment, pediatric OCD can severely divert the trajectory of normal development, leading to long-term deficits across many areas of functioning. Timely and effective intervention is therefore of the utmost importance.

Fortunately, significant advances in treatment have been made over the past decade and, as is the case with adult OCD, cognitive-behavioral therapy (CBT) has emerged as the initial treatment of choice for pediatric OCD (Abramowitz, Whiteside, & Deacon, 2005; March, Frances, Kahn, & Carpenter, 1997; POTS Team, 2004). The evidence for the efficacy of CBT has strengthened considerably in the past decade, lending further credence to experts' recommendation that families be vigorously encouraged to seek CBT for children and adolescents suffering from this often-disabling condition.

Medications, particularly serotonin reuptake inhibitors, also demonstrate evidence of effectiveness with OCD, both in adult and in pediatric populations. A comprehensive review of pharmacotherapy for OCD is beyond the scope of this chapter (for such a review, see Franklin & Simpson, 2005). By way of a general review, however, we can say that (1) large, multisite randomized studies clearly indicate that medications that affect the serotonergic neurotransmitter system (e.g., selective serotonin reuptake inhibitors or SSRIs, the tricyclic antidepressant clomipramine) are efficacious for OCD for children, adolescents, and adults; (2) the effects of these medications are far from universal or complete; and (3) side effects prevent some patients from reaching doses likely to be efficacious.

Cognitive behavioral therapy involving EX/RP has been found consistently superior to various control conditions, and either comparable to or superior to active pharmacotherapy. Recent evidence (POTS Team, 2004) indicates that combining medication with CBT can be particularly effective, but it is also notable that when the response criterion was defined as "excellent response," defined as OCD symptoms in the extremely mild to subclinical range, CBT alone was comparable to the combination of CBT with the SSRI sertraline. As such, the remainder of this chapter focuses exclusively upon the most-researched psychological treatment for youth with OCD: CBT involving EX/RP.

Theoretical Background

Our exposure-based OCD treatment is grounded in an understanding of the behavioral and cognitive environment in which OCD evolves. It draws upon relevant behavioral and cognitive theory in its design as it aims to reduce compulsive responding and therefore, indirectly, obsessive symptomatology. EX/RP was initially developed for the population of adult OCD sufferers and, as has typically been the case with all pediatric anxiety and mood disorders, was adapted for youth with OCD via an age-downward extension of this protocol, which had been found to be highly efficacious in adults (e.g., Hofman & Smits, 2008). Below, we review the relevant theory that contributed to the development of this particular treatment model.

Several cognitive behavioral theories about the development and maintenance of OCD symptoms have been put forward. Dollard and Miller (1950) adopted Mowrer's two-stage theory (1939, 1960) to explain the development and maintenance of fear/anxiety and avoidance in OCD. Mowrer's theory maintains that a neutral event stimulus (conditioned stimulus, or CS) comes to elicit fear when it is repeatedly presented together with an event that by its nature causes pain/distress (unconditioned stimulus, or UCS). The CS can be mental events, such as thoughts, and/or physical events, such as coming into contact with bathrooms and trash cans. After a fear/anxiety/distress response to the CS is acquired, OCD sufferers develop escape or avoidance behaviors – repeated compulsions or rituals – to reduce the anxiety.

Mowrer's theory not only adequately explains fear acquisition, but is also consistent with observations of how rituals are maintained. In a series of experiments, Rachman and colleagues (Hodgson, Rachman & Marks, 1972; Roper, Rachman & Hodgson, 1973; Roper & Rachman, 1976) demonstrated that obsessions increase distress and compulsions do indeed reduce it. This conceptualization of a functional relationship between obsessions and compulsions influenced the definitions of OCD in the DSM-III (DSM III; APA, 1980) and its successors.

In a seminal theoretical paper, Foa and Kozak (1986) proposed that OCD is characterized by erroneous cognitions. First, OCD sufferers assign a high probability of danger to situations that are relatively safe. For example, an individual with OCD will believe that if he touches public doorknobs without thoroughly washing his hands afterwards, the germs on the doorknob will cause serious disease to him and/or to people whom he might touch with his dirty hands. Second, individuals with OCD exaggerate the cost of the bad things that they imagine can happen – for example, perceiving contracting a minor cold as a terrible thing. For others with more abstract fears, the fear responses are associated with mistaken meaning rather than with a particular stimulus. For example, some patients who are disturbed by perceived asymmetry and reduce their distress by rearranging objects do not fear the objects themselves, nor do they anticipate disaster from the asymmetry. Rather, they are upset by their view that certain arrangements of stimuli are "not right." Foa and Kozak (1986) further suggested that individuals with OCD, in the face of lack of evidence that a situation or an object is safe, will conclude that it is dangerous. Therefore, OCD sufferers require constant evidence of safety. For example, in order to feel safe, an OCD sufferer might require a guarantee that the dishes in a given restaurant are extremely clean before eating in that restaurant. People without OCD, on the other hand, usually conclude that, if they do not have evidence that a situation is dangerous, it is safe. Thus, a person without OCD will eat from the dishes in the restaurant unless he has clear evidence that they are dirty.

The cognitive model posited by Salkovskis (1985) is also highly relevant to our conceptualization of OCD and our treatment approach. According to this model, intrusive, obsessional thoughts are stimuli that may provoke certain types of negative automatic thoughts. In particular, an exaggerated sense of responsibility and self-blame are central themes in the OCD belief system. Neutralization, in the form of behavioral or cognitive compulsions, can be understood as an attempt to reduce this sense of responsibility and to prevent blame. Salkovskis further proposed that dysfunctional assumptions characterize obsessive compulsives and differentiate them from persons without OCD. These assumptions include focus on the idea that thoughts are equivalent to actions – i.e., having a thought about harm is considered by the OCD sufferer to be the same as performing that harmful action. In addition, the youth with OCD is likely to believe that s/he can and/or should be able to control the content of thoughts, and that failing to neutralize a thought about harm or danger would indicate an actual wish for the harm/danger thought or image to become reality. Thus, while the obsession may be ego dystonic, the automatic thought that it elicits will be ego syntonic. This model suggests that treatment of OCD should focus on identifying the erroneous assumptions and modifying the automatic thoughts.

Treatments based on each of the aforementioned theoretical models tend to result in therapeutic approaches tied to the mechanism by which the OCD is understood to be maintained; for example, the more behavioral conceptualizations would lead therapists to emphasize reduction of all forms of passive and active avoidance to permit learning to occur, whereas the cognitive theories would yield a particular focus on challenging the underlying belief system to effect symptom change. Theories that blend cognitive and behavioral elements such as Foa and Kozak's Emotional Processing Theory (Foa & Kozak, 1986) combine the use of cognitive and behavioral treatment strategies, with the aim of providing the patient with corrective information about the world and about their own fear responses. The current manual used most often to guide EX/RP for children (March & Mulle, 1998) blends these cognitive and behavioral approaches to create a structured guide to treatment in a developmentally sensitive framework for child and adolescent OCD sufferers. A review of the extant evidence base for this treatment model is provided at the end of this chapter.

Therapeutic Goals and Methods

The current version of the pediatric OCD treatment manual (March & Mulle, 1998; POTS Team, 2004) typically involves 14 sessions over 12 weeks. The first four sessions focus on psychoeducation and cognitive training, with an emphasis on the externalization of the OCD as a neurobehavioral problem independent of the child's unique self. Using this knowledge – that OCD is "not me" but an external force that is vulnerable to the child's attempts to regain control – a hierarchy of exposure tasks is developed, starting with relatively easy ways to resist compulsions (e.g., touching a bathroom wall at home and not washing), and building up to very challenging exposure tasks (e.g., touching a toilet seat in a public restroom and not washing). The child is encouraged to "poke OCD with a stick" by doing activities that provoke OCD-related anxiety or discomfort, and then resist the ritual that their OCD leads them to believe will reduce this anxiety or discomfort. Exposures are completed in session and as homework, and the child charts his or her anxiety/discomfort level over time using a "fear thermometer" ranging from 1 (easy) to 10 (hardest ever).

As the child learns that the anxiety associated with obsessions is tolerable and remits over time regardless of ritual performance, more and more challenging tasks can be accomplished. The process of habituation that occurs during the exposures facilitates a sense of control for the patient, and also tends to reduce the frequency and intensity of obsessions and urges to ritualize. In many cases (up to a third of children treated with CBT only, and up to a half of children receiving CBT plus medication, as described by the POTS Team, 2004), subclinical status can be attained within the 12 weeks.

Pre-treatment assessment

Before beginning CBT for pediatric OCD, a full assessment of OCD symptomatology, as well as comorbid conditions, is indicated. For a review of assessment tools for pediatric OCD, see Merlo, Storch, Murphy, Goodman, Geffken (2005). In our view, an adequate assessment of pediatric OCD should include a comprehensive evaluation of current and past OCD symptoms, current OCD symptom severity and associated functional impairment, and comorbid psychopathology. The strengths of the child and of the family should also be considered, as well as their knowledge of OCD and its treatment.

Treatment and session structure

The treatment, consisting for four phases, extends for 14 sessions conducted over 12 weeks. Table 18.1 summarizes the treatment protocol, while Table 18.2 summarizes the structure of each session.

The treatment can be divided into four phases. Phase one involves psychoeducation around the nature and process of OCD, and takes place during the first two sessions, both conducted in week one. Phase two, beginning in week one and concluding in week two, focuses on cognitive training, or how to "talk back" to OCD. Phase three, also occurring in the double sessions in week two, is called "mapping OCD" and involves creating a fully developed account of the youth's OCD symptoms, including a hierarchy of symptom intensity. These first three phases serve to set up the final and longest phase: graded exposure and response prevention (EX/RP), practiced in

Table 18.1 Summary of the treatment protocol.

Visit	Goals
Pre-treatment	Assessment of OCD and comorbid conditions
Week 1 (two sessions)	Psychoeducation
	Cognitive training
Week 2 (two sessions)	"Mapping" OCD
	Cognitive training
Weeks 3–12	Exposure and response prevention (EX/RP)
Weeks 11–12	Relapse prevention
Visits 1, 7, &11	Parent sessions

Table 18.2   The structure of each session.

Session elements
Statement of goals
Review of preceding week
New information
Therapist-assisted practice
Homework assignment
Monitoring procedures

session and at home during weeks three to twelve. Each phase is further delineated below:

Phase one aims to enhance child and family understanding of the neurobiological nature of OCD and the structure and process of the cognitive behavioral treatment model for OCD. It explicitly focuses on OCD as a medical illness and uses this concept to focus the child and the family on forming an alliance with the therapist to fight back against OCD symptoms. In many families, parents enter treatment feeling that they are battling their child directly; this reframing process creates a significant change in family process, allowing for a team mentality and identifying OCD, not the child, as the problem. Developmentally appropriate interventions are used to support this conceptualization of OCD as external to the child, ranging from talking about "brain hiccups" or a malfunctioning "worry computer," to examining MRI scans of OCD sufferers in order to see the different process of the OCD brain.

Phase two begins to build up the cognitive "toolbox" of the child and family. These cognitive tactics focus on increasing a sense of personal efficacy, predictability, controllability, and self-attributed likelihood of a positive outcome for EX/RP tasks. Targets for cognitive training include (1) reinforcing accurate information regarding OCD and its treatment, (2) cognitive resistance ("bossing OCD"), and (3) self-administered positive reinforcement and encouragement. The purpose of these tools are primarily to support motivation for and participation in EX/RP rather than to reduce anxiety per se. We explicitly frame EX/RP as the strategy and the therapist and parents (and sometimes teachers or friends) as the allies in the child's "battle" against OCD. Approaching OCD in this way allows everyone to ally with the child in order to "boss back" OCD, and thereby provides a narrative scaffolding on which to hang family interventions. Constructive self-talk ("bossing OCD") and the use of positive coping strategies provide the child with a set of cognitive tools to use when preparing for and executing exposure and response prevention tasks, which in turn facilitate EX/RP compliance and effectiveness.

Phase three creates a comprehensive "map" of the child's OCD, including a detailed picture of specific obsessions and compulsions, triggers for symptoms, avoidance behaviors, and perceived consequences. Integrated within this map is a functional hierarchy of OCD symptoms which serves as a guide to graded EX/RP over the next phase of treatment. Depending on child preferences and cognitive style, the "maps" can range from full-blown detailed maps of island nations (including "contamination island," "checking island" and the patient's own island) to comprehensive lists of obsessions and compulsions, ranked by anxiety-provoking value. Crucial in the

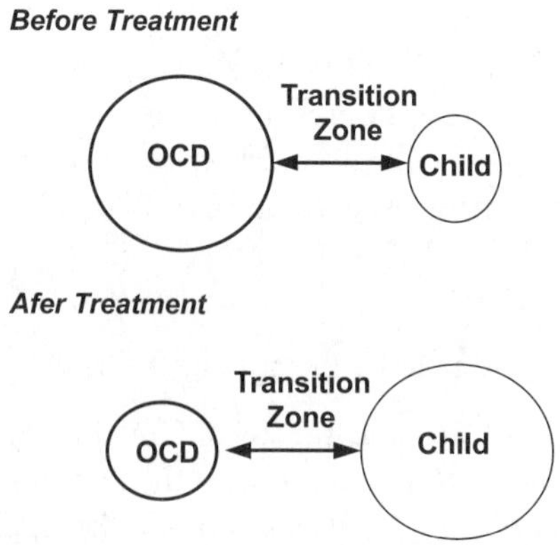

Before Treatment

Afer Treatment

Figure 18.1 Mapping OCD.

"mapping" phase is a well-described picture of what we call the "transition zone" (see Figure 18.1), which is the group of symptoms which the young patient can sometimes feel empowered to fight against or resist effectively. The "transition zone" is presented as the staging ground for taking back the child's "life territory" from OCD – by beginning exposures with this set of symptoms, which, in practice, make up the lower end of the stimulus hierarchy, the exposure intervention is likely to be well-tolerated and effective, generating enthusiasm for further work and higher levels of challenge.

Phases two and three include easy trial EX/RP tasks to gauge the patient's tolerance of anxiety, level of understanding, and willingness or ability to comply with treatment, while instilling the idea that it is possible to successfully resist and then "win" against OCD. These trial EX/RP tasks also demonstrate whether the transition zone has been accurately located, thereby avoiding disruptive "surprises" due to poorly targeted goals for exposure or response prevention.

Phase four fully implements the core of cognitive-behavioral psychotherapy for the anxiety disorders – namely, intensive graded exposure and response prevention (EX/RP), including therapist-assisted imaginal and *in vivo* EX/RP practice coupled with weekly homework assignments.

Exposure occurs when the child purposefully exposes herself to the feared object, action, or thought. Response prevention is the process of blocking rituals and/or minimizing the avoidance behaviors. Take, for example, the child with a "contamination" fear about touching doorknobs. In this case, since doorknobs trigger the obsession, the exposure task would require the child to touch the "contaminated" doorknob until his or her anxiety disappears. Response prevention takes place when the child refuses to perform the usual anxiety-driven compulsion, such as washing hands or using a tissue to grasp the doorknob.

For many families, it can be helpful to frame OCD as the enemy, against which all parties remain intransigent. However, since only the child can do the actual fighting of this enemy (via EX/RP), he or she remains in charge of choosing targets from the transition zone. As the child becomes more competent and successful at resisting OCD, her therapist begins each session by updating the transition zone, which moves incrementally up the stimulus hierarchy.

Carefully planned, hierarchical use of EX/RP in a supportive environment over time permits habituation to and eventual mastery of OCD symptoms, feelings, and behaviors. Finally, training in relapse prevention and judicious use of the skills from CBT combined with as-needed consult and booster sessions with the CBT clinician can prevent OCD from recurring at anything beyond a mild intensity.

The role of parents and family

Naturally, families affect and are affected by OCD. Research suggests that family accommodation of the child's OCD symptoms is the norm (Peris, Bergman, Langley, Chang, McCracken, & Piacentini, 2008; Storch, Geffken, Merlo et al., 2007a), and that family conflict and comorbid externalizing symptoms are worse when families attempt to refrain from accommodation (Peris et al., 2008). Some investigators have placed a strong emphasis on family work in the development of their CBT protocols (e.g., Piacentini, Bergman, Jacobs, McCracken, & Kretchman, 2002), and group cognitive-behavioral family CBT has been found to be as effective as individual CBT at reducing OCD symptoms (Barrett, Healy-Farrell, & March, 2004).

Though the amount of involvement should vary as a function of child development and type of OCD symptom, parents and family members are key players in the process from the very beginning of assessment and treatment. Parents provide their own perspective on OCD, related symptoms, and impairment in the assessment phase, which can add useful depth to the clinical picture (e.g., parents sometimes can provide information around more "automatic" rituals that the child may lack insight into). Parents are included to some extent in all sessions, and sessions 1, 7, 11, and 14 spend extensive time in collaboration with the parents. As a rule, parents check in with the therapist at the beginning and/or end of each session and we invite parents to comment on how the child is progressing in her struggle against OCD.

The extent of parental involvement should vary according to the degree of anxiety parents feel about their child's OCD. Early in treatment, parents who are heavily involved in their child's rituals often need extra understanding and encouragement. Reminding parents that OCD is an illness like any other can help alleviate the anxiety that comes from a sense of personal failure or responsibility for their child's OCD. At the beginning of treatment, parents may need some tools to cope with their own anxiety before they become involved in tracking their child's progress. The "battle" against OCD can only be won at the child's own pace. It is often the case that rituals involving parents occupy a space so sensitive they do not fall within the initial transition zone. In such cases, parental involvement in treatment should increase in intensity over the course of care as the child feels ready. Some children, however, especially young children, may prefer a higher degree of parental involvement throughout treatment. (Note: In a specialized treatment protocol for very young children with OCD, parents are involved in every session and essentially learn to conduct EX/RP with their children (Freeman, Choate-Summers, Moore et al., 2007)).

Therapists assess the needs of patients with regard to family involvement through-out treatment and should build enough flexibility into their approach to accommodate varying needs. Family sessions 7 and 11 focus on incorporating targets for parental response prevention with the child again selecting targets from the transition zone. Rarely, parents are encouraged to select targets for extinction, even when the child protests. More commonly, parents need to be instructed to stop giving advice or insisting on inappropriate exposure tasks. We also encourage parents to praise the child for attempts (successful or not) at resisting OCD, while at the same time refocusing their attention on positive elements in the child's life, an intervention technically termed differential reinforcement of other behavior (DRO). Sessions 13 and 14, which generally incorporate parents, focus on generalization training and relapse prevention.

Homework and between-sessions practice

Therapists give homework assignments each week with individualized cues to help the child successfully "boss back" OCD, making it clear from session 1 that practice at home will be a crucial component of treatment that cannot be omitted. Analogies to the importance of practice in sports or music may be useful here. The therapist emphasizes to the youth that the homework task will generally be created by him/her in collaboration with the therapist, and only those EX/RP tasks which s/he feels ready for will be assigned.

Positive reinforcers are used liberally for the completion of homework assignments, such as within-session praise and small goodies, such as pencils or gum, and between-session larger rewards, such as a trip for pizza with friends. In order to facilitate positive reinforcement and to extinguish punishment by adults and peers, we also make a special effort to help the youngster tell other people (such as friends, teachers, or grandparents) how she's successfully reduced OCD's influence over her life.

Important considerations/therapist competencies

While the theoretical concepts that guide EX/RP are clear and parsimonious, the implementation of treatment can often be complex and challenging. In this section we review some specific details of treatment implementation that we hope will be of use to the EX/RP practitioner.

Thought suppression. It is important that the therapist emphasize to the child the futility of thought suppression efforts, including distraction, because these efforts produce negative reinforcement and therefore can lead to increased obsessive symptoms. The goal instead should be to cultivate non-attachment – learning to simply notice obsessions and then to allow them to come and go of their own accord. In trying to underscore this point in a developmentally sensitive manner, we encourage pediatric patients to "*let* the thoughts go away instead of trying to *make* them go away." Outcome studies and experimental data show that, over time, a reduction in the frequency and intensity of these obsessions is likely to follow the elimination of thought suppression efforts. However, we take care to de-emphasize the goal of living "obsession-free," and instead underscore the importance of refraining from rituals and avoidance behaviors when obsessions do arise.

Avoidance. The skillful therapist must exercise vigilance in identifying avoidance when assessing and treating OCD. Children and adolescents with OCD may have a habit of avoidance that may not initially be identified as part of OCD, but which may have an impact on functioning and contribute to the continuation and exacerbation of OCD symptoms. Some forms of avoidance are obvious, such as never using public bathrooms or avoiding certain chores such as taking out trash. However, other forms may be more subtle, such as wearing slip-on shoes to avoid touching shoes with hands, or using drinking straws to reduce contact with potentially "contaminated" cans or glasses. Because these forms of avoidance may occur outside of patient awareness, a gentle approach to evaluation is important. To be effective, exposure tasks must be implemented without avoidance strategies in place, so careful planning is always required.

Although compulsive rituals are intended to reduce the distress associated with obsessions, patients sometimes report that the performance of these rituals is averse in itself. When certain compulsions become averse, some patients decrease the time they spend performing the ritual by increasing avoidance behaviors or by substituting other less time consuming rituals. In some cases, seemingly "new" rituals may develop during the course of treatment to fill the function of those previously identified and prevented. It is important to recognize and address such substitutions because, even if they are less time consuming and functionally impairing, they too serve the same negative reinforcing function Mowrer described. Therapists must remain alert to such shifts in ritualistic behaviors, and help patients to become alert to the possibility of such shifts as well.

Threat cues. Each OCD sufferer will have his own unique threat cues. For example, youths who fear contamination from toilets may fear all toilets or only those open to the public. One child may fear only the toilet itself, while another also fears bathroom floors, doorknobs, and faucets.

Images, impulses, or abstract thoughts that the child finds disturbing, shameful, or disgusting may also generate anxiety and distress. Examples of such cues include detailed images of oneself hurting a family member, thoughts of one's parent injured in an accident, or fear of shouting out an inappropriate word in school or church. Internal threat cues may be triggered by external situations such as the sight of a knife triggering the obsession of stabbing one's sibling. Some youth with OCD may become distressed when experiencing certain bodily sensations, such as minor aches and pains triggering the fear of having cancer.

For successful behavioral treatment of OCD it is important that the therapist conduct a thorough investigation of objects, situations, and places that evoke obsessional distress for the patient. In many cases, children may be reluctant to express their obsessive thoughts, either because they are ashamed of them or because they fear that expressing them will make the consequence more likely to occur. As with external cues, therapists have to recognize internal fear cues in order to understand the underlying fears.

Feared consequences: Many youth with OCD are afraid that something terrible will happen if they fail to perform their rituals. Some children have clearly defined negative consequences (e.g., "I will not be allowed to go to heaven unless I fix my thought about swearing in church") while others have only a vague notion of negative consequence (e.g., bad luck). Others do not fear catastrophes at all, but simply feel that they cannot tolerate the emotional distress they experience if they do not perform rituals. Data from the DSM-IV field trial indicated that approximately two-thirds of adult OCD patients identified consequences other than emotional distress that would follow from foregoing rituals (Foa, Kozak, Goodman, Hollander, Jenike, & Rasmussen, 1995). It is important to identify the details of the patient's feared consequences in order to plan an effective treatment program, since these consequences must be directly targeted in exposure and ritual prevention exercises.

Session-By-Session Delivery of Program

This section details the provision of the cognitive behavioral treatment for pediatric OCD in a session-by-session approach. As a general rule, flexibility in implementation as relevant to the youth's developmental stage and symptom presentation is essential. The tone, pace, and even the content of treatment may vary somewhat depending on the maturity level of the participating youth. The responsive therapist must adapt the level of discourse, including use of examples and metaphors, to fit the child's developmental level. For example, younger children may require more "play" time with the therapist and smaller doses of didactic information, while adolescents may need more attention to peer issues and more discussion of technical and medical details related to OCD. Likewise, the various types of OCD symptoms must be accommodated in treatment; while some patients will require extensive *in vivo* exposure, others will benefit from imaginal practice (especially those who suffer from obsessions that take the form of images, such as harm images, or those whose OCD occurs solely in the home or at specific times of day like bedtime). As noted, the level of family involvement and inclusion is also heavily dependent upon developmental stage and family involvement in OCD symptoms.

Again, the full treatment protocol for pediatric OCD is available in March & Mulle, 1998. For a case-based review of the protocol in action in a complex presentation of pediatric OCD, see Moore, Allard & Franklin (2006).

Week 1, Session 1: A Model for understanding OCD

Goals of this session, which generally includes parents, are to establish rapport with the child and family, to provide a neurobehavioral framework for understanding OCD, and to explain the process of treatment. We begin with a simple message at the beginning of treatment, focusing on the idea that the goal of treatment is to provide the youth with both the strategy for "bossing back" OCD and the support and allies he needs for this challenging job. It is crucial that the therapist clearly convey the message that s/he is on the side of the child and the family in their joint fight against OCD. In addition, it is useful for the therapist to conduct a "getting to know you" type of exercise that identifies the child's strengths and interests. Knowing details such as the child's skills in music or sports and their preferred learning process in school can be tremendously useful later in treatment. It can also be helpful in session 1 to identify any concerns related to previous ineffective treatments.

The next focus of session 1 is to provide a neurobehavioral framework for OCD. While remaining clear that OCD can be eliminated through behavioral means, we begin by stating that OCD is not simply a "bad habit" to be fixed. The therapist guides the family to the understanding that OCD is a neurological problem that cannot be construed as a simple behavioral issue that could be stopped through simple will power on the child's part. Metaphors for OCD such as "brain hiccups" or an overactive "worry chip" with a faulty "volume control" in the child's own computer (brain) that sends fear cues where none are needed or turns up the volume on very minor threatening stimuli can be useful.

Through the discussion of what OCD is (a medical issue) and is not (a behavior problem that the child should be blamed for), the therapist can educate the family also on the crucial components of OCD: obsessions, compulsions, and avoidance. The therapist illustrates these constructs using examples from the child's own OCD (e.g., "Your OCD starts by giving you an *obsession,* which is that there are germs on the railings of the school stairwells. You then engage either in *avoidance,* such as not touching the stairwells at all, or, if you do touch them, you may engage in *compulsions,* behaviors that are aimed at reducing the fear from the obsession, such as really scrubbing your hands, or using hand sanitizer.") Other information about OCD that may be helpful to the family can also be shared, including prevalence, neurobiology, or the synergy between medication treatment and CBT for OCD.

By the end of this session, the therapist should have succeeded in clearly defining OCD and making OCD (not the child) the problem of focus. One concrete and sometimes fun way to make this explicit for younger children is to have the child pick a nickname for OCD – something silly or slightly demeaning, such as "Ms. Bossy" or "Scrubby."

The final goal of session 1 is to explain how treatment will work. The core idea driving treatment is that the child will be "bossing back" or "saying no" to OCD. The child is told that he will be provided with allies and support (therapist, parents, friends) as well as a winning strategy (the techniques of CBT). We make it clear that the therapist will serve as "coach" but that the child will dictate the pace, thus avoiding the problem of the therapist simply telling the child what to do, which may feel like "just stop" to a sensitive child and/or may lead to misjudgments in EX/RP targets.

The two components of EX/RP, exposure and response prevention, are explained to the child, in the context of the question, "Who's the boss, you or OCD?" Exposure, which requires the child to confront feared stimuli such as touching a "contaminated" object, reduces anxiety over time, while response prevention is required to provide the adequate dose of anxiety provoked by the exposure. A third concept, extinction, is useful in family work for OCD, and is defined as the elimination of compulsive behaviors via removal of parental positive reinforcement. In this discussion, the therapist uses examples tailored to the child's symptom presentation, but is careful to present the time frame – the child will, by the end of treatment, be able to "boss back OCD," but there is no expectation that the child will do so today. The discussion of EX/RP is almost always stressful for the child and therefore the therapist is clear that (1) the child will be provided with coping strategies to use; and (2) the child will set the pace of treatment, although there must always be forward movement in treatment, lest treatment become part of the general avoidance picture. Use of humor (to tease OCD, never to tease the child) can be useful in this discussion and in any discussion about OCD; this helps to alleviate the embarrassment and demoralization that some children feel as a result of OCD symptoms.

Unless clearly contraindicated by the specific clinical situation, parents are included for the entire first session. This permits the therapist to give support, share information, and model the externalization of OCD for the parents. In addition, it provides an opportunity for the therapist to assess family accommodation of OCD symptoms. It is important for parents to hear that EX/RP is a gradual, collaborative process and to understand their dual roles as "cheerleaders" and, later, if indicated, "co-therapists."

If not completed in session, the homework assignment is for the child to choose a name for OCD. In addition, the therapist may ask the child to begin bringing his/her attention to how OCD affects his life on a day-to-day basis, with special attention to any times that the child "wins" against OCD.

Week 1, Session 2: Beginning to map OCD

Goals for this session include further work on "making OCD the problem," beginning the process of "mapping" OCD, and introducing the fear thermometer. The therapist begins with homework review, including the OCD name selection and a review of OCD symptoms. Helpful questions might include:

How has OCD bossed you around this week?

How does OCD mess things up for you in your life?

How have you "said no" to OCD this week?

Who or what helps you to boss OCD back?

The continued work to externalize OCD continues through this dialogue, as the therapist gathers information on the child's current symptoms and level of resistance.

The next goal of the session is working on "mapping" OCD. We review two basic "flavors" of OCD with the child, helping her to differentiate between OCD symptoms driven by negative affects (fear of harm, disgust, or guilt) and symptoms driven by a need to have things "just so." Both affects (negative and "just so") maybe present in a single patient. We next introduce a map metaphor that integrates the information from the Children's Yale-Brown Obsessive Compulsive Scale (CYBOCS) or other OCD assessment to create a clear picture of the territory of the child's life – the parts controlled by OCD, the parts controlled by the child, and the crucial "transition zone," in which the child is already successfully resisting OCD some of the time. The transition zone serves as a primary guide for selecting EX/RP targets.

While mapping OCD, the concept of the "feelings thermometer," a 1–10 rating scale for subjective units of distress, is introduced and used to measure the anxiety associated with each symptom on the map. This scale can also assist the child to rank specific symptoms for difficulty as designated EX/RP targets. For children who get caught up with numbers, particularly those who may have "unlucky" numbers or counting rituals, use of a color-oriented or similar scale may be useful. Creativity and artistic talent on the part of the child can sometimes be harnessed here in service of creating a hierarchy and/or a rating scale.

At this session, the child is assigned the homework task of acting as a "spy" or a "detective" to detect OCD triggers and note severity of symptoms, listing them and rating them using the fear thermometer.

Week 2, Session 3: Cognitive training and continued mapping

This session continues the psychoeducational and assessment-oriented components of the first two sessions, while beginning the process of cognitive training. As with all sessions, we begin with a review of homework, which is the list of triggers assigned last week. Successful completion is roundly praised. Completion of home practice is crucial for the success of this treatment, so early signs of non-compliance or struggle with homework completion must be addressed.

The triggers list and the child's completed CYBOCS together can be used at this point to further refine the map of OCD. Current obsessions and corresponding compulsions are specified. For each symptom, triggers, related avoidance behaviors, time spent on each symptom, distress/interference caused by the symptom, and motivation and current ability to resist are recorded. Incorporation of others into each symptom is also carefully assessed. Each symptom complex, consisting of trigger, obsession, and compulsion, is then ranked according to fear thermometer score and the child's perception of the difficulty of resisting or "bossing back" that particular symptom. The therapist should note that this portion of the treatment is the beginning of exposure – the child must imagine resisting specific OCD symptoms in order to generate a fear thermometer rating – and thus this task in and of itself is an imaginal exposure. Therefore, some frustration, resistance, or avoidance can be expected in this process. Using very specific questions that also can serve to alleviate the child's sense of isolation can be useful (e.g., "Other children who have this kind of OCD often use quite a lot of soap when washing – how about you?") The end goal of the mapping process is not only to provide information for subsequent EX/RP treatment, but to contribute to the child's hope and willingness to participate in treatment. By creating the map, OCD is no longer seen as an all-encompassing problem, but a geographically limited "enemy territory" that can be taken back into the child's own territory through the techniques of treatment.

Once the homework is reviewed and the map updated, the therapist begins the task of assessing and beginning to change the child's self-talk around OCD. The child is encouraged to argue with or "boss back" OCD, thereby continuing the externalization process and increasing motivation to comply with later EX/RP exercises. It is notable that direct, content-oriented "talking back" to OCD, such as saying "I DID lock the door before I went upstairs" tends to lead to a cognitive ping-pong match that the child will usually lose. (OCD will repeat the fear message, "Perhaps you forgot to check. . . . You really need to re-check" tirelessly). Instead, the child is trained to talk back in a more general way to OCD. Rather than engage the exact content of the OCD fear, it is enough to simply acknowledge that OCD is currently present, and that the child does not any longer plan to respond to OCD with a ritual. The developmental format of this response can range from "Go jump in a lake, OCD, I'm the boss!" to "This anxious feeling I am experiencing is just my OCD, and I no longer do what OCD tells me to do."

Self-talk around efficacy should be carefully assessed. Negative self-talk and maladaptive cognitions related to OCD (or to comorbid anxiety or depression) should be noted and alternative cognitions suggested or encouraged. Identifying and correcting negative self-talk is critical both to prepare the child to take on the challenge of EX/RP and to keep the externalization of OCD consistent. Positive self-statements such as "I can cope with OCD" or "OCD may make me upset, but I will feel better in a little while, even if I do not do a ritual" can help set the stage for successful tolerance of anxiety provoked by EX/RP.

As with all exposure-based treatments, motivation can be a concern. We find that virtually all children do better when *rewards* are incorporated into the treatment. These rewards can be as simple as verbal praise for the socially motivated patient to more complex token economy based rewards systems such as those described by Kazdin (2008). Rewards must always be focused on effort rather than results – the child who takes on a tough exposure should be rewarded for that willingness and work, whether or not the exposure task turns out to be a full success. Self-reward via accurate, positive self-talk focused on effort is also important – children must be able to give themselves credit (even "partial credit") for any and all attempts to fight OCD. Rewards for specific tasks completed in session, or assigned as homework between sessions, help to keep OCD identified as the problem, while at the same time increasing self-esteem and motivation.

Homework for this session assigns the child to continue the role of "detective" or "spy." Particular attention is focused on the times or symptom domains in which OCD wins only part of the time (e.g., times when the child sometimes is successful in saying no to OCD). This will be the groundwork for identifying the transition zone in the next session.

Week 2, Session 4: Transition zone, tool kit, and trial exposure

In this session, we finish up our preparation work in education and assessment, and begin the course of EX/RP with a trial exposure task. As always, we begin with a homework review. Depending on the child's success in identifying the *transition zone* (those times or symptom domains in which the child already has partial control), the therapist may simply give praise for identifying and resisting OCD. For children who have had with a harder time finding this zone, the therapist can work together with the child (and sometimes with parent assistance) to identify some symptom areas or situations in which resistance is either already happening or could potentially occur. These symptoms or triggers can be identified on the map by a lower thermometer rating. If the transition zone is particularly hard to find, a careful examination of events in the child's life where OCD and the child compete for influence, such as school or bedtime, can be useful. Looking for symptoms that used to be present but are no longer present can also be useful here.

It is important to note that the transition zone is a moving target during treatment; as the child reclaims more and more territory back from OCD, the transition zone will move up the stimulus hierarchy. Once the therapist and child co-locate the transition zone, a trial exposure task, and all future EX/RP tasks, can be identified from this zone.

For the last part of this session, the therapist and child pick out and execute a trial EX/RP task to illustrate the points covered in session and to prove to the child experientially that it is indeed possible to "beat up OCD." Selection of the specific task is extremely important. The therapist should pick a task that will create an anxiety level low enough to tolerate throughout the exposure (without ritualizing). The trial EX/RP can be completed in imagination (imaginal exposure) or "*in vivo*" – i.e., the child can imagine touching a "contaminated doorknob and not washing, or s/he can actually do that (if the thermometer rating is low enough). During the task, feelings thermometer ratings are taken at specified intervals (usually every two minutes). This creates numerical data that can then be used to illustrate the fact that anxiety will attenuate, rather than continue to rise, with prolonged exposure. The therapist can model "talking back" to OCD during the task if needed.

We wrap up the session by presenting the child with his/her "Tool Kit," which includes EX/RP, fear thermometer, "bossing back," the transition zone, and rewards. This can be done via a list, artwork, or verbal review. An analogy to a carpenter's belt or a tool bag can sometimes be useful in conveying the idea that the child is equipped with coping strategies as he begins the battle against OCD. EX/RP, as the most powerful tool, is supported in its implementation by the other tools.

The homework task for this week is daily practice of a trial exposure. The purposes of the trial exposure are to assess the accuracy of the stimulus hierarchy with respect to difficulty, to ascertain compliance, and to assess the child's ability to rate anxiety. The specific task chosen may be the one completed during the session, or another the child feels more ready to do in the home setting. *Caution* is indicated in selection of this task, as selecting a too-difficult task may make future EX/RP difficult to motivate. Without the therapist's assistance, fear thermometer ratings may be higher. Therefore, it is better to choose something "too easy" than something that seems borderline. To ensure greater effectiveness, planning a specific time each day for homework task completion is useful. During the exposure task, the child is encouraged to "talk back" to OCD, especially when feeling an urge to do a compulsion. The child should refuse to ritualize until the fear thermometer comes down to level 1–2. As in session, the child should rate his anxiety levels using the fear thermometer at 2–3 minute intervals throughout the exposure task.

Week 3, Session 5: Bossing OCD

We now move into the most challenging and most rewarding phase of the treatment process, as EX/RP begins in earnest. We utilize a consistent session format going forward which includes homework review (with rewards), update of hierarchy, continued imaginal or *in vivo* EX/RP, and assignment of home practice.

Homework review is particularly detailed in this session, as we are processing the first week of exposures attempted at home. The therapist uses the review to evaluate such issues as motivation, accuracy of anxiety level prediction, parental involvement, impact of comorbidities, and other obstacles. In exposure treatment, the therapist must always keep in mind the risk of the child "bailing out" of the EX/RP homework, thereby strengthening OCD and reducing motivation, and thus it is important to find tasks that the child can complete successfully. If a pattern of avoidance or bailing out is identified, it is likely that the chosen task was too difficult, and an easier task must be identified or designed.

Once the homework has been reviewed, attention turns to updating the symptom hierarchy – the child should review the list and indicate if any fear thermometer "temperatures" have changed or if there are any new symptoms she would like to add to the list. The therapist should be mindful of avoidance symptoms and may ask questions to identify the presence of avoidance. In addition, the role of parents and other family members is always assessed as the hierarchy is updated – e.g., we talk with the child about how OCD bosses around his/her parents and what fear thermometer ratings might result from changes in parental behavior (e.g., response prevention or extinction).

The crucial component of this and most of the following sessions follows: continued EX/RP. Each week, a new EX/RP target is chosen from the symptom hierarchy and practiced, either imaginally or *in vivo*, in the office. Once that is completed, EX/RP homework for the week is selected. Therapist-assisted EX/RP in session increases the likelihood that the child will succeed in the same task at home. One often-helpful component of EX/RP is therapist modeling – e.g., the therapist may touch a "contaminated" object and model "bossing back" before the child tries it. During EX/RP, the therapist routinely asks for fear thermometer ratings at regular intervals, and reminds the child to use her tool kit (bossing back, rewards). As a general rule, we recommend staying with the task and the continued ratings until the fear temperature has decreased by 75% or so (sometimes we simply tell children to do it until it becomes boring). In addition, the therapist is alert for subtle forms of avoidance (attempts at self-distraction, subtle wiping off of "contaminated" body parts or refusal to touch objects with these body parts, requests for reassurance). The aim is to assist the youth to fully engage with the anxiety provoked by the exposure task.

Homework for the week is daily practice of an EX/RP task selected from the hierarchy – it may or may not be similar to the one completed in session, depending on the child's situation. The therapist should remind the child to use "bossing back" and to record thermometer ratings at regular intervals, and be sure that rewards for effort (not for success) are included in the plan. Scheduling a between-session phone call can be useful in helping children to successfully complete daily EX/RP practice. The phone call can allow for between-session adjustment of too-hard or too-easy tasks, and can increase compliance and increase motivation and therapeutic alliance.

Week 4, Session 6: More bossing OCD

This week's session follows the same general format as the previous session, with the aim of consolidating success, troubleshooting any EX/RP failures or difficulties, and moving slightly upward on the hierarchy. Homework review is followed by therapist-assisted in-session EX/RP. Note that in-session tasks present an opportunity for a more advanced level of difficulty compared to assigned work at home, but difficulty still must be carefully titrated at this early stage of EX/RP.

Occasionally, there may be difficulty with in-session EX/RP, especially when challenging targets are selected. If a task shows itself to be too difficult, it is important to praise the child for his/her effort, and, if possible, to attempt re-exposure as soon as possible, generally at a substantially easier level. For example, if an exposure in which a child decides to touch the back of the toilet tank turns out to be too difficult and results in a washing ritual that the child feels unable to delay or modify, it would be valuable for the therapist to work with the child to find a "less contaminated" object in the bathroom to touch once the washing ritual is complete. Be sure to let the child know that, in trying the initial exposure, and in coming back and re-exposing himself, that he has "put OCD on notice" and that he has "had the last word" by finishing the exposure attempt on his own terms and without a ritual. In the case that the child is too demoralized to re-attempt, be sure to praise the effort and normalize the experience (examples of other children who have struggled with a hard exposure can be very useful here), while encouraging and incentivizing a plan for re-exposure at an easier level as soon as possible.

At the end of the session, the therapist again assigns a daily practice task. A parent check-in at the end of this session is advised. The therapist should encourage parents to praise their child for successes in resisting OCD, but to refocus their attention more generally on the positive aspects of the child's life. To prepare for session 7, we ask parents at the end of session 6 to reflect specifically on the ways that they are involved with OCD (rituals, avoidance) and to bring a list of these to the family session next week.

Week 5 – Session 7: Family session

OCD can have multiple impacts on families, all of which require attention in therapy. Parents or siblings may become entangled in compulsions (such as bedtime rituals) or in the support of avoidance. Parents may experience distress around the content of their child's obsessions, especially those involving harm or sexuality. Control struggles related to rituals are common and can be particularly problematic in adolescents. The purpose of this session, conducted in family format, is to focus on the family impact of OCD and to bring the family together to support the child in his battle against OCD.

This session begins with a review of the neurobehavioral framework for OCD, in order to re-orient the parents to the externalizing approach to OCD. Then, parental roles vis-à-vis the OCD are reviewed. Therapists work with parents to identify the ways in which parents are helping OCD, either wittingly or unwittingly, and to create a plan to begin withdrawing this help. In order to maintain the therapeutic alliance between child, family, and therapist, all changes in parental behavior that relate to OCD (e.g., withdrawal of reassurance) must be screened for difficulty using the feelings thermometer, and in most cases implemented only with child agreement.

Skillful assessment of parental attitudes toward OCD and early treatment progress is helpful in this session. In some families, especially those experiencing significant fatigue related to OCD rituals or avoidance, small improvements from early EX/RP practice engender a high level of pressure to "just stop" the rest of the ritualizing. Again, allowing the child to set the pace of treatment and to choose explicitly how and when parental behavior should change is extremely important. Focusing parental support as "cheerleaders" strictly upon the chosen EX/RP targets can also mitigate pressure on children to fight OCD all of the time or without regard to difficulty.

In the rare case where parents are enormously inconvenienced (e.g., a 4-hour bathroom ritual in a home with just one bathroom), and the child is unable to resist OCD at all, parents may pick an EX/RP target without the child's consent. This is almost always significantly distressing both to child and family, so therapists must help design a careful plan and strategy to manage behavior and emotional distress.

Ending the session on a positive note, we discuss ceremonies and/or notifications that are planned for the end of treatment. Ceremonies are special occasions that recognize the child's success in reducing OCD's influence in his/her life. Notifications are special letters or phone calls to inform friends and relations of the child's progress. In this session, we gather ideas for ceremonies and notifications that have meaning for the child. A homework task for the week is to set a goal for the first ceremony, and to plan for notifications.

As the session ends, we plan an EX/RP task for the coming week (either a repeat of last week's, if needed, or a new task). This session may have sharpened insight into family processes as they relate to the targeted OCD symptom(s), and may result in parental homework as well. At this point in treatment, parents may begin to assume the role of *co-therapist* with the child's consent, though this role should be carefully structured by the therapist and the child in session. We also ask the parents to continue to watch for new or previously unidentified ways in which they may support OCD. These can be discussed in depth at the next formal family meeting (session 11). Occasionally, this session may generate a referral for family or marital therapy in the case that family dysfunction or marital discord represent a constraint to effective OCD treatment. Again, a mid-week phone call is recommended to encourage EX/RP and troubleshoot any problems with practice.

Weeks 6–8, Sessions 8–10: More EX/RP practice

These sessions follow the same basic format as sessions 5 and 6. We conduct a careful homework review to be sure that home practice is as efficient and effective as possible. Sometimes it is useful to conduct imaginal exposures in session to prepare for or enhance performance on particularly challenging homework tasks. Continued use of rewards for effort is encouraged in order to maintain or enhance motivation. As EX/RP progresses, the excitement and relief of reclaiming territory from OCD is often "reward" enough for the child. This process should be celebrated via ceremonies either in or out of session. Certificates of achievement are presented for accomplishments, which the child is then encouraged to share as part of "notification" of friends or family members.

As the child works her way up the stimulus hierarchy into more and more challenging tasks, the therapist must be aware of comorbidity issues and ongoing therapy needs. Comorbid anxiety is common and, at times, may require its own treatment, either exposure based or skills based (e.g., relaxation). For example, a child with social phobia who needs to use a public bathroom as part of an OCD-focused EX/RP task might first need to expose herself to the bathroom in a way that does not bother OCD in order to reduce social anxiety in that context and allow the EX/RP task to occur.

As always, sessions end with a parent check-in focused on helping parents to support the child effectively. Sometimes, parental EX/RP targets may be picked (at the child's pace). Home EX/RP practice tasks are selected, and a mid-week phone call scheduled for encouragement and troubleshooting.

Week 9, Session 11: Family session

As with session 7, this session is conducted with parents and child together. Child and therapist together present a review of treatment progress, and therapists encourage parents to speak positively about improvements they have noticed and areas of the child's life that are now free of OCD. During this process, the therapist is mindful of the quality of the praise and aims to keep it accurate, specific, and short, as children may experience excessive praise as overwhelming or pressuring. Parents who are experiencing continued frustration with remaining symptoms may struggle with finding areas to praise and may require therapist assistance to do so. Concerns that parents bring up at this time can be deferred temporarily to the next phase of the session while the therapist works with the parents to find appropriate praise for work completed.

Once progress is acknowledged, work begins on "re-mapping" OCD, identifying the places in which OCD still "bosses" the child and/or the parents. The aim here is to re-establish the transition zone in order to identify current appropriate EX/RP targets that may include the parents. Parents may feel eager at this point in therapy to completely cease performing certain tasks that support OCD. However, this can sometimes create excessive anxiety for the child (i.e., the thermometer rating would be very high), and therefore, as before, the child should ideally collaborate on decisions regarding any change in parental behavior.

In this session, we can further develop the role of the parent as co-therapist, if the child consents. For example, a parent and child may decide that the parent will no longer re-wash dishes prior to eating, when previously the child's OCD had required this re-washing. In session, the therapist works with the parents and child to predict the expected anxiety rating, and to identify ways in which the parent can coach or support the child in use of cognitive techniques to manage the resultant anxiety.

At the end of the session, both child and parent EX/RP tasks are selected for daily practice. If the parent task presents a significant challenge for the child, she may continue with the previous week's practice, or may elect to focus exclusively on managing the anxiety around the parent task. Again, a mid-week call is planned to support the practice.

Week 10, Session 12: Reaching the top of the hierarchy

As we enter the last stretch of the 12-week treatment protocol, we turn our focus to consolidating gains while reaching for the maximum possible benefit via child and family EX/RP participation. This session begins with a review of homework and a particular focus on the child's reaction to the parents' chosen EX/RP task. A careful review of the symptom list and stimulus hierarchy is also important here, to gain a clear view of how much territory the child has regained and what challenges may still remain. At this point in treatment, the child should have made significant gains and may even have reached a plateau. Such a plateau should be addressed via a ceremony of graduation (to acknowledge progress made) and a discussion regarding the new focus of treatment. At these times, the transition zone must be re-identified for the new area of focus, and the child is asked to select a new aspect of OCD to attack. At this point in treatment, the new target often belongs to territory that the child had originally identified as unapproachable territory at the beginning of treatment – e.g., thermometer ratings of 8–10 +. The therapist should work with the child to identify a bold new target, still taking care to balance ambition with caution. The child remains the pace-setter, while the therapist reminds the child of his strengths and of successes and gains thus far.

It is important to note here the potential impact of comorbidity. At times, in children with comorbid presentations, the improvement gained in OCD symptoms can leave room for comorbid symptoms to become more central. While this can be frustrating for parents and child alike, the improvement in OCD and the child's hard work should not be overlooked. If further treatment or referral are needed, be sure to allow for completion of the present OCD treatment so as not to dilute its impact at this crucial point.

The parent check-in at the end of this session may be a bit longer, as additional parent EX/RP tasks may need to be assigned. In the case that there is a symptom area where the child is unwilling or unable to give parents permission to stop supporting OCD, the therapist and parents may work together to pick an EX/RP task despite the child's protests. If this approach is taken, the therapist must work with the parents to choose manageable targets and to provide parents with a strategy for managing child distress.

Homework is an EX/RP task chosen from the new territory discussed during this session. Imaginal in-office practice may be needed to prepare for home practice, and the mid-week phone call may be particularly important this week to support the new level of challenge.

Week 11, Session 13: Relapse prevention

At this point in treatment, the child is generally ready to begin to work with the concept of relapse prevention. Some children may not want to think about this possibility; however, explicit discussion about and readiness for relapse is an important exposure task. We sometimes use the term "hiccup" to refer to brief and expectable symptom flare-ups, and we distinguish these instances from a full relapse characterized by a substantial and persistent return of OCD symptoms. Therapist assures the child that the presence of a hiccup is not equivalent to the loss of treatment gains and can be prevented from turning into a relapse.

To prepare for the possibility of relapse, the therapist and the child discuss the ways in which the child expects that OCD might be most likely to try to reclaim territory, and specific and detailed plans are made for how to fight back against OCD in this case. The goal of the session is to help the child to fully internalize the CBT model so that, in the future, they may "automatically" do the opposite of what OCD demands. We use imaginal exposure to cement the learning process – the child is asked to imagine the hiccup as if it were really occurring and rate anxiety at 1- to 2-minute intervals using the fear thermometer.

The concept of relapse prevention can bring on questions and concerns for the child, who may wonder about the likelihood of relapse. The therapist should reinforce the fact that a full relapse is not likely due to the child's new stance toward OCD and the skills (toolbox) gained in therapy.

At the parent check-in, the therapist educates parents about hiccups and relapse (and the difference between the two) and coaches them on how to respond to hiccups effectively. Parents are encouraged to maintain an aware and matter-of-fact attitude about the possibility of relapse. In this meeting, we also plan any upcoming graduation ceremonies, including the one to occur in the next therapy session.

Homework this week consists of a relapse prevention exposure task completed imaginally (or *in vivo*, if applicable). The child may also pick an additional EX/RP task on the symptom hierarchy that s/he wants to complete before the end of treatment. The final mid-week phone session will offer support and encouragement with this final prescribed homework.

Week 12, Session 14: Graduation ceremony

This session focuses on the accomplishments made and effort expended throughout the treatment process. We encourage the child to review and celebrate the details of the specific territory reclaimed from OCD. We officially recognize the child's hard work through the presentation of a certificate of achievement. The therapist may also present the child with a letter of acknowledgement, highlighting instances in the treatment in which the therapist felt proud or was impressed by the child's hard work and/or skill. In this session, we explicitly acknowledge that OCD may try to reclaim territory, but we also emphasize the child's new ability to "boss back" OCD.

The child is encouraged to notify family and friends of her achievement, as this notification process can serve to solidify the child's confidence and sense of gains made against OCD. The treatment process and the child's experience now allow a significant reframe of the "story" of OCD in the child's life from a story of dysfunction or failure to one of the child's competence. If children are reluctant to tell others, that is acceptable, but we recommend encouraging the child to tell at least one peer of her accomplishments and new life "map."

Parents join the end of the session and are encouraged to provide feedback on progress. The therapist addresses any lingering concerns with the parents. Planning for relapse, including discussion of the possibility of booster sessions, is an important part of this last session, as severe OCD is likely to try to return at some point. The therapist reminds parents and children to focus on the new strategies and tools they have at their disposal to manage any new OCD symptoms; these skills will apply at any time and with any new OCD symptom presentation.

The final homework assignment is notification; many families choose to frame and/or display the child's certificate in their home.

Recent Empirical Findings

As noted at the beginning of the chapter, empirical work evaluating efficacious psychosocial treatment for pediatric OCD began with age-downward extension of established adult OCD protocols, then publication of single case studies, case series, and open clinical trials involving these protocols. Taken as a whole, the published uncontrolled evaluations (e.g., Franklin, Kozak, Cashman, Coles, Rheingold, & Foa, 1998; March, Mulle, & Herbel, 1994; Piacentini et al., 2002) showed remarkably similar and encouraging findings across settings and cultures: at post-treatment, the majority of patients were responders, with significant symptom reductions. This pilot work set the stage for randomized studies evaluating the efficacy of CBT, the first of which was published in the late 1990s (de Haan, Hoogduin, Buitelaar, & Keijsers, 1998). Since then a number of other randomized controlled trials have followed (Barrett et al., 2004; Bolton & Perrin, 2008; Freeman, Garcia, Coyne et al., 2008; POTS Team, 2004; Storch, Geffken, Merlo et al., 2007b; Williams, Salkovskis, Forrester, Turner, White, & Allsopp, 2010), and their collective outcomes further underscore that CBT involving EX/RP is an efficacious treatment for children and adolescents with OCD (Abramowitz et al., 2005; Barrett, Farrell, Pina, Peris, & Piacentini, 2008).

Which treatment for which patient?

In addition to the strong evidence base for the treatment as a whole, there have been recent advances in research on treatment and patient factors which may affect outcome. However, the evidence base in this area is in need of refinement.

Dose/treatment schedule. Most of the studies of CBT outcomes in pediatric OCD have employed a weekly therapy regimen. Franklin et al. (1998) found no differences between 14 weekly sessions over 12 weeks or 18 sessions over 4 weeks, but interpretation of this finding is hampered by the lack of random assignment. Storch et al. (2007b) found that patients respond well to CBT delivered either weekly or intensively. However, due to small samples sizes, both of these studies lacked sufficient power to examine predictors of response to one regimen or the other. Therefore, at this point, clinical judgment must be used to determine if a patient might need more than the standard weekly treatment.

Moderators and predictors of CBT response. Although many have suggested that the presence of comorbidity (especially with the tic disorders), lack of motivation or insight, and the presence of family psychopathology might predict a poor outcome in children undergoing CBT, there is as yet little empirical basis on which to predict treatment outcome in children undergoing psychosocial treatment.

In a recent review of existing treatment trials for youth OCD, Ginsburg, Kingery, Drake, and Grados (2008) reviewed the available evidence on moderators or predictors of treatment outcome. Higher OCD severity at baseline and increased family dysfunction were related to poorer outcome in CBT trials, whereas tics or externalizing symptomatology were associated with poorer response to medication. No effects were found for gender, age, OCD symptom type (e.g., checkers versus washers), or psychophysiological or neuropsychological factors. The authors noted a pressing need for improved research designs in order to allow for appropriate power to test hypotheses around moderation and prediction of treatment outcome.

Moderators of treatment are variables that interact with particular types of treatment in determining outcome, and can only be evaluated in studies with multiple treatment arms. The POTS I trial, with three active treatment arms (CBT, sertraline, and CBT + sertraline), provided a unique opportunity for evaluation of moderators of treatment. Within this dataset, we found that comorbid tic diagnosis predicted response to medication but not to CBT (March, Franklin, Leonard et al., 2007). In addition, positive family history of OCD seemed to reduce treatment effect size in general, but particularly in CBT (Garcia, Sapyta, Moore et al., 2010), where that form of treatment was six times less effective than it was for those without a positive family history.

In terms of more general predictors of treatment outcome that may not be specific to treatment type, POTS I data showed negative effects of high baseline severity, externalizing symptomatology, and family accommodation of OCD symptoms on outcomes for all treatment groups (Garcia et al., 2010). Similarly, Storch et al. (2007b) found that externalizing conditions such as oppositional defiant disorder (ODD) predicted poorer response to CBT.

Unfortunately, as noted by Ginsburg and colleagues (2008), sample sizes in all the treatment studies thus far have not yielded adequate power to test confirmatory hypotheses regarding predictors and moderators of treatment. Therefore, while the existing evidence provides some tentative guidelines for treatment (e.g., considering CBT monotherapy for comorbid tic sufferers; considering starting with medication only or a combination of medication and CBT for those with a family history of OCD), the current empirical base cannot offer definitive decision-tree guidelines for picking particular treatment modalities for specific patients.

Durability of treatment

Epidemiological studies suggest that OCD is a chronic condition. The three pediatric OCD pilot studies (Franklin et al., 1998; March, Mulle, & Herbel, 1994; Wever & Rey, 1997) and one recently published randomized trial (Bolton & Perrin, 2008) support the durability of EX/RP, with therapeutic gains maintained up to 9 months post-treatment. Moreover, since relapse commonly follows medication discontinuation, the finding of March et al. (1994) that improvement persisted in six of nine responders following the withdrawal of medication provides limited support for the hypothesis that CBT inhibits relapse when medications are discontinued. Follow-up data from Barrett et al.'s (2004) study further indicate the durability of gains made in CBT for pediatric OCD (Barrett, Farrell, Dadds, & Boulter, 2005).

Availability, acceptability and tolerability of CBT for pediatric OCD

Experts have recommended CBT as a first-line treatment for OCD in children and adolescents (March et al., 1997), yet several barriers may limit its widespread use. First, few therapists have extensive experience with CBT for pediatric OCD. Second, even when CBT is available, some patients and families reject the treatment as "too difficult." Once involved in CBT, some patients find the initial distress of confronting feared thoughts and situations while simultaneously refraining from rituals so aversive that they drop out of treatment. In our protocol, we use hierarchy-driven EX/RP, actively involve the patient in choosing exposure exercises, and include anxiety management techniques for those who need them. As a result, the drop-out rates in our pilot studies and in our clinical trials have been quite low, which in turn suggests that the vast majority of children and adolescents can tolerate and will benefit from CBT when delivered in a clinically informed and developmentally sensitive fashion.

CBT for pediatric OCD is unfortunately often difficult to find outside of the academic medical settings associated with the development and empirical evaluation of these protocols, most of which share the common elements of exposure and ritual prevention. Hence, many children with OCD do not have access to therapists who follow the Expert Consensus Guideline recommendations (March et al., 1997) to begin treatment with CBT or with combined treatment (COMB, or CBT plus a serotonin reuptake inhibitor). A recently completed open trial that examined the efficacy of CBT in community clinics as delivered by masters-level clinicians who were not OCD experts provides encouragement about the transportability of this treatment. Valderhaug and colleagues (2007) tested a "supervision of supervisors" model in providing the psychologists who were supervising these clinicians in rural Norway with access to expert supervision. Findings indicated both statistically significant and clinically meaningful reductions in OCD and related symptoms at post-treatment that were maintained at follow-up (11 months). Benchmarking these outcomes against findings from pilot studies conducted in our respective clinics (Franklin et al., 1998; March et al., 1994) demonstrates comparability of outcomes at both acute and follow-up assessment, and indicates that CBT can indeed be disseminated well beyond the academic context and hence transported to the kinds of clinical settings where most families who have a child with OCD will be able to access care. Larger, randomized studies with comparison conditions are needed to extend these findings and to continue to build this important bridge to improved access to CBT for families in need.

Current comparative treatment trials

Treatment research continues to be conducted in youth OCD; here we describe two research studies that are nearing completion, conducted by the collaboration between Duke, the University of Pennsylvania, and Brown University medical center.

POTS II. Despite the growing evidence base for CBT, for most pediatric OCD patients, the first-line treatment remains monotherapy with an SSRI. Unfortunately, recommended doses of these medications leave the great majority of patients with clinically significant residual symptoms (Freeman, Choate-Summers, Garcia et al., 2009) and the chances for excellent response (defined as CYBOCS score less than or equal to 12) are lower with medication alone – for example, POTS I indicated that the rate of excellent response in children treated with sertraline monotherapy was just 21%. Accordingly, our next phase of research was designed to address the issue of treatment augmentation (adding an additional treatment to a current treatment) as well as treatment transportability (developing a treatment in a research setting specifically for use in community clinical settings). In the POTS II study, we compare the relative efficacy of augmentation of (1) medication management (MM) provided by a study psychiatrist (MM only); (2) MM + OCD-specific CBT as delivered by a study psychologist (MM + CBT); and (3) MM + instructions in CBT (MM + I-CBT) delivered by the study psychiatrist assigned to provide MM. The primary questions of interest to be addressed are (1) can CBT augment medication management? and (2) is a more transportable treatment, in the form of MM + I-CBT, as effective as full CBT by a psychologist (MM + CBT)? We have recently completed recruitment of over 120 children and adolescents aged 7–17 who were already taking an SSRI for OCD and yet still experiencing clinically significant OCD symptoms, and results are being analyzed at this time. A description of the participating sample can be found in Freeman, Saptya, Garcia et al., 2011.

Family-based treatment of early childhood OCD. Recent work also supports the success of family-based CBT for young children (5–8) with OCD as compared to a family-based relaxation training protocol (RT; Freeman et al., 2008). Inclusion and exclusion criteria were identical to the other POTS trials described above except that at least one parent was required to participate in every session. Both treatment protocols (CBT and RT) consisted of 12 sessions delivered over the course of 14 weeks. Our family-based CBT program draws on extant approaches for older children, but contains novel elements that have been tailored to young children with OCD. These elements include (1) attention to developmental stage and concomitant levels of cognitive and socioemotional skills, (2) awareness of a child's involvement in and dependence on a family system, and (3) the incorporation of parent-training and behavior management techniques.

Using the intent-to-treat sample, 11 of 22 (50%) participants randomized to CBT were classified as achieving clinical remission after 12 weeks of treatment, as compared with 4 of 20 (20%) participants in the RT group; this difference in response rates was statistically and clinically significant. Using the completer sample, 11 of 16 (69%) participants randomized to CBT were classified as achieving clinical remission, compared with only 3 of 15 (20%) participants in the RT group, which was again statistically and clinically significant. Given the small sample size, the results were very encouraging and indicated that CBT was associated with a moderate and clinically relevant treatment effect (ITT ES=0.53). This is especially promising given that the control condition was also an active treatment and not a waitlist control as is common in treatment development studies. A multi-site replication and extension of that study is currently underway at Brown, Penn, and Duke universities, which will also allow examination of predictors of response with a much larger sample.

Directions for Future Research

Using the POTS collaborations as a stepping stone, current research efforts in the field of pediatric OCD are now (or shortly will be) focusing on the following key areas: (1) more controlled trials comparing medications, CBT, and combination treatment to determine whether medications and CBT are synergistic or additive in their effects on symptom reduction; (2) comparisons of individual and family-based treatments to determine which is more effective in which children; (3) development of innovative treatment for OCD subtypes, such as obsessional slowness or hoarding, that may not respond well to EX/RP; (4) developing treatment innovations to target specific factors, such as family dysfunction and externalizing comorbidity, that constrain the application of CBT to patients with OCD; (5) once past initial treatment, the management of partial response, treatment resistance, treatment maintenance, and discontinuation; and (6) exporting research treatments to divergent clinical settings and patient populations in order to judge the acceptability and effectiveness of CBT as a treatment for child and adolescent OCD in non-academic settings.

Summary and Conclusions

CBT for pediatric OCD has blossomed in the past decade into an empirically supported treatment for this often disabling condition, with randomized studies from around the world attesting to its efficacy relative to various comparison conditions and to active medication. As is the case in treatment studies for adults suffering from OCD, the effects of CBT for children and adolescents seem to be both robust and durable, with the follow-up studies we have available indicating that the effects of treatment last for up to one year after treatment has ended. Weekly treatment for approximately 12–14 weeks seems to be sufficient, although future studies should examine whether symptom severity, comorbidity, readiness for change, and case complexity (e.g., family problems) necessitate more intensive and/or long-term approaches. Both alone and in combination with serotonin reuptake inhibitors, CBT provides a viable treatment alternative to SSRIs alone, although the paucity of therapists trained in its use makes it difficult in some regions to heed the expert consensus guidelines recommendations to begin treatment with CBT alone or with COMB. Dissemination of CBT for pediatric OCD thus remains a pressing challenge to the field, although there are now encouraging data available suggesting that a "supervision of supervisors" model can yield impressive results comparable to those achieved in the academic medical settings that have developed the CBT protocol use with children and adolescents. A modified CBT protocol that centrally involves parents in the treatment of young children aged 5–8 with OCD has now been developed and its efficacy evaluated in a small initial study; findings from that randomized trial indicate that the treatment can be delivered effectively to this population as well, which might encourage earlier intervention for those whose symptoms are already evident in young childhood.

We are truly excited by the new possibilities that these and other initiatives will yield, and we look forward to another decade's worth of progress in identifying and treating OCD in young people before the illness disrupts developmental trajectories that are difficult to get back on track.

References

Abramowitz, J. S., Whiteside, S. P., & Deacon, B. J. (2005). The effectiveness of treatment for pediatric obsessive-compulsive disorder: A meta-analysis. *Behavior Therapy, 36,* 55–63.

Adams, G. B., Waas, G. A., March, J. S., & Smith, M. C. (1994). Obsessive compulsive disorder in children and adolescents: the role of the school psychologist in identification, assessment, and treatment. *School Psychology Quarterly, 94* (4), 274–294.

APA (1980). *Diagnostic and statistical manual of mental disorders,* 3rd edn. Washington, DC: American Psychiatric Association.

Barrett, P., Farrell, L., Dadds. M., & Boulter, N. (2005). Cognitive-behavioral family treatment of childhood obsessive-compulsive disorder: Long-term follow-up and predictors of outcome. *Journal of the American Academy of Child & Adolescent Psychiatry, 44,* 1005–1014.

Barrett, P. M., Farrell, L., Pina, A. A., Peris, T. S., & Piacentini, J. (2008). Evidence-based psychosocial treatments for child and adolescent obsessive-compulsive disorder. *Journal of Clinical Child & Adolescent Psychology, 37,* 131–155.

Barrett, P., Healy-Farrell, L., & March, J. S. (2004). Cognitive-behavioral family treatment of childhood obsessive-compulsive disorder: A controlled trial. *Journal of the American Academy of Child and Adolescent Psychiatry, 43,* 46–62.

Bolton, D. & Perrin, S. (2008). Evaluation of exposure with response-prevention for obsessive compulsive disorder in childhood and adolescence. *Journal of Behavioral Therapy and Experimental Psychiatry, 39,* 11–22.

de Haan, E., Hoogduin, K. A., Buitelaar, J. K., & Keijsers, G. P. (1998). Behavior therapy versus clomipramine for the treatment of obsessive- compulsive disorder in children and adolescents. *Journal of the American Academy of Child and Adolescent Psychiatry, 37,* 1022–1029.

Dollard, J., & Miller, N. (1950). *Personality and Psychotherapy: An Analysis in Terms of Learning, Thinking, and Culture.* New York: McGraw-Hill.

Flament, M. F., Whitaker, A., Rapoport, J. L., Davies, M., Berg, C. Z., Kalikow, K., et al. (1988). Obsessive compulsive disorder in adolescence: an epidemiological study. *Journal of the American Academy of Child & Adolescent Psychiatry, 27* (6), 764–771.

Foa, E. B., & Kozak, M. J. (1986). Emotional processing of fear: Exposure to corrective information. *Psychological Bulletin, 99,* 20–35.

Foa, E. B., Kozak, M. J., Goodman, W. K., Hollander, E., Jenike, M. A., & Rasmussen, S. (1995). DSM-IV field trial: Obsessive compulsive disorder. *American Journal of Psychiatry, 152,* 90–96.

Franklin, M. E., Kozak, M. J., Cashman, L. A., Coles, M. E., Rheingold, A. A., & Foa, E. B. (1998). Cognitive-behavioral treatment of pediatric obsessive-compulsive disorder: an open clinical trial. *Journal of the American Academy of Child and Adolescent Psychiatry, 37,* 412–419.

Franklin, M. E., & Simpson, H. B. (2005). Combining pharmacotherapy and exposure plus ritual prevention for obsessive compulsive disorder: Research findings and clinical applications. *Journal of Cognitive Psychotherapy, 19,* 317–330.

Freeman, J. B., Choate-Summers, M. L., Moore, P. S., Garcia, A. M., Sapyta, J. J., Leonard, H. L., et al. (2007). Cognitive behavioral treatment of young children with obsessive compulsive disorder. *Biological Psychiatry, 61,* 337–343.

Freeman, J. B., Choate-Summers M. L., Garcia, A. M., Moore, P. S., Sapyta, J., Khanna, M. S., et al. (2009). The Pediatric Obsessive-Compulsive Disorder Treatment Study II: Rationale, design and methods. *Child and Adolescent Psychiatry and Mental Health,* ArtID4. 15 pp.

Freeman, J. B., Garcia, A. M., Coyne, L., Ale, C., Przeworski, A., Himle, M., et al. (2008). Early childhood OCD: Preliminary findings from a family-based cognitive-behavioral approach. *Journal of the American Academy of Child and Adolescent Psychiatry, 47,* 593–602.

Freeman, J. B., Sapyta, J., Garcia, A., Fitzgerald, D., Khanna, M., Choate-Summers, M., et al. (2011). Still struggling: Characteristics of youth with OCD who are partial responders to medication treatment. *Child Psychiatry and Human Development, 42,* 424–441.

Garcia, A. M., Sapyta, J. J., Moore. P. S., Freeman, J. B., Franklin, M. E., March, J. S., et al. (2010). Predictors and moderators of treatment outcome in the Pediatric Obsessive Compulsive Treatment Study (POTS I). *Journal of the American Academy of Child and Adolescent Psychiatry, 49,* 1024–1033.

Ginsburg, G. S., Kingery, J. N., Drake, K. L., & Grados, M. A. (2008). Predictors of treatment response in pediatric obsessive-compulsive disorder. *Journal of the American Academy of Child and Adolescent Psychiatry, 47,* 868–878.

Hodgson, R. J., Rachman, S., & Marks, L M. (1972). The treatment of chronic obsessive-compulsive neurosis: Follow-up and further findings. *Behaviour Research and Therapy, 10,* 181–189.

Hofmann S. G., & Smits, J. A. (2008). Cognitive-behavioral therapy for adult anxiety disorders: a meta-analysis of randomized placebo-controlled trials. *Journal of Clinical Psychiatry, 69,* 621–632.

Kazdin, A. E. (2008). *the Kazdin Method for Parenting the Defiant Child.* Boston: Houghton Miflin.

March, J., Frances, A., Kahn, D., & Carpenter, D. (1997). Expert Consensus Guidelines: Treatment of Obsessive-Compulsive Disorder. *Journal of Clinical Psychiatry, 58* (Suppl. 4), 1–72.

March, J. S., Franklin, M. E., Leonard, H., Garcia, A., Moore, P., Freeman, J., et al. (2007). Tics moderate the outcome of treatment with medication but not CBT in pediatric OCD. *Biological Psychiatry, 61,* 344–347.

March, J., & Mulle, K. (1998). *OCD in Children and Adolescents: A Cognitive-Behavioral Treatment Manual.* New York: Guilford Press.

March, J. S., Mulle, K., & Herbel, B. (1994). Behavioral psychotherapy for children and adolescents with obsessive-compulsive disorder: an open trial of a new protocol-driven treatment package. *Journal of the American Academy of Child and Adolescent Psychiatry, 33,* 333–341.

Merlo, L. J., Storch, E. A., Murphy, T. K., Goodman, W. K. & Geffken, G. R. (2005). Assessment of pediatric obsessive-compulsive disorder: a critical review of current methodology. *Child Psychiatry and Human Development, 36*, 195–214.

Moore, P. S., Allard S. U., & Franklin, M. E. (2006). Obsessive-compulsive disorder in children and adolescents: Case based review. *Journal of Clinical Outcomes Management, 13*, 405–411.

Mowrer, O. H. (1939). A stimulus-response analysis of anxiety and its role as a reinforcing agent. *Psychological Review, 46*, 553–565.

Mowrer, O. H. (1960). *Learning Theory and Behavior*. New York: John Wiley & Sons, Ltd.

Peris, T. S., Bergman, R. L., Langley, A., Chang, S., McCracken, J. T., & Piacentini, J. (2008). Correlates of accommodation of pediatric obsessive-compulsive disorder: Parent, child, and family characteristics. *Journal of the American Academy of Child & Adolescent Psychiatry, 47*, 1173–1181.

Piacentini, J., Bergman, R. L., Jacobs, C., McCracken, J. T. & Kretchman, J. (2002). Open trial of cognitive behaviour therapy for childhood obsessive-compulsive disorder. *Journal of Anxiety Disorders, 16*, 207–219.

Piacentini, J., Bergman, R. L., Keller, M., & McCracken, J. (2003). Functional impairment in children and adolescents with obsessive-compulsive disorder. *Journal of Child & Adolescent Psychopharmacology, 13* (2, Suppl.), S61–S69.

POTS (Pediatric OCD Treatment Study) Team (2004). Cognitive-behavior therapy, sertraline, and their combination for children and adolescents with obsessive-compulsive disorder: The pediatric OCD treatment study (POTS) randomized controlled trial. *Journal of the American Medical Association, 292* (16), 1969–1976.

Rapoport, J. L., Inoff-Germain, G., Weissman, M. M., Greenwald, S., Narrow, W. E., Jensen, P. S., et al. (2000). Childhood obsessive-compulsive disorder in the NIMH MECA Study: Parent versus child identification of cases. *Journal of Anxiety Disorders, 14*, 535–548.

Roper, G., & Rachman, S. (1976). Obsessional compulsive checking: Experimental replication and development. *Behaviour Research and Therapy, 14*, 25–32.

Roper, G., Rachman, S., & Hodgson, R. (1973). An experiment on obsessional checking. *Behaviour Research and Therapy, 11*, 271–277.

Salkovskis, P. M. (1985). Obsessional compulsive problems: A cognitive-behavioral analysis. *Behavioral Research and Therapy. 23*, 571–583.

Stewart, S. E., Geller, D. A., Jenike, M., Pauls, D., Shaw, D., Mullin, B., et al. (2005). Long-term outcome of pediatric obsessive–compulsive disorder: a meta-analysis and qualitative review of the literature. *Acta Psychiatrica Scandinavica, 110*, 4–13.

Storch, E. A., Geffken, G. R., Merlo, L. J., Jacob, M. L., Murphy, T. K., Goodman, W. K., et al. (2007a). Family accommodation in pediatric obsessive-compulsive disorder. *Journal of Clinical Child and Adolescent Psychology, 36*, 207–216.

Storch, E. A., Geffken, G. R., Merlo, L. J., Mann, G., Duke, D., Munson, M., et al. (2007b). Family-based cognitive-behavioral therapy for pediatric obsessive-compulsive disorder: Comparison of intensive and weekly approaches. *Journal of the American Academy of Child and Adolescent Psychiatry, 46*, 469–478.

Valderhaug, R., Larsson, B., Götestam, K. G., & Piacentini, J. (2007). An open clinical trial of cognitive-behaviour therapy in children and adolescents with obsessive-compulsive disorder administered in regular outpatient clinics. *Behaviour Research and Therapy, 45*, 577–589.

Wever, C., & Rey, J. M. (1997). Juvenile obsessive compulsive disorder. *Australian and New Zealand Journal of Psychiatry, 31*, 105–113.

Williams, T. I., Salkovskis, P. M., Forrester, L., Turner, S., White, H., & Allsopp, M, A. (2010). A randomised controlled trial of cognitive behavioural treatment for obsessive compulsive disorder in children and adolescents. *European Child and Adolescent Psychiatry, 19*, 449–456.

19

Panic Disorder

Alexander H. Queen and Jill Ehrenreich-May

University of Miami, Florida, USA

Compared to treatment research for other youth anxiety disorders, panic disorder (PD) in adolescence has historically received less attention from clinical researchers, despite the debilitating and recurrent nature of this disorder (Birmaher & Ollendick, 2004; Keller, Yonkers, Warshaw, & Pratt, 1994; Ollendick, Birmaher, & Mattis, 2004; Ollendick & Pincus, 2008). Adolescents with PD utilize health care services more frequently than youth with other psychiatric conditions (Katerndahl & Realini, 1997), experience significant impairments in school, peer, and family functioning (Birmaher & Ollendick, 2004), and are at-risk for suicide in adulthood, likely due to increased comorbidity with depression symptoms over time (Weissman, Klerman, Markowitz, & Quellette, 1989). Although historically understudied compared to other anxiety disorders in youth, recent evidence suggests that PD in adolescence can be effectively treated using cognitive-behavioral treatment models (Pincus, Ehrenreich-May, Whitton, Mattis, & Barlow, 2010.

In this chapter, we review current research on psychosocial treatments for PD (and PD with agoraphobia [PD/A]) symptoms. We first present the phenomenology of PD in adolescence, including its typical symptom picture, onset, and differential diagnosis, followed by a review of pharmacological and psychosocial treatments. The majority of the chapter will then consist of a session-by-session delineation of a recent evidence-based treatment for PD in adolescence, Mastery of Anxiety and Panic for Adolescents (MAP-A; Pincus, Ehrenreich, & Mattis, 2008). This delineation will be followed by a case study to illustrate MAP-A's clinical application with an adolescent client.

Symptom Picture and Onset

According to the most recent version of the *Diagnostic and Statistical Manual of Mental Disorders* (DSM-IV-TR; APA, 2000), PD is characterized by recurrent, "out of the blue" (e.g., not clearly triggered by an identifiable external stimuli, etc.) panic

The Wiley-Blackwell Handbook of The Treatment of Childhood and Adolescent Anxiety, First Edition. Edited by Cecilia A. Essau and Thomas H. Ollendick.
© 2013 John Wiley & Sons, Ltd. Published 2013 by John Wiley & Sons, Ltd.

attacks, with at least 1 month of anticipatory anxiety about the occurrence of future attacks. Panic attacks are typically of short duration (e.g., less than 30 minutes) and can be distinguished from anxiety alone by the very intense nature of their physiological, emotional, and/or cognitive symptoms (Bouton, Mineka, & Barlow, 2001). Typical physical symptoms of a panic attack include breathlessness, rapid heartbeat, dizziness, and chest discomfort, and often include cognitive symptoms such as fears of dying, going crazy, or losing control (APA, 2000). At least four of these symptoms must be present to meet DSM-IV criteria for a panic attack. Panic attacks with less than four symptoms are referred to as *limited symptom* panic attacks. The most frequently reported PD symptoms among adolescents include heart palpitations, dizziness, shortness of breath, trembling, and sweating (Diler, Birmaher, Brent et al., 2004).

Youth PD typically emerges in mid to late adolescence (Kearney, Albano, Eisen, Allan, & Barlow, 1997; Kessler, Berglund, Demler, Jin, Merikangas, & Walters, 2005), and is more common in adolescent females than males (Thyer, Parrish, Curtis, Nesse, & Cameron, 1985). Additionally, retrospective evidence indicates that 40% of adults with PD began to experience symptoms in mid to late adolescence, further suggesting that this is an important developmental period for early treatment (Moreau & Follet, 1993). PD is very rare in children under 10 years old (Kearney et al., 1997). Some (e.g., Doerfler, Connor, Volungis, & Toscano, 2007; Nelles & Barlow, 1988) have theorized that younger children do not have the cognitive development necessary to make catastrophic attributions about internal stimuli; although the age at which such attributions typically emerge and subsequently become problematic is not clear. Given the typical age of onset for panic symptoms, conditioned fear to internal sensations may be hypothesized to occur sometime in early to mid adolescence, when youth have obtained the necessary abstract thinking abilities to elaborate on worries regarding the source and/or continuing nature of such sensations (Doerfler et al., 2007).

Comorbidty of PD with other psychological disorders is quite high. Frequently co-occurring anxiety disorders include generalized anxiety disorder (GAD) and separation anxiety disorder (Diler et al., 2004). Essau, Conradt, and Petermann (1999) found that 80% of adolescents with PD in a community sample also met criteria for major depressive disorder (MDD). Interestingly, Diler and colleagues (2004) found that adolescents with PD had higher rates of MDD than youth with non-anxiety disorders, although not significantly higher than youth with other anxiety disorders. Regardless of how unique this particular trajectory is amongst the anxiety disorders, youth with comorbid PD and MDD may be at particular future risk for suicide, school failure, marital dissatisfaction, and substance abuse (Birmaher, Ryan, & Williamson, 1996; Fleming, Offord, & Boyle, 1989; Gotlib, Lewinsohn, & Seeley, 1998; Weissman et al., 1989). Comorbidity with bipolar disorder, oppositional defiant disorder, and attention-deficit/hyperactivity disorder (ADHD) is also common (Birmaher & Ollendick, 2004; Diler et al., 2004).

Many adolescents with PD develop agoraphobia, which is the avoidance of places or situations in which the adolescent fears he or she will have a panic attack (APA, 2000). Often, the adolescent with PD/A fears that he or she will not be able to escape or get help if a panic attack occurs in these situations. Some of the most commonly avoided places reported by adolescents with PD/A include restaurants, crowds, elevators, parks, and school (Kearney et al., 1997). If the situation cannot be avoided, adolescents with PD/A will often go with a family member or friend or carry an object (e.g., cell phone, medication) with them. These are referred to as *safety people* or *safety objects*, as adolescents with PD/A believe they must be present in order to safely "get through" a situation.

Differential Diagnosis

In order to meet criteria for PD or PD/A, the adolescent must experience recurrent, "out of the blue" panic attacks with at least 1 month of anticipatory worry about having another panic attack (APA, 2000). During the assessment process, it is important for the clinician to determine the potential trigger(s) for such panic attacks, as panic may also occur in the course of other anxiety disorders, particularly phobic disorders (including social phobia). Adolescents with PD often report that panic attacks seem to come "out of the blue," although they are in reaction to an internal, physiological stimulus (e.g., noticing that one's heart is beating fast, etc.). In contrast, if an adolescent only has panic attacks within the context of an identifiable situation (e.g., a situationally-bound panic attack), such as when speaking in public, then another anxiety disorder diagnosis (in this case, social phobia) may be more appropriate. Furthermore, panic attack triggers cannot be solely attributed to trauma-related cues, as is characteristic of post-traumatic stress disorder (PTSD). Panic attacks also cannot solely be based on worry about non-panic-related current and future events, as may be the case in GAD. Therefore, in PD, it is the physical sensations themselves that trigger the fear response, as opposed to a phobic stimulus or situation. Such discriminations may be tricky at the outset for a clinician, as the adolescent and/or their parent(s) may not have insight about the source of panic-related triggers, furthering the need for functional assessment and/or a comprehensive diagnostic evaluation. Importantly, this differential diagnosis also has implications for treatment, as effective behavioral interventions for PD specifically target the adolescent's reactions to somatic sensations of panic, while other common treatments for other youth anxiety disorders (e.g., Kendall, Furr, & Podell, 2010, etc.) do not explicitly target these in their approach.

Evidence-Based Assessment

Current evidence-based assessment tools for adolescent PD include structured/semistructured diagnostic interviews and self-report measures of panic symptoms. Among diagnostic interviews, the Anxiety Disorders Interview Schedule for the DSM-IV, Child and Parent Versions (ADIS-IV-C/P; Silverman & Albano, 1996), has received extensive validation for anxiety disorder diagnoses among youth ages 7–17 years and includes PD and agoraphobia modules. In addition to assessing panic attack symptoms, frequency, and apprehension about future attacks, the ADIS-IV-C/P allows the clinician to assign a clinical severity rating (CSR) to capture the degree of interference for PD and agoraphobia symptoms. Ratings range from 0–8, with a CSR of 4 or higher indicating clinical levels of interference (Silverman & Albano, 1996).

Although demonstrating good reliability and validity, diagnostic interviews such as the ADIS-IV-C/P may be impractical for administration in many clinical and community settings, due to time for administration and need for sufficient clinician training. In such settings, brief self-report screening measures of panic symptoms may be more appropriate. Queen, Ehrenreich-May, and Hershorin (2012) validated a two-item screening tool for adolescent PD within primary care clinics, the Autonomic Nervous System Questionnaire (ANS; Stein, Roy-Byrne, McQuaid et al., 1999), which was originally developed for adults. In this study, the ANS demonstrated excellent sensitivity (Se = 1.00), although moderate specificity (Sp = 0.47), with regards to PD and agoraphobia diagnoses. In addition, compared to adolescents screening negative on the ANS, youth screening positive reported higher levels of panic symptoms, anxiety sensitivity, and functional impairment (Queen et al., 2012). Therefore, in settings in which time or resources may be limited (e.g., medical clinics), brief screening measures such as the ANS may offer clinicians the ability to quickly identify and provide further follow-up to youth with panic symptoms.

Finally, in addition to diagnostic interviews and self-report measures, symptom induction tasks, such as used with a Behavioral Approach Test (BAT; Craske, Barlow, & Meadows, 2000), allow clinicians to combine physiological and subjective reports. In the case of panic, this is accomplished by conducting exercises (e.g., spinning in a chair, breathing through a thin straw) to elicit panic sensations (e.g., dizziness, breathlessness; Bacow, May, Choate-Summers, Pincus, & Mattis, 2010), and then assessing (1) the adolescent's heart rate, and (2) the adolescent's subjective sense of distress through a rating scale. This method allows for a more "*in-vivo*" and theoretically objective assessment of the adolescent's symptoms, as well as the degree to which the youth perceives these sensations as distressing.

Evidence-Based Treatment

Despite generally poor outcomes for adolescents with untreated PD, clinical research into treatments for PD in adolescence has lagged behind other youth anxiety disorders (Birmaher & Ollendick, 2004), potentially due to perceptions about its relatively lower base rates. In contrast, PD treatment among adults has received considerable empirical attention. In this section, we review pharmacological interventions, with the vast majority of evidence stemming from trials of adults with PD, and psychosocial treatments, with a main focus upon cognitive-behavioral interventions.

Pharmacological treatment of panic disorder

Pharmacological treatment is often the first-line treatment for PD, especially within the primary care setting (Perugi, Frare, & Toni, 2007). One reason for this may be the high frequency with which individuals with PD first seek medical treatment for their panic symptoms (Katerndahl & Realini, 1997; Katon & Roy-Byrne, 1989). Although research into pharmacological treatments of PD in adolescents is quite limited, the two classes of psychiatric medication that show the most promise among adults with PD include selective serotonin reuptake inhibitors (SSRIs) and benzodiazepines. SSRIs are often the first choice for prescribing physicians and psychiatrists, as they are often better tolerated than other antidepressant medications (e.g., tricyclic antidepressants, etc.) and carry less risk of dependency compared to high-potency benzodiazepines (Kumar & Browne, 2002). Among the SSRIs, paroxetine (Paxil), sertraline (Zoloft), fluvoxamine (Luvox), and citalopram (Celexa) have all demonstrated efficacy in reducing PD symptoms relative to a placebo (Ballenger, Davidson, Lecrubier et al., 1998; Gorman & Wolkow, 1994; Lepola, Wade, Leinonen et al., 2001). Evidence for fluoxetine (Prozac) is more mixed, with some reports suggesting that fluoxetine may be less tolerable to patients with PD due to often-observed increases in anxiety in the initial weeks of treatment (Pollack, Lydiard et al., 1999; Schneier, Liebowitz, Davies, & Fairbanks, 1990). Furthermore, the US Food and Drug Administration's "black box" warning of possible increased risk of suicidal ideation for adolescents taking SSRIs may make this treatment approach less desirable, if other efficacious treatments are available or compliance with psychosocial intervention is likely.

High-potency benzodiazepines, including alprazolam (Xanax) and clonazepam (Klonopin), have also demonstrated efficacy in treating PD compared to placebo (Rosenbaum, Moroz, Bowden et al., 1997; Uhlenhuth, Balter, Ban, & Yang, 1998). Benzodiazepines are often better tolerated than SSRIs and also tend to act more quickly in reducing panic attacks (Perugi et al., 2007). However, high dosages of benzodiazepines are often needed to attain efficacy, and as a result, there is significant risk for dependency and withdrawal (Ballenger et al., 1998). Furthermore, benzodiazepines have not shown effectiveness in treating depressive symptoms and underperform in improving global functioning compared to SSRIs (Clum, Clum, & Surls, 1993; van Balkom, Bakker, Spinhoven, Blaauw, Smeenk, & Ruesink, 1997). This poses potential problems for adolescents with PD, given the high comorbidity with MDD (Diler et al., 2004). Even worse, there is some evidence for emergence of depressive episodes during the course of treatment with benzodiazepines (Cohen & Rosenbaum, 1987; Lydiard, 1988). Therefore, while benzodiazepines have demonstrated efficacy in PD treatment and may represent a viable option if SSRI treatment is unsuccessful or contraindicated, concerns about dependency and ineffectiveness in treating co-occurring depressive symptoms remain. Therefore, current recommendations include using benzodiazepines for only short-term management of symptoms (Perugi et al., 2007).

Despite the short-term effectiveness of SSRIs and benzodiazepines, there is little evidence for their long-term efficacy in treating PD (Perugi et al., 2007). In addition, there is significant risk for relapse of PD symptoms once treatment is discontinued. Most follow-up studies have found that approximately 50% of patients will experience a relapse of symptoms after discontinuation of pharmacological treatment (Faravelli, Paterniti, & Scarpato, 1995; Keller et al., 1994). This is in contrast to cognitive-behavioral therapy (CBT), which has demonstrated long-term gains and low risk for relapse among adult patients (Burns, 1990; Westen & Morrison, 2001). In addition, CBT has shown comparable efficacy to that of SSRIs in treating PD in adults (Mitte, 2005). Therefore, CBT seems to be a viable alternative or adjunctive treatment to pharmacological interventions for PD.

Psychodynamic treatment for adolescent panic

According to psychoanalytic theory, PD emerges from the interaction of unconscious drives, defense mechanisms, and relationships with significant others. This theory posits that individuals with PD often experience disruptive attachments with caregivers in early childhood, and as such, develop a "fearful dependency" on others (Shear, Cooper, Klerman, & Busch, 1993). When the individual perceives rejection or unavailability from the attachment figure, the person then experiences unconscious anger towards that caregiver. These feelings of anger towards the attachment figure elicit symptoms of anxiety, as the individual fears this emotion will further disrupt the relationship (Shear et al., 1993). Clinical observations have given some support to this theory, with individuals with PD demonstrating poor tolerance of anger towards others (Kleiner & Marshall, 1987).

Arising from this theory, panic-focused psychodynamic psychotherapy (PFPP; Milrod, Busch, Cooper, & Shapiro, 1997) was developed as a manualized, short-term form of psychoanalytic treatment for PD. The treatment is divided into three phases, with the goal of treatment to understand the meaning behind panic symptoms, gain awareness of defenses to suppress feared, unconscious feelings, fantasies, or wishes, and reduce the perceived threat of these feelings once brought into conscious awareness (Milrod et al., 1997). Preliminary evidence for psychodynamic treatments is promising. In a randomized controlled trial comparing PFPP to applied relaxation training (ART) in the treatment of adult PD, patients receiving PFPP showed greater response to treatment, as well as greater improvement in psychosocial functioning, compared to ART (Milrod, Leon, Busch et al., 2007). Although PFPP has yet to be directly compared to CBT, preliminary evidence suggests this treatment may be beneficial to adults with PD and a viable alternative to those who have not previously responded to pharmacological treatment or CBT. In addition, adaptations of PFPP are currently being applied to adolescents with PD (e.g., Milrod, Busch & Shapiro, 2004).

CBT for adolescent panic: Mastery of Anxiety and Panic for Adolescents (MAP-A)

MAP-A is an adolescent-focused adaptation of Mastery of Anxiety and Panic (MAP; Barlow, Craske, Cerny, & Klosko, 1989; Craske & Barlow, 2006), a cognitive-behavioral treatment for adults with PD. Similar to the adult protocol, MAP-A includes psychoeducation about panic, cognitive restructuring to target maladaptive thoughts, interoceptive exposure (exposure to panic-associated somatic sensations), situational exposure, and breathing retraining (Pincus et al., 2008). Developmental adaptations to the adolescent protocol include the use of handouts and metaphors (e.g., the term "watch dog" to describe apprehension about panic attacks) to concretize material. In addition, adolescent-friendly situations are commonly discussed (e.g., avoiding school or the mall, worries about having a panic attack in front of one's peer group). MAP-A is typically delivered in 11 sessions over the course of 12 weeks (Pincus et al., 2008). Table 19.1 illustrates the skills covered over the course of treatment with their accompanying sessions.

Table 19.1   Outline of 11-week version of MAP-A.

Session number(s)	Treatment components
1–2	Psychoeducation and three-component model
3–4	Cognitive restructuring
5–10	Interoceptive and *in-vivo* exposures
11	Relapse prevention and termination

Cognitive treatment components are based on Clark's (1986) model of panic, which posits that catastrophic interpretations about bodily sensations drive PD. For example, an adolescent who notices that his heart is beating fast may think "I'm having a heart attack!" as opposed to "My heart is beating fast because I just walked up a flight of stairs." A related cognitive construct targeted in treatment is anxiety sensitivity, or heightened awareness and reaction to anxiety-related somatic sensations (Reiss & McNally, 1985). These cognitive models have been supported with both cross-sectional and prospective evidence. Among community samples of adolescents, hypersensitivity to and fear of bodily sensations are predictive of panic symptoms (Calamari, Hale, Heffelfinger et al., 2001; Schmidt, Keough, Mitchell et al., 2010). Research with clinical samples of youth has yielded similar results, whereby youth with PD demonstrate higher anxiety sensitivity relative to controls (Ollendick, 1995) and youth with other anxiety disorders (Kearney et al., 1997).

Theories of conditioning and learning underlie the behavioral components of MAP-A treatment. Given that fear and avoidance of panic sensations are core features of PD, exposure to these sensations are purported to help patients "unlearn" the association between bodily sensations and the fear response. Common to CBT for other youth anxiety disorders, therapist-assisted and out-of-session situational exposure to avoided places (e.g., malls, subways) is conducted in a graduated manner, beginning with lower anxiety-provoking situations and progressing to higher anxiety-provoking stimuli. Interoceptive exposures, on the other hand, are unique to MAP-A, and are related to the fear of bodily sensations, which is a central distinguishing feature of PD.

A recently completed randomized controlled trial (RCT) of MAP-A is the first known RCT of a psychosocial treatment for PD and provides preliminary evidence for its efficacy. In this trial, 26 adolescents, ages 14–17 ($M = 15.75$ years, $SD = 1.10$), with a primary diagnosis of PD/A were randomized to an immediate treatment condition ($n = 13$) or a self-monitoring, delayed-treatment control condition ($n = 13$). In the control condition, subjects were instructed to monitor their panic and mood for 8 weeks prior to beginning treatment and met with a clinician for 30 minutes every other week. No hypothesized "active ingredients" of treatment were delivered in these meetings. Diagnoses were based upon administration of the ADIS-IV-C/P. Subjects with a psychotic disorder, pervasive developmental disorder, mental retardation, or current suicidal ideation were excluded. Stabilization periods of 1 month for benzodiazepines and 3 months for SSRIs were required before the initial evaluation (Pincus et al., 2010).

Results indicated a significant Time × Condition effect, with subjects in the immediate treatment condition showing significantly greater reductions in clinical severity ratings (CSRs) for PD/A diagnoses, as observed by an independent evaluator, compared to controls. Specifically, those in immediate treatment went from mean pretreatment PD/A CSRs within the clinical range ($M = 5.62$, $SD = 0.65$) to mean post-treatment CSRs in the subclinical range ($M = 3.31$, $SD = 1.36$). In contrast, mean CSRs in the control condition did not significantly change from pre-treatment ($M = 5.41$, $SD = 1$) to post-treatment ($M = 4.75$, $SD = 1.60$) and remained in the clinical range. Additionally, there was a significant Time × Condition effect on secondary measures of self-reported general anxiety symptoms, anxiety sensitivity, and depressive symptoms, with reductions favoring the immediate treatment condition.

Effect sizes for all reductions in secondary variables were large, with Cohen's *d* values ranging from 0.87 to 1.17 (Pincus et al., 2010). Therefore, treatment effects seemed to extend to other anxiety and depressive symptoms, which holds importance for generalizability, given the high comorbidity of PD with other anxiety disorders and with MDD (Diler et al., 2004).

Sessions 1–2: Psychoeducation about panic and the three component model

In these initial sessions, the therapist reviews prior assessment information, including the frequency of panic attacks, situations associated with panic attacks (which may be currently avoided), and the physical, cognitive, and behavioral symptoms the adolescent experiences during panic attacks. Similar to other models of CBT for anxiety disorders, the therapist then helps the adolescent identify triggers for his or her panic attacks. Since adolescents with PD report that attacks come "out of the blue," triggers for panic are often not external, as they may be in the case of other anxiety disorders (e.g., giving a speech, being near a feared object). Therefore, it is important that the therapist help the adolescent begin to pinpoint *internal* triggers for his or her panic attacks. These internal cues may be physical sensations (e.g., heart starts to beat fast) or cognitions (e.g., believing one is starting to go crazy). Through learning to identify these triggers, the adolescent is able to become an observer of his or her experiences, which aids in building his or her confidence to better manage panic. Helpful questions to ask the adolescent to identify these triggers include:

- "What do you feel in your body right before a panic attack starts?"
- "What is the first thing you think in your head right before a panic attack starts?"
- "What do you imagine happening when you start to feel panic?"

After the therapist has worked with the adolescent on identifying internal triggers, the next step is to help the adolescent "break down" the experience of anxiety into three components: *what I feel, what I think,* and *what I do.* The physical component of anxiety (*what I feel*) comprises the bodily sensations that occur when the adolescent experiences anxiety. Such sensations may include commonly reported symptoms of panic, including a racing heart, dizziness, and rapid breathing. Given the saliency of physical sensations in PD, many adolescents with PD may readily identify these bodily sensations, and thus the physical component of anxiety may be a good starting point when introducing this model. The cognitive component of anxiety (*what I think*) refers to the thoughts or images the adolescent has either immediately before or during the panic attack. For this component, it is important for the therapist to reiterate how individuals with PD look for potential threats once they notice their body is having an alarm reaction, yet cannot find any visible threat externally. In the absence of an outside threat, these individuals often turn their attention *inward*. As a result, panic thoughts may emerge, such as the aforementioned fears of losing control, dying, or going crazy. The final component (*what I do*) consists of behaviors that occur during or as a result of panic, and often are aimed at attempts to avoid the situation where the panic attack took place. This avoidance behavior is negatively reinforced because it reduces anxiety in the short-term. However, in the long-term, avoidance behaviors ultimately increase anxiety because they do not allow the adolescent to learn how to cope with their panic attacks.

Finally, it is important for the therapist to convey to the adolescent that anxiety and fear are natural and harmless emotions. The therapist should illustrate how anxiety can be adaptive, such as getting out of the way if one is about to be hit by a car. Therefore, the goal of treatment is not to remove all anxiety, but rather to learn how to handle fear and anxiety when it is not helpful or necessary. The message that the goal of treatment is not to suppress negative emotions may be particularly needed for adolescents with PD, as emotion research on adults with PD indicates they often "smother" emotions in attempts to control them, which only serves to increase physiological arousal (Campbell-Sills, Barlow, Brown, & Hofmann, 2006; Tull & Roemer, 2007).

After the three component model has been introduced, the therapist moves into discussing the physiological components of panic (*what I feel*). In line with the goal of normalizing emotional experiences, the therapist describes how the physical sensations the adolescent experiences during a panic attack are normal, natural reactions to perceived threat and are a result of the activation of the "fight-or-flight" system. It is helpful to describe how specific physical sensations are geared towards the body's goal of either fighting or fleeing from the perceived threat. For example, the reason adolescents experience a racing heart during a panic attack is because the heart must pump faster to get blood and oxygen to muscles to run or fight. Another example is sweating, which serves a dual purpose: first, to help the body cool down after activating the fight-or-flight system, and second, to make one more slippery from predators. After providing specific examples, it is important that the therapist explain that once the fight-or-flight system is activated, there is a "point of no return" at which the adolescent is not likely able to stop a panic attack from occurring; however, he or she can reduce the intensity of these attacks through behavioral strategies introduced in treatment.

Sessions 3–4: Cognitive restructuring

This section of treatment focuses on identifying and reappraising maladaptive cognitions commonly associated with PD. In particular, two types of "thinking errors" are identified and discussed throughout the treatment, as adolescents with PD frequently make them: *probability overestimation* and *catastrophic thinking*. Probability overestimation refers to an unrealistically high prediction of an unlikely event occurring, which causes the individual to unnecessary levels of anxiety. In the case of panic, these thoughts are often about having a panic attack when entering a situation (e.g., when going to the mall or at a school dance). Although the adolescent may realize that their prediction did not occur in these situations, they may attribute this to an avoidance or safety behavior (e.g., leaving the dance early) or to luck, believing that the next time they will not be as fortunate.

Catastrophic thinking involves thinking or imagining the worst possible consequence(s) occurring, often as a result of a panic attack. The adolescent believes that these consequences will be intolerable or dangerous, when in reality they may be only embarrassing or uncomfortable. Panic-related examples may include: "If I faint in front of other people, it would be the worst thing in the world," or "If I have a panic attack, I may die." Although the therapist should empathize with the adolescent that the identified situation may indeed be embarrassing, frightening, or uncomfortable, the key is to bring the adolescent to a greater understanding of both the actual likelihood of such consequences and their coping ability should certain consequences (e.g., having a panic attack) occur.

Once the therapist and adolescent have practiced identifying panic-related cognitive errors, the therapist introduces the concept of "thinking like a detective" to explain the concept of altering maladaptive thoughts. The therapist can explain that much like a detective uses clues to solve a mystery, the therapist and adolescent will gather "clues" and evidence to test the adolescent's thoughts. For an adolescent who fears they will have a panic attack and faint at a school dance, the following "detective" questions can help them gather evidence for their probability overestimation:

- "How many times have I fainted in the past when I have had a panic attack?"
- "What is the most likely thing that will happen?"
- "What evidence do I have that it will happen? What evidence do I have that it will not happen?"

It is often a useful activity to have the adolescent rate their prediction on a scale (such as from 0–100) *before* using detective questions, and then again immediately *after* they have examined the evidence for and against the prediction. Having the adolescent illustrate each prediction with a pie chart can often be a helpful visual aid. Similar steps are used when examining catastrophic thoughts. Using the same example of an adolescent who fears fainting in front of others, the following questions can help them examine the realistic consequences of the feared outcome:

- "What is the worst that can happen? Can I live through it?"
- "Could I cope? Have I been able to cope with embarrassment in the past?"
- "Is fainting in front of others really so terrible?"

Sessions 5–10: Interoceptive and in-vivo *exposures*

During these sessions, the therapist and adolescent target the third component of the model of panic (*what I do*). Interoceptive exposures focus on allowing the patient to fully experience somatic sensations of panic (e.g., racing heart, shortness of breath) and observe the process by which such symptoms naturally wane over time, as they would even in the context of a panic attack. *In-vivo* exposures are geared towards approaching feared situations associated with panic attacks and agoraphobic behaviors, most specifically (e.g., the mall, movie theater, subway train). With both forms of exposure, the goal is to have the adolescent eliminate avoidance behaviors that prevent full engagement in situations or with stimuli associated with panic symptoms.

As with other CBT protocols for youth anxiety, MAP-A uses a graduated approach to interoceptive and in-vivo exposures. Prior to conducting exposures, the therapist and patient construct a "fear hierarchy" that ranks somatic sensations and situations according to the level of anxiety elicited. In order to help the therapist and patient rank situations on the hierarchy, subjective units of distress (SUDS) ratings can be applied to each situation. Although MAP-A uses a SUDS range from 0 (no anxiety) to 8 (highest anxiety), the range is free to vary as the therapist sees fit. Situations with the highest SUDS ratings are ranked at the top of the hierarchy, while those with lower ratings are placed on the bottom of the hierarchy. With graduated exposures, the therapist and adolescent begin with items with lower SUDS ratings and progressively work towards higher anxiety-provoking situations. Although immediate exposure to the highest anxiety-provoking situations can be effective (i.e., flooding), graduated exposures may be more tolerable to the patient and allow for the patient to experience success with lower to mid-level hierarchy items before attempting the more difficult exposures.

The fear hierarchy should be as concrete and specific as possible when ranking stimuli. For example, if the adolescent reports "going to the mall" is the most anxiety-provoking situation, the therapist should help the patient describe qualifiers that lessen or increase anxiety. Using the example of going to the mall, the therapist should probe to see if anxiety is higher or lower if the patient goes to the mall by themselves versus with friends, if the mall is crowded or sparse, and so forth. In conjunction with helping the patient construct concrete and specific situations, the therapist should also look for "core fears" that be may be targeted in a variety of contexts. For example, if the patient's core fear is that he or she will have a panic attack in a crowded place and will not be able to escape, exposure to a multitude of crowded places (e.g., malls, elevators, subway train) will target this fear. Table 19.2 illustrates a sample fear hierarchy, with those situations eliciting the greatest fear (e.g., highest SUDS ratings) at the top of the hierarchy.

Before beginning exposures, it is important that the adolescent understand the rationale behind exposures. The rationale for interoceptive exposures can be explained through the concept of interoceptive conditioning, which is the pairing of somatic sensations with fear. The therapist can first use a general example of conditioning, such as pairing a certain food with disgust after getting sick from eating the food. The therapist can explain how a similar process occurs with panic, whereby these somatic sensations have been repeatedly paired with a fear response. Over time, the physical sensation itself (e.g., noticing one's heart is beating faster) may be sufficient to trigger fear. Therefore, the goal of interoceptive exposures is to allow the adolescent to experience these sensations, without engaging in avoidance, so that he or she can learn that these sensations are not actually harmful. With repeated practice, the adolescent's fear to these sensations will naturally decrease, and the association between somatic cues and fear will be weakened.

Table 19.2 Sample fear hierarchy.

Situation	SUDS (0–8)
Going to a crowded mall by myself	8
Riding on a crowded subway train by myself	7
Sitting in the middle of movie theater aisle during a crowded time	7
Riding on a crowded subway train with friends	6
Going to the mall when it is not crowded by myself	5

Another important concept underlining both interoceptive and *in-vivo* exposures is the concept of habituation. In the case of PD treatment, habituation refers to a reduced fear response to both the somatic sensations of panic as well as previously avoided situations. One useful metaphor to illustrate habituation is "riding the wave" of anxiety: similar to a wave in the ocean, which peaks but eventually falls, the adolescent's panic intensity and anxiety will eventually decrease over time (Pincus et al., 2008). Similarly, as the wave peaks are lower and lower as the wave approaches the shore, repeatedly practicing exposures results in eliciting lower and lower levels of anxiety over time (Pincus et al., 2008).

After explaining the rationale behind exposures, the therapist and patient should begin symptom induction exercises. Before having the adolescent complete these exercises, the therapist should first briefly demonstrate the exercise and give the patient specifics on the duration of the exercise. Immediately following the exercise, the therapist should collect the following information from the patient: (1) a description of the physical sensations elicited; (2) a rating ranging from 0 to 8 of the intensity of the sensations; (3) a rating (0–8) of the level of anxiety; and (4) a rating (0–8) of how similar the sensations elicited by the exercise were to the adolescent's actual panic attacks. Before beginning the next exercise, it is important to allow for the sensations to at least partially diminish to demonstrate that somatic cues do eventually subside in intensity. Furthermore, exercises should be conducted repeatedly to allow for habituation to occur. The exercises listed below are recommended for interoceptive exposures. Since some symptom induction exercises may cause more distress than others, it is important to have the patient perform all of these to determine which exercises elicit the most anxiety.

- Running in place for 1 minute (rapid heartbeat)
- Shaking head from side to side for 30 seconds (dizziness)
- Spinning quickly in a chair for 1 minute (dizziness)
- Breathe throw a thin straw (e.g., coffee stirrer) for 2 minutes with nostrils held together (hyperventilation)
- Hold breath for 30 seconds (difficulty breathing)
- Place head between knees for 30 seconds and then quickly lift to an upright position

After successfully conducting interoceptive exposures, the therapist and adolescent conduct *in-vivo* exposures based on the patient's fear hierarchy. As stated earlier, *in-vivo* exposures are conducted gradually, beginning with situations that provoke lesser amounts of anxiety and progressively working towards situations that elicit greater levels of anxiety. During therapist-assisted situational exposures, it is important for the therapist to observe overt as well as covert attempts to avoid experiencing anxiety. Covert attempts may be safety behaviors such as distraction (e.g., looking down at the floor, holding onto a railing, trying to engage in conversation), seeking reassurance (e.g., "I'm not going to have a panic attack, right?"), or carrying a safety object (e.g., cell phone, bottle of water). During situational exposures, the therapist should assist the patient in monitoring his or her level of anxiety through SUDS ratings and have the adolescent stay in the situation until his or her level of anxiety reduces by half. Although some research suggests that habituation may not be necessary in every instance for exposures to be effective (van Minnen & Foa, 2006), when working with youth clients, therapists should use their clinical judgment in determining whether allowing a client to end exposures prior to habituation would be harmful to therapeutic alliance or rapport.

In addition to therapist-assisted exposures, as with other CBT protocols, homework assignments are critical to ensure adolescents generalize skills outside of session. Out-of-session exposure assignments should be similar in intensity and duration to those conducted in session. It is important for the therapist to make the exposure assignment specific (e.g., "Go to the mall by yourself two times this week in the early evening and stay there for at least one hour"). Making the exposure assignment specific increases the likelihood that the task will be completed and will be of sufficient intensity.

Troubleshooting difficulties during exposure treatment   Since interoceptive and *in-vivo* exposures involve having the adolescent encounter somatic sensations and situations that elicit considerable anxiety, it is natural for resistance and hesitation about exposures to emerge. This is especially true for patients who have come to believe that the only way to "stay safe" is to avoid these stimuli. Resistance can manifest in many forms, such as missing sessions, giving numerous excuses (e.g., that one is too "stressed out" to do exposures), not completing homework exercises, or outright refusal to complete exposures. When resistance occurs, it is important for the therapist to understand the reasons for resistance. The reasons can be numerous, and may include fear of exposures, not understanding the rationale behind exposure, prior unsuccessful attempts at exposure, and beliefs that their PD symptoms will not improve.

After uncovering the reason behind the patient's resistance, it is crucial that the therapist effectively handle resistance to maximize the likelihood that exposures will be successful. Techniques behind motivational interviewing may be particularly helpful in these scenarios, such as helping the patient to weigh the pros and cons of change and evaluate potential long-term benefits of doing exposures (Miller & Rollnick, 2002). It is also important to convey the message of choice to the adolescent: although the therapist is there to encourage and "push" the patient to face feared stimuli, it is ultimately the adolescent's decision of whether or not to continue exposures. Allowing the adolescent to be an active participant in their exposures, such as giving the adolescent a few choices about which exposure to do on a given day, where possible (e.g., going to the mall or going to the subway train), is also helpful in managing resistance.

Although managing resistance and hesitation is common for exposure treatment cutting across all anxiety disorders, one often-reported concern perhaps unique to PD treatment is the patient's fear of having a panic attack while engaging in interoceptive and *in-vivo* exposures. If the patient reports this concern, it is important for the therapist to empathize with the adolescent's fear but not to encourage avoidance or safety behaviors. The therapist should acknowledge that having a panic attack is a possibility and may even indicate a successful exposure, given that the goal of exposures is to elicit the maximum amount of anxiety possible. Once the patient sees they can "survive" a panic attack without avoiding the situation, the fear of having a panic attack will ultimately diminish. If the patient experiences a panic attack during the course of an exposure, it is important for the therapist to remain calm, guide the adolescent in using his or her skills (e.g., cognitive restructuring) to manage their anxiety, and have the patient remain in the situation until the panic attack subsides. Although it may be helpful to acknowledge that the panic attack is not actually harmful, the therapist should be careful not to provide too much reassurance, as this may encourage safety behaviors.

In addition to managing the patient's distress, the therapist must deal with his or her own discomfort when conducting exposures. While exposures are difficult for both patient and therapist for any anxiety disorder, as they inevitably elicit distress in the patient, it may be particularly difficult for therapists treating adolescents with PD, given the high physical arousal they are likely to observe in the patient. During the course of treatment, the therapist and patient develop close emotional bonds, and it is natural for the therapist to experience discomfort when seeing the adolescent in distress. However, it is critical that the therapist realize that the long-term benefits of exposures for the patient (e.g., being able to effectively cope with panic attacks, improved quality of life) likely far outweigh any short-term distress. In addition to helping the therapist handle their own discomfort, discussing the long-term advantages of exposures to the patient may also lessen resistance.

Session 11: Termination and relapse prevention

This last session involves skill consolidation, reviewing accomplishments made in treatment, and planning for the future. At this point in treatment, the patient has learned all the skills they need to effectively manage PD symptoms, and in essence are ready to be their "own therapist." The therapist should briefly summarize the core skills learned in treatment, including cognitive restructuring and habituation to panic symptoms gained from interoceptive and *in-vivo* exposures. Allowing the adolescent to report what he or she learned from treatment and skills he or she found most helpful may help further consolidate treatment skills. It is also important to review treatment gains the adolescent has made, which may include being able to go to places previously avoided (e.g., the mall) or being better able to tolerate panic attacks. Having the adolescent re-rate his or her fear hierarchy is a concrete way for the adolescent to compare his or her anxiety levels before and after exposure exercises.

After reviewing skills and accomplishments, the therapist and adolescent should discuss a specific "practice plan" for the patient to continue conducting interoceptive and *in-vivo* exposures on his or her own. The therapist and adolescent should review the patient's fear hierarchy to determine areas needing further improvement. It is important to make the exposure assignments as specific as possible, including the frequency and duration of each exposure task. Making the exposure tasks specific and determining times for the adolescent to conduct these exercises maximizes the likelihood that these assignments will be completed and sufficiently challenging for the patient. Emphasizing the importance of repeated practice in real-life situations to continue gains in PD symptom reduction may help build motivation.

In addition to constructing a specific practice plan with the patient, the therapist should discuss relapse prevention. Upon treatment completion, many patients with PD may have the goal of never having another panic attack. However, given that panic attacks are relatively prevalent among adolescents (King, Gullone, Tonge, & Ollendick, 1993), it is likely that the adolescent may experience a panic attack during future periods of stress. Therefore, the therapist should discuss how symptom fluctuations are to be expected and how the adolescent can use his or her new skills to manage these symptoms. For example, the adolescent may have a panic attack when initially returning to the mall; however, how the adolescent copes with his or her panic attack (e.g., staying in the situation until the panic attack subsides) is more important than experiencing symptom fluctuation. Furthermore, the therapist should differentiate between a "lapse" and a "relapse," with the former representing a partial return and the latter a full return of avoidant behaviors. Encouraging the patient to recognize symptoms of a lapse and to use his or her coping strategies may help prevent a full-blown relapse. Through explaining how symptom fluctuations are lapses to be expected, the therapist can help prevent the patient from engaging in future catastrophic appraisals (e.g., believing one has lost all gains after experiencing an increase in symptoms).

Intensive Treatment Adaptation

Although the 11-week standard version of MAP-A has shown promising results (Pincus et al., 2010), for some adolescents with more severe PD symptoms and interference (e.g., inability to attend school), an intensive treatment approach may be indicated. With this in mind, Pincus, Spiegel, Mattis, Micco, and Barlow (2003) developed an 8-day intensive adaptation of MAP-A for families of adolescents with more severe agoraphobia, as well as for families traveling long distances for treatment. The pilot study involved 18 adolescents (mean age = 14.5 years; 66.6% female), most of whom were from outside the local area.

The treatment is delivered over 8 consecutive days and incorporates the same core elements found in traditional MAP-A, including psychoeducation, cognitive restructuring, and interoceptive and *in-vivo* exposures. Psychoeducation and cognitive restructuring are covered in the first three days of treatment, with the first three sessions lasting approximately 2–3 hours each. The fourth and fifth days involve therapist accompaniment on integrated interoceptive and *in-vivo* exposures for 5–7 hours for each session. The sixth and seventh days involve family accompaniment on exposure exercises, again for 5–7 hours for each session. The eighth day of treatment consists of a 2-hour final session reviewing treatment gains, discussing relapse prevention, and planning for future adolescent-directed exposures. Table 19.3 displays an outline of the intensive treatment.

Results from the pilot study suggested initial efficacy for the intensive adaptation. By the end of treatment, 14 out of 18 adolescents were subclinical in PD clinical

Table 19.3 Outline of 8-day intensive version of MAP-A.

Treatment day(s)	Treatment component	Typical session duration
1–3	Psychoeducation, cognitive restructuring, interoceptive exposure	2–3 hours
4, 5	*In-vivo* exposure with therapist accompaniment	5–7 hours
6, 7	*In-vivo* exposure with family accompaniment	5–7 hours
8	Relapse prevention and termination	2 hours

severity ratings (Pincus et al., 2003). This is particularly encouraging, as this sample had more severe symptoms than the 11-week treatment group (Pincus et al., 2003, 2010). At 1-month follow-up assessment, 17 out of 18 adolescents no longer met criteria for PD and reported no longer experiencing clinically significant interference. Furthermore, mean panic attacks reduced from a group average of 11.4 panic attacks per week at pre-treatment to 2.2 attacks per week at 1-month follow-up, and further decreases to 1.5 panic attacks per week at 3-month follow-up (Pincus et al., 2003). In addition, self-reported anxiety sensitivity significantly decreased from pre- to post-treatment and was maintained at follow-up assessments (Pincus et al., 2003). In addition to improved symptom functioning, participants and their families reported improved academic performance, peer and family functioning, and increased parental confidence to effectively manage their child's panic attacks (Pincus et al., 2003). Overall, these results suggest an intensive, 8-day adaptation of MAP-A may be a viable option for families of adolescents with greater PD severity or for those who live long distances from the treatment clinic.

Parental Involvement

In general, there is evidence that including parents in the treatment process of youth anxiety disorders can enhance effectiveness and maintenance of gains (Dadds, Heard, & Rapee, 1992; Ginsburg, Silverman, & Kurtines, 1995). Parents can be conceptualized as "co-therapists" who help the adolescent generalize skills to out-of-session experiences and provide positive reinforcement for approach behaviors. Reviewing treatment skills with the parent(s) can give the adolescent and parent a "common language" when managing panic symptoms, such as "using detective questions" or "riding the wave" of anxiety. Furthermore, since many adolescents with PD have anxious parents, reviewing treatment skills can help parents learn tools with which to manage their own anxiety.

One common concern of parents of adolescents with PD is witnessing their child's distress when experiencing a panic attack. It is important for the therapist to empathize with the parent and explain that this is a natural reaction, given that a parent's main role is to protect their child from harm. However, the therapist should discuss how certain behaviors (e.g., modeling anxious behaviors, allowing their adolescent to avoid situations that trigger panic attacks) may actually reinforce the adolescent's anxiety. The therapist should educate the parent that panic attacks are uncomfortable, but not harmful, and stress the importance that the adolescent "face the fear" to overcome the panic symptoms. This can be accomplished through both didactic information as well as having the parent witness their adolescent perform an interoceptive or *in-vivo* exposure. Having the parent involved in an exposure session can help the parent see that their adolescent indeed can tolerate and effectively cope with the panic symptoms without escaping the situation. Furthermore, teaching the parent how to effectively coach their adolescent through an exposure can improve the chances that exposures will be practiced outside of sessions and that gains will be maintained after treatment.

A final note about parental involvement is attending to the possibility that parents may fear a "loss" of closeness in their relationship with their adolescent. Although parents certainly do not desire for their children to experience panic symptoms, many parents may enjoy that their adolescent wishes to "stay close" to them out of fear of having a panic attack alone. Since a goal of treatment is to have the adolescent perform more tasks independently, it is natural for parents to mourn this loss of closeness with their child. However, the therapist, adolescent, and parent should discuss other ways they can remain close without encouraging avoidance behaviors.

Case Study: Lucia M.

Lucia M.[1] is a 17-year-old adolescent female that was referred by her mother to a University-based clinic specializing in anxiety disorders for treatment of panic disorder and agoraphobia symptoms. Lucia and her mother participated in an initial intake process using the ADIS-IV-C/P to assess current diagnostic status, followed by the intensive version of the MAP-A treatment program described above. Post-treatment and 6-month follow-up status was attained using a briefer version of the ADIS-IV-C/P that focuses primarily on status of previously assigned diagnoses and any newly reported concerns (often referred to as the Mini-ADIS). A summary of each stage of assessment and treatment are reported in chronological order below.

Initial assessment

Lucia and her mother each completed the ADIS-IV-C/P and a battery of question-naires at the intake meeting, with the goal of providing sufficient detail about her background, current symptoms, and functioning to assess fit with a variety of poten-tial anxiety and depressive disorder diagnoses. Prior to this intake meeting, a phone screening with Mrs. M relayed that Lucia was currently experiencing a number of difficulties which seemed potentially indicative of PD/A, including avoiding certain classes at her high school and spending these class sessions in the school nurse's office or guidance counselor's office. Mrs. M reported that Lucia had an initial panic attack, for which she received care at a local emergency room, approximately 6 months prior while on her school's grounds with a friend, and experienced other, seemingly less severe panic attacks since that time. Mrs. M indicated that Lucia had been increasing her dependence on Mrs. M to take her to places that she previously navigated inde-pendently, as Lucia refused to drive outside of a close radius of her family's home or take public transportation, activities she previously did without concern or complaint. During the phone screen and subsequent ADIS-IV-C/P, Mrs. M indicated that Lucia had a history of separation anxiety disorder, but no history of potentially exclusionary conditions for this clinic such as substance dependence, intellectual/developmental disability, significant suicidal/homicidal ideation or psychiatric hospitalization. Lucia previously received six sessions of reportedly effective psychosocial treatment at age 8 for separation anxiety symptoms; however, she had not received any other psychoso-cial treatments since that time. Notably, Lucia was prescribed a benzodiazepine by

---

[1]The case of Lucia M. is based on an amalgam of recent cases treated by the authors using the MAP-A approach and its intensive variant. All demographic and identifying information has been significantly altered to protect the confidentiality of client data.

an emergency room physician 6 months ago and a SSRI by her pediatrician approximately 3 months for her PD/A symptoms. Mrs. M indicated that Lucia was not taking either medication at the present time, as they made Lucia feel "weird" and did not immediately relieve her symptoms to a satisfactory degree for her to persist in their usage.

During the intake, Lucia presented as an intelligent, poised, and friendly adolescent female who was forthcoming, made excellent eye contact, and was generally insightful about her concerns. Her mother was also very open in discussing her daughter's difficulties at present. Both informants reported feeling overwhelmed and upset by Lucia's recent dramatic change in functioning at school, in particular. Lucia was in the 11th grade at a prestigious private high school. Mrs. M reported that Lucia was previously an "A student" at this school, but that her grades were significantly worse since the onset of panic symptoms (mostly Bs, with one C in an advanced calculus class) due to missed classes and difficulty managing her work without consistent, direct teacher feedback and instruction.

Lucia indicated that she was born in Argentina, but that her family relocated to the suburban, Northeastern U.S. town where she resided since age 3. Mrs. M was a full-time mother with a substantial volunteer commitment to a local community service agency. Her father, Mr. M, had a leadership position with an international business that required extensive travel. Lucia had a sister, Isabelle (age 22), who attended a Master's program in video production and film studies on the west coast of the USA and an older brother, Max (age 19), who attended a nearby, ivy league college. Lucia indicated that she was particularly close to her mother and older brother, but that her relationship with her father was "strained" as he reportedly held high academic standards for his children and exhibited poor tolerance of her current school challenges. Mrs. M concurred that her husband had "lost patience" with Lucia regarding her school avoidance behaviors and that they had frequent verbal disputes about it, causing a rupture in their formerly strong relationship. Mrs. M reported that she had a history of post-partum depression and anxiety, but no current symptoms of either. Lucia's sister also reportedly had a long history of anxiety and panic symptoms and was currently unable to fly home to see her family due to significant fears about air travel.

Using parent and child reports from the ADIS-IV-C/P, additional background information, and questionnaire data, the clinician conducting Lucia's intake assigned her the following diagnoses: panic disorder with agoraphobia (CSR = 7) and major depressive disorder, single episode, moderate, in partial remission (CSR = 3). Some symptoms of GAD were also noted related to worry about school performance, the future, her health and that of her family, but these appeared consistent with Lucia's PD/A symptom cluster at present. A past diagnosis of separation anxiety disorder (CSR = 4) was also assigned to account for historical reports of Lucia's significant fears and anticipatory worry about separations at school and social activities (e.g., play dates, camp, etc.) through age 8. Notably, the clinician found that Lucia continued to experience fears about long-term separations from her mother, in particular, in the course of her current panic disorder and indicated that Mrs. M served as the primary "safety person" from whom Lucia preferred to gain assistance when going someplace where she felt likely to experience panic, or when needing to leave a situation where she feared panic would occur, such as school or when in a less familiar location.

In terms of current PD/A symptoms, Lucia reported experiencing moderate to severe panic attacks approximately once a week, with limited symptom attacks occurring more frequently (2–3 times per week). Lucia reported that her symptoms of panic were most acute in the 10-minute interval following their onset and included trigger symptoms of heart palpitations, followed by shortness of breath, dizziness, sweating and nausea. Lucia reported that she feared fainting and ultimately dying while having a panic attack, although she was previously reassured that she had no heart or pulmonary condition underlying such symptoms by physicians. Lucia indicated that she primarily managed panic symptoms by leaving the situation she was in as soon as she noticed their onset and returning only if and when she felt "normal" again. Lucia discussed a strong fear of panic symptoms returning in situations where they previously occurred. She insightfully reported that due to her fears about panic recurrence, she was avoiding more and more situations and the people associated with them. Lucia indicated that while she had one close friend, Ashley, with whom she generally felt "safe" and "confident" when experiencing panic symptoms, she realized that she was avoiding more and more social opportunities with other friends. For instance, she had recently declined a trip into the city where her brother attended school (approximately 1.5 hours away) because her friends planned to take a train from their suburban town there together and she did not feel comfortable riding the train without her mother, despite Ashley's presence on the trip. In terms of agoraphobia symptoms, Lucia and her mother reported that Lucia avoided classrooms where she previously had panic symptoms, a portion of the school's outdoor courtyard where she had her first panic attack, driving to/from school or outside of the small town in which they lived at all (and would only drive within the town if her mother, brother or friend, Ashley, was in the car with her), taking public transportation without her mother (e.g., trains, buses, etc.), being in unfamiliar locations alone and, to a lesser extent, movie theatres and sporting events (where she indicated she might feel "boxed in" by a crowd of people and be unable to get help for panic/cardiac symptoms as needed).

Lucia and her mother both reported that Lucia recently experienced a depressive episode. Lucia indicated that she was feeling increasingly depressed about the pervasiveness of her panic symptoms and worried that such feelings would "never go away" or "could not be fixed". Mrs. M felt that both the initial PD/A diagnosis made by the emergency room physician and subsequent discussions with their pediatrician were frightening and depressing for Lucia, especially given her sister Isabelle's continuing struggles with similar problems. Lucia reported that her mood was not currently depressed every day or almost every day for the prior two weeks, but that she had experienced at least one two week period during the previous three months in which her mood was consistently sad and/or irritable. She also reported anhedonia, hopelessness, loss of appetite, poor sleep and thoughts about death (but no significant thoughts of self-harm or suicide) during that same two week interval. She indicated that such symptoms were currently slightly better and less consistent, as she was hopeful about treatment and had a renewed motivation to overcome her panic at present.

Course of treatment

Lucia and her mother were given a choice between a weekly application of the MAP-A protocol and its intensive format. Given her increasing levels of school-related avoidance, the family elected to participate in the 8-day intensive approach for these symptoms. The treating clinician theorized that Lucia's current depressive symptoms seemed closely tied to the course of her panic disorder and, therefore, prioritized the focus on PD/A symptoms, as it was believed that the MDD symptoms might abate with further amelioration of her panic. Lucia indicated that she was highly motivated for treatment and, while this was viewed as a positive treatment indicator, the clinician worked with Mrs. M and Lucia in advance of the first session to manage expectations for outcomes appropriately.

Intensive treatment days 1–2

At the onset of treatment, Lucia seemed eager and interested to learn psychoeducational information about anxiety and panic symptoms. In particular, she appeared to resonate with a greater understanding that her panic attacks were not solely due to something within the situations she avoided, but rather high levels of physiological symptoms and worry about engaging Lucia's "fight or flight response". In session, she relayed her initial panic attack in detail and its associated antecedents, as well as subsequent panic attacks. After reviewing the three component model, Lucia demonstrated increased awareness that her current avoidance behaviors were not preventing panic symptoms in the long-term, but conversely, reinforcing them, as she was unable to ascertain whether her panic-related physiological symptoms would worsen (as she predicted) or naturally decrease over time, should she remain in a fear-evoking situation. Lucia and the clinician also reviewed the common presentation of physiological symptoms associated with PD/A and their role in creating alarm-like reactions in the body, as well as facilitating the fight/flight response in the case of actual bodily threats. On Day 2, as time allowed for such, the clinician introduced the concept of "thinking traps" and how these might relate to Lucia's behavioral choices while experiencing panic symptoms. At the conclusion of both Days 1 and 2, a significant amount of time was spent with Mrs. M (and Mr. M on Day 2 only, given his work schedule) to both increase their familiarity with anxiety and panic and increase their knowledge about how best to support Lucia through what was likely to be a potentially stressful 8-day interval. Mr. M spoke directly about his frustrations with both Isabelle and Lucia's anxiety symptoms and his difficulty understanding how Lucia would potentially let such feelings interfere with her positive academic trajectory. The clinician discussed working to accept the past occurrence of such behaviors and working together as a team, with Lucia, to make successful changes in her approach to panic-related situations. These meetings were positive in tone, included Lucia's participation at times, and overall seemed to suggest good family support for future exposure activities.

Intensive treatment day 3

By Day 3, Lucia indicated an increased awareness that she was unlikely to be harmed by her panic symptoms and that her behavioral avoidance was serving to maintain such symptoms over time. However, she still expressed a high degree of anticipatory worry about the consequences of experiencing intense physical sensations and the exposure sessions she knew to be forthcoming. After an abbreviated review of cognitive restructuring techniques geared toward worry Lucia might experience in the course of upcoming panic-related *in-vivo* exposure sessions and in the context of panic symptoms more generally, the clinician elected to spend the remainder of Day 3 introducing the concept of interoceptive conditioning and exposure, followed by the development of a fear and avoidance hierarchy. Given that Lucia had multiple avoidance behaviors that might benefit from initial therapist-assistance in exposure (e.g., driving, school, public transportation, crowded places, etc.), this focus also allowed sufficient time for these varied and potentially time-consuming exposures to take place. Moreover, Mrs. M expressed some concerns about her ability to "say no" if Lucia pressed her to avoid or escape a planned exposure, especially with Mr. M working on Days 6 and 7 of treatment. Therefore, additional time was also planned to help Mrs. M increase her confidence that Lucia could achieve her exposure goals and foresee how best to support her approach-oriented behaviors.

The clinician commenced a discussion of interoceptive conditioning with Lucia and the role of habituation in exposure. Lucia was concerned about the use of symptom induction tasks to initially increase her experience of physiologic sensations associated with panic, but agreed to proceed with this exercise. Lucia, in fact, completed all of the symptom induction tasks assigned (e.g., breathing through a thin straw, shaking her head vigorously, spinning in a chair, etc.). Lucia was asked to use a "body scanning" technique to keep her focus on her bodily sensations in between tasks and report to the clinician when her Subjective Units of Distress level (SUDS; on a scale of 0–8) reduced by half of its intensity from the end point of the symptom induction task. Lucia was observed to have a strong visceral reaction to such tasks and often took a lengthy amount of time to experience a significant reduction in the intensity of such symptoms. At the end of this exercise, Lucia reported that she felt "tired" but generally more aware of the exposure process. She indicated that her fear of panic-related physiological symptoms also improved throughout the exercise and was assigned to practice several challenging symptom induction tasks for homework. Mrs. M was invited into session to also practice interoceptive exposures and to observe as Lucia demonstrated several of these tasks for her.

Finally, the clinician, Mrs. M, and Lucia completed an initial fear and avoidance hierarchy, ranking Lucia's stated fear level and degree of avoidance regarding situations in which she feared experiencing panic symptoms or otherwise exhibited agoraphobic avoidance. As the school had agreed to make several classrooms available to the clinician and Lucia the next day, the clinician and Lucia determined to first practice a couple of lesser-feared situations (involving crowded places and public transportation) then progress to school-related exposures that afternoon. The clinician indicated that she would be flexible with Lucia about the ordering and pace of exposures as the next 2 days progressed in order to be maximally responsive to both her fears and her energy level, given that intensive exposures can be tiring for the client. Mrs. M concurred with these plans and agreed to be available, as needed throughout both therapist-assisted exposure days to observe and include separation-oriented exposures within these contexts where appropriate.

Intensive treatment days 4–7

The clinician commenced *in vivo* exposure practice at the University's soccer field the next morning, where a collegiate match was taking place. The plan was for Mrs. M to walk with Lucia to the game, meet the clinician and then return to their hometown, while the clinician and Lucia conducted exposures in the crowded stands during the match, followed by a 30 minute train ride to their suburban train stop. Despite the early hour, the stands for this match were quite crowded and Lucia appeared visibly nervous upon approaching the clinician, stating that she "trusted" the clinician, but was unsure that she wanted her mother to leave. Upon discussion, Lucia indicated that she knew it was unlikely that she would require medical attention for her panic or related physiological symptoms, but felt uncomfortable that the clinician had not brought a car with her that day and did not want her mother to leave in hers, in case they required immediate assistance. Using the cognitive restructuring skills previously discussed, Lucia was able to identify her catastrophizing thoughts in this instance and vocalize alternative thoughts regarding her safety. After 5 minutes of discussion, Mrs. M did leave the soccer field and Lucia entered the field's stands, directed by the clinician to take seats in the middle of a crowded area. Lucia reported that her SUDS was then a 7 on a 0–8 scale, but this level reduced systematically within a 15-minute interval to a 3. Lucia indicated that this experience was illuminating, as she would normally leave such a situation immediately if her panic symptoms were similarly intense elsewhere. At this point, the clinician asked Lucia to give her any "safety objects" (e.g., cell phone, water bottle, etc.) and indicated that she would meet Lucia outside of the field area. Lucia's reported level then returned to a 6 and the clinician stated that she wanted Lucia to wait until her level was below a 3 before exiting the stands to find her. This task was challenging, but successfully accomplished and the clinician and Lucia left to board the train to her hometown.

At the train station, Lucia stated that she would find the exposure more challenging if the clinician was not immediately visible on the train ride. Therefore, it was deter-mined that a similar pattern of exposure practice would be conducted on the train as at the soccer field, with the clinician starting the exposure with Lucia, then mov-ing out of sight until her SUDS was suitably reduced. This exposure also went well. However, afterwards, Lucia began complaining of excessive fatigue upon approaching her mother at the station. On the car ride to get a quick lunch and subsequently on the way to her school, Lucia became increasingly vocal that she felt she had "done enough" for the day and did not want to participate in school-based exposures. The clinician reminded Lucia of her earlier achievements and empathized with her about her fatigue and concern, as the school was the site of her initial panic attacks and the source of near-daily reminders about panic. After arriving at the school, Lucia tearfully indicated that she would only proceed if her mother stayed in the parking lot with her cell phone ready, should she be needed. The clinician discussed this with Mrs. M and it was agreed that instead, Mrs. M would come into the school with Lucia and practice a similar fading procedure to the one conducted with the clinician earlier (e.g., starting the exposure with the clinician, then systematically repeating or continuing the exposure with the clinician away or out of sight). By doing so, sepa-ration from Mrs. M was more cohesively weaved into the *in vivo* exposure process. Although still notably tired and upset, Lucia stated that she found this idea agreeable as well.

School-based exposures included entering and remaining in classrooms that she frequently avoided and entering the area of the school courtyard where her first panic attack took place. Lucia handled these successfully, albeit more slowly than the morning's exposures, and the clinician was able to appropriately fade her mother's presence in such exposures. The next day centered on driving-related exposures, culminating in driving on the highway from her town to the nearby larger city where the clinician's office was located. Lucia first drove this route with the clinician in the same car, and then drove the route back on her own. Later in the day, the clinician returned to Lucia's high school to again practice school-based exposures with her, but without Mrs. M present. Lucia drove the clinician to the school, dropped her off then repeated the drive home and to school again alone, followed by independently entering her avoided classrooms and courtyard, while the clinician remained outside (with no cell phones or other safety signals in use). Lucia reported these exposures to be "exhausting", but felt that she was ready to attempt them independently over Intensive Treatment Days 6–7 and throughout the next school week.

On Days 6 and 7, the client and her parents were assigned to practice several of the previously attempted exposure activities, with appropriate fading of or no parent involvement, nor use of any safety signals during exposures. Additional exposure activities that were not attempted (e.g., riding the train/bus without clinician or parent, attending a movie at a crowded theatre, driving in more naturalistic settings alone and/or with less familiar people, etc.) were particularly targeted during this time, as were other opportunities for repeated practice and/or extensions of previous exposures. Mrs. M was explicitly coached on managing her own reactions to Lucia's distress and in how to encourage approach-oriented and independent coping solutions during this time.

Intensive treatment day 8

On Day 8, the client and her parents attended a 2-hour follow-up session after school was completed for the day. Lucia reported that she successfully conducted three exposures over the weekend prior, including taking the train into the city to see her brother alone, driving two friends to a movie and remaining for the entire show, and returning to the school courtyard for a repeat practice of that prior exposure. She had also attended all of her classes, though with a high level of distress in some instances, throughout that day. Both her parents praised Lucia for her perseverance, but also indicated that Lucia had been quite reluctant to practice exposures and required a good deal of reminders about cognitive restructuring and planned rewards (e.g., a new cell phone that they had promised her for completing the program) to motivate herself to continue. They reported some concern about how to keep Lucia motivated in the future when she experienced normal stressors or lapses in her panic symptoms. The clinician normalized Mr. and Mrs. M's concerns and reminded both Lucia and her parents that such fluctuations were normal, particularly when highly fatigued or otherwise stressed. Overall, continued practice was consistently emphasized as the route to a complete recovery from Lucia's PD/A symptoms. Although Lucia attempted nearly every exposure task requested by her parents or the clinician, she was further encouraged to make such exposure plans more so on her own and practice approach-oriented behaviors as soon as she became aware of any panic triggers or cues independently to further solidify her excellent treatment outcomes.

Post-treatment and follow-up assessments

Two days later, Lucia and her mother returned for a Mini-ADIS. An independent evaluator determined that Lucia's PD/A symptoms had reduced in intensity during this 8-day interval from a CSR of 7 to a 3, while her MDD symptoms remained at a CSR = 3, partially owing to Lucia's continued reports of anhedonia and fatigue. The clinician had prepared Mrs. M and Lucia to anticipate further improvements at a 6-month follow-up visit, should Lucia continue to practice her approach-oriented behaviors and other treatment techniques consistently. This was, in fact, the case. When Lucia returned for this 6-month follow-up assessment, her PD/A CSR = 2, while her MDD was deemed in full remission by the evaluator. The independent evaluator, however, did add a provisional GAD diagnosis at a sub-clinical level (CSR = 3) to account for excessive worry about schoolwork-related challenges, worry about the future (particularly college acceptances, which were arriving shortly), and the health of her sister and parents. The evaluator discussed these findings with the clinician, who subsequently conducted two booster sessions with Lucia to discuss her increase in worry symptoms. Lucia reported that as her panic symptoms decreased, she came to realize the degree to which her response to her panic had hurt her grades and school performance. She felt that she was under a high level of pressure to return to her former academic standing at school and attain entry to prestigious colleges. She also felt responsibility to "spread the word" about CBT for panic symptoms and particularly attempt to find similar assistance for her sister. In fact, soon after the second booster session, Lucia and her mother flew to the west coast to help her sister begin an intensive CBT program. Neither the clinician nor Lucia's family felt her GAD symptoms required further treatment, but rather were a natural outgrowth of her school-related stressors, high-achieving family, and her own personality style. Nonetheless, the clinician indicated that she was available for further treatment sessions should such worry symptoms or PD/A symptoms become problematic in the future.

References

APA (2000). Panic disorder. In *Diagnostic and Statistical Manual of Mental Disorders: DSM-IV-TR*, 4th edn. (pp. 433-441). Arlington: American Psychiatric Association.

Bacow, T., May, J., Choate-Summers, M., Pincus, D. B., & Mattis, S. G. (2010). Concordance between measures of anxiety and physiological arousal following treatment of panic disorder in adolescence. *Child & Family Behavior Therapy, 32* (4), 322–333. doi:10.1080/07317107.2010.515843

Ballenger, J. C., Davidson, J. T., Lecrubier, Y., Nutt, D. J., Baldwin, D. S., den Boer, J. A., et al. (1998). Consensus statement on panic disorder from the International Consensus Group on Depression and Anxiety. *Journal of Clinical Psychiatry, 59* (8), 47–54.

Barlow, D. H., Craske, M. G., Cerny, J. A., & Klosko, J. S. (1989). Behavioral treatment of panic disorder. *Behavior Therapy, 20* (2), 261–282. doi:10.1016/S0005-7894(89)80073-5

Birmaher, B., & Ollendick, T. H. (2004). Childhood-onset panic disorder. In Ollendick, T. H., & March, J. S. (eds.), *Phobic and Anxiety Disorders in Children and Adolescents* (pp. 306–333). Oxford University Press.

Birmaher, B., Ryan, N. D., & Williamson, D. E. (1996). Depression in children and adolescents: Clinical features and pathogenesis. In K. I. Shulman, M. Tohen, S. P. Kutcher, K. I.

Shulman, M. Tohen, & S. P. Kutcher (Eds.), *Mood Disorders Across the Life Span* (pp. 51–81). New York: Wiley-Liss.

Bouton, M. E., Mineka, S., & Barlow, D. H. (2001). A modern learning theory perspective on the etiology of panic disorder. *Psychological Review, 108* (1), 4–32. doi:10.1037/0033–295X.108.1.4.

Burns, L. E. (1990). Current progress in panic and phobic disorder research. *PsycCRITIQUES, 35* (6), 600–601. doi:10.1037/028725.

Calamari, J. E., Hale, L. R., Heffelfinger, S. K., Janeck, A. S., Lau, J. L., Weerts, M. A., et al. (2001). Relations between anxiety sensitivity and panic symptoms in nonreferred children and adolescents. *Journal of Behavior Therapy and Experimental Psychiatry, 32* (3), 117–136. doi:10.1016/S0005-7916(01)00026-X.

Campbell-Sills, L., Barlow, D. H., Brown, T. A., & Hofmann, S. (2006). Acceptability and suppression of negative emotion in anxiety and mood disorders. *Emotion, 6* (4), 587–595. doi:10.1037/1528–3542.6.4.587.

Cohen, L. S., & Rosenbaum, J. F. (1987). Clonazepam: New uses and potential problems. *Journal of Clinical Psychiatry, 48* (Suppl), 50–55.

Craske, M., & Barlow, D. H. (2006). *Mastery of Your Anxiety and Panic, Therapist Guide*. New York: Oxford University Press.

Craske, M. G., Barlow, D. H., & Meadows, E. (2000). *Mastery of Your Anxiety and Panic: Therapist Guide for Anxiety, Panic and Agoraphobia (MAP-3)*. San Antonio, TX: Graywind Psychological Corporation.

Clark, D. M. (1986). A cognitive approach to panic. *Behaviour Research and Therapy, 24*, 461–470.

Clum, G. A., Clum, G. A., & Surls, R. (1993). A meta-analysis of treatments for panic disorder. *Journal of Consulting and Clinical Psychology, 61* (2), 317–326. doi:10.1037/0022-006X.61.2.317.

Dadds, M. R., Heard, P. M., & Rapee, R. M. (1992). The role of family intervention in the treatment of child anxiety disorders: Some preliminary findings. *Behaviour Change, 9* (3), 171–177.

Diler, R., Birmaher, B., Brent, D. A., Axelson, D. A., Firinciogullari, S., Chiapetta, L., & Bridge, J. (2004). Phenomenology of panic disorder in youth. *Depression and Anxiety, 20* (1), 39–43. doi:10.1002/da.20018.

Doerfler, L. A., Connor, D. F., Volungis, A. M., & Toscano, P. F. (2007). Panic disorder in clinically referred children and adolescents. *Child Psychiatry and Human Development, 38* (1), 57–71. doi:10.1007/s10578-006-0042-5.

Essau, C. A., Conradt, J., & Petermann, F. (1999). Prevalence, comorbidity, and psychosocial impairment of somatoform disorders in adolescents. *Psychology, Health, and Medicine, 4* (2), 169–180. doi:10.1080/135485099106306.

Faravelli, C., Paterniti, S., & Scarpato, A. (1995). 5-year prospective, naturalistic follow-up study of panic disorder. *Comprehensive Psychiatry, 36* (4), 271–277. doi:10.1016/S0010-440X(95)90072-1.

Fleming, J. E., Offord, D. R., & Boyle, M. H. (1989). Prevalence of childhood and adolescent depression in the community: Ontario Child Health Study. *British Journal of Psychiatry, 155*, 647–654.

Ginsburg, G. S., Silverman, W. K., & Kurtines, W. K. (1995). Family involvement in treating children with phobic and anxiety disorders: A look ahead. *Clinical Psychology Review, 15* (5), 457–473. doi:10.1016/0272-7358(95)00026-L.

Gorman, J. M., & Wolkow, R. (1994). Sertraline as a treatment for panic disorder. *Neuropsychopharmacology, 10*, 35–197.

Gotlib, I. H., Lewinsohn, P. M., & Seeley, J. R. (1998). Consequences of depression during adolescence: Marital status and marital functioning in early adulthood. *Journal of Abnormal Psychology, 107* (4), 686–690. doi:10.1037/0021-843X.107.4.686.

Katerndahl, D. A., & Realini, J. P. (1997). Use of health care services by persons with panic symptoms. *Psychiatric Services, 48* (8), 1027–1032.

Katon, W., & Roy-Byrne, P. P. (1989). Panic disorder in the medically ill. *Journal of Clinical Psychiatry, 50* (8), 299–302.

Kearney, C. A., Albano, A. M., Eisen, A. R., Allan, W. D., & Barlow, D. H. (1997). The phenomenology of panic disorder in youngsters: An empirical study of a clinical sample. *Journal of Anxiety Disorders, 11,* 49–62. doi:10.1016/S0887-6185(96) 00034-5.

Keller, M. B., Yonkers, K. A., Warshaw, M. G., & Pratt, L. A. (1994). Remission and relapse in subjects with panic disorder and panic with agoraphobia: A prospective short interval naturalistic follow-up. *Journal of Nervous and Mental Disease, 182* (5), 290–296. doi:10.1097/00005053-199405000-00007

Kendall, P. C., Furr, J. M., & Podell, J. L. (2010). Child-focused treatment of anxiety. In J. R. Weisz, A. E. Kazdin, J. R. Weisz, A. E. Kazdin (Eds.), *Evidence-Based Psychotherapies for Children and Adolescents,* 2nd edn (pp. 45–60). New York: Guilford Press.

Kessler, R. C., Berglund, P., Demler, O., Jin, R., Merikangas, K. R., & Walters, E. E. (2005). Lifetime prevalence and age-of-onset distributions of DSM-IV disorders in the National Comorbidity Survey replication. *Archives of General Psychiatry, 62* (6), 593–602. doi:10.1001/archpsyc.62.6.593.

King, N. J., Gullone, E., Tonge, B. J., & Ollendick, T. H. (1993). Self-reports of panic attacks and manifest anxiety in adolescents. *Behaviour Research and Therapy, 31,* 111–116. doi:10.1016/0005-7967(93)90049-Z.

Kleiner, L., & Marshall, W. L. (1987). The role of interpersonal problems in the development of agoraphobia with panic attacks. *Journal of Anxiety Disorders, 1*(4), 313–323. doi:10.1016/0887-6185(87)90011-9.

Kumar, S., & Browne, M. (2002). Panic disorder. In S. Barton, S. Barton (Eds.), *Clinical Evidence Mental Health* (pp. 97–102). Williston, VT: BMJ Books.

Lepola, U. M., Wade, A. G., Leinonen, E. V., Koponen, H. J., Frazer, J., Sjödin, I., & Lehto, H. J. (2001). A controlled, prospective, 1-year trial of citalopram in the treatment of panic disorder. *Psychiatria Hungarica, 16* (Suppl1), 17–28.

Lydiard, R. (1988). Pharmacological treatment. *Psychiatric Annals, 18* (8), 468–472.

Michelson, D., Pollack, M., Lydiard, R., Tamura, R., Tepner, R., Tollefson, G., & Fluoxetine Panic Disorder Study Group (1999). Continuing treatment of panic disorder after acute response: Randomised, placebo-controlled trial with fluoxetine. *British Journal of Psychiatry, 174,* 213–218. doi:10.1192/bjp.174.3.213.

Miller, W., & Rollnick, S. (2002). *Motivational Interviewing: Preparing People for Change.* New York: Guilford Press.

Milrod, B. L., Busch, F. N., Cooper, A. M., & Shapiro, T. (1997). *Manual of Panic-Focused Psychodynamic Psychotherapy.* Arlington, VA: American Psychiatric Publishing.

Milrod, B. L., Busch, F. N., & Shapiro, T. (2004). *Psychodynamic Approaches to the Adolescent with Panic Disorder.* Malabar, FL: Krieger Publishing Company.

Milrod, B. L., Leon, A. C., Busch, F. N., Rudden, M., Schwalberg, M., Clarkin, J., & Shear, M. (2007). A randomized controlled clinical trial of psychoanalytic psychotherapy for panic disorder. *American Journal of Psychiatry, 164* (2), 265–272. doi:10.1176/appi.ajp.164.2.265.

Mitte, K. (2005). A meta-analysis of the efficacy of psycho- and pharmacotherapy in panic disorder with and without agoraphobia. *Journal of Affective Disorders, 88* (1), 27–45. doi:10.1016/j.jad.2005.05.003.

Moreau, D. L., & Follet, C. (1993). Panic disorder in children and adolescents. *Child and Adolescent Psychiatric Clinics of North America, 2,* 581–602.

Nelles, W. B., & Barlow, D. H. (1988). Do children panic? *Clinical Psychology Review, 8* (4), 359–372. doi:10.1016/0272-7358(88)90064-5.

Ollendick, T. H. (1995). Cognitive behavioral treatment of panic disorder with agoraphobia in adolescents: A multiple baseline design analysis. *Behavior Therapy, 26* (3), 517–531. doi:10.1016/S0005-7894(05)80098-X.

Ollendick, T. H., Birmaher, B., & Mattis, S. G. (2004). Panic disorder. In Morris, T. L. & March, J. S. (Eds.), *Anxiety Disorders in Children and Adolescents*, 2nd edn (pp. 189–211). New York: Guilford Press.

Ollendick, T. H., & Pincus, D. (2008). Panic disorder in adolescents. In R. G. Steele, T. D. Elkin, & M. C. Roberts (Eds.), *Handbook of Evidence-Based Therapies for Children and Adolescents* (pp. 83–102). Springer Books.

Perugi, G., Frare, F., & Toni, C. (2007). Diagnosis and treatment of agoraphobia with panic disorder. *CNS Drugs, 21*(9), 741–764. doi:10. 2165/00023210–200721090–00004

Pincus, D. B., Ehrenreich, J. T., & Mattis, S. G. (2008). *Mastery of Anxiety and Panic for Adolescents: Riding the Wave, Therapist Guide*. New York: Oxford University Press.

Pincus, D. B., Ehrenreich-May, J., Whitton, S. W., Mattis, S. G., & Barlow, D. H. (2010). Cognitive-behavioral treatment of panic disorder in adolescence. *Journal of Clinical Child and Adolescent Psychology, 39* (5), 638–649. doi:10.1080/15374416.2010. 501288.

Pincus, D. B., Spiegel, D. A., Mattis, S. G., Micco, J. A., & Barlow, D. H. (2003). Treatment of adolescents with panic disorder and agoraphobia: A comparison of an 8-day intensive treatment program and an 11-week treatment program. Paper presented at the annual meeting of the Association for Advancement of Behavior Therapy, Boston, MA.

Queen, A. H., Ehrenreich-May, J., & Hershorin, E. R. (2012). Preliminary validation of a screening tool for adolescent panic disorder in pediatric primary care clinics. *Child Psychiatry & Human Development 43* (2), 171–183. doi:10.1007/s10578-011-0256-z.

Reiss, S., & McNally, R. J. (1985). The expectancy model of fear. In S. Reiss & R. R. Bootzin (Eds.), *Theoretical Issues in Behavior Therapy*. New York: Oxford University Press.

Rosenbaum, J. F., Moroz, G., Bowden, C. L., & Clonazepam Panic Disorder Dose-Response Study Group (1997). Clonazepam in the treatment of panic disorder with or without agoraphobia: A dose-response study of efficacy, safety, and discontinuance. *Journal of Clinical Psychopharmacology, 17* (5), 390–400. doi:10.1097/00004714-199710000-00008.

Shear, M., Cooper, A. M., Klerman, G. L., & Busch, F. N. (1993). A psychodynamic model of panic disorder. *The American Journal of Psychiatry, 150* (6), 859–866.

Silverman, W. K., & Albano, A. M. (1996). *Anxiety Disorders Interview Schedule for DSM-IV: Child and Parent Versions*. San Antonio: Psychological Corp.

Schmidt, N. B., Keough, M. E., Mitchell, M. A., Reynolds, E. K., MacPherson, L., Zvolenksy, M. J., et al. (2010). Anxiety sensitivity: Prospective prediction of anxiety among early adolescents. *Journal of Anxiety Disorders, 24* (5), 503–508. doi:10.1016/j.janxdis.2010.03.007.

Schneier, F. R., Liebowitz, M. R., Davies, S. O., & Fairbanks, J. (1990). Fluoxetine in panic disorder. *Journal of Clinical Psychopharmacology, 10* (2), 119–121. doi:10.1097/00004714-199004000-00007.

Stein, M. B., Roy-Byrne, P. P., McQuaid, J. R., Laffaye, C., Russo, J., McCahill, M. E., et al. (1999). Development of a brief diagnostic screen for panic disorder in primary care. *Psychosomatic Medicine, 61* (3), 359–364.

Thyer, B. A., Parrish, R. T., Curtis, G. C., Nesse, R. M., & Cameron, O. G. (1985). Ages of onset of DSM-III anxiety disorders. *Comparative Psychiatry, 26*, 113–122. doi:10.1016/0010-440X(85)90031-8.

Tull, M. T., & Roemer, L. (2007). Emotion regulation difficulties associated with the experience of uncued panic attacks: Evidence of experiential avoidance, emotional nonacceptance, and decreased emotional clarity. *Behavior Therapy, 38* (4), 378–391. doi:10.1016/j.beth.2006.10.006.

Uhlenhuth, E. H., Balter, M. B., Ban, T. A., & Yang, K. (1998). International study of expert judgment on therapeutic use of benzodiazepines and other psychotherapeutic medications: V. Treatment strategies in panic disorder, 1992–1997. *Journal of Clinical Psychopharmacology, 18* (6, Suppl 2), 27S–31S. doi:10.1097/00004714-199812001-00006.

van Balkom, A. M., Bakker, A., Spinhoven, P., Blaauw, B. W., Smeenk, S., & Ruesink, B. (1997). A meta-analysis of the treatment of panic disorder with or without agoraphobia: A comparison of psychopharmacological, cognitive-behavioral, and combination treatments. *Journal of Nervous and Mental Disease, 185* (8), 510–516. doi:10.1097/00005053-199708000-00006.

van Minnen, A., & Foa, E. B. (2006). The effect of imaginal exposure length on outcome of treatment for PTSD. *Journal of Traumatic Stress, 19* (4), 427–438. doi:10.1002/jts.20146.

Weissman, M. M., Klerman, G. L., Markowitz, J. S., & Quellette, R. (1989). Suicide ideation and attempts in panic disorder and panic attacks. *New England Journal of Medicine, 321,* 1209–1214.

Westen, D., & Morrison, K. (2001). A multidimensional meta-analysis of treatments for depression, panic, and generalized anxiety disorder: An empirical examination of the status of empirically supported therapies. *Journal of Consulting and Clinical Psychology, 69* (6), 875–899. doi:10.1037/0022–006X.69.6.875.

20

Post-Traumatic Stress Disorder

William Yule, Patrick Smith, Sean Perrin,
and David M. Clark

Institute of Psychiatry, London, UK

Post-traumatic stress disorder (PTSD) was first recognized as a coherent diagnostic classification in 1980 (APA, 1980) when the puzzling symptoms presented by veterans of the Vietnam War were properly described. Three groups of symptoms or reactions were identified as occurring together: distressing intrusive images and memories; emotional numbing and avoidance of traumatic reminders; and increased physiological arousal. Initially it was asserted that children would not develop PTSD but that view had been based on an absence of information gathered from children themselves. By the end of the 1980s, studies by Pynoos in USA and Yule in UK had firmly demonstrated that children and adolescents can and do develop PTSD after significant life-threatening experiences.

However, from the very beginning, it was realized that children rarely report emotional numbing. Given that clients had to show evidence of three out of seven possible numbing/avoidance symptoms, this meant that it was more difficult for children than adults to reach the DSM criterion. This is a direct consequence of developing diagnostic criteria for children by downward extension of adult classificatory rules. Indeed, the younger the child, the less applicable the rules were. Even so, the articulation of the diagnosis drew attention to stress reactions in children. It became quickly evident that many children do react adversely to serious traumatic events and are socially handicapped by these reactions.

As always, the paucity of good studies of stress reactions in children reflects the low level of investment by many societies. Initially, clinicians and researchers did not ask children themselves how they had been affected. By relying on second-hand accounts from parents and children, they missed crucial evidence. Moreover, as it is more expensive to observe and interview children than simply to ask them to complete questionnaires, the latter approach was widely followed. Children under age 8 are generally unable to read and respond to questionnaires so that again the effects on very young children were ignored.

The Wiley-Blackwell Handbook of The Treatment of Childhood and Adolescent Anxiety, First Edition.
Edited by Cecilia A. Essau and Thomas H. Ollendick.
© 2013 John Wiley & Sons, Ltd. Published 2013 by John Wiley & Sons, Ltd.

To counteract these methodological problems, Scheeringa and colleagues (2011) developed a simplified algorithm that demanded fewer and more developmentally relevant symptoms. That algorithm has been found useful in other studies (e.g., Meiser-Stedman, Smith, Glucksman, Yule, & Dalgleish., 2008). Thus, the current situation in 2012 is that slightly modified criteria for the diagnosis of PTSD in children are now generally accepted. The range of stress reactions is better described and effective interventions are becoming available.

The UK NICE Guidelines (2005, and endorsed again in 2011) recommended that all UK National Health Service facilities for child mental health should make available Trauma Focused-Cognitive Behaviour Therapy (TF-CBT), and noted that EMDR "shows some promise". In the years since the publication of that guidance, the evidence for the value of both treatment regimes has been strengthened. The only other child-oriented therapy to receive endorsement through the publication of randomized control trial (RCT) evidence has been KID-NET – the child version of Narrative Exposure Therapy (Schauer, Neuner, & Elbert, 2011). The UK advice remains that pharmacological intervention is not recommended for children and adolescents, although on the basis of an open trial of fluoxetine (Yorbik, Dikkatli, Cansever, & Sohmen, 2001), the USA advice is that SSRIs can be "cautiously considered" (Cohen, Bukstein, Walter et al., 2010).

Incidence and Prevalence

PTSD is often considered a rare disorder. Most teachers, for example, will hardly ever encounter a child who suffers from it. When they do, they may be ill-prepared to deal with it. In addition, professionals in primary care frequently underestimate how often PTSD does occur in children (Ehlers, Gene-Cos & Perrin, 2009). However, it is important for all service providers and planners to remember the difference between *incidence* and *prevalence*.

Estimates of the incidence of PTSD in trauma-exposed children vary enormously, partly as a result of differing methodologies, and partly as a result of different types of traumatic event. Studies of the mental health of child refugees from war-torn countries find the incidence to be close to 67%. Sexual abuse results in high rates of PTSD (Salmon & Bryant, 2002), as does witnessing violence (Margolin & Gordis, 2000). In various studies on the effects of traffic accidents, rates of 15–30% are reported (e.g., Stallard, Salter, & Velleman, 2004). A study of 200 adolescent survivors of the sinking of the cruise ship Jupiter (Yule, Bolton, Udwim, Boyle, O'Ryan, & Nurrish, 2000) reported an incidence of PTSD of 51%. Most cases manifested within the first few weeks with delayed onset being rare. Following a nightclub fire in Gothenburg, 25% of the 275 adolescent survivors met DSM-IV criteria for PTSD 18 months after the fire (Broberg, Dyregrov, & Lilled, 2005). Overall, it has been estimated that 36% of children will meet criteria for PTSD following a range of traumas (Fletcher, 1996). This seems fairly constant across developmental levels. In other words, significantly increased demands will be made at all level of primary and secondary child and adolescent mental health services following major traumatic events.

Most epidemiological studies have been of older adolescents and adults. For example, Giaconia, Reinherz, Silverman, Pakiz, Frost, & Cohen (1995) report a lifetime prevalence of 6% in a community sample of older adolescents. More recently, Merikangas, He, Burstein et al. (2010) report a lifetime prevalence of 5% using data collected from adolescents (up to 18 years old) in the United States National Comorbidity Survey – Adolescent Supplement. A national sample of eighth grade Danish students estimated a 9% lifetime prevalence (Elklit, 2002). By contrast, the British National Survey of Mental health of over ten thousand children and adolescents (Meltzer, Gatward, Goodman, & Ford, 2003) report that only 0.4% of 11–15 year olds were diagnosed with PTSD, with girls showing twice the rate of boys. Below age 10, it was scarcely registered. This lower rate is, of course, a point prevalence estimate and is bound to be lower than a lifetime prevalence estimate. Moreover, the screening instrument was not specifically developed to screen for PTSD. The implication is that while the numbers of children and adolescents experiencing PTSD at any one point in time may be as low as 1%, this is still a significant level of morbidity in any community.

Risk and Maintaining Factors

Not all children exposed to trauma will develop PTSD, and of those who do, many will recover without treatment. Thus, factors other than exposure to trauma must influence the onset and maintenance of the disorder. Trickey, Siddaway, Meiser-Stedman, Serpell, & Field (2012) reviewed 64 studies involving over 32 000 children and adolescents and report on the effect sizes of 25 different risk factors. While there is a paucity of studies, and a variety of methodologies, it was possible to conclude that pre-trauma variables and objective aspects of the traumatic event had only small to medium population effect sizes on later PTSD. Peri-traumatic factors (such as perceived life threat and peri-traumatic fear) and post-trauma variables (such as thought suppression, distraction, blaming others, and social support) had medium to large effect size estimates. In other words, the peri- and post-event milieu is more important than the nature and severity of the trauma in determining the course of the disorder. Cognitive models of the disorder (e.g., Ehlers & Clark, 2000) provide a detailed elaboration of how these peri- and post-trauma variables – along with other factors – operate to maintain persistent PTSD.

Cognitive Model

PTSD is classified as an anxiety disorder within DSM. With adult patients, approaches based on successful interventions with other anxiety disorders initially predominated, foremost among these being prolonged exposure approaches. However, the application of findings from cognitive psychology drew attention to the changes in attribution and in memory function that were widely reported (Brewin, Andrews, & Valentine, 2000; Brewin, Andrews, & Rose, 2003) and PTSD was largely reformulated as a disorder of memory in the influential paper by Ehlers and Clark (2000).

The treatment presented in this chapter is based on Ehlers and Clark's (2000) cognitive model of PTSD and treatment protocol (Ehlers et al., 2003a, 2003b, 2005, in press), suitably adapted for children. Under this model, persistent PTSD is maintained by disjointed and poorly elaborated trauma memories; idiosyncratic misappraisals of the trauma and trauma-related symptoms; and dysfunctional (behavioral and cognitive) coping strategies. Adaptations of the model for children take into account the important role that parental reactions and coping strategies play in the maintenance of children's PTSD (Meiser-Stedman, Yule, Smith, Glicksman, & Dalgleish, 2005; Smith, Perrin, Yule, & Clark, 2010).

Nature of the trauma memory

Ehlers and Clark (2000) propose that trauma memories in individuals with persistent PTSD are poorly elaborated and inadequately integrated into an autobiographical memory knowledge base (also cf Dalgleish, Meiser-Stedman, & Smith, 2005). That is, trauma memories lack contextual (time, place, subsequent and previous information) and abstracted (event type, personal time period, related autobiographical themes) information. This has the effect that the memory of the worst moments of the trauma has not been updated with relevant information (e.g., "I did not die", "It was not my fault"). Furthermore, trauma memories in PTSD are heavily laden with sensory detail, and characterized by strong stimulus–stimulus and stimulus–response links, with strong perceptual priming (i.e., a reduced perceptual threshold) for trauma-related stimuli. Such memory characteristics can help to explain poor intentional recall, the sense of "now-ness" accompanying intrusive recollections, and the easy triggering of unwanted memories by physically similar or temporally associated cues. There is evidence that for adults, these sorts of memory characteristics do indeed predict persistent PTSD (e.g., Michael, Ehlers, Halligan, & Clark, 2005), and that characteristics of trauma memories (particularly their organizational quality) change during treatment for PTSD (Foa, Rothbaum, & Molnar, 1995). Evidence that trauma memory quality is related to PTSD symptoms in children is also emerging: trauma memories in children are characterized by being heavily sensory-laden (Meiser-Stedman, Dalgleish, Smith, Yule, & Glucksman, 2007), and disorganized (Salmond, Meiser-Stedman, Dalgleish, Glucksman, Thompson, & Smith, 2011).

Idiosyncratic appraisals

Central to the cognitive model of PTSD is the role of idiosyncratic appraisals (regarding the trauma and trauma-related symptoms) in generating a sense of serious current threat. First, in relation to the trauma itself, such misappraisals may take the form of over-generalisation of danger (e.g., an overestimate of the likely re-occurrence of a similar traumatic event, and/or an appraisal of normal activities as being more dangerous than they are). Mistaken beliefs about the causes of the trauma may lead to a sense of inflated responsibility and excessive guilt. Individuals may negatively evaluate the way they reacted during the trauma, leading to feelings of shame. Second, in relation to trauma sequelae, it is common for individuals with persistent PTSD to mis-appraise the meaning of PTSD symptoms. For example, individuals may believe the presence of distressing symptoms indicates that they are going crazy, that they cannot cope, that they are weak, that they have been permanently damaged. There is now accumulating evidence that such misappraisals play an important role in the maintenance of PTSD in children (Bryant, Salmon, Sinclair, & Davidson, 2007; Ehlers et al., 2003b; Meiser-Stedman, Smith, Bryant et al., 2009; Salmon, Sinclair, & Bryant,

2007; Stallard, 2003; Stallard & Smith, 2007). In line with this, changes to cognitive misappraisals during TF-CBT for childhood PTSD seemed to mediate the effect of treatment (Smith, Yule, Perrin, Tranah, Dalgleish, & Clark, 2007).

Unhelpful coping strategies

Frequent PTSD symptoms, accompanied by a sense of current threat, motivate a range of coping strategies. Typical coping strategies in individuals with persistent PTSD tend to be characterized by behavioral and cognitive avoidance. This may take a number of forms: pushing thoughts and memories out of mind, trying not to think about the event, staying away from trauma reminders, repeatedly scanning for danger in the environment (hypervigilance), and ruminating about the event and its consequences. Ehlers and Clark (2000) note that such strategies may be either intentional or habitual; that they make sense to the individual (i.e., they are meaningfully linked to appraisals and beliefs); and that they may provide short term symptom relief. Importantly, however, they have a number of unintended consequences which can maintain PTSD: they directly produce PTSD symptoms; they prevent changes to problematic appraisals; and they prevent changes to the nature of the trauma memory. As with adults (e.g., see Brewin et al., 2000), there is evidence from retrospective (Udwin, Boyle, Yule, Bolton, & O'Ryan, 2000) and prospective studies of children (Meiser-Stedman, 2002; Stallard, 2003) that cognitive and behavioral avoidance, and thought control strategies such as rumination and thought suppression, serve to maintain PTSD symptoms.

Parents and carers

Family factors in childhood PTSD have received relatively little attention to date. Available evidence suggests that maternal symptoms of PTSD and depression are related to child PTSD symptoms across a variety of settings and populations (e.g., Meiser-Stedman, Yule, Dalgleish, Smith, & Glicksman, 2006; Smith et al., 2010; Wolmer, Laor, Gershon, Mayes, & Cohen, 2000). Trickey et al. (2012) found in their meta-analysis that poor family functioning in the aftermath of trauma is also related to children's PTSD symptoms. The mechanisms by which PTSD is maintained within a family are not well understood. One possibility is that children and carers negatively reinforce each other for avoiding discussion of, or exposure to reminders of, the trauma. That is, parents and children may get locked into cycles of avoidance, each maintaining the other's maladaptive coping. Meiser-Stedman and colleagues (2006) found that parental endorsement of worry as a helpful strategy seemed to mediate the relationship between maternal depression and child PTSD. Further research is needed, but evidence to date implies that psychopathology and cognitive styles within the family play a significant role in maintaining children's PTSD.

Treatment Targets in Trauma-Focused Cognitive Therapy

Ehlers and Clark's (2000) cognitive model of PTSD as summarized earlier in relation to young people is helpful because it specifies key maintaining factors. Treatment aims to reverse the maintaining factors described previously. The following four treatment targets therefore follow from the cognitive model:

1. To reduce memory disjointedness and help the child to build a coherent narrative of the traumatic event.
2. To identify and modify unhelpful misappraisals of the trauma and reactions to it
3. To identify and change maladaptive cognitive and behavioural avoidance and other unhelpful coping strategies.
4. To recruit carers as co-therapists and to alter counter-productive patterns of inter-actions between the child and carer about the event.

Overview and components of trauma-focused cognitive therapy

A variety of techniques is used to reach these targets. Most of the techniques described below will be used in individual one-to-one sessions with the young person. Nevertheless, parents and carers may play a key role throughout treatment.

Each session lasts between 60 and 90 minutes, depending on the age of the young person, stage in therapy, and treatment components used in session. The first session focuses on engaging the child and parents, building trust, setting treatment goals, education, and normalization. Later sessions focus on updating the traumatic memory, and it is expected that the core of treatment to this end will be within-session imaginal reliving (achieved through talking, writing, and drawing), closely integrated with cognitive therapy techniques designed to counter misappraisals of the trauma and its consequences. Homework is set each week. Other therapy components such as image-work to enhance elaboration of the memory, stimulus discrimination techniques, and sleep-hygiene are used as necessary. The final session includes a review of therapy, and relapse prevention work – developing a "blueprint" for the future.

Assessment

Having received where possible a detailed description of the traumatic event in advance, the initial assessment should involve a brief joint parent and child meeting to describe the interview process. This is followed by asking parents and child separately to complete standardized, self-report measures, and then separate parent and child interviews. Children will frequently reveal details of what happened and how they reacted during their interview, details of which the parents are unaware. This first session ends with joint feedback and arranging, if necessary, for further assessment.

A great deal can be achieved in this first session. The therapist aims to engage the child and parents in therapy as well as assess problems for planning treatment. All too often, children are referred long after the traumatic event and will have built up patterns of avoiding discussing the trauma. The child often feels that their reactions are out of control and so the therapist must show that the child can get control over small aspects, such as deciding whether the child or parents are interviewed first. Every opportunity is taken even at this early stage to normalize the child's reactions – not dismissing them, but getting across the message that they are frequent and well understood. The information is used to set treatment goals and the child and parents are given the rationale for trauma-focused CBT which is outlined.

Formulation and rationale for treatment

Assessment also needs to clarify what may be maintaining the symptoms that were caused by the traumatic event. As described above, there are four potential maintaining factors in childhood PTSD, as understood in Ehlers and Clark's (2000) adapted cognitive model: the nature of the trauma memory; unhelpful appraisals of the event and its consequences; unhelpful coping strategies; and family factors. Maintaining factors are idiosyncratic and each should be identified in detail so that the broad treatment approach outlined below can be customized for the individual child.

Much of the key information about memory quality and misappraisals comes from the child's detailed account of what happened and how he or she reacted. In the early stage, the child may give a brief account in the past tense. As treatment progresses, the child is prompted to give greater detail of what was seen, heard, smelled as well as what thoughts they were having at that time. The therapist monitors the account closely, noting which points are difficult to relate, are most confused and so on. Together, this information indicates "hot spots" that have to be confronted, as well as misappraisals that will have to be updated. Information about parental reactions, and about interactions between carers and children, can be obtained from interviewing each individually, and by observing them together. Asking the child what they have tried to do to cope with the problems will usually elicit that they have tried to avoid talking about it or otherwise avoid the intrusive images. When asked if that helped, they will usually report that it only helped for a very short time, and then the images returned.

Establishing a solid rationale for treatment is essential, and often follows from a discussion about unhelpful coping. The therapist might discuss how avoidance is a very common strategy that is counterproductive. A thought suppression experiment can be used to illustrate this important point. Helpful metaphors to convey the rationale for treatment are described in detail in Smith et al. (2010, pp. 52–53).

Outline of trauma-focused cognitive therapy techniques

A flexible treatment package based on Ehlers' treatment protocol (e.g., Ehlers et al., 2005, in press) has been shown (Smith et al., 2007) to be very effective when delivered in up to 12 weekly 90-minute sessions. A brief outline of the main elements of TF-CT is provided below. For a fuller account of the treatment procedures, the reader is referred to the therapist manual (Smith et al., 2010). Not all of the techniques are needed in every case. The therapist selects which elements to use and in which order to use them, depending on the detailed case formulation.

Psycho-education and normalization

It is important that the child and parents learn more about PTSD and its treatment, dispelling any unhelpful beliefs they may have. The therapist explains that most people can be overwhelmed by a major, distressing, traumatic event and that while everyone reacts slightly differently, there are certain aspects in common. Foremost are the intrusive images and memories that can appear to come out of the blue but are often triggered by internal or external stimuli. Most people try to cope by pushing these away but that works only temporarily and so other ways of dealing with the distressing memories have to be learned. Handouts can be given to the child and parents at the first assessment session and then discussed to ensure the model has been understood in the second session. Examples are found in our text (Smith et al., 2010, Appendix B).

In this early part, the key message is that avoidance does not work. It keeps intrusions going. It actually makes them worse. So a chief goal is to stop avoiding and instead to deliberately recall what happened. This message needs to be repeated often.

The other message to get across to both child and parents is that the distressing symptoms are "normal" in the sense that they occur frequently; they can be treated; they are not signs that the child is going mad. Little wonder that some children think this. They may suddenly have very vivid flashbacks when they seem to be living the traumatic event all over again. Their heart races. Their skin sweats. They hear noises, even voices. Isn't that evidence that they are going mad? The therapist's job is to explain that such reactions are normal.

Reclaiming life

The child will have described how they have stopped doing many things they used to enjoy. The longer the gap between the event and coming for treatment, the more things they may have stopped doing and it will be a challenge to convince them to start doing them again. We help the child to reclaim their life, using techniques derived from behavioral activation. The aim is to lift mood and to counter the sense that "life is stuck in the past". The child is helped to develop a list of activities they previously enjoyed. The therapist helps them to decide which are most important and also which will be easiest attempt (and, of course, to experience an early success). This is one place where it is vital to have the parents understanding the point of the exercise and supporting the child in trying to do one of the activities at home. It helps to give the child an activity diary showing the goals, the days they will try to work toward them and so on.

Imaginal reliving

Imaginal reliving is a powerful technique because it relates to several of the maintaining factors described above. First, identification of hotspots during imaginal reliving allows misappraisals to be identified (and later modified). Second, reliving can promote coherence in the trauma memory by developing an ordered narrative. Third, reliving directly counters avoidance of the trauma memory, and can be set up as a behavioral experiment to test the feared consequences of recalling the event. That is, reliving is a powerful demonstration to the child that they can recall the trauma without going crazy or losing control.

Having agreed a rationale for reliving, the child is invited to tell what happened, in the first person, present tense, paying special attention to sensory impressions, thoughts, and feelings. It is important to allow enough time afterwards to hear what it was like for the child to recall the event in this way. In subsequent relivings, the clinician uses judicious prompts to enquire about sensory detail, peri-traumatic cognitions, and associated affect. As hotspots (emotionally charged moments in the memory) are identified, the child may be asked to hold the memory and to rewind it as if it were a tape. Often, the child has to be asked to slow down so that sufficient attention can be given to these more distressing hotspots. After a reliving, it is important to enquire about levels of anxiety to demonstrate its natural decline. When possible, relivings can be audiotaped and the child is asked to listen to them for homework.

For adolescents, writing is a helpful alternative or adjunct to imaginal reliving. This technique seems especially well suited to young people who are markedly avoidant, who have very chronic PTSD, or those whose trauma memory is particularly disjointed. For younger children, drawing is often used as an alternative to imaginal reliving: the child is supported in developing a "storyboard" of the event, as a means of accessing the traumatic memory and associated meaning.

Cognitive restructuring

Children may show misappraisals about the trauma itself (e.g., to do with responsibility, guilt, or others' reactions at the time) and/or about the consequences of the trauma (e.g., interpreting persistent symptoms as signs of weakness or madness).

Sometimes there is a spontaneous shift in these sorts of meanings after the application of the standard reliving techniques outlined about. However, spontaneous change to appraisals does not always occur, and in that case, cognitive restructuring is indicated. Following cognitive restructuring, it is important that new meanings are incorporated into the trauma memory by closely integrating reliving with restructuring.

Key cognitions may be identified during reliving or narrative work. As noted above, problematic meanings are often associated with emotional hotspots in the trauma memory. Once misappraisals have been identified, cognitive restructuring can be used to modify them. The aim is to help the child identify new information so that the trauma memory can be updated. There are many ways to achieve this. New information may be present in the trauma memory itself; may be obtained from talking to family, friends, and professionals; or may emerge following a site visit (see below). Broad cognitive themes such as guilt or shame can be addressed using a variety of CBT techniques including Socratic questioning, behavioral experiments, and surveys.

A striking feature of PTSD in young people is that despite re-appraisal on an intellectual level ("I now realize that it was not my fault"), there is a failure to incorporate this new information into the trauma memory ("When I recall what happened, I still feel guilty"). When this occurs, close integration of reliving with restructuring is needed. For example, in carrying out imaginal reliving, the young person is asked to verbalize the new information at the appropriate point; in constructing a narrative, new information is included in the script. This process can be repeated for various cognitions at different emotional hotspots.

Visiting the scene of the trauma

Avoiding exposure to the scene of a trauma is understandable, but does nothing to overcome the distress. Such avoidance is maintained partly by beliefs about the likelihood of current harm. Avoidance prevents the child from updating the trauma memory and having experiences that disconfirm their beliefs. *In vivo* exposure to the site of the trauma allows the child to break the link between the harmless trigger (i.e., the site of the trauma) and the trauma memory.

Visits to the site can yield unexpected and very helpful information, but are usually best left until the second half of treatment. Initially, children are simply too scared to return. With widely available phone cameras and video-cameras, it is possible to bring pictures and sounds of the site in to the treatment sessions earlier. This allows realistic work to be undertaken on the trauma memory.

In preparation for an actual site visit, the therapist can help set up a number of behavioral experiments – in other word get the child to predict how they will react and so be able to test out these predictions. "I will go crazy"; "I will faint"; "Another accident will happen" – all are testable hypotheses.

The child is asked to monitor all the similarities and differences between what they recalled and what they now see. During the visit, every opportunity is taken to correct distortions in the trauma memory. The child is encouraged to allow the memories and associated feelings to arise and not to suppress them. Memories are contrasted with the current reality. Predictions are evaluated and this helps disconfirm them. The therapist ensures that there is sufficient time for arousal to diminish before leaving the scene. It is helpful to have time to debrief after such a visit and reflect on what has been learned.

Stimulus discrimination – working with triggers

Children often report that distressing memories and images flood in out of the blue. This adds to their feelings of being out of control and of going mad. It is important that they come to realize that these intrusive thoughts are likely to have been triggered by stimuli in their environment (less frequently by internal triggers). Therefore they need to be alerted to what triggers their adverse reaction.

Once triggers have been identified, children can be deliberately exposed to them in order to break the link between the trigger and the trauma memory. Triggers may not be immediately obviously related to the event but rather may be sensory based. For example, after the sinking of the cruise ship *Jupiter*, many adolescents described how they felt afraid when they heard running water – as they had done when the ship's side was breached. Others got distressed when they smelled diesel – spread on the water when the ship sank. Sights, sounds, movement and smells can all trigger distressing memories. The child needs to learn that whenever they have such an experience they should try to identify the trigger. Once identified, it loses its potency.

Part of treatment is to identify the triggers and then to explain to the child how they can be mastered. Next, the child is encouraged to expose themselves to a previously avoided trigger, to note the thoughts and feelings that emerge, and to contrast the current context with the past events. Constantly reminding the child of what happened *then* and what is happening *now* reinforces the time-stamping of the memory. The child learns that the trigger itself is harmless in the current context.

Distressed children try hard to avoid situations where the distress may be triggered. Thus, survivors of nasty car accidents avoid travelling in cars. The safety-seeking behaviors can quickly become elaborated and so behaviors such as holding on to the seat or keeping a hand near the emergency brake need to be identified and dropped.

Working with images

Often after reliving, the images become less vivid and more like ordinary memories. Sometimes this does not happen completely and so the child is given direct ways of changing the images. There are a variety of ways of doing this and some work for some children and others with others. The child can be asked to imagine seeing the troublesome image as if projected on their palm. What happens if the hand moves very close? (The image gets blurred). What happens if the hand moves far away? (The image gets very small.) Imagine the image is on a TV screen and the TV is switched off. What happens? Both visual and auditory images can be manipulated in these simple ways and the child gets a sense of being able to control them. These and other techniques are more fully described in Dyregrov (1997a, 1997b) and Smith, Dyregrov, & Yule (1999).

Sleep hygiene and working with nightmares

After distressing intrusive images, one of the commonest complaints that children have is of disrupted sleep. Often this is related to experiencing scary dreams and nightmares connected to the traumatic event. Many children reason that if only they stay awake for as long as possible and get really tired, then they will fall asleep quickly and not have the dreams. Alas, this is counterintuitive and they still get the dreams but also less sleep. So they wake tired and have difficulty concentrating.

Poor sleep and nightmares are best tackled early on in therapy. Parents and children are advised to (re-)establish a regular routine at bed-time, with a wind down period. If necessary, children can be taught relaxation techniques to practice in bed as often they then naturally fall into a sleep. Caffeine based drinks and other stimulants should be avoided.

The nightmares can be tackled directly using two main techniques. Children are asked to draw or write about the dream in detail and to go over it until it gets boring. Doing this during the day is easier and it helps to tell it to someone else. Do not do it just before bed-time. There is now a substantial literature demonstrating that the endings of nightmares can be changed. Since the dream belongs to the child, they can take control over it and work out a positive ending. It might be that younger children see a super hero fly in to save them, or that the scary monster turns out to be a helpful big friendly giant. Imagination and humor can be let run riot. While the child is discussing alternative endings, inevitably s/he is exposing him/herself to the feared dream. By rehearsing the new ending during the day, then when the dream does recur, the ending is likely to change at night. For many children, both very young and teenagers, putting a "dream catcher" over their window seems to help, although we know of no RCTs to support this.

Parent work

Parents are always involved in their child's treatment to some extent. The therapist should make clear that the parent is important to their child's recovery and they will be involved in the treatment process at all times. It is useful to have the parent join in for the last few minutes of each session so they can be kept informed of progress and of any homework set for the following week. Generally 1 or 2 separate sessions to answer questions about the effects of trauma on their child, the nature of treatment, and what the parent can expect going forward are helpful. Therapists should be careful in these separate sessions *not* to run through a list of do's and don'ts of how to parent a traumatized child. Therapists need to recognize that parents often feel extremely guilty about their child's trauma and engage in quite a lot of self-blame. Such beliefs can drive responses to the child which may be unhelpful (e.g. overprotectiveness). Care needs to be taken that the parents does not interpret advice from the therapist that they are responsible for the child's PTSD or that studiously following the suggestions will lead to a more rapid recovery.

Whenever the therapist is alone with the parents, the sessions should always revolve around a shared formulation of specific problems and the interventions introduced should be evidence-based. At this stage, there is no set of evidence-based, parent-targeted interventions for children with PTSD – only general recommendations. To date there is no evidence to suggest that having the parents present during the entirety of the child's CBT session, or having separate parent-only sessions, is more effective in reducing the child's PTSD symptoms than seeing the child alone. There is evidence, albeit very limited, to suggest that regular sessions with the parents may facilitate greater overall adjustment in the child. Looking across treatment outcome studies, it seems that the best predictor of the child's overall adjustment post-treatment is the extent to which the therapist is able to reduce the PTSD symptoms.

The evidence base (both child and adult) strongly suggests that recovery from PTSD is dependent upon the repeated use of interventions which modify the trauma memory so that its overall structure more closely resembles those of life-events which do not intrude on consciousness, and which identify and weaken dysfunctional, trauma-related beliefs and the avoidance and safety behaviors these beliefs drive. Interventions aimed at these targets should be considered the *maximally active ingredients* in trauma-focused CBT. If a therapist involves the parents in treatment sessions (and there may be good reason for doing so), they need to take account of how much time is spent working with the parents' traumatic reactions, family conflicts and stressors, and how much time is spent using these maximally active interventions with the child.

Early in treatment, parents will often have many questions about what they should or should not do when their child exhibits symptoms of PTSD (e.g., "Should I try to get my child to talk to me about the trauma? Should I let my child sleep in my bed when they come at night after having a nightmare? Should I change the channel when programs come on and talk about similar traumas? My child won't let us go near where the trauma happened, should I allow this?"). Responses to these questions need to be considered on the basis of a good assessment of the child within that particular family, and should not be off-the-cuff suggestions. First and foremost, the therapist will help the parents to understand how they will play an important role in the child's recovery. Second, they should expect a reduction in requests for reassurance, to sleep in their parents' bed, and an increase in general confidence *after* the therapist has gained some traction using specialist interventions designed to reduce the PTSD symptoms. Third, these are interventions which cannot be sped up or easily replicated by the parent. Thus, the parent can be encouraged to allow a few weeks of therapy to occur before they try and alter their parenting style. Providing the child with support and tangible rewards for attending treatment and doing homework exercises will generally be sufficient at the early stages of treatment. Exceptions to this watch-wait-and-reward advice will occur when there is any evidence of self-harm behaviors, persistent physical aggression, or outright school refusal. Where such behaviors are present, the therapist will need first need to consider whether the child and family are ready to proceed to child-focused CBT. Nevertheless, great weight should be given to the fact that PTSD symptoms often drive comorbid problems and constantly delaying treatment of PTSD to address these comorbid problems can be a significant barrier to recovery. Where the comorbid problems can be managed alongside trauma-focused CBT, the therapist should allow for at least 30 minutes at the end of each session to meet with parents to manage comorbid difficulties.

It is important to recognize that sometimes parents do engage in behaviors, largely reflecting their own traumatization, which might be the subject of interventions in parent-only sessions. For example, some parents find it hard not to make catastrophic or characterological statements in front of their child (e.g., "It's a miracle you didn't die! I've told you a million times you must be more careful! It was the worst thing that ever happened! I will never forget this! I/we will never be the same! What happened to my happy, outgoing little child?"). Some parents will constantly monitor their child for signs they are upset and then quickly intervene to distract or comfort their child. Some parents will have significant symptoms of PTSD and depression and may largely withdraw from the child. The therapist should work with the parent to understand that changes in the parents' behavior towards the child are expected and often reflect the parents own traumatization. However, the solution is not for the parents to go about constantly self-monitoring to insure they don't upset their child with their own reactions, or to constantly monitor their child for signs of upset. The whole family sticking to routines around sleep, work, school, and activities is generally a good idea for the whole family but when the child is suffering acutely from symptoms of PTSD, a little parental flexibility goes a long way. Reassurance seeking, sleeping in the parents' bed, and avoidance will be time-limited if the parent brings the child regularly to treatment and encourages engagement in treatment. The therapist should work with the parents to help them effectively communicate that they care for and love the child, do not blame them for the trauma, that the child does not need to protect them from their own upset or try to manage the parents' upset. Finally, help the parent to communicate to the child that they are available at any time to listen, to talk if this is what the child wants, and sometimes not to talk and just to offer a reassuring hug.

One of the most important interventions aimed at parents early on in the child's treatment is to help the parent consider whether they need treatment themselves. Parents will often say that they might need treatment but are *completely focused on their child* and want to see their child get better first. This is understandable but we will point out the benefits to the child of the parent modeling treatment-seeking and treatment-compliance. We will also point out that the child wants the parent to feel better as much as the reverse, and that like the parent, the child can often sense when the parent is *faking it*. It should be noted that there is no evidence at present that children who receive trauma-focused CBT for PTSD are less likely to recover if they have a parent with PTSD who remains untreated and unwell throughout the course of the child's treatment. In almost all circumstances, therapy for the child should not be contingent upon the parents entering or completing treatment for their own traumatic reactions. Rather the posture of therapist towards the traumatized parents should be the same as any health professional under such circumstances: validate and normalize the parents' suffering; provide information about evidence-based treatments; and offers to help the parent access the appropriate care (e.g. writing to the GP or directly to the appropriate mental health service).

Relapse prevention

In research trials and routine clinical interventions, relapse appears to be rare among successfully treated children. However, by the very nature of the disorder, some symptoms may recur such as around the anniversary of the traumatic event. Individuals who have once developed PTSD are at an increased risk of developing similar symptoms if ever they are exposed to other traumatic life events.

At present there is no evidence-base in support of any particular set of relapse-prevention interventions in respect of childhood PTSD (or childhood anxiety disorders generally for that matter). In the first instance the best thing a therapist can do to prevent relapse is to make sure the child has *fully recovered from their PTSD*. It is important to remember that while traumatic intrusions may be significantly reduced or absent and the child seems to be fully re-engaged in everyday activities, subtle trauma-related, avoidance-like behaviors often remain (e.g., hyper-vigilance to threat, attempts to suppress feelings of anxiety/arousal, minimizing contact with traumatic reminders). Such behaviors are often tied to equally subtle (e.g., not verbalized in treatment) dysfunctional beliefs about the long-term effects of the trauma and to emotional upset ("If I get really upset, all of my nightmares and flashbacks will come back to me"), the likelihood of another trauma, and the value of avoidance behaviors in maintaining safety and calm. The presence of these trauma-related avoidance behaviors and beliefs leave the child vulnerable to relapse, particularly in the face of any further stressful events. Thus towards the end of treatment the therapist should take great care to probe (again) for such beliefs and avoidance behaviors, and to spend some time with the child outside the therapy office to do planned reliving and cue discrimination tasks which help elicit these beliefs and behaviors (e.g., "Show me you are better in the *real world*").

Nevertheless, at the end of treatment the therapist will spend time talking about relapse. The therapist will want to review what the specific symptoms of PTSD and have the child explicitly note these and what things have helped. The child can be asked to look back at the problems they had at the start of treatment and contrast these with how they feel at the end. They can then identify what has changed. What was previously keeping the problems going and how could they use that again in the future if they ever needed to. A helpful ruse is to ask them to think what advice they would give to other people if they ever developed similar stress reactions. In other words, make the helpful strategies explicit and part of the child's repertoire. Providing the child and the parents with a list of what symptoms were present before and after treatment, and what interventions were used which were helpful can serve as important prompt to use these interventions if the child or parent is concerned going forward. Finally, the therapist should help the child and the parents to articulate the difference between what might be normal, time-limited bouts of anxiety or sleeplessness (for example), and what constitutes relapse. There should be some discussion about a follow-up phone call from the therapist to see how things are going in 3–6 months, what facilities there are for the patient/parents contacting the therapist after treatment, and how the family can access care if the PTSD should relapse.

Recent Empirical Findings

The flexible Trauma-Focused Cognitive Therapy approach described above was subject to a randomized control trial (Smith et al., 2007). To our knowledge, this was the first RCT to evaluate individual TF-CT for PTSD in children affected by single traumatic events – in this case road traffic accidents and violence. Post-treatment, 11 of the 12 young people who received CBT no longer met criteria for PTSD compared with 5 of the 12 on the waitlist. Treated children also showed significant reductions in symptoms of depression and anxiety. The differences remained at 6-month follow-up. As predicted, therapeutic gains in the CBT group were mediated via changes in maladaptive cognitions.

These results are in line with a body of work from the USA which shows that TF-CBT is a highly effective treatment for childhood PTSD as a result of sexual abuse (e.g., Cohen, Deblinger, Mannarino, & Steer, 2004; Cohen, Mannarino, & Iyengar, 2011); and when delivered in a group format for young people exposed to violence (Stein, Jaycox, Kataoka et al., 2003).

There have been a number of recent reviews that summarize the published evidence, and they agree to a substantial extent on which studies are included in their reviews (Stallard, 2006; Feeny, Foa, Treadwell & March, 2004; NICE, 2005, endorsed 2011). In addition to CBT there are is evidence for the effectiveness of EMDR and a form of Narrative Exposure Therapy (KidNET) (Schauer et al., 2011).

EMDR

There are a number of case reports claiming effectiveness of eye movement desensitization and reprocessing (EMDR) in treating PTSD in children, but a dearth of published RCTs or even other group studies. De Roos, Greenwald, de Jongh, & Northoorn (2004) reported an RCT involving 52 children following the 2000 Enschede (Netherlands) fireworks disaster. Both EMDR and CBT produced significant lowering of stress symptoms, with EMDR doing slightly better in fewer sessions. The small literature has been reviewed in Rodenburg, Benjamin, de Roos, Meijer, and Stams (2009) and updated in Ribchester, Yule, and Duncan (2011). Despite the lack of a theoretical basis for EMDR, it seems that it can work very quickly and so should be considered as a possible treatment with children.

Narrative Exposure Therapy (NET)

Arising in part from South American methods of helping victims of torture and in part from a thoroughgoing analysis of the neurobiology of autobiographical memory and ways of completing fragmented memories, Schauer et al. (2011) have developed Narrative Exposure Therapy and used it in RCTs with adult refugees in the Sudan (Neuner, Schauer, Klaschik, Karunakara, & Elbert, 2005), war-affected children in Sri Lanka (Schauer, Kohila, Catani, Onyut, & Elbert, 2005), and child refugees living in Germany (Ruf, Schauer, Neuner, Catani, Schauer, & Elbert, 2010). Pennebaker (e.g., 1995) has long demonstrated that writing about emotional events in structured ways can have very positive effects, and so one can anticipate that structured writing therapies and NET will develop more in the near future.

Early intervention

Early intervention is attractive if it could be shown that it prevented later development of PTSD or other disorders as well as alleviating current distress but, as with adult studies, there have been few properly controlled trials of any early intervention. Stallard et al. (2004) compared a trauma focused discussion on an individual basis with a generally supportive talk. At follow-up, both groups of road traffic accident survivors had made good progress and both reported how helpful it had been to talk about the accident (presumably when establishing what happened and inadvertently validating reactions by asking about them systematically). However, there was no difference in PTSD symptoms between the debriefed children, and those in the control condition. The study had been designed when single, brief interventions were considered as possible ways of providing early intervention. It now is widely agreed that such one-off, brief, individually administered interventions do not help reduce later PTSD. The study demonstrated that children were not upset by talking about their traumatic accident, and this alone should help adults when uncertain about whether to talk to affected children or not. Kramer and Landolt (2011) reviewed four RCTs and three other early intervention studies and concluded that there were small to large beneficial effect sizes. Methodological rigor varied between studies, and further research is clearly needed.

Working with large groups after disasters

While the search for improved individual treatments for PTSD in children and adolescents proceeds slowly, many thousands of children are regularly badly traumatized by wars and natural disasters. These mainly affect poor countries where child mental health services may be sparse. There is no way that specialist individual therapy can be mobilized and offered to every survivor. There is, therefore, a great need to work with children in groups.

Until the late 1990s, many NGOs tried to ameliorate the effects of disasters on children by involving them in various child friendly activities. However, there was at times an antipathy towards recognizing that children developed stress reactions and little effort was expended in devising effective interventions. There have been some exceptions and the Foundation for Children and War was established in Norway to develop better evidence-based group interventions and to evaluate their use (see www.childrenandwar.org). The Foundation has now developed a number of manuals that can guide people in helping children develop better coping strategies to ameliorate the worst of their distress. This is not "therapy" in the traditional sense, but is intended to reduce distress to a level that permits children to benefit from support in school, family, and community.

To date, the *Teaching Recovery Techniques* manual has been used after a number of disasters and has been evaluated in RCTs in Thailand some years after the 2004 tsunami (J. Nuttorn, in preparation) and in the West Bank (Barron, Abdullah, & Smith, in press). This manual is based on effective CBT techniques adapted for presentation to groups of 15–20. The manual was adapted for use with adults by colleagues in Iran after the 2003 Bam earthquake and some 21 000 survivors were reported as benefitting substantially (Gudarzi & Yasamy, 2007).

The *Writing for Recovery* manual is based on the work of Pennebaker (1995) on the effect of writing about emotions on aspects of adjustment. Children are asked to write twice a day for 3 consecutive days. Each meeting lasts for only 15 minutes (a total of only 90 minutes of writing). Pilot studies have indicated a reduction in reported symptoms as well as a decrease in cortisol levels. Kalantari, Yule, Dyregrov, Neshatdoost, & Ahmadi (2012) report an RCT in which the Writing for Recovery manual, was used with bereaved adolescent Afghanian refugees. There was a significant drop in their reported traumatic bereavement symptoms.

Currently, there is considerable interest in developing better ways of helping children who have been traumatically bereaved. The Foundation has recently developed a group manual for this and that is being evaluated at present (Dyregrov, Yule, Straume, & Krause, 2012).

Closing Overview

Our understanding of the effects of major stress on children has developed greatly since the diagnosis, PTSD, was first formulated in 1980. From the initial assumption that PTSD would not occur in children, to the recognition that it does occur in children and can be effectively treated, reflects the efforts of many clinicians and researchers. However, it is still the case that developmental aspects require greater attention.

Trauma-focused CBT is currently the best evidence-based intervention with EMDR and KidNET showing considerable promise. The need now is for greater investment in services for children to ensure better recognition and faster treatment so as to mitigate the distressing reactions to traumatic events.

References

APA (1980). *Diagnostic and Statistical Manual of Mental Disorders*, 3rd edn. Washington, DC: American Psychiatric Association.

Barron, I., Abdullah, G., & Smith, P. (in press). Randomized control trial of a CBT trauma recovery program in Palestinian schools. *Journal of Loss and Trauma*. Available online 11 June 2012. doi:10.1080/15325024.2012.688712

Brewin, C. R., Andrews, B., & Rose, S. (2003). Overlap between acute stress disorder and PTSD in victims of violent crime. *American Journal of Psychiatry, 160*, 783–785.

Brewin, C. R., Andrews, B., & Valentine, J. D. (2000). Meta-analysis of risk factors for post-traumatic stress disorder in trauma-exposed adults. *Journal of Consulting and Clinical Psychology, 68*, 747–766.

Broberg, A., Dyregrov, A., & Lilled, L. (2005). The Goteborg discotheque fire: posttraumatic stress, and school adjustment as reported by the primary victims 18 months later. *Journal of Child Psychology and Psychiatry, 46*, 1279–1286.

Bryant, R., Salmon, K., Sinclair, E., & Davidson, P. (2007) A prospective study of appraisals in childhood posttraumatic stress disorder. *Behaviour Research and Therapy, 45*, 2502–2507.

Cohen, J., Bukstein, O., Walter, H., Benson, S. R., Chrisman, A., Farchione, T. R., et al. (2010). Practice parameters for assessment and treatment of children and adolescents with PTSD. *Journal of the American Academy of Child and Adolescent Psychiatry, 49*, 414–430.

Cohen, J., Deblinger, E., Mannarino, A. P., & Steer, R. A. (2004). A multi-site randomised controlled trial for children with sexual abuse related PTSD symptoms. *Journal of the American Academy of Child and Adolescent Psychiatry, 43*, 393–402.

Cohen, J., Mannarino, A., & Iyengar, S. (2011). Community treatment of PTSD for children exposed to intimate partner violence: an RCT. *Archives of Paediatrics and Adolescent Medicine, 165*, 16–21.

Dalgleish, T., Meiser-Stedman, R., & Smith, P. (2005). Cognitive aspects of posttraumatic stress reactions and their treatment in children and adolescents: an empirical review and some recommendations. *Behavioural and Cognitive Psychotherapy, 33*, 459–486.

De Roos, C., Greenwald, R., de Jongh, A., & Noorthoorn, E. O. (2004). EMDR versus CBT for disaster exposed children: A controlled study. Poster presented at International Society for Traumatic Stress Studies, New Orleans, November 2004.

Dyregrov, A. (1997a). *Barn og Traumer [Children and Trauma]*. Bergen: Sigma Forlag.

Dyregrov, A. (1997b). The process in psychological debriefings. *Journal of Traumatic Stress, 10,* 589–605.

Dyregrov, A., Yule., W., Straume, M., & Kraus, F. (2012) *Children and Grief: Teaching Life Skills – A Children and War Foundation Manual.* Bergen, Norway.

Ehlers, A., & Clark, D. M. (2000). A cognitive model of posttraumatic stress disorder. *Behaviour Research and Therapy, 38,* 319–345.

Ehlers, A., Clark, D. M., Hackmann, A., McManus, F., & Fennell, M. (2005). Cognitive therapy for PTSD: development and evaluation. *Behaviour Research and Therapy, 43,* 413–431.

Ehlers, A., Clark, D. M., Hackmann, A., McManus, F., Fennell, M., & Grey, N. (in press). *Cognitive Therapy for Posttraumatic Stress Disorder: A Therapist's Guide.* Oxford: OUP

Ehlers, A., Clark, D. M., Hackmann, A., McManus, F., Fennell, M., Herbert, C., & Mayou, R. (2003a). A randomised controlled trial of cognitive therapy, a self-help booklet, and repeated assessments as early interventions for posttraumatic stress disorder. *Archives of General Psychiatry, 60,* 1024–1032.

Ehlers, A., Gene-Cos, N., & Perrin, S. (2009). Low recognition of posttraumatic stress disorder in primary care. *London Journal of Primary Care, 2,* 36–42.

Ehlers, A., Mayou, R. A., & Bryant, B. (2003b). Cognitive predictors of posttraumatic stress disorder in children: results of a prospective longitudinal study. *Behaviour Research and Therapy, 41,* 1–10.

Elklit, A. (2002). Victimization and PTSD in a Danish national youth probability sample. *Journal of the American Academy of Child & Adolescent Psychiatry, 41* (2), 174–181.

Feeny, N. C., Foa, E. B., Treadwell, K. R., & March, J. (2004). Posttraumatic stress disorder in youth: a critical review of the cognitive and behavioral treatment outcome literature. *Professional Psychology: Research and Practice, 35,* 466–476.

Fletcher, K. E. (1996). Childhood posttraumatic stress disorder. In E. J. Mash, & R. A. Barkley (Eds.), *Child Psychopathology* (pp. 242–276). New York: Guilford.

Foa, E. B., Rothbaum, B. O., & Molnar, C. (1995). Cognitive-behavioral therapy of PTSD. In M. J. Friedman, D. S. Charney, & A. Y. Deutch (Eds.), *Neurobiological and Clinical Consequences of Stress: From Normal Adaptation to PTSD.* New York: Raven Press.

Giaconia, R. M., Reinherz, H. Z., Silverman, A. B., Pakiz, B., Frost, A. K., & Cohen, E. (1995). Traumas and posttraumatic stress disorder in a community population of older adolescents. *Journal of the American Academy of Child and Adolescent Psychiatry, 34,* 1369–1380.

Gudarzi, S. S., & Yasamy, M. T. (2007). Evolving epidemiology of the psychological conditions following Bam Earthquake. Paper presented at the 10th European Conference on Traumatic Stress, Opatija, Croatia, June.

Kalantari, M., Yule, W., Dyregrov, A., Neshatdoost, H., & Ahmadi, S. J. (2012). Efficacy of writing for recovery on traumatic grief symptoms of Afghani refugee bereaved adolescents: A randomized control trial. *Omega, 65* (2), 139–150.

Kramer, D. N., & Landolt, M. A. (2011) Characteristics and efficacy of early psychological interventions in children and adolescents after single trauma: a meta-analysis. *European Journal of Psychotraumatology, 2.* doi: 10.3402/ejpt.v2i0.7858.

Margolin, G., & Gordis, E. B., (2000). The effects of family and community violence on children. *Annual Review of Psychology, 51,* 445–479.

Meiser-Stedman, R. (2002). Towards a cognitive-behavioral model of PTSD in children and adolescents. *Clinical Child and Family Psychology Review, 5,* 217–232.

Meiser-Stedman, R., Dalgleish, T., Smith, P., Yule, W., & Glucksman, E. (2007). Diagnostic, demographic, memory quality and cognitive variables associated with acute stress disorder in children and adolescents. *Journal of Abnormal Psychology, 16,* 65–79.

Meiser-Stedman, R., Smith, P., Bryant, R., Salmon, K., Yule, W. Dalgleish, T., & Nixon, R. (2009). Development and validation of the Child Post-Traumatic Cognitions Inventory (CPTCI). *Journal of Child Psychology and Psychiatry, 50,* 432–440.

Meiser-Stedman, R., Smith, P., Glucksman, E., Yule, W., et al. (2008). The posttraumatic stress disorder diagnosis in preschool- and elementary school-age children exposed to motor vehicle accidents. *American Journal of Psychiatry, 165,* 1326–1337.

Meiser-Stedman, R., Yule, W., Dalgleish, T., Smith, P., & Glucksman, E. (2006). The role of the family in child and adolescent posttraumatic stress following attendance at an emergency department. *Journal of Pediatric Psychology, 31,* 397–402.

Meiser-Stedman, R., Yule, W., Smith, P., Glucksman, E., & Dalgleish, T. (2005). Acute stress disorder and posttraumatic stress disorder in children and adolescents involved in assaults or motor vehicle accidents. *American Journal of Psychiatry, 162* (7), 1381–1383.

Meltzer, H., Gatward, R., Goodman, R., & Ford, T. (2003). Mental health of children and adolescents in Great Britain. *International Review of Psychiatry. 15,* 185–187.

Merikangas, K. R,. He, J.-P., Burstein, M., Swanson, S. A., Avenevoli, S., Cui, L., et al. (2010). Lifetime prevalence of mental disorders in US adolescents: results from the national comorbidity survey replication adolescent supplement (NCS-A). *Journal of the American Academy of Child and Adolescent Psychiatry, 49,* 980–989.

Michael, T., Ehlers, A., Halligan, S. L., & Clark, D. M. (2005). Unwanted memories of assault – what intrusion characteristics are associated with PTSD? *Behaviour Research and Therapy, 43,* 613–628.

NICE (National Institute for Clinical Excellence) (2005). *Post Traumatic Stress Disorder: the Management of PTSD in Adults and Children in Primary and Secondary Care (Clinical Guideline 26).* London: Gaskell and the British Psychological Society

Neuner, F., Schauer, M., Klaschik, C., Karunakara, U., & Elbert, T. (2005). A comparison of narrative exposure therapy, supportive counselling, and psychoeducation for treating posttraumatic stress disorder in an African refugee settlement. *Journal of Consulting and Clinical Psychology, 72,* 579–587.

Pennebaker, J. W. (Ed.) (1995). *Emotion, Disclosure and Health.* Washington, DC: American Psychological Association.

Ribchester, T., Yule, W., & Duncan, A. (2011). EMDR for childhood PTSD after road traffic accidents: Attentional, memory and attributional processes. *Journal of EMDR Practice and Research, 4,* 138–147.

Rodenburg, R., Benjamin, A., de Roos, C., Meijer, A. M., & Stams, G. J. (2009). Efficacy of EMDR in children: A meta-analysis. *Clinical Psychology Review, 29,* 599–606.

Ruf, M., Schauer, M., Neuner, F., Catani, C., Schauer, E., & Elbert, T. (2010). Narrative exposure therapy for 7–16 year olds: a randomised controlled trial with traumatised refugee children. *Journal of Traumatic Stress, 23,* 437–445.

Salmon, K., & Bryant, R. (2002). Posttraumatic stress disorder in children: the influence of developmental factors. *Clinical Psychology Review, 22,* 163 – 188.

Salmon, K., Sinclair, E., & Bryant, R. A. (2007). The role of maladaptive appraisals in child acute stress reactions. *British Journal of Clinical Psychology, 46,* 203–210.

Salmond, C., Meiser-Stedman, R., Dalgleish, T., Glucksman, E., Thompson, P., & Smith, P. (2011). The nature of trauma memories in acute stress disorder in children and adolescents. *Journal of Child Psychology and Psychiatry, 52,* 560–570.

Schauer, E., Kohila, M., Catani, C., Onyut, P., & Elbert, T. (2005). Building local capacity for mental health service provision in the face of large-scale traumatisation: a cascade model from Sri Lanka. ESTSS (European Society for Traumatic Stress Studies), Stockholm, June 2005.

Schauer, M., Neuner, F., & Elbert, T. (2011). *Narrative Exposure Therapy: a Short-Term Intervention for Traumatic Stress Disorders after War, Terror, or Torture,* 2nd edn. Hogrefe & Huber.

William Yule et al.

Scheeringa, M., Zeanah, C., & Cohen, J. (2011). PTSD in children and adolescents: towards an empirically based algorithm. *Depression and Anxiety, 28,* 770–782.

Smith, P., Dyregrov, A., & Yule, W. (1999). *Children and War: Teaching Recovery Techniques.* Bergen, Norway: Children and War Foundation.

Smith, P., Perrin, S., Yule, W., & Clark, D. M. (2010). *Post Traumatic Stress Disorder: Cognitive Therapy with Children and Young People.* London: Routledge

Smith, P., Yule, W., Perrin, S., Tranah, T., Dalgleish, T, & Clark, D. M. (2007). Cognitive Behavior Therapy for PTSD in Children and Adolescents: A Randomized Controlled Trial. *Journal of the American Academy of Child and Adolescent Psychiatry, 46,* 1051–1061.

Stallard, P. (2003). A retrospective analysis to explore the applicability of the Ehlers and Clark (2000) cognitive model to explain PTSD in children. *Behavioural and Cognitive Psychotherapy, 31,* 337–345.

Stallard, P. (2006). Psychological interventions for post traumatic stress reactions in children and young people: A review of randomised controlled trials. *Clinical Psychology Review, 26,* 895–911.

Stallard, P., Salter, E., & Velleman, R. (2004). Posttraumatic stress disorder following road traffic accidents: A second prospective study. *European Journal of Child and Adolescent Psychiatry, 13,* 172–178.

Stallard, P., & Smith, E. (2007). Appraisals and cognitive coping styles associated with chronic post-traumatic symptoms in child road traffic accident survivors. *Journal of Child Psychology and Psychiatry, 48,* 194–201.

Stein, B. D., Jaycox., L. H., Kataoka, S. H., Wong, M., Tu, W., Elliott, M. N. et al. (2003). A mental health intervention for schoolchildren exposed to violence: A randomized controlled trial. *Journal of the American Medical Association, 290,* 603–611.

Trickey, D., Siddaway, A. P., Meiser-Stedman, R., Serpell, L., & Field, A. P. (2012). A meta-analysis of risk factors for posttraumatic stress disorder in children and adolescents. *Clinical Psychology Review, 32,* 122–138.

Udwin, O., Boyle, S., Yule, W., Bolton, D., & O'Ryan, D. (2000). Risk factors for long-term psychological effects of a disaster experienced in adolescence: Predictors of Post Traumatic Stress Disorder. *Journal of Child Psychology and Psychiatry, 41,* 969–979.

Wolmer, L., Laor, N., Gershon, A., Mayes, L. C., & Cohen, D. J. (2000). The mother-child dyad facing trauma: A developmental outlook. *Journal of Nervous and Mental Disease, 188,* 409–415.

Yorbik, O., Dikkatli, S., Cansever, A., & Sohmen, T. (2001). The efficacy of fluoxetine treatment in children and adolescents with posttraumatic stress disorder symptoms [in Turkish]. *Klin Psikofarmakol Bulteni, 1,* 251–256.

Yule, W., Bolton, D., Udwin, O., Boyle, S., O'Ryan, D., & Nurrish, J. (2000). The long-term psychological effects of a disaster experienced in adolescence: I: The incidence and course of post traumatic stress disorder. *Journal of Child Psychology and Psychiatry, 41,* 503–511.

21

School Refusal

David A. Heyne and Floor M. Sauter
Leiden University Institute of Psychology, The Netherlands

Theoretical Background

Classifying school attendance problems

At first glance, "school attendance problem" looks like a relatively straightforward phenomenon. However, considerable confusion and debate has surrounded the classification of school attendance problems. An initial issue concerns the distinction between school attendance patterns regarded as non-problematic and those which are best regarded as problematic. A second issue concerns the differentiation between types of school attendance problems.

The distress associated with school attendance is often regarded as normal when observed in a child starting school. Throughout the school years it is also common for students to be absent from school from time to time. Just how much distress or absence ought to be regarded as concerning or problematic? Being able to reliably distinguish between non-problematic and problematic distress and absence has practical benefits (e.g., providing an indication for parents about when to seek assistance; guiding school-based policy about when to intervene) as well as scientific benefits (e.g., consistency across studies examining the causes of school attendance problems; determining whether treatment has been successful). Kearney (2003) proposed a useful distinction between non-problematic and problematic absenteeism as follows: "Problematic absenteeism could refer to school-aged youths who (a) have missed most (i.e., >50%) school time for at least 2 weeks and/or (b) experience difficulty attending school for at least 2 weeks such that significant interference occurs in the child's or the family's daily life routine" (p. 59). The absences are not due to factors which parents and school officials regard as legitimate, such as illness or arrangements for home schooling. School-aged youth fulfilling criterion (b) may be those who "consistently skip certain classes, show frequent morning misbehaviours to try to miss

The Wiley-Blackwell Handbook of The Treatment of Childhood and Adolescent Anxiety, First Edition.
Edited by Cecilia A. Essau and Thomas H. Ollendick.
© 2013 John Wiley & Sons, Ltd. Published 2013 by John Wiley & Sons, Ltd.

school, and/or have considerable anxiety about school" (p. 59). The 2-week criterion is applied because temporary absenteeism is common and often not problematic.
More recently, Kearney (2008) proposed that criterion (a) be changed to "missed at
least 25% of total school time for at least 2 weeks" and that a third criterion be added,
namely "and/or are absent for at least 10 days of school during any 15-week period
while school is in session" (p. 265).

Regarding differentiation between types of school attendance problems, it is probably helpful to think in terms of two sub-classes: parent-motivated attendance problems
and child-motivated attendance problems (Kearney, 2003). The former sub-class sig-
nifies those problems which essentially arise out of a parent's ambivalence or opposi-
tion towards their child attending school, such that the parent exerts little or no effort
to secure their child's regular attendance. This problem has also been referred to as
school withdrawal (Kahn & Nursten, 1962). Reasons cited for not sending a child to
school have included: to keep a healthy or ill family member company (Hersov, 1990);
to help look after younger siblings or do housework or shopping (Galloway, 1985;
Hersov, 1990); supporting the family business (Amatu, 1981; Obondo & Dhadphale,
1990); parental conflict with school staff (Kearney, 2001); and socially deviant parents
not accepting their responsibilities (Berg, Butler, Hullin, Smith, & Tyrer, 1978).

When a school attendance problem is child-motivated, it implies that the resistance
to school attendance comes predominantly from the young person and not from the
parent[1]. Child-motivated school attendance problems may take the form of truancy,
school refusal, or occasionally a combination of the two. Definitions of truancy have
focused on a lack of parental knowledge about the child's absenteeism (Kearney,
2002) or the child's whereabouts when not at school (Berg, Casswell, Goodwin,
Hullin, McGuire, & Tagg, 1985), and a lack of parental consent for the child's
absence (Galloway, 1985). In short, truancy entails absence from school which is
not authorized by the parents. A distinction is often made between truancy and
school refusal, based on the notion that school refusal entails difficulty attending
school in association with emotional distress (e.g., King & Bernstein, 2001; Martin,
Cabrol, Bouvard, Lepine, & Mouren-Simeoni, 1999; Okuyama, Okada, Kuribayashi,
& Kaneko, 1999), it is not associated with serious antisocial behavior (e.g., Honjo,
Nishide, Niwa et al., 2001; McShane, Walter, & Rey 2001), and it involves the child
usually staying at home versus being elsewhere (e.g., Hansen, Sanders, Massaro, &
Last, 1998; Kameguchi & Murphy-Shigematsu, 2001). Further, Martin et al. (1999)
noted that in cases of school refusal the parents and child are convinced of the necessity
of school attendance.

Berg and colleagues' initial criteria (Berg, Nichols, & Pritchard, 1969) and revised
criteria (Berg, 1996, 1997, 2002; Bools, Foster, Brown, & Berg, 1990) help to identify
school refusal and distinguish it from truancy and school withdrawal. The criteria
include: (1) reluctance or refusal to attend school, often (but not necessarily) leading
to prolonged absence; (2) the child usually remaining at home during school hours,
rather than concealing the problem from parents; (3) emotional upset at the prospect
of attending school, which may be reflected in excessive fearfulness, temper tantrums,

---

[1] It is important to bear in mind, however, that multiple risk factors and processes may be associated with
the development and maintenance of a child-motivated school attendance problem, including individual,
family, school, and community-related factors (Heyne, 2006; Heyne, King, & Ollendick, 2004).

unhappiness, or possibly in the form of unexplained physical symptoms; (4) an absence of severe antisocial behavior, beyond the child's resistance to parental attempts to get them to school; and (5) reasonable parental efforts to secure the child's attendance at school, at some stage in the history of the problem. Researchers often operationalize the third criterion as the presence of an anxiety disorder and/or depressive disorder to provide a rigorous test of treatments under investigation. However, a young person can fulfill criteria for school refusal in the absence of such disorders.

Earlier studies support the differentiation between school refusal and truancy (e.g., Berg, Butler, Franklin, Hayes, Lucas, & Sims, 1993; Bools et al., 1990). For example, a study of 100 children with school attendance problems revealed that almost half of the truants had a conduct disorder while none of them had an emotional disorder, and that none of the school refusers had a conduct disorder while half of them had an emotional disorder (usually with anxiety and fearfulness, and occasionally with unhappiness; Bools et al., 1990). A more recent community-based study lends additional support to a differentiation between school refusal and truancy. Egger, Costello, and Angold (2003) found that school refusal was significantly associated with anxiety disorders and depression while truancy was significantly associated with disruptive behavior disorders and depression. Moreover, school-related fears and performance anxiety were significantly associated with school refusal and not with truancy, whereas lax parental supervision was significantly associated with truancy and not with school refusal.

Differentiation between types of school attendance problems helps isolate type-specific risk factors and processes which warrant attention in treatment. Indeed, emphases in the treatment of truancy are different to those for school refusal (e.g., Berg, 2002; Teasley, 2004). The current chapter preserves the distinction between school refusal and truancy, and conceptualizes school refusal according to Berg and colleagues' criteria as outlined above.

Understanding school refusal in relation to anxiety, depression, and externalizing behavior

School refusal is not a formal diagnosis in the *Diagnostic and Statistical Manual of Mental Disorders* (DSM) classification system but young people presenting with school refusal are often diagnosed with one or more internalizing disorders. In Bernstein's (1991) North American study of 96 referred school refusers (defined by "poor school attendance secondary to psychological symptoms without medical illness", p. 44), 28% had a DSM-III-R (APA, 1987) anxiety disorder only, 28% had a depressive disorder only, and a further 25% had both an anxiety disorder and a depressive disorder; as few as 19% had no internalizing disorder. McShane et al. (2001) reported on an Australian sample of 192 young people seen in a child and adolescent psychiatric clinic and classified as school refusers (based on parent reports of the young person's fear of school). Fifty-four per cent met DSM-IV (APA, 1994) criteria for an anxiety disorder and 52% met criteria for a depressive disorder. Among 33 school refusers (defined by Berg and colleagues' 1969 criteria) seen in a child and adolescent psychiatry service in India, 64% were diagnosed with a DSM-IV depressive disorder and 58% with an anxiety disorder (Prabhuswamy, Srinath, Girimaji, & Seshadri, 2007). Egger et al. (2003) also observed DSM-IV internalizing disorders among the 130 school refusers in their community-based North American sample, albeit to a lesser extent. Pure anxious school refusal was defined according to "school nonattendance (of at least a half-day's duration) due to worry/anxiety; staying home mornings from school because of anxiety; failing to reach school or leaving school and going home; and/or having to be taken to school because of worry and anxiety about attending school," at least once in a 3-month period (p. 799). Depression and separation anxiety disorder were the most common disorders (14% and 11% respectively). Other internalizing disorders included social phobia (3%), simple phobia (2%), and generalized anxiety disorder (2%)[2]. Egger and colleagues (2003) noted that the young people in their study had "fairly mild school refusal" (p. 804) which probably accounts for the lower rates of DSM internalizing disorders relative to the rates observed among referred samples of school refusers.

Even when full diagnostic criteria for a particular anxiety disorder are not met, the prominent phobic or anxious symptoms displayed by a school refuser may lead to a diagnosis of Anxiety Disorder Not Otherwise Specified (e.g., Heyne, King, Tonge et al., 2002; McShane et al., 2001). Yet other school refusers will experience fear or anxiety in relation to school attendance but at a level which is below the diagnostic threshold. In Egger and colleagues' (2003) sample of anxious school refusers, anxiety-related symptoms were reported by a larger proportion of young people than were diagnosed with an anxiety disorder (e.g., 17% were afraid that something would happen at home while they were at school, 18% worried about harm befalling a parent, 36% reported a fear specific to school, and 27% reported headaches or stomach-aches associated with separation or school attendance). Similarly, the depression-related symptom of fatigue was more prevalent among school refusers (32%) than was depression at the disorder level (14%). In an earlier review of depression and school refusal behavior[3], Kearney (1993) estimated that 31% of young people with school refusal behavior met diagnostic criteria for depression while as many as 52% of young people with school refusal behavior experienced symptoms of depression. Kearney argued that some young people with school refusal behavior will not be identified as depressed according to diagnostic criteria but will display symptoms warranting attention during treatment.

With respect to externalizing behavior, it is important to recall that Berg and colleagues' (Berg, 1996, 1997, 2002; Berg et al., 1969; Bools et al., 1990) definition of school refusal includes the criterion that there is an absence of severe antisocial behavior such as stealing and destructiveness. Thus, conduct disorder (CD) is typically not observed among school refusers. School refusal is sometimes associated with other externalizing behavior such as argumentativeness and aggression when parents try to get the young person to go to school (e.g., Berg, 2002; Hoshino, Nikkuni, Kaneko, Endo, Yashima, & Kumashiro, 1987). In some cases the presence of multiple externalizing behaviors over time will lead to a diagnosis of oppositional defiant disorder (ODD). Rates of ODD among clinic-referred school refusers include 9% (Prabhuswamy et al., 2007), 21% (Heyne et al., 2002), and 24% (McShane et al.,

---

[2]No composite rate of internalizing disorders was reported.

[3]Kearney (2003) uses the umbrella term 'school refusal behavior' to refer to the behaviors of the group of young people often regarded as truants, as well as the behaviors of the group of young people often regarded as school refusers.

2001). In Egger and colleagues' (2003) community-based study, which avoided the use of Berg and colleagues' criteria, 6% of school refusers were diagnosed with ODD and 5% with CD.

Given that school refusal is not a separate diagnostic category and is often associated with anxiety and/or depression, might it be sufficient to treat school refusal via a protocol for anxiety disorders or depressive disorders? Certainly overlap exists between the cognitive-behavioral therapy (CBT) components outlined in this chapter and the components in CBT interventions for anxiety in young people (e.g., Barrett & Turner, 2000; Chorpita, 2007) and depression in young people (e.g., Lewinsohn, Clarke, Hops, & Andrews, 1990; TADS Team, 2003). At the same time, there are several reasons why a treatment protocol specific to school refusal is preferable to a protocol for anxiety or depression. First, school refusal requires timely resolution (see "Emphasizing early increase in school attendance"), necessitating specific treatment content and process. By contrast, cases involving an anxiety disorder but no school refusal (e.g., specific phobia – natural environment type) or depression but no school refusal may involve less sense of urgency. Second, school refusal is decidedly heterogeneous with respect to etiology and presentation. It may be associated with one or more of the internalizing disorders together with externalizing behavior. Thus, in the treatment of school refusal, parents are encouraged to acquire and employ behavior management strategies relevant to the presentation of both internalizing and externalizing behavior. Third, anecdotal reports from clinical researchers suggest that anxiety-focused treatments fail to address co-occurring school attendance problems among young people presenting with anxiety disorders. Albano (1995) noted that school refusal presented "unique challenges" for clinicians who worked with socially phobic adolescents in a study of CBT for social phobia (p. 280). It was suggested that alternative treatment plans may be needed in cases involving concurrent social phobia and school refusal. Likewise, depression-focused treatments may fail to address co-occurring school attendance problems among young people presenting with depressive disorders. In the Treatment for Adolescent Depression (TADS) study, school refusal presented an obstacle to clinicians implementing the CBT protocol for depression (Kennard, Ginsburg, Feeny, Sweeney, & Zagurski, 2005).

Taking adolescent development into account

School refusal occurs for about 1–2% of young people (Egger et al., 2003; Heyne & King, 2004). It poses a threat to the young person's social, emotional, and academic development, and follow-up studies of referred school refusers indicate a risk for ongoing mental health problems in late adolescence (Buitelaar, Van Andel, Duyx, & Van Strien, 1994) and adulthood (Berg & Jackson, 1985; Flakierska-Praquin, Lindstrom, & Gillberg, 1997; McCune & Hynes, 2005). Further, a comparison between successfully and unsuccessfully treated school refusers indicated that those who did not return to school displayed more antisocial behavior and a trend towards poorer social adjustment at 7-year follow-up (Valles & Oddy, 1984). Thus, while school refusal is not highly prevalent relative to other problems in childhood and adolescence, it can have serious implications for a young person's longer-term well-being. Importantly, developmental differences have been reported with respect to the prevalence, presentation, and outcome of treatment for school refusal.

Hersov (1985) suggested that school refusal is more prevalent among secondary school students and referral rates in studies of school-refusing children and adolescents lend support to this contention (e.g., Last & Strauss, 1990; McShane et al., 2001). What is unclear is the extent to which differences in referral rates are related to a greater likelihood of onset in adolescence and/or a greater propensity to refer adolescent school refusers. Among non-referred anxious school refusers aged 9–16 years, Egger et al. (2003) found that the mean age of onset was 10.9 years and prevalence was significantly higher among younger children. Thus, the higher referral rates for adolescents relative to children might be better explained by the complexity of the problem in adolescence and not by a higher prevalence in this period.

Diagnostically, separation anxiety disorder is more common among younger school refusers, and older school refusers are more likely than younger school refusers to experience social phobia (Last & Strauss, 1990). Depressive symptoms are more likely among adolescent school refusers (e.g., Baker & Wills, 1978) and adolescents with school refusal behavior (thus, school refusal and truancy) are more likely than children with school refusal behavior to meet diagnostic criteria for depression (Kearney, 1993). Eisenberg (1959) observed that the adolescent school refuser is far more disturbed than the younger school refuser and this impression subsequently received empirical support (see review by Atkinson, Quarrington, & Cyr, 1985). Three studies (Hansen et al., 1998; Heyne, 1999; Prabhuswamy et al., 2007) have since reported significantly higher levels of school absenteeism among older school refusers relative to younger school refusers.

Treatment outcome has also been found to be inferior for older school refusers relative to younger school refusers (Heyne, 1999; Last, Hansen, & Franco, 1998; Prabhuswamy et al., 2007; Valles & Oddy, 1984). This might be explained by the type of internalizing symptoms experienced by adolescent school refusers (i.e., social phobia and depression are more common among this group). It might also be explained by the severity of school refusal in adolescence, inasmuch as school-refusing adolescents have poorer school attendance relative to school-refusing children. Related to this last point, two studies found that lower attendance at the start of treatment was significantly related to poorer functioning at the end of treatment (Last et al., 1998; Layne, Bernstein, Egan, & Kushner, 2003).

The nature of the tasks and transitions inherent to adolescence may also impact upon treatment outcome. Writing about anxiety in general, Southam-Gerow, Kendall, and Weersing (2001) suggested that the interference caused by anxiety-related difficulties may be especially troublesome in adolescence when young people are also facing challenging developmental tasks. Writing about school refusal in particular, Hansen et al. (1998) proposed that the complexity of the adolescent developmental period may present a heightened challenge for school-refusing adolescents as they endeavor to cope with fears of school. Relative to primary school, secondary school is usually a more complex and demanding environment, socially and academically. The increasing importance of peer influences and identity formation in adolescence may make it more difficult for a school-refusing adolescent to confront and overcome their difficulty attending school, relative to a school-refusing child. Hansen and colleagues also suggested that adolescents are more likely to resist – and are more physically capable of resisting – parents' and teachers' efforts to return them to school. Adolescent school refusers may prefer to decide for themselves about when and how they return to school, due to the drive towards independence which may fuel a defiance of external control and authority (Rubenstein & Hastings, 1980). Developmental factors also present specific challenges for clinicians endeavoring to engage adolescents in treatment (Sauter, Heyne, & Westenberg, 2009).

In all, adolescence is an important developmental period with respect to the referral, severity, and clinical presentation of school refusal, and with respect to treatment outcome. Following Holmbeck, Colder, Shapera, Westhoven, Kenealy, and Updegrove (2000), we contend that treatment for school refusal needs to account for the confluence of developmental issues arising during this period. In this chapter we present a cognitive-behavioral treatment designed to be sensitive to a range of developmental issues associated with school refusal in adolescence. The treatment was developed based on the authors' experience with treatment-resistant cases of adolescent school refusal and familiarity with the literature on developmental psychology, developmental psychopathology, and clinical child and adolescent psychology. Because the treatment was designed with the more challenging group of adolescent school refusers in mind, an abbreviated form of the treatment may well be sufficient when working with school-refusing children and with mild forms of school refusal in adolescence.

Therapeutic Goals and Methods

The aim of treatment for school refusal is to help the young person resume a normal developmental pathway via a reduction in emotional distress and a return to regular school attendance. In the absence of treatment, a small proportion of school refusers may experience a spontaneous recovery but the vast majority continues to display emotional distress and a problematic level of school attendance (King, Tonge, Heyne et al., 1998). The treatment approach described in this chapter is based upon the @school program, a developmentally-sensitive CBT for school refusal (Heyne, Sauter, & Van Hout, 2008). It is applicable to young people displaying school refusal as defined by Berg and colleagues (Berg, 1967, 1997, 2002; Berg et al., 1969; Bools et al., 1990; see "Classifying school attendance problems"). The school refuser's emotional distress may be manifest in clinical or sub-clinical levels of fear, anxiety, and depression. Externalizing problems in the form of oppositional and defiant behavior may also be observed at clinical or sub-clinical levels. The treatment has not been designed for or evaluated with school refusers displaying conduct disorder. We acknowledge that a small group of school refusers who display emotional upset at the prospect of attending school may also present with conduct disorder (e.g., Berg et al., 1993; Egger et al., 2003; McShane et al., 2001). The most effective intervention for this group awaits investigation. Similarly, the treatment has not been evaluated with school refusers presenting with intellectual disability (ID) or an autism spectrum disorder (ASD). The reader is referred to recent descriptions of CBT with clients with ID or an ASD to inform the adaptation and application of the @school treatment program (e.g., Karnezi & Tierney, 2009; Whitehouse, Tudway, Look, & Kroese, 2006; Wood, Drahota, Sze, Har, Chiu, & Langer, 2009).

Emphasizing early increase in school attendance

From a developmental perspective, the resumption of school attendance is critical. Vasey and Dadds (2001) noted: "To the extent that a child on a deviant developmental pathway is unable to enter developmental contexts in which important skills are learned or honed, adaptation to future developmental challenges is jeopardized" (p. 12). School refusers with problematic levels of non-attendance miss opportunities for developing their academic and social-emotional skills and, as noted earlier, are at risk of longer-term problems.

A key question for clinicians is: just how quickly should the school-refusing young person increase their school attendance? Authors have written about "early return" (e.g., Kennedy, 1965), "rapid return" (e.g., Leventhal, Weinberger, Stander, & Stearns, 1967), "immediate return versus later return" (e.g., Berecz, 1969), "rapid versus graduated re-entry" (e.g., King & Ollendick, 1989), and "much later school return" (e.g., Berecz, 1969). Adding complexity, these terms have been variably used to address two separate questions associated with increasing school attendance: (1) How soon after the commencement of treatment will the young person be expected to start increasing school attendance? and (2) How much time will the young person spend at school when he[4] starts increasing school attendance?

With the aim of promoting clarity we propose a distinction between "early full-time increase" and "early part-time increase." "Early" refers to a treatment plan in which the young person will start increasing school attendance within 4 weeks of the commencement of treatment. "Full-time" refers to a plan for the young person to attend school for the whole school day, for every school day, from the time of the planned increase in attendance. This resembles the behavioral technique of flooding inasmuch as exposure commences with the most anxiety-provoking situation – being at school full-time. "Part-time" is defined as attendance at school for anything less than the whole of the school day. It involves a step-wise approach to overcoming the discomfort or anxiety associated with school attendance and thus resembles the behavioral technique of graded *in vivo* exposure. Successive exposures to school attendance are usually organized around the amount of time the young person spends at school, but other factors may also be taken into account such as the amount of contact the young person has with peers at school or the extent of participation in academic activities. We use the term "delayed increase", whether it be "delayed full-time increase" or "delayed part-time increase", to describe those situations in which helping professionals do not intend for the young person to start increasing school attendance within 4 weeks of the commencement of treatment.

We return now to the first question about how soon after the commencement of treatment the young person will be expected to start increasing attendance. A minority of writers have argued in favor of delayed school return. For example, Waldfogel, Coolidge, and Hahn (1957) contended that a focus on school return interferes with the therapy process because the young person is prevented from solving internal emotional conflicts. On the other hand, Eisenberg (1959) argued that the clinician's failure to insist on a prompt return to school feeds neurotic patterns within the

---

[4]For convenience we use the masculine form when referring to the young person and the feminine form when referring to the clinician.

family; Berg (1985) argued that the approach of taking pressure off the child to go to school while providing home tuition and carrying out treatment for psychiatric disturbance has found little favor and should be stopped; and Bryce and Baird (1986) suggested that those who advocated against an early school return did not consider the possibility that it could be handled in a manner which is unlikely to be harmful to the young person. Indeed, emphasis upon an early increase in attendance has been a recurring theme in behavioral and CBT approaches (e.g., Blagg 1987; Blagg & Yule, 1984; Heyne et al., 2002; Kennedy, 1965; King, Ollendick, & Tonge, 1995; Mansdorf & Lukens, 1987), as well as in psychodynamic approaches (see review by Want, 1983) and family-focused approaches (e.g., Bryce & Baird, 1986; Framrose, 1978). The advantages commonly associated with an early increase in attendance include preventing anxiety being reinforced through avoidance (e.g., Hersen, 1971), preventing access to secondary gain (e.g., King & Ollendick, 1989), and warding off impairment in academic and social functioning (e.g., Want, 1983).

We turn now to the second question about how much time the young person will spend at school when he starts increasing school attendance. There has been no systematic evaluation of the effectiveness of "early full-time increase" relative to "early part-time increase" but it is accepted that some cases respond better to a part-time increase (King & Ollendick, 1989). Yule, Hersov, and Treseder (1980) proposed that both approaches can work in particular cases, adding that "the problem is to know before-hand which approach to try first with which cases" (p. 276). In the absence of empirically-derived guidelines, clinicians must weigh up the relative merits of full-time versus part-time increase in school attendance. We propose that considerable therapeutic leverage can be gained by eliciting the school refuser's preference. Some school-refusing young people prefer a full-time increase so that they do not have to also deal with potential questions from peers about partial attendance at school. Many others opt for a part-time increase (e.g., attending for one class on the first day, two classes the next day, etc.); it makes the process of increasing school attendance seem more achievable. Cases which involve chronic complete non-attendance and/or high levels of anxiety about increasing attendance may also respond better to a part-time increase. Further, it has been suggested that the part-time approach may help circumvent the problem of treatment drop-out which has been reported in relation to *in vivo* flooding with adults (Last & Francis, 1988).

Utilizing behavioral and cognitive interventions

Of the various interventions which have been reported for the treatment of school refusal (e.g., psychodynamic psychotherapy, family therapy, behavioral therapy, cognitive-behavioral therapy, pharmacotherapy), cognitive-behavioral therapy (CBT) has gained most empirical support. The cognitive-behavioral view of child and adolescent psychopathology has largely focused on learning processes and information-processing. It has acknowledged biological, neurological, and genetic factors while not elaborating upon them, and it has avoided exploration of unconscious conflicts (Kendall, Howard, & Epps, 1988). Family factors and broader systemic factors have increasingly gained attention in cognitive-behavioral conceptualizations of psychopathology in young people (e.g., Drinkwater, 2005; Dummett, 2006). In particular, the thoughts, feelings, and behaviors of parents have been associated with the maintenance of children's behavioral and emotional problems (e.g., Suveg, Roblek, Robin, Krain, Ascenbrand, & Ginsberg, 2006; White, McNally, & Cartwright-Hatton, 2003), and problematic patterns of family communication and problem-solving are regarded as important targets when treating youth anxiety (Ginsburg & Schlossberg, 2002) and depression (Restifo & Bögels, 2009).

There is no unified cognitive-behavioral theory of the development and maintenance of school refusal. Rather, there are various behavioral conceptualizations of its etiology (Burke & Silverman, 1987; King et al., 1995) and attention has also been given to the role of unhelpful cognition in the development and maintenance of the problem (Heyne, 2006; Maric, Heyne, de Heus, van Widenfelt, & Westenberg, 2012). Numerous studies support the role of parent and family factors in the etiology of school refusal (Atkinson et al., 1985; Bernstein, Warren, Massie, & Thuras, 1999; Kearney & Silverman, 1995) and the school context is another important etiological consideration (Kearney & Hugelshofer, 2000; Ollendick & Mayer, 1984; Thyer & Sowers-Hoag, 1986). In line with a developmental psychopathology perspective, we contend that the most apt understanding of the etiology of school refusal invokes multiple pathways representing different combinations of risk factors and processes. See Heyne (2006) for an account of the various individual, family, school, and community factors and processes which have been associated with the development and maintenance of school refusal.

Just as there is no unified cognitive-behavioral theory, the cognitive-behavioral approach to therapy is not a unitary approach. CBT is an umbrella term for a broad range of cognitive and behavioral techniques that are employed in different permutations (Drinkwater, 2005) and with different parties involved in treatment (e.g., the young person, their parents, and school staff). As such, there is considerable flexibility in addressing the risk factors and processes associated with school refusal. The @school treatment program described in this chapter is based on the principles of CBT. Thus, intervention with the young person and with the parents focuses upon thoughts, feelings, and behaviors. Intervention conducted jointly with the young person and parents focuses upon family communication and problem-solving skills. School consultation is also guided by the principles of CBT. Support for the utility of the various cognitive and behavioral interventions included in the @school treatment program comes from two randomized controlled trials (King et al., 1998; Last et al., 1998), two uncontrolled trials (Heyne et al., 2002; Heyne, Sauter, Van Widenfelt, Vermeiren, & Westenberg, 2011), one non-randomized comparative study (Blagg & Yule, 1984), two open clinical trials (Kearney & Silverman, 1990; Kennedy, 1965), a multiple baseline case series (Tolin, Whiting, Maltby et al., 2009), and many uncontrolled case studies (e.g., Chorpita, Albano, Heimberg, & Barlow, 1996; Mansdorf & Lukens, 1987; McNamara, 1988).

When implementing treatment with the young person and parents, the cognitive-behavioral clinician is mindful of processes characteristically associated with CBT, namely: collaboration in agenda-setting; providing a clear rationale when introducing a specific skill; making use of educational handouts; regularly checking out the client's understanding; engaging the client in self-monitoring (e.g., anxiety, depression, cognitions); facilitating collaborative problem-solving discussions; modeling skills; engaging clients in skills' rehearsal and providing positive and constructive feedback; and setting home tasks to strengthen and generalize skills learned in-session, and to gather information about progress to further inform treatment planning.

Several additional points about the implementation of the treatment program deserve mention. First, the treatment has been designed to increase effectiveness with adolescents. The clinician can utilize optional modules which have been included in the modularized treatment based on their relevance to school refusal in adolescence. The clinician working with an adolescent school refuser will also be mindful of adapting the manner in which CBT is delivered with adolescents vis-à-vis children, and with adolescents varying according to developmental level. The reader is referred to Sauter et al. (2009) for a discussion of ways in which to tailor the delivery of cognitive and behavioral therapeutic techniques with adolescents. Second, we recommend the use of a dual clinician model where possible, whereby one clinician works with the young person while another works with the parent(s). This model has practical advantages, such as a reduced need for the family to make twice as many visits to the clinic to see one clinician. It also serves important therapeutic functions. First, the clinician working with the young person may have a greater opportunity to establish a therapeutic alliance with him. Rather than seeing the clinician as aligned with the parents, the young person may perceive a greater alliance between himself and his clinician, thus facilitating openness and collaboration. Second, families benefit from the knowledge, expertise, and ideas of two clinicians and the clinicians have the opportunity to consult with and support each other.

Considering the role of empathy

The "T" in CBT can be seen as a reminder that CBT is about the implementation of cognitive and behavioral interventions within the context of a therapeutic alliance between the clinician and client. The quality of the therapeutic alliance is influenced by the clinician's ability to foster both a warm relationship and client participation. Empathy is a key ingredient for a warm relationship (Weersing & Brent, 2005) but it has received "remarkably little" discussion or research in the CBT literature (Thwaites & Bennett-Levy, 2007, p. 591).

Thwaites and Bennett-Levy (2007) help redress this shortcoming via their discussion of the nature and function of empathy in CBT, focusing on the key elements of empathic attunement, empathic stance, empathic communication, and empathy knowledge. Although their writing focuses on CBT with adults, there is no reason to believe that it is any less important for the field of CBT with young people. In fact, most young people participate in treatment because they are referred by others, so we could expect that empathy and its influence on the therapeutic alliance is even more important when working with young people. An indicator of the potential importance of the therapeutic alliance during CBT with young people is found in Kendall and Southam-Gerow's (1996) 2- to 5-year follow-up study of children and adolescents treated for anxiety. When asked to report on what was important for them during treatment, the most common response was the relationship with the clinician. More recently, Chiu, McLeod, Har, and Wood (2009) found that a stronger alliance early in treatment did not predict greater improvement in the anxiety symptoms of children and young adolescents following CBT. However, improvement in alliance over the course of treatment was associated with superior outcomes. Overall there is little research which points to the impact of the therapeutic alliance on the outcome of CBT for young people, but it seems that young people are more likely to complete treatment when a good therapeutic alliance is present (Manassis, 2009).

We believe that therapeutic empathy is highly important during all phases of CBT for school refusal. It is important from the outset (i.e., intake and assessment) because anxious and depressed school refusers have often come to regard themselves as "not normal" simply because they do not attend school regularly "like all the other kids do." The parents of school refusers are likely to have experienced a high degree of stress associated with the crisis-like presentation of school refusal and/or their inability to successfully resolve the problem of their own accord (Heyne & Rollings, 2002; Kearney, 2001). During the initial school consultation, an empathic stance towards the frustrations experienced by school staff can also help build a working alliance with this important treatment party.

Throughout treatment, CBT clinicians ask clients to engage in difficult and emotionally challenging tasks (Thwaites & Bennett-Levy, 2007), including CBT clinicians working with young people (Kendall & Ollendick, 2004). Because clients are asked to engage in such tasks, "therapeutic empathy becomes even more important" (Thwaites & Bennett-Levy, 2007, p. 592). In the behavioral treatment of anxiety and depression, emphasis is placed upon the difficult task of approaching rather than avoiding, or becoming active rather than withdrawing (Weersing, Gonzalez, Campo, & Lucas, 2008). Likewise, in the treatment of school refusal, emphasis is placed on the difficult and often emotionally challenging task of increasing school attendance, underscoring the importance of therapeutic empathy. Cognitive interventions also need to be implemented in the context of a warm therapeutic relationship (Beck, Rush, Shaw, & Emery, 1979). For example, the clinician will ideally show her understanding of the strong feelings associated with the school refuser's cognitions as they are detected, and respond empathically when making links between thoughts, feelings, and behaviors (Friedberg & McClure, 2002). Empathic communication of this kind relies upon the clinician's empathic attitude and attunement, together with her knowledge of the important function of empathic communication (Thwaites & Bennett-Levy, 2007).

Conducting assessment

A comprehensive multi-source and multi-method assessment provides the broad range of information needed to develop and test hypotheses about the development and maintenance of a specific case of school refusal, and thus to identify the most important treatment targets. Assessment typically incorporates clinical-behavioral interviews with the young person and their parents (e.g., Heyne & Rollings, 2002); diagnostic interviews with both parties to develop a profile of the nature and severity of difficulties for the young person; self-reports of emotional, social, behavioral, and family functioning via questionnaires and self-monitoring procedures; parent and teacher reports of the young person's functioning; parent reports of their own functioning and of family functioning; a review of the young person's school attendance record to detect non-attendance patterns that may signal maintenance factors (e.g., avoidance of a specific class or teacher; poor attendance following paternal access visits); consultation with school staff with regard to the young person's social, emotional, behavioral, and academic functioning at school, and to determine whether any of the young person's school-related fears and anxieties are reality based (e.g., bullying); consultation with other involved professionals (e.g., pediatrician; school guidance officer) to elicit useful information and to facilitate the implementation of a consistent management plan across all involved parties; and achievement and intelligence testing as indicated. An overview of relevant self-report and other-report measures can be found in Heyne and King (2004) and Kearney (2001).

Several instruments have been developed specifically for the school refusal population. The Self-Efficacy Questionnaire for School Situations (SEQ-SS; Heyne, King, Tonge et al., 1998) is a self-report measure in which the young person indicates the strength of his belief that he could or could not cope with situations associated with school attendance (e.g., school work; being asked about absence from school). To obtain further cognitive data that may be missed via a standardized measure like the SEQ-SS, Heyne and Rollings (2002) developed a Self-Statement Assessment – Youth Form. The young person is engaged in a think-aloud task that encourages a continuous monologue via a variation on the free association method (Genest & Turk, 1981). Responses derived from stimuli (e.g., "going to school in the morning"; "being away from your parents during the school day") are recorded, transcribed, and analyzed with respect to valence (positive, negative, neutral) and thinking style (e.g., overgeneralization; underestimation of the ability to cope) in order to identify targets for cognitively focused interventions. The Self-Efficacy Questionnaire for Responding to School Attendance Problems (SEQ-RSAP; Heyne, Maric, & Westenberg, 2007) is a new measure designed to assess parents' self-efficacy for dealing calmly and constructively with a child's difficulty attending school. It shows promising convergent validity and good temporal stability (Lavooi, 2010). The Self-Statement Assessment – Parent Form (Heyne & Rollings, 2002) can also be used to elicit parents' cognitions in response to stimuli such as "who ought to be most responsible for the young person's attendance at school" and "how quickly a young person should return to school after an absence due to school refusal." Finally, the School Refusal Assessment Scale – Revised (SRAS-R; Kearney, 2002) provides a descriptive functional analysis of school refusal behavior (school refusal and truancy). Parent and child reports are combined to determine which of four functional conditions (i.e., reasons for the maintenance of school refusal behavior) is strongest: (1) avoidance of school-related stimuli that provoke a sense of general negative affectivity; (2) escape from aversive social and/or evaluative situations at school; (3) pursuit of attention from significant others; or (4) pursuit of tangible reinforcement outside the school setting. As noted by Kearney (Kearney, 2001, 2006; Kearney & Albano, 2004), the SRAS-R is one element of a more comprehensive assessment process. When used in conjunction with other assessment information it may be useful for generating and (dis)confirming hypotheses based on learning theory about the maintenance of school refusal.

Following Blagg (1987), we spend considerable time conducting separate interviews with the young person and parents, allowing each the opportunity to freely discuss their views. We refrain from asking the young person about reasons for nonattendance too early in the process. Often, school refusers have been asked about why they have difficulty going to school by a host of well-meaning people, leading to increased frustration or resistance when unable to identify contributing factors. In two parent families, considerable emphasis is placed upon both parents attending assessment sessions. This yields richer information about the functioning of the young

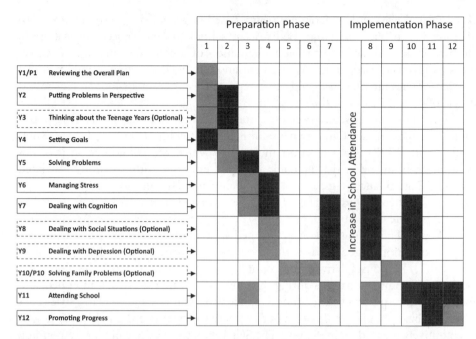

Figure 21.1 Guide for sequencing and pacing modules with the young person. (Black squares indicate the common timing of module introduction and continuation; grey squares indicate possible introduction or continuation of a module.)

person and family and it underscores from the outset the importance of both parents participating in treatment.

Treatment Delivery

In this section we describe a modularized CBT for school refusal. The selection, sequencing, and pacing of modules is based upon an individualized treatment plan. Modules are implemented with the young person, the parents, and pivotal school staff. Two modules are implemented jointly with the young person and parents, and these are presented in the section "Modules implemented with the young person". A guide to the common sequencing and pacing of modules with young people is presented in Figure 21.1, and the parent equivalent is presented in Figure 21.2.

Approximately one half of treatment is dedicated to preparing all parties for an increase in school attendance – the Preparation Phase. In this phase sessions are ideally conducted twice a week with the young person and parents to consolidate skill acquisition while not unnecessarily delaying an increase in attendance. The increase in attendance often occurs in the fourth week of treatment, but it may occur sooner (e.g., in cases where optional Modules are not indicated). Increase in attendance may occur somewhat later in cases requiring more attention to the optional modules, or when the cognitive developmental level of the young person calls for the clinician to work at a slower pace. The Implementation Phase commences with the planned increase in school attendance. During this phase treatment sessions are commonly held on a weekly basis to support skill implementation and to problem-solve arising difficulties.

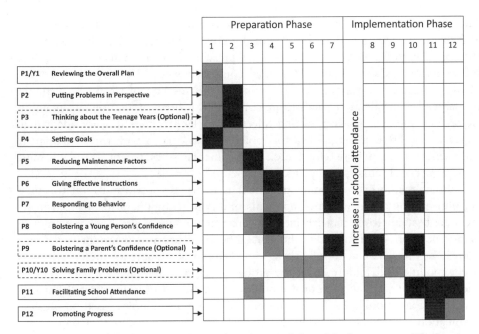

Figure 21.2 Guide for sequencing and pacing modules with the parents. (Black squares indicate the common timing of module introduction and continuation; grey squares indicate possible introduction or continuation of a module.)

As indicated in Figures 21.1 and 21.2, material associated with numerous modules will be included in the plan for a specific session (often three or four modules per session). An exception is when optional Module Y10/P10 is implemented, given the time that is needed to conduct communication and problem-solving training with the young person and parents together. Modules introduced in the Preparation Phase are also likely to be re-visited during sessions in the Implementation Phase. Treatment typically comprises 10–14 sessions with the young person and 10–14 sessions with the parents. Treatment is usually longer in cases of adolescent school refusal (i.e., closer to 14 sessions than 10 sessions) given that: (a) two optional modules are routinely indicated for cases of adolescent school refusal (Modules Y3/P3 and Y10/P10); and (b) the other two optional modules for young people (Modules Y8 and Y9) are more likely to be employed with adolescents than with children due to the rise in depression and in social anxiety during this developmental period. Sessions are commonly 1 hour long, except for joint sessions focused on family communication and problem-solving which are commonly 1.5 hours.

Treatment planning

The need to develop a sound strategy for determining treatment-relevant differences among school refusers was underscored in Burke and Silverman's (1987) review of models for classifying school refusal subtypes. Subsequently, Kearney and Silverman (1990) proposed and tested a functional analytic model of school refusal behavior, aimed at helping clinicians classify, assess, and treat this heterogeneous population.

The SRAS-R (Kearney, 2002; see "Conducting assessment") embodies the functional analytic model. Different combinations of cognitive and behavioral interventions with the young person and/or their parents are prescribed on the basis of the SRAS-R subscale scores. Case studies and a small controlled study (Kearney & Silverman, 1999) provide some support for the utility of this method of treatment planning but larger-scale evaluation needs to be conducted. Moreover, the four maintaining factors encompassed in Kearney and Silverman's (1990) model do not adequately represent the broader range of factors potentially associated with the development and maintenance of school refusal (e.g., developmental issues; parent attitudes toward managing school refusal; family functioning).

Another method for planning treatment is to use a case formulation to guide decision-making about which components of a multi-component manualized treatment are best employed in a specific case. Treatment components – often referred to as modules – are incorporated in the manual because theory supports their relevance in treating the problem. Ideally, there is also empirical support for the effectiveness of the module in helping to treat the problem. Standard modules are held to be of relevance to all cases and optional modules are relevant to specific cases. Clinicians make decisions about the selection of optional treatment modules based on the case formulation. The case formulation also guides decision-making about the sequencing and pacing of modules. As an example of the sequencing of modules in the @school program, Module Y7 (Dealing with cognition) might be scheduled early in treatment when the case formulation indicates that unhelpful cognition is a prominent maintaining factor and that the young person has the cognitive capacity to respond to the demands of cognitive therapy. As an example of variation in the pacing of modules, the clinician working with a parent who displays some competence in the planned ignoring of their child's inappropriate behavior may plan to devote less time to discussing and practicing this particular contingency management skill when implementing Module P7 (Responding to behavior). The case formulation method for selecting, sequencing, and pacing the modules of a modular manualized treatment was employed in the TADS study of treatment for adolescent depression (Rogers, Reinecke, & Curry, 2005) and is the method advocated by Chorpita (2007) for the treatment of anxiety in children and adolescents.

Given the complex array of factors potentially associated with a young person's refusal to attend school, we advocate the case formulation method for systematically planning individualized treatment. Qualitative and quantitative information derived from the multi-source and multi-method assessment is drawn upon to develop the case formulation. In the case formulation the clinician firstly specifies the central problems for the young person as well as problems experienced by the parents. Attention is then given to the factors hypothesized to be associated with the development of the presenting problems (predisposing and precipitating factors) and with the maintenance of the problems (perpetuating factors). These hypotheses address individual factors (e.g., problems with making friends; academic difficulties), family factors (e.g., parental anxiety/depression; incidental reinforcement of non-attendance; parent-child conflict), school factors (e.g., conflict with the teacher; inadequate policy or response to schoolyard bullying), and community factors (e.g., violence in the vicinity of the school; conflicting professional advice to parents about the management of school refusal). Targets for treatment are identified based on the hypotheses about the development and maintenance of the problem (e.g., a target is to help the young person manage depression). These targets are linked with specific treatment modules indicated for such targets (e.g., optional Module Y9 to address depression). The formulation specifies potential treatment obstacles together with possible responses in the face of such obstacles.

The positive qualities (protective factors) of the individual, family, school, and community are also specified in the case formulation and drawn upon when planning treatment in order to facilitate progress (Rogers et al., 2005). Rohde, Seeley, Kaufman, Clarke, and Stice (2006) found that the presence of coping skills at pre-treatment predicted faster recovery among depressed adolescents participating in CBT than among depressed adolescents participating in a placebo treatment condition. It was concluded that "CBT works best when it can capitalize on an adolescent's existing coping skills" (p. 86). Focusing on a client's former and current coping skills as well as their personal qualities may benefit treatment by enhancing self-efficacy and a sense of self-worth.

The hypothesis-forming aspect of case formulation is an ongoing process, from the time of referral until the last contact. As more information becomes available, hypotheses are confirmed or disconfirmed and new hypotheses are developed, calling for refinement of the treatment plan. In the TADS study, clinicians were encouraged to review progress midway through the acute stage of treatment and to adjust the treatment plan as needed (Rogers et al., 2005). Because of the nature of school refusal treatment, whereby increased school attendance is planned for half-way through treatment, progress reviews are recommended at one-third and two-thirds of the way through treatment (i.e., shortly before and shortly after the planned increase in attendance). At these points the two clinicians (and a supervisor if available) review the progress made, revise the case formulation in the light of new information, and determine whether adjustments need to be made to the current treatment plan with respect to the selection, sequencing, and pacing of treatment modules. Preliminary support for the efficacy of the case formulation method of planning treatment is found in the positive treatment outcomes observed in three school refusal treatment outcome studies in which the method was used (Heyne et al., 2002, 2011; King et al., 1998).

Modules Implemented with the Young Person

Reviewing the overall plan (Y1/P1)

A simplified version of the case formulation is shared with the young person and parents. This includes summative feedback about the assessment results and how the results connect with key hypotheses about the development and maintenance of school refusal and associated problems. Attention is also given to the range of protective factors noted during assessment. During this module the clinician creates a forum in which a number of objectives can be pursued: (1) to promote a shared understanding of the problems and the related targets for treatment; (2) to reinforce family members' sense that the treatment plan is based on the clinician's thorough understanding of the problems; and (3) to determine whether there are any changes since assessment which should be taken into account in the formulation and treatment plan. Presentation of the case formulation often involves the use of visual aids as well as sensitive reframing of presenting problems (e.g., "a hiccup in the young person's educational career"). Subsequently, the clinician invites the young person and parents to offer feedback. Discussion is facilitated around points of agreement, disagreement, misunderstanding, and new information, so that all parties can reach some consensus on a revised formulation. The objectives and process associated with this module reflect the collaborative problem-solving approach inherent to CBT, and can foster family members' motivation for treatment. The module can be implemented rather quickly (e.g., 20 minutes) but the length of time will vary based on the extent to which the parents and young person understand and (dis)agree with the formulation.

Putting problems in perspective (Y2)

After reviewing the case formulation together with the young person and parents, work commences with the young person alone. At first, the clinician may explore and empathically respond to the young person's experience of reviewing the case formulation. Then the clinician engages the young person in a psychoeducational process to further promote their readiness for CBT. The provision of information about psychological problems and treatment serves to correct misperceptions and to fill information gaps (Taylor, 2000). As noted by Kearney (2005), psychoeducation helps to build and maintain rapport, offer encouragement, enhance motivation, and ease tension. The clinician's psychoeducational work may be guided by the three main objectives of the module: "normalizing", "forecasting", and "linking".

First, the clinician helps to normalize the problem of school refusal (and anxiety or depression) by providing information about prevalence, variability in presentation, and the cognitive-behavioral conceptualization of why such problems exist (i.e., the links between thinking, feeling, and doing; the consequences of avoidance/approach in anxiety and of withdrawal/re-activation in depression). Normalizing the young person's difficulties may help reduce "self-downing" and secondary emotional problems (e.g., anxiety about anxiety), improve self-esteem, enhance family functioning as a result of reduced blaming, and enhance treatment compliance (Birmaher & Ollendick, 2004). Second, based on knowledge of the scientific literature, the clinician can forecast the potential positive outcomes of treatment in the short-term and long-term. Third, the clinician links the young person's problems with the indicated treatment modules, to enhance his understanding of the relevance of treatment. The young person and parents were already introduced to a general rationale for treatment during Module Y1/P1, but in the current module the clinician provides more information about how specific treatment components can alleviate specific difficulties experienced by the young person. The process of treatment can also be discussed (e.g., a skills-building Preparation Phase precedes a planned increase in attendance; the clinician serves as "coach" as the young person learns ways to deal with difficulties; between-session practice tasks help the young person to strengthen skills and effect desired changes). Because normalizing, forecasting, and linking involve a considerable amount of information, an interactive process is advisable (e.g., posing questions; inviting comments; self-disclosing; reviewing information sheets together).

Thinking about the teenage years (Optional, Y3)

When conducting treatment with school-refusing adolescents it is helpful to explore the impact that a range of developmental transitions and tasks ("changes and challenges") may have (had) on the presenting problems (e.g., the complexity of the secondary school environment relative to the primary school environment; worry about physical appearance; frustration with parents who provide little opportunity for adolescent decision-making). Sensitive exploration of the young person's experience of adolescence serves several purposes. It can enhance the young person's sense of being understood by the clinician, strengthening the therapeutic alliance. It may provide additional information for the case formulation and thus for treatment planning (e.g., the need to encourage school staff to consider special arrangements to help the young person feel more comfortable at school; cognitive therapy targeting cognitions related to self; greater emphasis on family communication and problem-solving). It also informs the need for psychoeducation to normalize difficulties associated with adolescence (e.g., adolescence is characterized by changes and challenges which are not always easy to deal with; increased prevalence of social anxiety in adolescence; increased parent–adolescent conflict about rules and expectations). This module is often conducted during the first or second session, and it may be revisited as developmentally related issues arise throughout treatment.

Setting goals (Y4)

Goal-setting underscores the collaborative nature of CBT, it suggests the possibility for change, it provides structure and focus in treatment, and it facilitates the evaluation of progress. A distinction can be made between goal-setting as a process in treatment and as the content of treatment. It is a process in treatment when the clinician helps the young person consider goals related to the presenting problems (e.g., feel more confident with other kids at school) and more general goals for themselves (e.g., being allowed to use the computer more). While the central goals of CBT for school refusal are a reduction in emotional distress and the resumption of regular school attendance, these may best be achieved by also giving attention to general goals that have more immediate appeal for the young person. Young people rarely initiate treatment, and any goals they have may be different to the goals of those who refer them. Thus a collaborative goal-setting process may help avoid non-compliance and discontinuation of treatment (Ralph, 1996). The clinician may need to creatively link the young person's general goals with the central goals of treatment (e.g., by advocating on the young person's behalf for parents to allow more time on the computer in exchange for efforts and achievements associated with school attendance).

Clinical experience suggests that some young people will nominate school-related goals when encouraged to think about the goals they have. In other cases the clinician will need to gently but clearly introduce school attendance to the agenda, modeling confidence in the young person's ability to learn how to cope with school attendance. At this point the clinician can explain that increased school attendance is usually scheduled around the third or fourth week of treatment, with sufficient time beforehand for the young person, parents, and school staff to become well-prepared. The clinician can also explain that the young person will be consulted on issues such as their preferred type of attendance plan (early part-time increase versus early full-time increase), which day of the week might be easiest for the first day back at school, and so on (Module Y11).

Sometimes the young person is hesitant to identify goals related to the presenting problems. This may occur when anxious avoidance provides relief and decreases motivation for change, or when depression-related cognition inhibits the capacity to imagine an alternative future. The clinician may need to address motivation for change by, for example, helping the young person develop a list of the ways in which avoidance has a negative impact on their life and a list of the ways in which life could be better without anxious avoidance. If a young person is generally resistant towards involvement in treatment the clinician may need to pay even greater attention to the general goals of the young person. It can also be helpful to acknowledge the normalcy of not being highly goal-focused in childhood and adolescence, and to reframe the notion of goal-setting (e.g., "getting-what-I-want plans"; "having a dream with a plan").

Goal-setting is the content of treatment when the young person receives information about setting and achieving goals (e.g., SMART goals are *S*pecific, *M*easurable, *A*ction-based, *R*ealistic, *T*ruly meaningful; short-term versus longer-term goals; dealing with potential obstacles; monitoring progress) and when he is provided with opportunities for guided practice in goal-setting.

Solving problems (Y5)

Failure to deal effectively with stressful situations has been associated with the development of school refusal, and improved problem-solving capacity is held to be a key treatment target (Place, Hulsmeier, Davis, & Taylor, 2002). Problem-solving is also regarded as a core component of CBT for the treatment of internalizing problems in young people (Weersing et al., 2008). When the young person is helped to develop or hone skills in independent problem-solving, problems can be faced with a greater sense of confidence and competence, the range of solutions available to the young person is broadened, and as noted by Weersing et al. (2008), chosen solutions can lead to a resolution of the problem or a lowering of arousal. This benefits the young person's functioning in general, it can enhance flexible thinking and decision-making, and it may help reduce unhelpful thinking such as catastrophizing (Seligman, 1995) or rumination.

After collaboratively exploring the strengths and soft-spots in the young person's current approach to solving problems, the clinician outlines four key skills involved in systematic problem-solving (problem definition, generation of alternatives, evaluation and decision making, and solution implementation and verification; Bell & D'Zurilla, 2009; Kendall, Chansky, Kane et al., 1992). It is usually easier for young people to learn and recall the skills when they are linked to a meaningful acronym (e.g., IPOD = *I*dentify the problem, *P*lay around with solutions; *O*pt for a good one, *D*evelop an action plan; WWW.problem-solved = *W*hat is the problem?, *W*hat are some options for solving the problem?, *W*hich will I choose?, Is the *problem-solved*?). These skills are modeled and rehearsed, using hypothetical problems as well as problems relevant for the young person. Throughout treatment the clinician fosters the young person's use of their problem-solving skills to address arising problems (e.g., inability to complete a treatment-related home-task) and to prepare for difficulties which might arise as the young person increases their attendance at school (e.g., emotional distress; questions from peers; teasing; social isolation; worrying about parents; study problems).

In some cases cognitive interventions may need to be employed to modify maladaptive attitudes towards problems so that the young person is more likely to make good use of problem-solving skills. Training in a positive problem orientation has been shown to substantially improve the efficacy of problem-solving training with depressed adults (Bell & D'Zurilla, 2009). A positive problem orientation is reflected in the following attitudes: seeing problems as opportunities, believing problems are solvable, having self-efficacy for solving problems, and being prepared to spend time and effort to solve problems.

Managing stress (Y6)

Relaxation is an important emotion-focused coping strategy for school refusers. According to Place and colleagues (2002), one of the coping mechanisms which school refusers lack is the ability to find ways to relax in potentially stressful situations. Like problem-solving, its cognitively-oriented counterpart, relaxation is regarded as a core component of CBT for internalizing problems in young people (Weersing et al., 2008). Via relaxation young people can manage the stress (negative emotional responses and physiological arousal) associated with problem situations. This is especially helpful when the problem itself cannot be solved because it is not under the young person's control (Lohaus & Klein-Hessling, 2003). In the case of school refusal, the young person does not have control over the legal requirement to attend school, and relaxation is a skill which he can use to manage the stress that occurs in attendance-related situations (e.g., getting ready to go to school; taking tests; giving a class talk; being around other children at school). Relaxation can also be used to manage stress arising from day-to-day activities or negative life events, and it may be employed as the anxiety-inhibitor during a desensitization procedure (Module Y11).

After exploring the young person's symptoms, sources, and responses to stress, and reinforcing the positive ways in which he currently manages stress, the clinician introduces relaxation as a stress management technique. Mirroring Weersing et al. (2008), the various relaxation procedures are framed as tools to relax the body (i.e., breathing retraining; progressive muscle relaxation training), to relax the mind (i.e., autogenic relaxation training; guided imagery), and to relax the world around us (soothing activities such as listening to music or taking a warm shower). Special attention is given to the tools to relax the body and mind, because with sufficient practice and pairing with a cue (e.g., saying the word "relax" as breathing out; intermittently tensing and relaxing the dominant hand), the young person can efficiently induce a sense of relaxation. The transportability of cue-controlled relaxation increases the likelihood that the young person can quickly respond to emotional and physiological signs of stress as they begin to appear. After a brief demonstration of the various tools for relaxing the body and the mind, the young person may choose the tool(s) regarded as having greater appeal and effect. These will become the focus of in-session and between-session practice. Providing choice facilitates motivation to engage in sufficient practice to the point of being able to induce cue-controlled relaxation. An overview of various relaxation scripts is presented in Heyne, King, and Ollendick (2004).

The module is a standard module because many young people can benefit from developing or honing skills in stress management. However, the pacing of the module is guided by the case formulation. For example, more time is devoted to practicing relaxation when there are frequent physiological responses to stress (e.g., headache; stomach-ache) or when severe anxiety indicates the value of employing systematic desensitization prior to the planned increase in attendance.

Dealing with cognition (Y7)

Unhelpful cognition has been linked theoretically with the development and maintenance of school refusal (e.g., Kennard et al., 2005; Mansdorf & Lukens, 1987; McNamara, 1988; Okuyama et al., 1999; Place, Hulsmeier, Davis, & Taylor, 2000). Further, in a recent empirical study, Maric (2012) found that school refusers reported significantly more negative cognition relative to a control group. It was suggested that negative thoughts of personal failure and the tendency to overgeneralize negative events contribute to the maintenance of school refusal and are two types of cognition which may need to be targeted during treatment. In an earlier study which examined the coping strategies of school refusers in the light of normative data, school refusers were found to be less able to maintain a positive outlook in the face of adversity (Place et al., 2002). Cognitive interventions thus seem to be a potentially important component of treatment for school refusal. Cognitive therapy is aimed at helping the young person modify unhelpful cognition and discover and employ more helpful cognition in order to effect a change in affect and behavior, thus helping to mobilize him towards school attendance.

The 7D mnemonic device (Heyne & Rollings, 2002) helps clinicians attend to key processes when conducting cognitive therapy: *D1 = Describing* key components of the cognitive therapy model to the point that the young person understands and tacitly accepts the model (e.g., the notion of self-talk; the impact that self-talk can have on feeling and behaving, for better and for worse; how we can influence the impact of self-talk); *D2 = Detecting* cognition (e.g., discussing, imagining, or role-playing situations [A's] associated with negative feelings [C's] in order to ascertain pertinent cognition [B's]; cartoons which depict problem-specific situations and include empty thought bubbles to be filled in by the young person; self-statement assessment; questionnaires assessing cognition; a diary for monitoring A's, B's, and C's); *D3 = Determining* which cognition to target (e.g., based on the frequency, interference, and believability of different B's); *D4 = Discrediting* targeted cognition (e.g., scientific analysis; alternative explanations; probability analysis; helpfulness analysis; third person projection; logical analysis; responsibility pie; continuum technique; behavioral experiments); *D5 = Discovering* helpful cognition (e.g., reviewing a list; collaborative brainstorming; reframing); *D6 = Doing* in-session and between-session practice tasks (e.g., cognitive rehearsal in the form of a "brain-game" [Seligman, 1995]; developing and using coping cards); and *D7 = Discussing* the outcome of the practice tasks.

Developmental sensitivity is highly important when conducting cognitive therapy. The clinician makes decisions about the selection and pacing of cognitive therapy techniques based upon formal and informal assessment of the young person's capacities. Even though adolescence is the period in which many of the cognitive capacities relevant to CBT are acquired, it is unhelpful to conclude that all adolescents are able to successfully engage in all cognitive therapeutic techniques (Sauter et al., 2009). Lower capacity suggests that D4 techniques would be paced slowly, and may even be omitted in favor of the less-demanding techniques associated with D5 (Stallard, 2005). Some young people require preparation for engagement in cognitive therapy in the form of emotional education techniques aimed at increasing the capacity for recognizing feelings, distinguishing between feelings of different type and intensity, and discussing feelings. Occasionally it is necessary to help the young person gain practice in distinguishing between thoughts, feelings, and actions via a worksheet inviting differentiation between thought-related sentences, feeling-related sentences, and doing-related sentences (Quakley, Reynolds, & Coker, 2004). When the young person is able to identify and articulate their thoughts and feelings with minimal clinician guidance, the clinician might spend less time helping the young person learn techniques for identifying unhelpful thinking and more time on complex discrediting strategies (Kingery, Roblek, Suveg, Grover, Sherrill, & Bergman, 2006), including Socratic questioning (Siqueland, Rynn, & Diamond, 2005).

The scheduling of this module is guided by the extent to which the cognitive component of the case formulation suggests that cognitive interventions are important for the treatment of school refusal, and by the young person's readiness for cognitive therapy interventions. The extent to which the module is implemented throughout treatment is guided by the pace at which the young person is able to acquire and employ selected cognitive interventions.

Dealing with social situations (Optional, Y8)

Schools are inherently social environments and are regarded developmentally as the second milieu after the family (Buitelaar et al., 1994). It can thus be expected that social-related problems would be associated with the development or maintenance of school refusal. Between 5 and 65% of school refusers in clinic-referred samples have been found to meet diagnostic criteria for social phobia (Heyne et al., 2002, 2011; Hoshino et al., 1987; King et al., 1998; Last & Strauss, 1990; McShane et al., 2001). Among a community sample of school refusers, just 3% met criteria for social phobia (Egger et al., 2003). However, 28% were shy with peers, 29% were bullied or teased, and 19% had difficulty making friends because of withdrawal. Each of these problems was significantly more prevalent among the school refusers than among young people without school refusal.

This optional module incorporates treatment components to address social-related difficulties that may be a cause, consequence, or correlate of school refusal, anxiety, or depression (e.g., difficulty forming and strengthening friendships; inability to deal assertively with bullying; anxiety about answering peers' or teachers' questions about absence from school). The problem-solving skills honed during Module Y5 are drawn upon as the clinician and young person generate ideas for how to respond to targeted social situations, evaluate these ideas, and select a preferred response. The clinician models variations on the response before engaging the young person in practice of the response. Across successive practices we aim to gradually increase the extent to which the social situation is realistic or challenging. The young person's success in responding to realistic and challenging practices strengthens self-efficacy for responding to the range of reactions that may occur in real-life social situations. Micro-skills (e.g., body language to show interest in another), macro-skills (e.g., keeping conversations going; assertiveness), and social-cognitive skills (e.g., perspective-taking; gauging the receptiveness of another) are targeted as needed. Consideration should be given to peer involvement, especially when working with adolescents because of the important role that peers play in the development of their psychosocial skills (Holmbeck, O'Mahar, Abad, Colder, & Updegrove, 2006). Unhelpful social-related cognitions (e.g., "they'll think I'm stupid") are addressed via the cognitive interventions included in Module Y7.

Dealing with depression (Optional, Y9)

A substantial proportion of school-refusing young people experience depression-related symptoms and disorders (e.g., Baker & Wills, 1978; Martin et al., 1999; McShane et al., 2001), and this is especially true for adolescents relative to children (Baker & Wills, 1978; Kearney, 1993). The presence of depression is held to interfere with the ability to participate in CBT for school refusal (Bernstein, Borchardt, Perwien et al., 2000). This module contains treatment components aimed at helping school refusers manage depression-related behaviors (e.g., withdrawal) and cognitions (e.g., "there's no point in trying to go back to school") that are likely to interfere with the effectiveness of CBT for school refusal. If depression was identified as a treatment target, psychoeducation around depression will have been addressed during Module Y2. During psychoeducation, personalized "downward and upward spirals" (Clarke, Lewinsohn, & Hops, 1990) may be developed to make the link between: (a) depressed mood, depressogenic behaviors, and depressogenic cognitions; as well as the link between (b) activity scheduling, dealing with depressive cognition, and a positive change in mood.

Activity scheduling is a "hallmark of behavioral treatment for depression" and has received empirical support as a stand-alone intervention (Kanter, Manos, Bowe, Baruch, Busch, & Rusch, 2010, p. 612). It aims to increase the depressed person's engagement in pleasurable and goal-directed activities to increase response-contingent positive reinforcement and thereby reduce negative mood. The problem-solving approach addressed in Module Y5 is used during activity scheduling with the young person. First, the problem is identified (i.e., a low frequency of activities which could positively influence mood). Second, the clinician and young person collaboratively develop a list of activities that may have a positive impact upon mood. This can be achieved in various ways: by reviewing the results of a self-monitoring exercise whereby the young person recorded activities engaged in and the impact they had upon mood; recalling activities which the young person used to do and enjoyed doing during times when he was not depressed; and by considering activities that others seem to enjoy and that might also be enjoyable for the young person (perhaps facilitated via review of the Pleasant Events Schedule; MacPhillamy & Lewinsohn, 1982). Third, the clinician and young person evaluate the activities in the list according to several key criteria (e.g., affordable; achievable; acceptable to parents) in order to select activities which can be introduced in activity plans. Parents may be encouraged to support the young person's engagement in the activities.

Unhelpful cognition linked to depressed mood is addressed as described in Module Y7. Implementation of the 7Ds takes account of the young person's depressed mood. During D1 for example, the depressed school refuser may find it difficult to believe that it is possible to change one's thinking, because of a tendency to attribute negative experiences to stable causes. The clinician can empathize with the young person's sense of hopelessness and explain that this style of thinking is expectable when someone is depressed. During D2 the clinician may need to be more directive if the young person has difficulty detecting cognition due to their depressive feelings (Friedberg & McClure, 2002). The young person may also have difficulty disclosing their thoughts for fear of feeling even more depressed. In this case the clinician might explore the thoughts associated with non-disclosure and help the young person disclose thoughts and feelings in a more graduated fashion (Friedberg & McClure, 2002). Decision-making about which cognition to focus upon (i.e., D3) can be guided by cognitive theories of depression and supporting research (e.g., selective abstraction is a common cognitive error; Maric, Heyne, Van Widenfelt, & Westenberg, 2011).

Solving family problems (Optional, Y10/P10)

In adolescent school refusal, family conflict has been identified as one of the major stressors associated with school refusal onset (McShane et al., 2001). Family stress and conflict is also likely to be a consequence of school refusal (Kearney & Bensaheb, 2006; McAnanly, 1986), and this may be especially true in adolescence if the young person's ideas about returning to school clash with the parents' ideas. According to Valles and Oddy (1984), the resolution of family conflict is a crucial factor in the treatment of school refusal. This conclusion was based on their observation that more conflict was present in the families of non-successfully treated cases of school refusal relative to successfully treated cases. Insufficient independence is another family-related factor that has been noted among school refusers (e.g., Hansen et al., 1998; Place et al., 2000, 2002; Place, Hulsmeier, Brownrigg, & Soulsby, 2005).

As would be expected, family-based interventions for school refusal have been recommended by those adopting a family systems perspective (e.g., Bryce & Baird, 1986). Family-based interventions have also been recommended by those who more typically employ a cognitive-behavioral approach to treating school refusal (i.e., Bernstein et al., 1999; Kearney & Silverman, 1995). Kearney and Silverman (1995) suggested that communication training and problem-solving are important for families characterized by conflict or detachment. Bernstein and colleagues (1999) suggested that the successful treatment of adolescent school refusal requires helping adolescents and parents in disengaged and rigid families to become more connected and flexible. The alteration of family interaction patterns is also regarded as important in the treatment of adolescent anxiety, with the aim of reducing parental overprotection and psychological control and facilitating the development of adolescent autonomy (Siqueland et al., 2005). Likewise, communication training and problem-solving are regarded as key components of treatment for adolescent depression (Restifo & Bögels, 2009).

Helping the family of an adolescent school refuser to hone and employ skills for effective communication and problem-solving may help to redress family-based factors that have been associated with the development or maintenance of school refusal (e.g., conflict; detachment/disengagement; rigidity/insufficient independence), anxiety, or depression. The skills are also directly relevant to the process of increasing school attendance. The parents and adolescent can more calmly and confidently discuss the process of increasing attendance. Reduced conflict and tension during such discussions may increase the adolescent's willingness and ability to follow through with plans for attending school.

The clinician engages the parents and adolescent in a review of their current strengths and soft-spots in communicating with each other, making decisions, and dealing with problem situations. Targets for effective communication are discussed (e.g., active listening; I-statements to express feelings, needs, and ideas), examples are provided via modeling and by drawing attention to spontaneous occurrences of effective communication, and family members are engaged in practice with the clinician, or directly with each other. Positive and constructive feedback is offered by the clinician and solicited from family members. Subsequently, family problem-solving is introduced as a systematic method via which families can respond to the changes that occur as children grow up (harking back to Modules Y3/P3), reduce conflict and tension, and ultimately "meet more of the needs of more of the people, more of the time." Because the young person has already learned the key steps in individual problem-solving (Module Y5), he may be invited to explain the steps to his parents. The clinician[5] introduces additional points unique to family problem-solving (e.g., the problem needs to be defined in such a way that all can agree that it is a problem for them). To gain practice, the family is engaged in solving a meaningful but not overly conflictual problem. The clinician provides prompts and reinforcement, ensures balanced participation of all family members, and aims to ensure that the family is able to achieve all steps of the problem-solving process during their first practice. Depending on the speed of skill acquisition and use, the clinician sets a home task to discuss and solve an issue related to school attendance, or to engage in further practice of communication skills. In the next session the family is engaged in further problem-solving of school attendance issues and the clinician fades her in-session prompts. Exemplary school attendance issues addressed by the family include: which school to attend; the ideal day of the week for increasing school attendance; evening-morning sleeping routines during the week versus in the weekend; and the best way for parents to provide support.

This is an optional module which is typically indicated for the treatment of adolescent school refusal. Pacing of the module varies according to the extent to which family factors are likely to be associated with the young person's school refusal and the rate at which family members acquire and employ the skills. Preferably, three sessions are held with the young person and parents together. The first is scheduled around session 5, to allow sufficient time for the respective clinicians to independently

---

[5]When working with two clinicians in the treatment of school refusal (one working with the young person and another with the parents), it is customary that both clinicians be involved in these family sessions. In effect, both treatment parties have their own 'support person' during family problem-solving, and clinicians are better placed to ensure balanced participation.

build a good therapeutic alliance with the young person or parents. The second session is scheduled as the very next session in order to explore the outcome of the family-related home task and to progress family discussion of important issues associated with school attendance. The third family session usually occurs after the planned increase in attendance to review and facilitate communication and problem-solving around arising issues.

Attending school (Y11)

A central component of CBT for school refusal is of course the development and implementation of a plan for the young person to increase school attendance. In cases involving anxiety, the increase in school attendance may be conceptualized as exposure, whether it be exposure to anxiety-provoking aspects of school or exposure to separation from parents. In cases involving depression, the increase in attendance may be conceptualized as behavioral activation. Collectively, exposure and activation have been regarded as engagement (Weersing et al., 2008). The notion of engagement befits the work done with anxious and/or depressed school refusers to help them increase their school attendance. Other therapeutic processes are also likely to be active when school attendance is increased, such as a reduction in positive reinforcement of school refusal, increased self-efficacy for facing situations associated with school attendance, and the modification of misperceptions about attending school.

Drawing on the problem-solving approach, the clinician helps the young person decide whether he would like to work towards a part-time or full-time increase in attendance. A part-time increase is often planned when anxiety is high, general activity levels are low, absence from school has been long-standing, self-efficacy is low, or misperceptions are firmly held. Under such circumstances the young person's motivation to attempt an early full-time return is usually low. The young person's preference is communicated to parents (Module P11) and school staff (Module S2) and they are encouraged to support the plan (e.g., parents may need to be available to pick their child up from school after he or she has attended for just 2 hours as planned). Attendance plans will vary considerably from one school refuser to the next. One young person may opt for several steps over 1 week (e.g., attending for two classes on Monday, and one extra class each subsequent day until full attendance is achieved on Friday) while another feels more confident to engage in smaller steps (e.g., meeting with the home-room teacher for 30 minutes on the first day; meeting with the home-room teacher and a peer for 1 hour on the second day; sitting in class for 1 hour, together with the same peer, on the third day; etc.). When a young person's anxiety is very high, imaginal desensitization may precede implementation of the attendance plan. With younger children, a developmentally sensitive variant of systematic desensitization may be employed, namely emotive imagery (see King, Heyne, Gullone, & Molloy, 2001). Some young people prefer that attendance occur on a full-time basis from the first day of the planned increase in attendance. In such cases, imaginal desensitization can be employed prior to the full-time increase in attendance.

The date for commencement of the attendance plan is discussed around the third session, permitting time to build first a therapeutic alliance with the young person. The clinician explains that the plan to increase attendance at about half-way through treatment ensures that there is sufficient time to be well prepared beforehand and sufficient time afterward to monitor progress and fine-tune the plan if needed. The clinician and young person identify possible obstacles to completion of the planned steps and use a problem-solving approach to identify ways to deal with such obstacles. Immediately prior to the planned increase in school attendance, the young person is encouraged to draw on his behavioral and cognitive coping skills to manage discomfort and bolster confidence. When the attendance plan does not go according to plan, the clinician provides liberal reinforcement for all efforts and partial achievements, and patiently and persistently explores the obstacles and works with the young person to modify the plan for the coming school days.

In cases involving severe anxiety or depression-related inactivity, the clinician helps the young person increase engagement in other situations prior to increasing school attendance. For example, when severe separation anxiety is present, the young person is gradually exposed to separation from parents across 1 or 2 weeks preceding a delayed increase in attendance. The clinician works together with the young person to develop a plan (e.g., a "separation plan" or "social contact plan") in the same way that the attendance plan was developed. This topic is also discussed with parents (Module P8).

Promoting progress (Y12)

Research on the short-term outcome of CBT for school refusal suggests that gains are maintained for at least 2–4 months post-treatment (e.g., Heyne et al., 2002, 2011; King et al., 1998). Several strategies are employed to help the young person increase the likelihood that gains will be maintained and reduce the likelihood that temporary setbacks (lapses) turn into intense and long-term difficulties (relapse).

The clinician engages the young person in a developmentally sensitive review of: (a) changes in functioning (including changes in thoughts, feelings, and behaviors); (b) changes in knowledge and skills; and (c) the link between changes in functioning and changes in the young person's knowledge/skills. To review changes in functioning, the clinician and young person can recall the goals identified during Module Y4, and discuss achievement of these goals. It is important to consider the degree to which goals have been achieved, especially when working with young people who tend to be black-and-white in thinking and regard moderate achievement as non-achievement. To review the knowledge/skills which the young person has acquired or honed during treatment, the clinician and young person can review the personalized "resource folder" in which skill-specific information sheets and homework sheets are stored. The link between changes in functioning and changes in knowledge/skills can be made by engaging the young person in a "Secrets to Success" or "My Commercial" activity (Kendall et al., 1992). The young person gets to share their ideas about how best to deal with school refusal, in the form of a poster, by playing the "expert in the field" during a make-believe interview or commercial which is recorded and reviewed, or by conducting a "motivational talk" for another clinician or family members. Throughout, the clinician draws attention to the young person's effort and success in applying their knowledge/skills to create positive change for themselves.

This prepares the young person for dealing with possible lapses by strengthening learning, identifying instrumental treatment components from the young person's perspective, and enhancing self-efficacy (Kendall et al., 1992) and self-esteem (Kearney

& Hugelshofer, 2000). Furthermore, the poster or recording may serve as a home-based prompt to use specific knowledge/skills when faced with temporary setbacks. The young person is invited to be on the look-out for signs of a setback (e.g., increased anxiety; low motivation) and to draw on the knowledge/skills which they have already found to be most helpful for them. The clinician and young person consider obstacles to the maintenance of gains (e.g., returning to school after a long holiday period) and use problem-solving to devise a plan for overcoming such obstacles. This module also provides the context for attending to the young person's thoughts and feelings about treatment termination.

Modules Implemented with the Parents

Reviewing the overall plan (P1/Y1)

This module is implemented with the parents and young person together, and is described in the section "Modules implemented with the young person".

Putting problems in perspective (P2)

The aims and process associated with this module closely mirror those of the equivalent module conducted with the young person (Module Y2). Several additional points warrant consideration. Psychoeducation about the nature of the young person's difficulties may foster greater commitment among parents who hitherto primarily regarded their child's school refusal as naughty behavior. "Normalizing" the occurrence of school refusal and its impact upon parents, couples, and families may help reduce parental stress and strengthen the therapeutic alliance. In some cases a parent may be minimally concerned about school refusal and have a nonchalant attitude towards treatment. In these cases less attention might be paid to "normalizing" and more to "forecasting" the possible outcomes in the absence of treatment. The "linking" component of psychoeducation involves linking specific presenting problems with specific treatment components. When working with parents, links are not only made between child-focused difficulties and interventions, but also between child-focused difficulties and parent- and family-focused interventions, and between difficulties for the parents (thoughts, feelings, and behaviors) and related treatment components. Throughout, the clinician employs a non-blaming stance while helping parents understand the valuable role they can play in helping their child. Sometimes parents remain focused on the question of causation. The clinician can empathize with the "desire to know" and advise that CBT emphasizes the development and use of skills in the here-and-now. If needed, a handout addressing a broad spectrum of contributing factors (see Heyne & King, 2004) can facilitate discussion aimed at achieving a consensus on causation and promoting readiness to move onto subsequent modules.

Thinking about the teenage years (Optional, P3)

Parents of adolescent school refusers are helped to explore the impact (positive and negative) that developmental transitions and tasks have had, currently have, or may yet have on their child, on his presenting problems, on themselves, and on their relationship with their child. Autonomy development may be a particularly important topic when an adolescent school refuser presents with anxiety given the association between over-protective parenting and youth anxiety (Sauter et al., 2009; Siqueland et al., 2005). During the exploration of developmental transitions and tasks the clinician provides information about adolescent development, as required.

The module serves similar functions to those indicated in the corresponding module for adolescent school refusers (Module Y3), including the normalization of clients' experiences. In addition, it supports parents in coping with the challenges associated with adolescent school refusal and with parenting an adolescent, and it fosters a parenting style befitting the developmental needs of an adolescent school refuser. Enhanced parenting and parent–adolescent relating may benefit treatment-specific processes (e.g., parent use of developmentally sensitive behavior management strategies; family problem-solving) and may foster secondary treatment outcomes (e.g., increased family harmony). The module is implemented during the first or second session and can be revisited as developmentally related issues arise throughout treatment.

Setting goals (P4)

The functions served by goal-setting with parents are similar to those described in Module Y4. Some differences in the process are apparent. Parents are quite easily engaged in the identification of treatment-related goals so it is not necessary to explore more general goals they may have for themselves. They are, however, helped to identify treatment-related goals for themselves (e.g., knowing what to do when the young person does not get out of bed; staying calm). This module also provides the context for the clinician to explain that increased school attendance is usually scheduled around the third or fourth week of treatment, allowing sufficient time beforehand for preparing the young person, parents, and school staff. The module is usually implemented in the second session but may commence in the first session to enhance the face validity of treatment when working with parents who are more sceptical or impatient.

Reducing maintenance factors (P5)

Parents are helped to consider the presence and influence of maintaining factors in three key domains: health, school, and home. For parents, reservations or worry about the young person's physical health or about the suitability of the current school may interfere with their willingness to implement strategies incorporated in subsequent modules. For the young person, positive experiences at home during school hours may make it harder for them to contemplate and attempt an increase in school attendance.

School refusal is often associated with somatic complaints like headaches and stomach-aches (Honjo et al., 2001) and in some cases a relationship seems to exist between school refusal and conditions such as chronic fatigue syndrome (Richards, 2000). Parents can arrange a medical examination to help clarify whether there is any medical basis to the young person's somatic complaints. It is helpful for all parties (parents, young person, school staff, and clinicians) to know to what extent the young person is physically able to cope with school attendance.

Parents' uncertainty about the suitability of their child's current class or school placement may stem from concern about the quality or type of education provided; conflict with school staff; a child's negative experiences with other students; and so on. Parents need to be confident in the class/school placement in order to be able to model confidence in the plans for increasing attendance in that class or school. The clinician facilitates a problem-solving discussion around the advantages and disadvantages of changing class or school. When working with school-refusing adolescents, such decision-making can take place during Module P10/Y10 (Solving family problems).

Home-based factors that may serve to maintain school refusal include an alternative evening-morning routine (e.g., being able to sleep in on school mornings; not showering or dressing until later in the day) and access to activities or things not typically available at school (e.g., watching television; playing computer games; pets; treats). Establishing a normal evening-morning routine and reducing access to those things not associated with school attendance help reduce the incidental reinforcement associated with not being at school, they convey the message that parents expect that the young person will increase school attendance, and they provide parents with the opportunity to practice behavior management strategies such as instruction-giving (Module P6) and positive reinforcement of appropriate behavior (Module P7). Instigating a suitable week-day routine also prepares the young person physically and mentally for the upcoming increase in school attendance.

Giving effective instructions (P6)

In the Preparation Phase parents often need to issue instructions about which activities the young person may and may not engage in when at home during school-time (Module P5). In the Implementation Phase, parents may need to actively facilitate their child's attendance at school (Module P11), including instructions about getting out of bed, getting ready for school, and leaving home to go to school. Effective instruction-giving has been associated with an increased likelihood of child compliance (Sanders, 1992) and reduced behavioral disorder in adolescence (Roberts, Lazicki-Puddy, Puddy, & Johnson, 2003).

The clinician discusses the value of effectively issuing instructions to young people (e.g., to help break the cycle of avoidance or inactivation), encourages the parents to reflect upon the nature and effectiveness of their approach to instruction-giving, and empathizes with the parents' disappointment or frustration when their child does not do what they have been asked to do. As required, training in instruction-giving makes use of educational handouts, clinician modeling, parent rehearsal, and feedback (Forehand & McMahon, 1981). Attention is paid to developmentally sensitive instruction-giving with adolescents. A link is made between the transitions and tasks discussed in Module P3 (e.g., striving for autonomy; increased capacity for alternative thinking) and the effect that these may have upon an adolescent's compliance with instructions. This helps normalize parents' experiences when asking adolescent children to do something and provides leads for adapting instruction-giving with adolescents. In two-parent families, consideration is also given to the respective roles of each parent in relation to the issuing of instructions.

In some cases the module can be covered quite efficiently (e.g., within about 15 minutes), such as when parents report and display helpful attitudes and skills associated with instruction-giving. In other cases more time may need to be spent on the material in this module (e.g., a whole session, with follow-up work in a subsequent session). This is indicated when parents display unhelpful attitudes (e.g., I mustn't be firm with my child) or require more in-session practice of the skills.

Responding to behavior (P7)

This module aims to help parents manage the consequences of the young person's behavior in order to increase desirable behaviors (e.g., use of coping skills; school attendance; doing homework) and reduce undesirable behaviors that get in the way of school attendance (e.g., tantrums; arguments; excessive reassurance-seeking). Adaptive changes may also occur in the parent–child relationship (Kearney & Silverman, 1995), such as a reduction in parent over-involvement with a child who ordinarily seeks and receives an excessive amount of reassurance.

The clinician and parents collaboratively specify which desirable behaviors will ideally be recognized and strengthened via positive reinforcement and which undesirable behaviors will ideally be extinguished via planned ignoring. Parents are helped to review the strengths and soft-spots in their use of these behavior management strategies and to identify targets for the refinement or development of skills. Key points associated with positive reinforcement include: the need to identify powerful and feasible reinforcers; the value of rewarding effort and small achievements in the interests of ultimately achieving larger goals; and the relative merits of contingency contracts vis-à-vis spontaneously administering reinforcement. Parents sometimes express reservations about the use of positive reinforcement (e.g., it is unfair because other children in the family are not rewarded for going to school; a child should attend school without having to be rewarded). The clinician can engage the parents in a problem-solving discussion to arrive at solutions they are comfortable with (e.g., temporarily employ reward systems to increase desired behaviors of other children in the family). Cognitive interventions may also be helpful (e.g., reframe the use of positive reinforcement for school attendance as "a short-term parental maneuver to achieve a return to normal family life"). In the case of planned ignoring, key points include: a reminder that parents are ignoring undesirable behavior and not the child themselves; the possibility of an extinction burst and the importance of persistent ignoring at this time; and balancing the use of planned ignoring with the scheduling of non-contingent positive interactions with the child. Planned ignoring is often practiced in-session to help parents be well-prepared to respond to the young person's distress-related undesirable behaviors when school attendance increases. In-session practice provides a rich source of information to guide the clinician's positive and constructive feedback to parents.

The module is introduced in the Preparation Phase and re-visited during the Implementation Phase to ascertain the use and effectiveness of the strategies and the need for fine-tuning.

Bolstering a young person's confidence (P8)

The young person is likely to find it easier to increase school attendance when he has already developed confidence in facing difficult or anxiety-provoking situations associated with school attendance. For example, the young person with clinical or sub-clinical separation anxiety can be gradually exposed to separation from parents prior to the planned increase in school attendance. Likewise, the socially anxious or isolated young person can be helped to increase social contact with school-based peers during the Preparation Phase. Young people with depression-related withdrawal can be helped to become more active prior to increasing school attendance.

Building on the psychoeducation material presented in Module P2, the clinician helps the parents understand the principles associated with facing rather than avoiding difficult situations, and the value of taking the time to help build the young person's confidence via preliminary engagement tasks. The case formulation guides decision-making about the likely focus of preliminary engagement tasks. Via a problem-solving discussion between the clinician and parents, viable options for engagement tasks are identified and an accompanying plan of action is developed (e.g., communicating with the child about the value of preliminary engagement; involving the child in the selection and sequencing of steps). Between-session tasks associated with prompting and facilitating the young person's preliminary engagement are a key aspect of this module. Parent involvement in facilitating preliminary engagement may bolster a parent's self-efficacy for increasing a child's school attendance. It may also reveal unhelpful cognitions (e.g., being firm is bad parenting; my child will not cope) to be addressed via Module P9. Some adolescents may prefer to attempt preliminary engagement without parent involvement. In any case, parents can employ the knowledge and skills discussed in Module P7 to reinforce the young person's efforts and success once they start re-engaging with difficult situations.

The module is introduced in the Preparation Phase, often beginning in the third session. The number of difficult situations and the chronicity and severity of avoidance will influence the pacing of the module.

Bolstering a parent's confidence (Optional, P9)

The parents of school refusers may also experience internalizing problems at clinical levels (Bernstein & Garfinkel, 1988; Last, Francis, Hersen, Kazdin, & Strauss, 1987). Other parents not meeting criteria for an anxiety disorder or depressive disorder nevertheless experience emotional distress associated with the challenging task of responding to a child's school refusal. This optional module focuses on behavioral and cognitive strategies that can help parents manage their own emotional distress and feel more in control. In this way, parents are better able to model non-anxious behavior when their child starts increasing school attendance, and they are better placed to employ the knowledge and skills acquired and honed during treatment. For example, when negative emotional responses such as extreme disappointment or excessive anxiety are managed, the parent may more readily perceive the merit in the small steps achieved by their child and proceed to positively reinforce such achievements. Research supports the role of parent anxiety management in enhancing outcomes for anxious children and young adolescents (Khanna & Kendall, 2009).

The behavioral strategies that can be employed with parents mirror those described in Module Y6 for the young person. The cognitive strategies also mirror those employed with young people in Module Y7. Cognitive errors that may be detected during D2 include an underestimation of the child's or parent's ability to effectively deal with school refusal, and expecting negative outcomes when the parent is firm (Mansdorf & Lukens, 1987). We have also detected unhelpful cognition such as "It's my child's responsibility for learning to cope with being at school" and

"I've tried everything and it doesn't work." Unhelpful cognition may fuel ambivalence toward learning and employing strategies aimed at helping the young person increase their school attendance. When working with the parents of adolescent school refusers, special attention may need to be paid to cognitions associated with parenting teenagers (e.g., "He's too big to listen to what I say").

The initial case formulation and subsequent revisions of the formulation at one-third and two-thirds of the way through treatment, guide decision-making about the selection, sequencing, and pacing of this module (i.e., hypotheses about the relative contribution of parental stress and unhelpful cognitions in the maintenance of the young person's school refusal). Specific assessment instruments may help to specify targets for cognitive therapy (e.g., the SEQ-RSAP and SSA-Parent introduced in the section "Conducting assessment"). In some cases it may be sufficient to encourage a parent to employ a relaxation technique already familiar to them and to develop several key coping statements (D5) for use at critical times. In other cases several sessions may be devoted to training in relaxation and/or cognitive techniques, with further attention paid to these skills during subsequent sessions.

Solving family problems (Optional, P10/Y10)

This module is implemented with the parents and young person together, as described in the section "Modules implemented with the young person".

Facilitating school attendance (P11)

A complex aspect of treatment concerns the role that parents will play in facilitating school attendance. Opinions have varied, including the standpoint that parents should enforce the young person's attendance at all costs (e.g., Kennedy, 1965), the suggestion that parents be involved in treatment if the young person's refusal to attend school is maintained by positive reinforcement (e.g., Kearney & Albano, 2007), and the preference for allowing the young person to decide when they are ready to return to school (e.g., Patterson, 1965). A similar lack of clarity exists with respect to the ideal role of parents in facilitating the exposure tasks of adolescents with anxiety disorders (Kendall, 2005). We contend that the best outcomes in the treatment of school refusal are likely to be achieved by taking account of developmental issues when considering the role of parents.

With children, parents can be more actively involved in steering the school attendance process. That is, "professionally condoned parental pressure" (Gittelman-Klein & Klein, 1971) may be applied if, following parents' clear instructions regarding attendance, the young person does not respond. Parent involvement in escorting the younger school refuser to school allows parents to block avoidance behavior, but the process requires good planning and support (Kearney & Roblek, 1998; Kennedy, 1965). With many adolescents, the developmental task associated with autonomy development points to the value in parents initially playing a "supportive role" in facilitating attendance, rather than a "steering role". The adolescent is given an opportunity across 1–2 weeks to make use of the knowledge and skills he has acquired and honed during treatment to cope with increased school attendance, independent of intensive parental involvement in facilitating school attendance. The parents employ a supportive, autonomy-granting role (e.g., gentle psychological prompts for the young person to employ coping strategies; positive reinforcement for effort and achievements). After 1–2 weeks, if required, the parents can employ a more steering, authoritative role, whereby they are more actively involved in getting the young person to school.

The following topics are commonly discussed during this module, some of them being more relevant to the "steering role" of parents and some to the "supportive role": (i) the parents' prior experience in responding to school refusal (e.g., what worked more/less effectively) and the clinician's experience (e.g., strategies effectively employed by other parents); (ii) principles from learning theory (e.g., blocking avoidance behavior); (iii) the therapeutic leverage gained by involving the young person in decision-making appropriate to them (i.e., because school attendance is difficult for the young person and because he is not involved in deciding whether attendance will be increased, it is important to be able to foster his motivation for engaging in the attendance plan by involving him in some decision-making about the process; involving the young person in decision-making about the steps associated with part-time return ensures that the successive steps are well-paced according to his capacity); (iv) feedback from the young person's clinician about the young person's preferences/planned steps; (v) the importance of parent flexibility during the planned increase in attendance (e.g., going to work a little later than usual so as to be able to support or steer the young person's attendance); (vi) helpful strategies when dropping the young person off at school (e.g., keeping farewells brief; refraining from contacting the child during the school day); (vii) using the knowledge and skills addressed in Modules P6 and P8; (viii) dealing with the young person's non-response to instructions (e.g., calmly and firmly guiding the young person in behaviors such as getting out of bed, getting ready for school, going into the school building); (ix) keeping in mind that it may take a little while before the young person's refusal behaviors decrease; and (x) drawing on their knowledge and skills for managing their own distress (Module P9).

Various decisions need to be made, such as: (i) the date of school return (e.g., which day of the week is likely to be easiest for the child; how and when to communicate the date to the child)[6]; (ii) who can serve as support person in the case of one-parent families (e.g., a relative, neighbor, or friend who can provide support in the face of difficult situations, remind about key strategies for facilitating attendance, and help in the process of escorting the young person to school); and (iii) how to respond to obstacles that might arise during the Implementation Phase (e.g., how to respond to the remote possibility that the young person will run away from school). The clinician's stance is one of consultant and coach; she discusses pertinent points and guides problem-solving in such a way that parents will adopt and employ strategies most likely to lead to increased attendance.

In the sessions following the planned increase in attendance a review takes place, addressing: (i) the extent to which steps in the attendance plan have been achieved; (ii) the way in which parents worked to facilitate attendance; (iii) liberal reinforcement of parent effort and achievements; and (iv) fine-tuning parent facilitation of attendance,

---

[6]With adolescents, the date for school return is discussed in the context of Module P10/Y10 (Solving family problems).

as required. In cases where parents initially employed a supportive autonomy-granting approach, consideration is given to the need to move to a steering, authoritative approach, and the timing for this.

The module is introduced early in treatment, at around session 3. At this time the focus is upon establishing a specific date for increasing school attendance, reviewing parents' prior efforts to facilitate attendance and the related outcomes, and helping parents develop a specific plan for their role in facilitating attendance. In the session prior to the planned increase in attendance the clinician and parents review the key strategies. After the planned increase in attendance the module is revisited as the clinician and parents review progress and engage in any necessary fine-tuning of the parent's involvement in facilitating attendance.

Promoting progress (P12)

Parents are helped to maintain treatment gains and prevent any lapses from turning into a relapse. First, the clinician engages the parents in a review of positive changes for the young person, parents, and family. The list of initial treatment goals can be used to facilitate the review. If an area of change has been less than ideal, problem-solving discussion takes place to determine the subsequent course of action. Second, parents are helped to recall the knowledge and skills they have honed or acquired by looking over the instructional handouts associated with each module. Third, parents are helped to identify links between positive changes and their use of specific knowledge/skills. This may strengthen parent self-efficacy for responding to lapses. Links between positive changes and the young person's use of knowledge/skills are also considered, to highlight areas for parental prompting and reinforcement after treatment has ended. Fourth, parents are helped to consider likely obstacles to the maintenance of gains and are engaged in a problem-solving discussion to determine how such obstacles can best be managed. They are encouraged to be alert to signs of a lapse and to make use of knowledge/skills identified as most helpful. Lapses may be observed in the young person (e.g., increased anxiety on school mornings) as well as in parent behavior (e.g., inadvertent reinforcement for non-attendance). The module is implemented in the last one or two sessions, during which time the parents have an opportunity to discuss issues related to treatment termination.

Modules Implemented with School Staff

Treatment-related consultation with relevant school staff commonly occurs during two school visits, one in the Preparation Phase and one in the Implementation Phase. Standard modules addressed during the first visit include an Orientation to the intervention (S1), Organizational issues (S2), and Emotional issues (S3). Module S1 incorporates a brief review of the case formulation; the rationale for selected CBT modules; and the respective roles of school staff, parents, young person, and clinician. Organizational issues addressed in Module S2 revolve around the planned increase in attendance (e.g., steps associated with a part-time increase; whether/how to advise peers of the young person's return to school; informing other staff about the plans for accommodating the young person's needs) and identification of a staff member who will coordinate the school-based interventions, monitor progress, and serve as the contact point between the school and the clinician working with the young person. Module S3 is routinely implemented because school refusers usually experience some degree of distress when increasing attendance. A problem-solving discussion around ways to support the young person may yield special temporary arrangements (e.g., allowing "settling in time" with the mentor if feeling distressed on arrival at school; permitting the young person to leave class at will to "check-in" with the mentor; not automatically sending the young person home if he complains of feeling unwell). Staff are also helped to identify feasible but powerful forms of reinforcement for the young person's effort in using their coping skills.

During the first and second school meetings, one or more of the following optional modules may be implemented as indicated by the case formulation: Behavioral issues (S4), Academic issues (S5), and Social issues (S6). These provide the context for problem-solving discussions around relevant topics (e.g., responding to disruptive behavior; temporary exclusion from gym class; special consideration when assessing school-work; initiating a buddy system). During the second meeting the standard module Promoting progress (S7) is implemented to facilitate discussion around the ways in which school staff can foster the maintenance of treatment gains and respond to lapses. In the Implementation Phase additional school consultation occurs during regular telephone and email contact, especially in relation to the fine-tuning of attendance plans. Some school staff profit from the supportive and optimistic attitude of the clinician given that student non-attendance often places a strain upon school staff (McAnanly, 1986).

Empirical Findings

Reviews of evidentiary support for CBT

In their review of CBT for school refusal, King, Tonge, Heyne, and Ollendick (2000) employed the criteria of Lonigan, Elbert, and Johnson (1998) to determine the level of evidentiary support for CBT. The criteria were applied to the two randomized controlled trials published at that time. The first of these was King and colleagues' (1998) study which demonstrated that a 4-week CBT condition (comprising six sessions with the young person, five sessions with the parents, and consultation with school staff) was superior to a waitlist control condition. The second was Last and colleagues' (1998) comparison of a 12 week CBT condition (comprising 12 sessions with the young person and some contact with parents and school staff) with an education and support therapy (EST; comprising 12 sessions with the young person). The CBT and EST conditions were associated with improved attendance and reduced emotional distress, and no significant difference was found between the conditions at post-treatment with respect to remission of the primary anxiety disorder. However, non-response was higher in the EST condition (40% of those in the EST condition showed no improvement in attendance at 4-week follow-up relative to 14% in the CBT condition). When these two studies were evaluated in relation to Lonigan and colleagues' (1998) criteria, it was concluded that CBT could not yet be described as a "well-established" or "probably efficacious" treatment for school refusal.

Subsequently another randomized trial of CBT was published. Heyne et al. (2002) randomly allocated 61 school refusal cases to a child/adolescent-focused CBT (eight sessions across 4 weeks), a parent-focused CBT (eight sessions across 4 weeks), or the combination of child/adolescent-focused CBT and parent-focused CBT (eight child/adolescent sessions and eight parent sessions across 4 weeks). All conditions were associated with increased school attendance and reduced emotional distress. Because the young people in this study all had an anxiety disorder at pre-treatment, the study was included in Silverman, Pina, and Viswesvaran's (2008) review of group-design studies evaluating psychosocial treatments for phobic and anxiety disorders in youth. The two randomized controlled trials reported above (King et al., 1998; Last et al., 1998) were also included in the review. Silverman et al. (2008) employed the criteria of Chambless and colleagues (Chambless, Sanderson, Shoham et al., 1996; Chambless & Hollon, 1998) to classify treatment for school refusal. Collectively the results of the three studies indicated that the classification "possibly efficacious" is applicable to child/adolescent-focused CBT (Heyne et al., 2002; Last et al., 1998), parent-focused CBT (Heyne et al., 2002), and the combination of child/adolescent-focused CBT and parent-focused CBT (Heyne et al., 2002; King et al., 1998).

Pina and colleagues (2009) conducted the most recent review of psychosocial interventions for school refusal. They identified 242 articles in English-language peer-reviewed journals which referred to "school refusal," and 67 of these were judged to be possible intervention articles. After excluding clinical anecdotal case studies and articles reporting on pharmacological interventions, 15 studies remained. These included eight single-case experimental design studies and six group-design studies[7]. All of the single-case design studies focused on behavioral interventions with the young person and/or parents, and one incorporated additional cognitive therapeutic techniques with the young person. Two of the group design studies involved an evaluation of CBT (Heyne et al., 2002; King et al., 1998), one involved evaluation of behavioral intervention alone or in combination with cognitive intervention (Kearney & Silverman, 1999), one compared 3 months versus 6 months of the combination of EST, social skills training, milieu therapy, and family therapy (Berg & Fielding, 1978), one compared behavior therapy with hospitalization and with the combination of home tuition and psychotherapy (Blagg & Yule, 1984), and one compared CBT with EST (Last et al., 1998). Based on their review, Pina and colleagues (2009) suggested that behavioral strategies alone or in combination with cognitive strategies "seem promising" given the observed increases in school attendance and reductions in symptoms associated with school refusal (e.g., anxiety, fear, depression, disruptive behavior) (p. 18).

Follow-up periods varied in length from as little as 1–6 months in some of the group-design studies (Heyne et al., 2002; Kearney & Silverman, 1999; King et al., 1998; Last et al., 1998) and between 12 and 24 months in two other group-design studies (Berg & Fielding, 1978; Blagg & Yule, 1984). The King, Tonge, Heyne et al. (2001) study reporting on a 3- to 5-year follow-up of subjects treated in the context

---

[7]The authors make reference to seven group design studies, but one of these so-called group design studies (i.e., King et al., 2001) was purely a long-term follow-up of subjects included in another of the studies (i.e., King et al., 1998).

of the King et al. (1998) study provides the strongest support for the durability of gains following CBT for school refusal.

More recent studies of CBT

Recently two more group-design studies have been reported. Both of these involved CBT for adolescent school refusal. Walter and colleagues (2010) reported on an observational study of inpatient CBT with 147 adolescents with attendance problems and concurrent anxiety or depression. Inpatient CBT lasted 8 weeks on average (ranging from 3 to 18 weeks) and often included cognitive interventions with the adolescent, social skills training, and parenting skill training. Results at 2-month follow-up were positive with respect to increased school attendance and reduced anxiety/depression. However, definitive conclusions about the effectiveness of CBT are limited by the variable combination of cognitive-behavioral interventions, psychopharmacological interventions, and other inpatient and outpatient interventions.

Our group reported on the efficacy of the developmentally sensitive manualized and modular CBT outlined in this chapter, based on its implementation with 20 school-refusing adolescents (Heyne et al., 2011). The average age of the adolescents was 14.6 years, and the average length of the current episode of school refusal was 6.5 months. Fourteen adolescents (70%) had not attended school at all in the 2 weeks prior to assessment and pre-treatment attendance across all 20 adolescents was just 15%. All adolescents met criteria for a DSM-IV anxiety disorder and most (60%) had two or more diagnoses. Treated adolescents showed significant improvements which were maintained at 2-month follow-up for primary outcome variables (school attendance; school-related fear; anxiety) and secondary outcome variables (depression; overall functioning; adolescent and parent self-efficacy). Effect sizes were medium to large. Importantly, the treatment was rated as acceptable by adolescents, parents, and school staff, which possibly explains the very low attrition rate. The treatment now awaits more robust evaluation in a randomized controlled trial. In the meantime it seems to be a promising treatment for the complex problem of school refusal – a problem which is often more complex and treatment-resistant among adolescents. To further inform the enhancement of treatment for school refusal in adolescence, future research could examine the relationship between developmental factors (e.g., cognitive development; psychosocial development) and the process and outcome of CBT.

References

Albano, A. M. (1995). Treatment of social anxiety in adolescents. *Cognitive and Behavioral Practice, 2,* 271–298.

Amatu, H. I. (1981). Family-motivated truancy. *International Journal of Psychology, 16,* 111–117.

APA (1987). *Diagnostic and Statistical Manual of Mental Disorders,* 3rd edn. Revised. Washington, DC: American Psychiatric Association.

APA (1994). *Diagnostic and Statistical Manual of Mental Disorders,* 4th edn. Washington, DC: American Psychiatric Association.

Atkinson, L., Quarrington, B., & Cyr, J. J. (1985). School refusal: The heterogeneity of a concept. *American Journal of Orthopsychiatry, 55,* 83–101.

Baker, H., & Wills, U. (1978). School phobia: Classification and treatment. *British Journal of Psychiatry, 132,* 492–499.

Barrett, P. M., & Turner, C. (2000). *FRIENDS for Children: Group Leader's Manual.* Bowen Hills, Australia: Australian Academic Press.

Beck, A. T., Rush, A. J., Shaw, B. F., & Emery, G. (1979). *Cognitive Therapy of Depression.* New York: Guilford Press.

Bell, A. C., & D'Zurilla, T. J. (2009). Problem-solving therapy for depression: A meta-analysis. *Clinical Psychology Review, 29,* 348–353.

Berecz, J. (1969). Phobias of childhood: Etiology and treatment. In S. Chess & A. Thomas (Eds.), *Annual Progress in Child Psychiatry and Child Development* (pp. 558–601). New York: Brunner/Mazel.

Berg, I. (1985). Management of school refusal. *Archives of Disease in Childhood, 60,* 486–488.

Berg, I. (1996). School avoidance, school phobia, and truancy. In M. Lewis (Ed.), *Child and adolescent psychiatry: A comprehensive textbook* (pp. 1104–1110). Baltimore: Williams and Wilkins.

Berg, I. (1997). School refusal and truancy. *Archives of Disease in Childhood, 76,* 90–91.

Berg, I. (2002). School avoidance, school phobia, and truancy. In M. Lewis (Ed.), *Child and Adolescent Psychiatry: A Comprehensive Textbook,* 3rd edn (pp. 1260–1266). Sydney: Lippincott Williams & Wilkins.

Berg, I., Butler, A., Franklin, J., Hayes, H., Lucas, C., & Sims, R. (1993). DSM-III-R disorders, social factors and management of school attendance problems in the normal population. *Journal of Child Psychology and Psychiatry, 34,* 1187–1203.

Berg, I., Butler, A., Hullin, R., Smith, R., & Tyrer, S. (1978). Features of children taken to juvenile court for failure to attend school. *Psychological Medicine, 8,* 447–453.

Berg, I., Casswell, G., Goodwin, A., Hullin, R., McGuire, R., & Tagg, G. (1985). Classification of severe school attendance problems. *Psychological Medicine, 15,* 157–165.

Berg, I., & Fielding, D. (1978). An evaluation of hospital in-patient treatment in adolescent school phobia. *The British Journal of Psychiatry, 132,* 500–505.

Berg, I., & Jackson, A. (1985). Teenage school refusers grow up: A follow-up study of 168 subjects, ten years on average after in-patient treatment. *British Journal of Psychiatry, 147,* 366–370.

Berg, I., Nichols, K., & Pritchard, C. (1969). School phobia: Its classification and relationship to dependency. *Journal of Child Psychology and Psychiatry, 10,* 123–141.

Bernstein, G. A. (1991). Comorbidity and severity of anxiety and depressive disorders in a clinic sample. *Journal of the American Academy of Child and Adolescent Psychiatry, 30,* 43–50.

Bernstein, G. A., Borchardt, C. M., Perwien, A. R., Crosby, R. D., Kushner, M. G., Thuras, P. D., & Last, C. G. (2000). Imipramine plus cognitive-behavioral therapy in the treatment of school refusal. *Journal of the American Academy of Child and Adolescent Psychiatry, 39,* 276–283.

Bernstein, G. A., & Garfinkel, B. D. (1988). Pedigrees, functioning, and psychopathology in families of school phobic children. *American Journal of Psychiatry, 145,* 70–74.

Bernstein, G. A., Warren, S. L., Massie, E. D., & Thuras, P. D. (1999). Family dimensions in anxious-depressed school refusers. *Journal of Anxiety Disorder, 13,* 513–528.

Birmaher, B., & Ollendick, T. H. (2004). Childhood-onset panic disorder. In T. H. Ollendick & J. S. March (Eds.), *Phobic and Anxiety Disorders in Children and Adolescents: A Clinicians Guide to Effective Psychosocial and Pharmacological Interventions.* New York: Oxford University Press.

Blagg, N. (1987). *School Phobia and Its Treatment.* New York: Croom Helm.

Blagg, N., & Yule, W. (1984). The behavioural treatment of school refusal: A comparative study. *Behaviour Research and Therapy, 22,* 119–127.

Bools, C., Foster, J., Brown, I., & Berg, I. (1990). The identification of psychiatric disorders in children who fail to attend school: A cluster analysis of a non-clinical population. *Psychological Medicine, 20,* 171–181.

Bryce, G., & Baird, D. (1986). Precipitating a crisis: Family therapy and adolescent school refusers. *Journal of Adolescence, 9,* 199–213.

Buitelaar, J. K., Van Andel, H., Duyx, J. H. M., & Van Strien, D. C. (1994). Depressive and anxiety disorders in adolescence: A follow-up study of adolescents with school refusal. *Acta Paedopsychiatrica, 56,* 249–253.

Burke, A. E., & Silverman, W. K. (1987). The prescriptive treatment of school refusal. *Clinical Psychology Review, 7,* 353–362.

Chambless, D. L., & Hollon, S. D. (1998). Defining empirically supported therapies. *Journal of Consulting and Clinical Psychology, 66,* 7–18.

Chambless, D. L., Sanderson, W. C., Shoham, V., Bennett Johnson, S., Pope, K. S., Crits-Christoph, P. et al. (1996). An update on empirically validated therapies. *The Clinical Psychologist, 49,* 5–18.

Chiu, A. W., McLeod, B. D., Har, K., & Wood, J. J. (2009). Child-therapist alliance and clinical outcomes in cognitive behavioral therapy for child anxiety disorders. *Journal of Child Psychology and Psychiatry, 50,* 751–758.

Chorpita, B. F. (2007). *Modular cognitive-behavioral therapy for childhood anxiety disorders.* New York: The Guilford Press.

Chorpita, B. F., Albano, A. M., Heimberg, R. G., & Barlow, D. H. (1996). A systematic replication of the prescriptive treatment of school refusal behavior in a single subject. *Journal of Behavior Therapy and Experimental Psychiatry, 27,* 281–290.

Clarke, G. N., Lewinsohn, P. M., & Hops, H. (1990). *Adolescent Coping with Depression Course.* Eugene, OR: Castalia Press.

Drinkwater, J. (2005). Cognitive case formulation. In P. J. Graham (Ed.), *Cognitive behaviour therapy for children and families,* 2nd edn (pp. 84–99). Cambridge: Cambridge University Press.

Dummett, N. (2006). Processes for systemic cognitive-behavioural therapy with children, young people and families. *Behavioural and Cognitive Psychotherapy, 34,* 179–189.

Egger, H. L., Costello, E. J., & Angold, A. (2003). School refusal and psychiatric disorders: A community study. *Journal of the American Academy of Child and Adolescent Psychiatry, 42,* 797–807.

Eisenberg, L. (1959). The pediatric management of school phobia. *Journal of Pediatrics, 55,* 758–766.

Flakierska-Praquin, N., Lindstrom, M., & Gillberg, C. (1997). School phobia with separation anxiety disorder: A comparative 20- to 29-year follow-up study of 35 school refusers. *Comprehensive Psychiatry, 38,* 17–22.

Forehand, R. L., & Mcmahon, R. J. (1981). *Helping the Noncompliant Child: A Clinician's Guide to Parent Training.* New York: the Guilford Press.

Framrose, R. (1978). Out-patient treatment of severe school phobia. *Journal of Adolescence, 1,* 353–361.

Friedberg, R. D., & Mcclure, J. M. (2002). *Clinical Practice of Cognitive Therapy with Children and Adolescents: the Nuts and Bolts.* New York: the Guilford Press.

Galloway, D. (1985). *Schools and Persistent Absentees.* Oxford: Pergamon Press.

Genest, M., & Turk, D. C. (1981) Think-aloud approaches to cognitive assessment. In T. V. Merluzzi, C. R. Glass, & M. Genest (Eds.), *Cognitive Assessment* (pp. 233–269). New York: The Guilford Press.

Ginsburg, G. S., & Schlossberg, M. C. (2002). Family-based treatment of childhood anxiety disorders. *International Review of Psychiatry, 14,* 143–154.

Gittelman-Klein, R., & Klein, D. F. (1971). Controlled imipramine treatment of school phobia. *Archives of General Psychiatry, 25,* 204–207.

Hansen, C., Sanders, S. L., Massaro, S., & Last, C. G. (1998). Predictors of severity of absenteeism in children with anxiety-based school refusal. *Journal of Clinical Child Psychology, 27*, 246–254.

Hersen, M. (1971). The behavioral treatment of school phobia: Current techniques. *The Journal of Nervous and Mental Disease, 153*, 99–107.

Hersov, L. (1985). School refusal. In M. Rutter & L. Hersov (Eds.), *Child and Adolescent Psychiatry: Modern Approaches,* 2nd edn (pp. 382–399). Oxford: Blackwell.

Hersov, L. (1990). School refusal: An overview. In C. Chiland & J. G. Young (Eds.), *Why Children Reject School: Views from Seven Countries.* New Haven: Yale University Press.

Heyne, D. (1999). Evaluation of child therapy and caregiver training in the treatment of school refusal. Unpublished doctoral dissertation. Monash University, Melbourne, Australia.

Heyne, D. (2006). School refusal. In J. E. Fisher and W. T. O'Donohue (Eds.), *Practitioner's Guide to Evidence-Based Psychotherapy* (pp. 599–618). New York: Springer.

Heyne, D., & King, N. J. (2004). Treatment of school refusal. In P. M. Barrett & T. H. Ollendick (Eds.), *Handbook of Interventions That Work with Children and Adolescents: Prevention and Treatment* (pp. 243–272). Chichester: John Wiley & Sons, Ltd.

Heyne, D., King, N. J., & Ollendick, T. (2004). School refusal. In P. Graham (Ed.), *Cognitive Behaviour Therapy for Children and Families,* 2nd edn (pp. 320–341). Cambridge: Cambridge University Press.

Heyne, D., King, N. J., Tonge, B., Rollings, S., Young, D., Pritchard, M., et al. (2002). Evaluation of child therapy and caregiver training in the treatment of school refusal. *Journal of the American Academy of Child and Adolescent Psychiatry, 41*, 687–695.

Heyne, D., King, N., Tonge, B., Rollings, S., Pritchard, M., Young, D., et al. (1998). The Self-Efficacy Questionnaire for School Situations: Development and psychometric evaluation. *Behaviour Change, 15*, 31–40.

Heyne, D., Maric, M., & Westenberg, P. M. (2007). *Self-Efficacy Questionnaire for Responding to School Attendance Problems.* Unpublished measure, Leiden University, Leiden, the Netherlands.

Heyne, D., & Rollings, S. (2002). *School Refusal.* Oxford: Blackwell Scientific Publications.

Heyne, D., Sauter, F. M., & Van Hout, R. (2008). *The @school program: Modular Cognitive Behavior Therapy for School Refusal in Adolescence.* Unpublished treatment manual, Leiden University, Leiden, the Netherlands.

Heyne, D., Sauter, F. M., Van Widenfelt, B. M., Vermeiren, R., & Westenberg, P. M. (2011). School refusal and anxiety in adolescence: Non-randomized trial of a developmentally sensitive cognitive behavioral therapy. *Journal of Anxiety Disorders, 25*, 870–878.

Holmbeck, G. N., Colder, C., Shapera, W., Westhoven, V., Kenealy, L., & Updegrove, A. (2000). Working with adolescents: Guides from developmental psychology. In P. C. Kendall (Ed.), *Child and Adolescent Therapy: Cognitive-Behavioral Procedures* (pp. 334–385). New York: The Guilford Press.

Holmbeck, G. N., O'Mahar, K., Abad, M., Colder, C., & Updegrove, A. (2006). Cognitive-behavior therapy with adolescents: Guides from developmental psychology. In P. C. Kendall (Ed.), *Child and Adolescent Therapy: Cognitive-Behavioral Procedures* (pp. 419–464). New York: Guilford.

Honjo, S., Nishide, T., Niwa, S., Sasaki, Y., Kaneko, H., Inoko, K., et al. (2001). School refusal and depression with school inattendance in children and adolescents: Comparative assessment between the children's depression inventory and somatic complaints. *Psychiatry and Clinical Neurosciences, 55*, 629–634.

Hoshino, Y., Nikkuni, S., Kaneko, M., Endo, M., Yashima, Y., & Kumashiro, H. (1987). The application of DSM-III diagnostic criteria to school refusal. *The Japanese Journal of Psychiatry and Neurology, 41*, 1–7.

Kahn, J. H., & Nursten, J. P. (1962). School refusal: A comprehensive view of school phobia and other failures of school attendance. *American Journal of Orthopsychiatry, 32*, 707–718.

Kameguchi, K., & Murphy-Shigematsu, S. (2001). Family psychology and family therapy in Japan. *American Psychologist, 56,* 65–70.

Kanter, J. W., Manos, R. C., Bowe, W. M., Baruch, D. E., Busch, A. M., & Rusch, L. C. (2010). What is behavioral activation? A review of the empirical literature. *Clinical Psychology Review, 30,* 608–620.

Karnezi, H., & Tierney, K. (2009). A novel intervention to address fears in children with asperger syndrome: A pilot study of the cognitive behavior drama (CBD) model. *Behaviour Change, 26,* 271–282.

Kearney, C. A. (1993). Depression and school refusal behavior: A review with comments on classification and treatment. *Journal of School Psychology, 31,* 267–279.

Kearney, C. A. (2001). *School Refusal Behavior in Youth: A Functional Approach to Assessment and Treatment.* Washington, DC: American Psychological Association.

Kearney, C. A. (2002). Identifying the function of school refusal behavior: A revision of the School Refusal Assessment Scale. *Journal of Psychopathology and Behavioral Assessment, 24,* 235–245.

Kearney, C. A. (2003). Bridging the gap among professionals who address youths with school absenteeism: Overview and suggestions for consensus. *Professional Psychology: Research and Practice, 34,* 57–65.

Kearney, C. A. (2005). *Social Anxiety and Social Phobia in Youth: Characteristics, Assessment, and Psychological Treatment.* New York: Springer.

Kearney, C. A. (2006). Confirmatory factor analysis of the School Refusal Assessment Scale – Revised: Child and Parent Versions. *Journal of Psychopathology and Behavioral Assessment, 28,* 139–144.

Kearney, C. A. (2008). An interdisciplinary model of school absenteeism in youth to inform professional practice and public policy. *Educational Psychology Review, 20,* 257–282.

Kearney, C. A., & Albano, A. M. (2004). The functional profiles of school refusal behavior: Diagnostic aspects. *Behavior Modification, 28,* 147–161.

Kearney, C. A., & Albano, A. M. (2007). *When Children Refuse School: A Cognitive-Behavioral Therapy Approach / Therapist's Guide,* 2nd edn. New York: Oxford University Press.

Kearney, C. A., & Bensaheb, A. (2006). School absenteeism and school refusal behavior: A review and suggestions for school-based health professionals. *Journal of School Health, 76,* 3–7.

Kearney, C. A., & Hugelshofer, D. S. (2000). Systemic and clinical strategies for preventing school refusal behavior in youth. *Journal of Cognitive Psychotherapy, 14,* 1–15.

Kearney, C. A., & Roblek, T. L. (1998). Parent training in the treatment of school refusal behavior. In J. Briesmeister & C. E. Schaefer (Eds.), *Handbook of Parent Training: Parents as Co-therapists for Children's Behavior Problems,* 2nd edn. New York: John Wiley & Sons, Ltd.

Kearney, C. A., & Silverman, W. K. (1990). A preliminary analysis of a functional model of assessment and treatment for school refusal behavior. *Behavior Modification, 14,* 340–366.

Kearney, C. A., & Silverman, W. K. (1995). Family environment of youngsters with school refusal behavior: A synopsis with implications for assessment and treatment. *The American Journal of Family Therapy, 23,* 59–72.

Kearney, C. A., & Silverman, W. K. (1999). Functionally based prescriptive and nonprescriptive treatment for children and adolescents with school refusal behavior. *Behavior Therapy, 30,* 673–695.

Kendall, P. C. (2005). Considering CBT with anxious youth? Think exposures. *Cognitive and Behavioral Practice, 12,* 136–150.

Kendall, P. C., Chansky, T. E., Kane, M. T., Kim, R. S., Kortlander, E., Ronan, K. R., et al. (1992). *Anxiety Disorders in Youth: Cognitive-Behavioral Interventions.* Boston: Allyn and Bacon.

Kendall, P. C., Howard, B. L., & Epps, J. (1988). The anxious child: Cognitive-behavioral treatment strategies. *Behavior Modification, 12,* 281–310.

Kendall, P. C., & Ollendick, T. H. (2004). Setting the research and practice agenda for anxiety in children and adolescence: A topic comes of age. *Cognitive and Behavioral Practice, 11,* 65–74.

Kendall, P. C., & Southam-Gerow, M. A. (1996). Long-term follow-up of a cognitive-behavioral therapy for anxiety-disordered youth. *Journal of Consulting and Clinical Psychology, 64,* 724–730.

Kennard, B. D., Ginsburg, G. S., Feeny, N. C., Sweeney, M., & Zagurski, R. (2005). Implementation challenges to TADS cognitive-behavioral therapy. *Cognitive and Behavioral Practice, 12,* 230–239.

Kennedy, W. A. (1965). School phobia: Rapid treatment of fifty cases. *Journal of Abnormal Psychology, 70,* 285–289.

Khanna, M. S., & Kendall, P. C. (2009). Exploring the role of parent training in the treatment of childhood anxiety. *Journal of Consulting and Clinical Psychology, 77,* 981–986.

King, N. J., & Bernstein, G. A. (2001). School refusal in children and adolescents: A review of the past ten years. *Journal of the American Academy of Child and Adolescent Psychiatry, 40,* 197–205.

King, N. J., Heyne, D., Gullone, E., & Molloy, G. N. (2001). Usefulness of emotive imagery in the treatment of childhood phobias: Clinical guidelines, case examples and issues. *Counselling Psychology Quarterly, 14,* 95–101.

King, N. J., & Ollendick, T. H. (1989). School refusal: Graduated and rapid behavioural treatment strategies. *Australian and New Zealand Journal of Psychiatry, 23,* 213–223.

King, N. J., Ollendick, T. H., & Tonge, B. J. (1995). *School Refusal: Assessment and Treatment.* Boston: Allyn & Bacon.

King, N., Tonge, B., Heyne, D., & Ollendick, T. (2000). Research on the cognitive-behavioral treatment of school refusal: A review and recommendations. *Clinical Psychology Review, 20,* 495–507.

King, N. J., Tonge, B. J., Heyne, D., Pritchard, M., Rollings, S., Young, D., et al. (1998). Cognitive-behavioral treatment of school-refusing children: A controlled evaluation. *Journal of the American Academy of Child and Adolescent Psychiatry, 37,* 375–403.

King, N., Tonge, B., Heyne, D., Turner, S., Pritchard, M., Young, D., et al. (2001). Cognitive-behavioral treatment of school-refusing children: Maintenance of improvement at 3- to 5-year follow-up. *Scandinavian Journal of Behavior Therapy, 30,* 85–89.

Kingery, J. N., Roblek, T. L., Suveg, C., Grover, R. L., Sherrill, J. T., & Bergman, R. L. (2006). They're not just "little adults": Developmental considerations for implementing cognitive-behavioral therapy with anxious youth. *Journal of Cognitive Psychotherapy, 20,* 263–273.

Last, C. G., & Francis, G. (1988). School phobia. In B. B. Lahey & A. E. Kazdin (Eds.), *Advances in Clinical Child Psychology* (pp. 193–222). New York: Plenum Press.

Last, C. G., Francis, G., Hersen, M., Kazdin, A. E., & Strauss, C. C. (1987). Separation anxiety and school phobia: A comparison using DSM-III criteria. *American Journal of Psychiatry, 144,* 653–657.

Last, C. G., Hansen, C., & Franco, N. (1998). Cognitive-behavioral treatment of school phobia. *Journal of the American Academy of Child and Adolescent Psychiatry, 37,* 404–411.

Last, C. G., & Strauss, C. C. (1990). School refusal in anxiety-disordered children and adolescents. *Journal of the American Academy of Child and Adolescent Psychiatry, 29,* 31–35.

Lavooi, M. (2010). Evaluation of the Self-Efficacy Questionnaire for Responding to School Attendance Problems. Unpublished Master's Thesis. Leiden University, Leiden, the Netherlands.

Layne, A. E., Bernstein, G. A., Egan, E. A., & Kushner, M. G. (2003). Predictors of treatment response in anxious depressed adolescents with school refusal. *Journal of the American Academy of Child and Adolescent Psychiatry, 42,* 319–326.

Leventhal, T., Weinberger, G., Stander, R. J., & Stearns, R. P. (1967). Therapeutic strategies with school phobics. *American Journal of Orthopsychiatry, 37,* 64–70.

Lewinsohn, P. M., Clarke, G. N., Hops, H., & Andrews J. (1990). Cognitive-behavioral group treatment of depression in adolescents. *Behavior Therapy, 21*, 385–401.

Lohaus, A., & Klein-Hessling, J. (2003). Relaxation in children: Effects of extended and intensified training. *Psychology and Health, 18*, 237–249.

Lonigan, C. J., Elbert, J. C., & Johnson, S. B. (1998). Empirically supported psychosocial interventions for children: An overview. *Journal of Clinical Child Psychology, 27*, 138–145.

MacPhillamy, D. J., & Lewinsohn, P. M. (1982). The Pleasant Events Schedule: Studies on reliability, validity, and scale intercorrelation. *Journal of Consulting and Clinical Psychology, 50*, 363–380.

Manassis, K. (2009). *Cognitive Behavioral Therapy with Children: a Guide for the Community Practitioner*. New York: Routledge.

Mansdorf, I. J., & Lukens, E. (1987). Cognitive-behavioral psychotherapy for separation anxious children exhibiting school phobia. *Journal of the American Academy of Child and Adolescent Psychiatry, 26*, 222–225.

Maric, M., Heyne, D. A., de Heus, P., van Widenfelt, B. M., & Westenberg, P. M. (2012). The role of cognition in school refusal: An investigation of automatic thoughts and cognitive errors. *Behavioural and Cognitive Psychotherapy, 40*, 255–269.

Maric, M., Heyne, D. A., van Widenfelt, B. M., & Westenberg, P. M. (2011). Distorted cognitive processing in youth: The structure of negative cognitive errors and their associations with anxiety. *Cognitive Therapy and Research, 35*, 11–20.

Martin, C., Cabrol, S., Bouvard, M. P., Lepine, J. P., & Mouren-Simeoni, M. C. (1999). Anxiety and depressive disorders in fathers and mothers of anxious school-refusing children. *Journal of the American Academy of Child and Adolescent Psychiatry, 38*, 916–922.

McAnanly, E. (1986). School phobia: The importance of prompt intervention. *Journal of School Health, 56*, 433–436.

McCune, N., & Hynes, J. (2005). Ten year follow-up of children with school refusal. *Irish Journal of Psychological Medicine, 22*, 56–58.

McNamara, E. (1988). The self-management of school phobia: A case study. *Behavioural Psychotherapy, 16*, 217–229.

McShane, G., Walter, G., & Rey, J. M. (2001). Characteristics of adolescents with school refusal. *Australian and New Zealand Journal of Psychiatry, 35*, 822–826.

Obondo, A., & Dhadphale, M. (1990). Family study of Kenyan children with school refusal. *East African Medical Journal, 67*, 100–108.

Okuyama, M., Okada, M., Kuribayashi, M., & Kaneko, S. (1999). Factors responsible for the prolongation of school refusal. *Psychiatry and Clinical Neurosciences, 53*, 461–469.

Ollendick, T. H., & Mayer, J. A. (1984). School phobia. In S. M. Turner (Ed.), *Behavioral Treatment of Anxiety Disorders* (pp. 367–411). New York: Plenum Press.

Patterson, G. R. (1965). A learning theory approach to the treatment of the school phobic child. In L. P. Ullmann & L. Krasner (Eds.), *Case Studies in Behavior Modification* (pp. 279–285). New York: Holt, Rinehart & Winston.

Pina, A. A., Zerr, A. A., Gonzales, N. A., & Ortiz, C. D. (2009). Psychosocial interventions for school refusal behavior in children and adolescents. *Child Development Perspectives, 3*, 11–20.

Place, M., Hulsmeier, J., Brownrigg, J., & Soulsby, A. (2005). The Family Adaptability and Cohesion Evaluation Scale (FACES): An instrument worthy of rehabilitation? *Psychiatric Bulletin, 29*, 215–218.

Place, M., Hulsmeier, J., Davis, S., & Taylor, E. (2000). School refusal: A changing problem which requires a change of approach? *Clinical Child Psychology and Psychiatry, 5*, 345–355.

Place, M., Hulsmeier, J., Davis, S., & Taylor, E. (2002). The coping mechanisms of children with school refusal. *Journal of Research in Special Educational Needs, 2*, 1–10.

Prabhuswamy, M., Srinath, S., Girimaji, S., & Seshadri, S. (2007). Outcome of children with school refusal. *The Indian Journal of Pediatrics, 74*, 375–379.

Quakley, S., Reynolds, S., & Coker, S. (2004). The effect of cues on young children's abilities to discriminate among thoughts, feelings, and behaviours. *Behaviour Research and Therapy, 42*, 343–356.

Ralph, A. (1996). The importance of setting and measuring individual treatment goals for adolescents learning improved prosocial behavior. *Australian Journal of Guidance and Counseling, 6*, 77–88.

Restifo, K., & Bögels, S. (2009). Family processes in the development of youth depression: Translating the evidence to treatment. *Clinical Psychology Review, 29*, 294–316.

Richards, J. (2000). Chronic fatigue syndrome in children and adolescents: A review article. *Clinical Child Psychology and Psychiatry, 5*, 31–51.

Roberts, M. C., Lazicki-Puddy, T. A., Puddy, R. W., & Johnson, R. J. (2003). The outcomes of psychotherapy with adolescents: A practitioner-friendly research review. *Journal of Clinical Psychology, 59*, 1177–1191.

Rogers, G. M., Reinecke, M. A., & Curry, J. F. (2005). Case formulation in TADS CBT. *Cognitive and Behavioral Practice, 12*, 198–208.

Rohde, P., Seeley, J. R., Kaufman, N. K., Clarke, G. N., & Stice, E. (2006). Predicting time to recovery among depressed adolescents treated in two psychosocial group interventions. *Journal of Consulting and Clinical Psychology, 74*, 80–88.

Rubenstein, J. S., & Hastings, E. M. (1980). School refusal in adolescence: Understanding the symptom. *Adolescence, 15*, 775–782.

Sanders, M. R. (1992). *Every Parent: a Positive Approach to Children's Behaviour.* Sydney: Addison-Wesley.

Sauter, F. M., Heyne, D., & Westenberg, P. M. (2009). Cognitive behavior therapy for anxious adolescents: Developmental influences on treatment design and delivery. *Clinical Child and Family Psychology Review, 12*, 310–335.

Seligman, M. (1995). *The Optimistic Child: a Revolutionary Approach to Raising Resilient Children.* Sydney: Random House.

Silverman, W. K., Pina, A. A., & Viswesvaran, C. (2008). Evidence-based psychosocial treatments for phobic and anxiety disorders in children and adolescents. *Journal of Clinical Child and Adolescent Psychology, 37*, 105–130.

Siqueland, L., Rynn, M., & Diamond, G. S. (2005). Cognitive behavioral and attachment based family therapy for anxious adolescents: Phase I and II studies. *Journal of Anxiety Disorders, 19*, 361–381.

Southam-Gerow, M. A., Kendall, P. C., & Weersing, V. R. (2001). Examining outcome variability: Correlates of treatment response in a child and adolescent anxiety clinic. *Journal of Clinical Child Psychology, 30*, 422–436.

Stallard, P. (2005). Cognitive behavioural therapy with prepubertal children. In P. J. Graham (Ed.), *Cognitive Behaviour Therapy for Children and Families* (pp. 121–135). Cambridge: Cambridge University Press.

Suveg, C., Roblek, T., Robin, J., Krain, A., Aschenbrand, S., & Ginsburg, G. S. (2006). Parental involvement when conducting CBT. *International Journal of Cognitive Psychotherapy, 20*,191–203.

Taylor, S. (2000). *Understanding and Treating Panic Disorder: Cognitive-Behavioral Approaches.* New York: John Wiley & Sons, Ltd.

Teasley, M. L. (2004). Absenteeism and truancy: Risk, protection, and best practice implications for school social workers. *Children and Schools, 26*, 117–128.

Thwaites, R., & Bennett-Levy, J. (2007). Conceptualizing empathy in cognitive behavior therapy: Making the implicit explicit. *Behavioural and Cognitive Psychotherapy, 35*, 591–612.

Thyer, B. A., & Sowers-Hoag, K. M. (1986). The etiology of school phobia: A behavioral approach. *School Social Work Journal, 10*, 86–98.

Tolin, D. F., Whiting, S., Maltby, N., Diefenbach, G. J., Lothstein, M. A., Hardcastle, S., Catalano, A., & Gray, K. (2009). Intensive (daily) behavior therapy for school refusal: A multiple baseline case series. *Cognitive and Behavioral Practice, 16*, 332–344.

TADS (Treatment for Adolescents With Depression Study) Team (2003). Treatment for Adolescents With Depression Study (TADS): Rationale, design, and methods. *Journal of the American Academy of Child and Adolescent Psychiatry, 42,* 531–542.

Valles, E., & Oddy, M. (1984). The influence of a return to school on the long-term adjustment of school refusers. *Journal of Adolescence, 7,* 35–44.

Vasey, M. W., & Dadds, M. R. (2001). An introduction to the developmental psychopathology of anxiety. In M. W. Vasey & M. R. Dadds (Eds.), *The Developmental Psychopathology of Aanxiety* (pp. 3–26). Oxford: Oxford University Press.

Waldfogel, S., Coolidge, J. C., & Hahn, P. B. (1957). The development, meaning and management of school phobia. *American Journal of Orthopsychiatry, 27,* 754–780.

Walter, D., Hautmann, C., Rizk, S., Petermann, M., Minkus, J., Sinzig, J., et al. (2010). Short term effects of inpatient cognitive behavioral treatment of adolescents with anxious-depressed school absenteeism: An observational study. *European Child and Adolescent Psychiatry, 19,* 835–844.

Want, J. H. (1983). School-based intervention strategies for school phobia: A ten-step 'common sense' approach. *The Pointer, 27,* 27–32.

Weersing, V. R., & Brent, D. A. (2005). Psychological therapies: A family of interventions. In P. J. Graham (Ed.), *Cognitive Behaviour Therapy for Children and Families,* 2nd edn (pp. 48–63). Cambridge: Cambridge University Press.

Weersing, V. R., Gonzalez, A., Campo, J. V., & Lucas, A. N. (2008). Brief behavioral therapy for pediatric anxiety and depression: Piloting an integrated treatment approach. *Cognitive and Behavioral Practice, 15,* 126–139.

White, C., McNally, D., & Cartwright-Hatton, S. (2003). Cognitively enhanced parent training. *Behavioural and Cognitive Psychotherapy, 31,* 99–102.

Whitehouse, R. M., Tudway, J. A., Look, R., & Kroese, B. S. (2006). Adapting individual psychotherapy for adults with intellectual disabilities: A comparative review of the cognitive-behavioural and psychodynamic literature. *Journal of Applied Research in Intellectual Disabilities, 19,* 55–65.

Wood, J. J., Drahota, A., Sze, K., Har, K., Chiu, A., & Langer, D. A. (2009). Cognitive behavioral therapy for anxiety in children with autism spectrum disorders: A randomized, controlled trial. *Journal of Child Psychology and Psychiatry, 50,* 224–234.

Yule, W., Hersov, L., & Treseder, J. (1980). Behavioural treatments of school refusal. In L. Hersov & I. Berg (Eds.), *Out of School* (pp. 267–301). Chichester: John Wiley & Sons, Ltd.

22

Anxiety Prevention in School Children and Adolescents: The FRIENDS Program

Cristina Akiko Iizuka, Paula Barrett, and Kate Morris

Pathways Health and Research Centre, Queensland, Australia

Anxiety disorders are frequently described as one of the most commonly diagnosed psychiatric conditions among school-aged children and adolescents (Chavira, Stein, Bailey, & Stein, 2004; Costello & Angold, 1995; Rapee, Schniering, & Hudson, 2009). Current prevalence rates range from 4% to 25%, with an average rate of 8% within school-aged children (Boyd, Kostanski, Gullone, Ollendick, & Shek, 2000; Cole, Peeke, Martin, Truglio, & Seroczynski, 1998; Tomb & Hunter, 2004). However, the actual rate of prevalence is likely to be even higher, with many children and adolescents remaining unidentified and untreated (Neil & Christensen, 2009).

If left untreated, anxiety disorders in childhood and adolescence can lead to reduced career choices (due to absenteeism and lower school grades), increased medical use, depression and substance abuse in adulthood (Donovan & Spence, 2000; Rapee, Kennedy, Ingram, Edwards, & Sweeney, 2005). Given the high prevalence rate, costs of pediatric depression, and the difficulty in treating depression once it has developed, efforts to prevent youth anxiety and depression are unquestionably necessary (Gladstone & Beardslee, 2009).

The pertinence of prevention is further reflected in research that indicates that only 25–34% of children and adolescents with a diagnosable psychological disorder (e.g., anxiety, depression, or another mental health problem) receive clinical treatment. Many children and adolescents who receive treatment terminate the intervention prematurely or fail to respond to it (Donovan & Spence, 2000; Essau, 2005; Farmer, Burns, Phillips, Angold, & Costello, 2003; Farrell & Barrett, 2007). According to Donovan and Spence (2000), the failure to respond to treatment often occurs when treatment is offered too late and the adverse effects associated with the disorder become ingrained and difficult to reverse.

Additionally, research suggests that children who suffer from high anxiety are more likely to experience anxiety when they become adults (Mattison, 1992). According to Kessler, Berglund, Demler, Jin, & Walters (2005), half of adult mental disorders begin before the age of 14, and early intervention can prevent and reduce more

The Wiley-Blackwell Handbook of The Treatment of Childhood and Adolescent Anxiety, First Edition.
Edited by Cecilia A. Essau and Thomas H. Ollendick.
© 2013 John Wiley & Sons, Ltd. Published 2013 by John Wiley & Sons, Ltd.

serious consequences later in life (WHO, 2004). Early anxiety intervention programs have been shown to reduce the number of children and youth who develop anxiety disorders (Barrett, Farrell, Dadds, & Boulter, 2005; Dadds, Spence, Holland, Barrett, & Laurens, 1997; Lock & Barrett, 2003). These programs are cost-effective as they can reduce the cost for future professional services as well as target large groups of individuals over a short period of time.

The past few decades have seen a large shift in focus from treatment to prevention and early intervention in the late childhood/adolescent years (Greenberg, Sisitsky, Kessler et al., 1999). Early intervention programs are necessary and beneficial for individuals, families, and communities to prevent the development of anxiety and depression. This can be achieved by increasing emotional resilience and promoting positive coping skills before more serious emotional difficulties may be manifested (Barrett & Ollendick, 2004).

According to Whitman, Aldinger, Zhang, & Magner (2008), the majority of children and adolescents with disorders worldwide who received care were identified and referred by schools. This suggests that schools are greatly overlooked and underutilized when it comes to their potential in the area of mental health promotion and prevention of disorders. The expansion of the role of schools worldwide is critical, since the school system is an ideal avenue for the promotion of prevention and early intervention programs for anxiety (Masia-Warner, Nangle, & Hansen, 2006). School-based programs delivered as part of the formal school curriculum or as an after-school endorsed activity targeting schoolchildren can ameliorate many of the common barriers to treatment in the community such as time, location, stigmatization, transportation, and cost. This can be achieved by offering convenient, low-cost, and non-threatening alternatives (Barrett & Pahl, 2006; Masia-Warner et al., 2006).

In a literature review conducted by Schoenfeld and Janney (2008), the authors state that school-based intervention for anxiety disorders is effective. Students with anxiety disorders who participate in cognitive-behavioral intervention at school emerged with fewer symptoms than non-participants, and show similar effects to peers who participate in off-campus interventions.

Mental health professionals have an important role to play in strengthening the capacity of schools in addressing both student and staff about this important issue. This role can be fulfilled by means of advocacy, policy development, teaching, professional development for clinicians and educators, research, as well as creation of new models of service for resource-poor sites (Whitman et al., 2008).

Three types of prevention and early intervention programs tend to be offered in schools, all of which exhibit a number of advantages and disadvantages (Mrazek & Haggerty, 1994). Universal programs are presented to all students regardless of symptoms and are often designed to build resiliency or enhance general mental health (Barrett & Turner, 2001). Selective programs target children and adolescents who are at risk of developing a disorder for being exposed to particular risk factors (e.g. being children of an anxious parent or divorced parents) (Spence, 1996). Indicated programs are delivered to students with early or mild symptoms (e.g. anxiety disorder) (Mrazek & Haggerty, 1994).

Schools can play a fundamental role in the promotion of social-emotional development in children by implementing universal intervention programs focused on increasing social-emotional learning. As presented in Figure 22.1, universal

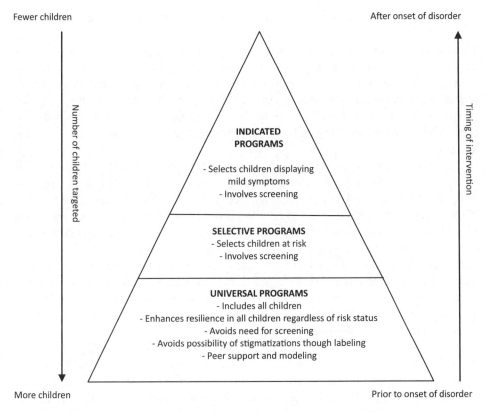

Figure 22.1   Common types of prevention and early intervention offered in schools.

programs are designed to include all children (e.g. in a classroom), and schools are an important setting to reach millions of students and adult staff. In 2005, worldwide, 84% of all children of primary school age were enrolled in school. This percentage decreases to 59% when it comes to secondary school age children enrolled in school (UNESCO, 2005).

According to Strein, Hoagwood, and Cohn (2003), specific aspects of the public health model that have particular relevance for schools include: (1) applying scientifically derived evidence to the delivery of psychological services, (2) strengthening positive behavior rather than focusing exclusively on decreasing problem behavior, (3) emphasizing community collaboration and linked services, (4) using appropriate research strategies to improve the knowledge base, and (5) effectively evaluating school psychological services.

Therefore, the school as a setting to deliver mental health programs and services has the potential to impact positively on the mental health of millions of young people. This chapter presents a review of the importance of building social-emotional skills in school-aged children so as to increase academic success and decrease the likelihood of later life pathologies. The FRIENDS for Life program (Barrett, 2008a, 2008b, 2010a, 2010b, 2010c, 2010d) will be introduced as a universal intervention program to teach social-emotional skills to children and adolescents in order to prevent the onset of emotional and behavioral difficulties (e.g. anxiety and depression).

Theoretical Background of the Intervention Program

The FRIENDS for Life program has a strength-based approach that ensures that the focus is on people's capabilities. It is based on a resilience promotion framework which focuses on the interactions between the individual and his/her surrounding systems/contexts including the community and the family (Garmezy, 1985; Werner & Smith, 1982, 1992). The program uses a multisystem, person–environment approach by actively involving children, families, teachers, and schools in the intervention process.

The specific goal of the program is to promote emotional resilience. Emotional resilience is an individual's capacity to recover from the extremes of trauma, deprivation, threat or stress in healthy and constructive ways (Atkinson, Martin, & Rankin, 2009). According to Goldstein and Brooks (2005), it refers to positive outcomes and adaptation in the face of significant risk, adversity, or stress. These authors describe resilience as an outcome, rather than a psychological construct in and of itself. This has led to efforts to identify variables that can be used to predict resilience. The factors that lead to resilient outcomes are referred to as protective factors, and are defined as characteristics or processes that moderate or buffer the negative effects of stress, resulting in more positive behavioural and psychological outcomes than would have been expected in their absence.

In a theoretical framework presented by Werner and Smith (1982, 1992), the authors stated that protective and vulnerability processes affecting children at risk operate on three levels: community (e.g. social support, neighborhood), family (e.g., parental warmth), and the child (e.g., social skillfulness or intelligence). The FRIENDS program uses this multisystem approach by involving children, families, teachers, and schools in the intervention process. Children, parents, and teachers are taught the program's skills, aiming to prepare them to overcome life challenges and adversities.

No child is immune from the pressure of our fast-paced and stressful society. Even children who are not faced with significant adversity or trauma will probably experience some pressure around them (Goldstein & Brooks, 2005). The FRIENDS program is based on the conception that most children will feel pressure at some stage in their lives and it is important to provide them with effective coping skills. When they face a challenging situation (e.g., changing schools or parents' divorce), they have the skills (e.g., problem solving, positive thinking, relaxation, self-soothing among others) to help them to overcome the situation.

In addition to a resiliency framework, the FRIENDS program is also grounded in cognitive-behavioral therapy (CBT). CBT is a form of psychotherapy that blends strategies from traditional behavioral treatments with various cognitively oriented strategies. The difference between CBT and other forms of psychotherapy (e.g., traditional psychodynamic psychotherapies) is that CBT focus on the modification of behaviors and cognitions that are considered to be currently maintaining a problem (here and now), rather than uncovering historical antecedents of maladaptive behavior or thought patterns (Hersen & Rosqvist, 2005).

CBT is one of the most extensively researched forms of psychotherapy (Hollon & Beck, 1994). According to these authors, over 120 controlled clinical trials were added to the literature in the 8 years between 1986 and 1993 and this proliferation has continued. According to Butler, Chapman, Forman, and Beck (2006) there are now over 325 published outcome studies on cognitive-behavioral interventions. This growth is in part because of the ongoing adaptation of CBT to a wide range of disorders and problems (Beck, 1997; Salkovskis, 1996).

According to Hersen and Rosqvist (2005) there are structured treatment protocols based on CBT principles for most psychological disorders (e.g., anxiety disorders). In a meta-analysis conducted by Gloaguen, Cottraux, Cucherat, & Blackburn (1998), the authors found that the effectiveness of CBT for generalized anxiety disorder was substantially superior to waitlist or no-treatment controls, non-directive therapy, and pill placebo. Furthermore, CBT treatment effects were maintained for substantial periods beyond the cessation of treatment.

Over the past 15 years, a number of studies have indicated that CBT is effective in reducing anxiety and emotional distress in children and adolescents (Barrett, Dadds, & Rapee, 1996; Kendall, 1994). A large number of these studies have examined the effectiveness of the FRIENDS program in reducing anxiety and depression in individual and group treatments (Barrett, 1998; Barrett et al., 1996; Barrett, Duffy, Dadds, & Rapee, 2001a; Shortt, Barrett, & Fox, 2001).

CBT for children emphasizes a skills building approach; it is often action-oriented, directive, and frequently educative in nature (Seligman & Ollendick, 2005). The FRIENDS program incorporates several important components from CBT which co-exist with areas of social-emotional learning. It focuses on teaching children cognitive problem-solving skills (e.g. for dealing with interpersonal challenges); recognizing and dealing with body clues (e.g. having control of physiological arousal); cognitive restructuring (e.g. recognizing and changing unhelpful thoughts into helpful thoughts); attention training (e.g. looking for the positive aspect of a situation); graded exposure to fears (e.g. creating a coping step plan); and family/peer support. Social-emotional learning interventions help children accumulate knowledge and skills that facilitate the optimal emotional processing of, and response to, their social context (Zins, Elias, & Greenberg, 2003).

As shown in Figure 22.2, there is an interaction among different processes intervening for the success of the intervention program. For example, if a child thinks that going to a new school is a threatening situation (cognition), his/her body will respond accordingly with sweaty palms, butterflies in the stomach or increased heart rate (physiology). This situation may lead this child to avoid having contact with other children (attachment), which can prevent him/her from learning how to cope properly and enjoy the situation (learning). The FRIENDS program seeks to address each one of the processes individually – attachment, cognitive, learning and physiological – by teaching specific skills and techniques.

Therapeutic Goals and Methods of the FRIENDS Program

The underlying philosophy of the FRIENDS program is strength-based. It empowers families to make positive changes in their lives, and values the unique knowledge and experiences that parent, siblings, and children bring to the group (Pahl & Barrett, 2010a).

The key to the success of the FRIENDS program is for each participant to learn that they have the power to control their thoughts, emotions and to feel good.

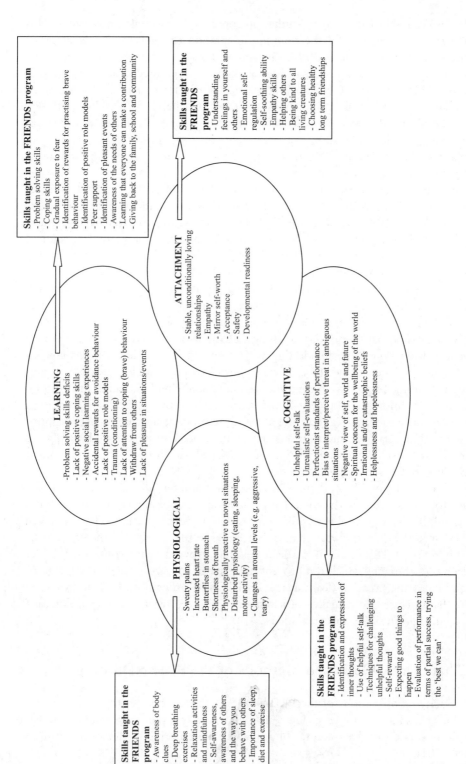

Figure 22.2 The theoretical model for the prevention and early intervention of anxiety (Barrett, 2010b, p. 7). The arrows illustrate how the FRIENDS program relates to each one of the processes.

A variety of group-leader skills are useful for implementing the FRIENDS program. These include:

Positive reinforcement: involves providing encouragement and praise for desirable behavior (e.g. group participation and applying newly learnt skills to situations). This may be in the form of non-verbal communication (such as head nods and eye contact), or verbal communication. The group-leader should use positive reinforcement every time a desirable behavior is shown. For example: "Thank you for sharing your ideas on self-talk (child's name)."

Specific feedback: clear specific feedback should be provided to participants. This helps them understand what they have done well. It also gives them the sense of achievement and encourages them to continue to try hard. For example: "(child's name), I really liked the way you used deep breathing and positive self-talk when you faced the first step of your Coping Step Plan."

Self-disclosure: personal information can be disclosed to help convey examples directly relevant to the course content. This helps to build rapport among the group, as well as aid participants in understanding core concepts. For example: "When I feel worried I get butterflies in my stomach and sweaty palms."

Empathy: refers to the group leader's ability to identify with the participants' feelings, their ability to emotionally put themselves in the place of another person. The attendant skills of paraphrasing, summarizing, and reflecting are strongly involved in developing empathy (Ivey, 1994). Empathy helps to build a therapeutic relationship with the participants – an essential ingredient to success of the FRIENDS program. Encourage empathy between group participants – understanding of other people's feelings.

Paraphrasing: paraphrasing feeds back to the speaker the essence of what they have been saying by shortening and condensing their comments. This communicates to participants that they have indeed been heard. For example: "It sounds as though you think you're not good enough to make the football team. Is that what you are saying?"

Summarizing: summarizing is similar to paraphrasing but covers a longer period of time. The skill of summarizing involves attending to the key concepts of the conversation and then relaying these concepts back to the speaker. For example: "Let me see if I've heard you correctly so far. You often find yourself feeling nervous when you are around people you don't know very well; you get sweaty palms and butterflies in your stomach. But when you are around people you know well, you don't seem to worry as much. Is that right?"

Reflecting: reflecting involves observing participants' emotions and feeding key feelings back to them. This helps participants to clarify their own feelings and indicates that they have been heard correctly (Ivey, 1994). For example: "It sounds like you're feeling pretty upset and worried about your exam next week." Once familiar with the content of the sessions, the group leaders are encouraged to adjust their sessions to suit particular group requirements, such as age range, regional, or cultural characteristics.

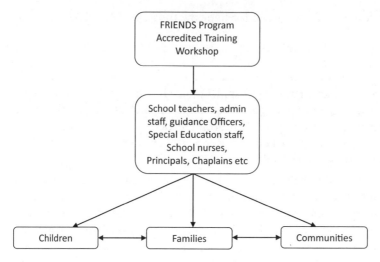

Figure 22.3 Model of the FRIENDS program as a universal preventive intervention implemented at schools.

Delivery of the Program

The FRIENDS program (Barrett, 2008a, 2008b, 2010a, 2010b, 2010c, 2010d) is a 10-session intervention designed to meet the different developmental needs of pre-school children (Fun FRIENDS 4–6 years), early primary school aged children (FRIENDS for Life 7–10 years), and senior primary and high school aged children (My FRIENDS 11–17 years). Although the core of the program is similar across the age groups, each program caters for the developmental differences in children's abilities. This is reflected in each session's content and activities.

The program is designed to permit easy implementation at all levels of the prevention continuum, and also through to early intervention and treatment. It is recommended that the FRIENDS program last from an hour to two hours on a weekly basis across two school terms, and utilizes one or two group leaders depending upon group size.

There are two "booster sessions" to review the central components of the FRIENDS program and to help participants to maintain the skills learnt throughout the sessions. It is advised that the first booster session is implemented 1 month after the 10-session program has been completed, and the second booster session to be implemented 3 months after the end of the program. Booster sessions are extremely important for long-term maintenance of skills. Teachers can utilize these sessions to prepare in advance for any challenges (e.g. carnivals, music performances, exams, camping trips) or to debrief difficult life events (e.g. hospitalizations, illness, accidents).

The program is very cost-effective, involving a group leaders' manual and a participant activity book for each age group. After-school personnel (e.g. teachers, school counselors, chaplains, or nurses) attend an accredited training workshop, the program can be implemented within the classroom as a universal preventive intervention.

The group leader's manual[1] is a user-friendly guide that describes in detail all the information necessary for facilitating the FRIENDS program successfully on a session-by-session basis. The content covered in the manual is: (1) general theoretical information about childhood development and basic knowledge about risk and protective factors for childhood anxiety and depression, (2) the rationale behind the FRIENDS program, (3) the aims of each session and its agenda, (4) the approximate time to be spent in each activity, (5) the materials required for each session, and (6) the major learning for each session.

The participant's activity book[2] contains exercises to be done during the sessions, as well as information for participants to read with their families, and home-based activities. Every participant should have their own FRIENDS activity book as this will allow them not only to write their private information but also keep a record for themselves of all the information learnt during the program.

The FRIENDS program is positively focused, with the content designed to enhance and develop skills and competencies in children and youth. The program integrates key elements from a cognitive-behavioral perspective and combines those with useful strategies from both family therapy and interpersonal approaches. The family and interpersonal components include the establishment and utilization of a social support network, conflict management, and learning the importance of helping other people. The content and process of each session is specified in the group leaders' manual (Barrett, 2008a, 2010b, 2010d), supported by participants' activity books (Barrett, 2008b, 2010a, 2010c). The common thread that runs though the program is the enhancement and/or development of skills and competencies which can be utilized in facing difficult situations, whether they are fears and worries, daily challenges, or aversive and stressful life events.

The program is developed around the acronym FRIENDS to help participants to remember and use the skills taught in the sessions. Each letter of the word stands for a different skill and each skill builds upon the skills previously presented:

Fun FRIENDS	FRIENDS for Life and My FRIENDS
F = Feelings	**F** = Feelings
R = Relax	**R** = Remember to relax. Have quiet time
I = I can try!	**I** = I can do it! I can try my best!
E = Encourage	**E** = Explore solutions and coping step plan
N = Nurture	**N** = Now reward yourself!
D = Don't forget to be brave	**D** = Don't forget to practise
S = Stay happy	**S** = Smile! Stay calm for life!

[1]All FRIENDS program's materials can be found at Pathways Health and Research Centre Website: www.pathwayshrc.com.au

[2]All FRIENDS program's materials can be found at Pathways Health and Research Centre Website: www.pathwayshrc.com.au

Two parent sessions are suggested for those parents interested in their child's involvement in the FRIENDS program. The sessions last approximately 2 hours each. The parent program is designed to educate parents on childhood development, the development and transition of normal fears and worries, and basic knowledge about risk and protective factors for childhood anxiety. It also aims to help parents to manage anxious children and recognize/modify any negatively reinforcing parenting practices. Despite the evidence for the importance of family factors in the development and maintenance of childhood anxiety and depression, few programs incorporate such knowledge into their contents. It is suggested that the first parent session occurs at the beginning of the program and the second parent session half way through the program. These sessions are flexible and may need to be broken into greater or fewer sessions, according to the needs of the group.

The guidelines for the parent sessions are included at the end of the group leaders' manual. It is highly recommended that parents be encouraged to take part in the program and to facilitate practicing the skills as a family for 10–15 minutes daily. This helps to improve the chances of their child learning effective resilience coping skills, and using them in real-life situations within the context of family and school friendships. The FRIENDS program has been designed so that it can be implemented by both teachers in classrooms and clinicians in clinical settings. In this chapter we will focus on the program in schools facilitated by a class teacher.

Session-by-Session

Although the core components of the programs are similar across the three different age groups, and they all follow the FRIENDS acronym, the method of delivery varies to cater for the developmental needs of each age group.

The Fun FRIENDS (4–6 years old) has a large focus on play-based, experiential learning within a CBT framework. Multiple activities lasting approximately 5–10 minutes each are administered to teach the skills to promote resilience in children.

The FRIENDS for Life (7–10 years old) still has a large focus on play-based activities and experiential learning but its activities rely on the more developed cognitive abilities of older children.

The My FRIENDS (11–17 years old) program encourages lots of discussion among the participants about the topics covered. Additionally, it fosters participants' empathy and critical thinking.

Following is the description of the sessions' content and goals of the FRIENDS program for each age group. Group leaders are encouraged to adapt the activities according to their student's specific need. However, it is fundamental to maintain the program's structure and sequence.

Session One

The goal of the first session of the program is to introduce participants to each other, and explain the aims and rationale of the FRIENDS program.

Fun FRIENDS	FRIENDS for Life	My FRIENDS
The first session aims to teach sense of identity to the participants. The concept of being brave by looking people in the eyes, using a brave voice, standing up tall and smiling is introduced. To promote a positive self-identity, children are taught to accept that there are similarities and differences between people and places. Social skills training is covered throughout games. Children are provided with a reward chart to encourage brave behaviors.	The first session aims to help children to understand feelings in themselves and others, and to learn to help others as well. The major learning of this session is helping participants to recognize and share their feelings. The concept of being brave is introduced. To promote a positive self-identity, children are taught to accept that there are similarities and differences between people and places. The importance of working together is also highlighted. Participants are also encouraged to think about happy experiences and set personal goals.	The first session aims to help participants to understand feelings in themselves and others, and to learn to help others as well. The major learning of this session is helping participants to understand that the skills taught in the program are important life-skills that will help them to try their best in all situations. Also, it helps participants to understand that all people are different, and to learn tolerance, empathy, and appreciation of differences. Participants are encouraged to think about different aspects of their lives and set personal goals.

Session Two

Fun FRIENDS	FRIENDS for Life	My FRIENDS
F = Feelings The major learning for this session is to normalize all feelings and teach participants that they can make positive feelings grow.	*F = Feelings* The major learning for this session is having participants to understand and show their feelings, and to care about feelings in others (empathy).	*F = Feelings* The major learning for this session is having participants to understand and show their feelings, and to care about feelings in others (empathy).

(continued)

Fun FRIENDS	FRIENDS for Life	My FRIENDS
	Participants show an understanding of a range of feelings experienced by themselves and others (including animals). They also understand that there are different triggers for different feelings.	This session also aims to teach participant to develop physiological self-awareness as a response to different feelings. They are taught the link between what happens to their bodies when they feel excited, happy, nervous, worried, sad, or angry.

Session Three

Fun FRIENDS	FRIENDS for Life	My FRIENDS
The goal is to teach participants to recognize and understand feelings in other people. Empathy training (how to help other people feel better) is introduced.	**R = Relax** The goal is to enhance participants' awareness of body cues and introduce relaxation activities to them. In this session, participants learn to recognize different signs that their body gives when they feel nervous or worried and some of the situations that make them feel worried. Participants also learn that relaxation activities can help them to calm down and feel more confident. Relaxation activities are presented in this session and participants are encouraged to think about activities that make them feel good.	The goal is to focus on confidence. This session involves enhancing participants' confidence through recognition of their strengths, and developing awareness of how participants can boost the confidence of others. The major learning for this session is for participants to recognize the benefits of having high levels of self confidence. It teaches participants how they can build their own confidence, and help them to understand how social constraints can limit people's ability to make confidence-boosting statements and decisions, as well as accept people's compliments.

Session Four

Fun FRIENDS	FRIENDS for Life	My FRIENDS
R = *Relax*	**I** = *I can do it! I can try my best!*	**R** = *Relax*
In this session, participants learn to recognize different signs their bodies give when they feel nervous or worried (e.g. heart beats fast, butterflies in stomach).	This session helps participants to understand the concept of self-talk and learn to think in positive ways.	The goal of the fourth session of the program is to introduce relaxation activities to the participants.
Participants also learn that relaxation activities can help them to calm down and feel more confident.	Self-talk is described in terms of two different kinds: green helpful thoughts and red unhelpful thoughts.	The major learning outcome for this session is for participants to be able to recognize that relaxation and mindfulness are effective methods of becoming more aware of themselves, of others and of their environment.
Relaxation activities, such as diaphragmatic breathing, progressive muscular relaxation, and visualization are taught in this session.	The analogy with the traffic light is introduced. Green means go and red means stop.	It also teaches participants that relaxation is a positive way of overcoming unhelpful emotions such as stress and worry that affect their physical and psychological health, as the movement from tension to relaxation helps them to gain control over their bodies and manage feelings and difficult situations more effectively.
	The session also encourages participants to learn how they can change their negative thoughts into more positive or "helpful" thoughts. The link between thoughts and feelings is also introduced.	

Session Five

Fun FRIENDS	FRIENDS for Life	My FRIENDS
I = I can try This session helps participants to understand the concept of self-talk and the difference between feelings and thoughts. Self-talk is described in terms of two different kinds: green helpful thoughts and red unhelpful thoughts. The analogy with the traffic light is introduced. Green means go and red means stop. They also learn to think in positive ways.	This session builds upon the content on the previous session by encouraging participants to learn how they can change their unhelpful red thoughts into more helpful green thoughts. They learn how to challenge unhelpful red thoughts and come up with alternative helpful green thoughts.	*I = I can do it! I can try my best! Inner helpful thoughts* The goal is to introduce participants to the idea that positive thoughts are a powerful way to change negative inner thoughts and self-talk. This session helps participants to understand the concept of self-talk and learn to think in positive ways. The analogy with the traffic light is introduced: green means go and red means stop. It also encourages participants to recognize that there are many different ways of thinking about the same situation and that some ways of thinking are going to help them to cope better than others. Participants learn how they can change their unhelpful thoughts into more helpful thoughts as well. The link among thoughts, feelings and behaviors is also introduced.

Session Six

Fun FRIENDS	FRIENDS for Life	My FRIENDS
The goal of this session is to encourage participants to learn how they can change their negative (red) thoughts into more positive or (green) thoughts. They learn how to challenge unhelpful red thoughts and come up with alternative helpful green thoughts.	*E = Explore solutions* This session helps participants to explore ways to solve problems. One way is to break down difficult situations into smaller, more manageable steps (graded exposure hierarchies called "Coping Step Plan").	This session builds upon the content on the previous session by encouraging participants to learn how they can change their unhelpful red thoughts into more helpful green thoughts.

Session Seven

Fun FRIENDS	FRIENDS for Life	My FRIENDS
E = Encourage This session helps participants to set goals and explore ways to solve problems, such as by doing things one step at a time and breaking hard thing down into lots of little steps (graded exposure hierarchies called "Coping Step Plan"). Children are taught how to create a basic step plan. Parents and teachers are encouraged to create step plans for their children.	The goal is to build upon the content on the previous session by encouraging participants to feel confident, brave, and explore further solutions to difficult situations. The major learning outcome for participants in this session is the development of problem-solving skills. Participants learn the importance of social support by identifying role models for them. Also, they are encouraged to identify their own social support team, which will be there to help them to use their problem solving skills they have learnt.	*E = Explore solutions* This session helps participants to set realistic goals for their problems, and explore ways to solve them. One way is to break down difficult situations into smaller, more manageable steps (graded exposure hierarchies called "Coping Step Plan").

Session Eight

Fun FRIENDS	FRIENDS for Life	My FRIENDS
The goal is to teach participants the importance of being friendly and how to make new friends. It introduces the importance of smiling, sharing, helping, and listening.	The goal is to continue with step 4 of the Friends plan: Explore Solutions. In this session, participants are presented with more different ways to explore solutions.	The goal is to continue exploring solutions to difficult situations and to learn about Support Teams (what they are, their importance, and how to build them). It also teaches the importance of role models and suggests participants to think about a role model for themselves.

Session Nine

Fun FRIENDS	FRIENDS for Life	My FRIENDS
In this session, participants are encouraged to plan a party for the last session using the Coping Step Plan.	*N = Now Reward Yourself! You've done your best!* *D = Don't forget to practice!* *S = Smile! Stay Calm and talk to your Support Networks!* The major learning of this session is for participants to focus on the process rather than on the outcome. Participants learn how to reward themselves for trying hard, and are reminded about practice using the steps of the FRIENDS plan they have learnt. It also teaches the importance of having support groups and encourages participants to think about their own support team at home, at school and in the wider community.	*N = Now Reward Yourself! You've done your best!* The goal is to help participants to keep looking at the Coping Step Plans they have built to cope with challenging situations. It introduces participants to leadership skills in Peace making, and teaches different ways to handle conflicts and manage bullying. It also teaches participants the importance of rewarding themselves and how they can do that.

Session Ten

Fun FRIENDS	FRIENDS for Life	My FRIENDS
N = *Nurture* The goal is to teach participants the importance of having role models in their lives. It is suggested that participants think about a role model for themselves.	The goal is to establish strategies to maintain participants' coping skills for use in the future. It also aims to congratulate the participants for the completion of the program and the hard work they have done. The major learning of this session is for participants to learn how to maintain their new skills and that these skills can be used in the future, should they experience any further challenges.	**D** = *Don't forget to practise* **S** = *Stay Strong Inside* The first goal is to remind participants the importance of practicing the skills learnt during the program. Participants are encouraged to share the skills learnt with family and community. The second goal of the session is to encourage participants to start using the FRIENDS plan in real-life situations that they may face. It also encourages participants to help others to feel good about them and to build school, family and community spirit.

Booster Session 1

Fun FRIENDS	FRIENDS for Life	My FRIENDS
D = *Don't forget to be brave* The goal is to show participants the importance of having support groups and to think about their own support team at home, at school and in the wider community. It also teaches participants that they can help other people.	The major learning for this session is to help participants to see the benefits of taking a positive approach to difficult situations and remembering that all situations give opportunities for improvement. This session also aims to help participants to identify alternative solutions and ideas if they are faced with challenges.	The aim of this session is to help participants to remember what they have learnt throughout the program and remind them how they can use the Friends plan in their day-to-day life and in the future.

Booster Session 2

Fun FRIENDS	FRIENDS for Life	My FRIENDS
S = Smile, Stay happy! The last session in the Fun Friends program is a party previously organized by the participants. The components of the Friends plan are reviewed with different games.	The major learning for this session is to encourage participants to continue engaging in positive behaviors and to identify alternative plans if difficult situations arise while implementing their Friends plans.	The major learning for this session is to encourage participants to continue engaging in positive behaviors and to identify alternative plans if difficult situations arise while implementing their Friends plans

Recent Empirical Findings

Evaluation of the efficacy of the FRIENDS program has been a priority for Barrett and colleagues for the past 15 years. A multiple informant and multi-method approach is highly recommended when assessing the FRIENDS program efficacy. Usually, clinical interviews with the child and his/her parents (when possible), and self-report measures are used before and after the end of the intervention. Assessments 6 and 12 months following the treatment are included always when possible.

An initial controlled clinical trial was conducted in 1994 and 1995 to evaluate the program as a clinical intervention for children and youth diagnosed with DSM-IV anxiety disorders (Barrett et al., 1996). The 14-session program formerly known as the Coping Koala Program was offered as individual treatment to anxious children, and parents attended concurrent sessions. Children aged 7–14 who fulfilled diagnostic criteria for anxiety were randomly allocated to three treatment conditions: CBT, CBT + family management, and waiting list. Results at the end of the intervention indicated that, across treatment conditions, 69.8% of children no longer fulfilled diagnostic criteria for an anxiety disorder, compared with 26% of the waiting list children. Twelve months after the intervention, 70.3% of the children in the CBT group and 95.6% of the children in the CBT + family did not meet criteria and have remained so for up to 6 years following the intervention. Results of the 6-year follow-up study indicated that 85.7% no longer fulfilled diagnostic criteria for any anxiety disorder (Barrett, et al., 2001a).

Following on from the successful results achieved in treating anxious children the intervention was later tested in a group format as a family-based, group cognitive-behavioral treatment. In the first controlled trial of a group CBT, Barrett (1998) randomly assigned 60 children aged 7–14 years into three treatment conditions: Group CBT, Group CBT + family management, and waitlist control. Results showed that after the intervention, 56% of the children in the Group CBT and 71% of the children in the Group CBT + family, and 25% of the children in the waiting list no longer met criteria for any anxiety disorder diagnosis. Twelve months after the intervention, 65% of the children in the Group CBT and 85% of children in the Group CBT + family were diagnosis free. These results suggested that CBT family interventions for childhood anxiety disorders can be effective when administered in a group format.

The FRIENDS program was then created. Shortt et al. (2001) conducted the first randomized clinical trial evaluating the efficacy of the FRIENDS program for children. Seventy-one children ranging in age from 6 to 10 years who met diagnostic criteria for an anxiety disorder were randomly assigned to the FRIENDS group or waitlist control. Children in the treatment group participated in 10 weekly sessions in addition to two booster sessions that occurred 1 and 3 months following treatment. Results indicated that children who completed the program showed greater improvement than the waitlist condition. Sixty-eight percent of the children who completed the family group CBT were diagnosis free, as compared to 6% of the children in the waitlist condition. At 12-month follow-up, treatment gains were maintained with 76% of the children in the treatment group diagnosis free. These results were positive and demonstrated the efficacy of the FRIENDS program with family involvement in decreasing anxiety immediately following program implementation and over time.

The FRIENDS Program as an Indicated School-Based Intervention

In 1997 the program was first trialed as an indicated school-based intervention (Dadds et al., 1997). Children were selected for participation following a four-stage screening process that involved measures related to reports of children, teachers, and parents. Screening resulted in an initial cohort of 1786 children, being reduced to a final sample of 128 children aged 7–14 years. The participating children were then randomly assigned to either the intervention group or a monitoring control group. All participating schools were matched for size and socio-demographic variables. A clinically trained psychologist, assisted by a graduate student, facilitated all sessions. Diagnostic status was the primary outcome measure. As a group, children who received the intervention emerged with lower rates of anxiety disorder at a 6-month follow-up, compared to those who were identified but monitored only. In terms of preventive efficacy, from the children who had features of, but no full disorder at pre-intervention, 54% progressed to a diagnosable disorder at the 6 month follow up in the monitoring group, compared with only 16% in the intervention group. These results indicate that the intervention was successful in reducing rates of disorder in children with mild to moderate anxiety disorders, as well as preventing the onset of anxiety disorder in children with early features of a disorder. The intervention effect remained 2 years later (Dadds, Holland, Laurens et al., 1999).

This study was later replicated with an independent research group in the Netherlands (Muris & Mayer, 2000; Muris, Mayer, Bartelds, Tierney, & Bogie, 2001). Four hundred and twenty five children from grades 5–8 across four schools completed childhood anxiety questionnaires during regular classes. Of the 42 children who were invited to participate in the intervention on the basis of elevated scores, 85.7%

consented. The intervention successfully prevented 75% of children from developing an anxiety disorder.

More recently, Liddle and Macmillan (2010) also conducted an indicated preventative study involving 95 children aged 8–14 years in a Scottish setting. Participants were allocated to an intervention group or a waitlist group. The 10-week FRIENDS program was delivered in small settings by educational psychologists. Using standardized self-report measures of anxiety, mood, and self-esteem, the study found significant improvements in all of these measures following the intervention. The results were sustained 4 months later.

The FRIENDS Program as a Universal School-Based Intervention

In addition to being an indicated school-based intervention for anxiety (Dadds et al., 1997; Liddle & Macmillan, 2010; Muris & Mayer, 2000; Muris et al., 2001), the FRIENDS program has provided successful results in decreasing anxiety symptoms as a universal school-based intervention when compared with monitoring participants (Barrett, Farrell, Ollendick, & Dadds, 2006; Barrett & Turner, 2001; Lowry-Webster, Barrett, & Dadds, 2001; Lowry-Webster, Barrett, & Lock, 2003; Pahl & Barrett, 2010b; Rose, Miller, & Martinez, 2009; Stallard, Simpson, Anderson, Carter, Osborn, & Bush, 2005; Stallard, Simpson, Anderson, & Goddard, 2008; Stallard, Simpson, Anderson, Hibbert, & Osborn, 2007).

Universal prevention strategies have the potential to be of enormous benefit in terms of reducing the prevalence of childhood anxiety, as these disorders are one of the most prevalent forms of psychopathology in children and youth. Lowry-Webster and colleagues (2001, 2003) conducted a 12-mont follow-up to their universal anxiety prevention program in seven schools in Australia; where 594 children were randomly assigned to receive the FRIENDS program or a control group. Participants were classified as either "at risk" or "not at risk". Results indicated that although the children's anxiety scores improved significantly from pre-test to post-test, irrespective of whether they had received the intervention or not, the improvement was greater among children who had received the intervention. At post-test, 75.3% of at risk children who had received the intervention were no longer at risk, compared to 42.2% of at risk children who had not received the intervention. At one year follow-up, the anxiety scores among children who had received the intervention remained significantly lower than the scores among the children who had not received the intervention. A further comparison of the anxiety scores at post-test and at follow-up among the children who had received the intervention showed a further significant decrease in anxiety scores from post-test to follow-up.

Barrett and Turner (2001) also investigated the effectiveness of the program when implemented as a universal school-based intervention run by different leaders (psychologists or teachers). In this study, participants were classified as either "at risk" or "healthy" and the schools were randomly assigned to one of three treatment conditions: two intervention conditions (one conducted by a psychologist with 188 participants), and one conducted by a teacher with 263 participants), and a non-intervention, monitoring condition (with 137 participants). Results indicated statistically significant reductions in anxiety symptoms among the children in both intervention conditions compared to the children in the monitoring condition. At post-intervention, "at risk" children in the intervention conditions were more likely to have moved into the "healthy" range compared to "at risk" children in the monitoring condition.

When it comes to when is the best time to intervene, Lock and Barrett (2003) suggested that the earlier the better. The authors conducted a longitudinal study of developmental differences using the FRIENDS program as a universal preventive intervention at schools with 737 participants aged 9–16 years. Their results showed that primary school children reported the greatest changes in reducing anxiety symptoms.

In relation to the long-term effects of the program, Barrett et al. (2006) found that children who had undergone a FRIENDS program demonstrated significantly greater reductions in anxiety 3 years later, for both a 9- to 10- and a 14- to 16-year-old cohort, compared to control groups. Interestingly, they also found stronger prevention impacts at a 4-month follow-up than immediately after the intervention.

More recently, Pahl and Barrett (2010b) found that the program can be used as a school-based universal preventative intervention program for preschool aged children as well. Two hundred sixty three children aged 4–6 attending preschool in Australia were randomly allocated into an intervention group or a waiting list control group. In a 12-month follow-up, parent report data revealed improvements on anxiety levels, behavioral inhibition and social emotional strength in the intervention group. Teachers' reports revealed significant improvements after the intervention on behavioral inhibition and social emotional strength for the children who received the program.

Additionally, the FRIENDS program has shown promising results when used as a universal intervention in schools in countries other than Australia. Stallard et al. (2007) used the program in the UK with children aged 9–10 years. Anxiety and self-esteem levels were recorded as stable for 6 months prior to the program commencing. Three months after completing the FRIENDS program, rates of anxiety had decreased and self-esteem increased, both significantly. In a 12-month follow-up study, the authors found that the significant improvements in emotional health identified 3 months after the intervention were maintained. That is, 67% of the children initially identified as high risk had moved into the low-risk category after 12 months, and none of the low-risk children had become high risk (Stallard et al., 2008).

Likewise, Rose et al. (2009) found reduced levels of anxiety when the program was used in Canada.

These intervention effects were demonstrated equally across psychologist-led and teacher-led interventions, suggesting that the FRIENDS program can be successfully implemented by lay providers, such as teachers within existing systems. Most encouraging were the positive effects shown for children who displayed high levels of anxious symptomatology before the intervention. In comparison to the monitoring condition, the intervention condition resulted in a significant reduction in the number of children who reported clinical levels of anxious symptomatology after the intervention. Additionally, if the intervention can be successfully delivered within existing systems and resources (by school teachers within the classroom, for example), their cost-effectiveness is improved and sustainability is enhanced.

More recently, strength-based measures (e.g., happiness, resilience, and coping skills) have been added to evaluate the effectiveness of the intervention in terms of its ability to enhance participant happiness, and promote more positive, proactive coping strategies. Additionally, social validation of the FRIENDS program has been conducted to establish not only whether the intervention works, but also whether participants consider the program to be beneficial and worthwhile (Barrett, Shortt, Fox, & Wescombe, 2001b). Parents, children, and adolescents were surveyed over time on their global satisfaction with the program, the acceptability of the treatment components, and the completion of homework tasks. Results indicated a high level of satisfaction with the FRIENDS program and high completion rate of homework tasks.

Summing up, an increasing body of evidence shows that CBT school-based interventions seeking to prevent childhood depression and anxiety have large potential to improve the lives and well-being of both participants and their families. It is the role of clinicians, researchers, and teachers to advocate for the importance of children's social and emotional development as a way not only to prevent mental health problems, but mainly to promote their general well-being.

References

Atkinson, P. A., Martin, C. R., & Rankin, J. (2009). Resilience revisited. *Journal of Psychiatric and Mental Health Nursing, 16*, 137–145.

Barrett, P. M. (1998). Evaluation of cognitive-behavioral group treatments for childhood anxiety disorders. *Journal of Clinical Child Psychology, 27* (4), 459–468.

Barrett, P. M. (2008a). *Fun Friends: a Facilitator's Guide to Building Resilience in 4 to 7 Year Old Children*, 2nd edn. Brisbane: Barrett Research Resources Pty Ltd.

Barrett, P. M. (2008b). *Fun Friends: Family Adventure*, 2nd edn. Brisbane: Barrett Research Resources Pty Ltd.

Barrett, P. M. (2010a). *Friends for Life: Activity Book for Children*, 5th edn. Brisbane: Barrett Research Resources Pty Ltd.

Barrett, P. M. (2010b). *Friends for Life: Group Leaders' Manual for Children*, 5th edn. Brisbane: Barrett Research Resources Pty Ltd.

Barrett, P. M. (2010c). *My Friends Youth Resilience Program: Activity Book for Youth*, 5th edn. Brisbane: Barrett Research Resources Pty Ltd.

Barrett, P. M. (2010d). *My Friends Youth Resilience Program: Group Learders' Manual for Youth*, 5th edn. Brisbane: Barrett Research Resources Pty Ltd.

Barrett, P. M., Dadds, M. R., & Rapee, R. M. (1996). Family treatment of childhood anxiety: A controlled trial. *Journal of Consulting and Clinical Psychology, 64* (2), 333–342.

Barrett, P. M., Duffy, A. L., Dadds, M. R., & Rapee, R. M. (2001a). Cognitive-behavioral treatment of anxiety disorders in children: Long-term (6-year) follow-up. *Journal of Consulting and Clinical Psychology, 69* (1), 135–141.

Barrett, P. M., Farrell, L., Dadds, M., & Boulter, N. (2005). Cognitive-behavioral family treatment of childhood obsessive-compulsive disorder: Long-term follow-up and predictors of outcome. *Journal of the American Academy of Child and Adolescent Psychiatry, 44* (10), 1005–1014.

Barrett, P. M., Farrell, L. J., Ollendick, T. H., & Dadds, M. (2006). Long-term outcomes of an Australian universal prevention trial of anxiety and depression symptoms in children and youth: An evaluation of the friends program. *Journal of Clinical Child and Adolescent Psychology, 35*(3), 403–411.

Barrett, P. M., & Ollendick, T. H. (2004). *Handbook of Interventions That Work with Children and Adolescents: Prevention and Treatment* (Vol. XVII). New York: John Wiley & Sons, Ltd.

Barrett, P. M., & Pahl, K. M. (2006). School-based intervention: Examining a universal approach to anxiety management. *Australian Journal of Guidance and Counselling, 16* (1), 55–75.

Barrett, P. M., Shortt, A. L., Fox, T. L., & Wescombe, K. (2001b). Examining the social validity of the FRIENDS treatment program for anxious children. *Behaviour Change, 18* (2), 63–77.

Barrett, P. M., & Turner, C. (2001). Prevention of anxiety symptoms in primary school children: Preliminary results from a universal school-based trial. *British Journal of Clinical Psychology, 40,* 399–410.

Beck, A. T. (1997). The past and future of cognitive therapy. *Journal of Psychotherapy Practice and Research, 6,* 276–284.

Boyd, C. P., Kostanski, M., Gullone, E., Ollendick, T. H., & Shek, D. T. L. (2000). Prevalence of anxiety and depression in Australian adolescents: Comparisons with worldwide data. *Journal of Genetic Psychology, 161* (4), 479–492.

Butler, A. C., Chapman, J. E., Forman, E. M., & Beck, A. T. (2006). The empirical status of cognitive-behavioral therapy: A review of meta-analyses. *Clinical Psychology Review, 26*(1), 17–31.

Chavira, D. A., Stein, M. B., Bailey, K., & Stein, M. T. (2004). Child anxiety in primary care: Prevalent but untreated. *Depression and Anxiety, 20* (4), 155–164.

Cole, D. A., Peeke, L. G., Martin, J. M., Truglio, R., & Seroczynski, A. D. (1998). A longitudinal look at the relation between depression and anxiety in children and adolescents. *Journal of Consulting and Clinical Psychology, 66* (3), 451–460.

Costello, E. J., & Angold, A. (1995). Epidemiology. In J. S. March (Ed.), *Anxiety Disorders in Children and Adolescents* (pp. 109–124). New York: Guilford Press.

Dadds, M. R., Holland, D. E., Laurens, K. R., Mullins, M., Barrett, P. M., & Spence, S. H. (1999). Early intervention and prevention of anxiety disorders in children: Results at 2-year follow-up. *Journal of Consulting and Clinical Psychology, 67* (1), 145–150.

Dadds, M. R., Spence, S. H., Holland, D. E., Barrett, P. M., & Laurens, K. R. (1997). Prevention and early intervention for anxiety disorders: a controlled trial. *Journal of Consulting and Clinical Psychology, 65* (4), 627–635.

Donovan, C. L., & Spence, S. H. (2000). Prevention of childhood anxiety disorders. *Clinical Psychology Review, 20* (4), 509–531.

Essau, C. A. (2005). Frequency and patterns of mental health services utilization among adolescents with anxiety and depressive disorders. *Depression and Anxiety, 22* (3), 130–137.

Farmer, E. M. Z., Burns, B. J., Phillips, S. D., Angold, A., & Costello, E. J. (2003). Pathways into and through mental health services for children and adolescents. *Psychiatric Services, 54* (1), 60–66.

Farrell, L., & Barrett, P. M. (2007). Prevention of childhood emotional disorders: Reducing the burden of suffering associated with anxiety and depression. *Child and Adolescent Mental Health, 12* (2), 58–65.

Garmezy, N. (1985). Stress-resistant children: The search for protective factors. In J. E. Stevenson (Ed.), *Recent research in developmental psychopathology* (pp. 213–233). Oxford: Pergamon.

Gladstone, T. R. G., & Beardslee, W. R. (2009). The prevention of depression in children and adolescents: a review. *Canadian Journal of Psychiatry-Revue Canadienne De Psychiatrie, 54* (4), 212–221.

Gloaguen, V., Cottraux, J., Cucherat, M., & Blackburn, I. M. (1998). A meta-analysis of the effects of cognitive therapy in depressed patients. *Journal of Affective Disorders, 49* (1), 59–72.

Goldstein, S., & Brooks, R. B. (2005). *Handbook of Resilience in Children.* New York: Kluwer Academic/Plenum.

Greenberg, P. E., Sisitsky, T., Kessler, R. C., Finkelstein, S. N., Berndt, E. R., Davidson, J. R. T., et al. (1999). The economic burden of anxiety disorders in the 1990s. *Journal of Clinical Psychiatry, 60* (7), 427–435.

Hersen, M., & Rosqvist, J. (2005). *Encyclopedia of Behavior Modification and Cognitive Behavior Therapy.* Thousand Oaks, CA: Sage.

Hollon, S. D., & Beck, A. T. (1994). Cognitive and cognitive-behavioral therapies. In A. E. Bergin & S. L. Garfield (Eds.), *Handbook of Psychotherapy and Behavior Change,* 4 edn (pp. 428–466). New York: John Wiley & Sons, Ltd.

Ivey, A. E. (1994). *International Interviewing and Counseling: Facilitating Client Development in a Multicultural Society,* 3rd edn. Belmont: Brooks-Cole.

Kendall, P. C. (1994). Treating anxiety disorders in children: Results of a randomized clinical trial. *Journal of Consulting and Clinical Psychology, 62* (1), 100–110.

Kessler, R. C., Berglund, P., Demler, O., Jin, R., & Walters, E. E. (2005). Lifetime prevalence and age-of-onset distributions' of DSM-IV disorders in the national comorbidity survey replication. *Archives of General Psychiatry, 62* (6), 593–602.

Liddle, I., & Macmillan, S. (2010). Evaluating the FRIENDS programme in a Scottish setting. *Educational Psychology in Practice, 26* (1), 53–67.

Lock, S., & Barrett, P. M. (2003). A longitudinal study of developmental differences in universal preventive intervention for child anxiety. *Behaviour Change, 20* (4), 183–199.

Lowry-Webster, H. M., Barrett, P. M., & Dadds, M. R. (2001). A universal prevention trial of anxiety and depressive symptomatology in childhood: Preliminary data from an Australian study. *Behaviour Change, 18* (1), 36–50.

Lowry-Webster, H. M., Barrett, P. M., & Lock, S. (2003). A universal prevention trial of anxiety symptomology during childhood: Results at 1-year follow-up. *Behaviour Change, 20* (1), 25–43.

Masia-Warner, C., Nangle, D. W., & Hansen, D. J. (2006). Bringing evidence-based child mental health services to the schools: General issues and specific populations. *Education and Treatment of Children, 29* (2), 165–172.

Mattison, R. E. (1992). Anxiety disorders. In S. R. Hooper, G. W. Hynd, & R. E. Mattison (Eds.), *Child Psychopathology: Diagnostic Criteria and Clinical Assessment* (pp. 179–202). New Jersey: Erlbaum.

Mrazek, P. J., & Haggerty, R. J. (1994). *Reducing Risks for Mental Disorders: Frontiers for Preventive Intervention Research.* Washington, DC: National Academy Press.

Muris, P., & Mayer, B. (2000). Vroegtijdige behandeling van angststoornissen bij kinderen (Early treatment of anxiety disorders in children). *Gedrag-and_Gezondheid: Tijdschrift voor Psychologie and Gezondheid, 28,* 235–242.

Muris, P., Mayer, B., Bartelds, E., Tierney, S., & Bogie, N. (2001). The revised version of the screen for child anxiety related emotional disorders (SCARED-R): Treatment sensitivity in an early intervention trial for childhood anxiety disorders. *British Journal of Clinical Psychology, 40,* 323–336.

Neil, A. L., & Christensen, H. (2009). Efficacy and effectiveness of school-based prevention and early intervention programs for anxiety. *Clinical Psychology Review, 29* (3), 208–215.

Pahl, K. M., & Barrett, P. M. (2010a). Interventions for anxiety disorders in children using group CBT with family involvement. In J. Weisz & A. Kazdin (Eds.), *Evidence-Based Psychotherapies for Children and Adolescents,* 2 edn (pp. 61–79). New York: Guildford.

Pahl, K. M., & Barrett, P. M. (2010b). Preventing anxiety and promoting social and emotional strength in preschool children: A universal evaluation of the Fun FRIENDS program. *Advances in School Mental Health Promotion, 3* (3), 14–25.

Rapee, R. M., Kennedy, S., Ingram, M., Edwards, S., & Sweeney, L. (2005). Prevention and early intervention of anxiety disorders in inhibited preschool children. *Journal of Consulting and Clinical Psychology, 73* (3), 488–497.

Rapee, R. M., Schniering, C. A., & Hudson, J. L. (2009). Anxiety disorders during childhood and adolescence: Origins and treatment. *Annual Review of Clinical Psychology, 5,* 311–341.

Rose, H., Miller, L., & Martinez, Y. (2009). Friends for Life: The results of a resilience-building, anxiety-prevention program in a Canadian Elementary School. *Professional School Counselling* (1216), 400–407.

Salkovskis, P. M. (1996). *Frontiers of Cognitive Therapy.* New York: Guilford Press.

Schoenfeld, N. A., & Janney, D. M. (2008). Identification and treatment of anxiety in students with emotional or behavioral disorders: A review of literature. *Education and Treatment of Children, 31* (4), 583–610.

Seligman, L. D., & Ollendick, T. H. (2005). Children behavior therapy. In A. Freeman (Ed.), *Encyclopedia of Cognitive Behavior Therapy.* New York: Springer.

Shortt, A. L., Barrett, P. M., & Fox, T. L. (2001). Evaluating the FRIENDS program: A cognitive-behavioral group treatment for anxious children and their parents. *Journal of Clinical Child Psychology, 30* (4), 525–535.

Spence, S. H. (1996). The prevention of anxiety disorders in childhood. In P. Cotton & H. Jackson (Eds.), *Early Intervention and Prevention in Mental Health* (pp. 87–107). Melbourne: Australian Psychological Society.

Stallard, P., Simpson, N., Anderson, S., Carter, T., Osborn, C., & Bush, S. (2005). An evaluation of the FRIENDS programme: A cognitive behaviour therapy intervention to promote emotional resilience. *Archives of Disease in Childhood, 90* (10), 1016–1019.

Stallard, P., Simpson, N., Anderson, S., & Goddard, M. (2008). The FRIENDS emotional health prevention programme: 12 month follow-up of a universal UK school based trial. *European Child and Adolescent Psychiatry, 17* (5), 283–289.

Stallard, P., Simpson, N., Anderson, S., Hibbert, S., & Osborn, C. (2007). The FRIENDS emotional health programme: Initial findings from a school-based project. *Child and Adolescent Mental Health, 12* (1), 32–37.

Strein, W., Hoagwood, K., & Cohn, A. (2003). School psychology: a public health perspective I. Prevention, populations, and systems change. *Journal of School Psychology, 41* (1), 23–38.

Tomb, M., & Hunter, L. (2004). Prevention of anxiety in children and adolescents in a school setting: The role of school-based practitioners. *Children and Schools, 26* (2), 87–101.

UNESCO (2005). *Global Education Digest.* Montreal: Institute of Statistics.

Werner, E. E., & Smith, R. S. (1982). *Vulnerable but Invincible: a Study of Resilient Children.* New York: McGraw-Hill.

Werner, E. E., & Smith, R. S. (1992). *Overcoming the Odds: High Risk Children from Birth to Adulthood.* Ithaca, NY: Cornell University Press.

Whitman, C. V., Aldinger, C., Zhang, X. W., & Magner, E. (2008). Strategies to address mental health through schools with examples from China. *International Review of Psychiatry, 20* (3), 237–249.

WHO (2004). *Prevention of Mental Disorders: Effective Interventions and Policy Options.* Geneva, Switzerland: World Health Organization.

Zins, J., Elias, M., & Greenberg, M. (2003). Facilitating success in school and in life through social and emotional learning. *Perspectives in Education, 21* (4), 55–67.

23

Prevention of Anxiety in Children and Adolescents with Autism and Asperger Syndrome

Tony Attwood[1] and Kate Sofronoff[2]

[1]The Asperger's Syndrome Clinic, Australia
[2]The University of Queensland, Australia

The impact of an autism spectrum disorder (ASD) is increasingly recognized with 1 in 150 children currently diagnosed (Chakrabarti & Fombonne, 2005). The social emotional impairments, language and communication difficulties, and repetitive and restricted behaviors and interests are also relatively well recognized. What has lagged behind is the recognition of the psychological sequelae that is likely to accompany the diagnosis, not least of which is the debilitating anxiety that besets many of these children, adolescents and adults.

There have been many estimates of the rate of anxiety experienced by children with ASD. In clinical settings, referrals for anxiety-based problems are among the most common for children and adolescents with ASD (Ghaziuddin, 2002). To date there are no reported large-scale epidemiological studies on the rates of anxiety disorders in ASD but a recent review paper reported rates of 11–84% (White, Oswald, Ollendick & Scahill, 2009). For example, de Bruin, Ferdinand, Meester, de Nijs, and Verheij (2007) found that 55% of their clinic sample met criteria for at least one anxiety disorder while Simonoff, Pickles, Charman, Chandler, Loucas, and Baird (2008) reported that 42% of a population sample met criteria for an anxiety disorder. These rates are significantly higher than rates of anxiety reported for children in the typically developing population; we do not have rates of anxiety for adolescents with ASD but they are likely to be higher than for children (White et al., 2009).

Many of the difficulties faced by young people with ASD are exacerbated if not caused by anxiety symptoms. The school setting is especially anxiety-provoking and teacher reports of anxiety frequently reflect greater severity than parent reports (Guttman-Steinmetz, Gadow, DeVincent, & Crowell, 2010). The relationship between anxiety and repetitive behaviors has been the subject of ongoing research efforts (Gadow, Roohi, DeVincent, Kirsch, & Hatchwell, 2010; Wood & Gadow, 2010) with suggestions that anxiety is likely to exacerbate repetitive and stereotypic behaviors (Joosten, Bundy, & Einfeld, 2009). Issues with anxiety are also likely to increase social interaction impairments (Beaumont & Sofronoff, 2008) and this in

The Wiley-Blackwell Handbook of The Treatment of Childhood and Adolescent Anxiety, First Edition.
Edited by Cecilia A. Essau and Thomas H. Ollendick.

turn can leave the child vulnerable to bullying and teasing from peers (Sofronoff, Dark, & Stone, 2011).

Interventions for Anxiety

The evidence base for interventions for anxiety in the typically developing population is strong and the non-pharmacological treatment of choice is cognitive-behavior therapy (CBT; Kendall, Aschenbrand, & Hudson, 2003; Ollendick, King, & Chorpita, 2006). CBT for anxiety in children typically includes the use of graded exposure techniques, relaxation strategies, cognitive restructuring, modeling, and reinforcement (Kendall & Hedtke, 2006).

CBT for anxiety with children with ASD

In the past decade there has been a growing literature devoted to cognitive-behavioral interventions for anxiety in children with ASD. There have been a number of single case studies (e.g., Reaven & Hepburn, 2003), several small group intervention studies (e.g., Sze & Wood, 2007) and an increasing number of randomized controlled trials (e.g., Chalfant, Rapee, & Carroll, 2007; Sofronoff, Attwood, & Hinton, 2005; Wood, Drahota, Sze, Har, Chui, & Langer, 2009). Each of these programs has been based in a cognitive-behavioural theoretical framework and each has underscored the need for modifications to suit the cognitive profile of a child with ASD. The "Cool Kids" program (Lyneham, Abbott, Wignall, & Rapee, 2003) was adapted for a trial with children with ASD (Chalfant et al., 2007). The program was extended over a longer time frame (12 × 2-hour sessions over 6 months), greater use of visual materials was introduced, and more emphasis was placed on concrete exercises. Results indicated that the program was effective in reducing child-, teacher- and parent-reported anxiety. Wood et al. (2009) suggested that CBT should be *expanded* rather than adapted to suit the cognitive profile of a child with ASD. They adapted the "Building Confidence" program (Wood & McLeod, 2008) for use with children with ASD and also included additional modules for children, parents and teachers to address areas such as social skill deficits, adaptive skills, circumscribed interests, and other problem behaviors. There were 16 weekly 90-minute sessions that focused on anxiety management with 30 minutes spent with the child and 60 minutes with parents. The results from the program demonstrated very positive outcomes based on parent-report measures of anxiety.

Moree and Davis (2010) have provided a good review of the trends in modification of CBT programs for anxiety in children with ASD. The predominant trends include developing disorder specific hierarchies, using more concrete and visual strategies to explain concepts, including the child's specific interest where possible, and engaging actively with parents. The notion of creating hierarchies that account for the cognitive profile of the individual child is central to a program and clearly differentiates it from a program for typically developing children. Anxiety is treated, therefore, within the context of the cognitive profile of ASD – incorporating social and communication skills and taking account of difficulties with perspective taking that a child may have.

We would also emphasize the need to take a positive and strengths-based approach in which the positive attributes of the child are celebrated and the talents and special interests are used to increase motivation and understanding.

The "Exploring Feelings" program (Attwood, 2004) was developed specifically for children with ASD and the following section provides a detailed explanation of the adaptations made and the session content.

Adaptations for children with an ASD

Typical children have an intuitive ability to perceive emotions within others and themselves, an extensive vocabulary to precisely describe those emotions, and a wide range of emotion repair mechanisms. Children with an ASD have difficulties with all these abilities (Attwood, 2007). The psychological term Theory of Mind describes the ability to recognize and understand the thoughts and emotions of other people – in other words, "mind reading." There is now considerable literature that confirms that children with an ASD have impaired Theory of Mind. However, this can include impaired theory of own mind, that is, perceiving and conceptualizing inner thoughts and feelings, or self-reflection. Impaired Theory of Mind can also lead to dysfunctional beliefs and cognitive distortions regarding the intentions of others, for example falsely believing malicious intent, leading to an irrational fear of harm. While research on Theory of Mind abilities has identified the problems children with an ASD have "reading" emotional states, clinical experience and research has also confirmed characteristics of alexithymia, namely a diminished vocabulary to describe the different levels of emotional experience, especially the more subtle or complex emotions (Hill, Berthoz, & Frith, 2004). Research on the cognitive abilities of children with an ASD has also identified cognitive inflexibility; in particular, not having a wide range of problem-solving strategies. This can restrict the range of emotion repair mechanisms available to the child. Thus, the affective education and cognitive restructuring components of CBT are particularly important for this population.

Children with an ASD usually have hyper- or hyporeactivity to sensory input. Indeed, this characteristic is being proposed as one of the diagnostic criteria for ASD in DSM-V. Sensory experiences that are innocuous to other children, such as the noise of a vacuum cleaner, can be perceived as distinctly aversive for a child with an ASD. This can create a heightened sense of anxiety that is associated with specific sensory experiences. Clinical experience has also identified that children with an ASD are prone to developing an almost pathological fear of failure or errors and a tendency to "catastrophize" or "hit the panic button" in situations that should be associated with a relatively mild level of anxiety (Attwood, 2007). Clinical experience has also identified that children with an ASD are less likely than typical children to use other strategies such as affection, disclosing feelings in a conversation, relaxation, and reflection to alleviate anxiety. There is also a greater tendency to primarily rely on destruction, solitude, and using the special interest as a means of "thought blocking" to manage anxiety. Thus, during the assessment phase of CBT for a child with an ASD, the clinician will need to examine aspects of Theory of Mind abilities, alexithymia, and sensory sensitivity, and also be aware of intense emotional overreactions and a limited repertoire of emotion repair mechanisms.

We also recognize that children with an ASD are at risk of comorbid ADHD and Oppositional Defiant Disorder. A dual diagnosis will impact on the design and application of a CBT program. While in research studies, subjects are randomly allocated to an experimental or control group, in clinical practice this is not required, and careful consideration can be made with regard to the personalities and abilities of group participants that can affect group dynamics and the rate of progress. It is also important to consider each child's learning profile. Children with an ASD are more responsive to programs that are highly structured and appeal to the logical or scientific thinking associated with ASD. The cognitive profile can include remarkable visual reasoning abilities such that activities are enhanced with the use of pictures and drawing, thereby placing less emphasis on conversation. Due to problems with generalization associated with ASD, role plays and practice in real-life situations need to be included in the program to a greater extent than would occur with a typical child. It is also important that the clinician has an understanding of other characteristics of children with an ASD, such as a tendency to make literal interpretations so that idioms and metaphor could be confusing; and that such children are at greater risk than their peers of being the victim of bullying and teasing.

Therapeutic goals and methods

The main modifications to a conventional CBT program for children with an ASD are a greater emphasis on affective education and an increase in the range of emotional repair mechanisms. The theme of the Exploring Feelings program was to encourage the participants to be scientists investigating why we have emotions, discovering how to identify and measure emotions, and new strategies that can alleviate feeling anxious. This approach appeals to the logical thinking of children with an ASD. Due to problems with Theory of Mind, there needs to be a greater component, compared to typical children, on how to discover the salient cues that indicate feeling anxious, especially internal physiological signals and changes to thinking and behavior. Sometimes children with an ASD are the last to be aware of their own increasing levels of anxiety, with parents and teachers more able to identify the cues that indicate the rising levels of emotion. A strategy specifically designed for children with an ASD to improve Theory of Mind abilities is the use of Social Stories and Comic Strip Conversations which have been developed by Carol Gray (Gray, 1998; Karkhaneh, Clark, Ospina, Seida, Smith, & Hartling, 2010). Social Stories enable adults to understand the perspective of the ASD child and why he or she feels anxious, and the stories can incorporate CBT treatment components. Comic Strip conversations use simple drawings with stick figures, and thought, speech and emotion bubbles to illustrate events and emotions. They are particularly useful in correcting inaccurate or dysfunctional perceptions of social situations.

The affective education component of CBT is also important in improving the vocabulary of the child with an ASD to describe emotions, thereby diminishing the effects of alexithymia. The approach adopted in the Exploring Feelings program was to quantify the degree of expression such that if the precise word was elusive, the child could calibrate and express his or her degree of anxiety using a thermometer or numerical rating. To accommodate a fear of failure, there was an emphasis on positive reinforcement. Some children who have an ASD have a fascination with machinery and are eager to repair items in the home and at school. To increase cognitive flexibility, there was a conceptualization of emotional repair using a "tool box" with many different types of tool or strategy to fix or repair feelings of anxiety.

The Exploring Feelings program included a workbook for participants to record information, although this was deliberately kept to a minimum due to the authors' recognition that children with an ASD often have poor handwriting skills and prefer to watch and do rather than take notes. At the end of each session the project to be completed before the next session was explained, and then discussed at the start of the subsequent session. The project was designed to obtain more information or data and to apply strategies in real situations. The clinician had trainers' notes for each session that provided information on time allocation, resources needed for each session and the rationale and details needed for each activity. The program ran for six sessions with each session lasting 2 hours. The participant's manual and trainers' notes are available commercially (Attwood, 2004).

Session 1

Children with an anxiety disorder can become anxious at the mere thought of having to talk about anxiety, knowing the emotion will be experienced again. The first session explored two positive emotions to reassure the child that the sessions were not going to be unpleasant and to demonstrate the types of activity that can be used to explore feelings and which could subsequently be applied to anxiety. The first emotion in the program was happiness, followed by relaxation. There were several activities employed to measure, experience, and compare positive emotions in specific situations.

Children with an ASD often develop special interests and these were identified in session 1. The interest can become an effective emotion repair mechanism in the "tool box" and be used to improve conceptualization with examples taken from a special interest (Attwood, 2007); if the child has a fascination with Harry Potter, for example, he or she could be encouraged to be brave in adversity by imagining what Harry would do in a particular situation.

The project to be completed before the second session included identifying situations that elicit feelings of happiness, a happiness diary and a pleasures book, which included a brief description of why specific activities, experiences, thoughts, and sensations are associated with happiness. Resources to be used in the program were to be collected, such as pictures of people in various states of relaxation; and a rating scale to identify specific situations associated with different levels of anxiety was to be completed.

Session 2

This session started with the exploration of feelings of anxiety, and the recognition of the changes that anxiety creates in the body, thinking, behavior, and speech. An explanation was given of the survival value of anxiety in precipitating the fight or flight response and the release of energy to overcome or escape predators. The concept of an emotional toolbox with many different types of tool to repair feelings of anxiety was introduced. One type of tool in a mechanic's toolbox is a hammer, and this was used to represent physical activities that use a quick release of intense energy to repair feelings of anxiety. The constructive release of energy is very important for children with an ASD, as many of their preferred activities are sedentary, and they often choose not to engage in active games in the playground or at home. They are also frequently excluded from active play with peers due to their being clumsy. An addition to the program could be to seek advice from a personal trainer to design a range of vigorous physical activities that suit the body type, interests, and personality of the child. Another tool in the toolbox is a brush to brush away the dust; this represents tools that help the child relax. The project for this session was to identify with family members and friends both physical and relaxing tools that could be added to their personal emotion repair tool box.

Session 3

The third session explored social tools, in other words, how other people can help fix your feelings using words and gestures of affection. However, children with an ASD can be tactile defensive, and a hug can be perceived as an unpleasant experience. It is important to use expressions of affection that are pleasurable, relaxing, and comforting for the child with an ASD, and these may be unusually moderate expressions that would not be sufficient for a typical child. Sometimes an effective emotional repair strategy for a child with an ASD is solitude, with no social interaction for a time. The section on social tools also explored how the child could help fix the anxious feelings of someone in the family or a friend at school. This section also included how animals can help the child relax, since children with an ASD are often more able to relate to and enjoy the company of animals than people. Thinking tools were introduced into the toolbox as a means of repairing anxious feelings. To avoid a tendency of children with an ASD to catastrophize, the value of putting things in perspective and a reality check was explored. Other thinking tools included ways to encourage being brave and feeling self-confident, and the use of imagination.

Other tools explored in session 3 were special interests, humor, and acting. The special interest is not only an enjoyable intellectual and emotional experience for a child with an ASD, it can also serve as a thought blocker that may act as a barrier to anxious thoughts. Because children with an ASD have few alternative strategies to escape feelings of anxiety, they can become quite agitated if they are denied access to their special interest. The approach in the Exploring Feelings program is not to eliminate the special interest but to ensure that there are alternative emotion management strategies. Sometimes the special interest originally began as a means of using knowledge to overcome fear. For example, one child had a fear of spiders. Whenever she saw a spider at home, she ran not to her mother for comfort, but to the bookshelves to read about spiders in order to understand them rather than be afraid of them – a very intelligent strategy. The more she read about spiders, the more fascinated she became regarding their abilities, and she then began to collect spiders. Arachnophobia became arachnophilia. Another tool that can be used is humor to release emotional energy through laughter, for example, while watching a favorite comedy show or reading a humorous book or comic. Some children with an ASD can be encouraged to use acting as a way to deal with their anxiety; they become their favorite hero, or someone they know and admire, who they believe would be able to cope with an anxiety-provoking situation. This provides the child with a role model and script.

This session also explores the concept of inappropriate repair tools, such as using a sledge hammer to fix a computer. Inappropriate tools included becoming excessively controlling at home, using threats and emotional blackmail to avoid situations associated with anxiety; the excessive use of routines and rituals to relax; or an excessive amount of time spent in solitude or engaged in the special interest. Also, the discharging of emotional energy by fighting and tormenting siblings was explained as an inappropriate tool. The clinician may also examine the tools used by adults to check if they are appropriate, or should be removed from the emotion repair tool box. The project for session 3 was for the child to create with parents his or her personal tool box, and to start using the tools discovered in the current and previous sessions.

Session 4

The fourth session focused on a measuring instrument for anxiety, starting with a length of rope on the floor as a "thermometer" to measure the degree of anxiety. Situations were proposed that elicit anxiety for all the participants and each participant was asked to stand on the rope at the position that represented his or her level of anxiety. The person who indicated the least anxiety was asked how he or she seemed more able to cope with that particular situation. This became the basis for discussion, with the participants offering advice to each other. The next activity was to use role plays of each participant's situation to practice strategies generated by the group. The project between sessions was to draw a thermometer on a very large piece of paper. The participant was asked to think of situations that create various levels of anxiety, and to write each situation on a Post-it, which was then placed at the point on the thermometer that represented the degree of anxiety associated with it. The participant was also to consider and put into practice strategies from the personal emotional toolbox to deal with a situation identified in session 4 that was associated with a relatively mild expression of anxiety.

Session 5

The fifth session introduced the Social Stories component of the program. This was to improve social and emotional knowledge and combine the tools in a written plan or Social Story. There needed to be some guidance from the clinician in writing a Social Story based on the recommendations of Carol Gray (2010). The other activity in session 5 was to create antidotes to poisonous thoughts. First, the participants were required to read a list of thoughts and identify which would be helpful (an antidote) or unhelpful (poisonous) in managing anxiety. Then, as a group, they were to suggest antidotes to specific poisonous thoughts, such as "Everyone hates me." The project was to write a Social Story with parents regarding one of the situations that elicit anxiety, create a list of personal "poisonous thoughts" and explore potential antidotes.

Session 6

The main focus for session 6 was for the participants to design a CBT program for themselves and other members of the group. The participants worked in pairs creating emotional repair tools for each other, writing a Social Story as a plan of what to do and a list of antidotes to poisonous thoughts. At the conclusion of session 6, the participants were asked to identify the key points they had learned during the course, and the assessment instruments for anxiety were completed to identify changes in clinical profile and knowledge.

Postscript to the program

The participants were able to provide personal comments on the program. One of the motivating factors was the opportunity to validate feelings with peers who share the same experiences and emotions, which led to a sense of group identity, mutual support, and empathy. These experiences can be elusive for children with an ASD who feel isolated and different from typical peers. The groups actually facilitated friendships beyond the duration of the program and elicited in the participants feelings of self-worth from being able to contribute to the well-being of fellow participants. The parents commented that the program had also improved their son's or daughter's quality of life due to feeling more confident and motivated to engage in social and community activities and be more independent. Some children with an ASD, due to aspects of his or her personality, would achieve greater success if the program was conducted using one-on-one sessions rather than a group design. However, there were many advantages practically, financially, and socially in using a group format.

The program was of limited duration and the participants and parents were informed that it would be worthwhile reviewing and possibly repeating the program and strategies as the person matures. This could be especially valuable during the emotional storms associated with adolescence, or should new circumstances occur such as parental separation, or the adolescent experimenting with alcohol and drugs as a means of alleviating anxiety.

While the research evaluation of the program requires no variation in the content and resources used, in clinical practice there can be modifications. Since the Exploring Feelings program was designed and evaluated, new resources have become available that could be incorporated into the sessions. The *Mind Reading Interactive Guide to Emotions* developed by Simon Baron-Cohen and colleagues at Cambridge University is an interactive DVD that can be used in the Affective Education component of CBT for children with an ASD. The Cognitive Affective Training resources, or *CAT-kit*, developed by Tony Attwood, Kirsten Callesen and Annette Moller-Nielsen in Denmark provides valuable resources that could be incorporated into the Exploring Feelings program. The *Secret Agent Society* developed by Renae Beaumont and Kate Sofronoff in Brisbane includes games and activities to express and cope with anxiety. It is also interesting that there are now two books on managing anxiety written by adults who have ASD (Dubin, 2009; Lipsky, 2011). The insight and strategies described by adults with ASD would have great credibility for children with an ASD.

Evaluation of "Exploring Feelings"

Following the development and piloting of the "Exploring Feelings" program, a randomized controlled trial was conducted (Sofronoff et al., 2005). Seventy-one children aged between 10 and 12 years were recruited to participate in the program and were randomly assigned to one of three conditions. Twenty-three children were assigned to condition 1 in which the children participated in the 6-week intervention with minimal parent involvement; 23 children were assigned to the waitlist treatment as usual group; and 25 children were assigned to condition 2 in which parents attended a concurrent parent session while the children participated in the child sessions. There were 6 weekly 2-hour sessions. The child sessions were conducted by postgraduate clinical students who had been trained to deliver the program and received weekly supervision. The groups consisted of three children and two therapists and a senior clinical psychologist conducted the large parent group.

Measures

Child anxiety was measured using the Spence Children's Anxiety Scale – Parent version (SCAS-P: Nauta, Scholing, Rapee, Abbott, Spence, & Waters, 2004) and also the Social Worries Questionnaire – Parent version (Spence, 1995). The child's knowledge of strategies to manage anxiety in a difficult social situation was measured using "James and the Maths Test" (Attwood, 2004). This is a hypothetical scenario that requires the child to generate appropriate strategies.

Results

The three groups (child only vs child + parent vs waitlist) were compared on the measures at three time points – pre-intervention (before the program), post-intervention (immediately on completing sessions), and again at 6-week follow-up. There were significant differences found on all measures between the pre-intervention scores and the follow-up scores for the two intervention groups. This showed that over time the parents reported significantly lower levels of anxiety and fewer social worries in their child. There was also a significant difference between the two intervention groups and the waitlist group that demonstrated that the children who had received the intervention were described as much less anxious and socially worried than the group who had not completed the program. This relationship is depicted in Figure 23.1.

The results above demonstrate a difference on the total score of the SCAS-P. This measure also has six subscales that capture different types of anxiety – separation anxiety, social anxiety, obsessive-compulsive disorder, panic, personal injury fears, and generalized anxiety. The intervention groups showed significant changes on parent-report on all of these subscales, indicating that the program seemed to be able to target individual anxiety problems.

A major focus of this evaluation was to determine whether the active inclusion of parents would add significantly to the benefits derived from the program by the children. The results showed significant differences between the two intervention groups such that the scores from the child + parent condition reflected greater improvement than the scores from the child only group. It seems that parent involvement resulted in greater use of strategies at home and greater familiarity with the program also gave parents an opportunity to recognize and reward the efforts of their child. The differences can clearly be seen in the results from the child measure "James and the

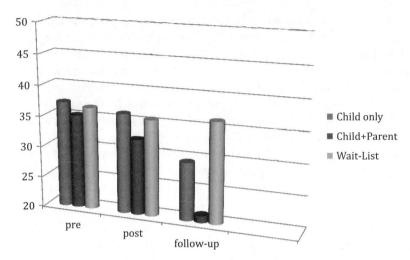

Figure 23.1 Total scores for parent-reported child anxiety by intervention type and time.

Maths Test" where the group with parent involvement went from strength to strength throughout the program (Figure 23.2).

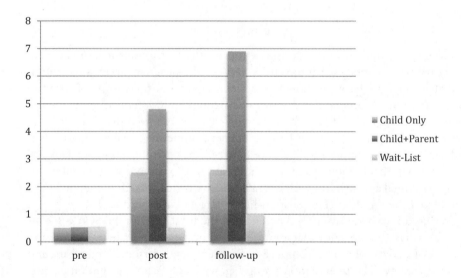

Figure 23.2 Child strategies for 'James and the Maths Test' by intervention type.

Qualitative findings

In setting up an evaluation of a new program it is not always possible to anticipate which specific measures will capture the changes produced by the intervention. In this case we assumed that we would see a change in parent-reported child anxiety and in the child's ability to generate more positive strategies to manage their own anxiety.

This did prove to be the case for many of the children who were involved. We were also interested, however, to know of any other changes, either positive or negative, that parents attributed to attending the program and so we developed a questionnaire that allowed parents to give qualitative comments. When we analyzed these comments we found that parents mentioned some occurrences that we had noted, such as some children forming friendships and staying in contact outside of the groups, and some parents forming friendships and helping one another out in a variety of ways. Some parents also indicated that they now had a common language with which to talk to their child about anxiety or about distress in general, and that this was a positive outcome because it resulted in issues being managed earlier and therefore lower levels of general distress. Other parents reported that their children now became distressed more slowly and recovered more quickly, especially when they were encouraged to use strategies that they had learned and were rewarded for doing so.

Concluding Remarks

The outcomes from the Exploring Feelings program and also from the other programs that use similar strategies and approaches, suggest that a cognitive-behavioral approach to anxiety management with children with high-functioning autism spectrum disorder is effective when the program uses the adaptations outlined. This is a very significant and positive finding because anxiety is common for these children and if left unmanaged will interfere with a child's capacity to function optimally. It remains for us the further improve our programs and to extend the reach of such programs to adolescents and adults.

References

Attwood, T. (2004) *Exploring Feelings: Cognitive Behaviour Therapy to Manage Anxiety*. Arlington, TX: Future Horizons.

Attwood, T. (2007) *The Complete Guide to Asperger's Syndrome*. London: Jessica Kingsley Publishers.

Beaumont, R., & Sofronoff, K. (2008). A multi-component social skills intervention for children with Asperger syndrome: The Junior Detective Training Program. *Journal of Child Psychology and Psychiatry, 49* (7), 743–753.

Chakrabarti, S., & Fombonne, E. (2005). Pervasive developmental disorders in preschool children: Confirmation of high prevalence. *The American Journal of Psychiatry, 162* (6), 1133–1141.

Chalfant, A., Rapee, R., & Carroll, L. (2007). Treating anxiety disorders in children with high-functioning autism spectrum disorders: A controlled trial. *Journal of Autism and Developmental Disorders, 37,* 1842–1857.

de Bruin, E. L., Ferdinand, R. F., Meester, S., de Nijs, F. A., & Verheij, F. (2007). High rates of psychiatric co-morbidity in PDD-NOS. *Journal of Autism and Developmental Disorders, 37,* 877–886.

Dubin, N. (2009) *Asperger Syndrome and Anxiety: A Guide to Successful Stress Management*. London: Jessica Kingsley Publishers.

Gadow, K. D., Roohi, J., DeVincent, C. J., Kirsch, S., & Hatchwell, E. (2010). Brief Report: Glutamate transporter gene (SLC1A1) single nucleotide polymorphism (rs301430) and repetitive behaviors and anxiety in children with autism spectrum disorder. *Journal of Autism and Developmental Disorders, 40,* 1139–1145.

Ghaziuddin, M. (2002). Asperger syndrome: Associated psychiatric and medical conditions. *Focus on Autism and Other Developmental Disabilities, 17,* 138–144.

Gray, C. (1998). Social stories and comic strip conversations with students with Asperger syndrome and high-functioning autism. In E. Schopler, G. Mesibov & L. J. Kunce (Eds.), *Asperger's Syndrome or High-Functioning Autism?* New York: Plenum Press.

Gray, C. (2010). *The New Social Story Book.* Arlington, TX: Future Horizons.

Guttman-Steinmetz, S., Gadow, K. D., De Vincent, C. J., & Crowell, J. (2010). Anxiety symptoms in boys with autism spectrum disorder, attention-deficit hyperactivity disorder, or chronic multiple tic disorder and community controls. *Journal of Autism and Developmental Disorders, 40,* 1006–1016.

Hill, E., Berthoz, S., & Frith, U. (2004). Cognitive processing of own emotions in individuals with autistic spectrum disorder and in their relatives. *Journal of Autism and Developmental Disorders, 34,* 229–235.

Joosten, A. V., Bundy, A. C., & Einfeld, S. L. (2009). Intrinsic and extrinsic motivation for stereotypic and repetitive behavior. *Journal of Autism and Developmental Disorders, 39,* 521–531.

Karkhaneh, M., Clark, B., Ospina, M. B., Seida, J. C., Smith, V., & Hartling, L (2010). Social stories to improve social skills in children with autism spectrum disorder: A systematic review. *Autism, 14,* 641–662.

Kendall, P. C., Aschenbrand, S. G., & Hudson, J. L. (2003). Child-focused treatment of anxiety. In A. E. Kazdin & J. R. Weisz (Eds.), *Evidence-Based Psychotherapies for Children and Adolescents.* New York: Guilford Press.

Kendall, P. C., & Hedtke, K. (2006). *Coping Cat Workbook,* 2nd edn. Ardmore, PA: Workbook Publishing,.

Lipsky, D. (2011). *From Anxiety to Meltdown: How Individuals on the Autism Spectrum Deal with Anxiety, Experience Meltdowns, Manifest Tantrums, and How You Can Intervene Effectively.* London: Jessica Kingsley Publishers.

Lyneham, H. J., Abbott, M. J., Wignall, A., & Rapee, R. (2003). *The Cool Kids Family Program –Therapist Manual.* Sydney, Australia: Macquarie University.

Moree, B. N., & Davis, T. E. (2010). Cognitive-behavioral therapy for anxiety in children diagnosed with autism spectrum disorders: Modification trends. *Research in Autism Spectrum Disorders, 4,* 346–354.

Nauta, M. H., Scholing, A., Rapee, R. M., Abbott, M., Spence. S. H., & Waters, A. (2004). A parent-report measure of children's anxiety: Psychometric properties and comparison with child-report in a clinic and normal sample. *Behaviour Research and Therapy, 42,* 813–839.

Ollendick, T. H., King, N. J., & Chorpita, B. F. (2006). Empirically supported treatments for children and adolescents. In P. C. Kendall (Ed.), *Child and Adolescent Therapy: Cognitive-Behavioral Procedures,* 3rd edn (pp. 492–520). New York: Guilford Press.

Reaven, J., & Hepburn, S. (2003). Cognitive-behavioral treatment of obsessice-compulsive disorder in a child with Asperger syndrome: A case report. *Autism, 7*(2), 145–164.

Simonoff, E., Pickles, A., Charman, T., Chandler, S., Loucas, T., & Baird, G. (2008). Psychiatric disorders in children with autism spectrum disorders: prevalence, comorbidity, and associated factors in a population-derived sample. *Journal of the American Academy of Child and Adolescent Psychiatry, 47,* 921–929.

Sofronoff, K., Attwood, T., & Hinton, S. (2005). A randomized controlled trial of a CBT intervention for anxiety in children with Asperger syndrome. *Journal of Child Psychology and Psychiatry, 46,* 1152–1160.

Sofronoff, K., Dark, E., & Stone, V. (2011). Social vulnerability and bullying in children with Asperger syndrome. *Autism, 15*(3), 355–372.

Spence, S. H. (1995). *The Social Worries Questionnaire. Social Skills Training: Enhancing Social Competence with Children and Adolescents.* Windsor: Nfer-Nelson.

Sze, K. M., & Wood, J. J. (2007). Cognitive-behavioral treatment of comorbid anxiety disorders and social difficulties in children with high-functioning autism: A case report. *Journal of Contemporary Psychotherapy, 37* (3), 133–143.

White, S., Oswald, D., Ollendick T., & Scahill, L. (2009). Anxiety in children and adolescents with autism spectrum disorders. *Clinical Psychology Review, 29* (3), 216–229.

Wood, J. J., Drahota, A., Sze, K., Har, K., Chui, A., & Langer, D.A. (2009). Cognitive behaviour therapy for anxiety in children with autism spectrum disorders: A randomized controlled trial. *Journal of Child Psychology and Psychiatry, 50* (3), 224–234.

Wood, J. J., & Gadow, K. D. (2010). Exploring the nature and function of anxiety in youth with autism spectrum disorders. *Clinical Psychology: Science and Practice, 17* (4), 281–292.

Wood, J. J., & Mcleod, B. D. (2008). *Child Anxiety Disorders: a Family-Based Treatment Manual for Practitioners.* New York: W.W. Norton & Co.

Further resources

Mind Reading: The Interactive Guide to Emotions. Distributed by Jessica Kingsley Publishers, London. The program uses an interactive DVD and can be used with children from age six to adults. More information available from www.jkp.com.

Secret Agent Society: Solving the Mystery of Social Encounters. Developed by Renae Beaumont and Kate Sofronoff with more information available from www.sst-institute.net.

The CAT-kit Cognitive Affective Training developed by Tony Attwood, Kirsten Callesen and Annette Moller Nielsen. Published by Future Horizons in Arlington Texas with more information available from www.catkit-us.com.

24

CBT Intervention for Anxiety in Children and Adolescents with Williams Syndrome

Cecilia A. Essau[1] and Elena Longhi[2]

[1]University of Roehampton, UK
[2]Università degli Studi di Milano-Bicocca, Italy

Williams syndrome (WS) is a rare genetic disorder which occurs in 1 in 20 000 live births. It was identified in 1961 and is caused by a microdeletion of at least 25 genes on chromosome 7q11.23 (Donnai & Karmiloff-Smith, 2000). WS syndrome is characterized by a distinctive facial dysmorphology, including puffiness around the eyes, a short nose with a broad nasal tip, wide mouth, full cheeks, full lips, and a small chin. People with WS are also likely to have a long neck, sloping shoulders, limited mobility in their joints, and curvature of the spine (Donnai & Karmiloff-Smith, 2000). Individuals with WS are often of short stature, with the average height for females being 5 ft and for males 5ft 6 in.

Individuals with WS are highly sociable (Dilts, Morris, & Leonard, 1990), never going unnoticed in a group (Dykens & Rosner, 1999), warm, cheerful, and friendly (Udwin & Yule, 1991). Jones, Bellugi, Lai et al. (2000) described individuals with WS as behaving 'as if everyone is their friend'. Numerous authors have described WS individuals as often friendly, social, outgoing, and empathic (Gosch & Pankan, 1997) – features which are likely to be related to their strengths in expressive language and in facial memory and recognition. According to Udwin and her colleagues (1987), about 64% of parents and teachers spontaneously talk about the friendliness of children with WS towards adults. The overly friendly behavior of individuals with WS extends to unfamiliar people as well (Jones et al., 2000). The positive social disposition of individuals with WS is reported to be present from infancy. For example, during laboratory experiments, infants with WS were found to show a strong interest in engaging the experimenter using eye contact, smiling, and cooing; and when unable to complete a task they played with the table or waved to their parents, instead of becoming upset as a normal child might (Jones et al., 2000). Parents of individuals with WS also rated their children as being more empathetic and sensitive compared to parents of typically developing children or individuals with other developmental disorders (Doyle, Bellugi, Korenberg, & Graham, 2004; Jones et al., 2000; Klein-Tasman & Mervis, 2003).

The Wiley-Blackwell Handbook of The Treatment of Childhood and Adolescent Anxiety, First Edition.
Edited by Cecilia A. Essau and Thomas H. Ollendick.
© 2013 John Wiley & Sons, Ltd. Published 2013 by John Wiley & Sons, Ltd.

The downside of being so eager to interact with others is that sometimes they come across as socially inappropriate; in addition, they seem to have poor social judgment and approach others indiscriminately. Moreover, individuals with WS show over-enthusiastic manners of interaction and intense eye contact which could contribute to social difficulties and may reflect their poor understanding of environmental cues. Children with WS have been reported to experience difficulties establishing and maintaining friendships with their peers (Davies, Udwin, & Howlin, 1998; Einfeld, Tonge, & Florio, 1997; Udwin & Yule, 1991). These difficulties tend to persist into adulthood with the same or greater frequency (Davies et al., 1998). As reported by Davies et al. (1998), almost all of the participants in their study reported having difficulties making or maintaining friendships, and about three-quarters of them reported being socially isolated. Additionally, most of them continued to be socially disinhibited, overly friendly, and too trusting of others in adulthood. They have also been reported to have problems in some forms of communication such as greeting behaviors, topic maintenance, and question answering (Semel & Rosner, 2003). In about half of these individuals, there were reports of them being physically overly demonstrative to other people such as touching, hugging, and kissing (Davies et al., 1998); such behavior could make individuals with WS vulnerable to sexual exploitation and abuse during adolescence and adulthood. In fact, at least 20% of the participants in Davies et al.'s study (1998) had been victims of sexual abuse.

Individuals with WS can easily initiate social contacts, but they often lack understanding of "unwritten" rules of social interactions and discourse (Semel & Rosner, 2003). Their tendency to be open, direct or personal when communicating with others, together with their lack of inhibition, may lead them to say things that could be uncomfortable for other people. Such behavior is usually not intentional or malicious, but rather it is due to their difficulties in understanding social nuances and the social implications of their behavior. On the other hand, their inability to understand the subtleties of social interactions, and a tendency to take language literally, could result in them becoming easily offended or upset. Thus, sociability is an important component of the behavior of individuals with WS and in order to remain a strength, it needs to be appropriately guided.

Medical and Developmental Problems

Many children and adolescents with WS have medical and developmental problems, which need to be taken into account when doing prevention/intervention work with them. Some of the most common problems include: heart and blood vessel problems, irritability, kidney abnormalities, and hernias; in their infancy, they often suffer hypercalcemia and feeding problems (Black & Bonham-Carter, 1963; Semel & Rosner, 2003). One of the most common medical problems is hyperacusis, which is defined as over-sensitivity to particular sounds. This includes being sensitive to sound or noise with high volume, as well as to specific sounds or noises regardless of volume and strength. Over 90% of individuals with WS show some hypersensitivity to sounds, particularly to sudden "explosive" sounds such as drills and fireworks, but also to vacuum cleaners, food processors, and washing machines (Semel & Rosner, 2003). Even people's voices or laughter could sometime lead to high level of anxiety. Hyperacusis seems to be less problematic with increasing age. There is a general tendency of females with WS to report higher rates of fears and hyperacusis compared to males with WS (Blomberg, Rosander, & Andersson, 2006). Moreover, Bloomberg and colleagues (2006) reported a significant correlation between fears and hyperacusis. In particular, it has been suggested that hyperacusis is related to a general and a hyper-arousal tendency in the sympathetic nervous system, which could lead to fight-flight reactions. In this respect, hyperacusis is connected to fear and anxiety irrespective of sound or noise. Although hyperacusis appears to improve with age, about 50% of adults continue to experience significant problems with hypersensitivity to noise. In coping with this problem, individuals cover their ears or try to avoid distressing sounds by leaving the room. A common consequence of hyperacusis is also avoidance of social activities (Johnson, Comeau, & Clarke, 2001). Others may respond to the discomfort caused by sounds with panic attacks and aggressive outbursts.

WS is also marked by some degree of learning disability, with IQs generally ranging between 50 and 60 (Semel & Rosner, 2003). Studies have also shown that most children with WS tend to show language delay (e.g., Grant, Valiant, & Karmiloff-Smith, 2002; Jarrold, Baddeley, & Hewes, 1998; Laing, Butterworth, Ansari et al., 2002; Thomas, Grant, Barham et al., 2001; Udwin & Yule, 1998). More than 80% of parents reported their children with WS as "language delayed" on the William Syndrome Association (WSA) Checklist (Semel & Rosner, 2003). Children with WS have also shown some delays on expressive language compared to children without WS (see for example, Singer Harris, Bellugi, Bates, Jones, & Rossen, 1997; Udwin & Yule, 1990). Although their language is initially delayed, individuals with WS seem precocious in their use of unusual words and conversational flourishes (Semel & Rosner, 2003). Young children with WS often experience developmental delays; walking, talking, and toilet training are often achieved later than normal.

Anxiety and Depression in Young People with WS

Given their language abilities, friendliness, and absence of social inhibition, people with WS seem to be rather good in social interactions (Meyer-Lindenberg, Hariri, Munoz, et al., 2005). However, this overshadows their behavioral and emotional problems which are characterized by preoccupation and obsessions as well as high levels of anxiety and fears (Dykens, 2003). As reported in several studies, about 81% of the adolescents with WS meet the criteria for at least one psychiatric disorder (Dykens, 2003; Leyfer, Woodruff Borden, Klein Tasman, Fricke, & Mervis, 2006), most commonly an internalizing disorder such as anxiety or depression.

In a series of studies, Einfeld and colleagues (1999) reported that a significantly higher percentage of parents of children in the WS group, compared to parents of children without WS, described their children as being: tense or anxious, overly affectionate, overactive, obsessed/preoccupied with idea or activity, with short attention, covering ears or avoiding particular sounds, wandering aimlessly, repeating words or phrases, not to mix with own age groups preferring instead adult company, and to be inappropriately happy or elevated. Eight years later, the total behavior problems score decreased significantly compared to those obtained during the first interview (Einfeld, Tonge, & Rees, 2001). Significant decreases were obtained in three of the five subscales: disruptive/antisocial, self-absorbed, and anxious. The communication disturbance subscale was significantly higher in the WS than in the community control group. These findings were interpreted as suggesting behavioral problems to be persistent among individuals with WS, although they became less severe with age.

In the study by Dykens (2003), caregivers of 51 individuals with WS, aged 5–49 years, were interviewed for the presence of anxiety disorders in their offspring. The prevalence of specific types of anxiety disorders among individuals with WS were: specific phobia (35%), generalized anxiety disorder (GAD; 16%), separation anxiety disorder (4%), and obsessive-compulsive disorder (2%). Leyfer and colleagues (2006) extended Dyken's study by including a wide range of other psychiatric disorders. In this study, a sample of 119 parents of children aged 4–16 years with WS was interviewed. Most children (80.7%) were reported to have at least one psychiatric disorder. The most common disorders were that of ADHD (64.7%) and specific phobia (53.8%). Among those who had specific phobia, the most common situation they were afraid of was loud noises (27.7%; i.e., hypersensitivity to specific sounds), including those that were related to startling sounds (e.g., fire drills, sirens, thunder), motor sounds (e.g., lawn mowers, weed whackers, vacuum cleaners, blenders), noisy settings (e.g., concerts, ball games), fireworks, crying, and screaming. About 60% of the children with hypersensitivity to specific sounds also had at least one other specific phobia. Other common phobias were shots and/or blood tests, and doctors/dentists unrelated to shots and blood tests. It was argued that the fear of doctors and blood tests/shot may be related to the physical problems often associated with WS which make them more frequently exposed to these situations. About 12% of the sample had GAD, and the 11–16 year olds had significantly higher rates of GAD than those in the youngest group. The authors also reported that a high percentage of children with WS worry in anticipation of a wide range of events; however, this worry seems to dissipate once the events begin.

Our own research that involved a face-to-face interview with 10 young people, aged 15–26 years, with WS and their parents confirmed the high frequency of anxiety and depressive disorders (C. Essau & E. Longhi, in preparation). All 10 of them met the diagnosis for at least one DSM-IV anxiety disorders, the most common being that of GAD and specific phobia disorder. The latter was related to fear of noises such as children's crying and hearing fireworks. Individuals with this fear generally avoided the places where such noises might occur such as in restaurants or parks. Worries among those with GAD varied across life domains; among older adolescents, most worries tended to focus on employment and independent living. Among those with an anxiety disorder, most of them also had a depressive disorder. In these individuals, anxiety usually came first followed by depression. Of the 10 individuals with WS that we interviewed, four were already seeking professional help and were taking antidepressant medications.

Anxiety problems may result from many different situations or events. According to Udwin and Yule (1991), among people with WS, anxiety may arise in relation to three primary areas:

(a) *Excessive demands.* Their good verbal abilities can lead others to overestimate their general ability. This often results in them being exposed to situations in which they are unable to cope. If the presence of excessive demands persists, individuals with WS may withdraw and lose interest in activities and/or relationships, which, in turn, may lead to depression.

(b) *Change and uncertainty*. Anticipating something new or different from normal routine may cause anxiety. Studies have reported that between 38 and 47% of individuals with WS reported fear of new experiences (Semel & Rosner, 2003).

(c) *Threat*. Many individuals with WS have difficulty understanding the complexities of social interactions; therefore, the outside world is often perceived by them as being hostile and frightening. They can also be very protective of the people they care of and may become anxious if they think that someone or something is threatening them. Moreover, as reported in several studies (e.g., Dykens, Hodapp, & Finucane, 2000; Scheiber, 2000), many WS individuals worry excessively about other people's health and safety.

Emotional and Social Skills Training for Individuals with WS (ESST-WS)

Despite the high prevalence of anxiety disorders among adolescents and young adults with WS, to our knowledge there is no intervention program designed specifically for anxiety disorders in this population. Therefore, it is important to develop an intervention program for anxiety for young people with WS. In order to get useful information that is specific for the WS and which could be integrated in the ESST-WS, an unstructured interview was conducted with 10 adolescents and young adults with WS and their parents; these 10 individuals with WS were the same group of individuals who participated in the study that examined the frequency of anxiety and depressive disorders as described earlier. In addition, a focus group was also conducted with three carers of young adults with WS who live in homes for people with special needs. The aim of this interview was to obtain information about worries, anxieties, and other psychological problems that those with WS may have, and in the way in which they coped with these problems. Each individual with WS was interviewed separately from their parents and their carers. All interviews were video-recorded and were analyzed offline. Information from the interviews helped the development of the ESST-WS, a program based on the principles of cognitive-behavioral therapy (CBT).

In developing the ESST-WS, the following medical and psychological problems of young people with WS were taken into consideration: (a) learning difficulties; (b) short attention span and distractibility; (c) difficulty in controlling emotions; (d) the presence of medical problems such as heart problems, kidney abnormalities, and hernias; (e) impaired motor functioning such as gross motor deficits, balance problems and problems with sports activities (Semel & Rosner, 2003) (for the latter, studies have indicated that children with WS have problems doing sports such as catching or kicking a ball); (f) problems with spatial orientation such establishing a directional orientation (Atkinson, Anker, Braddick, Nokes, Mason, & Braddick, 2001; Farran, Bades, Boucher, & Tranter, 2010); (g) difficulty building friendships and in social interaction; (h) love of animals; and (i) high anxiety around unexpected changes in routines (Semel & Rosner, 2003).

In order to address the presence of these medical and psychological problems, it has been important for the ESST-WS to be conceptualized as follows: (1) to be

Figure 24.1 A story used in the ESST-WS.

written in simple language and to be easy to understand; (2) to use visual illustrations such as drawings of animals to illustrate the main principle of CBT, in which stories are also used to teach the patients how to react in fearful situations; (3) to include homework assignments and in-session activities that do not involve a high level of physical activities; (4) to split the 45-minutes session into two if needed to keep the patient's attention; (5) to contain a structured description of each session, and accordingly to the participant's level of cognitive functioning, visual illustrations may be needed; (6) to use repeated direct instructions and reminders; and (7) to include two sessions on social skills training. Finally, the individuals need to be reminded of their next session (e.g., the number of night sleeps).

The ESST-WS consists of six sessions, each lasting 50–60 minutes. However, as the program is designed to be implemented in individual sessions and depending on the individual's concentration level, it is possible to split each session into two resulting in 12 sessions. As most of the young people with WS love animals, many illustrations have animal characters (Figure 24.1).

Session 1: Introduction

The first session focuses on building rapport between the "therapist" and the individual with WS to develop a trusting and supportive relationship. This is followed by providing the aims of the ESST-WS and an overview of the program. Other topics covered in this session include talking about the experience of anxiety, where it is explained that it is normal to feel this way and that everyone feels anxious or worried from time to time. They are then introduced to the cognitive-behavioral treatment conceptualization of anxiety. Specifically, it is explained that anxiety or fear usually shows itself in three ways:

(1) bodily reactions (e.g., heart beating fast, stomach aches, sweating),

(2) thoughts (e.g., "I might get hurt"), and

(3) actions or behaviors (e.g., avoiding the feared situation or object).

At the end of this session, the importance of having self-esteem is discussed. As argued by several authors (Werner & Johnson, 2004), the promotion of self-esteem is one of the key ingredients in many effective intervention process.

Session 2: Feelings

This session focuses on the feelings of anxiety, the changes that take place in the body, the thought and behaviors that are related to the experience of anxiety. It is made clear that anxiety feeling is natural and that everyone experience anxiety and fear from time to time, and that it is biological adaptive. It is also explained that anxiety has a survival value in precipitating the fight or flight response.

The participants are introduced with the idea that we can get clues about how people feel from their facial expressions, body postures (e.g., they way they stand or sit; eye contact) and what they say and do. Several techniques are helpful in teaching participants about feelings, like telling stories that outline the different feelings, or using "feeling cards" which show pictures of faces with various facial expressions (see Figure 24.2) as well as taking photos of the participants displaying various naturally occurring feelings. With some participants, "feeling cards" (i.e., cards showing happy, sad, angry, worried, or anxious faces) are used when they are asked to best describe how they feel when they are, for example, in certain places (e.g., in school, supermarket).

During this session, participants also learn to recognize their body signals when they feel worried, nervous, or scared. It is important for them to be able to make the connection between physical symptoms of anxiety and anxiety-provoking events. For example, a person who feels sick before attending an important event is unlikely to be feeling sick due to a physical illness. This sick feeling may be the way in which the person's body is giving them a 'clue' that they are feeling worried. This is followed by

Figure 24.2   Feeling cards.

discussing some of the signals associated with feeling worried or anxious or frightened (e.g., red face, headache, heart beats faster, sweaty hands, shaky voice). The participants are then asked about the types of signals they experience when they feel anxious, worried, or frightened.

Session 3: Thoughts

This session covers issues regarding the process of thinking experienced by the participants. In particular it is explained to them that: (a) every one of us has thoughts; (b) different thoughts run through our mind all the time; (c) many of our thoughts are describing the way we see ourselves (e.g., "I am so stupid"), or the way we judge what we do (e.g., "I cannot do anything right"), or about the way we view our future (e.g., "I can never find a best friend").

Differences between unhelpful and helpful thoughts are discussed and illustrated using drawings and stories. In addition, participants are asked to generate a list of positive things they could say to themselves to make them feel good, such as "I can do it"; "I can cope with it".

Session 4: Linking thoughts, feelings, and behavior

The main aim of this session is to explain how thoughts, feelings, and behavior are related to anxiety, and how anxiety occurs. Given the fact that some participants have problems in differentiating between thoughts, feelings and behaviors, these participants are given the cues that are used to determine how to discriminate among thoughts, feelings and behaviors. That is, following the work of Quakley, Reynolds, and Coker (2004), participants are given three sentences, written on a card, which describe a feeling (e.g., Christmas was coming and Mary was very excited), a thought (e.g., Mary wished that Father Christmas would bring her a new puppy), and a behavior (e.g., Mary made a home for the puppy with a blanket and a cardboard box). Then they are given three boxes with photos on them (one that illustrates thought, one feeling, and one behavior), and they are asked to put each sentence in the correct box.

This session also involves teaching the participants different ways to relax. This includes: deep breathing; using humor; calming pictures; absorbing activities; visualization.

Another topic covered in this session is on skills development by taking small, graduated steps. Specifically, in developing a particular skill, the participants are asked to take three steps: (1) set a goal (i.e., list the type of skill that they wish to develop); (2) plan what is needed to reach a goal in small steps, and (3) practice the small steps, one at a time, until the goal is reached.

Sessions 5 & 6: Social skills training

Individuals with WS often have difficulties in establishing and maintaining peer relations. These difficulties are related to topic maintenance and turn-taking during social interaction, as well as their inability to accept criticism, and difficulty with social crowding (i.e., invade other people's personal space) by standing too close to them

(Semel & Rosner, 2003). Therefore, these sessions cover basic social skills such as conversations and listening skills that are designed to improve social competence across various dimensions. Participants also learn to use the Problem-solving steps technique to solve social problems. Specifically, they are taught to use three steps:

Step 1: Say what the problem is (i.e., paying attention to our feelings and those of other people).

Step 2: Think of possible solutions (i.e., think of ways to solve the problem and to examine each solution by looking at the good and bad aspects of each one).

Step 3: Try the best solution (i.e., use social skills to carry out the chosen solution).

Below we describe a case study in the implementation of the ESST-WS in an adolescent girl with Williams Syndrome.

The Case of MJ

The present case describes an 18-year-old female with WS who will be referred to as "MJ". MJ's mother wanted her daughter to participate in the ESST-WS because of her frequent complaints of chronic anxiety, fatigue, insomnia, stomach distress, and low mood, all of which had increased in the 2 months prior to referral.

MJ was diagnosed with WS when she was 3 years old. As a child, she used to suffer from several health problems including hernias and cardiac problems for which she had to undergo surgery. She was close with her immediate family; she was the eldest of three children and currently lived with her parents. However, she hoped to be able to get a place at a residential home for young people with special needs. She used to attend a mainstream school, but decided to quit at the age of 17 years. She does a volunteer job once a week, selling vegetables at a small store that sells organic foods. She communicates with some of her friends through face-book. She used to attend a yoga class once a week, but has not done so recently. MJ enjoyed listening to soft music and reported having a hot bath as a way to relax.

MJ participated in an ESST-WS group. Before the assessment and the first treatment, the leader (CAE) made phone calls to MJ to discuss the procedures involved. This was deemed necessary as any unplanned activities normally made MJ highly anxious. Details of MJ's clinical presentation and results of intervention progress will next be discussed.

Assessment

Assessments were conducted at pre-treatment (1 week prior to treatment), mid-treatment (immediately before the start of the third treatment session), post-treatment, and follow-up (3 months following the last treatment session); the Penn State Worry Questionnaire, the Columbia Impairment Scale, and the Depression, Anxiety, and Stress Scale were administered.

Because of MJ's writing and reading difficulties, these questionnaires were read to her by an independent assessor. A diagnostic interview schedule (The Composite International Diagnostic Interview) was also administered by an independent assessor at the pre-treatment and at the follow-up assessment. In addition to these tests, MJ was also requested to monitor her mood on a daily basis.

Instruments

The Composite International Diagnostic Interview (CIDI) was used to assess anxiety (agoraphobia, social phobia, specific phobia, panic disorder, GAD, obsessive-compulsive disorder) and depressive disorders based on DSM-IV criteria (APA, 1994). The CIDI also provides rating of impairment related to anxiety and depression. Both the reliability and validity of the CIDI diagnoses have been examined in numerous studies in different centers throughout the world, as part of the World Health Organization field trials. Findings of these field trials have shown the CIDI to have good cultural appropriateness, excellent inter-rater reliability, and good test–retest reliability (Wittchen, Robins, Cottler, Sartorius, Burke, & Regier, 1991).

The Penn State Worry Questionnaire (PSWQ) (Meyer, Miller, Metzger, & Borkovec, 1990) is a 16-item inventory designed to assess the pathological worry characteristic of GAD. Items of the PSWQ are rated on a Likert scale ranging from 1 ("not at all typical to me") to 5 ("very typical of me"). It too has been shown to have good internal consistency with samples from various settings (Beck, Stanley, & Zebb, 1995; Meyer et al., 1990). It has demonstrated good test–retest reliability over 8–10 weeks (Meyer et al., 1990).

The Depression, Anxiety, and Stress Scale (DASS; Lovibond & Lovibond, 1995) was used to assess depressive, anxiety, and stress symptoms. Respondents indicate how much the statements apply to them over the past week, using a 4-point Likert scale ranging from "did not apply to me" (0) to "applied to me very much or most of the time" (3).

The Columbia Impairment Scale (CIS) is a 13-item scale that can be used to measure four major domains of functioning or impairment: interpersonal relations, broad areas of psychopathology, functioning at school or work, and use of leisure time. Items of the CIS are rated on a Likert scale ranging from 0 (no problem) to 4 (a very big problem). The CIS total score and their subscales scores can be obtained by summing scores on relevant items. The CIS has been found to show excellent psychometric properties.

Treatment

MJ received 6 weeks of individual ESST-WS. As described above, this treatment protocol was developed specifically for individuals with WS, in terms of its delivery, choice of tasks for the homework and the in-session activities, explanation of CBT principals (e.g., using scripts with animals characters) . Because of MJ's level of concentration, all the six sessions were split into two 25-minute sessions, with a break of about 60 minutes between the two slots. Intervention techniques included cognitive restructuring (e.g., using cue cards as proposed by Quakley et al., 2004), role-playing, *in vivo* exposure exercises, social skills training, and homework assignments.

Overall, MJ had no problems with understanding the concepts that are used in the ESST-WS, for example, the difference between feelings and thoughts, or doing cognitive restructuring.

Table 24.1 Hierarchy for MJ's fear of children.

Step	Description
1	Going to a recreational park through its back entrance and walk for 10 minutes in the park
2	Going to a recreational park through the main entrance and walk for 10 minutes in the park
3	Going to a recreational park through the main entrance and walk 200 meters towards the playground, before turning back to the entrance.
4	Going to a recreational park through the main entrance and walk 50 meters towards the playground, and see the children playing before turning back to the entrance.
5	Going to a recreational park through the main entrance and played for 10 minutes at the playground, and say "hello" to some of the children before turning back to the entrance.
6	Going to a recreational park through the main entrance and played for 20 minutes at the playground; say hello to some of the children before turning back to the entrance.

Because of her fear of children and avoidance of places with children, and to prevent her from being housebound, the ESST-WS was slightly modified to include an emphasis on:

- Establishing a fear-hierarchy by going to places with children (i.e., recreation park). As shown in Table 24.1, a fear hierarchy related to going to a recreation park was established, starting off with the least to the most frightening ones. Subjective Units of Discomfort (SUDS) elicited by going close to the children (with 5 representing distress and 0 representing no or little distress), were gathered throughout each of the exposure tasks.
- Increasing her level of pleasant activities that included activities that she used to enjoy such as contact with friends, swimming, yoga, etc.
- Cognitive-restructuring that was used to deal with her uncontrollable worries (e.g., excessive worries about her future, health, mum, future living arrangement, employment), and cognitive dysfunction (e.g., what other people would think of her as having WS and learning disability).

After each task, MJ completed thought-listing forms and provided a rating of her anxiety on a 0 to 5 SUDS.

Results

Pre-assessment

The baseline assessment confirmed that MJ met the diagnoses of DSM-IV GAD and specific phobia. She also reported high scores on depression; however, the criteria for a major depressive disorder were not met. MJ was very cooperative and open about disclosing her worries and fear during the assessment. At times, she seemed fidgety – playing with her fingers and rocking back and forth.

GAD: According to MJ, she had been having anxiety and worry about numerous topics as long as she could remember; however, it was worst in the last few months. She reported that she would spend several hours a day "in her head," worrying about her family and friends, and their health. For example, she stated that almost every day she would worry about her grandmother, how she was doing at home, whether she was able to get out of her house, and if she was eating a proper meal. Her other constant worries were related to her future (e.g., employment and accommodation opportunities), and to the way in which other people might judge her because of her WS. She often said "They will know right away that I have WS and that I have a disability. I am sure they will say 'Look at how ugly that girl is. I am also convinced that she is very stupid'."

MJ recognized that her worries were excessive and uncontrollable. Often she had difficulties stopping herself from worrying, experiencing a chain effect where one worry lead to another, and she was not able to control it to the point that she would feel "very sick." Her worries and anxiety were so pervasive that she also felt very tense and irritable, causing tension with her family. She reported that her worries and anxiety caused her considerable distress in her life.

Specific phobia: As a child, she used to be very scared of loud noises such as fireworks, vacuum cleaners, and "noisy" places (e.g., supermarkets). With age, her fear of these situations decreased. However, in the past year, she had been avoiding going to places where there may be children. This fear developed after being in a bus with some children who were crying and screaming. Since then, she refuses to go to places where there is the possibility that there may be children such as restaurants or parks. Even the anticipation of going to places where there is the possibility of the presence of children has often lead her to have a panic attack. Because of this fear, she was almost house-bound.

Depression: MJ also reported having mood swings, for which she was taking an antipsychotic medication for the past 2 years. Although she initially had some benefit from taking this medication, she complained about gaining weight, and that the medicine made her "very fat and ugly." She also reported feelings of worthlessness and guilt. She felt she took so much of her parent's time because of the health problems related to her WS. And she felt guilty for not being as "good and smart" as her two sisters.

She had no sleeping problems. In fact she reported sleeping too much and that she often had to "drag" herself out of bed. She also felt constantly tired and had no energy. She ate well, and loved eating Chinese food.

Post- and follow-up assessments

Three months following treatment, MJ no longer met diagnostic criteria for GAD and specific phobia. Questionnaire data revealed consistent decreases in symptoms of worry, as well as depressive, anxiety and stress symptoms on the DASS throughout the course of treatment. As seen in Figure 24.3, there was a steady decline in worry scores on the PSWQ, as well as on depression, anxiety and stress subscales on the DASS at post-treatment and at follow-up. All the scores remained well within the normal range. Self-report ratings of impairment also indicated improvement. Moreover, the

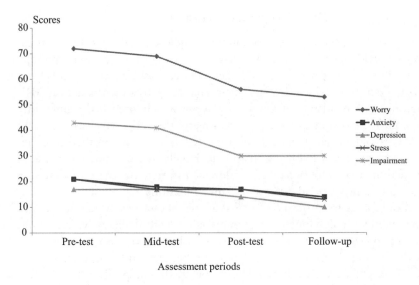

Figure 24.3 Worry, anxiety, depressive, and stress symptoms by assessment periods.

number of activities that MJ did with her friends increased over the course of treatment (Figure 24.4).

Positive statements were noted on MJ's thought-listing forms at follow-up, including thoughts such as "I enjoy watching children playing near our recreational park", and "Being in a place where there are lots of children was not as bad as I expected it to be." By the end of treatment, MJ had expanded her activity by volunteering in a "Kids Club" in her church; this club provided special children's provision every Sunday morning alongside morning service.

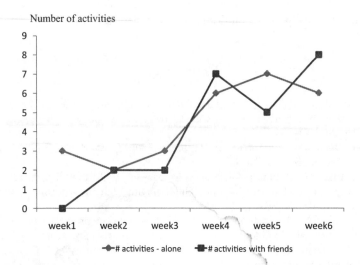

Figure 24.4 Number of activities with friends and alone.

Discussion and conclusion

The results suggest that CBT was successful in reducing anxiety, depressive and stress symptoms in an individual with WS who was diagnosed with GAD and specific phobia. Three months following treatment, MJ no longer met diagnostic criteria for GAD and specific phobia. There was evidence of the maintenance of treatment gains, as MJ's anxiety symptoms and avoidance of going to places with children had significantly decreased 3 months following treatment. In summary, the ESST-WS was successful in reducing MJ's avoidant behaviors and self-reported worry level. Furthermore, her approach behaviors increased following treatment. Finally, these improvements generalized to situations that were not directly addressed in treatment (e.g., eating in a restaurant, going to a playground, attending family functions).

The overall outcomes from the ESST-WS that uses the principles of the CBT to anxiety management with high functioning young people with Williams Syndrome was effective when the program used the adaptations as outlined above. Specifically, visual aids such as the feeling thermometer and picture schedules outlining each session, and the use of scripts were incorporated into the treatment package to facilitate comprehension of therapy tasks.

The results of this study also demonstrate a difficulty in treatment adherence with respect to homework completion. Manualized treatments for fear and anxiety often include exercises that the person can complete at home. These exercises serve to provide additional practice of skills taught during the treatment session, as well as to promote generalization and relapse prevention (Albano & Kendall, 2002). Because many individuals with WS have learning disabilities, it is a challenge for them to do the homework assignment on their own. It is therefore important to get their parents or their carers to help them with their homework.

To conclude, ESST-WS is effective in reducing anxiety. This is an important result because of the high frequency of anxiety experienced by individuals with WS, and left untreated could lead to a negative course and outcome. Our next step will be to conduct further studies of our newly developed ESST-WS to a large group of young people with WS, ideally with a randomized controlled trial.

References

Albano, A. M., & Kendall, P. C. (2002). Cognitive behavioural therapy for children and adolescents with anxiety disorders: Clinical research advances. *International Review of Psychiatry, 14,* 129–134.

APA (1994). *Diagnostic and Statistical Manual of Mental Disorders,* 4th edn. Washington: American Psychiatric Association.

Atkinson, J., Anker, S., Braddick, O., Nokes, L., Mason, A., & Braddick, F. (2001). Visual and visuospatial development in young children with Williams syndrome. *Developmental Medicine & Child Neurology, 43,* 330–337.

Beck, J. G., Stanley, M. A., & Zebb, B. J. (1995). Psychometric properties of the Penn State Worry Questionnaire in older adults. *Journal of Clinical Geropsychology, 1,* 33–42.

Black, J. A., & Bonham-Carter, R. E. (1963). Association between aortic stenosis and facies of severe infantile hypercalcemia. *Lancet, 2,* 745–748.

Blomberg, S., Rosander, M., & Andersson, G. (2006). Fears, hyperacusis and musicality in Williams syndrome. *Research in Developmental Disabilities, 27,* 668–80.

Davies, M., Udwin, O., & Howlin, P. (1998). Adults with Williams syndrome. Preliminary study of social, emotional, and behavioural difficulties. *The British Journal of Psychiatry, 172,* 273–276.

Dilts, C. V., Morris, C. A., & Leonard, C. O. (1990). Hypothesis for development of a behavioural phenotype in Williams syndrome. *American Journal of Medical Genetics, 6,* 126–31.

Donnai, D., & Karmiloff-Smith, A. (2000). Williams syndrome: From genotype through to the cognitive phenotype. *American Journal of Medical Genetics, 97,* 164–171.

Doyle, T. F., Bellugi, U., Korenberg, J. R., & Graham, J. (2004). "Everybody in the world is my friend": Hypersociability in young children with Williams syndrome. *American Journal of Medical Genetics, 124A,* 263–273.

Dykens, E. M. (2003). Anxiety, fears, and phobias in persons with Williams syndrome. *Developmental Neuropsychology, 23,* 291–316.

Dykens, E. M., Hodapp, R. M., & Finucane, B. M. (2000). *Genetics and Mental Retardation Syndromes: A New Look at Behavior and Interventions.* Baltimore: Brookes.

Dykens, E. M., & Rosner, B. A. (1999). Refining behavioral phenotypes: Personality-motivation in Williams and Prader–Willi syndromes. *American Journal on Mental Retardation, 104,* 158–169.

Einfeld, S., Tonge, B., & Florio, T. (1997). Behavioral and emotional disturbance in individuals with Williams syndrome. *American Journal of Mental Retardation, 102,* 45–53.

Einfeld, S., Tonge, B., Turner, G., Parmenter, T., & Smith, A. (1999). Longitudinal course of behavioural and emotional problems of young persons with Prader–Willi, Fragile X, Williams and Down syndromes. *Journal of Intellectual and Developmental Disability, 24,* 349–354.

Einfeld, S., Tonge, B., & Rees, V. (2001). Longitudinal course of behavioral and emotional problems in Williams syndrome. *American Journal of Mental Retardation, 106,* 73–81.

Farran, E. K., Blades, M., Boucher, J., & Tranter, L. J. (2010). How do individuals with Williams syndrome learn a route in a real-world environment? *Developmental Science, 13* (3), 454–468.

Gosch, A., & Pankau, R. (1997). Personality characteristics and behavioral problems in individuals of different ages with Williams syndrome. *Developmental Medicine and Child Neurology, 39,* 327–533.

Grant, J., Valiant, V., & Karmiloff-Smith, A. (2002). A study of relative clauses in Williams syndrome. *Journal of Child Language, 29,* 403–416

Jarrold, C., Baddeley, A. D., & Hewes, A. K. (1998). Verbal and nonverbal abilities in the Williams syndrome phenotype: Evidence for diverging developmental trajectories. *Journal of Child Psychology & Psychiatry & Allied Disciplines, 39,* 511–523.

Johnson, L. B., Comeau, M., & Clarke, K. D. (2001). Hyperacusis in Williams syndrome. *The Journal of Otolaryngology, 30,* 90–92.

Jones, W., Bellugi, U., Lai, Z., Chiles, M., Reilly, J., Lincoln, A., et al. (2000). II. Hypersociability in Williams syndrome. *Journal of Cognitive Neuroscience, 12* (Suppl. 1), 30–46.

Klein-Tasman, B. P., & Mervis, C. B. (2003). Distinctive personality characteristics of children with Williams syndrome. *Developmental Neuropsychology, 23,* 271–292.

Laing, E., Butterworth, G., Ansari, D., Gsdol, M., Longhi, E., Panagiotaki, G., et al. (2002). Atypical development of language and social communication in toddlers with Williams syndrome. *Developmental Science, 5,* 233–246.

Leyfer, O. T., Woodruff-Borden, J., Klein-Tasman, B. P., Fricke, J. S., & Mervis, C. B. (2006). Prevalence of psychiatric disorders in 4 to 16-year-olds with Williams syndrome. *American Journal of Medical Genetics B: Neuropsychiatric Genetics, 141,* 615–622.

Lovibond, P. F., & Lovibond, S. H. (1995). The structure of negative emotional states: Comparison of the Depression Anxiety Stress Scales (DASS) with the Beck Depression and Anxiety Inventories. *Behaviour Research and Therapy, 33,* 335–343.

Meyer, T. J., Miller, M. L., Metzger, R. L., & Borkovec, T. D. (1990). Development and validation of the Penn State Worry Questionnaire. *Behaviour Research and Therapy, 28,* 487–495.

Meyer-Lindenberg, A., Hariri, A. R., Munoz, K. E., Mervis, C. B., Mattay, V. S., Morris, C. A., et al. (2005). Neural correlates of genetically abnormal social cognition in Williams syndrome. *Nature Neuroscience, 8,* 991–993.

Quakley, S., Reynolds, S., & Coker, S. (2004). Visual cues and age improve children's abilities to discriminate between thoughts, feelings and behaviours. *Behaviour Research and Therapy, 42,* 343–356

Scheiber, B. (2000). *Fulfilling Dreams – Book I: a Handbook for Parents of Williams Sndrome Children*. Clawson, MI: Williams Syndrome Association.

Semel, E., & Rosner, S. R. (2003). *Understanding Williams Syndrome Behavioral Patterns and Interventions*. Mahwah, NJ: Lawrence Erlbaum Associates.

Singer Harris, N. G., Bellugi, U., Bates, E., Jones, W., & Rossen, M. L. (1997). Contrasting profiles of language development in children with Williams and Down syndromes. *Developmental Neuropsychology, 13,* 345–370.

Thomas, M., Grant, J., Barham, Z., Gsodl, M, Laing, E., Lakusta, L., et al. (2001). Past tense formation in Williams syndrome. *Language and Cognitive Processes, 16* (1–2), 143–176.

Udwin, O., & Yule, W. (1990). Expressive language of children with Williams Syndrome. *American Journal of Medical Genetics Supplement, 6,* 108–114.

Udwin, O., & Yule, W. (1991). A cognitive and behavioral phenotype on Williams syndrome. *Journal of Clinical and Experimental Neuropsychology, 13,* 232–244.

Udwin, O., & Yule, W. (1998). *Williams Syndrome: Guidelines for Parents*. Tonbridge, Kent: The Williams Syndrome Foundation.

Werner, E. E., & Johnson, J. L. (2004). The role of caring adults in the lives of children of alcoholics. *Substance Use and Misuse, 39,* 699–720.

Wittchen, H. U., Robins, L. N., Cottler, L. B., Sartorius, N., Burke, J. D., & Regier, D., 1991. Cross-cultural feasibility, reliability and sources of variance of the Composite International Diagnostic Interview (CIDI): Results of the Multicenter WHO/ADAMHA Field Trials (Wave I). *British Journal of Psychiatry, 159,* 645–653.

Index

The Wiley-Blackwell Handbook of The Treatment of Childhood and Adolescent Anxiety, First Edition.
Edited by Cecilia A. Essau and Thomas H. Ollendick.
© 2013 John Wiley & Sons, Ltd. Published 2013 by John Wiley & Sons, Ltd.